UNLESS THE LORD
BUILDS THE HOUSE

ALSO BY JEFFREY E. FORD

Books published under the pseudonym Kirk Adams:

Left on Paradise

The Electronic Mother

The Trouble with Girls

Hundreds of Reflections: 100 Psalms Explored in 100 Words

Measures of Insight: Moral Reflections for Daily Life

Husbandry

UNLESS THE LORD BUILDS THE HOUSE

MARRIAGE, HOUSEHOLD, AND SEX IN THE
CHRISTIAN TRADITION FROM ANTIQUITY TO
TODAY

DR. JEFFREY E. FORD

❧

Front Cover Art: *The Marriage at Cana* by Master of the Catholic Kings, c.1495/97. *Courtesy National Gallery of Art, Washington D.C. (Open Access).*

Back Cover Art: *The Visitation with Saints Nicholas and Saint Anthony Abbot* by Pietro di Cosimo, Florence, c. 1489/1490. *Courtesy National Gallery of Art, Washington D.C. (Open Access).*

Kirk Adams Books, PMB #219 / 45591 Dulles East Plaza, Suite 132 / Sterling, VA 20166

❀ Formatted with Vellum

CONTENTS

SUPPLEMENTARY MATERIAL

To Pam, with whom I have enjoyed the love and delight of Christian marriage for many years, and without whom this book would not have been written.

Unless the LORD builds the house,
those who build it labor in vain.
Unless the LORD watches over the city,
the watchman stays awake in vain.
It is in vain that you rise up early
and go late to rest,
eating the bread of anxious toil;
for he gives to his beloved sleep.

Behold, children are a heritage from the LORD,
the fruit of the womb a reward.
Like arrows in the hand of a warrior
are the children of one's youth.
Blessed is the man who fills his quiver with them!
He shall not be put to shame when
he speaks with his enemies in the gate.

—Psalm 127 (ESV)—

PREFACE: WISDOM FROM THE PAST

The words of the wise are like goads, and like nails firmly fixed are the collected sayings; they are given by one Shepherd. My son, beware of anything beyond these. Of making many books there is no end, and much study is a weariness of the flesh.[1]

There are thousands of books about marriage, both online and in bookstores, with many of them written from the perspectives and experiences of Christian authors. Is it really necessary for yet another such work to be published, or is it possible that I, too, have contributed to the ceaseless writing of unread books observed by Solomon? I pray not, for God reveals that those who presume to be teachers among his people will be strictly judged. Still, our Lord has also declared that anyone who buries his talents out of laziness and fearfulness will lose the blessing he might otherwise have received.[2] Because the Lord led me in my youth to church service, Christian activism, and graduate study at a prestigious university and later to marriage, fatherhood of four children, and a professional career that improved my writing, I step forward in faith—hoping that the Lord who previously called me to draft the initial version of this book

---

1. Ecclesiastes 12:11–12, *Holy Bible, English Standard Version* (Wheaton, Illinois: Crossway, 2001. Quotations and citations from this version hereafter are marked (ESV).
2. James 3:1; Matthew 25:14–30.

during graduate school now calls me to revise my efforts in light of later learning and experience. I pray that this expanded version will prove helpful to believers seeking divine guidance amidst a lost generation. I should note that I have discerned God's call only through my gifts, education, experience, and evaluation of a pressing public need. May the Lord forgive any presumption on my part.[3]

In 1996, I earned my Ph.D. in European History at the University of Wisconsin. Historical study is broadening, leading students into a world quite unlike the modern one. Old ideas are rediscovered and new perspectives are molded, with differences of time proving as consequential as those of distance and language. This is nowhere more true than with an examination of marriage, household, and love, which are critical topics for study in the contemporary university (at least, they were when I was educated). Still, despite much study and book-making, many modern men and women, particularly our public intellectuals and academics, have deceived themselves regarding the experience of family life in the past. Far too many scholars and pundits assume previous generations lived unfruitful, unhappy, and unfortunate lives in a world that lacked modern contraception, legalized abortion, sexual freedom, no-fault divorce, and women's equality. They project current cultural debates into the past and label those who lived differently than they do today as ignorant, oppressed, or evil. Such historians are quite simply wrong.[4]

While every generation has its particular vices and virtues, I have come to suspect that the world of our forefathers possessed more insight, indeed wisdom, in the governance of family and sex than does our age. Marital and sexual morality were questions of overriding concern in

---

3. Regarding my academic qualifications, my dissertation focused on marital law in sixteenth-century France, and my advisor was a leading expert on Reformation-era Geneva and France. I studied antiquity, medieval Europe, early modern Europe, and modern Europe at Indiana University Bloomington and the University of Wisconsin–Madison.

4. Key among such historians have been the following: Philippe Ariès, who believed past ages lacked a concept of a childhood distinct from adult life; Lawrence Stone, who doubted that affective marriages existed before the early modern era; Georges Duby, who viewed medieval marriage as a social strategy that ignored the needs of women; and Edward Shorter, who doubted women's emotional and sexual satisfaction before the rise of modern ideals and material culture. Many historians cited in this book challenged such pernicious pessimism and the misrepresentations of the human past associated with such historiography. Philippe Ariès, *Centuries of Childhood: A Social History of Family Life*, trans. Robert Baldick (New York: Vintage Books, 1962); Lawrence Stone, *Family, Sex, and Marriage: 1500–1800* (New York: Harper and Row, 1979); Georges Duby, *Medieval Marriage: Two Models from Twelfth-Century France* (Baltimore, Maryland: Johns Hopkins University Press, 1978); Edward Shorter, *A History of Women's Bodies* (New York: Basic Books, 1982).

many historical epochs, and numerous books that have survived the centuries bear witness to this fact. From Augustine of Hippo's treatises on marriage to G. K. Chesterton's celebration of conventional Christian family life, Christians have written about the meaning of flesh and family from a theistic perspective. Still, too few modern students are aware of the plethora of books written to address the ethics of the household, and even fewer incorporate the wisdom of the past into their ethics and worldview. Even religious authors frequently are so poorly informed about historical views of the household that they adopt an implicitly modern point of view, baptizing it as Christian while mistaking the dictates of contemporary fashion for the truth of eternal righteousness. This book attempts to remedy that deficiency by bringing to the forefront the Christian tradition of household writings and associated biblical commentary. Someone needs to remind modern readers, for better or worse, how our ethics regarding marriage, family, and household have departed from the traditional consensus of Christianity.[5]

Observant readers will notice that this work is neither a scholarly monograph nor a popular manifesto. I have aimed to write a book that is conceptually and theologically worthwhile while remaining accessible to readers both inside and outside academia. I have drawn from a serious academic education under a prominent scholar to summarize Christian doctrine for pastoral care and personal piety. I can only pray that I have achieved the necessary balance to do so, since nothing would please me more than to learn that pastors, elders, and laypersons are using my work. Such men and women are the flock of Christ, on whose behalf every servant of the Lord is granted ability and authority. I hope to enable Christian churches to better stand for sexual purity, marital fidelity, and household charity in an epoch during which such traditional virtues have

---

5. As one example from the 1990s, Lewis B. Smedes discussed human sexuality to counter those so enamored with techniques of sexual pleasure that they were describing *how* to audiences of single men and women on Christian college campuses. Smedes's ethics, however, were so compromised by modern mores that he made worse problems than those he opposed. At nearly every point of ethical judgment, Smedes exchanged traditional Christianity's uncompromising sexual morality for a gospel of sexual freedom. For just one example, he allowed gay marriage for "law-abiding and Christ-loving people [in] committed and faithful monogamous relationships with each other if they cannot change their condition and do not have the gift to be celibate." While some problems in his book are editorial, his belief that the primary purpose of sexual conduct is to establish emotional intimacy (rather than to produce children) framed Smedes's mistaken conclusions. Lewis B. Smedes, *Sex for Christians: The Limits and Liberties of Sexual Living* (Grand Rapids, Michigan: William B. Eerdmans Publishing Company, 1994), 92–93, 238–242.

fallen from favor. I pray that Christian leaders will reestablish the importance of household morality in the churches, as it was from the beginning. Indeed, I sometimes fear that much of modern piety attempts to build spiritual fervor on a very shaky foundation of the biblical understanding of household governance. This should not be, for New Testament writers interwove personal piety and church prayers with godly government of the household. To master the best books about spiritual discipline while remaining estranged from a spouse, disrespecting a parent, or fornicating with a neighbor is to accomplish nothing worthy before the Lord, no matter how religious a person might feel or believe himself or herself to be.

What this book is, then, is an exercise in personal ethics and church government more than disinterested scholarship. Although I have worked hard to understand and accurately portray historical knowledge, this book does not pretend to be an academic treatise. Nor does it aim to discuss the conventions and methods of contemporary scholarship. I intend to review historical context and precedent to make reasonable generalizations regarding the interpretation of Scripture and the attainment of Christian piety. I aim to summarize the consensus held by believers in the past by examining historical differences and striving toward universal truth. While I will paint with broad brush strokes and leave detailed examination of specifics to others, I have worked hard to document my findings, thereby providing readers with access to the biblical and historical sources required to delve deeper into a Christian understanding of marital and sexual ethics.[6] To that end, I have included both a *Glossary of Cited Authors* and a *For Recommended Reading* section. These describe the sources cited in this book and provide a list of books helpful for additional study, as well as for the equipping of institutional or individual libraries. I urge my readers to consider purchasing several of these books, helping such publishing to continue despite the economic challenges of digitalization.

Many current books about marriage serve as apologetic defenses of

---

6. In introducing Athanasius's *On the Incarnation,* C.S. Lewis observed two salient facts. First, new books must be tested "against the great body of Christian thought down the ages." Second, there must be a standard of "plain, central Christianity... which puts controversies of the moment in proper perspective." Lewis believed this standard comes from historical study since "every age has its own outlook" that requires the reading of old books to transcend. St. Athanasius, *On the Incarnation: The Treatise De Incarnatione Verbi Dei,* trans. C.S.M.V., intro. C.S. Lewis (New York: St. Vladimir's Seminary Press, 1993), 4.

Christian marriage against contemporary problems and practices, typically emphasizing two primary points. First, they observe how Christian marriage brings more happiness than modern immorality. Second, they teach how sexual life in marriage is ordained by God and should be considered *good*. Regarding the first point, such practical apologetics play a legitimate role in explaining Christian marriage to a generation raised in the sorrow, shame, and separations of the sexual revolution, with personal testimony working to illustrate the virtues and humanity of Christian doctrine. As for the second point, I honestly do not understand the need to make this assertion, nor can I understand the audience for whom it is intended. Because it has been centuries since any major branch of Christianity seriously devalued marriage, this seems to be an argument being made to ascetic ghosts of centuries past. Insofar as contemporary authors argue that God created sex, they are right enough, but who doubts that fact? I do not see the monasteries of Christendom being flooded with men and women begging to take vows of celibacy before they are dragged off to a honeymoon.[7] To me, such an emphasis appears to be an attempted Christianization of the sexual revolution and modern rootlessness, with a serious risk of the worldliness so forcefully rebuked by Jesus in the first chapters of the book of Revelation.[8] At the very least, it is a mistaken pastoral effort to deal with the grip of shame in individual couples (since deep shame more often flows from sinful experiences and current indulgences than from misguided theology).

I do not aspire to innovate. My approach to Christian marriage is not new. For centuries, Christians have looked to Holy Scripture and the Christian tradition to glean insight into the governance of morals and marriage. Relevant citations from church fathers were compiled and expounded during the Middle Ages (in extracts and collections called *florilegia*), and various Protestant Reformers likewise drew inspiration from Scripture and key works of Christian antiquity. I have tried to do the same, citing numerous authors and texts to familiarize readers with the broad current of Christian ethics, law, and doctrine regarding marriage, sex, and family life. After all, the fundamental problems that

---

7. This line plays off of a G.K. Chesterton quote.
8. I am speaking of Western culture and civilization. Much of the non-Western world shares in the chaste courtships, arranged marriages, and multi-generational households (in which grown men with children live under the authority of their fathers) that similarly marked Western history. People of the modern West dare not presume to be the model for all cultures since our society is the anomaly.

sinful conduct brings between man and woman are common to every age. In many ways, this book can be described as a compendium of key thoughts and texts drawn from Scripture and Christian history, collected here to catalog a consensus of Christian churches regarding marital and household ethics. In this, I have drawn from law, pastoral practices, theology, and confessions of faith, primarily focusing on what a broad range of churchmen have believed and taught. Additionally, I have added footnotes and references that shed light on biblical texts through comparison with medieval and early modern European customs, which seem closer to the biblical world than to our own era. My training in social history provided me with invaluable context for a better understanding of many commentaries and biblical texts.

I should note that very few thoughts in this book are my own, beyond a few nuanced opinions and occasional footnoted comments. Most ideas have been drawn from earlier Christian authors, an approach easily demonstrated through my citation of a multitude of sources. Even those few insights I might claim to have refined are the fruit of meditating on Scripture and reflecting over many years on the Christian consensus regarding household duties. Contemporary believers would do well to draw from our long heritage as we struggle with the temptations of the spirit of our age—a spirit of unbelief and immorality. Our generation surely includes many of those about whom the apostle Paul warned in the New Testament: deceivers who "creep into households" to capture those "burdened with sins and led astray by various passions, always learning and never able to arrive at a knowledge of the truth."[9]

Please understand that I have attempted to write about sexual purity with as much reverence as can be managed while bringing to the forefront matters of morality that must be discussed. Some professedly Christian books on sexuality and marriage are nearly pornographic works, violating both the spirit and the letter of Scripture with words and illustrations that writers should hesitate to display before their children, let alone to strangers. Since the apostle Paul declared it shameful "even to speak of the things [the ungodly] do in secret," I will follow his advice by refraining from public discussion of intimate details, sticking as closely as possible to the principles required for making moral and spiritual decisions. Still, propriety is as much substance as form, so it is better to present the full biblical position than to sidestep embarrassing issues

---

9. 2 Timothy 3:6–7 (ESV).

from misplaced modesty. While Moses was painfully frank in his discussion of sexual prohibitions, he required that the law of God be read aloud to the assembled people of Israel (man, woman, and child) every seven years. Such public reading included explicit passages from the book of Leviticus regarding sexual prohibitions, some of which even I am too embarrassed to discuss in this book. The same is true of many Old Testament prophets, who frequently used coarse language to condemn sin.[10]

Much has changed since I completed the first edition of this work in the 1990s, not only in the world but also for me. Regarding the world, same-sex marriage has become widely accepted in Western society, and there have been strong undercurrents suggesting efforts to normalize polygamy and close relative marriages. Progressive mores are prevalent in many public and corporate settings, and traditional Christian morals have been challenged, even in the relatively traditional United States. At the personal level, I left academia for public service and raised four children with my wife of thirty-seven years. I also became a better writer than I was straight out of university, and my earlier studies have been tested and tempered by decades of living. If not yet wise, I have certainly grown wiser than I was three decades ago, although the passing of the years leaves me unconvinced that I am a better person than I was when I first undertook this project. If I am not an objectively worse person than I was three decades ago (which I believe I am), I have at least gained greater awareness of the enduring flaws in my character. That noted, this book is rooted in the precepts and practices of the historical Christian tradition rather than in my virtues, and the past has not changed, even if modern iconoclasts topple its markers and cease to venerate its insights.

I would also like to confess that while my initial writings and subsequent life choices have not led to a sinless and easy existence for my family or me, our traditional faith has shielded us from many of the temptations and sorrows of our generation. God has defended my family from many of my particular faults and sins as a husband and father, for which I am grateful—and has forgiven the many sins that I did not forsake as thoroughly as I should have. No one should open this book and judge that I have attempted to write a definitive recipe for raising a family or running a successful household, for I would not presume to write such a book.

---

10. Ephesians 5:12 (ESV); Deuteronomy 31:10–13 (American Standard Bible, 1901; hereafter unmarked). We can see in Leviticus 18:24 and Ezekiel 16:20–21 examples of such explicit language.

What I have done is glean wisdom and truth from the insight and faith of past generations (some of which I have lived out in faith and some of which demand further repentance on my part) and gathered it into one place for meditation and application, as well as for the government of God's household. Just as Western society must repent of its apostasy or falter before its enemies (perhaps to be torn down, then resurrected by God's grace), so I have fallen short of the Lord's word in ten thousand acts of personal apostasy.

Despite my sins, I confess that Christ has redeemed my life from the chaos of the broken household in which I was raised and to whose sorrows I contributed, then blessed me with a good-sized family, graced with a measure of faith and joy amidst our sins and sorrows. Still, like King David (who was personally guilty of committing adultery and murder, as well as leading a household whose sins included rape, incest, treason, and murder), I am a sinner who has fathered sinners. Nevertheless, like David after repentance, I understand that "salvation belongs to the LORD," and I believe that I am allowed to "teach transgressors [God's] ways" in light of God's grace in my life. Similarly, King Solomon, the son of David, was called to share wisdom and godly precepts with all mankind in several books of the Bible, even though he himself did not always live according to God's righteousness in his household matters. Therefore, it is with my own sins and failures in mind that I pray the Lord will use this book to bless both those raised in Christian homes and those who have found God's holiness after being plagued by sexual immorality, divorce, and unfaithfulness to God's revealed will. The Lord brings greater good to his believing children than any of us deserve, good or bad alike, for God's word brings faith, hope, and love to sinners.[11]

I have revised and republished this work for several reasons. To begin with, the previous publisher (whose earlier support I will always be grateful for) did not aspire to the broader audience I would prefer, a matter I hope to resolve through republication under a new title and for a reduced price. Second, my writing has improved since I left academia, so I want to clean up my earlier scribblings. Years of professional writing have helped mitigate several problems, and writing fiction has helped with my paragraphing. Third, a few of my passages do not read with the same tone

---

11. Psalm 3:8; Psalm 51:13, *Holy Bible, New American Standard Bible* (La Habra, California: Lockman Foundation, 1995). Quotations and citations from this version hereafter are marked (NASB).

I intended in the 1990s. Words change meaning over time, and tone grows obsolete in a few short years. While I want to challenge modern readers with morality grounded in eternal truth as experienced during past generations, I am not permitted to forget the apostle's reminder to instruct "with gentleness," lest the devil ensnare our spiritual and moral opponents.[12] Finally, new scholarship and new translations of primary sources provide additional insight and access into both Scripture and the past, deepening any review of the Christian household grounded in the doctrines, practices, and traditions of the Christian churches.

All of these factors noted, I have altered no essential doctrine nor adjusted my teachings to court popularity; very little of my substantive understanding of marital ethics has changed. Because I have continued my studies only as an amateur (rather than a professional scholar), I will revise and reformat this previously published work with modest changes. While I would prefer to rewrite the entire book, the leisure of graduate school and vigor of youth have passed, and I have time only for editing, amplifications, and several new chapters. Ultimately, I am pursuing this project because a well-read, pious, and orthodox friend observed that my original book provided a unique perspective on marriage that filled a niche in the Christian book market, such that a revised edition might be of value. I pray to the Lord that he is right. If not, any folly and sin is mine, for I am the one who presumes to share my musings.

Initially, I approached this project as an evangelical Protestant of the Reformed tradition (albeit with an appreciation for the broader Christian tradition) and remain so in life and doctrine three decades later. As a conservative Presbyterian, I confess the Reformed Protestant tradition coming out of Zurich and Geneva, before making its way through France, England, Scotland, New England, and elsewhere. As a spiritual child of the 1970s evangelical revival, I confess the need for personal piety beyond received doctrinal statements and liturgical practices, as well as a full commitment to the inerrancy of Scripture in everything the Bible teaches. I, however, am inerrant neither in doctrine nor life and pray the Lord will correct my errors and forgive my faults as he leads me through the republishing of this book and the final chapters of my own life. May the Lord have great mercy on our sinful generation, leading us to a rebirth of life and righteousness.

Beyond whatever errors of history or doctrine I have made (and I

---

12. 2 Timothy 2:25–26 (ESV).

pray these be few), I confess that I find it challenging to get the tone of this book right. Teaching the clarity of the word of God is difficult enough in itself, especially in a perverse generation filled with divorce and sexual immorality. It is humbling (even shaming) to draft and edit so many points of doctrine and ethics that I myself frequently fall short of. Both Scripture and my own words convict me as the hypocrite condemned by Paul in the book of Romans, for I pass judgment while doing the things that I condemn in others.[13] Not only is God's law difficult to face, but it is also painful to discuss sensitive matters like divorce, abortion, sexually transmitted diseases, and other sorrows in a manner that upholds the wisdom and blessing of the Lord's path while preaching redemption to fellow sinners. How to condemn the sorrows brought by the sexual revolution without pouring salt into the wounds of those who have suffered its evils is beyond my character and capacity—and for this, I am sorry. I can only say that I sprinkle salt in these pages not to inflict gratuitous pain but for the medicinal and preservative good that spiritual salt can bring to open wounds and damaged spirits. May Christ use the salt of his word to do good to those in need, while both admonishing and forgiving me for any lack of compassion in my messaging. If this book helps even one sinner receive God's blessing in our lost world, every expense and effort involved in its writing will have been justified.

For the record, in drafting this book, I used multiple versions of the Bible. Still, I selected the American Standard Version of the Bible (1901) as my primary reference, and used both the New American Standard Bible 1995 (NASB) and the English Standard Version (ESV) for many of my quotations (with citations from the King James Version of 1611 in several instances). My criteria for choosing a version ranged from a particular preference to consistency with other passages. I also tried maintaining the book's flow as I moved between various versions. I appreciate the generous rules of use allowed by both publishers for their respective translations and pray that the Lord will bless those who share his word. I encourage my readers to purchase copies of both the New American Standard Bible 1995 and the English Standard Version translations, thereby supporting publishers who share God's word in this gracious manner. Scripture reminds us to share a portion of our wealth with those who make God's word available—and that should include generous publishers as well as apostolic messengers.

---

13. Romans 2:1.

Regarding the style of the present edition, I apologize for any inconsistencies and errors. Footnotes were double-checked, and the book was reviewed multiple times for consistency; yet, there can be no doubt that a book of this length will include errors and leave room for improvement. Most notably, I find it difficult to weave between verb tenses when discussing historical texts that retain current authority (both Scripture and later commentators). The past event is historical, while the current authority of a text often requires the use of the present tense. I would also note that there is some repetition throughout the work. This is frequently intentional, as I firmly believe in reiteration and review when sharing complicated information. Occasionally, I sought a pretext to include a cited author or footnote, as I genuinely believe that the most significant contribution of my book lies in its sharing of historical context and commentary with contemporary readers (many of whom lack access to research libraries or the time to consult them). My objective is to direct our generation toward the wisdom and writings given to God's holy servants long before we were born. These are the goads (i.e., spiked sticks used to herd livestock) that drive all of us toward repentance.

My heartfelt thanks go to my wife, Pam, with whom Christian marriage has been a delight, and to my children Joshua, Samuel, Hannah, and Benjamin. To this day, each of you suffers the loss of your father as he dedicates himself to rewriting a book almost beyond his ability. And to my daughters-in-law, Morgan and Jhosselin, may you see the teachings of Scripture lived in the family you have joined and which you blessed through marriage to my sons. Finally, to my grandchildren, whom I have lived to see by the Lord's specific grace (having providentially been spared from a dangerous cancer twenty years ago), may the Lord bless you and any other descendants whom the Lord grants to Pam and me.

I also thank Joe Ford, Cliff Bajema, David Wegener, and Phil Meade for their editorial assistance and substantive revisions in the first edition of this book, as well as David M. for his early feedback and assistance with this revision. I thank my readers for acquiring this book and ask that they improve what is lacking in my education, life, and talents. May the reader overlook my many mistakes and sins, focusing solely on God's revelation in Scripture and our Lord's providential work through many generations.

Dr. Jeffrey E. Ford

January 2026

PART I

THE LORD AS THE MAKER OF MARRIAGE

~

Christians confess that marriage has been made to reflect the glory of God and is ordained for eternal purposes rather than temporal ones. This understanding distinguishes the essentials of Christian doctrine from the perspectives of many unbelievers—who view human marriage as similar to the amoral copulations of animals. Believers teach that through marriage, humanity can better understand who God is and more perfectly reflect the divine image. This is true even though Christ himself—who perfectly reflects his Father's glory—remained single his entire life, as do many Christians (and all of us for part of our lives). Matrimony was not established merely for human convenience, happiness, or reproduction (though all of these are components of the institution as the Lord has designed it), but to lead people to a greater love and experiential knowledge of God.

Therefore, the first task of an inquiring Christian is to discover why the Lord created marriage in the first place. Every idea and ethical perspective regarding matrimony should be based on the answer to this fundamental question. The second task of the believer is to understand the specifics of marriage as God has revealed them. Christians must appeal to biblical perspectives and passages regarding marriage to ensure that these frame their theology and ethics. It is insufficient to appeal to nature, myth, or even history to uncover the purposes of marital life (since God's perfect revelation defines what Christians believe about marriage, in general, and how they govern their households, in particular). It also must be remembered that the very first chapters of the Bible discuss how marriage came into being and reveal its most important obligations. God allows no confusion regarding the purposes and duties of wedlock. Nor does the Lord allow family life to be treated as unimportant.

This section provides a doctrinal framework upon which specific ethical positions can be founded. It begins with a discussion of how and why mankind was made to reflect the image of God, as well as detailing specific moral attributes like purity and charity (which human marriage and sexuality were created to reveal). Next, the section examines the particular duties of marriage, how family life and ethics have been altered by the human race's fall into sin, the nature of God's governance over human affairs, and the Lord's guidance of his people through mortal life. Finally, this segment discusses how both individuals, the churches, and broader society can differentiate between those men and women called by God to serve through marriage and those called to serve in singleness.

1

THE RULE OF FAITH

The only rule of ordering the family is the written word of God. By it David resolved to govern his house when he said, "I will walk in the uprightness of my heart in the midst of my house." [1]

THE FIRST PROBLEM in determining how best to govern household relationships and sexual appetite is to establish a legitimate right to do so in light of competing claims to ultimate authority. Some people rely on the assertions of human reason unaided by divine revelation, while others try to imitate the world of nature or bow before the consensus of civilization. Even Christians have been divided into several camps. Mystics have sought direct personal experience of God, and more scholarly Christians accept the consensus of Christian academia. I believe God has spoken to his people through the original, inerrant text of the Old and New Testaments, understood as originally intended (albeit with poetry, prophecies, and divine mysteries interwoven into its various books) by believers living according to God's holy call. That is, the Lord speaks through the Bible as accepted (and judged complete) by many generations of Christians.

Traditional Roman Catholics generally argue that the Pope speaks for

1. William Perkins, "Christian Economy," in Joan Larsen Klein, ed., *Daughters, Wives, and Widows: Writings by Men about Women and Marriage in England, 1500–1640* (Urbana, Illinois: University of Illinois Press, 1992), 157.

the faith in interpreting the Bible in light of the Christian tradition, whereas orthodox Protestants believe that individual believers can understand Scripture directly (without the Pope or church tradition), holding that the rule of faith is *sola scriptura* (i.e., Scripture alone). Protestants believe that the Bible alone speaks for the Lord in directing God's people and all mankind toward true doctrine, piety, and love. In the above quote, William Perkins presented the standard Protestant position in his treatise on the Christian household—a book that provided guidance for the governance of the private family (based on biblical instruction) and the discipline of the Christian church. As an evangelical Protestant, that approach will be the foundation for my work. While I am not a trained theologian, I understand that Scripture was not given as a mystery to be interpreted by a priestly caste, but provided to all of God's people for their shared use and mutual edification.

Before William Perkins, Martin Luther, the first Protestant leader, approached the government of the household with an appeal to Scripture and wrote influential marriage treatises in which he argued for revised marriage laws, declaring that the Roman Catholic consensus was in error at several points.[2] Of course, Luther understood how strange it looked that an unmarried monk (as he remained when he first began to write on marital matters) should preach to all Christendom how and when to marry—that one lowly clergyman should challenge centuries of doctrine, practice, and tradition. In response to his critics, Luther appealed to *sola scriptura* as his rule of faith, stating: "I base my remarks on Scripture, which to me is surer than all experience and cannot lie."[3] *Sola scriptura* meant not only that Luther did not appeal to the Pope, church tradition, or canon (ecclesiastical) lawyers for rules of marriage, but also that he appealed to a standard more reliable than his own limited experience.

C.S. Lewis, the English apologist and writer, did the same when he authored several works discussing marriage and love, even though Lewis remained unmarried through much of his life. Some might find it odd that a bachelor wrote books that touch on marriage, sexuality, and romantic love. They should not, for anyone who reads the books of C.S.

---

2. Despite objections to Roman Catholic restrictions regarding clerical marriage and remarriage after divorce (as well as the breadth of existing impediments to marriage), Protestants preserved the core of medieval marital law. For a review of Luther's debt to medieval law, see Virpi Mäkinen, ed., *Lutheran Reformation and the Law* (Leiden: Brill, 2006).

3. Martin Luther, "The Estate of Marriage (1522)," in *Luther's Works*, vol. 45, ed. Helmut T. Lehman (Philadelphia: Fortress Press, 1962), 43.

Lewis must agree that he provides considerable insight into the realities of love, marriage, and family life. The source of his wisdom was not only his own childhood, good sense, and keen observation, but also ethics and doctrines revealed in Scripture and the Christian tradition, which Lewis studied for many years as a medieval and Renaissance scholar. Interestingly, Lewis observed that some who might criticize him for writing about marriage from the vantage of a bachelor had acquired their ideas about marriage from novels and films rather than from experience.[4]

An appeal to Scripture does, however, create difficulties. One of the most important is the vexing matter of interpretation: who has the final determination in understanding the Bible? While some believers have given this authority to church councils (i.e., majority rule), others have ceded this authority to the Papacy or mystical revelations. Egalitarians, extreme democrats, and levelers might favor a more democratic interpretation of the Bible, taking a political principle (*vox populi, vox dei*) as gospel truth. For these, God's voice is found among ordinary believers rather than with trained clergy. Traditional Protestants claim that biblical teaching is straightforward and can be understood by ordinary Christians as they live piously, read accurate translations, and interpret Scripture in its context (through the lens of Scripture itself). When disagreements and disputes arise over key passages, final judgment must be based on examining the Greek and Hebrew manuscripts of the Bible closest to the original text (since only the original manuscript was inspired by the Holy Spirit). Authoritative interpretation of Scripture also requires a conscientious effort to understand the Bible in its historical context, carefully examining the circumstances in which biblical writers lived and wrote. This approach requires theologians and scholars who can read and interpret biblical passages in accordance with the author's intent, as expressed through the meaning of the original language.[5]

Protestants understand biblical interpretation as more than an academic exercise, believing that only those teachers moved by the Holy Spirit

---

4. C. S. Lewis, *Mere Christianity* (New York: HarperOne, 1980), 109–110.
5. Stephen B. Clark discussed the cultural context of New Testament texts regarding household ethics, setting key passages in a specific historical context while linking them to an overarching theological perspective. Clark wrote: "The key texts of the New Testament concerning the roles of men and women present a consistent teaching. Each text has its own point of origin and its own perspective and content, but together they sketch out what can be accurately described as the New Testament approach." Stephen B. Clark, *Man and Woman in Christ: An Examination of the Roles of Men and Women in Light of Scripture and the Social Sciences* (Ann Arbor, Michigan: Servant Books, 1980), 255.

will interpret Scripture rightly and only students called by Christ to new life will confess the truth of God's word. For that reason, a strident atheist will never discern the meaning of the life and death of Christ since the unbeliever will necessarily twist facts and ignore truths that would force a reevaluation of his or her relationship with God. Even the best seminary education will do an unbeliever little good insofar as the unbeliever willfully persists in unbelief. To this end, Jesus revealed how only those whose eyes have been opened by the Holy Spirit can understand the meaning of his spiritual teachings and atoning sacrifice.[6] Without the Spirit of God, nothing truly spiritual may be discerned—neither the simplest parable nor the shortest proverb.

Bible-believing Protestants, however, must remember that God's Spirit has been given to the church across all generations rather than to one isolated pastor, scholar, congregation, or denomination. No one should imagine they stand above the human fray: understanding the depths of the word of God perfectly, comprehensively, or exclusively. In fact, Protestants who reformed Christian churches in the name of Scripture during the Reformation appreciated the historical Christian tradition; they believed it worthwhile to examine ancient and medieval authors to acquire fuller insight into the ways of God. While only the Bible was thought to speak with absolute authority, those churchmen confessed how God had spoken through Scripture to many generations of Christians and that biblical truth is possessed by the whole body of Christ, not being limited to self-ordained cliques of schismatics and fanatics. They confessed the faith of the second-century Apostles' Creed, which declared belief in the "holy catholic church."[7]

What I mean to say is that few Protestants were foolish enough to argue that God had been entirely silent among the churches before Martin Luther, Ulrich Zwingli, and John Calvin began their respective ministries. Most reformers believed God worked in the lives and words of John Chrysostom, Augustine of Hippo, Anselm of Canterbury, Bernard of Clairvaux, and many others—holding that the Lord had established

---

6. John 16:13.

7. Medieval theologian Anselm of Canterbury wrote: "For even the Fathers, because 'the days are short' [cf. Job 14:1], were not able to say all that could have been said if they had lived longer; and the logic of the truth is so copious and profound that it cannot be exhausted by mortals. Moreover, the Lord, who promised to be with the Church 'until the end of the world' [Matt. 28:20], does not cease to bestow his gifts within it." Anselm, "Why God Became Man," in Brian Davies and G.R. Evans, eds., *Anselm of Canterbury: The Major Works* (Oxford: Oxford University Press, 1988), 260.

his church across the centuries, even if the church of their generation required renewal, revival, and reform. And since the church of Christ was nothing less than the ongoing work of the Lord over many generations, Protestant Reformers found it useful to share the works and ideas of previous commentators, whose interpretations of the Bible might prove as insightful as their own. Most Protestant Reformers possessed sufficient spiritual humility and breadth of understanding to listen to earlier generations of believers, unless these proved inconsistent and incompatible with a plain reading of Scripture.[8]

Beyond this historical truth, we should remember the promise of Christ that even when his disciples suffer persecution, poverty, or other evils, the Lord's church will never suffer a lack of God's Spirit, and it is precisely in the interpretation of Holy Writ that God has promised to be with his people, preserving them from both devils and apostasy.[9] To repeat: the Spirit of the Lord always has been, and always will be, with his people in striving toward truth and righteousness, and at Pentecost the churches were given a visible sign confirming the Lord's promise to guide his people in preaching the word of God to the nations. Surely, this promise included the understanding and transmission of God's moral law to all mankind? Surely, this oath included God's providential guidance through ancient persecutions and heresies, the rise of Christian culture, the divisions of Christendom, and every challenge of modern secular society?

For this reason, I believe it is prudent to review modern debates about sexual and marital ethics in light of church tradition, as well as to consider some former doctrinal confessions and ethical controversies that are seldom discussed today. Whenever and wherever there has been consensus regarding the teachings, morals, and ceremonies of Christian marriage, it can be assumed that the Lord has spoken to his people and all mankind alike. In such circumstances, it would not only be divisive but almost schismatic to separate oneself from the settled beliefs of the people of God. Such self-segregation would be particularly egregious if Christians in past ages lived far more righteously in marital and sexual

---

8. As one instance, John Calvin objected that the heretic Michael Servetus dared to "repudiate as absurd all that was taught by the Fathers ever since the Apostolic Age itself, and accepted by all believers all down the course of the ages." John Calvin, *Concerning Scandals*, trans. John W. Fraser (Grand Rapids, Michigan: William B. Eerdmans Publishing Company, 1978), 66.
9. John 14:26.

matters than modern believers do, which seems to be the case. Far too many contemporary believers justify unbiblical preferences while categorically insisting that every major thinker from Clement of Alexandria to Charles Hodge has been misguided or mistaken. Such pride of life and disdain for the past is the hallmark of the modern mind, and one of the reasons that our world has stumbled into great sin. In contrast, the humble turn to others for guidance, even collecting the sayings of earlier believers as the "embedded nails—given by One Shepherd," referred to by Solomon.[10] And while I personally am not as humble as God calls me to be, I will, nevertheless, dare to collect the insight of the people of the Lord into one book and share it for the contemporary reader's use.

We must remember how Scripture was formed: that the Old and New Testaments were written and collected over extended periods. The Hebrew Scriptures required nearly a thousand years to complete; the New Testament took around fifty years to write, and even longer to gather into its authoritative form. Given the Lord's patient manner of compiling Scripture through many generations, there is no reason to doubt that he brings forth the fullest understanding of his ways over decades and centuries. Consequently, the tradition of the churches should not be set against Scripture as a rival authority but must be seen as the living work of the Lord who breathed into life both Scripture and his people's obedience to his word. While the Christian tradition is filled with sins and errors (just as each individual Christian sins daily), and neither the people of God nor their principal spokesmen speak with inerrant authority, neither is the work of God among mankind a mere collection of fables like Edith Hamilton's *Mythology* or any ancient compendium of pagan lore. Instead, it is the account of a holy God using sinful men and women to build his kingdom, thereby revealing his goodness, power, and grace for all to receive and enjoy.[11]

It will be worthwhile, then, to examine the traditions of the church in the framing of marital and sexual ethics, trying to glean from the past insight about morality and immorality alike. This seems doubly necessary when we remember how the repudiation of conventional moral standards by church liberals and modern atheists has corresponded to the decline of sexual chastity and familial harmony. The beliefs and opinions

---

10. Ecclesiastes 12:11 (ESV).
11. Edith Hamilton, *Mythology: Timeless Tales of Gods and Heroes* (New York: Black Dog and Leventhal Publishers, 1942).

of the past do not (and never will) exist on par with Holy Writ, for Scripture alone binds consciences and churches alike. Yet, both the Old and New Testaments present true religion as a body of truths that must be protected against innovations in doctrine and practice. The Old Testament prophesies a Messiah, and the New Testament testifies to Christ as the promised Messiah. Anything and anyone after this is antichrist and deception, whether adding new books to Scripture, removing controversial elements of the Bible, improperly translating God's word, or reinterpreting that to which the church has testified.

In this spirit, the Bible warns believers to hold fast to revealed truths about the Triune God and to live the virtuous life he has ordained. However, ideas of marriage, sex, and love honored and accepted by the Christian tradition for two millennia are being swept away in an orgy of lawless hedonism. False teaching and impious living have so overcome the church during recent decades that even Christian youth seldom marry without prior sexual sin, and believing couples make unbiblical divorces. Like the Israelites of old, modern Christians have rejected the Lord's law and stand in danger of judgment if God does not have mercy on us with reformation, renewal, and revival. As the apostle John warned near the end of Revelation, believers must hold fast to God's word. This includes not only the prophecies given to John in his vision of the apocalypse but also to all of Scripture and the divine law:

> *Blessed is the one who reads aloud the words of this prophecy, and blessed are those who hear, and who keep what is written in it, for the time is near... I warn everyone who hears the words of the prophecy of this book: if anyone adds to them, God will add to him the plagues described in this book, and if anyone takes away from the words of the book of this prophecy, God will take away his share in the tree of life and in the holy city, which are described in this book.* [12]

---

12. Revelation 1:3, 22:18–19 (ESV).

2

MANKIND AND MARRIAGE IN THE IMAGE OF GOD

We must, therefore, say that in man there exists the image of God, both as regards the Divine Nature and as regards the Trinity of Persons; for also in God Himself there is one Nature in Three Persons.[1]

> *So God created man in his own image,*
> *in the image of God he created him;*
> *male and female he created them.*[2]

MANKIND WAS MADE in the image of God. When people look at fellow human beings, whether little babies or mature adults, they see a creature unlike any mere animal. Humanity mirrors the glory of the eternal God in a way dogs and dolphins (among the most human-like animals) do not. What does this mean? How exactly does the human race resemble the eternal God? This core reality must be understood if marriage is not to be misunderstood or misused. And since the household is a feature of human nature that mirrors the likeness of God, family life must be governed by a clear understanding of what it means for

---

1. Thomas Aquinas, *The Summa Theologica*, vol. 1, trans. Daniel J. Sullivan (Chicago: Encyclopedia Britannica, Inc. and William Benton, 1952), 495.
2. Genesis 1:27 (ESV).

mankind to be made in the divine image. Moreover, because God is Spirit, it is certain that the image of God does not refer to a person's physical size or shape but to invisible qualities of personality and character that separate human nature (and family life) from the amoral baseness of animal sexuality. It is not in its biological origins that family life resembles the nature of God, but in qualities more enduring than temporal life.

God is a living being overflowing with infinite personality, reason, will, purpose, presence, emotion, goodness, holiness, and love. For that reason, for the sake of his own essence, God does not create anything (or anyone) inconsistent with his morally perfect purposes but governs everything according to his righteous and eternal plan. The Lord is utterly transcendent, omnipresent, omniscient, omnipotent, immutable, infinite, and ineffable (i.e., unknowable unless he chooses to reveal himself). Every divine act is part of an eternal design, with even moral and physical evil used by God to bring forth a greater good for the evildoer and the innocent alike. This is the glory of the crucifixion of Christ, through which God used the most evil act of mankind to establish infinite perfection and ultimate joy. When God used the ignorant and evil purposes of Jewish and Roman authorities to crucify Jesus, the Lord was making everything conform to his will, although without compromising himself with the wickedness of this world. Each of us was involved in that great evil, for we are the evildoers represented by those who conducted an illegal Jewish trial and implemented an unjust Roman execution, and we are the people for whose sins Christ was put to death. Nevertheless, what mankind did with evil intent (to kill God and human righteousness), the Lord used to atone for sin and resurrect spiritually dead mankind.

This is difficult for many people to understand or accept. How, some argue, can a good God bring forth his purposes by the unjust actions of sinners? A good answer can be found by comparing God's providence to the actions of human government. During the American Civil War, Abraham Lincoln's federal government enlisted and drafted both dedicated abolitionists and racial bigots to fight slavery; there were Union soldiers who cursed both slaves and abolitionists as they sacrificed their lives for the anti-slavery cause. Yet, the edicts and constitutional amendments abolishing servitude in the United States were compromised neither by the vileness of men who put them into effect by pen and sword nor by the revisionism of modern activists and historians—with the righteous objective of emancipation achieved (albeit imperfectly in a world of fallen men) despite bad intentions being found on both sides of the Mason-Dixon line. Just as President Lincoln could use bigots and evil men for good purposes, so, too, the Lord makes everything in creation conform to his eternal justice, for the Lord is not weaker than Abraham Lincoln. In his *Second Inaugural Address,* Lincoln himself acknowledged how he and the Union cause were mere instruments in the hands of God Almighty for divine punishment of the injustice of tolerating slavery.[3]

Not only is God purposeful, but he is loving and good. It is not misery that comes from the hand of the Lord, but joy. It is not death that God ordains, but life. It is not evil that the Lord establishes, but goodness. At the final judgment, the wisdom of God's actions will be proven right, although it is already demonstrable in this life that the Lord is good. For example, God not only preserves the life of sinful mankind but does so with food that is enjoyable to eat. The Lord also clothes mountains and forests with beauty and ordains the delights of human love, as well as the strength of honorable men and the grace of beautiful women. Everything we celebrate as good, happy, or beautiful comes as a gift from God. Because the Lord is the one who created this world and continues to fill it with beauty and delight, we must remember two important facts. First, God's goodness endures despite human sin. Neither demon nor sinful man can make God suffer or prevent him from bringing good to the sons and daughters of mankind. Second, although our immutable and eternal Creator is himself unaffected by human evil, the Lord is not a distant ruler unconcerned with the fate of his handiwork. Christ revealed how God grieves over the fate of unrepentant sinners, even as he ordains their judgment. As Jesus said of Jerusalem, the city whose people would be scattered for unjustly crucifying the Son of Man, so God feels for every nation, tribe, and race. We see this in the lamentation that our Lord cried out for the very city soon to murder him:

Jerusalem, Jerusalem, who kills the prophets and stones those who are sent to her! How often I wanted to gather your children

---

3. Per the *Wikipedia,* Lincoln's *Second Inaugural Address* declares: "If we shall suppose that American slavery is one of those offenses which, in the providence of God, must needs come, but which, having continued through His appointed time, He now wills to remove, and that He gives to both North and South this terrible war as the woe due to those by whom the offense came... fervently do we pray, that this mighty scourge of war may speedily pass away. Yet, if God wills that it continue until all the wealth piled by the bondsman's two hundred and fifty years of unrequited toil shall be sunk, and until every drop of blood drawn with the lash shall be paid by another drawn with the sword... still it must be said 'the judgments of the Lord are true and righteous altogether.'"

together, the way a hen gathers her chicks under her wings, and you were not willing![4]

These are not the cries of a distant father but the pleas of a lover and husband begging his unfaithful wife to return to her own house and children. The mourning of Jesus over the fate of the very people who would soon strike him dead shows how the Lord loves and suffers with those who grieve and mourn, for whatever reason. Dare we imagine that he who knows all things can see the depth of our sorrows and remain aloof and unaffected? Heaven forbid. Human sentiment was created to reflect the reality of God's deep emotions. Because the feelings of mankind (for joy and sorrow) were made as windows into the heart of God, it is not only permissible but even desirable for men and women to respond to one another, as well as to their own joys and troubles, with deep emotions. The sheer delight that a mother feels for her baby is godlike, and so is the raging jealousy a man feels for his unfaithful bride. From a biblical perspective, those who scorn the joys and sorrows of life as if they stood above the human fray are unbiblical and almost inhuman. While many philosophers have attempted to drive mankind toward a passionless ideal of stoic behavior, equally unmoved by life and death, this is wrong. As John Calvin once observed, mankind is made in the image of a passionate God, not in the image of an unfeeling stone.[5]

Human sexuality—the creation of mankind as man and woman distinct from each other and reunited as one flesh—is made to reflect the burning passion of the Lord. People do not mate mechanically or unemotionally (as do many less human-like animals). It is not by mistake that God compares his love for the godly with the jealous love of a husband. Nor is it a mere coincidence that God's greatest act of love, namely the crucifixion of Christ, traditionally has been called *the Passion*. The Son of God suffered in body and soul to redeem fallen humanity, showing that

---

4. Matthew 23:37–38 (NASB).
5. John Calvin wrote: "[To patiently] bear the cross is not to be utterly stupefied and to be deprived of all feeling of pain. It is not as the Stoics of old foolishly described 'the great-souled man': one who, having cast off all human qualities, was affected equally by adversity and prosperity, by sad times and happy ones—nay, who like a stone was not affected at all... Now, among Christians there are also new Stoics, who count it depraved not only to groan and weep but also to be sad and care ridden... We have nothing to do with this iron philosophy which our Lord and Master has condemned, [for] he groaned and wept both over his own and others' misfortunes." John Calvin, *Institutes of the Christian Religion*, vol. 1, ed. John T. McNeil, trans. Lewis Ford Battles (Philadelphia: Westminster Press, 1960), 709.

God's love is not detached or abstract but deeply emotional and intense. Ancient and medieval Christian thinkers sometimes idealized a sexual passion lacking in ardor, arguing that (before human sin) the first couple controlled their sexual passion like any other member of the body: by intellect and will. Insofar as they are struggling against the uncontrolled lusts found in fallen mankind, they were both right and insightful (the older I grow, the more convincing I find the pessimism of Augustine regarding human sinfulness and concupiscence). But to suggest that unfallen man would have approached unfallen woman without deep desire, as if sexual intimacy would have been as passionless as bending a finger, is to forget the deep love of God for his church and each one of us born into his church—a love beyond human reason. Moreover, the Lord conceived each of his eternal children as a planned person from his infinite passion and immeasurable joy for our life and existence.

This is not to celebrate unthinking feelings or blind lust as often is done today. Nor do the Scriptures reveal a pop psychology ethos. As noted before, God is purposeful and rational: even the joy of God is directed by his mind as much as his will is inspired by his heart. This is why men and women should no more celebrate unreasoned emotions than they should indulge in unemotional reasoning. To be made in the image of God is to have both a heart and a mind. It is also to have a will, which means not only that human beings should imitate God by choosing to live as God has life in himself, but also that men and women must choose to live in accord with the perfect moral character of God. In fact, humanity's moral nature is our most distinctively human attribute. Although beasts may think and feel, they do not differentiate good from evil. Nor do they attain spiritual intensity that transcends the cold logic of a math equation. In fact, when the first human couple, Adam and Eve, were tested in the Garden of Eden, it was their morality that was put to the test. It was through their ethical choices that they were to respect or reject the image of God, thereby bringing blessing or curse upon themselves and their descendants. All men and women and boys and girls are called to do the same: to love God and do what is right for ourselves and our heirs.

Yet another feature of mankind's divine likeness is that people resemble God in creating beauty and life in this world. While this includes human arts and industry, this trait particularly refers to the begetting of sons and daughters in human likeness. Just as human beings are made to resemble God, so they are enabled by God to beget sons and daughters to resemble themselves. Many psychologists and philosophers throughout the ages (and not a few politicians and activists today) have wondered why people seek parenthood, particularly since few men or women procreate from an abstract sense of social or biological duty in the manner that they pay taxes or submit to an administrative process. The human heart runs deeper than blind appetite and conscious reasoning in our desire for new life. Aristotle, for instance, believed that men sought to have sons to achieve a type of immortality for themselves.[6] Is this true? Is humanity driven to parenthood from our fear of mortality? Is it in their offspring that human beings find life after death? Probably not.

What the Scriptures teach is that mankind was called to procreate even *before* humanity was subjected to the penalty of death.[7] Mankind reproduces in imitation of the life-giving qualities of the Lord, and an essential part of bearing God's image is to possess sufficient love and grace to reproduce life by assuming the joys and risks of parenthood, just as the immutable God brought joy and sorrow to himself in some inexplicable manner through his creation of soon-to-fall mankind. It is not in scripted reality television productions or nostalgic sitcoms that we see men and women best reflect the glory of God, but in taking chances, making dares, and knowingly accepting the tribulations of parenthood (while working to repair and redeem resulting sins and sorrows)—just as omniscient God chose to give life to mankind in full awareness of every evil that we would choose. Human parents are called to reflect God's image by loving other people (even non-existent and unknown others) enough to share love and life in the hope of eternal joy. In the book of Genesis, Moses used the same words to describe God's creation of humanity and humanity's creation of other humans. Moses wrote:

> *When God created man, he made him in the likeness of God. Male and female he created them, and he blessed them and named them Man when they were created. When Adam had lived 130*

---

6. Aristotle, "Politics" (Book 1: Chapter 2), in Richard McKeon, ed., *The Basic Works of Aristotle* (New York: Random House, 1941), 1127–1128.

7. Peter Lombard explored what sexual intimacy and parenthood might have been like had mankind not sinned. Peter Lombard, *The Sentences, Book 2: On Creation*, trans. Giulio Silano (Toronto: Pontifical Institute of Medieval Studies, 2008), 86–92 (Distinction XX). C.S. Lewis does likewise in his novel *Perelandra*. See C.S. Lewis, *Perelandra* (New York: Scribner Classics, 1974).

*years, he fathered a son in his own likeness, after his own image,
and named him Seth.*[8]

Finally, God is Triune. Although the Lord is one being, with a single
unchanging will, mind, and heart, he is also three persons, coequal in the
divine nature. Father, Son, and Holy Spirit are not three gods but One,
and there is no more division in God than in any normal human mind. It
is the demon-possessed and the schizophrenic who are divided into separate personalities (although these retain a single soul); healthy people
experience life with one mind, one heart, and one conscience. Likewise,
the Lord God is one being, yet three persons who share that divine nature
completely. This is a profound mystery to finite and flawed man, for it
reveals the essential nature of the infinite God, who is vaster and greater
than all things of the universe added together and multiplied by themselves without end.[9] The Lord exceeds our mathematical equations and
logical formulas, even as he has revealed something profoundly true of
himself to us. We see a reflection of this in the reality of human social life,
wherein people live both as individuals and as part of differentiated
communities. Our very name itself reminds us that we are all of common
stock, regardless of our particular differences. Multiple men are *mankind*
or *humanity* in a way that several dogs do not seem to compose *dogkind*.
And each person stands alone as a representative of humanity, rightly
called *man* by himself. As the Lord God is three in one, humanity is one
from many. In this, man reflects the glory of the Trinity.

Among our differences, none is more important than God's creation
of the two sexes. It was as male and female that mankind was created in
God's image.[10] As we see in the book of Genesis, man and woman were
made together in the image of God. Even in paradise, man was incomplete and alone without woman, and woman was made to live in the love
of man. That is, they were created from the outset to be both different
and together, equal representatives of human nature. Man was not made

---

8. Genesis 5:1–3 (ESV).
9. Peter Kreeft wrote: "Because we are made in God's image, our love images his. Thus, a
mother and a father love a baby into existence by giving themselves to each. This is an image
of the Father and the Son loving each other so fully that the Holy Spirit proceeds from their
union. The common feature is that a third person comes from the love of two other
persons. The difference is that with a human family, the process has a before-and-after
sequence in time... But the likeness is as real as the difference." Peter Kreeft, *The God Who
Loves You* (Ann Arbor, Michigan: Servant Books, 1988), 80.
10. Genesis 1:27 (ESV); Genesis 2:20-24 (ESV).

to be by himself, and woman was not made to be independent of man. Only united in holy love and joyful delight do men and women fully represent the divine image.

Historically, this divine mandate was often thwarted by those who considered men as the reflection of God's glory and women as lesser, imperfect, or even flawed copies. Today, the divine mandate is rejected by those who would make women their own masters and mistresses by seeking their fullness of life within the sphere of women alone. Neither of these positions reflects the biblical understanding, which emphasizes that God completed his creation of mankind only when the life of woman was separated from man, then reunited with man in holy love. Moreover, this reality is not simply for the married, but is true of all relationships between the differing sexes: brothers and sisters in the family, men and women working together, and boys and girls on the playground. Even those who never marry or live in strict segregation of the sexes live within a broader framework of sexual differentiation. One author noted:

> *Whether within marriage or outside of it, this distinction in unity [of man and woman] forms an integral and inescapable part of human reality. It denotes the broader relation of the sexes in which no male can exist without the female and no female without the male... God has made sexuality in this wider sense an essential element in being human. No one can escape it.*[11]

Not only must we rejoice in God's work in making mankind both male and female, but we must be thankful that the Lord individually made each of us as man or woman. It is a great blessing that we are called to enjoy being who we ourselves are—never required (or permitted) to be another sex, nationality, ethnicity, class, generation, or individual.[12] I can rejoice in being a grown man (and having once been a mud-covered boy playing in a Midwest woods) while my wife equally can celebrate having been a quiet little girl who is now the mother of four grown children and

---

11. Geoffrey W. Bromiley, *God and Marriage* (Grand Rapids, Michigan: William B. Eerdmans Publishing Company, 1980), 2.
12. Herman Bavinck wrote: "No one [may] despise this sexual difference, either within one's own identity or in that of another person. It has been willed by God and grounded in nature. [God] is the sovereign Designer of sex; men and women have God to thank [for] their different sexes and natures." Herman Bavinck, *The Christian Family*, trans. Nelson D. Kloosterman (Grand Rapids, Michigan: Christian's Library Press, 2012), 5.

a grandmother of two (at present). We are individually and together who the Lord made us to be, and for this we are grateful. This means that neither of us can expect the other to be anyone other than who God has made them to be. We dare not confuse our natures or demand that one become more like the other (except in better reflecting the image of the Triune God who made us man and woman). Is it not a type of unnatural desire for a husband to enjoy his wife's physical beauty but wish for her to think like a man? Or for a wife to enjoy the strength of her husband's physical love, but expect him to be as soft as a little girl? Our minds and bodies are intertwined, and they separate man from woman and woman from man until the two sexes come together in human society (whether as a single household or a great civilization) as surely as husband and wife are joined together as one flesh through sexual intimacy.

No social relationship reflects the divine nature of the Triune God more than marriage and family life. The very names for household relationships mirror those of the Triune God, namely Father and Son. This is no accident, as if the Lord searched his creation for a randomly evolved analogy to reveal himself, like a poet scouring a thesaurus for a word he does not yet know. Rather, the Lord created this world to reflect his nature, intentionally designing fatherhood and sonship to demonstrate something of the relationship of the first and second persons of the Trinity.[13] Moreover, marriage was also made to foreshadow the eternal union of Christ to his bride, the church. In the book of Ephesians, the apostle Paul declared how marriage is a pattern of how Christ pledged—or rather, pledges—to love his people for eternity. Therefore, as husbands and wives (and parents and children) serve each other with humility and charity, they imitate and reveal the eternal qualities of the Triune God.[14]

---

13. One modern theologian wrote: "The Father, as the fount of deity, eternally begets the Son. Differentiated or ordered equality again characterizes the relationship which serves as a further model for the relation between man and woman (and husband and wife)." Geoffrey W. Bromiley, *God and Marriage*, 72.

14. Saint Augustine warned against misusing Trinitarian analogies, writing in Book 12:4 of *On the Trinity*: "They do not seem to me to advance a probable opinion, who lay it down that a trinity of the image of God in three persons, so far as regards human nature, can be discovered and completed in the marriage of male and female and in their offspring; in that the man himself, as it were, indicates the person of the Father, but that which has so proceeded from him as to be born, that of the Son; and so the third person as of the Spirit, is, they say, the woman, who has so proceeded from the man as not herself to be either son or daughter, although it was by her conception that the offspring was born." Whitney J. Oates, ed., Augustine, *Basic Writings of Saint Augustine*, vol. 2 (Grand Rapids, Michigan: Baker Book House, 1980), 810.

Fathers and sons reflect the essence of the divine nature, while husbands and wives embody the enduring love that the Lord has for his people. It is for such eternal ends that the family has been made, bringing forth a far greater harvest of goodness than even the intimacy of marital love and the fertility of the nuptial bed.

And, I must add, this love is far greater than duty and obligation, for it includes deep and abiding joy. The love of groom for bride, husband for wife, parent for child, and brother for sister is not simply a matter of duty or mutual assistance, but (in the appropriate manner) includes enjoyment, pleasure, fun, merriment, laughter, and everything else that makes life worthwhile. For different cultures, this joy may look different. In one society, people may make music together, and in another, they may play games on a weekend night. For one family, laughter may be the teasing between brother and sister, and for another, it may be a fierce (yet friendly) basketball competition between cousins. Such differences are inconsequential in themselves, for what matters is that family life includes such profound joy that the Christian household is not simply a rightful place to exercise piety but also the deep desire of those who do not believe—who wish their practices and perspectives would lead to the ordered joy of the godly Christian home, that they might be included in the blessings of God. However, Scripture is clear that God's blessing comes from reflecting his glorious image, and family life must reflect the joy of the holy Trinity. As one modern book has observed:

> *Genesis 1 also indicates that the family was designed to be the clearest demonstration of what is meant by the expression the image of God. Here we need to be careful. Each individual man and woman is the image of God in that each is a person... [but] God's personality cannot be considered apart from his diversity; three persons constitute the one true God.*[15]

---

15. Ranald Macaulay and Jerram Barrs, *Being Human: The Nature of Spiritual Experience* (Downer's Grove, Illinois: Inter-Varsity Press, 1978), 171.

3

THE LAW OF LOVE

If the supreme Spirit loves himself, no doubt the Father loves himself, the Son loves himself, and the one the other; since the Father separately is the supreme Spirit, and the Son separately is the supreme Spirit, and both at once one Spirit. And since each equally remembers himself and the other, and conceives equally of himself and the other, and since what is loved, or loves in the Father, or in the Son, is altogether the same, necessarily each loves himself and the other with an equal love.[1]

BECAUSE MEN and women are made in the likeness of God, they are created to give and receive love. For this reason, it is as essential for the heart to love and be loved as it is for the stomach to be filled with food and the lungs to breathe air—even more so. But what is love, and where does it come from? This is one of the most profound questions of human existence, and how it is answered will shape many of the most critical decisions in human life. A man who mistakes sexual passion for love will seduce (and abandon) as many lovers as he can to satisfy the desires that drive him; a woman who believes that love is dependent on flowers and candlelight dinners will seek endless romance; and saints who

---

1. Anselm of Canterbury, "Monologium," in *St. Anselm: Basic Writings*, trans. S. N. Deane (La Salle, Illinois: Open Court Publishing Company, 1962), 160–161.

believe that love requires charitable service will lay down their lives in sacrifice and martyrdom. Whatever a person believes about love ultimately determines how he or she will behave in establishing and maintaining that quality. Definitions matter, just as the apostle John taught when he inspired early Christians to love with the following command: "Beloved, let us love one another, for love is from God... God is love."[2]

God has neither body nor physical passion, yet experiences and expresses absolute love. While animals have bodies and sexual desires, they cannot love in the ultimate sense, which is critical to remember since much modern thought conflates love with sexual passion. Still, the fact that the two qualities are utterly distinct can be recognized from the reality that the incorporeal God loves, while corporeal animals do not. As for mankind, a man can possess the bed of a woman he does not care for, and a woman may endure carnal union with a man she loathes. What else are prostitution and rape? In contrast, affectionate husbands sometimes refrain from intimate embraces with their wives to ensure the well-being of their beloved (as with cancer patients), and many of the strongest bonds of human love entirely lack sexual intimacy (such as parent and child, brother and sister, friend and friend). Likewise, love in heaven will be without a sexual component if Christ's words, "in the resurrection they neither marry nor are given in marriage," are to be understood in their most obvious and literal sense—that is, if Jesus intended prophetically to reveal rather than prophetically to conceal.[3]

The point is this: no one should confuse what delights the eyes, pleases the senses, or satisfies sensual needs with what is truly divine in origin, for the love that comes from God is eternal and will exist when mortal marriage is no more. No matter how scientific or sophisticated it may seem to believe that love is based on man's animal nature and social needs, such reasoning stands in stark contrast to the teachings of Scripture: that real human love comes from God and reflects his eternal nature rather than temporal needs and desires. Love is the quality through which mankind was made and through which we are called to enjoy God. Medieval theologian Bernard of Clairvaux (one of the great teachers regarding Christian charity) rightly noted that love is a spiritual quality that flows from and is nourished by the Lord himself. Although God is Spirit without sexual need or selfish desire, he is the fount of every act of

---

2. 1 John 4:7–8 (NASB).
3. Matthew 22:30 (NASB).

love and kindness that has ever blessed or ever will bless creation. Bernard
of Clairvaux observed:

> *[Love] comes from a noble family. Indeed its birth is of God. There
> it is born, there it is nourished, and there it grows… Love is given by
> God alone, and love continues to exist in Him. Love is due to no one
> else but to God and for God.*[4]

Because real love flows from the mind and will of a perfect and
harmonious God, it never conflicts with equally divine attributes such as
holiness and moral purity. This is crucial to remember, as modern culture
often divorces the law of love from the letter of the moral law. In this
spirit, 1960s situation ethics advocate Joseph Fletcher attempted to navigate his way between hedonistic mores and moral absolutes by positing
that love should not be confused with either legalism or self-indulgence.
While objecting to the notion that codes of justice (such as the Ten
Commandments) are absolutely binding at all times, Fletcher simultaneously did not want people to act like moral swine in their behavior. What
Fletcher posited is that the duty to love is mankind's only governing law
and that works of love are best judged within a specific situation rather
than by transcendent codes of ethics. To that end, Fletcher claimed
people must be prepared to set aside traditional moral codes "in the situation," if love seems better served by doing so. Even marital infidelity
might be justified, Fletcher posited, if an adulterer acts from a loving
disposition.[5]

What Fletcher failed to consider is how biblical love differs from mere
motive and good intent. From the biblical optic, love is not a feeling but a
standard of behavior with specific obligations and duties that remain
fixed and defined. John recorded in his gospel how the apostles received
from Jesus (on the eve of our Lord's passion and crucifixion), teaching
that only those who possess and obey Christ's commandments truly love
him. Similarly, inspired by God's Spirit, John taught the same many
decades later when he wrote that we have come to know God "if we keep
His commandments."[6] Placing these words in the context of a self-giving

4.   Bernard of Clairvaux, *The Love of God and Spiritual Friendship*, ed. James M. Houston
(Portland, Oregon: Multnomah Press, 1983), 64.
5.   Joseph Fletcher, *Situation Ethics: The New Morality* (Philadelphia: Westminster Press,
1966), 26.
6.   John 14:21 (NASB); 1 John 2:3 (NASB).

sacrifice that Jesus himself prayed to avoid (if possible) makes clear how love reflects moral characteristics and obligations rather than emotional intent and feelings. Love and moral rectitude come from the same God.

Joseph Fletcher, like many modern people, contrasted love with duty. Such a divorce of love from law is a perversion of what otherwise remains a valid consideration: that real love is joyful and springs from the heart rather than from slavish fear or unfeeling obligation. The apostle John taught that love shows no fear because "perfect love casts out fear, because fear involves punishment, and the one who fears is not perfected in love." The entire New Testament reveals how our love for God must be distinguished from the terrified impulses prevalent in pagan religion. God's people must trust rather than dread him; we are called to have songs in our hearts while serving the Lord (and one another). Like devoted children, we must love our heavenly father as well as obey him, and we must love our brothers and sisters in the same spirit. Indeed, the word *devotion* brings us to the reverent and willing dedication at the heart of biblical love. Just as men and women *devoted* sacrifices and gifts to the Lord in the Old Testament law, so, too, they now *devote* themselves to their wives and children, for Christ's sake. While *devotion* includes sacrifice and duty, it also contains pure passion and holy love.[7]

The very apostle who reminded believers that biblical love is joyful and law-abiding rather than fearful or lawless also recorded a rebuke by Jesus of an unloving, yet otherwise obedient, Christian congregation. In his revelation to the church in Ephesus, John observed how disappointed and angry Jesus was with those believers who were serving him from a cold formality—who obeyed his teachings on the surface, but did not love God from the depths of their heart and soul. These professed believers did not offer to the Lord joyful and willing service in gratitude for the new life Christ provided to them when he gave his own life on the cross. Jesus judged such unloving, so-called obedience to be disobedience requiring repentance. To repeat: even congregants following the teachings and implementing the specific moral and doctrinal instructions of Scripture regarding church life were warned that they must serve the Lord with joyful passion and zealous love rather than pursue piety in cold formality. Christ specifically called (and still calls) such churches and

---

7. 1 John 4:18 (NASB). Leviticus 27:28 (ESV) reads: "But no devoted thing that a man devotes to the LORD of anything that he has, whether man or beast, or of his inherited field, shall be sold or redeemed; every devoted thing is most holy to the LORD."

believers to repent with the language of a man chastising his bride for having lost her initial passion for her husband. Jesus said:

> *I know your works, your toil and your patient endurance, and how you cannot bear with those who are evil... I know you are enduring patiently and bearing up for my name's sake, and you have not grown weary. But I have this against you, that you have abandoned the love you had at first.*[8]

The Old Testament likewise stressed this point, with Hebrew prophets warning God's people to return to their first love—the Lord God. That is to say, God wills to be a husband and father to human beings, not an oriental despot before whom his subjects bow in abject terror. The laments and praises of the Psalms make it clear how the law of God must be obeyed with a sincere heart, and the words of Moses commanded men to obey the Lord from love rather than from abject fear. Moses warned believers to love the Lord God "with all your heart and with all your soul and with all your might." The second commandment of the Decalogue specifically declared that to love God is to obey his commandments. Because the believer is called to have a heart that is zealous and devoted to God, a merely formal obedience is no more acceptable than a wife's frigid fulfillment of marital passion. Is any husband happy with a wife who meets his sexual needs without emotion or affection, with pro forma duty? Do not teenage boys and unmarried men make sport of and fear marriage to such women? Nor will God accept external obedience any more than a man will delight in intimacy with a woman whose heart remains cold and uncaring. Love must come from the heart and should never be confused with grudging obedience to God's law; it remains far more than sentiment, feeling, or passion.[9]

In conclusion, men and women who wish to test the quality of their love must examine neither the intensity of emotion nor the strength of romantic and sexual desire, since these do not define love. Because love is

8. Revelation 2:2–4 (ESV).
9. Deuteronomy 6:5 (ESV); Exodus 20:6 (NASB). Francis Schaeffer noted how loving God involves obeying him. Schaeffer wrote: "Loving a superior is different from loving an equal. Take, for example, the love of a child for a parent. If a child constantly says, 'I love you,' and yet at the same time is constantly and openly disobedient, the parent can say, 'Your actions do not indicate your love.'" Francis Schaeffer, "Genesis in Space and Time," in Francis Schaeffer, *The Complete Works of Francis Schaeffer*, vol. 2 (Westchester, Illinois: Crossway Books, 1982), 48.

the attitude that reflects the good and self-giving character of the Triune God, the man who loves after the manner of God will do as God does, and the woman who loves as God will share in the Lord's charitable heart and righteous conduct. Nor has the Lord left the definition of real love to the selfish imaginations of the sinful human heart—whether great poet, profound philosopher, learned theologian, modest mechanic, or poor peasant. Rather, God has specifically defined the characteristics of real love. Inspired by the Holy Spirit, the apostle Paul described with perfect clarity the qualities of God-like love:

> *Love is patient and kind; love does not envy or boast; it is not arrogant or rude. It does not insist on its own way; it is not irritable or resentful; it does not rejoice at wrongdoing, but rejoices with the truth. Love bears all things, believes all things, hopes all things, endures all things.*[10]

---

10. 1 Corinthians 13:4–7 (ESV).

4

THE PURPOSES OF PURITY

Throughout the Ten Commandments we should consider, not just what we should do, but what God himself is, for he has set before us this mirror, namely the Ten Commandments, that we may learn of his nature and strive to be like him... Men are not to run about like beasts who know no difference between chastity and unchastity. God is a pure, chaste, orderly being, and wants us to acknowledge him as such; and while we cannot see him physically and may not embrace him physically, he nevertheless wants us to keep him in our hearts as a pure, chaste, orderly being and to distinguish him from all irrational, unprincipled, impure natures, from beasts, from devils, and from men.[1]

LOVE REFLECTS WHO GOD IS. Few doubt that God is gracious, generous, and kind. Still, it remains difficult for many modern men and women to understand how purity likewise reflects the Lord's eternal character. Although there are many reasons for this blindness, one of the more significant is that contemporary men and women generally base their ethics on mere utility—with the good act being that which brings pleasure rather than pain to the greatest number of people. As a result,

---

1. Philip Melanchthon, *Melanchthon on Christian Doctrine*, ed. Clyde Manschreck (New York: Oxford University Press, 1965), 100–101, 112.

while modern people might condemn deceit or coercion in pursuit of sexual gratification, rarely do they find fault with consensual sexual liaisons between adults. Why? Because they believe what is good is that which brings pleasure. Only when sex is abusive is physical intimacy anathematized in the modern world, and the fact that it might be unnatural or unclean is judged to be of little consequence.[2]

Contemporary people also seek to hide the sense of shame that comes from rejecting traditional morality, for morality and conscience are real and cannot be entirely suppressed. The slightest moral condemnation of abortion, homosexuality, and divorce stirs anger and opposition from those guilty of such sins (and their companions)—just as John the Baptist was persecuted by King Herod and the king's wife, Herodias, because John condemned their marriage as a violation of the Mosaic code.[3] To be clear: John was not preaching holy war, fostering political rebellion, or challenging Herod's secular authority in any manner, only preaching that the king was living in sin and under divine condemnation. For that prophetic message, the king and his wife silenced John before their consciences, compatriots, and subjects. For upholding the holiness of marriage, John the Baptist was martyred. We should note how God's law was considered binding for every man and woman in Israel, even a half-pagan ruler and his foreign wife.[4]

In striking contrast to the immorality of King Herod and many contemporary people, the Lord God is a holy and pure fire who consumes wickedness and faithlessness. In the Sermon on the Mount, Christ made it clear that ethical notions based on pain and pleasure are wrong when he revealed that men can be cast into eternal hell for the sin of one impure thought. A man who willfully wallows in desire for the wife of his neighbor will be forever damned, though neither his wife nor the desired woman suspected his unfaithful thoughts. The reason for

---

2. Pierre Viret likewise wrote: "For, just as [the Lord commands] righteous deeds [and forbids] wicked actions [that He might] reveal to us that He is of a pure and holy essence and nature who holds all vileness and wickedness in abomination, so He also does the same in this commandment in which He declares to us how much chastity pleases Him and how much all uncleanness displeases Him, which is as contradictory to His nature as chastity and purity are suitable to it." Pierre Viret, *Exposition of the Ten Commandments*, vol. 2, trans. R.A. Sheats (Monticello, Florida: Psalm 78 Ministries, 2020), 129.
3. Mark 6:18 (ESV).
4. Charlie Kirk was martyred as I completed the final draft of this book, and for the same reason as John the Baptist: for preaching God's holy law against abortion, transgenderism, and other moral sins. Sadly, the world has not changed since the days of Herod.

such strict holiness is that God expects humanity to reflect his moral splendor and to be his faithful bride, submitting to her divine husband in flesh and spirit. The Lord demands fidelity, modesty, and purity from the heart (as do husbands and wives). It is for this reason that sexual deeds and marital arrangements must not be called good because they are productive and pleasurable, but should be considered lawful pleasures only as they prove to be morally good. Holiness and purity matter, and Christ revealed how God will punish every hidden sinful act and thought. In the Sermon on the Mount, Jesus declared:

> You have heard that it was said, 'You shall not commit adultery.' But I say to you that everyone who looks at a woman with lustful intent has already committed adultery with her in his heart. If your right eye causes you to sin, tear it out and throw it away. For it is better that you lose one of your members than that your whole body be thrown into hell. And if your right hand causes you to sin, cut it off and throw it away. For it is better that you lose one of your members than that your whole body go to hell.[5]

Sexual purity—like other forms of human righteousness (such as truthfulness, justice, honesty, and reverence)—is one way in which human nature reflects the radiance and goodness of the Lord's eternal being. Just as God is love, so also he is righteousness and light, as the prophet Isaiah observed after seeing a vision of the Lord on his throne, with nearby angels declaring: "Holy, holy, holy, is the LORD of hosts; the whole earth is full of his glory!" Overwhelmed by God's moral splendor, the prophet Isaiah recognized and confessed his sin, and an angel revealed God's atonement for the prophet's sinful nature. In the New Testament, the holiness of the Lord likewise is so absolute that the same apostle who most forcefully spoke of God's love also emphasized the depths of the Lord's righteous character, writing: "God is Light, and in Him is no darkness at all."[6]

We must call to mind how the persons of the Trinity are ever perfect, faithful, and righteous in their relationship with one another, and that the orderly nature of the Triune God never changes or falls into corruption. The Son is eternally and immutably begotten of his Father, and the

---

5. Matthew 5:27–30 (ESV).
6. Isaiah 6:1–7 (ESV); 1 John 1:5 (NASB).

Father eternally begets his Son. Likewise, the Spirit of God proceeds perfectly from Father and Son. There is not the slightest hint either of change or disorder in the nature and character of God: the Lord is a perfect being whose infinite and eternal nature is a perfect manifestation of reason, order, goodness, beauty, and holiness. He is truth and purity, righteousness and love. Such are the very characteristics which the Lord has ordained human marriage and sexuality to express as he manifests his wisdom before the rulers and authorities of all creation in filling our world with love and life through the marital union of two different persons called to live according to his righteousness and love.

Many ancient pagans thought that mankind could imitate the gods by indulging in orgies and immorality, as the gods themselves were said to do. While pagans mistakenly fashioned their gods in the image of human lust, Christians do just the opposite: subordinating human sexual desire to piety by imitating the virtuous qualities of the eternal God. Christians believe that people reflect God's nature when they bring to light his invisible qualities through lawful use of the sexual appetite. When a man or woman treats other people modestly, faithfully, and charitably, he or she becomes as generous and fair-minded as the creator of all mankind. When men and women treat the plain and the attractive alike as their merits deserve, they imitate the Lord, who shows no favoritism, except to reward good and punish evil. And when human beings limit the expression of their passions to one lawful mate, they remind the world that God loves mankind selflessly, neither using human beings for selfish and obscene purposes (as the pagan gods were said to do) nor abandoning them as seducers do. The Lord remains faithful to his own.

For this reason, Christians are called to be perfectly chaste—they must use their bodies to reflect their Lord's perfect love and absolute purity. The apostle Paul warned believers how "sexual immorality and all impurity or covetousness must not even be named among you, as is proper among saints." Paul also wrote that Christians should engage in neither "filthiness nor foolish talk nor crude joking, which are out of place, but instead let there be thanksgiving."[7] Augustine of Hippo, consistent with the warnings of Christ, observed that purity is violated not only by the words of the mouth but also by the looks of the eyes. In the following quote, Augustine gets to the heart of sexual attraction,

---

7. Ephesians 5:3–4 (ESV).

which is revealed through stolen glances and secret thoughts as much as by open flirting and immoral acts. Augustine noted:

> *For it is not only by affectionate embraces that desire between man and woman is awakened, but also by looks. You cannot say that your inner attitude is good if with your eyes you desire to possess [a person], for the eye is the herald of the heart. And if people allow their impure intentions to appear, albeit without words but just by looking at each other, and finding pleasure in each other's passion, even though not in each other's arms, we cannot speak any longer of the true chastity which is precisely that of the heart.*[8]

Each person, therefore, is called to resemble God by living a life of ordered sexual purity. This means that brides and grooms must aspire to enter marriage sexually untouched whenever possible, and married couples should embrace each other only with holy passion. Still, chastity requires far more than external virginity or formal fidelity: it is a spiritual quality that goes beyond the sanctity of the flesh since it requires moral discipline to bring lustful thoughts and promiscuous desires under control. Eyes must be kept to the ground rather than on the spouses of others; clothing must be selected to express modesty rather than to stir sexual desire; the married must keep their bodies holy during inevitable periods of abstinence due to absence, menstruation, sickness, pregnancy, and prayer. Couples are not permitted to use the marriage bed to satisfy every desire that entices corrupted flesh. Instead, they must govern themselves by God's grace to fix their hearts on maintaining a pure and exclusive physical relationship with the one spouse whom the Lord has provided. The single likewise must refrain from coveting their neighbor's husband or wife (or son or daughter), and must treat every Christian with the modesty of a brother or sister unless called to the equally demanding requirements of holy marriage with that person.

When it is written in the New Testament that believers are sisters and brothers in the household of God, those labels are far more than arbitrary names; they are prophetic realities. Sexual appetite presumably no longer exists in heaven; and because the redeemed will become brothers and

---

8. Augustine of Hippo, *The Rule of Saint Augustine: Masculine and Feminine Versions*, ed. Tarscicius J. Van Bavel, trans. Raymond Canning (London: Darton, Longman, and Todd, 1984), 16, 30.

sisters as God's adopted children, they will no more look at each other in vile lust than brothers and sisters (even among the ungodly) do in this mortal life. In heaven, every man will rejoice in the perfect purity of women, and every woman will rejoice in the blazing righteousness of men. Life without marriage will bring greater joys, passions, and pleasures than marriage and sexual intimacy do in the present age. As Paul taught in his letter to the Corinthians: "No eye has seen, nor ear heard, nor the heart of man imagined, what God has prepared for those who love him."[9] While some religions promise a heaven filled with eternal marriage, pleasure-filled harems, or the swapping of wives, we may be thankful this is not our future, for the Lord has not made mankind to live forever in pagan polygamy, jihadist sensuality, or hippie-like promiscuity. He will not allow the lusts and lies of this world to taint his eternal kingdom. Rather, Jesus taught that heaven will be a place of absolute purity and unending righteousness, and we may prophetically attest to this holy joy by living modest and chaste lives. To that end, the Westminster Larger Catechism summarized the duties of purity:

> *The duties required in the seventh commandment are, chastity in body, mind, affections, words, and behavior; and the preservation of it in ourselves and others; watchfulness over the eyes and all the senses; temperance; keeping of chaste company; modesty in apparel; marriage by those that have not the gift of continence; conjugal love, and cohabitation; diligent labor in our callings; shunning all occasions of uncleanness, and resisting temptations thereunto.*[10]

---

9. 1 Corinthians 2:9 (ESV).
10. *The Larger Catechism of the Westminster Assembly* (Philadelphia: Presbyterian Board of Publication and Sabbath-School Work, 1912), 245–246.

5

THE DESIGN OF CREATION

To those, on the other hand, who under a pious cloak blaspheme by their continence both the creation and the holy Creator, the almighty, only God, and teach that one must reject marriage and begetting of children, and should not bring others in their place to live in this wretched world, nor give any sustenance to death, our reply is as follows. We may first quote the word of the apostle John: "And now are many antichrists come, whence we know that it is the last hour..." If it is the view of these people who themselves owe their existence to sexual relations that such relations are impure, must not they be impure? But I hold that even the seed of the sanctified is holy.[1]

WHEN THE LORD declared the world to be *very good* in the Garden of Eden, he pronounced his blessing on the work of his hands and revealed that his work was perfectly suited to accomplish its appointed ends. The Lord's creation is teeming with life and form rather than with emptiness and formlessness, and it is a world that matters: one that has deep and abiding spiritual significance. The Lord not only blessed what he initially created, but also what he would bring forth through replication and

---

1. Clement of Alexandria, "On Marriage," in *Alexandrian Christianity*, ed. John Ernest Leonard Oulton and Henry Chadwick (Philadelphia: Westminster Press, 1954), 61–62.

reproduction in a world flooded with new life and subject to constant change. God's original blessing was, however, on a world conforming to his moral will and eternal purposes—a world in which mankind was not yet subject to sin and death.

The structure of God's world can be seen in everything from the laws of physics to the unfolding of particular genetic codes. Everything the Lord does has purpose, since God does not create simply for something to do in his spare time: to play as a child might carelessly make a mud pie. Rather, the creation was fashioned before time was ordained in the mind of an immutable God to bring forth good that would flourish for a moment, then immortalize into eternity—for the Lord ordained a temporal order in which the most profound spiritual blessings would flow from the humblest physical beginnings, just as the human soul is born with a physical body and will exist for all eternity in conjunction with a resurrected body. Even the vastness of differences in the creation mirrors the infinite nature of the eternal God. When God pronounced the world *good*, he did not mean simply that life is pleasurable and enjoyable, but that the entire creation is woven together as a magnificent tapestry of flesh and spirit and holiness and love to bring forth the glory of God and the eternal glory of the creation itself.[2] What I mean is that our world is not *good* in the way that a woman looks good or a candy bar tastes good (though the world can be beautiful and enjoyable), but is *good* in the way that a *good* man sacrifices his life in war against an evil enemy or a *good* mother denies herself rest for the welfare of her children. The world is a tapestry for such God-like giving of self in sacrificial love.

Since, however, the human mind has been dulled by iniquity and ignorance, it is not always easy for us to see this truth. And because human evil has affected nature, it is not always possible to comprehend the ultimate good of the world in which we find ourselves. This is why Christians await an eternal salvation in which both mankind and nature will be redeemed from sin and its destructive effects.[3] Nevertheless, even the most unimaginative human being must see how physical reality frequently produces moral good, even in this marred and mortal life. As one example, when a man and woman marry, their hearts are entwined by the mingling of their flesh, and their union produces children as the couple changes from mere husband and wife to becoming parents,

---

2. Genesis 1:31 (ESV).
3. Romans 8:19.

building and strengthening their marital bonds as they create a far more selfless love than even the holy passions of wedlock. The mingling of physical bodies and sowing of seed produces a harvest of moral and spiritual fruit that lasts forever, both in the new children and in the growing maturity of parental love as parents learn to set aside their own enjoyments and interests to meet the needs of babbling and bawling babies (just as Christ submitted himself to service and suffering to save the foolish men and women we have become).

Few things are as marvelous as the body of a mother. Not only does a woman's body nurture and care for her child *in utero*, but as soon as the baby is delivered, she produces antibodies and milk to protect and feed her newborn child. The woman's very body is transformed (even consumed) to serve another person. Then, even as she gives her breasts to her baby for physical life and strength, she provides caresses and kisses that feed the little one's heart and mind. From her body and mind come life and love for the soul and flesh of her child. The whole life-giving quality of motherhood sometimes seems almost automatic, so deeply is it rooted in the biological realities of human life, but this is precisely why we must confess how the human body has been ordained by its Creator to produce a crop of charity and moral good, culminating in eternal joy. Centuries ago, Augustine of Hippo pointed out how our mortal natures signify something far greater than perishable flesh, writing:

> *All these things [are] to be enjoyed which we have described as being eternal and immutable; others are to be used so that we may be able to enjoy those. In the same way we who enjoy and use other things are things ourselves. A great thing is man, made in the image of God, not in that he is encased in a mortal body, but in that he excels the beasts in the dignity of a rational soul.*[4]

Scripture does not command a woman to nurse her babies, nor does the Bible explicitly prohibit a kindergartener from marrying. Still, just as the care of a child is considered a natural law of motherhood, so have theologians judged the marriages of children to be unnatural and immoral, basing their denunciations on the physical changes required by

---

4. Saint Augustine, *On Christian Doctrine*, trans. D. W. Robinson, Jr. (Upper Saddle River, New Jersey: Prentice Hall, 1958), 18.

puberty.[5] Using similar reasoning, theologians and other moralists have condemned various human practices, including the unnatural use of the marital bed, artificial forms of birth control, and household organization that fails to recognize the distinct natures of men and women. While the merits of particular arguments may be disputed, what cannot be denied is how Christian theologians have seldom hesitated to draw ethical prescriptions from natural functions. The realities of biology and the duties of ethics cannot be divorced entirely from one another—not if the Lord is the actual maker of both realms.

Two consequences follow. First, it becomes necessary to appeal to the evident purposes of nature to resolve some ethical disputes. On certain occasions, humans must make moral judgments based on how the human body functions. Second, we must remember that the *good* of human sexuality is not to be found in sensations and thrills of pleasure. Like the human soul, the human body was made to be a window into such intangible qualities as purity, fidelity, and charity. The highest purpose of the body is a moral one, as marriage is ultimately intended to demonstrate divine qualities that cannot be adequately revealed through purely spiritual beings like angels or unreasoning ones like birds. In mankind, flesh and spirit are ordained to work together to reveal the character and goodness of our Creator, which is revealed in the Incarnation of our Lord as human flesh. Just contemplating baby Jesus—*very God of very God*, as the Nicene Creed confesses—suckling at Mary's breasts in a stable in Bethlehem reveals the profound depth of God's love in a manner no sermon ever will. How could a dictionary define such divine humility, or a philosopher pontificate regarding eternal wisdom born into time? What treatise can stir the soul, or bring tears to the eyes, like a Christmas Eve singing of *What Child Is This?*

Of course, many modern thinkers separate biology and morality. Some do so by denying there are such qualities as absolute right and wrong, while others are even more subtle, and more dangerous, as they define mankind as an amoral animal rather than an eternal being—denying that a Creator has designed nature and arguing how it was shaped into its present form through random mutations rather than by

---

5. Medieval canon law allowed parents to arrange an engagement as early as age seven. Such engagements required subsequent ratification by the couple if their betrothal was to remain lawful. Church officials frequently defended the right of minors to later refuse marriages made against their wishes. See Raymond of Penyafort, *Summa on Marriage*, trans. Pierre Payer (Toronto: Pontifical Institute of Medieval Studies, 2005), 17, 22.

divine design. As such, such religious skeptics and doubters believe that the world of men and beasts reflects mere survival instincts rather than purposes more noble and enduring than mortal life. For such men and women, human marriage does not exist to reveal the spiritual nature of the Triune God; it is simply a more sophisticated version of what animals do behind bushes (or even in plain sight). It is a physical act unrelated to any transcendent, eternal, or moral purpose.

In the spirit of unbelief, Charles Darwin, the father of evolutionary thought, was quite explicit in reducing human love to the mating of beasts. He wrote that birds *court* each other, even as he described human marriage as mere *mating*, thereby inverting Victorian-era language about the meaning of marriage and denying distinctive human morality in the process. Moreover, in a system of thought in which sexual selection was the key to the entire paradigm, this was not an incidental mistake. While Darwin would have described himself as an observer of nature, I would observe that Darwin's primary error stemmed not from his keen observations regarding the natural order but from his dubious evaluation of human nature. He reduced mankind to a more sophisticated version of chimpanzees in heat and denied the transcendent and moral purposes that frame our hearts and souls. Darwin's thinking was more worldly than outright sexual immorality and promiscuity. Better a street prostitute or a *Playboy* pinup girl than the scientific obscenity of Darwin that descended men into beasts through its discussion of mating and morality.[6] No promiscuous girl born of faithless mankind ever defiled sexual morality more than the scientist who wrote the following:

> *[Reproduction] is strikingly the same in all mammals, from the first act of courtship by the male to the birth and nurturing of the young... There is no fundamental difference between man and the higher animals in their mental facilities... the difference in mind between man and the higher animals, great as it is, is certainly one of degree and not of kind.*[7]

---

6. This is not hyperbole. A woman selling herself on the street or the Internet might defile hundreds or even thousands of men, but Darwin's amorality has wrecked entire churches, cultures, countries, and civilizations. If the pinup girl is to be judged (as she will), so much the man whose amorality and unbelief first fathered and fostered her immorality.

7. Charles Darwin, *The Descent of Man and Selection in Relation to Sex* (Princeton, New Jersey: Princeton University Press, 1981), 13–14, 35, 105.

In contrast, when Christians seek to understand the meaning of marriage and sexuality, they confess how the world of flesh and blood is ordained to reveal the truths of the spiritual realm, and that morality and natural function are associated, given that a morally perfect Creator designed his creation to reveal his character and share in his goodness. As just one example, nothing in Scripture requires mothers to nurse their children: there is no such command in the Bible, only statements that attest to the naturalness of maternal love. Nevertheless, the idea of using a surrogate nurse (a wet nurse) for convenience rather than necessity seems contrary to good motherhood and has been condemned by Christian teachers throughout the generations—just like mothers leaving their children with strangers so they can party with friends.[8] While correcting some of his congregants who had deserted their elderly parents, Ambrose of Milan portrayed the natural love of mother for child, explaining how the most dutiful and devoted among his listeners had not yet repaid their aged mothers for the challenges and suffering the women endured when their children were infants. Ambrose declared:

> *[Congregants have not repaid] the nourishment which [their mother] gave with tender compassion, milking her breast into your lips; ye have not recompensed the hunger which she bore for you, lest she eat something which would be harmful to you, lest she drink something which would poison her milk.*[9]

It is the same in Scripture: natural realities are praised and exalted more than commanded. As noted, there is no commandment for a

---

8. Valerie Fildes observed how medieval and early modern physicians and preachers commonly objected to the use of wet nurses, with Puritan preachers urging women to "feed their own babies because it was a duty to their children and to God." Per Fildes, some medieval preachers also complained of women "too delicate or too haughty" to endure the inconveniences of nursing, as well as rich ladies who "scorn to suckle" their own infants. Valerie Fildes, *Wet Nursing: A History from Antiquity to the Present* (Oxford: Basil Blackwell, 1988), 42, 68; Valerie Fildes, *Breasts, Bottles, and Babies: A History of Infant Feeding* (Edinburgh: Edinburgh University Press, 1986), 47. Medieval theologian Gratian considered it a "depraved custom" when woman hand their children to wet nurses so that they might more quickly resume sexual relations. Gratian, *The Treatise on Laws (Decretum DD. 1–20) with the Ordinary Gloss*, trans. James Gordley (Washington, D.C.: The Catholic University of America Press, 1993), 18 (Dist. 6:1).

9. Saint Ambrose of Milan, *Exposition of the Holy Gospel According to Saint Luke, with Fragments on the Prophecy of Esaias*, trans. Theodora Tomkinson (Etna, California: Center for Traditionalist Orthodox Studies, 2003), 366.

woman to nurse her children, except the commandment of natural love. There is no biblical mandate that a woman not leave her child with others while she parties, except the mandate of maternal affection. Human nature is a drama in which we all participate, with the script written in flesh and blood more than in words and lines. The Lord created such natural realities as parental love, marital passion, and familial love not only to create good things for temporal life, but as windows into his eternal and infinite goodness. This world did not evolve by chance mutation as Darwin posited, but was structured by its divine playwright— who scripted every scene, every character, and every line to establish his spiritual and moral purposes. So, yes, we must remember the sufferings of our parents and be grateful, as Ambrose teaches, but we must also not forget how our mothers were created (how motherhood itself was brought into existence) by the Lord God to reveal the great salvation we are being born into. This is why the prophet Isaiah compared God's salvation of his people, Jerusalem, to a woman who has given birth:

> *"Shall I bring to the point of birth and not cause to bring forth?"* says the LORD... *"Rejoice with Jerusalem [that] you may nurse and be satisfied from her consoling breast... Behold, I will extend peace to her like a river, and the glory of the nations like an overflowing stream; and you shall nurse, you shall be carried upon her hip, and bounced upon her knees. As one whom his mother comforts, so I will comfort you."* [10]

---

10. Isaiah 66:9–13 (ESV).

6

THE NATURE OF MARRIAGE

But for Adam there was not found a helper fit for him. So the
LORD God caused a deep sleep to fall upon the man, and while he
slept took one of his ribs and closed up its place with flesh. And the
rib that the LORD God had taken from the man he made into a
woman and brought her to the man. Then the man said,

> *"This at last is bone of my bones*
> *and flesh of my flesh;*
> *she shall be called Woman,*
> *because she was taken out of Man."*

Therefore a man shall leave his father and his mother and hold
fast to his wife, and they shall become one flesh... And God blessed
them [and] said to them, "Be fruitful and multiply and fill the
earth and subdue it"... God saw everything that he made, and
behold, it was very good.[1]

---

1. Genesis 2:20–24 (ESV); Genesis 1:28, 31 (ESV). Protestant theologian Girolamo Zanchi emphasized that Eve was created from Adam's very flesh, so that man would love his wife as he loves himself. Even modern believers who hold Scripture to be inerrant have lost much of the wonder and poetry of this passage due to the pernicious presence of Darwin in the back of our minds. Girolamo Zanchi, *The Spiritual Marriage between Christ and His*

THE FIRST CHAPTER of the book of Genesis reveals how God ordained his creatures to help fulfill the Lord's creative work. God did not create the world complete with every being that would ever live. Life was made to beget itself, multiply, and fill the face of the earth. Animals were created to reproduce animals and plants to make plants, and the harvest cycle, which begins anew every day, was established by its creator. Genesis goes on to reveal how mankind, too, was made in this fashion: not as a completed race of human beings but as one couple from whom all human life would flow, with marriage being the means to do so in perfect purity and charity. The call to marry and reproduce was the Lord's first explicit blessing upon the human race. Mankind's most important work and greatest earthly joy were to be the same.

Biblical passages discussing human marriage make it clear that male and female are differentiated from one another, both for the delight of romantic passion and the sake of human reproduction. We see the former in the overwhelming joy with which Adam greeted his bride, and we see the latter in the first chapter of Genesis, where God ordained nature to reproduce after its kind: plant, fish, bird, animal, and human. Indeed, male and female are the categories by which much of the natural world, including mankind, was created to extend life. Still, whereas brute beasts procreate by instinct or impulse, humanity is called to proliferate in willing obedience to the word of God, for the Lord *commanded* Adam and Eve to "be fruitful and multiply and fill the earth" in a way that he did not *command* the natural kingdom to procreate. Animals are not made to act upon the word of God in moral obedience, but to reproduce themselves by natural impulse rather than through spiritual faith.[2]

People, on the other hand, have been created with the ability to honor God's wisdom and will by deliberately bearing their young in holy wedlock. Human parents are called to reflect the glory of their heavenly Father, from whom every human household receives its existence, purpose, and authority.[3] We are given the ability to choose to love our Father in heaven by obeying him, just as our children show their love for us by respecting our judgments and obeying our commands. Humanity has been given the opportunity either to ratify the sound morals, good sense, and wise faith with which we were endowed initially (or might

---

Church and Every One of the Faithful, trans. Patrick J. O'Banion (Grand Rapids, Michigan: Reformation Heritage Books, 2021), 24–26.
2. Genesis 1:26 (ESV); Genesis 1:28 (ESV).
3. Ephesians 3:14.

attain) or to reject those good qualities in favor of blind passion, unwise planning, and untrusting anxiety. Mankind was given the gift of free will to enable us to resemble God in choosing good (rather than evil), just as the Lord eternally chooses righteousness. As with the commandment not to eat from the tree of the knowledge of good and evil, mankind was commanded to fill the earth with progeny. Adam sinned in the former, while many of his descendants fail with the latter. And just as Eve was deceived into eating from the forbidden fruit, so many of her daughters have fallen prey to lies and confusion against making a family, to similar sorrow and regret.

The book of Genesis also makes it plain that reproduction is not the only purpose intended for marriage. In the second chapter of Genesis, Moses provided a more comprehensive picture of how man and woman are to be differentiated from each other, and then returned to each other in marriage. Procreation is not mentioned in that key passage, showing that marriage is not simply for reproduction but also for the spiritual and social friendship of the sexes. After all, mankind could have been made to reproduce asexually had God so willed. Yet, the Lord did not make men and women like amoeba, but created them to marry. Man was made to cherish his wife as if she were his own body, taking care of her in all circumstances, no matter the cost to himself—even to the loss of his life. And woman was made to be man's helper in preserving life, establishing human authority, and learning to both lose and find herself in the love of her husband and children. Man and woman would be suited to each other in that their relationship would not be that of servant to master or worker to co-worker, but of husband to wife and wife to husband. No matter what use mankind later made of marriage (whether slavery or prostitution), such was its holy purpose ordained by the Lord: something more romantic than chivalry, more sacred than kindness, more passionate than pleasure, and more devoted than a binding contract.

Scripture reveals how male and female are naturally attracted to one another to fulfill the deepest longings of each other's heart and flesh.[4] While Adam was first called by God to tend his garden and to name the

---

4. Henry Bullinger believed marriage was made for procreation and (his words) *avoiding whoredom*, but noted that its primary purpose is to make life *pleasanter* and more *commodious* (as Bullinger's translator writes). Bullinger cited pagan authors to frame marriage as both a divine and natural institution. Henry Bullinger, *The Decades of Henry Bullinger, First and Second Decades* (The Parker Society), trans. H.I. (Cambridge: The University Press, 1849), 397–402.

animals of the world (to celebrate them like a poet and categorize them like a scientist), he yearned for something more than physical and intellectual vocation and labor, even in his unfallen state. While the work of Adam was not yet cursed, work was not enough to fulfill his deepest longings (though the Lord does call men to develop their particular gifts and interests while supporting their families). Even the deep joy Adam drew from his untarnished love for God did not remove his need for love with a human touch—and not only a human touch but specifically a woman's touch. As Genesis reveals, Adam found himself in enraptured joy only when he beheld his bride. Dietrich Bonhoeffer wrote of the humility that men should observe in receiving the gift of a wife:

> *Thus Adam knows that this creature, whom God has shaped with his assistance, out of his flesh, is unique, but he sees this action of his upon the other entirely as a gift of God. The fact that Eve derives from him is in Adam's eyes not a cause for glorification, but for gratitude.*[5]

Sexual intimacy augments this deep attraction between the sexes, linking the reproductive, affective, and pragmatic functions of the human household together as an inseparable whole. In the biblical view, sexual closeness should never be divorced from the overall purpose of the home, whether to make children or to conceive marital affection. C.S. Lewis observed that sexual intimacy outside of marriage is a "monstrosity" precisely because those who indulge in it are attempting to "isolate one kind of union (the sexual) from all the other kinds of union which were intended to go along with it and make up the total union."[6] Physical pleasure, emotional attachment, practical support, and conceiving children are intended to flow from the undying love of man and woman for each other. For that reason, sex must never become an indiscriminate affair as it was for many of the ancients, but must always remain a choice of holy love for one beloved spouse. While the mythology of the pagan gods was filled with rapes and passionate intrigues, and pagan religious rites frequently were tainted by both homosexual and heterosexual prostitution, Scripture reveals that rightful sexual experience should transpire

---

5. Dietrich Bonhoeffer, *Creation and Fall/Temptation*, trans. John C. Fletcher (New York: Macmillan and Company, 1959), 60.

6. C.S. Lewis, *Mere Christianity*, 104–105.

only between husband and wife: between those who have permanently assumed the mantle of exclusive fidelity and the obligations of intimate charity toward one another. God blesses neither faithless love nor loveless coitus.[7]

The account of Adam and Eve shows how exclusive love is intended to be, for the first couple married, loved, and were utterly happy with each other, even though no other human beings yet lived. They were completed as a couple even before they were blessed with offspring. Their absolute and perfect monogamy is a reminder that lawful sexual experience is restricted to one man and one woman, as well as how absolute purity must reign over wanton lust. Scripture does not bless every sexual pursuit: the love of Adam and Eve remained free of every illicit passion and impure desire. Not until the corruption of human nature by sin were sexual desires disordered and tainted by selfishness and immoral inclinations—a reality best revealed in the fact that it was the sinful descendants of Cain rather than the lineage of the godly who first introduced polygamy into human society. That is, any marriage less than the model of complete devotion of man to his wife and joyful obedience of woman to her husband falls short of what the Lord intends marriage to be.

Traditional commentators have drawn from the biblical texts three purposes for human marriage: procreation, mutual assistance in sustaining life, and lawful sexual experience. From these first principles come all marital ethics, such as the duties to reproduce, support one's household, and abstain from illicit sexual contact. Biblical rules for marital and family life are not arbitrary impositions but logical extensions of the purposes for which the household has been ordained. It is important to realize that the book of Genesis teaches that every human marriage (including those established today) is called to follow the pattern set by Adam and Eve.[8] When that creation narrative revealed that sons and daughters must leave their parents to cleave to their spouse in

---

7. Early Christian apologist Athenagoras attacked pagan myths as lewd, noting how Zeus "had children from his mother, Rhea, and his daughter Kore, and married his own sister." Athenagoras, "A Plea Regarding Christians by Athenagoras, the Philosopher," in *Early Christian Fathers*, ed. Cyril C. Richardson (Philadelphia: Westminster Press, 1953), 336.
8. Dietrich Bonhoeffer wrote of Genesis 2:24: "It could be said here that the narrator is obviously stumbling. How can Adam, who knows nothing of a father or a mother, say such a thing? We could also say this is the narrator's practical application of the story, or something of the kind. Really, though, we recognize a basic fact here which has so far been hidden and which has now, as it were unintentionally, come to light. We ourselves are the Adam who speaks." Bonhoeffer, *Creation and Fall*, 62.

marriage, it is evident that the text was written for us rather than the first couple (who did not have human parents from whom to depart). Passages relating to Adam and Eve exist for our salvation and edification. Notice, too, that sexual intercourse is revealed to have a dual purpose in the biblical texts, existing for both reproduction and marital intimacy alike. John Calvin declared:

> *Hence is refuted the error of some, who think that the woman was formed only for the sake of propagation, and who restrict the word "good" [to] the production of offspring [and who] do not think that a wife was personally necessary for Adam because, he was hitherto free from lust; as if she had been given to him only for the companion of his chamber, and not rather that she might be the inseparable associate of his life.*[9]

Calvin was reacting against the ancient and medieval ascetic belief that human sexuality avoids moral taint only when approached with the intent of conceiving a child. He believed that marital intimacy is also to be considered *good* insofar as it fosters a charitable, modest, and affectionate relationship between husband and wife. Hence, any marriage lived in genuine love for God's glory is morally fruitful. Such matrimony remains good if it brings forth a crop of love and devotion even when it fails to produce children, since marital harmony is a rightful purpose in itself. Calvin reminded his readers that marriage was created before sin entered the world and that Adam married before he was faced with the nearly uncontrollable sexual urges common to sinful humanity, male and female alike.[10] The household was (and remains) ordained by God as a natural human state in the perfection of Eden, and wedlock should not be scorned as unsuitable either by misogynists or feminists. As the author of the book of Hebrews wrote, everyone must honor marriage as an estate that brings much good to the world.[11]

Marriage not only brings forth temporal good but at the same time serves as a mirror into the mind of the Triune God. Marital love enables humanity to experience the exclusive love which the Lord has for his eternal bride, the Church, while the physical fruit of marriage (namely,

---

9. John Calvin, *Genesis*, trans. John King (Grand Rapids, Michigan: William B. Eerdmans, 1948), 131.

10.

11. Hebrews 13:4 (ESV).

children) allows human beings to experience the unconditional love through which the Lord rules his family, even calling prodigal children like ourselves to share in his eternal inheritance. Family life allows us to understand from the depths of our hearts and minds the meaning and nature of divine love, far transcending what unreasoning animals can experience. Animals may contend for the right to mate, but they do not experience jealousy or passion. Unthinking beasts may fight to protect their young from predators, but they can never know what it is to love a lost child. Fish do not grow despondent over separation from a mate. Nor do squirrels mourn empty nests, crows grieve lost chicks, or buffalo organize family reunions. Whales do not establish nursing homes for their elderly.

In establishing a biblical framework, we must not overspiritualize our marriages. The Lord does not intend marriage to be a church sermon, a university lecture, or an economic arrangement, but the union of two very different people in consummated joy, helpful service, and willing sacrifice. Commenting during a historical epoch when many churchmen spiritualized and denigrated marriage as too sensual for the pious, Martin Luther reflected on the playful behavior in which middle-aged Isaac engaged with his wife in the sight of King Abimelech—noting how friendly, even silly, Isaac was in comforting and enjoying Rebekah. In contrast, Luther castigated men who are "surly, peevish, and harsh" toward their wives, giving "no indication of love and affection either in word or deed." In response to such unfriendly husbands, Luther highlighted the "words of warm praise and expressions of joy from women whenever they see a husband living pleasantly and harmoniously with his wife." While the world fantasizes (Luther uses the word *dreams*) of marriage as little more than sexual intercourse and intimate embraces, Christian marriage is to be one of hearts as well as bodies, to include silliness, laughter, and play. Luther summarized his thoughts by declaring that it is because marriage is sacred that "[we] are permitted to laugh and have fun with, and to embrace, our wives, whether they are naked or clothed. But we should abstain from the wives of others."[12]

Animals know neither intimate charity nor romantic passion since only mankind has been made in the image of God.[13] It is our duty, then,

---

12. Martin Luther, "Lectures on Genesis (Chapters 26–30)," in *Luther's Works*, vol. 5, ed. Jaroslav Pelikan (Saint Louis, Missouri: Concordia Publishing House, 1968), 29–37.
13. Lactantius wrote: "God made the woman, alone of all the animals, submit to her

to love our parents, children, spouses, and siblings in such a way that we make clear to our fellows how deep the love of God is: how self-giving and other-focused the Lord is in his love for mankind (made in his image and called to be his eternal heirs and children). In our relationships, we must model the life-giving charity through which our Lord died as a man to adopt into his eternal household a race of fallen rebels, and we must show God's holy love to be the deep joy all men and women desire. That is the eternal and divine objective for which every marriage is created and to which every single marriage is called, not just as a demonstration but as reality in and of itself. The apostle Paul declared:

> *Husbands, love your wives, as Christ loved the church and gave himself up for her, that he might sanctify her, having cleansed her by the washing of water with the word, so that he might present the church to himself in splendor, without spot or wrinkle or any such thing, that she might be holy and without blemish. In the same way husbands should love their wives as their own bodies. He who loves his wife loves himself. For no one ever hated his own flesh, but nourishes and cherishes it, just as Christ does the church, because we are members of his body. "Therefore a man shall leave his father and mother and hold fast to his wife, and the two shall become one flesh." This mystery is profound, and I am saying that it refers to Christ and the church. However, let each one of you love his own wife as himself, and let the wife see that she respects her husband.*[14]

---

husband, although he willed that the other [female] animals should retreat from the males after conceiving a fetus. This was done so that desire would not force the men to look elsewhere, if their wives rejected them, and thus forfeit the glory of chastity. Furthermore, the woman would not achieve the virtue of purity, if she were unable to sin. For who would say that a dumb animal is chaste, when it rejects the male after conceiving a fetus? The animal does this because it will experience pain and danger if it allows penetration. There is no praise in not doing what you are unable to do. That is why people are praised for purity, because it is not natural but voluntary." Lactantius, "Divine Institutes 6," in David G. Hunter, ed., *Marriage and Sexuality in Early Christianity* (Minneapolis, Minnesota: Fortress Press, 2018), 105.

14. Ephesians 5:25–33 (ESV).

7

———

FAMILY LIFE AFTER THE FALL

*So when the woman saw that the tree was good for food, and that it
was a delight to the eyes, and that the tree was to be desired to make
one wise, she took of its fruit and ate, and she also gave some to her
husband who was with her, and he ate. Then the eyes of both were
opened, and they knew that they were naked. And they sewed fig
leaves together and made themselves loincloths.*[1]

THE SIN of Adam and Eve dramatically altered the conditions of human
life. Not only were selfishness and concupiscence inherited from our first
parents, but death, disease, pain, and toil also came into the world of men
and women following the fall of mankind into sin and evil. The human
household was not left untouched by this moral and physical catastrophe.
Eve was punished for her role as a temptress by facing increased labor
pains and intensification of her natural subordination to her husband,
while Adam brought wearisome toil in earning a living to himself and his
descendants, as well as the terrible curse of death, following his decision
to plunge humanity into ruin.[2] Worst of all, the descendants of Adam

---

1. Genesis 3:6–7 (ESV).
2. While human sexuality was disordered by sin, the fault of the first couple was in their
prideful desire to become as wise as God through foolish disobedience to the divine
command. They were like schoolyard cheaters trying to gain good grades (i.e., wisdom)
without the patient work and moral obedience required to become good students. Their sin

were made to inherit their father's moral wickedness so that no person conceived by a human father would be born into moral innocence, regardless of how pure newborn children might appear to human eyes. Whatever hymen protected the purity of the human heart was pierced, and its blood stained humanity with moral guilt as irreversible as the loss of virginity.[3]

The introduction of sin into the human heart quickly corrupted human society. Relationships of purity and charity were replaced by ones of violence and lust, with Adam's own family becoming contaminated by human evil. His son, Cain, murdered his brother, then dared to justify himself by declaring that he was not Abel's keeper. Generations later, a descendant of Cain went even further, for the Bible reveals that Lamech murdered a man in passionate revenge of himself, then justified his violence to his two wives (having broken the pattern of monogamy to which God had called Adam and Eve and established the unfortunate example of polygamy).[4] As with the fall of any household, sin's terrible effects became obvious both immediately and over the following generations. Even today, one generation's sin is inevitably visited upon its children and grandchildren, unless God gives his grace to repent and restore righteousness.

The godly are not called to imitate the brutality and sensuality of violent and lustful Lamech. The church father Tertullian observed that "plurality of marriage started with a man who was cursed."[5] By the time of Noah, matters were so bad that God destroyed nearly the entire human race because of sin. The Bible links the shortening of the human lifespan to the reality that people were joining together with little respect for God's will, simply coupling as they pleased, regardless of divine instructions and patterns. The customs of mankind had become *the world* about whose evils New Testament writers would later warn: what

---

had nothing to do with sex. Francis Schaeffer observed: "[We] find here a complete rejection of the common notion that the Fall was sexual in nature, that taking the fruit was actually a reference to the first sexual act. God looks upon man and woman together and says, 'All of this is good,' and in Genesis 1:28 he tells them to have children." Francis Schaeffer, "Genesis in Space and Time," in *The Complete Works of Francis Schaeffer*, vol. 2, 38. For a review of how Augustine established the doctrine of the fall of mankind in the Latin West, see Peter Brown, *The Body and Society: Men, Women, and Sexual Renunciation in Early Christianity* (New York: Columbia University Press, 1988), 399–405.

3. Genesis 3:16–19; Romans 5:1.
4. Genesis 4:19.
5. Tertullian, "An Exhortation to Chastity," in Hunter, ed., *Marriage and Sexuality in Early Christianity*, 51.

we might call human society and civilization bound together by, and founded upon, human selfishness, fleshly desires, and sinful attitudes and actions. People began to live faithlessly and promiscuously, or in domestic tyranny (which promotes their own self-pleasing lusts and restricts similar selfish passions found in others). Moses declared of the ancient world, which God condemned to destruction:

> *When man began to multiply on the face of the land and daughters were born to them, the sons of God saw that the daughters of man were attractive. And they took as their wives any they chose. Then the LORD said, "My Spirit shall not abide in man forever, for he is flesh: his days shall be 120 years."* [6]

While mankind was judged and punished for its perversions, the purposes of marriage remained as they were established in the beginning. Marriage was neither eliminated nor its essential purposes redefined, although the Lord became so grieved over the sin of fallen humanity that he destroyed mankind, leaving alive only a small, righteous remnant. Following the flood, God reiterated the command first issued in Eden when he reminded mankind to "be fruitful and multiply and fill the earth." The Lord repeated his command to reproduce three times, making its continued significance and authority clear. To repeat: even though God knew perfectly well how the "intention of man's heart is evil from his youth" and realized that mankind would fill the earth with suffering, sorrow, and shame, the Lord commanded (and still commands) sinful humanity to marry and beget children. The omniscient and infinite God sees before his eyes every war, massacre, enslavement, and assault that has (or ever will) occur, yet calls mankind to fill the earth with people despite his foreknowledge that the immoral monsters and miscreants of this world must rise from soiled and selfish mankind—even the tyrants and antichrists who plague us in our countries, communities, and homes. Of course, the Lord also foresees the courage and charity of those who resist tyranny and injustice and the everlasting glory that will crown humanity with such perfect and eternal joy that these days of evil will seem but few in number and light of burden. [7]

---

6. Genesis 6:1–3 (ESV).
7. Genesis 9:1, 7 (ESV); Genesis 8:17 (ESV); Genesis 9:11–12 (ESV). Pastor Phil Boender of the Christian Reformed Church in Fort Wayne, Indiana, preached on Labor Day (1997)

As with the ancient world judged by the Lord, there remain heretics and dissenters who preach and live in infidelity and polygamy.[8] Yet, some have also scorned marriage in protest of the evils of this mortal life. For instance, there were early Christians who doubted whether children should be brought into this wicked world, filled as it is with perversity and violence. Such doubters hoped that the conversion of the Gentiles and cessation of conception would bring to an end the evils of human history. Their reasoning was not God's, at least not as the Lord expressed himself to Noah when commanding sinful mankind to reproduce. Though fearful and selfish mankind prefers to pull the plug on suffering and shame, the Lord's way is to redeem what has been lost through the cross of Christ to bring forth a better resurrection. It is for this reason that the command to fill the earth through monogamous marriage and parenthood has not been rescinded by any divine revelation—and remains in full force.

In fact, following the fall of mankind into sin, another good reason to marry came into being: the need to tame and subdue the disordered passions of the flesh. The reasonable affections and spiritual passions once found in Eden were corrupted, and human nature was enslaved to its selfishness and lust.[9] None of us is as we ought to be, and all of us must repent of our folly, impurity, and greed to return to God's wisdom, holiness, and love. As a concession to human weakness, the Lord now instructs men and women unable to subdue their sexual appetite alone to do so with a spouse in holy marriage. The Lord does not require human beings to purify themselves of all sin before enjoying the blessing of matrimony, but has revealed that marriage is a necessary and effective means of restraining sexual temptation. The apostle Paul wrote in 1 Corinthians that the reality of sexual temptation means that "each man should have his own wife and each woman her own husband."[10]

---

on how the command to reproduce preceded the command to work the earth. As much as we are called to work, we have a greater obligation to reproduce.

8. For an account of polygamy in early modern European society, see John Cairncross, *After Polygamy Was Made A Sin: The Social History of Christian Polygamy* (London: Routledge and Kegan Paul, 1974).

9. Though self-controlled, Edenic passion would have been more passionate rather than less so, just as unfallen intellect would have been keener rather than duller and the unfallen body stronger rather than weaker. It also seems to me that the struggle of sexual temptation in fallen men and women comes less from the vigor of our sexual desire than from the weakness of our moral will.

10. 1 Corinthians 7:2 (ESV).

What Scripture is teaching is that anyone and everyone distracted by sexual desire must resist sexual temptation at a given moment, but also seek marriage (or prepare to seek marriage), if possible, as the best remedy against persistent sexual temptation. In other words, a remedial purpose for marrying has been added to the original purposes for matrimony, and Scripture is clear that both men and women need to use marriage as a remedy to the burning of the flesh (since male and female alike are sexual beings). While marriage does not eliminate sexual temptation and sin, it does provide a lawful outlet and thereby mitigates sexual passion's worst evils. Martin Luther confirmed the apostle Paul's teaching, observing that marriage is "not without its imperfections and uncleanness," but is a far better means of fighting sexual immorality than celibacy, monastic vows, and other feats of spiritual willpower. Luther wrote:

> *He commands you to choose for yourself one woman who pleases you and with whom you should spend your life. Of course, there is sin. "But I leave it to you," says God, "To play and laugh with your own wife and to keep away from the wives of others."* [11]

However, the use of marriage to help men and women progress in piety and faith goes far beyond resisting sexual temptation. Too often, sinful men and women are complacent about their personal selfishness. Blinded by pride, vanity, and greed, we do not see what self-centered and self-serving creatures we truly are. Family life teaches humility and service in a way nothing else can do—as the apostle Paul noted in the second chapter of 1 Timothy. When Paul declared how women are saved in childbirth *if they keep faith and love and sanctity*, he was not giving an ironclad promise that no Christian woman would ever die giving birth, but was reminding women (and men) that their faith must be lived in the challenges of daily life. Paul was likely alluding to God's promise after the fall of mankind to use the offspring of fallen woman to combat and destroy the evil one who had brought ruin to God's creation. Even in divine judgment, the Lord brought hope to mankind, revealing the great value of women who trust God amidst the suffering of childbearing. [12]

Not only was Paul reminding Christian women of their role in God's redemption, but he was also liberating women from traditional Jewish

---

11. Martin Luther, "Lectures on Genesis (Chapters 26–30)," in *Luther's Works*, vol. 5, 34.
12. 1 Timothy 2:15 (ESV); Genesis 3:15 (ESV).

and pagan beliefs that wrongly threatened divine judgment during child-birth beyond what Scripture revealed, thereby aggravating common fears and apprehensions with religious manipulation and base superstition. Instead of succumbing to such false teachings and customs, Scripture calls women to have reverent hearts that are devoted to serving their husbands, children, and relatives. For their part, men are commanded to be gentle and loving with their wives, praying without anger or disputing, since it does a man no good to pray to God while he is quarreling with his wife.[13] Peter made a similar point when he warned husbands that their prayers will remain unanswered if they mistreat their wives. Peter reminded wives to be reverently obedient if they wish to share in the righteousness that blessed Sarah. In short, marriage provides human beings with an opportunity to humble themselves for the good of others, all to God's glory and the redemption of mankind.[14]

This principle holds with children, though it is not always easy to deal with children, who are as morally flawed as their parents and far less mature. Often, babies are worse sinners than their elders since neither law nor grace has tempered their open expressions of selfishness and sin. Every parent has experienced the hateful stare of an infant who would strike his parent a mortal blow if only the baby wielded such power—and for no greater cause than a nose wiped, a diaper changed, or a feeding momentarily delayed. Moreover, the sinful parental heart does not always respond with patience to the needs of hungry, sick, or stubborn infants. Few mothers take pleasure in scrubbing dirty diapers, and even fewer fathers willingly humble themselves by forsaking public prestige for the unrecognized toil of parenthood. For this reason, ordinary household service can become an act of faith.

While Martin Luther was careful not to let his readers imagine they can earn their salvation through domestic good works, he observed that laundry, feedings, and household toil are part of the salvation that the Lord graciously bestows: the good works resulting from faith and demonstrating God's sanctifying work. Though such humble service was as despised in Luther's world as in our own, Martin Luther changed the

---

13. The *Mishnah*, which codified Jewish beliefs from this period, gives an example of false teaching not found in the law of Moses and of the very type rejected by the apostle Paul: "For three transgressions do women die in childbirth: for heedlessness of the laws of the menstruate, the Dough-offering, and the lighting of the [Sabbath] lamp." Herbert Danby, ed., *The Mishnah* (Oxford: Oxford University Press, 1991), 102 (Shabbath II:2:6).
14. 1 Timothy 2:15; 1 Peter 3:6–7 (ESV).

contemporary insult for a hen-pecked husband (i.e., *a diaper changer*) into a mark of spiritual humility and piety when he reminded readers how the eyes of faith must never judge through the values of the world. While the worldly seek comfort, glory, and power, Christians are called to charitable service. For that reason, there is no better way to receive a rich blessing in God's household than by willingly accepting the self-denial required in the troubles of family life, including washing diapers—even when one is mocked for doing so (perhaps, especially when one is so mocked). Such humble service is the true good that family life produces in a fallen world. Luther wrote:

> *[Christian faith] opens its eyes, looks upon all these insignificant, distasteful, and despised duties in the Spirit, and is aware that they are all adorned with divine approval as with the costliest gold and jewels. It says, "O God, because I am certain that thou hast created me as a man and hast from my body begotten this child, I also know for a certainty that it meets with thy perfect pleasure. I confess to thee that I am not worthy to rock the little babe or wash its diapers, or to be entrusted with the care of the child and its mother. How is it that I, without any merit, have come to this distinction of being certain that I am serving thy creature and thy most precious will? O how gladly will I do so, though the duties should be even more insignificant and despised. Neither frost nor heat, neither drudgery nor labor, will distress or dissuade me, for I am certain that it is thus pleasing in thy sight."*[15]

---

15. Martin Luther, "The Estate of Marriage (1522)," in *Luther's Works*, vol. 45, 39–40. One work of German art history shows a satirical woodcut from the 1530s that mocks a henpecked man washing diapers while his wife enforces power over her husband with a stick. Keith Moxey, *Peasants, Warriors, and Wives: Popular Imagery in the Reformation* (Chicago: University of Chicago Press, 1989), 103–108. Given the browbeating of modern men, it must be noted that Luther never intended to excuse proud, lazy, or abusive women, only to remind men to willingly help their wives and children with humble service in Christ-like humility and love.

8

THE GOVERNMENT OF GOD

Then God said to Noah, "Go out from the ark, you and your wife, and your sons and your sons' wives with you. Bring out with you every living thing that is with you of all flesh—birds and animals and every creeping thing that creeps on the earth—that they may swarm on the earth and be fruitful and multiply on the earth." [1]

JUST AS THE Lord called creation into existence, he continues to govern what he fashioned. After the Flood, the Lord gave (through Noah) a direct command to all mankind to reestablish the fullness of human life. Centuries later, the Lord called one man, Abraham, to leave his homeland in Mesopotamia and travel to what is now known as Israel, as part of God's plan to build a holy people through the patriarch Abraham. Abraham was told to conceive a child through whom a great people would come into existence. The descendants of Abraham were subsequently called to go first to Egypt and later to emigrate from Egypt to establish a sacred nation founded on the laws of the Lord. Throughout the many generations that followed, God guided his people through various trials and tribulations, raising prophets and peasants alike to build a new nation to serve him during their mortal lives and then to become his eternal sons and daughters. The Lord called into existence a

---

1. Genesis 8:15–17 (ESV).

genealogical line that included a repentant prostitute and a converted pagan, culminating in the capstone of human history: the birth of Jesus Christ, Son of David and Son of God. Through Christ, many peoples and kingdoms of the earth have converted to the faith of God.

An Internet site calculates the odds against any of us having come into existence as 1 in $10^{2,685,000}$. Given that the total number of atoms in the known universe is estimated at 10^{80}, such an astronomical number is beyond human comprehension.[2] What it signifies is that if a single couple in the Middle Ages had not married or a husband in antiquity had approached his wife an hour later than he did, not just one person but the vast majority of the people of our world would never have been conceived. If a single couple in the tenth century had not kissed and made up following a quarrel behind the hayrick, not a single person with the slightest European ancestry who presently lives would exist—and it is the same if an eighth-century African husband had fallen ill to malaria a few days before he fathered his fourth son or a sixth-century Asian toddler (and future mother) had not been pulled from a local pond before she drowned. We can consider as many scenarios as we can imagine, but we must recognize that our lineage is fragile and fortuitous, humanly speaking. Our existence depends on a precise chain of ancestors.[3]

Even on that bed on which we ourselves were conceived—whether through virtuous love, vile lust, or violent rape—there were as many as one billion potential boys or girls to be made in that single union of our parents. We were just one less-than-slim chance of conception (since a man includes in his body billions of different potential children at any given time).[4] A slim chance, unless the Lord specifically created not simply Jesus of Nazareth but also Abraham Lincoln, William Shakespeare, Joan of Arc, and every unknown or forgotten person in human history, to include each of us. Either chaos rules everything that matters

---

2. Jacinta Bower, "What Are the Odds You Exist?" *ScienceAlert*, (December 17, 2015).
3. The population of medieval Europe may have included as many as 52 million people in the year 1000 and 75 to 80 million people by the early fourteenth century. N.J.G. Pounds, *A Historical Geography of Europe* (Cambridge: Cambridge University Press, 1990), 121, 150.
4. The human male produces 100 million sperm each day and deposits up to one billion sperm inside a woman to conceive a human child with her (typically) single egg. Men's bodies store two or three billions of sperm at a time, and there may be as many as seventy trillion genetic combinations in a sperm cell, not to mention mutations and genetic combinations in women's eggs. Such staggering numbers express the nearly endless possibilities in our bodies, making plain the unlikeliness that any of us might come to exist if considered individually. [This information was provided with the assistance of OpenAI's ChatGPT.]

most (the people who exist), or the Lord specifically called each of us into being before the foundation of the creation, deciding who should come to be from the myriad paths of the possible. Unless the world is a massive super-lottery generating random genetic combinations without rhyme or reason, it is a living play in which the Lord deliberately creates every single human being who has, does, or ever will exist. This providential government of the Lord's creation is the confession of Scripture and Christian churches throughout the ages: the very ages that have brought forth the men and women needed to conceive each of us.[5]

A discussion of God's relationship to the world in all of its details is an undertaking beyond the scope of this book. What must be said here is that the Lord God of Scripture is not the absent landlord or distant watchmaker preached by the Deists of the Enlightenment. The Lord did not make the world like a wind-up watch and set it free from his control, but every day conceives life, blesses work, brings friendships, and judges rebellious humanity with disease and death. Given that the human family is at the foundation of all things—of life itself—it is impossible to consider how God could not be both interested and involved. That is, the human race began with one couple and grew from that humble beginning to become billions of people now on the planet, just as each of us is at the beginning or end of a story of millions of people created through other such couples. Even the Lord's Prayer calls God our *Father* and speaks of the Lord's daily care for his children in spiritual and temporal matters alike.[6] Heaven forbid that we consider the Lord to be like irresponsible philanderers that we see throughout our society, or the divine deadbeat dad portrayed by deist thinkers: philanderers and philosophers who, in practice and theory, show little regard for the lives they conceive, yet dare slander the Lord as being the same.[7]

Rather than being distant and unapproachable, the Lord is our Father who subjects himself to deep suffering to adopt us as his children. The writer of Hebrews revealed how he who "sanctifies and those who

---

5. Ephesians 1:4.
6. Matthew 6:1–2 (King James Version, 1611). Quotations and citations from this version hereafter will be marked (KJV).
7. I write elsewhere: "Many people take an essentially deistic view of God, seeing him less as a wise, powerful Father who governs his household well than a deadbeat dad who makes [illegitimate children] and lets them wander unloved and unsupported. No one should mistake the Triune God for the conceptions of eighteenth-century philandering philosophers or irresponsible modern men." Kirk Adams, *Measures of Insight: Moral Reflections for Daily Life* (Kirk Adams Books, 2021), 76, (n.16) 116.

are sanctified are all from one Father" and that Jesus is "not ashamed to call them brothers." Indeed, the entire New Testament makes plain that believers will be adopted as the children of God. Heaven itself is to be the household of the Lord and we its heirs of eternal salvation, not of some ghost-like spiritual world, but of this earth resurrected, renewed, and perfected: a world with a great city and pristine nature restored to a right-eousness more perfect than mere innocence—just as a wives, mothers, and even repentant prostitutes are far greater women than naive girls and untested virgins. In the book of Revelation, the Lord proclaims of the redeemed: "I will be his God and he will be My son."[8]

Yet, the Lord is our God here and now, too. The book of Hebrews declares how the Holy Spirit calls to us: "Today if you hear His voice, do not harden your hearts." Hebrews also reveals how the Old Testament and New Testament God is the same God: that Jesus Christ is the "same yesterday and today, and forever." In the context of this divine reality, believers are made heirs of the promise to Abraham. Just as that patriarch begat descendants as "innumerable as the sand which is by the seashore," so, too, we have the promise of building the kingdom of God through our families.[9] The Lord remains active both in fulfilling his ancient oaths and building new worlds (which each of us is). While the Lord could have created the human race in another manner, he chose sexual repro-duction through generations of human parentage because it most perfectly reveals his wisdom and love—or rather, in his wisdom and love, God chose this approach. Martin Luther once observed that the Lord chose "your father to beget you and your mother to nurse you, although He would have been able to create and to nourish you without parents." Luther continued that while God can "nourish the infant without milk, He does not want to do so."[10]

Though Abraham was past the age of begetting children and his wife Sarah was elderly and barren, God made Abraham a father through Sarah, who conceived in her old age because she "considered Him faithful who had promised."[11] This is the New Testament interpretation of the covenant the Lord made with Abraham two thousand years earlier, and it is a promise to contemporary believers that as we imitate the faith of Abraham, the Lord will be with us just as he was with that great patriarch

---

8. Hebrews 2:11 (NASB); Ephesians 2:19; Revelation 21:7 (NASB).
9. Hebrews 3:7–8 (NASB); Hebrews 13:8 (NASB); Hebrews 11:12 (NASB).
10. Martin Luther, "Lectures on Genesis (Chapters 26–30)," in *Luther's Works*, vol. 5, 173.
11. Hebrews 11:11 (NASB).

of the faith. This understanding and acceptance that the Lord is personal to each of us is a great revelation of Scripture: one that begins with the first chapters of Genesis and continues through the final chapters of Revelation into eternity, for it is a promise without limit or cessation. Several psalms make plain how the Lord is personal to everyone who calls his name. One psalmist revealed how God protects those who lack human defense, and settles the lonely in families, while pouring out his judgment against everyone who forsakes his law:

> *Father of the fatherless and protector of widows*
> *is God in his holy habitation.*
> *God settles the solitary in a home;*
> *he leads out the prisoners to prosperity,*
> *but the rebellious dwell in a parched land.*[12]

Moreover, with great joy, we confess how this promise is not only given to us as individuals but also extended to our families. On the day of Pentecost, the apostle Peter preached that the promises of God are for "you and your children." Similarly, the apostle Paul later told a jailer to believe in Christ so that the man could be saved, both he and his household.[13] To state the matter bluntly: the Lord God has come to dwell with men and women, and promises to be with believers and their children. Just as the Lord makes each man and woman from the trillions upon quadrillions of quintillions (and far beyond) of uncountable possibilities, so God reveals himself to each of them that they might know him and live as his adopted children, forever in joy and peace.[14] For those who believe, the Bible reveals how the blessings of this mortal life are included in God's promises.

The Lord not only builds families and people but also establishes secular governments and churches. Scripture reveals how the Lord calls the state (human government) into existence and also miraculously and providentially establishes his people among the nations of the earth: first in the form of a holy nation (ancient Israel) and now as a holy people drawn from all peoples of the earth (the Christian church). Just as the

---

12. Psalm 68:5–6 (ESV).
13. Acts 2:39 (NASB); Acts 16:31 (NASB).
14. No one is born into God's family. The spiritual reality that all of us are adopted into God's household should be some comfort for those among us who struggle with the haphazard nature of their conception by parents who may have preferred otherwise.

Lord revealed his person and power directly to Adam at the commencement of human history and revealed himself to Noah at the reconstitution of human history, so the Lord speaks to mankind through holy Scripture and today exercises his power indirectly through family, state, and church.[15] Our Lord remains at work in every household, government, and Christian congregation that bears his name—across every epoch and in every land. He is also at work among those who deny him, or even make war on his law.

While human institutions change over days, weeks, months, years, decades, centuries, and millennia, each has been called to its own sphere of power and is used by the Lord to govern fallen humanity in his restraint of evil and in bringing forth good. Some rulers wittingly and willingly serve the Lord, while others are unwitting and unwilling instruments in his hand.[16] Not only does God raise specific men and women to rule the nations, but he also changes kingdoms and empires over decades and centuries. Exactly how and why God uses both dramatic and gradual changes in human affairs to build his kingdom is as unanswerable as why he fills the human race with so much differentiation in appearance, language, achievement, and culture, or why he has chosen each of us from the billions of possibilities at the moment of our conception. But it is the reality we face, to the glory of the infinite God.

Let us return to the main point: God's active government of the human household. Already, we have seen how the Lord called Abraham to the miraculous making of a child—a son who himself was given a similar path to fatherhood when facing the initial barrenness of his wife, providentially (and specifically) led to him. Scripture declared how Isaac prayed to God "on behalf of his wife, because she was barren," then "Rebekah his wife conceived." Here, we see God directly involved in

---

15. Protestant Reformer Henry Bullinger observed: "No small parcel of the first and most excellent book of the bible, called Genesis, is spent in rehearsing the marriages of holy men." Bullinger, *The First and Second Decades,* 395. Martin Luther spent considerable time discussing the marriages of holy men in his commentary on Genesis, mostly notably those of Isaac and Jacob. Martin Luther, "Lectures on Genesis (Chapters 26–30)," in *Luther's Works,* vol. 5.

16. One thinks of Nero, who was the Emperor when Paul named the state as God's servant (Romans 13:4). It is difficult to imagine a man more opposed to Christ than Nero: a tyrant associated with sexual perversion and oppression. Nero is infamous for murdering his mother and persecuting Christians as scapegoats after the great fire of Rome in 64 A.D. (which Nero was rumored to have caused in his effort to make space for an architectural project), leading to the executions of Paul and Peter in Rome. Still, it was not long before God's providence sent a rebelling army to drive Nero to suicide and eternal judgment.

human affairs, leading a human couple through the flux of biology and history to create those persons whom the Lord conceived in his mind before the foundation of the world. And this leading of God in human affairs is not restricted to the Old Testament. In his preaching to the cultured and philosophical Athenians, the apostle Paul observed how God's providential control of life remains true throughout history, noting how God made humanity from one man, "having determined their appointed times and the boundaries of their habitation."[17]

The Lord God is the ruler of this world, but not as an uncaring potentate, impersonal force, or deadbeat dad. He is the Father who intentionally conceives and providentially cares for his children more than any of us will ever care for our sons and daughters. Although our love for our own families is real enough, it does not compare to the love the Lord has for our loved ones and us. This is what Jesus meant when he explained that we, though evil at heart, feed our hungry children fish and eggs (meat and potatoes for those of us raised in the Midwest) rather than scorpions and snakes. His point was not to praise our weak and corrupt love, but to remind believers how much greater God's care is for his children. While we may provide perishable food to our children, the Lord gives his very self to us, if only we ask for grace like the children of God we are called to be.[18] God's government of the world is merciful, and Christ heals our diseases, bears our sins, and delivers us from evil—gifts far greater than our daily bread. This is the mysterious, wonderful, and awesome government of our God.

> *Fools, because of their rebellious way, and because of their iniquities were afflicted... Then they cried out to the LORD in their trouble... He sent His word and healed them, and delivered them from their destructions... He sets the needy securely on high away from affliction, and makes his families like a flock. The upright see it and are glad; but all injustice shuts its mouth.*[19]

17. Genesis 25:21 (NASB); Acts 17:26 (NASB).
18. Luke 11:11–13.
19. Psalm 107: 17, 19–20, 41–42 (NASB).

9

THE LEADING OF THE HOLY SPIRIT

And [Ruth] went, and came and gleaned in the field after the reapers [to] the portion of the field belonging unto Boaz, who was of the family of Elimelech.

[Boaz said] unto his servant that was set over the reapers, Whose damsel is this? And the servant that was set over the reapers answered... It is the Moabitish damsel that came back with Naomi out of the country of Moab: and she said, Let me glean, I pray you... So she came, and hath continued even from the morning until now.

Then said Boaz unto Ruth, [Go] not to glean in another field, neither pass from hence, but abide here fast by my maidens, [for] have I not charged the young men that they shall not touch thee?

[Ruth] fell on her face, and bowed herself to the ground, and said unto him, Why have I found favor in thy sight, that thou shouldest take knowledge of me, seeing I am a foreigner? [1]

Boaz answered and said unto her, It hath fully been showed me, all that thou hast done unto thy mother-in-law since the death of thy husband; and how thou hast left thy father and thy mother, and the land of thy nativity, and art come unto a people that thou knewest not heretofore. [Now may] a full reward be given thee of

Jehovah, the God of Israel, under whose wings thou art come to take refuge.[1]

AS WE WILL DISCUSS LATER, the Israelites were forbidden to marry unbelievers (including Moabites), so Elimelech of Bethlehem presumably sinned by marrying his sons to Moabite women after emigrating to Moab during a famine.[2] Still, the curse of the law was not the end of the story, for his widowed daughter-in-law, Ruth, turned from her own people's pagan customs to the God of Israel (we do not know when she converted) and subsequently returned with her impoverished mother-in-law, Naomi, to join God's people in Bethlehem. Despite evident sin in that family, God honored the faith of Naomi and Ruth by providentially directing Ruth toward a field in which her diligent loyalty to her mother-in-law and trust in the Lord was noticed by a godly man, Boaz, who pitied the difficult circumstances of the impoverished family and honored the young woman's faith. Boaz and Ruth married and conceived a child from whom King David descended, and from David came the Son of David, Jesus Christ.[3]

The book of Ruth tells the story of a struggling family and reveals its final blessing: a blessing exalted by Matthew in his gospel. There are no miracles or prophecies in the book of Ruth, only a family that sinned and repented with such genuine faith that a pagan woman converted to the Lord and began a godly lineage. God was at work in this household as much as in any book of the Bible, but for those who lived through its famine, death, shame, and poverty, the Lord must have at times seemed distant and indifferent. There were no great miracles as during the exodus from Egypt, nor visions and dreams promising God's leading—only hard duty to be endured under a seemingly silent heaven. Still, the Lord God is not the deadbeat dad of the deists, and he did not abandon his loved ones to ruin. Instead, God gave Naomi a dedicated daughter-in-law and made Ruth herself an ancestor of the promised Messiah. Over many years, and then decades and centuries, the Lord built his kingdom and blessed his servants as they waited in quiet patience for his salvation.

This is how the Lord leads most of us through our lives. If we keep

---

1. Ruth 2:3–12.
2. Later Jewish custom allowed men to marry foreign women, but forbade Jewish women from marrying foreign men. I cannot reconcile this latitude with the texts and intent of Deuteronomy 23:3 and Ezra 9:2.
3. Ruth 4:21–22; Matthew 1:1, 5–6, 17.

the persistent faith of Naomi and Ruth through difficult times, the Lord protects us and leads us to the purpose of our lives, even when we have no idea what blessing he will choose or find ourselves in circumstances born of sin. In the New Testament (where God's revelation is made more plain to us than it was to Naomi and Ruth), the apostle Paul noted how the Spirit of God leads the sons of God as we cry to our Father as God's children.[4] Christians are to count themselves as God's beloved offspring rather than as servants, soldiers, or devotees to his religion; we are to have faith that the Lord is with us, whether we recognize his work or not, and we must understand that even our faith is his providential gift of grace. In that spirit, early twentieth-century theologian B.B. Warfield emphasized that God's promise of help is available to every believer rather than just a few privileged saints. Everyone who calls to the Lord as Father is guided by God's Spirit through mortal life to eternal joy. While God does not necessarily ensure our "worldly safety, worldly comfort, even worldly profit," he is working to redeem our mortal lives and secure our eternal salvation. Warfield observed:

> *[The leading of the Spirit of God] has but one end in view, the saving from sin, the leading into holiness; but it affects every single activity of every kind—physical, intellectual, and spiritual— bending it toward that end. [Since] it is nothing other than the power of God unto salvation, it must needs abide with the sinner, work constantly upon him, enter into all his acts, condition all his doings, and lead him thus steadily onward toward the one great goal [i.e., conforming the man to the image of Christ].*[5]

Ruth did not confuse faith with worldly success, and neither should we. There are many evils in life (especially in family life, I hasten to add) where we shall be spared much grief if we serve the Lord with truth and humility, though all believers remain subject to death, disease, and disappointment in this valley of tears, and the Lord does not always reveal his most important and enduring purposes for our lives before our days are

---

4. Romans 8:14–15.
5. B.B. Warfield nuanced his instruction: "Nor do I say that the gracious Lord has no care for the secular life of His people." Warfield also observed how godly living saves people from many evils in temporal life. B.B. Warfield, "The Leading of the Spirit," in B.B. Warfield, *Biblical and Theological Studies,* ed. Samuel G. Craig (Philadelphia: Presbyterian and Reformed Publishing Company, 1968), 546–547.

spent. Naomi and Ruth understood during their mortal lives how they had been rescued from poverty and the shame of childlessness—nothing more. It was not revealed to them how their grandchild would become the king of Israel (there were no Hebrew kings during their lives) or that their future heir would be the promised Messiah a thousand years later, just as none of us know whether our biological and spiritual descendants will be lifted up or cast down. For that reason, we must never evaluate our lives only by what we see, for the Lord is not restricted to our few years as he works across generations to call a holy people to himself.

Because we are not deists, we confess how the Lord answers prayer. Jesus certainly healed the sick mother-in-law of one disciple and raised to life the deceased loved ones of those who trusted in him. He miraculously provided wine to honor a wedding and cured menstrual bleeding in a sick woman.[6] In all such affairs of household, marriage, and sexual life, the Lord remains interested and active, never far from us and always seeking to save. He has the power and intent to preserve and bless his people according to the purposes of his eternal kingdom, and often allows us to suffer only to resurrect us better and stronger. If this nearness and power of God were not the case, the Lord's prayer would represent nothing more than a pious platitude—a pointless and meaningless charade. But God does answer prayer, and Jesus spoke truth when he taught us to believe that the Lord changes the course of events for those of his children who cry out to him. Such is the meaning of the Lord's prayer.

Our Father which art in heaven,
Hallowed be thy name.
Thy kingdom come,
Thy will be done in earth,
as it is in heaven.
Give us this day our daily bread.
And forgive us our debts,
as we forgive our debtors.
And lead us not into temptation,
but deliver us from evil:
For thine is the kingdom,
and the power,
and the glory, forever.

---

6. Matthew 8:14–15; Matthew 9:25; John 2:1–11; Matthew 9:20–22.

Amen.[7]

Nearly all believers are so familiar with the Lord's prayer that it has become as commonplace as the pledge of allegiance to a classroom of American children. This is not the case with one of the least modern passages in the entire Bible. In Numbers 5, a religious rite was established through which a man who suspected his wife of adultery could bring the accused woman (along with an offering) before a priest of the Lord for providential judgment from God.[8] If the accused woman maintained her innocence, the priest was to declare an oath which simultaneously exonerated the woman if she spoke the truth and threatened divine condemnation if she lied. While this passage was intended as a semi-public ritual for ancient Israel and is not directly applicable to the Christian era (as a rite of the church), the text revealed something important: that the Lord is the defender and judge of individual people amidst human affairs, both of good husbands from unfaithful wives and innocent wives from jealous husbands.[9] The Lord is God to every Christian as he was to Abraham and David, the sacred prophets, and the holy apostles—his promises are not simply to nations and churches but to Christian families and individual believers, to lead them in righteousness to salvation. To that end, we must remember how the Lord sent a vision to guide Joseph to do the right thing when the latter learned that his fiancée, Mary, was inexplicably pregnant. That is, God upholds the cause of all who call on him rather than turning to false religion or taking matters into their own hands. Just as Christians are not theological deists regarding the creation, so they should not be practical deists regarding their own lives.

What sets the Numbers passage apart is how the individual couple was called to submit themselves to the direct leadership of the Lord God. For her husband trapped in circumstances where he suspected, but was unable to confirm, the adultery of his wife, there was (and still is) a

---

7. Matthew 6:9–13 (KJV).
8. Numbers 5:11–31. For Jewish commentary on this passage, see Jacob Milgrom, *The JPS Torah Commentary: Numbers* (Philadelphia: Jewish Publications Society, 1989), 37–43.
9. The English scholar and jurist John Selden provided extensive commentary on this passage in his *Uxor Hebraica,* in which he examined how Jewish custom ritualized it with nuances and qualifications that reduced it (in my judgment) to mere form. Whereas this passage clearly appeals to God's providential, if not supernatural, intervention in human affairs, Jewish custom reduced it to a ritual process to segregate women from men and to extract confessions from fear of blasphemy. John Selden, *John Selden on Jewish Marriage Law: The Uxor Hebraica*, trans. Jonathan R. Ziskind (Leiden: E. J. Brill, 1991), 346–358.

terrible moral dilemma: any man who closes his eyes to the infidelity of his wife becomes complicit in her sin, even foolishly and willfully blind. And if his unfaithful wife remains unrepentant and dishonest, little basis for continued marriage exists. In such circumstances, human decency and divine holiness alike demand divorce. If, however, the accused wife is guiltless and yet harangued as guilty, her jealous husband will destroy their marriage as he shames an innocent woman before her friends and family, poisoning what is supposed to be an affectionate relationship. Moreover, a man will not sleep with an accused wife until the matter is resolved, thereby building tension for husband and wife alike through rejection, isolation, and sexual frustration. The slightest hint of adultery by a wife, even a misguided accusation, sets off a course of events that can destroy a marriage.

Since marital infidelity and false jealousy equally destroy biblical marriage, the Lord's law in the book of Numbers protected marriage in two ways. First, a jealous husband was to take his case to a priest, who presumably would question the man regarding the evidence and hear the wife's defense (just as medieval churchmen similarly reviewed evidence before authorizing trial by ordeal).[10] Because this vow was a holy oath, its appeal was made to God through a priest rather than through a judge for secular judgment—a process that enhanced impartiality and privacy. Moreover, because the appeal required a sacrifice of property to bring suit, trifles of jealousy were suppressed in jealous husbands prone to making unfounded accusations. If an accusation continued following a priest's examination, an appeal was made directly to the Lord, whose law required the jealous husband to wait for God's providential disposition of the case. That is to say, the accusing husband was obligated to wait for God to reveal the matter on God's timetable rather than his own (since no man controls the judgments of the Lord).

Meanwhile, the imperiled marriage remained valid until God's providence disposed of the case, with duties regarding support, intimacy, and respect remaining intact. Scripture declared the husband free from guilt

---

10. For accounts of medieval ordeals, see Hincmar of Rheims *De Divortio* and Eric Jager's *The Last Duel*. The first tells of Frankish King Lothar II's accusation of his wife of sordid sexual crimes; the second is a modern history drawing from legal archives to narrate the last trial by ordeal in European history—a duel between two nobles over an accused rape of one man's wife. Hincmar of Rheims, *The Divorce of King Lohar and Queen Theutberga: Hincmar of Rheims's De Divortio*, trans. Rachel Stone and Charles West (Manchester: Manchester University Press, 2016); Eric Jager, *The Last Duel: A True Story of Crime, Scandal, and Trial by Combat in Medieval France* (New York: Broadway Books, 2004).

in continuing his expected duties, even if his wife later proved to have been unfaithful. As for the wife, if guilty of adultery, the Lord swore to punish her sin, but if innocent, she remained under God's protection from a husband who might wish her evil. Having made his appeal to the Lord through the priesthood, the man was bound to wait for God's judgment rather than to take matters into his own hands—which protected mistaken husbands from doing wrong and limited the power of evil ones. After all, both majestic kings and common husbands have been known to fabricate charges against guiltless wives of whom they have grown tired, and good men have been known to make terrible mistakes based on misunderstood and incomplete evidence.[11]

The Lord is our God, and he leads us through our years, even when his work remains hidden—bringing forth divine purposes that sometimes align with our mortal objectives but, more often, are greater than we can imagine. The Lord's providential leading is given to those raised in the faith and those converted after faithlessness, immorality, and idolatry. Indeed, there is far more to this world than we can imagine. Ruth was not the only woman in Israel who was an ancestor to Messiah, for many Hebrew women shared in that honor, just as some contemporary wives and mothers will become the ancestors of great men and women born many generations in the future (we must remember that every living person of European ancestry is descended from every person living in Europe in the year 1000 who produced still-living descendants). Still, the Lord called out Ruth for the honor of such recognition in Scripture, explicitly naming her as a great-grandmother of King David, for whom the coming Son of David was named. One ancient Christian poet wrote of Ruth:

> *Ruth, burning under the heat in the field as she went over the stubble. Proving herself worthy of the hand of Boaz, and being taken in pure wedlock she conceived and gave birth to the family of Christ, David's royal line, and numbered God along with her mortal descendants.*[12]

---

11. The Numbers 5 passage is significant to me since it was the means through which the Lord protected my own marriage of over thirty years when my wife and I were presented with an inexplicable and incorrect medical diagnosis that was later reversed.
12. Prudentius, *Prudentius*, vol. 1, Loeb Classical Library (Cambridge, Massachusetts: Harvard University Press, 2006), 259–261.

10

THE CALL TO MARRIAGE

For as in those days before the flood they were eating and drinking, marrying and giving in marriage, until the day when Noah entered the ark, and they unaware until the flood came and swept them all away.[1]

TO LIVE LIFE WITHOUT REFLECTION—SIMPLY eating, drinking, and marrying is both foolish and dangerous. The men and women of this world who live for sensual pleasure are always struck down in deadly surprise when the judgment of God falls upon them. It is far better to live as both Christ and his servant Paul warned us to do: in prudent godliness. In the passage above from the Gospel of Matthew, Jesus told his listeners that people often have been distracted by the desire for marriage and everyday life to their eternal loss, and Paul made the same point in 1 Corinthians, when he warned Christians with wives to live "as though they had none." Paul was not denigrating marriage but reminding believers to make use of the world "as though they had no dealings with it."[2] Like Jesus, he warned each of us not to fall into the trap of those who remain concerned only for worldly affairs. Rather, Christ calls all of those who bear his name to live for eternity.

---

1. Matthew 24:38–39 (ESV).
2. 1 Corinthians 7:29, 31 (ESV).

How this is to be done is relatively straightforward. In 1 Corinthians 7, the apostle Paul explicitly reminded his readers that no believer must live without a sense of God's direction: each man and woman must have a call from God that they must follow. The apostle wrote that everyone should live the life which "the Lord has assigned to him, and to which God has called him," for no man or woman should drift through life without understanding where the Lord has called him or her to serve.[3] This teaching was presented in the context of discussing marriage, suggesting that in marriage (of all things), men and women must act according to the specific call of God. They must seek God's will, discern his paths, and study the Lord's word since these indicate what it is to be led by the Spirit of the Lord. Nonetheless, those who rush into marriage and only later realize their folly dare not declare such marriages invalid, for their marital obligations remain intact as with any other hasty or foolish contract.

As a side note, it must also be noted that Paul's teaching regarding God's call was not intended to drive believers into unceasing self-doubt, paralyzing introspection, or bitter remorse as they face a past that cannot be changed and a present that is constrained. When Paul reminded believers that they must be content with where God has placed them, he understood that many of the Corinthians came from difficult and unholy backgrounds, bringing with them suffering and shame to be redeemed and overcome in Christ. Some were divorced, facing separation from a spouse and children; others were perhaps diseased from prostitution or traumatized from sins committed against their physical bodies. God's call is one of hope and salvation, for it is a promise to be with us exactly where we now find ourselves, even after sin and sorrow.

After reminding the Corinthians of their sinful backgrounds, Paul then wrote how every category of believer (man or woman, Jew or Gentile, slave or free, married or single) must pursue the life God has given to them, subject only to the normal growth and changes of life as lived in piety and prudence. What Paul demanded—and what our Lord still requires—is that we realize who we are called to be and where God has placed us. Believers are to patiently wait for the Lord to redeem the sorrows we have suffered and the foolish decisions we have made, albeit on the Lord's timetable rather than our own. Christians must accept that the Lord's providence has led us from our conception to where we are at:

---

3. 1 Corinthians 7:17 (ESV).

where we must live God's faith, love, and wisdom. We must not dwell in a past that cannot be changed, but must serve Christ in the present moment with faith and hope in the redeemed future that the Lord promises to provide.

Three consequences follow from this instruction that Christians must live in light of God's providence and his call upon their lives. First, people must marry only a person God has judged lawful to wed. Second, they must decide to marry only when they are convinced that the Lord has called them to do so. Third, they must marry expecting to live a biblical marriage in sexual fidelity, mutual assistance, and the procreation of children. Nothing must be done apart from faith since "none of us lives to himself, and none of us dies to himself."[4] Only when people carefully consider marriage in light of God's divine word (taking the dictates of Scripture seriously) can they be fully assured that they are pursuing matrimony in an edifying fashion rather than thoughtlessly plunging into obligations they do not understand, as unbelievers did in the day of Noah and continue to do today. Such folly leads to sin and suffering, providing no foundation for a life of biblical piety and Christian charity.

Determining the call of God to marriage is no different than deciding the Lord's will in choosing a vocation, considering military service, or exercising political authority: the explicit teachings of Scripture must be sought in an attitude of humble submission and prayer.[5] Biblical doctrine, not emotions, circumstances, or individual preferences, must be considered the authoritative voice of God. People who rely on their impulses and emotions are ensnared by falsehood and self-deception whenever a momentary passion for a particular man or woman overwhelms moral and spiritual reasoning, or when an unreasonable demand for romantic feelings (based more on films and novels than grounded in biblical wisdom and real life) causes them to spurn a suitable suitor. Some couples even justify unwise marriages by pleading that God arranged the initial circumstances that brought them together, thereby confusing and conflating their personal greed and lust with the holy providence of the Lord. On the other hand, men and women who fear marriage because of childhood trauma or adult anxiety also allow the consequences of human

---

4. Romans 14:7 (ESV).
5. For a helpful work that reviews and critiques traditional evangelical approaches to seeking God's will (especially in dating and marrying), see Garry Friesen, *Decision Making and the Will of God: A Biblical Alternative to the Traditional View* (Sisters, Oregon: Multnomah Publishers, 2004).

sin to subvert the Lord's blessing and natural desire to be married. These, too, may fail to seek the will of the Lord or to trust that God's grace, power, and salvation are greater than the guilt and grip of their sin—although none of us should cast stones at them in their distress.

All such misunderstandings are best resisted by clinging to the word of God: marrying or giving in marriage only in accord with the teachings of the Bible. No one should seek to marry unless convinced the Lord has called them to do so, and no one should hesitate to enter into a marriage that Scripture blesses (admittedly, some people presume to know God's hidden plans, and others refuse to believe his revealed word). Believing Scripture alone allows the single to desire and hope for marriage, even when few suitors are available, for it is a mistake to believe that a person should not desire marriage just because he or she is not currently married. This is to foolishly try to discern God's will in the flux and flow of mutable events rather than in the firmness of God's revelation, blessing, and willingness to answer prayer. In 1 Corinthians 7 (one of the clearest biblical expositions regarding marriage and celibacy), the apostle Paul reminded the unmarried that they are free to seek marriage, and he provided acceptable reasons for doing so. Paul's instructions are worth a detailed review and serve as the framework for evaluating our longings if we find ourselves numbered among the unmarried.

To begin with, because marriage is the only appropriate place for sexual intimacy, Paul revealed that it is lawful to marry to live a chaste life.[6] He explained to both the unmarried and the widowed that those unable to control their sexual urges should marry. Not only should couples actually fornicating contract immediate marriage, but anyone of any age plagued with lust in thought or deed should seek, or prepare to seek, a lawful mate since marriage is the God-given remedy to tame the temptations of the mature flesh and distractions of the lustful heart.[7]

---

6. Jesus taught that looking at a woman lustfully (even without physical contact) is spiritually equivalent to physical adultery, declaring that a man should rather lose an eye or hand than use it for sexual sin. Both overt acts and hidden sexual desires outside of lawful marriage are prohibited. See Matthew 5:27–30 (ESV).

7. Hans Rookmaaker wrote of prudish ideals: "Toward the end of the eighteenth century the bourgeois world [began] to build up a defensive attitude toward sex that later became known as Victorian. We [can] no longer really understand what it was like in pre-Victorian times—how people knew that the fact that they had bodies and sexual urges was because they were human... Out of this grew the notion of 'romantic love', pure and beautiful and eternal, virgin-white and virtually sex-less... Reality, alas, is different. Biblical marriage is designed for men and women as they really are." Hans Rookmaaker, *Modern Art and the Death of a Culture* (Wheaton, Illinois: Crossway Books, 1994), 77–78.

While such reasoning does not sound particularly romantic to modern ears, it is entirely realistic and helpful advice since human beings truly are sexual beings. It is the Lord himself who made the sexual impulse strong enough to drive mankind toward marriage, thereby ensuring that human beings will continue to love and procreate, notwithstanding the indisputable hardships that marriage and parenthood bring in a fallen world. Sixteenth-century Protestant Edwin Sandys wrote:

> *[Be] the cares [of marriage] never so many and great, it is better to marry than burn, and even to be burdened with ordinary and honest cares than to be destroyed through unordinary and dishonest carelessness... He who sees a woman and in his heart has a lewd desire for her has defiled his heart and is in truth unchaste. If every man judged himself according to this rule precisely, he shall see a disease in himself that requires remedy. [It is his own fault if he ignores] medicine with an honorable title that draws us to it. The danger of not using it [is] death—for harlots and adulterers the Lord shall judge.*[8]

Even today, because of common pressure to postpone courtship and marriage, sexual passion pushes many young people into sexual immorality. Yet, the Lord desires chaste courtship and legitimate children, so marriage remains the appropriate remedy for every temptation of the flesh, and anyone tempted to sexual impurity should accept the responsibilities of marriage rather than using birth control and other protective measures to forestall pregnancy and prevent disease. Still, advice to seek marriage is not the same as encouraging lustful youth (unwilling and unready to live as adults) to wed, for marriage brings responsibilities as well as rights; it is to be used to control passion rather than to legitimize every base desire. While the apostle Paul advised unmarried believers to remain unmarried (like himself) for the sake of greater spiritual service, he simultaneously authorized marriage for those virgins and widows who "cannot exercise self-control," observing that "it is better to marry than to burn with passion." We must remember that Paul did not send those

---

8. Sandys also wrote: "It is true that all have not need for this remedy, because all are not subject to the danger and peril of the disease." Edwin Sandys, "The Sixteenth Sermon: A Sermon Preached at a Marriage in Stausborough," in *Sermons and Miscellaneous Pieces by Archbishop Sandys*, ed. Rev. John Ayer (The Parker Society) (Cambridge: Cambridge University Press, 1841), 316–317. I have edited this text for clarity.

tempted with sexual desire to prostitutes, paramours, or any other solution except matrimony and its attendant responsibilities.[9]

The apostle Paul also permitted marriage as a matter of the normal course of life. In 1 Corinthians, he wrote that a man might marry his betrothed simply because he is not treating her properly (one translation declared the virgin to be "past her youth").[10] In other words, it is proper to marry at the appropriate season of life, so people should not act dishonorably by stringing along a suitor (or oneself, for that matter), both extending temptation and ruining the other person's opportunity to marry and conceive children at an appropriate age. This suggests that men and women should seek marriage while they are still young and fertile. Moreover, when Paul warned his readers not to postpone marriage, he was referring to women in their twenties or younger; he certainly was not discussing women in their thirties or forties. In the Roman world of Paul's day, laws sometimes required powerful men to marry young and penalized those who remained childless. The Jewish world also expected women, at least, to marry as teenagers. The delayed age of modern marriage (with associated sexual immorality) does not reflect biblical commands, values, or expectations, but seems to be associated with an unwarranted delay in social maturity for many young men and women in our culture.[11]

While the age at which men and women marry may differ by culture and circumstance (based on the age of social maturity and the legitimate requirement to make a living), the obligation of men and women to be charitable toward each other remains unchanged. Even in a society like ours in which many people prefer later marriages, Christians must consider not only their own preferences, but also the needs and desires of the other sex in their planning—lest they court too long or marry too late. Men and women alike are obligated to think not simply about themselves, but also about the other sex in their consideration and planning of their timelines regarding engagement and marriage. A Christian man ought to hurry himself toward marriage to serve a single woman who longs for a family (whether young or reaching an age where pregnancy may be more challenging to achieve), and a woman ought to make herself available to marry a Christian man who desires a wife in his bed. Both

---

9. 1 Corinthians 7:8–9 (ESV).
10. 1 Corinthians 7:36 (NASB). Older translations also focus on the aging of the girl.
11. Surveys of Greek and Roman family life are found in Ken M. Campbell, ed., *Marriage and Family in the Biblical World* (Downer's Grove, Illinois: InterVarsity Press, 2003).

should regard the needs of the other sex more than themselves, for no one should live for himself or herself until their wedding day, and only then begin to think about what it means to serve the other sex. Intentional and deliberate efforts to understand and serve a person unlike oneself should start earlier, perhaps with the play of children.[12]

Paul made allowances to delay marriage in times of extreme crisis (perhaps plague, famine, war, or persecution), although his advice is not presented as authoritative and remains subject to his previous guidance that lust should be controlled through marriage and that timely decisions should be respected. In the epistle of 1 Corinthians, Paul allowed that the Corinthians were in a time of turmoil and should consider delaying marriage, given the troubles in which they found themselves.[13] One thinks of couples who came of age during the Second World War. In many instances, it was better for such couples to delay marriage until peace returned to avoid starting households that would be torn asunder by military service, armed invasions, and combat casualties. Still, we must remember that the apostle Paul was addressing a specific situation, as the rest of the New Testament (and Paul's other epistles) reveal that marriage remains the norm for most men and women. Just as the delayed marriages of the Second World War eventually fed into the Baby Boom of the 1950s, so Paul allowed a temporary delay in marriage during a time of crisis. And it was right that Paul did so, for in declaring that more pressing concerns might sometimes limit sexual fulfillment in marriage, the apostle was subordinating the impulses of lust and desire to the authority of wisdom and prudence as a general principle for the government of the entire household. This is divine wisdom embedded in practical advice.

In 1 Timothy, Paul used such wisdom to declare that young widows should seek a husband so they might contribute to the common good by bearing children and managing household affairs. Not only does such work keep women (and the men who marry them) from idle gossip and illicit sensual indulgence, but it also provides them with the ability to serve their extended families and the broader Christian communities. By taking on the responsibility to marry and bear children, such couples equip themselves to progress in the virtues of love, obedience, and service.

---

12. I do not mean the segregation of toys between the sexes (though the sexes do indeed differ from the womb), but the interaction of boys and girls such that modesty, affection, and respect are fostered between the sexes from their earliest days.
13. 1 Corinthians 7:26–27 (ESV).

Please note that this passage was written on the heels of the apostle's instruction that Christian widows ought to care for their elderly relatives (since possession of a stable home allows for care of the needy), which is why Paul advised younger widows to "marry, bear children, manage their households, and give the adversary no occasion for slander."[14] The duties of piety and charity require a house and household, if relatives (and strangers) are to be cared for. The holy call of marriage is far greater than romantic infatuation and sexual attraction.

Christian men and women who wish to know whether they have been called to marriage need look only as far as Scripture to hear the word of God. Is sexual temptation a distraction, or sexual intimacy deeply desired? Do the everyday rhythms of life make this time prudent to seek marriage? Is it a good time to establish a household for the birth of new life and care of elderly parents? Are there no spiritual or moral impediments to marriage with a particular suitor? If any or all of these reasons exist, and if the Lord has not called the man or woman to a celibate life by an abiding desire for charitable service which requires celibacy, marriage should be pursued, insofar as the Lord opens the door. With such pious motives, believers can be assured they marry according to God's will. In fact, if these criteria for considering marriage exist, and if there has not been a specific call by the Lord to celibacy, then a man or woman is not at liberty to remain single, particularly if distracted by sexual temptation, but must subordinate their hopes and dreams to the need to marry, or otherwise prepare themselves to marry. Thomas Cranmer observed that we are not free to decide for or against marriage based on our preferences, whims, or desires. He noted that we must seek the will of God rather than our own choices, writing:

> *Now good children consider this, that it is not in your own liberty whether you will be married or not. And thus I speak for this purpose, that you should be the more diligent to learn in time some craft, way, or science, whereby you might keep your house and get your living honestly, for both yourself, your wife, and your children, for God wills all those to use marriage that cannot live continently.*[15]

---

14. 1 Timothy 5:14–16 (ESV).
15. Thomas Cranmer, *A Catechism Set Forth by Thomas Cranmer*, ed. G. E. Duffield (Oxford: Sutton Courtenay Press, 1978), 67. I have edited the original English for clarity.

11

THE CALL TO CELIBACY

The disciples said to [Jesus], "If such is the case of a man with his wife, it is better not to marry." But he said to them, "Not everyone can receive this saying, but only those to whom it is given. For there are eunuchs who have been so from birth, and there are eunuchs who have been made eunuchs by men, and there are eunuchs who have made themselves eunuchs for the sake of the kingdom of heaven. Let the one who is able to receive this receive it." [1]

THE ANCIENT HEBREWS stressed the importance of marriage so much that they often regarded the unmarried and childless as second-class citizens. That was a terrible mistake. Not only does God use his unmarried and childless servants for some of his most important work, but when the Lord became a man, he remained unmarried for his entire life, thereby blessing the celibate life as fully pleasing to God. Moreover, when the disciples of Christ were scandalized by their Lord's refusal to compromise with the easy divorces of his day, they sharply responded to their teacher's uncompromising standard of absolute fidelity. "Well, if that's the case," they replied to his restriction of divorce (my paraphrase), "no one should get married at all!" That is, the disciples suggested singleness to be preferable to marriage without the possibility of divorce. In response, Jesus

---

1. Matthew 19:10–12 (ESV).

sternly reminded his disciples that celibacy is a gift from God, which must be considered as carefully and thoughtfully as a marriage might be planned. No one may either marry or remain single without a specific call from God; everyone is bound to consider carefully whether they are called to be celibate or married.

When Jesus responded to his disciples in Matthew 19, he distinguished between two classes of people who remain single in this world: the accidental and the intentional. According to Christ, some people endure singleness because of the wounds of natural or human evil, while others practice abstinence in willing obedience to God, although they might otherwise be well-suited for marriage. The physiologically impotent, for instance, are unable to be adequate spouses based on physical or biological injuries that render them unsuitable for marriage. One Puritan writer noted that it is "unlawful to make a contract with such a person as is unfit for the use of marriage, either by natural constitution of body [or by] the deprivation of the parts belonging to generation."[2] Jesus himself revealed how some people are rendered unmarriageable through acts of human violence. In ancient times, this might refer to servants castrated to guard a master's harem. Today, men wounded during combat (or by accident) and women traumatized by violent and indecent acts (such as rape or incest) number among such celibates—enduring singleness as tragedy and trauma. To such men and women, God promises demonstrable love in this life and an eternal heritage in the next. These are the eunuchs to whom Old Testament prophets promised a better inheritance than sons and daughters, if they patiently wait for God's deliverance.[3]

Jesus mentioned a second category of celibates: those who have willingly renounced marriage for the sake of God's kingdom, referring to the prophets and their successors. God called men such as Jeremiah, John the Baptist, and Paul to lives of service that precluded the responsibilities of marriage and parenthood. For them, to marry would have been practically difficult and spiritually harmful. The prophet Jeremiah was even

---

2. William Perkins, "Christian Economy," in Larsen Klein, ed. *Daughters, Wives, and Widows*, 161.

3. Inspired by the Holy Spirit, one prophet declared in Isaiah 56:3–5: "Let not the foreigner who has joined himself to the Lord say, 'The LORD will surely separate me from his people.' Nor let the eunuch say, 'Behold, I am a dry tree.' For thus says the LORD: 'To the eunuchs who keep My sabbaths, and choose what please Me, and hold fast My covenant, to them I will give in My House and within My walls a memorial, and a name better than than of sons and daughters; I will give them an everlasting name which will not be cut off.'"

told not to marry. Such celibate prophets were not indulged with easier lives than those called to family responsibilities, but were called to more difficult service as guardians of the Lord's house. They were made fathers (even *church fathers*) in the greater household of God's church, being called to harder service rather than lesser tasks.[4] Because their calling brought more humility than changing dirty diapers and more sleepless concern than tending ill children or ailing wives, we must never imagine that the renunciation of marriage is permitted to succeed in a career, enjoy a hobby, or pursue affluence. Christians in Roman antiquity were not exempted from marriage to tour the beaches of Hispania, the vineyards of Tuscia, and the mountains of Macedonia. Nor were they freed from the spiritual discipline of marriage to enjoy the library at Alexandria, the Colosseum in Rome, or the villas of Pompeii.

The apostle Paul traveled extensively throughout the Roman Empire, just not for pleasure. Rather, he lived a life as full of suffering as any man ever has, enduring nearly every form of pain and hardship that a person can experience. By his testimony, Paul suffered prison, stoning, beatings, floggings, shipwrecks, banditry, persecution, hunger, wandering, cold, nakedness, and the pressure of dealing with heresy and dissension in the churches he had planted.[5] Given the reality of his life, when Paul wrote to the Corinthians about the advantages of celibacy, he was not advising them to take an easy path, but to consider denying themselves the rigors of marriage for the sake of suffering more challenging hardships than the troubles of family life. Paul was teaching that the household of God needs hard-working fathers and anxious mothers as much as any mortal family does. The apostle declared:

> *I want you to be free from anxieties. The unmarried man is anxious about the things of the Lord, how to please the Lord. But the married man is anxious about worldly things, how to please his wife, and his interests are divided. And the unmarried or betrothed woman is anxious about the things of the Lord, how to be holy in body and spirit. But the married woman is anxious about worldly things, how to please her husband. I say this for your own benefit,*

---

4. Jeremiah 16:1–2.
5. 2 Corinthians 11:24–28.

not to lay any restraint upon you, but to promote good order and to secure your undivided devotion to the Lord.[6]

Elsewhere, Paul posited that he, like the other apostles, possessed "the right to take along a believing wife," if he so chose, just like the other apostles, brothers of Jesus, and Peter himself.[7] Though granted the gift of celibacy, the apostle Paul claimed the right to marry if he preferred. This is precisely what Jesus meant when he taught that any man who is willing to accept the gift of singleness should do so. Christ's words were not intended to bind men and women who desire marriage to a manner of life they find unendurable, only to remind believers how the renunciation of marriage is to be made freely rather than imposed as enslavement or tragedy (as impotence and castration are).[8] As for the apostle Paul, just as he gave up his right to receive financial support from churches during his missionary work, so he surrendered his freedom to take a wife on his dangerous journeys—and the Lord granted Paul grace both to fashion tents to financially support himself and to accept the spiritual gift of celibacy. Like Christ, the apostle freely chose to bear a cross for the good of the men and women around him. To repeat: when Jesus told believers that those who could accept celibacy should do so, he did not impose on anyone a spiritually distracting and emotionally destructive singleness, particularly if sexual temptation or the desire for companionship or children remain intense and pressing problems. Our Lord was revealing the lawfulness of men and women to freely choose to remain single for all (or part) of their lives to serve God, his church, or those in need. Only they must remain completely and contentedly chaste.

In our era of selfish singleness, it is essential to reiterate that Jesus did not exempt anyone from the rigors of marriage so they can preserve their freedom, affluence, lifestyle, comfort, or solitude. Men and women are called to remain intentionally single only as their singleness prepares them to serve outside of a household at a higher cost to themselves than through family life. Why? Because family life provides excellent discipline for curing character flaws and teaching spiritual qualities such as obedience, patience, and forgiveness. Since no one can learn such virtues by

---

6. 1 Corinthians 7:32–35 (ESV).
7. 1 Corinthians 9:5 (ESV).
8. The use of monasteries and convents for involuntary celibacy led to much sin, including sexual sin. For a portrayal of such problems, see Mary Laven's *Virgins of Venice: Broken Vows and Cloistered Lives in the Renaissance Convent* (New York: Penguin Books, 2002).

themselves, such characteristics must be learned as human beings struggle through the frustrations, difficulties, injustices, and temptations of living in close quarters with others. For that reason, Protestant Reformers insisted that the apparent spirituality of the convent or monastery was a poor substitute for family life in the building of Christian character, and often observed how it is far easier to be a monk at prayer or a nun in a quiet cell than a father laboring in the fields or a mother of babies in a noisy house. Protestant Reformers frequently rebuked those whose personal *call* to the celibate life was not genuine: men and women who proved more interested in avoiding the challenging task of raising a family than in adopting the even more demanding duty of serving God's people with the undivided strength of their hearts and hands.[9]

Modern social reformers and activists make the same mistake as medieval monks and nuns, convincing themselves that they have forsaken the comforts of family life in exchange for a life devoted to serving a cause, a charitable organization, or an educational institution.[10] Yet, no matter how many funds might be raised or political reforms launched, such self-denial is a facade, giving an appearance of charity rather than the reality of serving others. All too often, such lives are devoted to ambition, glory, and pleasure and do not include Christ-like service of others: the washing of feet and the suffering of splinters and spikes from a cross. Frequently, they do not even include chastity of mind or body. Such men and women only pretend to live in public service and personal sacrifice.

In contrast, those who serve others with their own hands grow in true humility and charity. Mother Teresa, for instance, was no mere activist: celibacy enabled her to serve more people than she might have done as a natural mother, having adopted the most despised of the despised as her spiritual children, washing their sores and wounds with her own hands. She cleansed the filth of the poor, following faithfully the call of the Lord Jesus Christ, who healed the diseased and washed the feet of his servants with his own hands. Our Lord requires his followers to do likewise, whether in the streets of Calcutta or the privacy of their homes.

---

9. The former monk Luther claimed that monasticism frequently was unchaste and permitted a "lazy, secure life." In contrast, Luther wrote how married people "never have any peace from their children or servants, and are never without work day or night. It is among such people you will find those who believe." Martin Luther, "An Answer to Several Questions on Monastic Vows (1526)," in *Luther's Works*, vol. 46, 150.
10. Some forsake parenthood because they believe the world to be evil and overpopulated, but God has not rescinded his command (Genesis 9:7–8) for sinful mankind to reproduce.

What matters before God is that we devote ourselves to the service of other human beings, so that we might increase our measure of love and faith, glorifying God and fulfilling our call to love others. No one should use celibacy to satisfy their self-indulgence. John Calvin declared:

> *[It] is not given to every man to keep chastity in celibacy, even if he aspires to it with great zeal and effort, and that it is a special grace which the Lord bestows only upon certain men, in order to hold them more ready for his work... Let no man long for celibacy unless he can live without a wife. Also, let him not provide in this state for the repose and convenience of the flesh, but only that, freed of this marriage bond, he may be more prompt and ready for all the duties of piety.*[11]

Of course, not everyone has the opportunity to marry. Our disordered and sinful world is as cursed with undeserved loneliness and unfulfilled desire as it is with death and disease. Sometimes, the Lord uses such hardships as the means of his fatherly discipline, just as he also uses death and disease to draw his servants to himself. In other cases, unwanted singleness results from the aftermath of human sin, as people suffer unsought celibacy resulting from having afflicted their bodies with diseases or squandered the most promising years of youth pursuing pleasure, ambition, or wealth. Others endure singleness from the effects of human evil or as a form of true martyrdom, rightly refusing to date, court, or marry any of the unbelievers among whom they live. For these, singleness is a cross of Christ as real as persecution, poverty, or disease. It was in this spirit of accepting sorrow for God's faith that Ruth left her pagan homeland and traveled with her widowed mother-in-law, Naomi, despite believing that her opportunity for marriage among the Israelites would be restricted due to her Moabite heritage. Despite that very real possibility, Ruth followed the Lord even though her devotion endangered her best chance to remarry and bear children, judging it better to

---

11. Calvin, *Institutes*, vol. 1, 406–407. I also would note that while nations and civilizations rise and fall, each individual human being is destined for eternal life, so it will not do for a person to devote himself (or herself) to any lesser cause (whether a sack of gold or society as a whole) than taking care of other people. Edward John Carnell noted: "If the *individual* is not infinitely worthy, then a society (which is composed of other unworthy people) is not any more valuable." Edward John Carnell, *A Philosophy of the Christian Religion* (Grand Rapids, Michigan: Baker Book House, 1952), 247.

live as a daughter-in-law to Naomi in Israel than to become a wife and
mother among the pagans of Moab.[12] Ruth decided it was better to live
alone, and even to die a lonely old woman, in the Lord's church than to
become the mother of an unbelieving family apart from God's holy
people.

All men and women who live in undesired singleness should consider
themselves free to marry as long as they can fulfill the obligations of
marriage and are afforded the opportunity to do so. Still, anyone who
cannot find a spouse should no more waste their life in self-pity than the
married should despair when they are confronted with everyday human
hardships like abuse, disease, and death. The truth is that no one, single
or married, is exempt from suffering in this world of war, famine, disease,
infertility, slavery, rebellion, immorality, injustice, and death. Those who
call to God and live by his word while facing unsought and undeserved
singleness should count themselves among the holy martyrs—if they
remain steadfast amidst the temptation to ignore the Lord's law for the
sake of their desires. Indeed, following the great persecutions of the early
churches (at the toleration of the Christian faith under Constantine),
some believers began to count among holy martyrs those ascetics who
fled the corruptions of Roman society in utter dedication to the Lord via
celibacy. While I have serious doubts that the ascetic ideal was prudent
and biblical, it remains true that those so devoted to the Lord that they
would rather suffer unsought and undesired singleness than make an
unbiblical marriage are to be counted among the martyrs of the faith
(and with a sorrow patiently endured year after year rather than in a
single act of courage). Jesus declared:

> *"Truly, I say to you, there is no one who has left house or wife or
> brothers or parents or children, for the sake of the kingdom of God,
> who will not receive many times more in this time, and in the age to
> come eternal life."*[13]

On the other hand, some people do not marry because unrealistic
demands regarding prospective mates have clouded their thinking. Some
men and women are given several opportunities to marry but refuse to
commit to any of their suitors, finding physical, moral, financial, or

---

12. Ruth 1:8.
13. Luke 18:29–30 (ESV).

emotional fault with each one (sometimes from vanity and greed; at other times from particularity and fretfulness). This does not imply that men and women should marry suitors whom they despise, but only to say that many contemporary men and women have unrealistic expectations about beauty, charm, compatibility, and achievement in a potential husband or wife. When a man refuses to court the pious, but plain, woman the Lord has brought to his notice, he makes a mistake that may cost him his best chance at marriage. When a woman rejects a hard-working suitor because his work carries little prestige, she has only herself to blame if she remains childless and alone for the rest of her life. After all, a starving man who continually refuses bread because he prefers croissants deserves the hunger he suffers, and death through starvation if he continues in his fastidious folly. God's word calls us to pray for our daily bread, accepting God's daily provision with gratitude and spurning every desire to have a better life than others.

Martin Luther once complained about how evildoers and devils try to break up impending marriages by using false rumors to question the virginity of a betrothed woman (so important was virginity in his culture). Similarly, it is the devil's work today to deceive modern people into making unreasonable expectations of potential mates. Contemporary men and women have come to expect too much from suitors, unaware of what marriage entails and how marital affection is best achieved. Rather than limiting themselves to biblical perspectives regarding the ability of potential spouses to provide sexual companionship, produce children, and provide for a growing household, they also demand that their potential spouse possess some particular skill, interest, or ability that is not essential to the core purposes of marriage. Some foolishly seek relationships resembling those found in obscene matchmaking television shows. Such approaches to marriage most emphatically do not obey Jesus in renouncing marriage for the kingdom of God, for they spurn chastity and charity for the kingdom of man. These men and women sin greatly as they stumble through sexual temptation or otherwise live selfish and worldly lives rather than seeking to serve a spouse, child, and family before the best opportunity to do so is lost. In this way, unwise demands and evil thinking subvert holy marriage as surely as a false rumor about a particular suitor. Martin Luther wrote:

> *To pay attention to evil suspicion or wicked fancy or even evil tongues which secretly slander such a [pious] girl is contrary to God*

and right. Satan himself has deprived many a good person of marriage through such wicked fancies and evil tongues, or where he could not prevent the marriage, he has embittered and ruined it with the darkest kinds of suspicion.[14]

---

14. Martin Luther, "On Marriage Matters (1530)," in *Luther's Works*, vol. 46, 300.

PART II

THE MAKING OF A LAWFUL MARRIAGE

❦

Just because men and women are convinced that God has called them to marriage does not give them the right to marry whomever they might choose. Both the Old and New Testaments include specific instructions regarding who may be married rightly, making it evident that God restricts the marriage pool. The Christian tradition often made the discussion of what are called "marital impediments" a matter of overriding concern as biblical ethics were taught and lived amidst cultures converting from moral laxness, pagan practices, and unbiblical customs. In Paul's first letter to the Corinthians (the very letter in which he sets forth significant teachings about the call to marriage and celibacy), the apostle Paul revealed that not every marital union is morally valid or spiritually lawful among God's people. Drawing on Old Testament instructions regarding marital impediments, the apostle insisted that believers use spiritual discernment in making a marriage: a call that makes clear that the idea of a spiritual (or natural) impediment to marriage is closely related to the notion that some marriages might be unwise, even prohibited.

Though the discussion of impediments might seem obscure or unimportant, nothing could be further from the truth. According to Scripture, the ancient world of Noah was destroyed in large part because mankind was marrying and giving in marriage without sufficient consideration for morality and spirituality. If this is true, then the modern world is facing the wrath of God as entire communities bless same-sex marriages and drift toward polygamous and incestuous marriages (following open promiscuity before marriage). This unbiblical drift is not only morally anathema to believers but is also a contradiction in terms. Whatever such liaisons are, they can never be called marriage by the tenets of Christian doctrine. Hence, in understanding the nature of marital impediments, the godly are brought to face-to-face confrontation with unbelievers in the public arena— hardly an obscure matter.

This section begins with a discussion of the nature of marital impediments in general, then examines particular impediments in fuller detail, including those concerning close blood relationships, authority, parental authority, nature, sexual purity, and criminality. Several factors wrongly feared by some to impede or taint marriage are also discussed in those chapters. Additionally, the ethics of courtship are examined as the section compares biblical customs of courtship with modern dating customs and notions of romantic love. There is also a discussion of the precise moment at which marriage occurs, as that is the moment at which marital duties become ethically obligatory, regardless of whether individuals, societies, or states recognize such obligations. The section concludes by examining the celebration of nuptials and the moral purposes weddings should reflect.

~

12

THE NATURE OF IMPEDIMENTS

*When man began to multiply on the face of the land and daugh-
ters were born to them, the sons of God saw that the daughters of
man were attractive. And they took as their wives any they chose.
Then the LORD said, "My Spirit shall not abide in man forever, for
he is flesh: his days shall be 120 years."* [1]

IN THE DAYS before Noah's flood, marriage was treated with far less
reverence than as a divine institution—with an indiscriminate intermin-
gling of men and women in marriage. Both the book of Genesis (above)
and Christ's discussion of the antediluvian world reveal that marriage was
treated more casually than as a holy calling. [2] The biblical text declares
that the *sons of God* (believers) went as far as to betroth themselves to the
daughters of men (unbelievers). People were too engrossed in their
worldly lives to govern themselves by the will of God, but married and
copulated as they pleased, without fear of God or respect toward religion
and morality. It was this sin that set the stage for the orgy of wickedness
that ended only when God destroyed the people of the ancient world
with a terrible flood. Such gross sin also overwhelms the modern world,
as men and women mate as they see fit, without respect for the laws of

---

1. Genesis 6:1–3 (ESV).
2. Matthew 24:38 (ESV).

the Lord or the faith into which they were born. None of us should, however, forget that God's holy character does not change. We, too, will face complete destruction if we do not repent of our sins. Violating God's law comes at a terrible cost.[3]

As will be discussed in the following chapters, Scripture warns of specific impediments (moral and spiritual obstacles) to the making of a legitimate marriage. These impediments determine when marriage and consequent obligations exist in the Lord's eyes, and when they do not. We must remember that even our secular society establishes impediments to the lawful marriage of some couples. For instance, a man cannot legally marry a minor or his sister, and a woman cannot marry her father or an already married man. Neither can they marry dead persons, unreasoning animals, inanimate objects, or themselves (though a few people attempt non-legally binding "marriage" in several such categories). In fact, few of us doubt that at least some marriages should be prohibited, with even the most ardent moral relativists preventing parents and children from marrying each other, if for no other reason than to prevent public scandal. Every code of law establishes at least some impediments to lawful marriage, and we all agree with many such obstacles.

The discussion of marital impediments centers not on the existence of impediments but on their origin and nature. While Jews and Christians have restricted marriage between close family members since God revealed the Mosaic law (there also are prior precedents against such relationships), many unbelievers repudiate, reject, or ignore the biblical tradition—restricting incest only for genetic reasons and permitting easy divorce and remarriage, or even open marriage, as natural outgrowths of human sexuality. In recent decades, increasingly secularized courts and legislatures have struck down laws restricting the marriages of same-sex couples, and some Western activists and governments are changing marital impediments away from those ideals rooted in thirty-five hundred years of Judeo-Christian custom, particularly laws against marrying close relatives and multiple partners.

---

3. Martin Luther observed that once the First Table of the Law (dealing with duties to God) has been repudiated, the Second Table of the Law (dealing with duties to mankind) will be similarly rejected. Luther wrote: "After the First Table has been cast aside, the Second Table, too, is cast aside, and lust takes over the first or principal position. Lust becomes utterly bestial and looks down upon the procreation of children... When lust becomes supreme in this way, [all of God's commandments] lose their power." Martin Luther, "Lectures on Genesis (Chapters 6–14)," in *Luther's Works*, vol. 2, 9.

In response to these challenges, Christians are called to imitate John the Baptist, who was martyred for upholding a biblical impediment to marriage. John was executed for condemning King Herod's incestuous marriage with Herodias (the wife of Herod's living brother) in accord with Mosaic law when he preached to the king and to all who could hear: "It is not lawful for you to have your brother's wife." These uncompromising words required that the law of God be respected by a half-pagan king who ruled primarily through Roman power, regardless of whether God's word conformed to the political and legal principles of the Roman Empire, Herod's government, or Jewish expediencies. Just as John the Baptist served as a prophetic witness against moral evil, so should we. Even where Christians lack sufficient political strength to influence public policy and common culture, we must uphold the Lord's law within his churches and raise prophetic voices in the broader community: even preaching judgment to half-pagan tyrants. The fact that Herod did not recognize the authority of John the Baptist's faith in no way changed the prophet's duty to preach and live the Lord's moral law before Herod and the Jewish people.[4]

Animals mate without the use of reason or morality, copulating with biological siblings and offspring without scruples. Apart from a few exceptions, such as wolves and perhaps a few birds, most beasts are not particularly monogamous, and it is certain that none take the wedding vows of mankind. In both plant and animal life, nature seeks prolific and indiscriminate reproduction (just as the Lord ordained for those creatures not made to reflect his moral splendor). However, moral impediments among human beings remind us that the universe has a spiritual order that must not be ignored. The Lord is so insistent that mankind differentiate human nature from the amorality of the natural world that he commanded ancient Israel to treat both nature and human custom in a holy manner, forbidding the Hebrews from cross-breeding animals, cross-sowing fields, and cross-manufacturing different materials into their clothing. Mankind was not to cross the boundaries established by God—who ordained every plant and animal to reproduce after its kind, thereby

---

4. Mark 6:18 (ESV). Fourth-century historian Eusebius observed: "[Josephus] mentions Herodias [and] tells how though she was his brothers's wife Herod married her, discarding his existing lawful wife—daughter of King Aretas of Petrea—and separating Herodias from her husband, who was still alive. For her sake, [Herod] put John to death and was involved in war with Aretas." Eusebius, *History of the Church from Christ to Constantine*, trans. G.A. Williamson; ed. Andrew Louth (London: Penguin Books, 1965), 28.

establishing how our world must continue until the cessation of mortal life.

Now, it certainly was not the case that the God who created every plant in the world was offended by the existence of fields in which wheat was mixed with barley during the sowing of seed. After all, God mixes all sorts of plants in the wilds of nature, and there are many fields where God has sent winds and rain to mix seeds and grow different grains together, contrary to what Moses allowed the Hebrews—and undoubtedly there were such fields in ancient Israel. Therefore, this law's purpose was less to separate the growing of differing types of grain seed than to remind mankind that the world of nature, especially the natural instincts of humanity, is to be ordered according to God's moral purposes rather than by brute desire or untamed impulse. This law calls us to remember that mankind originally was called not to live in the wild, but to tend a garden and harvest ordered beauty from raw nature. What mankind has accomplished with decorative gardens at Versailles, grain farms in Kansas, rice paddies in Vietnam, cattle ranches in Argentina, coffee estates in Kenya, and vegetable and flower gardens in American suburbs comes far closer to who we are called to be than what mankind can achieve through wandering tribes foraging and scrounging forests and fields without putting down roots or cultivating the earth. All of us are called to stand above nature as caretakers, and each of us is called to reflect the holy nature of the Lord God while doing so. That is why Leviticus reminded us to cultivate nature, but always while acknowledging and respecting all natural differences ordained by the Lord.[5]

Moreover, restrictions placed on the use of nature are intended as symbols for enduring spiritual purposes. This is especially the case regarding human sexual impulses. The relationships of parent, child, spouse, sibling, and stranger must never be confused with one another. A father is not a husband, and a brother is not a son; nor is a daughter-in-law a stranger or an aunt a cousin. Each relationship is of its own kind. Nor must human seed be sown so that parentage is unacknowledged: with children suffering the lack of a legitimate father because seed was

---

5. Genesis 2:15; Leviticus 19:19. Regarding these restrictions, one Jewish commentator observed: "The most favored explanation for the prohibition against mixtures is that it is a violation of the order God brought into the world by separating the species (Gen 1) and, hence, a symbol of disorder, the reversal of creation." Jacob Milgrom, *Leviticus 17-22: A New Translation with Introduction and Commentary* (New Haven, CT: Anchor Yale Bible, 2000), 1659.

indiscriminately mingled in a woman so that parentage became unseen or uncertain. Above everything else, the Lord desires that households be governed by purity and love rather than promiscuous desires and unreasonable couplings. Though ancient and modern libertines have preferred the dark lust of the orgy to the visible purity of love and holiness, God hates such gross wickedness and blesses only a clear distinction of persons and relationships, each of which has been instituted to reveal a different facet of his abundant goodness.

Like the many facets of a diamond, each human relationship reveals a different dimension of God's multi-faceted character: a man is given birth by his mother, grows up with his sister, marries a wife, and begets his daughter—and he has a unique set of obligations toward (and joys received from) each different class of woman. Honor is due to a mother, and fatherly concern is owed to a daughter. Fraternal friendship and innocence belong to a sister, and intimate purity and romantic passion to a wife. Modest friendship may be owed to an unmarried (widowed or divorced) neighbor and compassionate kindness to a needy stranger. Every human being is involved in a complex set of distinct relationships that reveal who God is: relationships that must never be crossed or confused. In addition, the Lord arranges matters so that the varied nature of human relationships works to unite humanity more closely, even as the differences among persons work to separate individual family members from one another into growing families and new responsibilities. By prohibiting marriage to close relatives, the Lord extends the reach of charity to distant strangers, now united to another family through the association of wedlock. Augustine of Hippo noted:

> *[Mankind], among whom concord is honorable and useful, should be bound together by the various relationships. When, therefore, a man has one person for his father, another for his father-in-law, friendship extends itself to a larger number.*[6]

The book of Leviticus established penalties and punishments for those who would defy God's created order by indiscriminately marrying and mating without regard for moral propriety. Incestuous and other perverted sexual unions were punished by death. If Scripture is true and

---

6. Augustine of Hippo, "The City of God (Book XV, Chapter 16)," in *Basic Writings*, vol. 2, 296–297.

historical (as Christians confess it to be), this was no empty threat, for the
Jews were reminded how they had been given the promised land precisely
because its previous inhabitants became a stench in the Lord's nostrils
through their idolatry and sexual perversion (among other sins). Moses
warned God's people how the Lord would reject them as he did the
Canaanites and the entire antediluvian world if they followed the evil
example of their pagan predecessors, who sinned to such an extent that
the Lord utterly destroyed them.[7] Such divine teachings must not be
factored from our thinking, and we must not imagine that the Lord's
immutable character has changed, or that God has repented of his
unbending laws of holiness and who he declares himself to be. The Lord
did not condemn incest and adultery under Moses with severe penalties,
only to change his mind under Christ, and turn a blind eye to infidelity
and impurity under the apostolic church.

Modern Christians would do well to remember that the Lord still
ordains impediments to marriage, the violation of which brings both illegitimacy and judgment. Though most people find it intuitively repulsive
to hear of a brother and sister sleeping together as husband and wife, our
culture seems to be sinking so spiritually low that even the incest taboo is
being directly challenged, and not just on sordid television talk shows.
Anyone who knows anything about animal sexuality understands that it
is not natural impulses that preclude incestuous promiscuity, for animals
from the same litter will mate if not separated from one another. That is
why those who reduce human nature to its merely natural components
lose not only their sense of the distinction between humanity and
animals but also come to believe that men and women should mate like
beasts. Some theorists argue that the sexual rites of stags and sows (more
accurately, bonobos and birds) should be adopted by mankind. It is as if
these immoral ethicists wish for our society to become as polluted by
incest as it already has been by fornication, adultery, and divorce. Is it not
bad enough that drunkards, drug addicts, and perverts abuse their children? Must unnatural lust also find its public apologists?

Marvin Harris, an influential anthropologist read by thousands of
university students during recent decades, once wrote that in our era of
"sexual liberation and experiment," sexual intimacy between brothers
and sisters is "probably on the verge of becoming just another 'kinky'

---

7. Leviticus 18:6–25; Leviticus 20:1–5, 22–24; Deuteronomy 8:19–20.

sexual preference of little interest to society."[8] Since Harris first penned these words, there has been even further drift toward acceptance of close relative sexual unions, something unimaginable in my youth. But so was the notion of legalized same-sex marriage that changed in a few short years. Who can be certain that the barriers against nuclear family incest will not be dismantled and discarded? Already, we see Ivy League professors confessing affairs with grown daughters, as well as American states and European countries reconsidering the legitimacy of legal prohibitions against sleeping with and marrying close relatives.[9]

Before we actually open the floodgates to such perversion, it is crucial that we understand that prohibitions against immoral sexual and marital unions are as binding today as they were in antiquity, just like injunctions against murder, rape, and kidnapping. God has not changed—if we indulge in the sins of Sodom and Canaan, we will share in the fate of those perverse lands and perish from the earth. The city-state of Sodom suffered destruction by brimstone, and the Canaanites were destroyed by the sword. Contemporary Americans may feel prosperous and secure, but we must remember that the land given to our forefathers will vomit us out if we become as godless as the heathen natives who once dwelled in the Americas proved to be. I am afraid that our forefathers (Puritan and Church of England alike) would repudiate and damn us if they knew what has happened to their legacy; they clearly understood that impediments rightly existed in the making of a holy marriage and recognized how the God of the New Covenant expresses his wrath against ungodly mating just as he did in the ancient world. The writer of the epistle to the Hebrew Christians not only warned believers to keep their marriage beds pure but also attached to his warning a threat that the Lord will judge the sexually immoral.[10]

Elsewhere in the New Testament, the apostle Paul chastised the

---

8. Marvin Harris wrote of the decriminalization of brother-sister incest in Sweden: "The Great Taboo, in other words, is greatly overrated. It is not just one thing but a set of sexual and mating preferences and avoidances that are selectively subject to change during the evolution of culture." For the record, Harris did object to parent-child incest on the grounds of statutory rape and child abuse. Marvin Harris, *Our Kind: Who We Are, Where We Came From, Where We Are Going* (New York: Harper Perennial, 1989), 206.

9. A Columbia University professor was criminally charged in 2010 for his relationship with his grown daughter (though he had many online defenders). William Saletan, "Incest Is Cancer—The David Epstein Incest Case: If Homosexuality Is OK, Why Is Incest Wrong?" *Slate*, December 14, 2010, https://www.slate.com/id/2275994/.

10. Hebrews 13:4 (ESV).

Corinthians for tolerating the incestuous relationship of a man with his father's wife, for a believer had taken up with his stepmother: either in open adultery before his father or following the death of his father (a relationship forbidden by both the law of Moses and the customs of pagan Rome). If this scandalous act drove Paul to fury, it cannot be doubted that he would be driven to righteous frenzy by our legalization of same-sex marriages, increasing toleration of incest, and allowance of lawful sexual relationships between stepmothers and stepsons. Like the previously mentioned ancients during the time of Noah, we are marrying with little regard for any ethical standard.[11] Whatever our amoral society says of such wrongs, the apostle Paul, inspired by God's Spirit, declared the following words of godly wrath against the sexual immorality in a church of his generation:[12]

> *It is actually reported that there is sexual immorality among you, and of a kind that is not tolerated even among pagans, for a man has his father's wife. And you are arrogant! Ought you not rather to mourn? Let him who has done this be removed from among you... When you are assembled in the name of the Lord Jesus and my spirit is present, with the power of our Lord Jesus, you are to deliver this man to Satan for the destruction of the flesh, so that his spirit may be saved in the day of the Lord.*[13]

---

11. One historian wrote: "Paul was drawn into the topic of sexual comportment by a scandal within his Corinthian community that had shaken the small circle of the faithful... A man had begun to cohabit with his stepmother, probably widowed. The two may not have been so far apart in age. Such scenarios were the material for much ribald comedy in Greek and Roman cultures. For Paul, the relationship was intolerable." Kyle Harper, *From Shame to Sin: The Christian Transformation of Sexual Morality in Late Antiquity* (Cambridge, Massachusetts: Harvard University Press, 2013), 99.

12. When revising this chapter, I randomly searched the Internet for stepmother and stepson liaisons, finding a rumored relationship of a famous Hollywood actor with his stepmother, as well as a recent Frenchman who married his stepmother following her divorce from his still-living father: the very relationship condemned by Paul. These modern examples may even be worse, for it is unclear from Scripture whether the husband and father wronged by a Corinthian congregant remained alive.

13. 1 Corinthians 5:1–2, 4–5 (ESV).

13

IMPEDIMENTS OF NATURE

Every person who is able to consent to conjugal affection and union of the flesh can contract marriage, unless expressly prohibited. I said "who is able to consent" because should a boy, although below the lawful age, that is under fourteen, or a girl under twelve, say the words appropriate to contract marriage, nonetheless, because they are not able to consent there is no marriage. A man who lacks both testicles cannot consent. Similarly, if a raving man or insane person should say the words he does not contract marriage because he is unable to consent mentally.[1]

WHEN DISCUSSING CELIBACY, Jesus indicated that some people remain unmarried because of a natural defect. In Matthew 19, Christ revealed that impotence is a natural hindrance to the making of marriage since men and women unable to enjoy sexual intercourse cannot take upon themselves an obligation to provide conjugal rights.[2] It is for this reason that both ecclesiastical and secular matrimonial law codes (such as the above medieval church law) have permitted the annulment of marriages left unconsummated because of sexual dysfunction. It is why Christians limit marriage to men and women rather than broadening the

---

1. Raymond of Penyafort, *Summa on Marriage*, 22.
2. Matthew 19:12 (ESV).

definition to include same-sex relationships: every marriage lawful before the Lord must be rooted in those natural realities that accomplish the divine purposes to which marriage is called (lawful procreation, sexual intimacy, mutual assistance, and natural compatibility). Not just in the obvious matter of reproduction, but in the complementary concerns of sexual intimacy, emotional interaction, and physical support, a marriage must include both man and woman to reach its highest purposes, particularly in representing the spiritual nature of God to mankind.

Over the centuries, most church laws and codes allowed immediate annulment for apparent physical defect in man or woman, while treating more cautiously any performative sexual dysfunction that remained unchanged after a set period of trial (sometimes for years).[3] This is not an easy teaching for contemporary people to understand or accept, for few modern people would repudiate a spouse for whom they had begun to care prior to marriage. Admittedly, it was simpler to annul an unconsummated marriage in epochs during which emotional love typically was kindled after marriage rather than before the wedding. It was also easier to do so when people believed that sexual intimacy, procreation, and mutual assistance were more important reasons to marry than romantic infatuation—when practical concerns mattered as much as impassioned emotions. Today, however, many couples enjoy sexual intimacy prior to marriage, separating the lifelong commitment of man and woman to each other from their sexual experience of one another. For that reason, questions of sexual dysfunction are frequently identified and addressed prior to marriage.

Annulling a marriage because of failed sexual intimacy implies that an unconsummated marriage is no marriage at all, suggesting that procreation and sexual companionship are so essential to marriage that their absence voids marriage from the outset. Christian churches have allowed release from vows (even when marriage was defined as the actual verbal vow), not only because sexual intimacy and the possibility of procreation

---

3. Steven Ozment wrote: "Both the Zurich and Basel courts recognized that chronic impotence could develop after marriage either for physical reasons or from growing hostility and repulsion between spouses. This was *impotentia superveniens*, impotence relative to circumstances created by the marriage, as distinguished from *impotentia antecedens* or impotence that existed before a marriage and prevented its consummation. Whereas Luther follows canon law in recognizing only *impotentia antecedens* as a valid ground for divorce, Bucer and Zwingli sanctioned both types." Steven Ozment, *When Fathers Ruled: Family life in Reformation Europe* (Cambridge, Massachusetts: Harvard University Press, 1983), 95.

are at the core of marriage, but also because Jesus was clear that eunuchs should not marry. Puritan theologian William Perkins argued nothing unusual when he observed that "impossibility of intercourse" is a bodily defect (which includes male frigidity, female constriction, castration, or even bewitchery) that prevents marriage from occurring.[4] Perkins posited that clearly observable problems with the genitals necessitate immediate annulment of the marriage, while observing that performative issues may take much longer to ascertain: a position consistent with earlier medieval custom.[5] While modern laws regarding the annulment of marriage for lack of consummation differ by jurisdiction, medieval and Protestant churchmen authorized annulment per the teachings of Christ. As William Perkins wrote:

> *[It] is unlawful to make a contract with such a person as is unfit for the use of marriage, either by natural constitution of body or by accident. For example, in regard of sickness, or of frigidity, or of the palsy incurable, or lastly of the deprivation of the parts belonging to generation. These and such like impediments are of force, though a contract should already be made. [God] makes known his will [that] he approveth not of such espousals, but would have [them] be dissolved.*[6]

Legal annulment is a remedy for sexual dysfunction at the outset of a marriage since no marriage has been consummated. But what is to be done with marriage if both husband and wife accept a non-sexual relationship? Are couples allowed to make non-sexual spiritual or fraternal marriages? This has been debated in the past, and the answer likely depends on individual circumstances and motives. The core concern is whether companionship without sexual intimacy fulfills enough of the

---

4. Witchery as a cause of impotence now seems comical but was no laughing matter in early modern Europe. For discussion of a marriage that included accusations of witchcraft as the cause of impotency (a marriage that failed in such a spectacular way that the story is the basis for a Hollywood movie), see Natalie Zemon Davis, *The Return of Martin Guerre* (Cambridge, Massachusetts: Harvard University Press, 1983).
5. William Perkins, "Christian Economy," in Larsen Klein, ed., *Daughters, Wives and Widows*, 160–162. Raymond of Penyafort, *Summa on Marriage*, 64–68. The delay in annulment presumably afforded couples the opportunity to mature into their conjugal obligations; it also prevented couples unwillingly enjoined to each other from colluding to separate under the pretext of impotence or frigidity.
6. William Perkins, "Christian Economy," in Larsen Klein, ed., *Daughters, Wives, and Widows*, 161.

purposes of marriage (since children can be adopted) to allow non-sexual unions to continue, or whether such marriages are prohibited because they do not provide an appropriate outlet for the sexually healthy partner. While it is hard to judge between the two camps, the words of Jesus suggest that no one can be required to remain married to a person unable to consummate physical intimacy. For this reason, impotence discovered after marriage vows is grounds for either partner to request an annulment. I would add only that there is the very modern possibility that medical treatment will resolve many issues of sexual dysfunction and, therefore, allow many struggling couples to remain married.

During antiquity, there existed a sect of Christians who slept naked with persons of the opposite sex (supposedly to prove their moral purity and spiritual willpower).[7] I suspect most readers will recognize the folly in this practice, since the Lord does not necessarily defend those who put him to the test. But how different is it to marry someone who can arouse but never satisfy desire? God may honor the subsequent fidelity of such men and women, just as he honors fidelity in an existing marriage when one spouse is stricken with a debilitating disease, but such victory is won at high cost to both persons.[8] Protestant Reformer Peter Martyr Vermigli observed that Roman and medieval church law permitted, but did not require, annulment of a marriage that cannot be consummated. Even though Vermigli believed unconsummated nuptials might remain valid, he still questioned the wisdom of making and continuing in such unions, asking what type of marriage can exist if made neither "for procreation of children, nor for the avoiding of whoredom?" [9]

Infertility, on the other hand, renders a man or woman unable to have children, but does not disqualify anyone from marriage since matrimony is equally directed toward companionship and reproduction. When Jesus spoke about the indissoluble nature of the marital union, he did so to Jewish men who believed that infertility justified divorce. Christ

---

7.   Philip Schaff, *History of the Christian Church*, vol. 2 (Grand Rapids, Michigan: William B. Eerdmans, 1950), 402–403.

8.   G.K. Chesterton chided modern people for being so obsessed with sex that no one can escape the sensuality of our culture, writing: "[There] is no escape for anyone. The lame and the halt, the doddering and the infirm" are "called upon somehow to squeeze out of their frail flesh the requisite response. It is the flesh which quickeneth, the spirit profiteth for nothing." Cited in George Roche, *A World Without Heroes: The Modern Tragedy* (Hillsdale, Michigan: Hillsdale College Press, 1987), 76–77.

9.   Peter Martyr Vermigli, *The Common Places of the Most Famous and Renowned Divine Doctor Peter Martyr* (London: n.p., 1583), 467.

declared otherwise. As will be discussed in a later chapter, our Lord restricted lawful separation to the cause of marital infidelity, separating the gift of fertility from that of marriage. This makes sense since it is not in human power to open or close the womb, for no one can foretell the fertility or infertility of a prospective spouse (especially a virgin). Such knowledge belongs to God alone, and the Lord's command is that we be willing to reproduce, not that we always succeed in doing so. Moreover, the Bible is filled with the stories of barren couples whose marriages were blessed by God before they conceived children (including the patriarch Abraham, whose wife miraculously conceived a son long after the onset of menopause). In several instances, the couple patiently endured years, and even decades, of infertility (without divorcing to conceive children with other spouses). Church father John Chrysostom once reminded Christians that marriage has two purposes, procreation and the preservation of chastity, and believed that "the purpose of chastity takes precedence," since marriage "does not always lead to child-bearing."[10]

Men and women who are unable to consummate a marriage cannot be considered binding marital partners, even if respect for the vows of marriage has led some to permit such couples to remain together as man and wife. Because it has traditionally been expected that people fulfill the purposes of marriage, young children have not been allowed to wed (or consummate planned marriages). While the Bible does not establish a minimum age for marriage, can anything be imagined to be more absurd than letting schoolchildren wed? No one can marry unless they can fulfill the responsibilities of marriage (sexual intimacy, mutual assistance in raising children and running a household, and a lifelong commitment to love), with puberty being the earliest age at which the responsibilities and challenges of marriage (physical, vocational, and emotional) may be safely handled. Marriage is for grown adults, just as mating is restricted in the animal kingdom to males and females who have ripened in their sexuality. This is the law of nature binding upon all mankind by the rule of the purposes of marriage and the laws of common morality.[11] As the Song of Solomon declared of girls who had not yet entered puberty:

---

10. John Chrysostom, "Sermon on Marriage," in John Chrysostom, *On Marriage and Family Life*, trans. Catherine P. Roth and David Anderson (Crestwood, New Jersey: St. Vladamir's Seminary Press, 1986), 78.

11. Many who condemn teenage marriage simultaneously encourage teenage sexual experimentation, which is inconsistent and absurd. Sexual experimentation outside marriage, particularly for the young, brings the same risks found in marriage, though without any of

We have a little sister, and she has no breasts.
What shall we do for our sister
on the day when she is spoken for?[12]

The fact that the Bible does not explicitly forbid children to marry reminds us that the laws of marriage and sexuality are founded not only on written commandments but also established through the purposes of marriage and the laws of human nature. If this were not true, an elementary school pupil could be married in the sight of the Lord, as could toddlers and kindergarteners. On the other hand, acknowledging how nature and maturity provide ethical direction leads to unforeseen conclusions. For instance, because the elderly often cannot fulfill every duty of marriage, some Christian thinkers have questioned the legitimacy of their marriages. Though few confessions of church discipline have banned such unions outright, many preachers have considered it scandalous for the elderly to contract marriage. As with everything, though, individual motives and circumstances matter. Though the use of holy matrimony as a tax shelter or to gain a larger Social Security check may be an abuse (since unholy greed is no more permissible for the elderly than for the young), it is just as prudent for the old to join households in marital friendship as for the young to do so, particularly since mutual assistance and companionship are numbered among the purposes of marriage.[13]

Moreover, beyond doctrinal statements regarding marriage, Scripture openly blesses the marriage of the aged. Abraham's remarriage after the death of Sarah furnishes a good example for the elderly to follow, for it was a marriage blessed by God. That widowed patriarch married in his old age, yet possessed sufficient virility to conceive children and govern a household the size of a small village. It was a real marriage with real children and a real household to tend to, not a tax shelter or mere facade. Even with the promise of God for a son (through whom future offspring

---

the advantages and protections that marriage brings for husband, wife, and children—and without the honor, romance, and adventure. Experimentation without permanent commitment reduces what might have become a seed of lifelong love to a spark of lust that burned for a short time.

12. Song of Solomon 8:8 (ESV).
13. Per one historian, at least some church courts proved unsympathetic with the plight of young brides who married elderly men (the age of sixty-five was mentioned in one instance), with officials hesitating to annul such marriages on the grounds of impotency since impotency was to be expected. Pierre Darmon, *Trial by Impotence: Virility and Marriage in pre-Revolutionary France,* trans. Paul Keegan (London: The Hogarth Press, 1985), 54–56.

would be as numerous as the stars) fulfilled, Abraham lived a life of hard work and daring faith, both marrying and begetting children after the death of his wife, Sarah (through whom the primary purpose of his life was fulfilled).[14] Such hard work, evident piety, and generous faith toward children who otherwise would not have been given life do not impede lawful marriage. Scripture declares:

> *Sarah lived one hundred and twenty-seven years... Sarah died in Kiriath-Arba (that is, Hebron) in the land of Canaan... Abraham took another wife, whose name was Keturah. She bore to him Zimran and Jokshan and Medan and Midian and Ishbak and Shuah.*[15]

Similar reasoning applies to the physically or mentally incapacitated. This goes beyond the question of impotence since some of the mentally challenged retain a strong sexual drive. The issue is whether such men and women can function as husbands and wives, not merely as sexual partners. Is it lawful to assume complicated and burdensome duties that a person cannot understand or fulfill? Probably not. Anyone who cannot raise the children they might conceive or cannot comprehend the nature of their marital vows must not marry. Nor can they depend upon parents to assist, since there is no guarantee that their parents will live long enough to raise grandchildren to maturity. This also holds for men and women whose minds are intact but whose bodies are unsuitable for running a household. This is not to restrict every marriage of moderately impaired persons (circumstances and conditions must weigh their cases), only to observe that severely handicapped men and women are not suited for marriage in some instances. Friendship may exist between the handicapped, or between disabled people and the unimpaired, but no one should marry who cannot both understand the duties of marriage and function as a spouse.[16]

---

14. There has been debate over whether these marriages took place before or after the death of Sarah. John Calvin allowed that they may have been prior, with the text inserted out of chronological order. Calvin wrote of the offspring of Keturah: "Many nations of considerable importance descended from [Abraham's] other sons [though] the spiritual covenant [remained] the exclusive possession of Isaac." Calvin, *Genesis*, vol. 2, 32–35.

15. Genesis 23:1–2 (NASB); Genesis 25:1–2 (NASB).

16. William Perkins wrote: "The fourth essential sign [of legitimate marriage] is a sound and healthful constitution of body, free from diseases incurably contagious [such as] leprosy, the French pox, and such like. For seeing there cannot be any matrimonial use of

Age differences should be mentioned. Is it lawful for men and women to marry spouses of vastly dissimilar ages? Is it necessary for a man to be older than his bride? Scripture gives no instructions or prohibitions concerning age, though it includes many instances of marriage between older men and younger wives. The ages of Ruth and Boaz are not specified in the book of Ruth, though it seems likely that Boaz was advanced in years (based on his wealth and authority), while his bride was a younger woman (which is why Boaz commended Ruth for seeking a marriage that honored her family rather than chasing after money or looks in a young husband).[17] Likewise, older women may marry younger men as long as they take seriously the purposes of marriage, including the duty to procreate. Typically, a husband should not exempt himself from the obligation to have children simply because his still-fertile wife did so before she married him. The commandment to reproduce was given to man and woman alike and should be considered for every marriage of those able to procreate. And having made such marriages, couples must approach marriage as a lifelong promise, even when the turning of the calendar brings to a woman a husband maturing more slowly than she wishes or to a man a wife whose hair has grayed far sooner than his own. None of this is to deny that similarity of age may be the ideal for marriage (were not Adam and Eve created at the same time?); it is only to observe that differences of age do not necessarily impede lawful matrimony.

While Christian churches (and godly governments) have generally allowed men and women of dissimilar ages to marry as long as the marriage was made for godly, chaste, and orderly purposes, there have been Christian governments that restricted or even prohibited marriages between couples of significantly dissimilar ages. As just one example, under the influence of John Calvin and his peers, early modern Geneva passed laws that forbade women under forty from marrying men ten or more years younger than themselves and women over forty from marrying men more than five years younger. Men over sixty were forbidden to marry women less than half their age.[18] The ancient Jewish

them that are tainted with such contagious diseases without apparent danger of infection, [such] marriages cannot be undertaken with good conscience." William Perkins, "Christian Economy," in Larsen Klein, ed., *Daughters, Wives and Widows,* 162.

17. Ruth 3:10 (ESV).

18. The Genevan ordinances were passed in 1566. Émile Rivoire, ed., *Les Sources du Droit du Canton de Genève: Tome Troisième de 1551 à 1620* (Genève: H.R. Sauerländer & Cie., 1933), 336. Witte and Kingdon discuss Calvin's objection to disparity in age in Witte and

philosopher Philo of Alexandria went to exegetical extremes by arguing that Eve was made from Adam's rib (and therefore younger than her husband) specifically to establish that men must marry wives younger than themselves, writing that men "who marry wives more advanced in years than themselves deserve blame, as having overturned the law of nature."[19] Even modern Christians have judged age dissimilarity to be troublesome, if not an actual impediment to marriage. Though Lutheran theologian Walter Maier observed that Martin Luther's wife was fifteen years younger than her husband" and admitted that "their married life was happy," he nevertheless refused to bless such unions of middle-aged men with younger wives, preferring compatibility in age, with the husband being the same age as his bride or only slightly older (preferably no more than a decade) or wives not much older than their husbands. Maier feared that age differences would foster marital discord.[20]

Despite the preference of some churchmen, the broad consensus of church history has not prohibited marriages between those of disparate ages. Nor have upper age limits been enforced to the degree that lower ones have been (since the latter are protecting children from exploitation). Neither Moses nor Paul explicitly restricted the marriages of the elderly, though both insisted that every marriage be made for godly purposes. As with Boaz and Ruth, Scripture insists that couples court and marry in honorable ways and for godly purposes rather than in blind lust or calculating greed. They must establish unions whose love directs even strangers to the glory of the Triune God. Still, whatever authority past governments possessed to govern the marriages of men and women of disparate ages, few states considered such restrictions to be impediments precluding lawful marriage: only temporal matters meriting good government and pious rules.[21]

Kingdon, *Sex, Marriage, and Family in John Calvin's Geneva* (Grand Rapids, Michigan: William B. Eerdmans Publishing Company, 2003), 278–281.

19. While I cite Philo for reference, I do not find his words to be authoritative or indicative of biblical teachings. Philo of Alexandria, "Questions and Answers on Genesis, 1," in *The Works of Philo*, trans. C. D. Yonge (Peabody, Massachusetts: Hendrickson Publishers, 1993), 796.

20. Walter A. Maier, *For Better, Not for Worse: A Manual of Christian Matrimony* (St. Louis, Missouri: Concordia Publishing House, 1939), 220–222.

21. To reiterate why I do not discuss the impediment of sexual differentiation (which would rightly belong in this chapter), I would note that the distinction of man and woman is so central to marriage (and Mosaic restrictions against same-sex intimacy so plain) that the matter does not require explanation, justification, or defense in a book focused on pastoral concerns rather than an apologetical defense of Christian marriage.

As for Scripture, the Bible sometimes blesses the marriages of older men with younger wives, as the marriage between Boaz and Ruth is presumed to have been. Men are not necessarily wrong in seeking much younger wives to build families, and women do not necessarily sin to marry honorable men beyond their years. Of course, being motivated by base lust or covetous greed is not the same as establishing a household, and it is in the desire for children that both men and women in such relationships can best ponder their deepest motives. When old men steal the beauty of women while robbing the latter of their rightful inheritance of sons and daughters, there is wrongdoing. Likewise, when young women trade their beauty to enjoy the lifestyle and possessions of an old man rather than to build a home in which to raise a large family, there is sin. A biblical perspective evaluates marriage for its significance in building faith and piety in both husband and wife, and seeks God's will in establishing his purposes across generations, as he did once with Boaz and Ruth.

> *[Boaz said to Ruth when she offered herself to him in marriage]*
> *"May you be blessed by the LORD, my daughter. You have made this last kindness greater than the first in that you have not gone after young men, whether poor or rich. And now, my daughter, do not fear. I will do for you all that you ask, for all my fellow townsmen know that you are a worthy woman."* [22]

---

22. Ruth 3:10–11 (ESV).

14

IMPEDIMENTS OF RELATIONSHIP

Jesus said to [the Samaritan woman at a well], "Go, call your husband, and come here." The woman answered him, "I have no husband." Jesus said to her, "You are right in saying, 'I have no husband'; for you have had five husbands, and the one you now have is not your husband. What you have said is true." [1]

[Jesus said], "But I say to you that everyone who divorces his wife, except on the ground of sexual immorality, makes her commit adultery, and whoever marries a divorced woman commits adultery." [2]

THE MOST OBVIOUS impediment to marriage is that one cannot marry someone already married. Since marriage is intended to be an exclusive relationship between one man and one woman, it is impermissible to marry someone already bound by wedlock. The pattern for matrimony, first established by Adam and Eve, is monogamy. Adam did not take two or three wives, only one. Of course, many of the men of the Old Testament violated this ideal, and God blessed them despite their polygamous marriages. The lesson to be drawn from this sad reality is that everyone is a sinner saved by grace, not that polygamy is spiritually blessed or morally

---

1. John 4:16–18 (ESV).
2. Matthew 5:32 (ESV).

defensible, for the law of Moses nowhere explicitly condoned the practice of taking multiple wives as ideal. God's law tolerated polygamy as an unfortunate reality while placing restrictions on its practice to ensure equal treatment of wives, just as with divorce.[3] Both practices were tolerated for the hardness of men's hearts (historically, men have been responsible for such vices more often than women have).

To mitigate the evil found in polygamy, Moses commanded that husbands must treat each wife fairly, not favoring one woman over the others, thereby placing limits on the spread of polygamy rather than giving men a license to marry every woman they might desire, regardless of the consequences for the women, their children, and their religious faith. A Hebrew man who chose to marry a second wife (typically, a man sought a younger wife as his first one aged) was not allowed to reduce in any fashion the right of his first wife to food, clothing, and sexual intimacy (representing all common rights women possess in marriage). To reduce any of these below the level to which every wife is entitled, and to which the specific wife was accustomed, authorized the first wife to leave the marriage, taking her dowry and property with her. As a practical matter, the taking of a second wife generally authorized the first wife to leave the marriage because her husband had deserted the marriage bed, reduced material support, and alienated some of his affection (since few, if any, men can take a second wife without denying their first wife at least a portion of what she is owed and has enjoyed).[4]

To repeat: it is evident to anyone who sits down to think the matter through that it is difficult enough to please one wife, let alone two or three, in a manner that does not diminish what is given to each. There is not a man on earth who can adequately tend to the spiritual, emotional, material, and sexual needs of a single wife after the fashion of Christ, let alone properly (and equally) love a harem of women with pious, self-giving love; and who could begin to care for the horde of children conceived in a polygamous household? What man can give himself entirely to the service of two women? It was not without reason that ancient nobles used eunuchs to guard the women of their harems from

---

3. One of the most perplexing revelations from God is found in 2 Samuel 12:7–8, in which God responded to David's adulterous affair by noting how he had given David multiple wives. Before we question God's justice in tolerating polygamy, we should consider Christ's toleration of remarriage after unlawful divorce among us. Does God not bless many contemporary people despite them being remarried into unbiblical remarriages?
4. Exodus 21:10.

sexual infidelity, or that children born into such unholy circumstances often plotted not only against rival siblings, but against their fathers.

Not only is polygamy an abuse of women and children, it is also the acceptance of a lesser marriage for men, for the husband who multiplies wives divides himself between families, and will never enjoy the fidelity and devotion that the husband of one wife receives. A polygamist does not receive an affectionate marriage two or three times over (as he naively and foolishly desires) but something altogether unexpected: disappointment, discord, and dissatisfaction. After a lifetime with hundreds of wives (many of them young and beautiful), Solomon observed how blessed it is for a man to enjoy life with his one wife, writing: "Enjoy life with the wife whom you love, all the days of your vain life that he has given you under the sun." Such is the voice of true wisdom.[5]

The New Testament is far more direct than the Old Testament in its condemnation of polygamy, not limiting itself to restrictions and indirect abolition of the institution. Christ explicitly declared that monogamy is the ideal established by God, with mankind made male and female and "no longer two, but one flesh" from the outset of human existence. When God became man, he made clear the original intent that he himself had established for human marriage at the outset, as well as for every marriage made since the beginning. In the spirit of monogamy being the divine ideal, the first letter of the apostle Paul to Timothy restricted men with multiple wives from serving in church leadership: instructions repeated in the apostle's epistle to Titus.[6] While the Lord did not annul every polygamous marriage, this undoubtedly was because divorce would have been even worse than polygamy. Instead, God put the men in such marriages under a lifelong penalty, even for marriages made prior to conversion. However much God may have suffered polygamy for a time (and for whatever reason), he no longer does so, and the Christian church has been consistent through the centuries in its upholding of our Lord's holy word. Monogamy is the rule of marriage that God originally instituted, and Christ expects men and women to uphold it. Church father Methodius observed that "contracting of marriage with several wives has been done away with" since the time of the prophets of Israel.[7]

The third chapter of 1 Timothy forbids church office to men who

---

5. Ecclesiastes 9:9 (ESV).
6. Matthew 19:5 (ESV); 1 Timothy 3:2; Titus 1:6.
7. Methodius, "Discourse 1: Marcella," in *Ante-Nicene Church Fathers*, vol. 12, trans. Philip Schaff (Grand Rapids, Michigan: Astern Press, 2014), 338.

possess more than a single wife. Polygamy was outlawed, as was another manner of possessing more than one wife: what has been called *serial polygamy*.[8] Just as a man is wrong to take two (or more) wives at once, so he is wrong to take two (or more) women in succession while an earlier wife yet lives. Such behavior is adulterous, as Christ made plain when he reminded the Samaritan woman (in the passage at the beginning of this chapter) how her existing relationship was not a valid marriage before God. Amidst a dispute regarding true religion, Jesus rather abruptly told the woman to fetch her husband, indicating that the woman's theological quarrel was diverting attention from the personal nature of her real problem with God: marital and sexual infidelity. In response, the Samaritan woman denied she had a husband (though she evidently was living with a man in some common-law arrangement). Christ declared her lie to be true, noting that the woman had known several men and her present partner was not a rightful husband.[9] Elsewhere (as I will discuss later in the book), Jesus revealed the doctrine behind his rebuke, explaining that remarriage after illicit divorce is adultery in God's sight. Since marriage establishes an exclusive unity that cannot be torn apart, no believer can marry someone still married in God's sight—even if divorced through the laws of the state. Only death ends a marriage and frees the survivor to remarry (as will be discussed later).[10]

Not only is it wrong to take more than one spouse at a time, but it is also forbidden to marry a blood relative. This obviously cannot refer to every distant cousin, or no one could ever marry, since we are all descendants of the first couple. The issue is a close blood relationship and the natural associations of the human household. Leviticus chapters 18 and 20 list those close relatives with whom it is forbidden either to marry or to have sexual relations (on penalty of death). Moses instructed Hebrew men and women not to marry their parents, stepparents, parents-in-law, children, stepchildren, children-in-law, grandchildren (to include half-grandchildren and even step-grandchildren raised as close relatives), aunts

---

8. Governments do not always possess the power to prevent de facto polygamy. For instance, some American states are unable to effectively regulate thousands of polygamous marriages enacted through religious ceremonies rather than civil ones. Florence Williams, "A House, 10 Wives: Polygamy in Suburbia," *New York Times*, Thursday, December 11, 1997.

9. 1 Timothy 3:2; John 4:16–17 (ESV).

10. Each of us should take the remarks of Jesus to this woman as personal rebukes of our own sin. As Christ spoke to this sinful woman in gentle forcefulness that exposed her sin before the Lord, so Jesus speaks to us through his word.

and uncles (by blood or marriage), siblings, half-siblings, or step-siblings raised with them in their own home. Traditionally, these prohibitions have been extended to men and women alike, both up and down the genealogical ladder (so that restrictions against marrying the daughter of one's son would also include one's grandchildren and great-grandchildren).[11] Moses also revealed that a person cannot marry the brother or sister of a spouse while the latter remains alive, or both a woman and her daughter. One could not marry a woman, then either her mother or daughter, following the woman's death.[12]

Moses forbade men (and women) to marry close relatives and in-laws. The aforementioned passages in Leviticus also prohibited marriage to the close relatives of those with whom sexual intimacy has been experienced. Not only was a stepdaughter forbidden, but so was the daughter of a woman with whom a man had enjoyed sexual relations. Moses commanded: "You shall not uncover the nakedness of a woman and of her daughter, and you shall not take her son's daughter or her daughter's daughter to uncover her nakedness; they are relatives; it is depravity." Later passages made clear that such unholiness cannot be sanctified through marriage. Moses wrote: "If a man takes a woman and her mother also, it is depravity; he and they shall be burned with fire that there may be no depravity among you." The experience of sexual intimacy, both married and unmarried alike, creates an enduring relationship that restricts marriage with close relatives of one's partner.[13]

Medieval church law expanded the definition of a close relative (rooting its teachings in passages from Augustine and other church fathers) so that prohibitions resulting from sexual intercourse resembled

---

11. Leviticus 18:6–20; Leviticus 20:10–21. I once read of a woman who married an aged Confederate soldier, then married the man's grandson after the veteran died. Unless the grandson was a stepchild, this was likely unbiblical.
12. While Mosaic law allowed marriage of first cousins, Christian churches have prohibited such marriages since antiquity. Sixteenth-century John Calvin observed that while it is wrong to question God's law (which allows first-cousin marriages), it was "accepted by long usage, however, that first cousins should not marry." John Calvin, *Calvin's Ecclesiastical Advice,* trans. Mary Bath and Benjamin W. Farley (Louisville, Kentucky: Westminster John Knox Press, 1991), 121. This sensitivity seems limited to Christian cultures since the marriage of first cousins remains common in countries like Pakistan and India. I agree with Calvin that marriage between first cousins should be prohibited to avoid scandal. Based on this principle, as well as the genetic disadvantages of marrying cousins, I believe that governments are authorized to restrict such marriages if they choose to do so. However, because this is a matter of cultural and legal expediency rather than biblical law, we cannot doubt the moral legitimacy of such marriages or their offspring when made.
13. Leviticus 18:17 (ESV); Leviticus 20:14 (ESV).

broader restrictions against marrying in-laws and blood relatives. More-over, the sibling of a sexual partner might be a prohibited spouse just like the sibling of a husband or wife, although there was debate as to precisely which specific types of sexual relations restricted future marriage (e.g., can a man or woman marry the close relative of someone they have kissed, as long as there was no sexual intercourse? What about fondling that leads to completion or caressing that does not?). Such amplifications of the Lord's law are too extensive and complicated for this short work. It is enough here to cite the direct commandments received from Moses and to note that such commandments likely have a wider application. We must remember how strict ancient Jewish customs were, which should make plain that any ambiguity must be resolved on the side of modesty and holiness. The breadth of language in Leviticus denoting sexual activity—from *uncover nakedness* to *lie down* with—suggests broad restrictions.[14]

Levitical codes remain binding for Christians today and have not been superseded by the establishment of the New Testament: a fact established beyond question by the previously noted discussion of incest in the first letter to the Corinthians.[15] When Paul rebuked the Corinthians for wrongly tolerating a man who married his father's wife, he spoke of a man who had married (or was living with) his stepmother. The man had violated Levitical codes of marital impediment, though Paul observed that even pagan Romans rejected such iniquity.[16] As noted, passages in Leviticus 18 and 20 also indicated that individuals cannot marry the parent or child of someone with whom they once experienced sexual relations. Whoever the man in the Corinthian church was (whether Jewish or Gentile), the man had sinned against Moses (and consequently against Christ and his holy apostles), and God's judgment was severe. No doubt such marriages exist within modern churches and should be subjected to the same spiritual discipline and anathema that Paul declared so long ago,

---

14. Leviticus 18:7; 20:12 (NASB). One recent historian provided a succinct description of medieval laws prohibiting marriage to blood relatives (based on Roman law), in-laws, and spiritual relatives—as well as the expansion of these prohibitions to more distant relatives under church law. Paul B. Newman, *Growing Up in the Middle Ages* (Jefferson, North Carolina: MacFarland and Company, Inc., Publishers, 2007), 247–252.

15. 1 Corinthians 5:1–5 (ESV).

16. Many legal impediments are increasingly being challenged. One author observed: "Various relationships created by a former marriage ('affinity') continue to be considered incestuous in a minority of jurisdictions and there is a continuing decline of such prohibitions." Harry D. Krause, *Family Law* (St. Paul, Minnesota: West Publishing Company, 1986), 42.

regardless of their acceptance in secular law or modern practices of church-state relationships.

Scripture insists that human beings related by blood ties, sexual experiences, or household bonds cannot marry one another. However, outside of such household obligations, differences of education, class, race, or nationality are not impediments to legitimate marriage, even when they bring temporal penalties (such as forfeiture of citizenship for offspring). A king may marry a pauper, and an African may wed a European. An American can marry an Indonesian, and a Ph.D. can marry a high school dropout. Because these non-essentials are not impediments to biblical marriage, it is absolutely wrong to deny the validity of matrimony based on such racial or social factors.[17] Not only does Scripture nowhere restrict such marriages, but the Bible includes many examples of people who crossed social and racial barriers in selecting spouses and were not condemned for having done so.

That said, in some instances, marrying couples may have to accept hardships resulting from their decisions. If an Australian marries an Indonesian during a vacation in Bali, a biblical marriage does not necessarily bind Australia or Indonesia to grant the alien newlywed the right to residency. In the same manner, disobeying family by marrying outside of one's own race or class may require considerable patience in restoring broken relationships. The fact that the couple is justified before God in their union provides more reason to imitate the meekness of Jesus by turning the other cheek to wrong responses from their communities and families, rather than giving less reason to be forgiving. This is not to deny either the moral lawfulness or prudence of such marriages; it is only to remind readers how believers are called to utter humility and forgiveness in all situations, and that many societies have had such strictures and prejudices that require principled gentleness in opposition. One cannot grow to hate one's neighbor and family for the love of a stranger.[18]

---

17. Roman Catholicism established impediments for godparents and Islam for wet nurses. Regarding the former, one historian observed how a rape accusation in medieval France necessarily included an incest accusation since the rapist was the godparent to a child of the victim's husband. Eric Jager, The *Last Duel: A True Story of Crime, Scandal, and Trial by Combat in Medieval France*, 108. As for incest via wet nurse, Valerie Fildes noted: "This legally-recognized relationship between wet nurse and their nurse children has not been found in other major world religions and may be peculiar to Islam. It is still a feature of Arab and other Muslim societies today." Valerie Fildes, *Wet Nursing*, 29.

18. The mixed Germanic and Roman law of the ancient Burgundians declared: "If indeed a Roman girl, without the consent or knowledge of her parents, unites in marriage with a

Regarding ethnicity and race, Moses explicitly permitted Jews to marry ethnic non-Jews, insisting only that foreign brides first undergo a public conversion to the religion of the Hebrews. Indeed, Moses himself married a foreign woman from Cush (modern Ethiopia and Sudan). In like manner, the book of Deuteronomy allowed the marriage of Hebrews to Egyptians and Edomites, albeit with delayed citizenship for their offspring. The only exception to this freedom regarded marriage to Canaanites (whom the Lord specifically marked for judgment because of their moral perversity, religious idolatry, and human sacrifice)—as well as some restrictions regarding the children of marriages with Moabites and Ammonites due to their treatment of God's people during the exodus from Egypt. This, however, was a matter of religious and political animosity rather than race, and individual Canaanites could be married if they converted to the Hebrew faith. That is how Rahab (a harlot from the Canaanite city of Jericho) was not only spared destruction but even blessed to become an ancestor of David, and through King David of the Lord Jesus Christ. The same blessing occurred with the Moabite woman Ruth, who became the great-grandmother of David after her conversion to the faith of Israel.[19]

Similar freedom is granted to marry across class or economic barriers: the lowly shepherd David married his king's daughter, thereby rising above his humble roots. In the New Testament, it is important to remember that the apostle Paul did not establish (or mention) a single marital restriction based upon class or blood, even though he taught about marriage in the racially and socially diverse Roman Empire (and in a society that generally did not permit its slaves to engage in civil marriage). Had God mandated impediments of class or race, Paul surely would have discussed them.[20] Several centuries later, church leader John Chrysostom warned Christians to remember that God is more concerned with religion and character than with nationality and race in the making

---

Burgundian, let her know she will have none of the property of her parents." Katherine Fischer Drew, *The Burgundian Code: Book of Constitutions or Law of Gundobad, Additional Enactments* (Philadelphia: University of Pennsylvania Press, 1949), 31.

19. Deuteronomy 21:10–13 (ESV); Numbers 12:1; Deuteronomy 23:7; Deuteronomy 7:3 (ESV); Deuteronomy 23:3; Matthew 1:5–6; Ruth 4:21–22.

20. Phillip L. Reynolds discussed church fathers like Callistus (who allowed Roman patrician women to marry freedmen and slaves) and churchmen who required social equality and prohibited slave marriages. See "Chapter VIII: The Impediment of Inequality," in Phillip L. Reynolds, *Marriage in the Western Church: The Christianization of Marriage during the Patristic and Early Medieval Periods* (Leiden: E.J. Brill, 1994).

of marriage. Marriage is made to build faith and family in the love of God, not for lesser purposes (such as establishing a great household in the eyes of the world). Chrysostom explained the criteria that Christian parents ought to use in selecting a son-in-law (which would be equally suitable for the choosing of a daughter-in-law):

> *When your daughter is to be married, don't look for how much money a man has. Don't worry about his nationality or his family's social position. All these things are superfluous. Look instead for piety, gentleness, wisdom, and the fear of the Lord, if you want your daughter to be happy.*[21]

---

21. John Chrysostom, "Homily 12," in *On Marriage and Family Life,* 72.

15

IMPEDIMENTS OF AUTHORITY

When a man sells his daughter as a slave, she shall not go out as the male slaves do. If she does not please her master, who has designated her for himself, then he shall let her be redeemed. He shall have no right to sell her to a foreign people, since he has broken faith with her. If he designates her for his son, he shall deal with her as with a daughter. If he takes another wife to himself, he shall not diminish her food, her clothing, or her marital rights. And if he does not do these three things for her, she shall go out for nothing, without payment of money. [1]

THE OLD TESTAMENT laws of slavery and servanthood are troubling for modern Americans to read. The terrible injustice of American slavery frames our thinking so profoundly that it is nearly impossible to ponder biblical notions of servanthood without filtering the texts through our national calamity. Still, a careful reading of the Old Testament makes clear how these were different types of slavery and servanthood, as well as that the law of God placed strict limits on all slavery and servanthood—for the Lord did not deliver Israel from the taskmasters of Egypt to hand them over to the callousness and cruelty of fellow Hebrews. The restrictions against slavery in Israel were so strict that the enslavement of fellow

---

1. Exodus 21:7–11 (ESV).

Hebrews was more like the indentured servanthood practiced in colonial America than chattel slavery in which guiltless men and women were taken from their homelands in iron chains. In Israel, both servants and slaves possessed legal and moral rights, and senseless physical violence was prohibited. For instance, if a master knocked out the tooth of a Hebrew slave, the slave was to be freed for the sake of the injury.[2]

In the same manner, the book of Exodus (which describes the emancipation of Israel from Egyptian slavery and presents the key tenets of God's law) commands that female servants be provided legal protection against sexual abuse. Unlike enslaved African women in antebellum America, who could be exploited at the discretion of a master, enslaved Hebrew women were granted the rights of a wife if sexually approached by their owner (or his son), with subsequent children granted the rights of an heir rather than being sold down the river for profit. Female Hebrew slaves could marry into their master's household as a daughter-in-law, gaining through their husband a portion of the master's property. The slavery of Hebrew women had strict limits, and a slave woman who was sexually taken advantage of gained the rights of a Hebrew wife. If later divorced, she was to be freed without cost to herself.[3]

Another obvious passage regarding marriage and slavery is found in Deuteronomy 21, in which a man was permitted to marry a woman captured in war (a slave is how she should be described as a point of fact, if not also in name). Though the Lord no more desires that slavery exist in his creation than that wars be fought, both are unfortunate realities in our sinful world, and the Lord makes clear his will regarding women so captured. If a man wished to marry a beautiful woman taken captive, he was to convert her to the religion of Israel in a ceremony that trimmed her beauty for a time (so that the man himself recognized a higher and holier purpose to their marriage than sexual desire). The man was to permit the woman an appropriate period of mourning for her lost family. Only then was he allowed to take her in marriage, providing her with the same rights possessed by every other wife in Israel. The woman was to receive kind treatment, sexual intimacy, physical protection, material provision, and even an appropriate inheritance for herself and her children.[4] Moses commanded:

---

2. Exodus 21:27.
3. Exodus 21:7–11.
4. God did not allow the Hebrews the brutal rights of conquest that ancient armies

When you go out to war against your enemies and the LORD *your God gives them into your hand and you take them captive, and you see among the captives a beautiful woman, and you desire to take her to be your wife, and you bring her home to your house, she shall shave her head and pare her nails. And she shall take off the clothes in which she was captured and shall remain in your house and lament her father and mother a full month. After that you may go in to her and be her husband, and she shall be your wife. But if you no longer delight in her, you shall let her go where she wants. But you shall not sell her for money, nor shall you treat her as a slave, since you have humiliated her.*[5]

As for those in slavery and servitude, Exodus 21 taught that a Hebrew servant could not be robbed of his household. If a slave brought his wife into slavery, she and their children were to be set free with him after a maximum of seven years of enslavement. Nor could a master do to the woman or her children anything he pleased during her husband's servitude. Laws against violence, rape, and adultery preserved the rights of the enslaved and imposed stringent penalties against abusers.[6] Still, Moses acknowledged that the household is composed of both property and persons, both of which are necessary to sustain family life. Utopian dreamers like Plato and Marx (and confused British rock stars from the early 1970s) may imagine a world without possessions and possessiveness, but Moses knew better. His laws upheld the right to material goods and familial associations that every home requires to exist—for without the right to its property, the family becomes a slave to the state (it is no coincidence that a *house* may be either a household or a physical dwelling; how could one exist without the other?).[7] And in the ancient world, the fact of slavery was a reality to be dealt with, just as modern courts uphold contracts that place individuals in constricted circumstances and authorize prison sentences that are de facto slavery within barred walls.

The law of Moses required Hebrews to treat their slaves fairly and

---

accepted as common custom. Entire Greek tragedies were based on the plight of women forced into rape, prostitution, and slavery after capture during war.

5. Deuteronomy 21:10–14 (ESV).

6. Exodus 21:7–11 (ESV).

7. For one description of Plato's utopian reorganization of family life in light of household relationship to state and property in classical Athens, see W.K. Lacey, *The Family in Classical Greece* (Ithaca, New York: Cornell University Press, 1968).

permitted lawful marriage to slaves (so that slaves would not live promiscuously), yet also secured the right to property that every household
needed, poor and rich alike. Before anyone protests the unfairness of this,
we must remember that slavery in the biblical system was used to punish
crime, pay off debt, and spare the lives of those captured in war. Not even
modern America allows an unrestricted right to marriage for prisoners,
homeless debtors, and military detainees. Nor did biblical slavery allow
lifelong servitude or authorize slavery to be passed as an ugly inheritance
from father to son (seven years was the maximum length of Hebrew
slavery—the same term that Jacob willingly worked for each of his two
wives). However, Moses did require slaves to seek permission to marry,
instructing that wives and children provided to a slave by his master
remained the master's property when the enslaved husband was emancipated from servitude. Though this sounds harsh, if slaves had been
allowed to emancipate wives and children acquired during enslavement,
many masters would have denied marriage to their slaves to prevent loss
of property, whether or not such mean-spiritedness was godly. After all, if
a man was enslaved for stealing, it was hardly his master's obligation to
provide the thief with a wife at the master's expense. What would be the
penitential purpose of such slavery? What would be its value as public
punishment?[8]

Moses allowed servants to marry and keep their families intact by
continuing service with a vow of permanent loyalty. Such an arrangement was sensible since it was in the interest of everyone concerned to
secure a well-ordered household, the building block of society. This
voluntary oath of lifelong fealty did not suspend standard protections for
servants, nor did it allow masters to separate families now sworn to their
care. We must purge from our minds the pernicious practices of American slavery. Those slaveowners in the United States who used biblical
rules regarding slavery to justify their peculiar institution will be judged
not only for doing to slaves what they did not want done to free men like
themselves, but (far more seriously) for using biblical restrictions to
defend the existence of slavery while ignoring the moral content of such

---

8. Moses authorized slaves marriages (and punished the seduction of slaves) when he
wrote: "Now if a man lies carnally with a woman who is a slave acquired for another man,
but who has in no way been redeemed nor given her freedom, there shall be punishment;
they shall not, however, be put to death, because she was not free. He shall bring… a ram for
a guilt offering. The priest shall also make atonement… his sin which he has committed, and
the sin which he has committed will be forgiven him." Leviticus 19:20–22 (NASB).

biblical injunctions. Such men blasphemed both the Declaration of Independence and the law of God and are rightly judged for their hypocrisy and callousness. In contrast, Moses wrote:

> *When you buy a Hebrew slave, he shall serve six years, and in the seventh he shall go out free, for nothing. If he comes in single, he shall go out single; if he comes in married, then his wife shall go out with him. If his master gives him a wife and she bears him sons or daughters, the wife and her children shall be her master's, and he shall go out alone. But if the slave plainly says, 'I love my master, my wife, and my children; I will not go out free,' then his master shall bring him to God, and he shall bring him to the door or the doorpost. And his master shall bore his ear through with an awl, and he shall be his slave forever.*[9]

Slavery has been abolished in America, we may thank the Lord, and labor is freely contracted today.[10] No one needs to ask an employer for permission to marry. Still, other institutions do exist that demand deference and respect. The government, for instance, regulates marital and family life. While certain Christians believe so strongly that marriage is a divine institution that they doubt rightful state jurisdiction in matrimonial matters, they are mistaken. Not only does the New Testament give public authorities the right to reward good and to punish evil, but Moses quite clearly placed the laws of marriage under the jurisdiction of temporal authorities.[11] It was the judges and elders of the city, not the priests of the temple, who settled seduction disputes or required a man to return his wife's dowry if he divorced her. Christians must accept the authority of the state reverently, even regarding the most intimate marital and sexual matters, for God has given government the right to rule human affairs, only demanding adherence to biblical commandments and natural law.

Moreover, the only real restriction modern states place on marriage, beyond upholding a few indisputable impediments, is the requirement to

---

9. Exodus 21:2–6 (ESV). The enslavement of Hebrews was for seven years only, with slaves to be freed if harmed or abused. This passage would go on to note that a woman sold into slavery (and treated as a wife) would retain all rights of a wife. If dismissed, she was to be emancipated without cost to herself. See Exodus 21: 7–11 (ESV).
10. For further discussion, see *Appendix 1: Charles Hodge and Slave Marriages.*
11. Romans 13:4.

sign a marriage license (i.e., contract), which is not an unreasonable burden for modern believers since the use of marriage licenses is designed to prevent violations of codes against bigamy and incest (or at least punishing them when violations do occur). Besides, a waiting period of a few days after an application to marry is considerably shorter than the weeks-long waiting periods frequently required by Christian churches and governments in the past. It is also true that some states require medical examinations. This practice, too, is reasonable as long as it is not directed against the right to procreate (as several European states and American state governments during the 1920s and 1930s used medical certification before marriage to prevent deaf, blind, or feebleminded persons from conceiving children). Such eugenics campaigns were (and remain) a grave danger to moral health and spiritual stability that transgresses biblical boundaries for the exercise and administration of moral and lawful state authority.[12]

Government has the duty to govern marriage according to divine law rather than through worldly insight. However, that is a discussion about how temporal authority ought to be exercised, not about whether the state has the right to rule matrimony at all. Americans presently live in a nation where the laws of the land uphold the value of family life. Except in a few controversial matters, as will be discussed in due time, American government structures civic obligations and exemptions to strengthen the household, which is why a housewife can receive her deceased husband's Social Security earnings. It also explains why elite combat units (who live directly under state authority in a manner few of us experience) do not claim the right to annul the marriages of soldiers. Enlisted men may be ordered to seek permission to marry from their officers, but failure to do so brings military punishment, not the annulment of a contracted and consummated marriage. Moreover, family men are exempted from compulsory military service in all but the most pressing national emergencies. Like the law of Moses, modern American law (reflecting its historical Christian roots) generally subordinates the political aspirations of rulers to the needs of the human household. Rulers are not permitted to draft every recruit or raise every tax that they may desire, just as Moses placed limits on state power when he declared:

12. For a discussion of pre-Second World War American laws with racial and eugenics overtones, see Stefan Kühl, *The Nazi Connection: Eugenics, American Racism, and German National Socialism* (Oxford: Oxford University Press, 2002).

*[Military officers] shall speak to the people, [saying] 'And is there
any man who has betrothed a wife and has not taken her? Let him
go back to his house, lest he die in the battle and another man take
her.'* [13]

The state has the right and duty to uphold public morality, and
believers must subordinate themselves to its efforts. However, when the
state passes immoral laws, there is no longer a duty to obey. Most obviously, American federal and state courts currently recognize the legitimacy of same-sex marriage, which no Christian can confess to be morally
right. No believer may bless with the name of holy matrimony what the
Lord refers to as sin on par with adultery and bigamy. Such wrongdoing
must be resisted by every moral means, even if doing so brings ostracism
and persecution—though always with the holy compassion of Christ and
humble confession that each of us sins in an equal, if not greater,
measure. Whereas the state has the right to enforce love and purity in
marriage, it does not have the authority to promote immorality. A
government may flog wife-beaters, and it should imprison men who rape
their dates, but it cannot call wrong right and right wrong, or require
believers to bless sin. Countries and communities may exile adulterers or
execute bigamists (as was done in the past), but no society can call holy
what God calls impure. What the nature of Christian disagreement and
resistance should be is a discussion for another book. Still, it is undeniable that believers must condemn as sin what Scripture prohibits. Even
when laws otherwise compel believers to serve within a worldly system (as
in paying taxes or providing insurance benefits), believers cannot violate
their conscience: that inner spirit to which God speaks his word. When
we consider the New Testament in the context of Jewish customs and
Roman culture, we see a prophetic witness against many wrongs of the
ancient world.

Impediments of authority are not particularly onerous in modern
America. Slavery has been abolished, and government laws are reasonable
as they, for the most part, enforce morality and justice. The various states
generally frame their respective laws not to uphold class interests, racial
divisions, or state power but to establish a reasonable protection of
marriage. While federal courts imposed same-sex marriage and some
federal and state courts are edging toward allowing close relatives to

---

13. Deuteronomy 20:5, 7 (ESV).

marry, the modern state otherwise does well in core legal principles enforced on the majority of marriages (it does much worse with what is not enforced). In many instances, the government upholds Christian concepts of marriage, whether it intends to or not, and therefore poses no challenge to the authority of the Lord. Such laws must be respected as the instrument of God's work. Biblically-consistent laws in Indiana in force during the 1990s, for instance, stated:

- *Section 1. Before two individuals marry each other, they shall obtain a marriage license.*
- *Section 2. Only a female may marry a male. Only a male may marry a female.*
- *Section 3. Two individuals may not marry each other if they are more closely related than second cousins.*
- *Section 4. Two individuals may not marry each other if either individual has a husband or wife living.*
- *Section 12. Individuals who intend to marry each other shall present a marriage license that is issued under this chapter to an individual who is authorized to solemnize marriages.*[14]

---

14. *Indiana Code, Titles 31 to 35* (Indiana Legislative Council, 1993), 189–190, 194.

16

IMPEDIMENTS OF PARENTAL AUTHORITY

If a son or daughter, or other, has their heart stirred to the desire of marriage, they are bound to give that honor to the parents that they open unto them their affection, asking of them counsel and assistance [and] how that motion which they judge to be of God, may be performed. If the father, friend, or master, deny their request, and have no other cause than the common sort of men have: namely, lack of goods, or because they are not so highly born as they require; yet the parties whose hearts are stirred must still not make any covenant till further declaration be made unto the Church of God.[1]

THERE IS nothing made more clear in the Bible and human experience than the right and need of parents to govern the marriages of youthful children. Both divine and human law have given fathers and mothers the legal right to veto the marriages of minor children. Even today, teenagers are typically not allowed to marry without parental permission. However, every human government has also recognized that a man must leave his father and mother to marry (as Scripture declares in Genesis). That is, marriage is the uniting of persons to build a distinct household separate

---

1. John Knox, "Book of Discipline," in *The Works of John Knox,* vol. 2, ed. David Laing (Edinburgh: Bannatyne Club, 1848), 246. I have edited this text for clarity.

from that of the couple's respective parents. How this should happen when more mature sons and daughters disagree with their parents in choosing a spouse is a matter to be worked through with sensitivity, tact, and impartial fairness. Over the course of our lives, we must provide the same respect we demand and permit the same freedoms we request.

Nearly all marriage laws have limited the scope of parental authority after an established age and often have placed restrictions on the exercise of parental power before the child's maturity. Generally, the discussion has been precisely on where to establish the proper age of emancipation. During the Protestant Reformation, Protestants typically aimed to set that age in the late teens or early twenties, whereas their Roman Catholic opponents upheld medieval church law, which established ages of emancipation at fourteen for boys and twelve for girls.[2] Both sides agreed that parents sometimes could veto the marriages of their children, and children sometimes could ignore the preferences of their parents; the issue was to decide whether to give a greater say to children or parents by placing emancipation at a younger or older age.[3] That noted, in those societies in which parents possessed formal authority in the arranging of marriages for their children, there were also mandatory rules for passing dowries and inheritances to those same children, even to support grown children in making a living and marrying. Such parental obligation is the backdrop to parental authority, for parents were selecting a son-in-law or daughter-in-law whom the parents might be required to assist, like it or not, for the rest of their lives. In contrast, modern parents have few rights in arranging their children's marriages, but likewise have few legal or social obligations to support those same children into adulthood. Modern (Western) culture leaves it to parental preference whether the latter will support their grown children's educations, provide dowries and inheritances, or even contribute to wedding costs.[4]

---

2. Early ages of marriage observed during the Middle Ages were rooted in Roman law and the medieval economic boom (linked to a climate warming period and consequent population growth). As with nineteenth-century and 1950s America, the availability of land, jobs, and food allowed uncommonly early marriage. For an introduction to the demographic realities that underlay European society, see Michael W. Flinn, *The European Demographic System, 1500–1820* (Baltimore: Johns Hopkins University Press, 1981).

3. For a good comparison of Protestant and Roman Catholic approaches to marriage, see Thomas Max Safley, *Let No Man Put Asunder: The Control of Marriage in the German Southwest: A Comparative Study, 1550–1600* (Kirksville, Missouri: The Sixteenth Century Journal Publishers, Inc., 1984).

4. Though Ravi Zacharias fell short of the Christian ideals he espoused, I find his book on marriage to bring a unique perspective to discussing arranged marriages from the optic of a

Where to set the precise age of emancipation is a concern of the temporal government since neither the Old Testament nor the New Testament specifies an exact age of legal emancipation. However, both Hebrew and Roman law provided parents with considerably more authority than does modern jurisprudence, which absurdly allows young people the right to marry before they can legally participate in their own wedding toast. While temporal government has the right to establish a reasonable age before which parental power may not be ignored, the corollary of such law is that there comes a point after which parental authority no longer binds. Both Moses and Paul permitted children to marry through either parental arrangement or personal initiative, at least in select circumstances. Jesus himself observed that parents and children each could make marriages when he noted how the men and women of this world both "marry and are given in marriage." The Bible is filled with instances of both parentally arranged and freely contracted marriages. Isaac married a bride chosen for him by his father through a household servant, while his son Jacob met and married a wife of his choosing. Both custom and individual preference are allowed in these matters, as long as the rights of parent and child alike are upheld.[5]

Even when historical codes of marriage permitted an age of legal emancipation after which sons and daughters were free to marry without parental consent, it remained true that Christians were expected to win the approval of parents in making their marriages rather than asserting their independence in a confrontational and disrespectful manner. Thus, while traditional Roman Catholic laws of marriage typically allowed the marriages of adolescents to stand as spiritually and legally uncontested (even if parents disapproved), Roman Catholic theologians simultaneously insisted that it was sinful to defy (or otherwise ignore) the will of one's parents in the making of a marriage, insofar as the parents themselves were not sinning against the Lord with their guidance. Shakespeare's fictional couple in *The Tragedy of Romeo and Juliet* may have made a legally binding clandestine marriage in Roman Catholic Italy, but they certainly sinned while doing so. Although their marriage remained valid, they were wrong to make it as they did.

This is not to say the young should have little say in their own lives—

non-Western culture that still practices such marriages. Ravi Zacharias, *I, Isaac, take Thee, Rebekah; Moving from Romance to Lasting Love* (Nashville, Tennessee: Thomas Nelson Publishers, 2004).

5.   Luke 20:34 (ESV); Genesis 24:2–4, 29:18.

only that parents and children should work out such vital matters in a spirit of charity and mutual respect. Children must not rebel against their parents, and parents must honor their children's preferences, even those of inexperienced children still maturing in life and faith (since growing into wisdom through making moral choices is a core element of human nature). Modern customs should not outweigh the moral principles of God's law and biblical guidance. Traditional churchmen firmly defended the right of parents to veto the marriages of legal minors and expected children to honor their parents in making marriages. Still, such leaders and pastors also understood how some parents had so wrecked their own lives as to be incapable of giving spiritual guidance to their children. In such circumstances, church leaders frequently permitted public authorities (church or state) to substitute for (and otherwise overrule) recalcitrant and unbiblical parents. John Knox, for instance, declared that a minister or magistrate could "enter in the place of the parent" when the "work of God" was being hindered by the "corrupt affections" of worldly parents.[6]

Parental responsibility to help their offspring marry appropriately is the flip side of a child's obligation to submit to father and mother (as the citation by John Knox at the beginning of the chapter shows). Martin Luther feared that many parents risked the sexual purity of their grown children to ensure future wealth and comfort.[7] Strasbourg Reformer Martin Bucer went further than Luther, arguing that parents err through simple inattention and insisting that parents prepare grown children to wed. Regarding children, Bucer advised maturing sons and daughters not to be too embarrassed to tell their parents of their "desire for marriage" since it was "hardly fitting for children to be ashamed to ask a chaste and holy marriage of their parents."[8] Similarly, an advice manual written in early modern Russia declared that parents are religiously and morally bound to help maturing children find spouses, judging parents culpable for the sexual sins of mature children who had not been provided a suitable mate. The manual stated:

Every parent ought to arrange a marriage for his son when he has grown up, at fifteen years, and for his daughter at twelve. This is

---

6. Knox, "Book of Discipline," *Works*, vol. 2, 246.
7. Martin Luther, "The Estate of Marriage (1522)," in *Luther's Works*, vol. 45, 36–37.
8. Portions of Bucer's "De Regno Christi," are included in *Melanchthon and Bucer,* ed. Wilhelm Pauck (Philadelphia: Westminster Press, 1969), 323.

*the true law. If, by the parent's inattention, either a son or a
daughter who is of legal age happens to engage in sexual intercourse, this is the parents' sin.*[9]

In the modern world, money-driven dating services, online media
platforms, youthful peers, and unproven theorists are allowed to set up
dates, offer advice, and encourage the pursuit of marriage. At the same
time, parents are isolated from the lives of their beloved sons and daughters. This is a perverse inversion of the affectionate guidance that the
Lord ordained for parents to provide to their offspring. When a contemporary father gives his daughter away at her wedding, the ceremony is
little more than a stage play since few daughters would postpone
weddings if their father voiced disapproval—and even fewer parents
would insert themselves into their children's private affairs, even to forestall calamity. In many instances, the only parental involvement in a
child's dating and courtship is the unbiblical, yet far too common,
request that young couples delay marriage while using birth control to
prevent pregnancy (along with discussions regarding parental contribu-
tions to wedding costs). Moreover, even parents who themselves married
young, bore several children, and lived happily with each other, grow
timid and fretful as their children approach the age of marriage. Sometimes, this anxiousness comes from genuine doubt that a given marriage
is biblical or that a specific partner is suitable. At other times, however,
such concerns come from a lack of faith and a lust for worldly success.

As for the obligation of sons and daughters to respect and even obey
parents in marital matters, Scripture is filled with such instruction. Some
of its more direct passages include the following: children are to honor
their parents, fathers retain the right to refuse the marriage of a daughter
to her seducer, and children are to obey parents in the Lord "in all
things." Moreover, King Solomon advised sons to listen to fathers and
mothers alike in marital matters and (more authoritatively yet), Jesus
allowed that lawful marriage sometimes results from having been "given
in marriage" (a reference to parental arrangement of marriage).[10] While
modern martial customs need not be the same as ancient ones (as if a

---

9. The passage notes how sexual sins committed by minors under the ages of fifteen and
twelve belong to the child rather than the parent. Eve Levin, *Sex and Society in the World of
the Orthodox Slavs, 900–1700* (Ithaca, New York: Cornell University Press, 1989), 187.
10. Exodus 20:12 (ESV); Deuteronomy 5:16; Exodus 22:16; Ephesians 6:1–3 (ESV); Colossians 3:20 (NASB); Proverbs 1:8–9, Proverbs 5:8–15; Matthew 22:30 (ESV).

custom is better because it is older), nor even those of a single generation in the past, Scripture gives parents far more authority than they typically exercise in today's world. If non-emancipated children rightly obey their parents in making marriage decisions, emancipated sons and daughters also face no undue hardship in heeding their rightfully concerned parents, when asked to reconsider an intended marriage for the sake of faith and good character. Sons and daughters should also reflect on the wise guidance of their parents when the latter remind them how to plan for a happy and productive life, since the Lord calls such parents to such affectionate leadership in imitation of divine love.

Martin Luther, born into an age in which fathers possessed significant authority to foster or restrict the marriage of their sons and daughters, struck the right balance when he wrote of Jacob's quest for a wife. Luther observed that Isaac did not force Jacob to take a wife whom the latter disliked, but still expected his son to seek an honorable marriage. In this request, the father provided guidance, and the son heeded the instruction. Still, Luther noted how a grown son should be free to engage the girl he loves and a father should not object to such a request since this is "the true and orderly way to contract a marriage."[11] Sons and daughters beyond the age of emancipation may freely marry within biblical parameters, with their independence limited only by the moral obligation to be reverent and respectful to their parents in all godliness.

Nevertheless, children who have not yet attained legal emancipation should not be without defense against stubborn and wrong-headed fathers and mothers. However, this is less of a problem in Western society than in lands where parental control is tighter (and ages of emancipation higher) than in our society.[12] I should add that where parents exercise authority and expect obedience, their children should anticipate material support consistent with biblical injunctions and human fairness. Similarly, where parents have generously enabled sons or daughters to acquire an independence of life that makes early marriage possible, such children should show gratitude and respect in humbly accepting any reasonable and biblical guidance offered by such generous and pious parents. Anything else is ingratitude and a desire for control that such children will not willingly grant to their own (future) sons and daughters.

---

11. Martin Luther, "Lectures on Genesis (Chapters 26–30)," in *Luther's Works*, vol. 5, 195.
12. God's revelation was framed not simply for the needs of modern Western society but for all cultures and eras.

Seventeenth-century Swiss theologian Francis Turretin provided a balanced approach toward exercising parental authority in establishing marriages for their children. Turretin believed that the biblical concept of parental authority included an age of emancipation, freedom from coerced marriages, and parental obligation to preserve the chastity of their children. Turretin focused not on parental rights but on parental responsibilities, insisting that parental authority was granted to secure the interests and piety of offspring. Parents are called to exercise their authority in a spirit of helpfulness and Christian love, not to fulfill their own thwarted aspirations but to help their sons and daughters live productive and joyful lives. In this, I would note that parents are called to imitate their father in heaven, who provides abundantly and generously for the eternal and temporal good of his adopted children, both working his will in them to do well and calling his sons and daughters to the freedom of the children of God. Turretin wrote:

> *[The Fifth Commandment] does not concern children freed and in their majority, who have already gone from under parental power (whom no one doubts to be independent), but especially concerns minors, who are still in every way constituted under parental authority. We confess that where parents, morose and avaricious and through sheer obstinacy, will not consent to the proper marriage of children and cannot give sufficient reasons for their dissent after the request has been made by their children that the latter are not absolutely bound to their will, but it is right for them to apply to a superior power to whom a judgment concerning the justice or injustice of the dissent belongs.*[13]

---

13. Francis Turretin, *Institutes of Elenctic Theology*, vol. 2, ed. James T. Dennison Jr. (Phillipsburg, New Jersey: Presbyterian and Reformed Publishers, 1994), 108. Please note how traditional approaches to disagreement involved appeal to a higher power (in church or state) than a parent, rather than allowing a child to rebel against or ignore parental authority.

17

IMPEDIMENTS OF SPIRITUAL IMPURITY

You shall not intermarry with them, giving your daughters to their sons or taking their daughters for your sons, for they would turn away your sons from following me, to serve other gods. Then the anger of the LORD would be kindled against you.[1]

A wife is bound to her husband as long as he lives. But if her husband dies, she is free to be married to whom she wishes, only in the Lord.[2]

ONE OF THE most obvious impediments to Christian marriage is that both persons must be believers. Otherwise, a specifically Christian marriage cannot exist at all, at least not as a reciprocal calling. Churches, since the earliest days of our faith, have stressed this teaching, and church councils have frequently condemned those who ignored such admonitions. Ultimately, the precept to marry in the faith is rooted not simply in Mosaic commandments that God's holy people must marry among themselves, for we can see throughout the book of Genesis how godly men and women were led to marry brides and grooms who shared in their faith—and this occurred long before God gave his laws to Israel at

---

1. Deuteronomy 7:3–4 (ESV).
2. 1 Corinthians 7:39 (ESV).

Mount Sinai. Did not Abraham marry Sarah hundreds of years earlier, with Sarah being a woman eventually commended by God for her faith in the Lord's power to fulfill his promise to conceive life in her barren body? Likewise, Isaac married the pious Rebekah, who left family and homeland to marry a husband who served the Lord from the heart.[3]

I have begun this chapter poorly in many ways, for I started with a prohibition, with *no* rather than *yes*. While this is an inescapable hazard in any instruction regarding impediments (which are restrictions by definition), perhaps it is best to step back from the breakage of law to the building of faith. While Scripture commands that believers should marry fellow believers and restricts them from marrying unbelievers, it does so as a means of bringing a blessing. Just as the prohibition against eating from the Tree of the Knowledge of Good and Evil was intended to direct mankind to the Tree of Life and its eternal blessings, so, too, the avoidance of marriage and childbearing with unbelievers is the flip side of the blessing to marry and raise children in the Lord: a blessing that brings life and joy, while avoiding many sorrows in family life.

What God designed for mankind from the beginning was marriage in which to conceive and raise godly children who would grow up to share in the image of God and parent alike, building a type of deep friendship within the bonds of affectionate authority and kind-hearted government. The Lord planned that children born into such marriages would mature in peace and love, growing to exercise godly gifts of learning, courage, strength, kindness, beauty, and everything else that is human and good. In turn, such sons and daughters would honor their parents and serve the Lord, bringing great blessings and filling the earth with the industries and arts observed throughout human history, culminating in the eternal civilization prophesied at the end of the book of Revelation.[4] Still, in this sinful and mortal life, the godly family remains the place where the most profound human blessings of human life are to be found, as one psalm revealed:

> *Your wife will be like a fruitful vine*
> *within your house;*
> *your children will be like olive shoots*
> *around your table.*

---

3. Hebrews 11:11; Genesis 24:50–67.
4. Revelation 21:1–3.

Behold, thus shall the man be blessed
who fears the LORD...
May you see your children's children! [5]

Russian novelist Leo Tolstoy famously introduced his novel *Anna Karenina* with the declaration: "All happy families resemble one another, every unhappy family is unhappy after its own fashion."[6] Tolstoy could not have been more wrong, for it is the healthy plant that grows strong and tall, differentiated to the utmost of its capacity, and the healthy animal that runs fast and free. Even in our fallen world, we see how it is orderly families who nourish musicians, strengthen athletes, and inspire poets. It is good families that toughen soldiers, create builders, and prepare prophets. In contrast, where the Lord is not present to bless by his Spirit, the qualities of chaos, sorrow, and despair prevail. Sins of the flesh (drunkenness, drug addiction, sexual immorality) and sins of the spirit (greed, pride, and irreligion) ruin family life so that it produces not the crop of godliness and love that the Lord desires but bitterness, desperation, and resentment. Families break apart, and children are abandoned to themselves, whether in the impoverished slums of large cities, the tidy immorality of the suburbs, the neighborly irreligion of small towns, or the hay-hidden sorrows of the countryside, does not matter. Even when unbelieving families avoid utter moral chaos, they fail to produce the full growth of temporal and spiritual fruit for which mankind was made and to which every family is called.

It is not sorrow, loneliness, and suffering that the Lord wants for mankind, but blessing and its fruits in God's world. To this end, Moses revealed that the people of God were to impress the commandments of God on their children from dawn to dusk, and the apostle Paul reaffirmed this teaching when he observed how his coworker in ministry, Timothy, was raised to salvation from infancy through nourishment in the holy Scriptures.[7] Beyond the message of spiritual redemption, the Bible also includes rules of godly prudence. For instance, the book of Proverbs translates the laws and wisdom of God into parables and poetry suitable both for living as an adult and training children (the many proverbs teaching wisdom to youth are too numerous to mention here).

---

5. Psalm 128:3–4, 6 (ESV).
6. Leo Tolstoy, *Works of Leo Tolstoy: Anna Karenina,* vol. 1 (New York: The Century Company, 1911), 5.
7. Deuteronomy 6:6–7; 2 Timothy 3:15.

Even more directly, the prophet Malachi specifically rebuked those who disrupt the fruit of the human household through divorce and infidelity. Malachi wrote:

> *Did he not make [husband and wife] one, with a portion of the Spirit in their union? And what was the one God seeking? Godly offspring. So guard yourselves in your spirit, and let none of you be faithless to the wife of your youth. "For the man who does not love his wife but divorces her, says the LORD the God of Israel, covers his garment with violence, says the LORD of hosts. So guard yourselves in your spirit, and do not be faithless."*[8]

In rebuking men who abandon their wives and children, often for other women, the Lord used military imagery to describe his authority and power to judge such desertion. He is the *Lord of hosts* who destroys those faithless men who divorce faithful wives and break faith with obedient children. The fact that believers are called to build godly and loving households in which husband and wife enable each other to better love God with all of their heart and strength is why Christian believers are forbidden to marry heretics and apostates. In the theocracy of ancient Israel, it was deemed a treasonous capital crime to marry into pagan nations and tribes conducting spiritual and military war against God's people.[9] Moses prohibited such unions and warned how such illicit relationships would cause Israel to desert the Lord to follow false gods and pagan practices if the people of God and their children made intimate alliances with infidels.[10] Throughout the Old Testament, such marriages were condemned.

Such unions were also forbidden in the New Testament. The apostle Paul allowed Christians to marry as they judged best, only insisting that they marry fellow believers. And though the New Testament gives no rule regarding the appropriate discipline to be administered to those who

---

8. Malachi 2:15–16 (ESV).
9. Though some might consider the struggle between biblical Israel and ancient paganism was a mannerly dinner table debate between Episcopalian priests and United Methodist ministers, the grim reality was a no-quarter war. Like Arabs of the 1940s (who would have returned Jewish emigrants to the furnaces of Auschwitz rather than share land with them), the ancient people of Canaan preferred to force Israel back to the slavery of Pharaoh rather than to share their country. Nor would the pagans repent of their idolatry, sexual immorality, and human sacrifice, for which cause the Lord was forfeiting their claim to the land.
10. Deuteronomy 7:3–4 (ESV).

marry unbelieving mates (just as it does not specify the spiritual punishment to be meted out to murderers and rapists), it is clear that admonition and excommunication have been used throughout church history
against unfaithful people among God's holy congregation. The history of
Israel showed how dangerous it is to tolerate unbelief in the community
of the godly, for Jews who married pagans did indeed compromise true
religion with heathen practices and idols. Pagan women used sexual
immorality to entice Hebrews from the unadulterated worship of the
Lord and bring false gods to Israel (along with judgment on themselves
and the compromised people of God). Moses openly declared how such
women tempted "the people of Israel to act treacherously against the
LORD in the incident of Peor, and so the plague came among the congregation of the LORD."[11] In the same way, believing men and women must
not be led through sexual immorality into marriages with unbelievers.
Even after sexual intimacy has been indulged wrongly, the command to
marry *in the Lord* remains authoritative. Only if the partner converts can
a marriage take place.

In like manner, there are spiritual sins that render men and women
unfit partners for Christian marriage. For instance, the apostles Paul and
John warned Christians to avoid heretics and grossly immoral persons
who have professed but not lived the Christian faith. Instead, believers
were instructed neither to share in the ministry of such sinners nor to
break bread with them in the name of Christian fellowship. If the faithful
are unable lawfully to eat a meal with apostate and renegade Christians,
can they ever be free to select such persons for marriage? This is particularly true for sinners under church discipline following scandalous
behavior or false doctrine. Still, it is critical to remember that God's
forgiveness is real and gracious. Once repentance has been made, there
remains no reason a man or woman previously false in life or doctrine
should not marry a faithful Christian (though it seems to me that
medieval theologians were spiritually reckless in allowing engagement to
heretics on the promise of conversion).[12] True repentance and confession
of faith are nothing less than God's work in a man or woman, and
bearing the fruit of God's Spirit is proof that a marriage is made *in the
Lord*.

God does not allow his people to marry unbelievers, heretics, and

---

11. Numbers 31:16 (ESV).
12. Raymond of Penyafort, *Summa on Marriage*, 51–53.

apostates, but what about denominational differences? While it seems evident that a Christian must not marry an atheist, a Muslim, or a Hindu, what of the differences found in divided Christendom? Should Southern Baptists marry Roman Catholics or Missouri Synod Lutherans marry Old Order Mennonites? Should an icon-venerating Greek Orthodox wed an iconoclastic Presbyterian? Should a tongue-speaking Pentecostal marry a tradition-venerating Episcopalian? The differences between denominations are not insignificant and frequently represent sharp historical differences regarding essential doctrines, and even terrible persecutions. Not all Christian traditions are of equal weight: a fact we see both in the congregations addressed in Paul's epistles and, more notably, in the seven churches addressed by Christ himself.[13] Some churches were blessed for their faith and good works, while others were judged as of little worth. The lesson to be drawn is that the church's history is marked by apostasy, heresy, and sin, as well as renewal, reformation, and restoration. Even today, Christ judges his people, so professing believers must carefully evaluate their differences in doctrine and practical piety before marrying across denominations, and they must always be motivated by faith rather than worldly desires.

That is to say, each of us, man and woman alike, is spiritually obligated to practice that "circumcision" which the apostle Paul calls "of the heart, by the Spirit." Where we are most intimate and most vulnerable, the Lord must be placed first and foremost. Since the apostolic command to marry *in the Lord* is given to individual believers, it is individual men and women who bear the responsibility to evaluate the fruit of the Spirit and assess the spiritual confession (doctrine and piety) of those who profess Christ—no matter what tradition, denomination, congregation, or household a suitor might come from. Only those who confess the name of the Lord and bear the fruit of righteousness in their inner being (moving them to repentance and revival throughout their earthly lives) will be blessed in Christian marriage. Only those men and women who live together in pious love raise godly children for their Creator.[14]

---

13. Revelation 1:10–11.
14. Romans 2:29 (ESV); 1 Corinthians 7:39 (ESV); Galatians 5:22–23; 1 John 4:1–3. While some churches follow the Lord's teachings and structure more closely than others, no denomination or congregation is without fault. The New Testament epistles reveal how the churches planted by the apostles included flawed human beings, and the warnings of Jesus to the seven churches in the book of Revelation showed how serious sin had grown in a single generation, to the point that some churches no longer were faithful to Christ in any meaningful sense. Moreover, even when a given denomination (or congregation) professes

The biblical command is to marry in the faith so that a believing couple can first love each other in pious love, but also that they may raise godly children, if children are entrusted to them. It seems that a cautious approach ought to be taken in marrying outside one's heritage, and that denominational loyalty should not be transferred to another church only because such membership brings an attractive woman or an industrious man. We must also acknowledge the unfortunate reality that many denominations have drifted from historical Christianity and can no longer be considered Christian at all, despite their steeples once towering over great cities, their seminaries once housing zealous prophets, and their sanctuaries previously echoing God's inerrant word. Likewise, some cults should not be considered the fruit of biblical Christianity, and some established traditions of Christendom remain filled with error and abuse. However, even with churches less at variance with each other in doctrine and life, denominational differences must still be recognized, as husband and wife must attend church together and raise their children under one roof and within a common faith. If a couple cannot attend church together, it seems apparent that they should not marry. What our Lord taught in another context certainly applies to the family itself: "If a house is divided against itself, that house will not be able to stand."[15]

Marriage outside the faith has been treated as a serious matter in the churches (including some marriages with congregants in rival denominations). Based on apostolic commands and the seriousness of the prohibition against marrying pagans, Christian leaders and councils have prohibited many marriages and disciplined those who made them. Given that marriage is supposed to foreshadow the love of Christ for his church and to make godly children for the Lord, how could it be otherwise? John Calvin shed light on the importance of this command when presenting it as the very foundation on which the idea of a people holy to God must exist. The church of God is not an association or a club of a few self-chosen members (like a monastic community or a modern club), but a great people of men and women and girls and boys called by their God and made holy through his word. It is for this reason that John Calvin observed the following about marriages made by the sons of God (believers) with the daughters of men (unbelievers) before the flood:

Christ faithfully in doctrine and good works, not every individual congregant demonstrates true faith.

15. Mark 3:25 (ESV).

It seems at first sight frivolous, that the sons of God should be so severely condemned, for having chosen for themselves beautiful wives from the daughters of men. But we must know first, that it is not a light crime to violate a distinction established by the Lord; secondly, that for the worshippers of God to be separated from profane nations, was a sacred appointment which ought reverently to have been observed, in order that a Church of God might exist upon earth.[16]

---

16. John Calvin, *Commentaries on the First Book of Moses Called Genesis*, vol. 1, trans. Rev. John King (Grand Rapids, Michigan: Baker Books, 2005; reprint), 238.

18

IMPEDIMENTS OF SEXUAL IMPURITY

You shall be a crown of beauty in the hand of the LORD... you shall be called My Delight Is in Her, and your land Married; for the LORD delights in you, and you land shall be married. For as a young man marries a young woman, so shall your sons marry you, and as the bridegroom rejoices over the bride, so shall your God rejoice over you. [1]

GOD CREATED MARRIAGE TO REPRESENT, foreshadow, and even prophesy his eternal marriage to his church. When the Lord's bride is married, she shall be as holy as a willing virgin: her spiritual and moral purity restored through the lifeblood of Christ himself. From the beginning, the Lord made marriage to demonstrate in human flesh a spiritual love beyond all flesh, beyond mortal desire and imagination. As Christ is righteous and will consummate his marriage with his unsullied bride when they join in eternal union, the Lord calls men and women to be spotless and holy when they enter mortal marriage. How could he do otherwise? And even when we cannot be utterly holy in thought and desire, we are called to honor charity and chastity in abstaining from sexual relations with each other prior to marriage. Of this Scripture leaves no doubt—not Moses, not the prophets and apostles, not Christ himself.

---

1. Isaiah 62:3–5 (ESV).

What then is to be done when men and women find themselves attracted to a person who has indulged in sexual intimacy prior to marriage and no longer embodies this ideal (which is true for many men and women in our culture)? As discussed in the previous chapter, spiritual apostasy and unbelief render men and women unfit for Christian marriage, though it is important to note that unbelief does not necessarily dissolve marriages made prior to conversion. What about sexual apostasy and unbelief? Does sexual sin become an impediment to Christian marriage? In like manner, must a believer (at least a younger one making a first marriage) select a virgin for holy matrimony, or may he (or she) marry someone widowed, divorced, or previously unchaste? While questions about divorce and remarriage following the death of a spouse will be addressed in subsequent chapters, here we will examine a question before marriage: must a believer, male or female alike, select only a sexually inexperienced and innocent partner for marriage?[2]

Virginity was the norm for young women in the law of Moses and ancient Israel. The law of the Lord God (who inspired every word) was, and remains, uncompromisingly righteous and holy. In the book of Deuteronomy, the Lord declared that a man who falsely accused his bride of not having been a virgin was to be fined one hundred shekels of silver (a common laborer earned one shekel per month, so this fine represented over eight years of labor in a society that limited slavery to seven years) and never allowed to divorce the slandered woman—which meant the man could not disinherit any children they conceived together. For her part, the woman was not required to tolerate further evil from her husband and retained common remedies against additional mistreatment. But if an accused bride was found not to have been a virgin, she was to forfeit her life. Virginity and honesty were taken seriously, and the woman who falsely professed to be a virgin essentially perjured herself during the legal vow of marriage. As we shall see, this passage discusses fraudulent claims of virginity more than virginity itself, since the Mosaic

---

2. No one marries as truly righteous before the Lord; each of us is the filthy object mentioned in Lamentations 1:17 (and associated in at least one older translation with menstruation). Protestant Reformer Pierre Viret noted: "[If] a person would consider this as it ought to be [and] make a comparison of himself with God, what horror would he have of appearing before so pure, so clean, so holy and perfect a majesty and nature, not only if he is debauched in body and spirit by adulteries, but even if he is only tainted by the least thought and desire which might exist in him, seeing that he must answer to Him who [knows] all and who is so clean, so pure, and so perfect?" Viret, *Exposition*, vol. 2, 133–134.

law elsewhere required marriage for violating virgins, not death. In this particular passage, Moses commanded:

> *[If a man accuses his bride of misconduct], saying, 'I took this woman, and when I came near her, I did not find in her evidence of virginity,' then the father of the young woman and her mother shall take and bring the evidence of her virginity to the elders of the city in the gate... Then the elders of that city shall take the man and whip him, and they shall fine him a hundred shekels of silver and give them to the father of the young woman... But if the thing is true, that evidence of virginity was not found in the young woman, then they shall bring out the young woman to the door of her father's house, and the men of her city shall stone her to death with stones, because she has done an outrageous thing in Israel by whoring in her father's house. So you shall purge the evil from your midst.*[3]

Throughout most of Christian history, the virginity of young brides was assumed, and corresponding chastity in men as well.[4] To dismiss the lack of virginity as a small matter was judged morally culpable, and to marry a woman who had not been chaste was often considered folly. While punishments were not as severe as in the holy commonwealth of ancient Israel, there were consequences in ancient, medieval, and early modern Christianity for unchastity.[5] We see at the beginnings of Christianity itself (in the first weeks after the conception of the Incarnate Christ) how Joseph planned to repudiate Mary, both for lack of virginity and for the more serious sin of betrothed adultery. When Mary was found to be with child before the lawful consummation of her marriage

---

3. Deuteronomy 22:13–21 (ESV). Please note that the deceived husband retained the right to accept his bride's impurity and deception with sin and forgiveness; he was never explicitly *commanded* to prosecute her, only permitted to do so, if needed.

4. Cyprian believed a woman could lack virginity even if her hymen were intact, suggesting many types of sexual intimacy defiled the spirit of virginity (for both sexes, I would add). He considered a lack of virginity to represent "adultery against Christ." Cited in Michael Rosenberg, *Signs of Virginity: Testing Virgins and Making Men in Late Antiquity,* 183–186 (New York: Oxford University Press), 186.

5. One medieval friar complained that his contemporaries wrongly believed that "simple fornication [i.e., sexual intercourse with a widow, prostitute, or concubine] is not a mortal sin because it is a natural act." Even so, the friar observed a common judgment against the violation of virgins. Siegfried Wenzel, ed., *Fasciculus Morum: A Fourteenth-Century Preacher's Handbook* (Philadelphia: University of Pennsylvania Press, 1989), 669, 677.

to her betrothed husband, Joseph decided to dismiss her for infidelity, and Scripture judged him a *righteous man* because he sought to discreetly end their engagement rather than to indulge sin or call for public disgrace (whether by ancient custom or Internet exposure).[6]

Here, we must separate the matters of virginity and adultery in what became a precedent-setting act of piety. By Hebrew custom and Mosaic law, the period of engagement (betrothal) was as binding as marriage (in some ways, it was considered marriage).[7] For that reason, Joseph judged Mary guilty not just of premarital impurity, which was serious enough, but of betrothed adultery: a sin far more serious than simple fornication and one that merited death by Mosaic law. It was for this reason that Joseph sought to rid himself of Mary, refusing to reward a surmised adulteress with the dignity of marriage or to raise a child he believed belonged to another man. However, just as Jesus would do three decades later, Joseph proved unwilling to subject an accused woman to public disgrace and sought to divorce Mary quietly since the laws of Roman occupation rather than the laws of holy Israel were in effect—until an angel revealed to Joseph how Mary's pregnancy represented God's holy love for his people rather than a man's unholy seduction of an unmarried girl. Nor should we condemn Joseph for his stern righteousness, for even men of our immoral age repudiate fiancées who became pregnant by other men. Nor does any woman with a shred of good sense marry a man who has been unfaithful (even without pregnancy) during their engagement.

The law of Moses was plain: if a man lay with the wife of another man or with a betrothed woman, both man and woman were judged guilty of a capital crime. The book of Deuteronomy revealed that a man who raped a married or betrothed woman should be put to death, while he who raped an unbetrothed virgin was to be fined and married to the girl (if her father approved), without right to divorce. In contrast, the

---

6. Matthew 1:18–25 (NASB). John Chrysostom wrote: "If her husband has intercourse with her, he becomes as impure as she is, since both of them become one body." John Chrysostom, "Homily 19," in *On Marriage and Family Life*, 29. Basil the Great tempered this moral purity with Joseph-like mercy and discretion, writing: "Our fathers did not order women to be exposed if they had committed adultery and dutifully confessed their faults or were convicted by other means, so that we might not be the cause of their death after their conviction." Basil the Great, "Letter 119 to Amphilochius," in Hunter, ed., *Marriage and Sexuality in Early Christianity*, 241.

7. Yifat Monnickendam's *Jewish Law and Early Christian Identity: Betrothal, Marriage, and Infidelity in the Writings of Ephrem the Syrian* (Cambridge: Cambridge University Press, 2020) examined Christian customs in light of Jewish and Roman betrothal laws.

book of Exodus revealed that a man who seduced an unbetrothed virgin must marry the woman and treat her with the rights of a bride, unless her father objected, in which case the man still had to pay the full bride price for a virgin to the girl, even if she was withheld from marriage by her father (who represented his daughter). The law was clear: a Hebrew who seduced a virgin was responsible for making amends for all that he took from the woman, to include providing a full dowry through which she could make a living or marry another man (who would not be required to pay the financial penalty for the seducer's sin). These passages make plain that the Lord judged sexual sin during betrothal as a violation of marriage. They also made clear that God considers sexual intimacy to be a matter that brings with it profound and undeniable responsibilities as consequential as those of marriage itself. Being required to provide a dowry to a virgin, even if she (through her father) refused marriage, might prevent the seducer from ever marrying, or reduce the man to slavery to pay his debt. It appears that the Lord gave the advantage to women in cases of seduction, likely to restrain the lusts of men.[8]

Returning to the problem at hand, we must determine if the lack of virginity impedes marriage, given both the laws of Moses and New Testament injunctions and church customs.[9] Historically, many believers have taken a strict approach to marriage, insisting that women marry as virgins. This was not an utterly inflexible rule since widows were allowed to marry, but it sometimes precluded the marriages of unchaste women, at least for some stricter Christians. Seventeenth-century Puritan William Perkins, for instance, believed it forbidden to marry "a harlot, a defamed

---

8.　Deuteronomy 22:22–29 (ESV); Exodus 22:16–17. We must remember that the penalty of rape fell on the rapist. The rapist was required to marry his victim if she so chose (without right of divorce), but the girl's father was not required to give his daughter to such a man, but could take the large fine (potentially leaving the rapist enslaved to pay the debt). If the rape involved abduction or bloodshed, there might be even more serious penalties. For an example in Renaissance Venice of some type of rape (which includes several categories of mistreatment even in modern law) that led to marriage, see Guido Ruggiero, *The Boundaries of Eros: Sex, Crime, and Sexuality in Renaissance Venice* (New York: Oxford University Press, 1985), 31.

9.　While rape brings many unfortunate consequences to a woman, it does not bring moral or spiritual pollution. After the sack of Rome in 410 A.D., Augustine of Hippo defended the moral innocence of the many women violated by Visigoth invaders. One historian noted: "[Augustine] insisted that female purity was a mental, intentional, and not an objective, physical state... He insisted, in short, that sin, rather than shame, provided the only real scale of sexual values... The lust of another, he defiantly claimed, could not 'pollute' one's purity" [and] a woman whose body was forced into sex [kept] her chastity intact." Kyle Harper, *From Shame to Sin*, 172.

woman [i.e., non-virgin], or one that comes of infamous parents, though she be repentant." Perkins forbade the marrying of a non-virgin, though I am unsure his prohibition reached the level of an impediment that made marriage illicit and impossible, as with incest.[10]

The problem with such strictness is twofold. First, passages in Exodus gave fathers the right of veto over the marriages of seduced daughters, leaving open the possibility that such women could seek a different marriage, now funded with the seducers' bride price (which is a sharp punishment of seducers who must pay for another man's marriage or face enslavement to raise the money to do so). Second, while virginity was and remains the biblical ideal, and Moses provided rules to address its violation, though Moses did not explicitly require brides to be virgins. One English legal theorist who lived a generation after William Perkins noted that Jewish law restricted marriage to only the most abandoned women.[11] John Selden observed how ancient historian Josephus commented on the Mosaic prohibition:

> We have from Josephus a prohibition, seemingly Mosaic, not to marry a harlot or a prostitute... God does not permit them holy matrimony.[12]

Perhaps the best way to judge the differences between the rigorist Perkins and the somewhat laxer Selden is to review biblical demands for the marriages of the Levitical priesthood (upon whose codes John Selden was commenting). While many passages of the Old Testament law assume virginity as an ideal, it was only in providing regulations for the marriages of Levitical priests that the Lord specifically commanded marriage to virgins. Moses required Jewish high priests to marry virgins, not allowing such high priests to marry even pious widows. Ordinary

10. William Perkins permitted men with concubines to marry if they repented and renounced their consort, which represented a double standard for sexual conduct. Perkins, "Christian Economy," in Larsen Klein, ed., *Daughters, Wives, and Widows,* 162–164.
11. At least one ancient Christian writing resembled the words of William Perkins, with a modern writer noting: "The *Apostolic Constitutions* added that a cleric could be married only once and only to a virgin, and that marriage to a widow was prohibited." Yifat Monnickendam, *Jewish Law and Early Christian Identity,* 42–43.
12. John Selden, *The Uxor Hebraica,* 94–95. One historian described Selden's book on the Hebrew wife as "dauntingly detailed historical scholarship." Margaret R. Sommerville, *Sex and Subjection: Attitudes to Women in Early-Modern Society* (London: Arnold, 1995), 192. Selden noted that medieval scholastic theologians distinguished between unrepentant women and those who returned "to chaste ways." Selden, *Uxor Hebraica,* 359.

priests were given more latitude, forbidden only to marry women previously divorced, seduced, or prostituted. These rigorous laws allowed no deviation, yet were not given to the entire people of God, only to those men born into the strict regulations of the Levitical priesthood—who were a caste of men separated from ordinary life, dedicated to the sacrificial priesthood and restricted from common customs beyond their choices in marriage. For instance, priests were not allowed to touch or approach the dead bodies of anyone, but the closest family members, and the high priest was forbidden to mourn even his parents by nearness to their dead bodies. God made his priests a holy caste of men subject to stringent regulations to represent his divine righteousness to the people of Israel and the Gentile world.[13]

Perkins went far beyond Moses by requiring brides to be virgins, and even Selden's more carefully nuanced arguments wrongly extended a regulation intended for the Levitical priesthood to the entire Hebrew laity. I am convinced that this approach fails to recognize the distinctive place of the Jewish priesthood in the law of God and the freedom that Christian clergymen, not to mention Christian laity, have from the purely ceremonial, ritualistic, and illustrative aspects of Jewish law. Moses revealed who was unsuitable for marriage and minced no words in expressing God's will. If sexually active men and women were disqualified from marriage, the matter would have been evident. But Moses empowered the fathers of seduced and ravished daughters to withhold their daughters from marriage to their violators, seemingly to marry such women to another man at a later date. He commanded only a select group of priests to restrict their marriages to virgins. Why? Because these men lived as typologies of God's holy character and love for his people, and were required to be ritually and morally holy before him. They were to be unblemished in body and soul alike (without sin, disease, defect, or injury) just as an animal sacrificed at God's altar was to be unblemished. This rule of faith bound no one else, and it would have been sacrilege for any Hebrew not born into the ritual priesthood to presume to live as if he had been born a Levite. Non-Levitical Hebrews were not permitted to assume responsibilities to which the Lord had not called them at birth. In many circumstances, such presumption was to be severely punished.

This less restrictive understanding of Mosaic law is evident in the New Testament. Paul's message was clear: marriage is not only permitted

---

13. Leviticus 21:13–14; Leviticus 21:7; Leviticus 21:1–4, 11.

for fornicators but required for everyone troubled by sexual desire. The apostle granted former sinners the right to marry when he called the Corinthians to marriage, even though he indicated that some of them previously were sexually immoral, adulterers, prostitutes, and homosexual offenders. While these were the kinds of people Perkins and Selden forbade believers from marrying, the apostle Paul (speaking with divine authority) instructed such converts to find spouses if tempted to return to the sexual immorality of which they had repented. Best practices may look different in cultures more chaste than our own, but among us, the apostolic response to the immoral culture of Corinth provides a good pattern to follow. The only restriction Paul imposed was that the unjustly divorced could not remarry since they already had husbands or wives with whom to reconcile.[14] The separated were told to restore the rightful marriages to which the Lord initially called them, since it is not permitted to maintain sexual purity through marital infidelity—to avoid the lesser sin of fornication through the more serious one of adultery. The gist of Paul's message is clear: those once corrupted by sexual immorality are called to holy wedlock in God's kingdom. Such men and women, it would seem, have a particular and pressing need to use God's provided remedy against the evil of sexual fornication. As a general rule, marriage must not be ignored or despised.[15] The apostle Paul wrote:

> *Do not be deceived: neither the sexually immoral, nor idolaters, nor adulterers, nor men who practice homosexuality, nor thieves, nor the greedy, nor drunkards, nor slanderers, nor swindlers will inherit the kingdom of God. And such were some of you. But you were washed, you were sanctified, you were justified in the name of the Lord Jesus Christ and by the Spirit of our God.*[16]

Someone might use Paul's subsequent teaching in 2 Corinthians that

---

14. Francis Schaeffer wrote about those with broken backgrounds: "I must frankly say that as I get older, I personally would not [object to marrying] a woman just because she had been married before. It is fine to marry a woman who is a virgin if she is the one the Lord directs you to. But I do not think the emphasis on marrying a virgin should become so great that the thought of marrying anyone else is less than best." Francis Schaeffer, *Letters of Francis Schaeffer*, ed. Lane T. Dennis (Westchester, Illinois: Crossway Books), 178–179.

15. The rule of charity would preclude marriage for a pedophile, for whom marriage (and parenthood) aggravates temptation rather than resolving it by placing the pedophile near his own children and their friends.

16. 1 Corinthians 6:9–11 (ESV).

believers and unbelievers should not be *unequally yoked* (as the King James Version translates 2 Corinthians 6:14) to require compatibility in sexual experience: to argue that chaste men should marry virgin women and that chaste women should marry sexually inexperienced men. This would be to abuse Paul's words (or rather, the words of Christ through Paul) since the apostle was not discussing sexual compatibility or even marriage, but distinguishing believers from unbelievers rather than differentiating sinful backgrounds among God's people. While there may be many reasons for the chaste (or unchaste) to prefer someone with a similar background, if they have the opportunity to make such a choice, selecting a spouse is not like shopping at a mall or a flea market: those seeking marriage typically must decide yea or nay regarding that single person God's providence has set before them, or take a chance in waiting for an unknown future.

Moreover, when men and women are pressed with sexual temptation, delay may be imprudent or wrong. Also, because repented sexual sin is not a revealed impediment to marriage, overemphasis on this one quality may lead to sin against charity and humility. Francis Schaeffer once observed how Jesus castigated "self-righteous people of His day" who harshly judged prostitutes, "because they had not committed these particular sins."[17] I would add that I have known outstanding Christian men and women at one time tainted with all sorts of sexual sin: men and women who subsequently lived fruitful and righteous lives before the Lord, and became great parents of well-raised sons and daughters of faith.

Often, discussions of sexual immorality focus on women more than men, or have done so historically, even though men are more likely than women to have sexual relations before marriage.[18] While Christian cultures sometimes have lacked impartiality, it is not the case that our Lord has indulged men in the matter of sexual immorality, for the Lord God tolerates no double standard.[19] As just one example of divine equity,

---

17. Francis Schaeffer, *Letters*, 205.

18. We must remember how Hebrew men brought family land and years of toil as their bridal gift: land and wealth to support their wife and children in the event of death (or divorce). Given this investment, men rightly expected honesty from women regarding any relationship with other men, for grooms were giving to their brides everything most of them would ever have to offer. Even we moderns would feel more compunction about honest character were we required to provide a bride price representing years of personal savings and decades of family labor—a one-time gift that could never be repeated.

19. Even if Roman and barbarian culture held men and women to different standards, Christian preachers generally did not. Judith Evans Grubbs wrote: "Christian apologists

a prophet of God called out the sacrilege and contempt of the Lord's worship by the sons of the priest Eli when those men slept with servant women tending to God's tent of worship. Scripture says nothing about the fate of the women, but the men were providentially killed for their unholy behavior. The reality of male headship in marriage and leadership among the Lord's people mandates higher standards of behavior for men than for women, and the prophet Hosea revealed how the Lord refused to punish sexually immoral women in Israel because "the men themselves go aside with prostitutes and sacrifice with cult prostitutes." To explore this further, while women are undoubtedly accountable for their moral choices and judged by God, the Lord first seems to deal with those sinful men (who bear ultimate responsibility for their families) who lead their households astray.[20]

Though no one can deny that there have been misogynist elements among Christian people (especially among ascetics who feared women as stumbling blocks to clerical celibacy), it must be noted that as a matter of church law, church leaders frequently have pressed for a consistent standard of sexual behavior for man and woman as Christian churches gained authority over pagan philosophy and religious customs, even when secular laws did not consistently implement a Christian ethos. In that spirit, one fifteenth-century text vigorously admonished contemporaries who chided women's infrequent extramarital affairs while tolerating men's common philandering (hypocrisy to the point that a married man's affair with a servant was judged a trifle). While we cannot review every ancient, medieval, or early modern sermon calling out such hypocrisy, it will suffice to point out how Reformation-era Geneva (the epitome of Protestant moral rigor) approached sins of the flesh with consistency regarding sexual morality, favoring neither man nor woman in the upholding of biblical law.[21] One modern historian has written that

---

from the second century on also stressed that husbands were held to the same standard of marital fidelity as wives." Judith Evans Grubbs, *Law and Family in Late Antiquity: The Emperor Constantine's Marriage Legislation* (Oxford: Clarendon Press, 1995), 70.

20. 1 Samuel 2:22, 27, 34; Hosea 4:14 (ESV).

21. One medieval author observed that women were created from a rib near the heart of man to establish love and differentiate marriage from serfdom and slavery. When discussing Augustine's opinion that adultery is worse in men than in women since men hold authority, the author observed: "[Men] are bolder and more cunning in passing off their sin, while they practically all support each other in it. It is men who are witnesses, judges, and enforcers of punishment against adultery in women. And because they are deeply guilty of it themselves, they are more or less unanimous in their efforts to back up their promiscuity."

Reformation-era Genevan authorities treated male and female fornicators with similar moral fervor. Both men and women were expected to do right; neither was indulged sins of the flesh.[22]

The notion that men and women (whether teenagers, middle-aged, or elderly) should be held to the same standard of sexual propriety is a Christian doctrine that disarms protests and complaints that traditional moral teachings are tools of oppression against women. It may be that some past laws have discriminated against women, and many men excuse their sexual immorality while denouncing the slightest indiscretion in women. I myself heard an unbelieving man living an unchaste life declare how he hoped to marry a virgin. Such hypocrisy should not be. There is room in Christian teaching for mercy and grace toward all who have sinned, man and woman alike. But there also must be equity and fairness. This has been the standard of the Christian faith since the beginning. One thousand years before Protestant Geneva disciplined sinning men and women by an equal standard of judgment, the church father John Chrysostom made a similar plea for consistency in upholding sexual morality, writing:

> *Do not tell me about the laws of unbelievers, which drag the woman caught in adultery into court and exact a penalty, but do not demand a penalty from the married men who have corrupted servant girls. I will read to you the law of God; which is equally severe with the woman and the man, and which calls the deed adultery.*[23]

See "Dives and Pauper," in Alcuin Blamires, ed., *Woman Defamed and Woman Defended: An Anthology of Medieval Texts* (Oxford: Clarendon Press, 1992), 260–264.

22. Jeffrey R. Watt wrote: "Authorities pursued male and female fornicators with the same aggressiveness—males actually comprised almost 60 percent of those convoked for fornication or adultery in Geneva for the years 1568–1582—and usually assigned the same penalties to them." Jeffrey R. Watt, *The Consistory and Social Discipline in Calvin's Geneva* (Rochester, New York: University of Rochester Press, 2020), 101.

23. John Chrysostom, "Sermon on Marriage," in *On Marriage and Family Life*, 79–80.

19

IMPEDIMENTS OF DISEASE AND ILLEGITIMACY

A promise of marriage made between those whereof the one hath a disease so loathsome as the other upon good ground cannot possibly endure familiar society... is unlawful. Of this sort is leprosy, the French pox [i.e., syphilis], and such like. For seeing there can't be any matrimonial use in them that are tainted with such contagious disease without apparent danger of infecting each other and those also which have society with them... and by this means the issue of their bodies growing of a corrupted seed are even born to perpetual misery... such marriage cannot be undertaken with good conscience.[1]

EARLY MODERN EUROPE was an era of disease—with cycles of contagious diseases (often generically identified as plague) depopulating cities and countryside alike during several hundred years of global cooling, religious turmoil, and political instability. Weakened by famine and poor weather, the population growth and economic boom of the Middle Ages faltered under the blows of shortened growing seasons and demographic catastrophe. This period of history also identified gonorrhea as an endemic concern and faced a destructive outbreak of syphilis. While

---

1. William Perkins, "Christian Economy," in Larsen Klein, ed., *Daughters, Wives, and Widows*, 161–162.

every epoch of human history is comprised of far more than what ails it, the impact of disease on the people of early modern Europe was profound, so it is not surprising that they (like their medieval ancestors dealing with the scourge of leprosy) required pastoral guidance regarding disease as an impediment to marriage.[2] Given the ugly aftershocks of the sexual revolution during the past sixty years, it is equally unsurprising that we, too, require similar counsel and guidance.

In the quote cited above, William Perkins (whose lifetime included two major cycles of bubonic plague in his native England) mentioned both plague and sexual disease as impediments to marriage. While discussing leprosy (perhaps a category inclusive of several debilitating diseases) as an impediment to marriage, Protestant Reformer John Calvin once commented how the wife of a man afflicted with leprosy "ought to be allowed to live as a widow, after a legal investigation by judges." Calvin's allowance for separation (although without the right to remarriage) freed the affected woman from conjugal obligations, suggesting that such disease should be considered an impediment to any future marriage of the diseased person. Moreover, Calvin was protective of wives despite his understanding that (what he called) leprosy caused the afflicted to possess enhanced sexual desire.[3] Regarding specifically sexual diseases, Calvin's compatriot Pierre Viret observed how excesses of food and alcohol debilitate the body far less than the "defilement and diseases and horrors which follow sexual immorality."[4] Sexually transmitted diseases and diseases with sexual implications are not new to the world.

Scripture does not directly address disease as an impediment to marriage, and we must not overstate what binds (or frees) consciences before the Lord. This is particularly the case since modern medicine mitigates the worst effects of many diseases, whether potentially mortal ones such as heart disease and cancer or sexually transmitted ones such as

---

2. For a review of climate cooling's impact on Europe after the medieval warming period, see Emmanuel Le Roy Ladurie, *Times of Feast, Times of Famine: A History of Climate Since the Year 1000,* trans. Barbara Bray (New York: Farrar, Straus & Giroux, 1988). Ladurie discusses the impact of eons-old cycles of global warming and cooling during the medieval and early modern periods. His book has implications for contemporary climate discussions.
3. Calvin, *Ecclesiastical Advice,* 133–134. The terms leprosy and syphilis could be confused or interchanged in early modern Europe. One physician wrote of syphilis found in a French army: "The French had contracted this malady by unclean relations with a leprous woman when they were crossing a mountain in Italy." Paul Lacroix, *History of Prostitution among All the Peoples of the World, from the Most Remote Antiquity to the Present Day,* vol. 2, trans. Samuel Putnam (New York: Civici Friede Publishers, 1931), 948.
4. Viret, *Exposition,* vol. 2, 162, 192.

syphilis and herpes. Modern couples often face fewer inconveniences from serious disease under modern medical treatment than our forefathers faced from rotted teeth, poor vision, and broken bones. Of course, if a sexually transmitted disease has damaged the reproductive system so that offspring cannot be begotten, both the desire and obligation for children may render a given marriage imprudent or necessitate consideration of adoption. In such instances, a transparent and honest confession of affliction is required at an appropriate time prior to engagement. After all, a wedding day or honeymoon night is not a good time to initiate a discussion or make a confession. Before emotions and obligations are stitched together, the receiving partner should be afforded a fair chance to make a discreet and gentle judgment—and opportunity to choose marriage in the face of costly risk and sacrifice, thereby demonstrating a deep faith in God's calling and uncommon love of their beloved. Any deceit, as with fraudulent claims of virginity or masking sexual impotence, presumably allows annulment and dissolution of the marriage on the grounds of the indecency mentioned by Moses.[5]

The biblical demand for premarital chastity is so natural and healthy that men and women who live chastely may prefer to marry someone who has lived the same way and is suited to live with them, sharing the demands of marriage and parenthood. Regarding disease, they may prefer not to accept the consequences of someone else's wrongdoing (though they should be particularly generous in body and spirit if they have sinned in the same way, even if they themselves were impacted differently). What I mean to say is no suitor can obligate a virgin (or otherwise undiseased woman) to accept a husband with a lifelong disease, for the woman has the freedom to choose otherwise. Nor can a woman insist that a man marry a wife who may pass him a disease. Both charity and humility require each of us to accept the consequences of our sin.

Though some men and women might *prefer not* to be married to a spouse afflicted with the consequences of sin, human preferences are not necessarily God's holy and charitable calling. The apostle James reminded believers that we must be willing to go wherever the Lord wills rather than seeking to control our lives too carefully, and the lives of the prophets, apostles, and saints are filled with examples of men and women led to lives they once tried to avoid.[6] As one such example, the prophet

5. Deuteronomy 24:1 (NASB).
6. James 4:15.

Hosea was specifically commanded by God to marry and conceive children with a prostitute. Later, the woman broke faith with her husband and conceived two of her three children with other men. Yet, the Lord God commanded Hosea a second time to "love a woman who is loved by her husband, yet an adulteress," so Hosea purchased his wife from the slave market (where she was being sold for cheap) and took her home, only warning the woman to live right.[7] Whatever the outcome of their life together, it is doubtful that Hosea entered manhood desiring illegitimate children born of an unfaithful wife. Still, his life was specifically ordained to the glory of God and the good of God's people: for a greater purpose than the happiness of Hosea himself. Hosea revealed in his own shame and sorrows the sufferings of God from the sin of unfaithful Israel, revealing God's love in a type of performance art that resonated far deeper than any modern theatrical production or interpretive dance. This was prophecy embedded in the throes of real life.[8]

While Hosea's marriage was a type of living prophecy, with Hosea representing the love of the Lord for his people, Israel, and Hosea's wife representing Israel's spiritual adultery with the pagan god Baal, it was also a flesh-and-blood marriage with tears, anger, and betrayal—along with reunion, renewal, and restoration. Hosea's wife, Gomer, was a lost soul, and the Lord not only taught Israel a lesson of holy love but saved Gomer from the streets, seemingly twice over, showing both the people of Israel and Gomer herself how the Lord overflows with compassion for lost souls. Despite Hosea's prophetic calling, no one should imagine the sacrifices of Hosea to be any greater than those to which each of us has been called. In like manner, the prophet Isaiah revealed how the Lord's suffering servant (that is, Christ) bears our sorrows and griefs, having been "pierced through for our transgressions" and "crushed for our iniquities." And the apostle Paul used Christ's willing sacrifice to reveal how husbands are to lay down their lives for their wives.[9]

In this spirit—in the power of the Holy Spirit of the Lord—some men and women may choose, through the freedom born of Christian love, to sanctify and love by sharing in a spouse's diseases, or risk thereof. To be affected with a disease from sinful fornication and adultery may be

---

7. Hosea 1:2–3 (NASB); Hosea 3:1–5 (NASB).
8. My understanding of the account of Hosea and his wife is based on H.H. Rowley, "The Marriage of Hosea," *Bulletin of the John Rylands Library* 39, no. 1 (September 1956): 200–233. Reprinted in *The Marriage of Hosea* (Manchester: 1956).
9. Isaiah 53:3–5 (ESV); Ephesians 5:26–27 (ESV).

shameful, but to share in the affliction of a spouse in imitation of Christ seems no impediment to Christian marriage unless the disease brings inescapable madness, debilitation, or death (as syphilis did when Viret, Calvin, and Perkins provided their pastoral guidance) or irreversible infertility for those still requiring children.[10] But when medical treatment can mitigate the worst effects, or any inconvenience of the disease is otherwise acceptable, marriage to an afflicted spouse need not be impeded since it subverts neither the essential purposes of marriage nor the holy calling of love found in the book of Ephesians. Because most wedding vows include a public oath to love one's spouse *in sickness and health,* it seems no exaggeration to say that Christ-like love sometimes involves bearing the grievous sins of others, just as Christ suffered our sins and moral contagion in his flesh. Moreover, what any undiseased husband or wife endures from the flesh of a diseased spouse is always far less harmful than what every spouse must endure from the sinful soul of their husband or wife. What tempts our souls to sin is far worse than what threatens our bodies with defilement and destruction.

I will add that no person should be evaluated for marriage only based on their sins and diseases. These can and often do matter, so it is necessary to honestly discuss faults and flaws that might represent impediments to marriage (especially if hidden). But it is equally important that suitors consider people in the totality of who they are. An untouched virgin may bring purity of the flesh, but if she is self-centered and stubborn, she will make a far less suitable Christian wife than a good-willed and family-oriented woman tainted by the mistakes of her past. Likewise, a compassionate and hard-working man who once soiled his body with a sexually transmitted disease (or his soul with the marks of sexual sin) will make a better candidate for Christian marriage than a man with a chaste body and an unkind disposition—or a man who wishes to play like a teenager or to be taken care of like a child. We must discuss these painful topics for the sake of conscience, yet without forgetting that many virtuous, admirable, and enjoyable people carry these afflictions: people who matter to God and should matter to the men and women of God more than their sins and diseases. Many believers with embarrassing diseases

---

10. One historian has described syphilis in premodern Europe: "A patient entering tertiary syphilis bobs in and out of sanity, as the victim's body sinks into paralysis. To be diagnosed with tertiary syphilis in the days before antibiotics was to be condemned to wakeful damnation." Kyle Harper, *Plagues Upon the Earth: Disease and the Course of Human History* (Princeton, New Jersey: Princeton University Press, 2021), 255–257.

would make suitable spouses if given the opportunity and ought to be considered for marriage by sensible and pious suitors, although they must demonstrate the reality of their repentance to a potential spouse. They must show repentance for having dishonored God's law more than mere regret for having caught a disease.

Sexual intimacy outside of marriage also leads to the birth of illegitimate children, at least in those situations in which fathers refuse to marry the women they have impregnated. Historically, there have been Christians who doubted whether believers should marry men or women of illegitimate birth, and early Judaism established something of a caste system regarding children born of forbidden unions. While discussing this sensitive matter, we must remember passages in the book of Ezekiel that "the son will not bear the punishment for the father's iniquity" and "when a wicked person turns away from his wickedness which he has committed and practices justice and righteousness, he will save his life." With God, there is always forgiveness and new life, regardless of past sins. Still, there are spiritual and natural consequences for sin, including for sexual and marital sins. With that in mind, the New Testament placed restrictions on church leadership for men whose past includes divorce or wrongful remarriage, and the Old Testament prohibited marriage to those born of illicit marriages and sexual unions.[11] Moses declared:

> *No one born of a forbidden union may enter the assembly of the LORD. Even to the tenth generation, none of his descendants may enter the assembly of the LORD.*[12]

The command of Moses was quite clear and was interpreted in Jewish tradition to signify that those born of forbidden unions were restricted from public leadership among God's people and ought to marry only those of similar descent. While Jewish custom generally focused on those born of adultery, incest, prostitution, and pagan unions, later Christians sometimes extended this to include those born before wedlock.[13] As with the command for Hebrews to marry within

---

11. Ezekiel 18:20, 27 (NASB).
12. Deuteronomy 23:2 (ESV). The NASB (1995) uses the word *illegitimate birth*.
13. The Hebrew word for such children is *mamzer*. One historian explained: "Hebrew, *mamzer*, meaning the child of adultery or incest, i.e., of a sexual union that is illicit because of an impediment to marriage between the partners (owing to the fact that the woman is legally married to someone else or by consanguinity, or affinity, between the partners). The

their tribes and for Levitical priests to marry from their own lineage, Israel was called to demonstrate in the flesh the holiness of God through ceremonial and symbolic purity. In a pagan world filled with ritual prostitution, sexual slavery, intimacy between close relatives, and other vile practices, the nation of Israel was called to make clear what holiness is and what it involves. This is a point worth repeating: Israel was called to establish a ritual and moral holiness that would grow into a language of faith through which the Lord would reveal himself to the various peoples and cultures of the Gentile world. While God's grace and mercy remained active for individuals, the Lord upheld his law so that divine mercy could take root among pagan nations when the Son of God was revealed, which the law of Moses accomplished. God was saving individuals, nations, and entire civilizations, demonstrating his righteous character to a pagan world enslaved to sin, suffering, and shame.

The aforementioned passage in Deuteronomy was public law for Israel, intended to govern marriage for society as a whole, and was included alongside commands not to practice religious prostitution or allow the Jewish temple to profit from harlotry (as well as to refuse to collect interest from fellow Israelites). These commandments were not personal ethics but public commands to ensure that the Jewish people pursued holiness in an observable manner before the pagan peoples of the ancient world—so that Israel would become the proverbial city on a hill, displaying the virtues of God's law. Protective marital laws were just one feature of this broad revelation. Nor were the laws of legitimacy in Israel unique in the ancient world. Athenians and Romans of antiquity also limited marriage to their countrymen, refusing citizenship to children conceived with foreigners, slaves, and disreputable persons. While the limitation of rights for those born of illicit births stands against modern legal customs, it is more than a little arrogant for modern men and women to condemn most previous civilizations based on the dictates of amoral Western legal principles.[14]

---

status of *mamzer* carries with it grave disabilities, including ineligibility to marry a normal Israelite. This disqualification ... retains vital importance in Jewish marriage law to this day." Judith Romney Wegner noted how slaves, captives, Samaritans, raped women, and proselytes fell into this category. Judith Romney Wegner, *Chattel or Person? The Status of Women in the Mishnah* (New York: Oxford University Press, 1988), 22–26, 224 n. 60.
14. Deuteronomy 23:3. One orator justified strict Athenian laws requiring marriage to Athenians on the grounds that no Athenian would have married a deflowered girl if legally permitted to marry a non-Athenian, but the laws allowed defamed Athenian girls to offer citizenship to their offspring. S.M. Baugh, "Marriage and Family in Ancient Greek Society,"

Indeed, in a modern world where many nations have out-of-wedlock birth rates near (or over) fifty percent of all births, it is a serious temptation for all of us to wish these commands away, for they draw attention to the extent of contemporary sin and shame. Nevertheless, we cannot ignore these commandments, preferring that the holy call of ancient Israel be refashioned in the image of modern immorality. We must rejoice not only that the people of God were called to limit the evils of slavery and usury (which they were), but also that they were called to overthrow evils rising from unbridled sexual passion: the itches and urges that led to temple prostitution, incestuous marriages (whether with a sister by Egyptian Pharaohs or a with a sister-in-law by King Herod), polygamy, serial divorce, and other great evils that flourished in the ancient world. If religion is to be more than a few hermits, monks, and Amish households fleeing society to keep themselves pure without regard for the damnation of the many, the public laws the Lord gives to govern society must be considered just and necessary.[15]

At the same time, we rejoice that the Lord himself atones for our many sins after breaking divine commands regarding marriage and sexual intimacy, whether we have done so publicly, in the shadows of our hearts, or were conceived by parents who sinned while making us. We must never forget that Moses included laws of atonement and purification in his commandments, making it plain how the Lord understands that fallen mankind requires mercy and cleansing amidst judgment. Even as God calls us to holiness, he understands how we suffer from original sin, family faults, and personal vices, and that his righteous commands are beyond our capacity to obey fully. He who established laws of sexual morality, separating clean from unclean, also provided a remedy for sin so that he can adopt as his holy children everyone who confesses his name, leaving behind none who would repent of their sins (or those of their parents). All who call upon the name of the Lord will be saved, whether they have been born of an immoral prostitute or a pious wife.

The Old Testament required a holy people, but also demonstrated compassion for all men and women created by the Lord, for the law was

---

in Campbell, *Marriage and Family in the Biblical World*, 105. Susan Treggiari's essay, "Marriage and Family in Roman Society," makes similar points about Roman marriages.

15. One historian reported an increase in European illegitimate births during the eighteenth century to four (and as much as seven) percent of births. To reduce modern percentages to this threshold would require a momentous religious revival. Michael W. Flinn, *The European Demographic System, 1500–1820*, 81.

given to bring Jew and Gentile alike to God's salvation. As noted, laws of atonement were included in the Mosaic law, and we see in the various Psalms what it looks like when unholy people are cleansed of their sin through the Lord's atonement. One psalmist condemned the extent of Israel's rebellion in murmuring against God, worshipping idols, marrying prohibited pagans, and shedding the blood of innocent children via human sacrifice. "Nevertheless," the psalmist declared, "[the Lord] looked upon their distress when He heard their cry [and] relented according to the greatness of His lovingkindness." Another psalm speaks of those humbled with hard labor, who stumbled before calling to the LORD in their trouble, and the LORD saved them from "darkness [and] the shadow of death." The reality of God's grace, forgiveness, and new life is as real as his laws of marriage and sexual morality.[16]

Though God's mercy is foreshadowed in the law of Moses and the prophets, it is most perfectly revealed in Christ and the holy apostles. In sending the apostles into the Gentile world to convert heathen cultures filed with degradation and vice (for paganism was not the rarified world of ancient philosophers and poets whose books we still admire, but the ugliness of temple prostitution, exposure of unwanted children, and oppression of wives and daughters), our Lord did not just call believers to live holy lives in their own houses and hometowns, but commanded them to baptize the nations and bring God's holy love to every corner of the world. Believers also were explicitly commanded to bring into God's house the "poor and crippled and blind and lame." Why? Because the Lord opens his doors to the broken, diseased, sinful, and outcast and expects us to do the same. To that end, while some of God's churches have limited the rights of those born out of wedlock, Christian leaders far more often have been generous and protective of those so born.[17]

The epistle of 1 Corinthians explicitly reveals that a believing spouse sanctifies an unbelieving one and makes their children holy (rather than the unbeliever defiling the children of a Christian), though it does so without condemning children born into unclean circumstances through no fault of their own. The writer of the epistle of Hebrews likewise observed that Christians have not come to "the sound of a trumpet and a voice whose words made the hearers beg that no further message be

---

16. Psalm 106:19, 25, 35, 38, 44–45 (NASB); Psalm 107:10–14 (NASB).
17. Deuteronomy 23:17–18; Hebrews 1:1–3; Luke 14:21 (ESV). Temple prostitution exists in modern India, with the Internet showing devotees of the goddess Devi (*devadasi*) practicing something ancient and terrible.

spoken to them, [for] they could not endure the order that was given."
Rather than such old covenant strictures, new covenant believers come to
"the assembly of the firstborn who are enrolled in heaven [and] to Jesus,
the mediator of a new covenant."[18] Even those once forbidden to enter
the assembly of God's people in ancient Israel are welcomed with open
arms into God's new assembly, the church of Christ, for which we all
must rejoice—for who among us does not count great sin and unbelief
even to the tenth generation of our ancestors? One scholar wrote that
several persons of illegitimate birth were among the ancestors of Jesus,
not to speak of the other sins and crimes of Christ's forefathers. And in
the long lineage that made each of us (no matter our class, race, religion,
or nationality), there are tyrants, thieves, murderers, rapists, adulterers,
prostitutes, traitors, rebels, slavers, cowards, and blasphemers, along with
the honorable men and women whose ancestry we proudly confess.[19]

It was in the spirit of Christ that church father Methodius of
Olympus mentioned children conceived in irreligious and unholy
circumstances, declaring how "very many who are begotten of unrighteous seed are not only numbered among those who are gathered into the
flock of the brethren, but are often called even to preside over them." He
also noted how those "who are so begotten, even though it be in adultery,
are committed to guardian angels."[20] While Christians rightly heed the
words of Paul that "the unrighteous will not inherit the kingdom of
God... neither the sexual immoral... nor adulterers, nor men who practice
homosexuality," we also heed Paul's equally authoritative words of hope
and joy in which the apostle declared: "Such were some of you. But you
were [washed, sanctified, and justified] in the name of the Lord Jesus
Christ and by the Spirit of our God."[21] Writing more than one thousand
years after Methodius, Pierre Viret echoed similar words of this hope and
joy in his review of the Deuteronomy passage, writing:

*If this passage meant that they weren't to be received into the
Church at all, [this] law would be horrible. But, for those who
examine this passage diligently and who compare it with many*

18. 1 Corinthians 7:14 (ESV); Hebrews 12:19–20, 23–24 (ESV).
19. John Witte, Jr., *The Sins of the Fathers: The Law and Theology of Illegitimacy Reconsidered* (Cambridge: Cambridge University Press, 2009), 6. For comparison, I was born in
1960, and I have tenth-generation ancestors born before the American Revolution.
20. Methodius, "Discourse II, Theophilia," in *Ante-Nicene Church Fathers,* 343–343, 346.
21. 1 Corinthians 6:9–11 (ESV).

others in Scripture, [it's] easy to see that it must be understood as being received amongst people of Israel to be admitted to public offices both in the Church as well as in the state... For seeing the Lord has no respect of persons as men do but looks to the faith and the truth which is within the heart, [the Lord] receives illegitimate children into the communion of His Church and of His Son Jesus Christ no less than He receives legitimate children, provided that they have faith... If we have faith, by which both illegitimate and legitimate children are all legitimate and acknowledged by God as His own legitimate children. Without this, all of us—even those who were born from a lawful marriage according to the flesh—are considered by God as illegitimate and sons of the devil.[22]

---

22. Viret, *Exposition*, vol. 2, 152–153. In light of contemporary challenges to traditional morals, see *Appendix 2: The Legitimacy of Illegitimacy?*

20

IMPEDIMENTS OF CRIMINALITY
AND SIN

*If it be here alleged that the sin of adultery dissolves the bond both
of contract and marriage, and therefore much more doth idolatry
or infidelity [lack of faith], which is a sin far more detestable than
adultery, I answer, that the question is not [which] of these is the
greater sin or more heinous in the sight of God but which of them is
more repugnant to the nature and condition of wedlock. Now the
sin of adultery is that alone which breaks the bond and renounceth
the troth plighted in marriage, and is the cause of a divorce, and
not idolatry or infidelity.*[1]

AN EVEN MORE PERPLEXING issue than the matters of spiritual and
sexual impurity is that of sin and criminality: is a man or woman (convicted of a serious crime) free to marry? The Old Testament penal system
allowed petty criminals to marry, since the punishment for theft and
other property crimes in the law of Moses was repayment, albeit with a
substantial penalty, of the stolen goods. If a man paid his fine, he was free
of prison or other penalties that might restrict marriage. However, if a
man could not pay his fine, he was sold into slavery to raise money to pay
his debt. And, as already discussed, a man sold into slavery could wed

---

1. William Perkins, "Christian Economy," in Larsen Klein, ed., *Daughters, Wives, and
Widows,* 162–163.

with the permission of his master. If Moses allowed convicted criminals and slaves to marry in a strict theocracy, there is no reason for modern believers to place burdensome restrictions on men and women convicted of criminal activity. A man who has stolen a car and paid his debt to society can freely marry; a woman who has sold drugs and been paroled is a suitable candidate for Christian courtship, insofar as she has truly repented of her sin and is living a new life in Christ. It seems reasonable to assume that most crimes can be judged under this rule. Hence, repentant criminals may marry and be given in marriage today, just as permitted under the law of Moses.[2]

Capital crimes are more challenging to sort out since the modern state rarely executes anyone, let alone every murderer, kidnapper, pedophile, rapist, and adulterer whom the law of Moses would have put to death—and not only Moses but (in some instances) the command of God given to all men and women after the flood. Even worse, modern penal systems frequently release convicts after a few short years of prison, and some criminals serve no jail time at all.[3] One notorious woman who murdered her young children in 1994 becomes eligible for parole in a few years, still in her fifties. Will a Christian man be free to marry her if she converts to God's truth upon release? Or are all suitors bound by the book of Proverbs, which warns the wise not to support fugitives burdened with the guilt of innocent blood? In a similar manner, can a woman marry a repentant rapist who deserves to die by a strict application of Mosaic law but who has been released from prison after only a few years? What about the kidnapper who was never charged and whose crimes have exceeded the statute of limitations? What of a man who confesses to a murder for which he was once acquitted? Or for which he was never charged?

To push matters further, can a man or woman marry someone

---

2. Exodus 22:3.

3. Old Testament penalties appear harsh to modern men and women accustomed to judicial systems that extend every possible mercy to criminals beyond what nearly every civilization in the past would have tolerated. What we must remember is that God punishes all sin, mortal and venial alike, with death, and has done so since the beginning of human history. God gives life, even eternal life, to those who obey him, but brings death, even eternal death, to those who forsake his life-giving ways. Natural death itself comes as punishment from God against the sins of the human race. The laws of Moses do judge sin with death, but this is the reality each of us faces every day. Perhaps notorious sinners face capital punishment and reckless ones end their days early in drunken wrecks and drug overdoses, but even those with everyday sins face ordinary deaths. Moses was making a profound and necessary theological point: life is found in God and death in forsaking him.

involved with an abortion as either patient, partner, or medical professional? That particular sin is not even a crime in most modern law, but a
championed right.[4] While the Bible does not directly address all of the
consequences of the legal and moral self-indulgence that mars our society, Scripture does provide principles on which we can build reasonable
answers. Moreover, it is necessary to address this matter since tens of
millions of Americans have been involved with sins that were capital
crimes in ancient Israel. Those guilty of such sins need to know whether
they are morally free to take a spouse or must live in self-exiled solitude,
while those innocent of such sins need to know that they are permitted to
marry the forgiven without fear of forsaking the path of righteousness.

In the Old Testament, crimes such as adultery, homosexuality, and
idolatry were punishable by death. In 1 Corinthians, the apostle Paul
noted how some Corinthians were guilty of such sins before they became
Christians. As previously mentioned, the apostle did not instruct spouses
to divorce such men and women, but commanded believers to remain
married even to idolatrous spouses to testify to unbelievers about God's
love and truth. Someone might object that while Paul allowed marriages
with pagans to continue, he prohibited such unions from being made in
the first place—which is a valid point since marriage must not be
contracted with an unbeliever, even if the marriage would remain
binding once made. Likewise, some might posit that no one should
marry a man or woman who remains unrepentant of a grave sin such as
murder or abortion, for we are called to marry *in the Lord*, and a lack of
repentance demonstrates a person to be in the flesh and the world rather
than of the Lord. That, too, seems clear enough.[5]

Yet, the Lord also gives new life, and this is where the matter becomes
more difficult to untangle. There have been teachers and theologians who
argued that moral or legal guilt in a capital offense allows an innocent
mate to divorce and remarry, reasoning that a man properly executed for
murder or rape would leave his widow freedom to remarry. Therefore, if
a state refuses to do what God commands, the Lord does not expect
innocent spouses to bear a burden the wider community refuses to shoulder, so the innocent spouse can be treated as if widowed.[6] This position

---

4. Genesis 9:6; Proverbs 28:17.
5. 1 Corinthians 6:9–11; 1 Corinthians 7:39 (ESV).
6. Scottish Reformer John Knox judged it prudent for the church to do work left undone
by an indulgent government, believing it necessary for church officials to declare the civil
death of a sinner whose capital crime has been left unpunished by the state, with an inno-

not only gives the spouse of a criminal (or someone guilty of sins punished prior to modernity) the freedom to divorce and remarry, but also implies that such criminals and sinners are not free to marry. Why? Because if they are marriageable, their original marriage should not have been dissolved. The Protestant Reformer Ulrich Zwingli (and his allies) adopted such reasoning into a marriage code that Zwingli helped to frame: a code in which Zwingli declared that the principle of divorce for adultery could be extended to various capital sins and other serious faults. Protestant-inspired Zurich law declared:

> *Likewise, greater reasons than adultery, as destroying life, endangering life, being mad or crazy [and other such cases]—these cases the judges can investigate, and proceed as God and the character of the cases shall demand.*[7]

Though such reasoning seems compelling, it is safer to argue from the direct evidence and examples presented in the Bible. In 1 Corinthians, the apostle Paul claimed the right to marry a believer, though we know from his own account that he previously was a persecutor of Christians (a man who had blood on his hands). While not a murderer by law, by any moral standard, he was a murderer of believers via unjust judicial persecution. Paul did not claim that apostles could marry, but that he himself was free to do so. And Moses, the human instrument through whom the Lord gave his law at Mount Sinai, began his public ministry with a wrongful killing. Having seen an Egyptian overseer strike a Hebrew slave, Moses killed the Egyptian before fleeing as a fugitive from Egyptian justice. While the Lord nowhere condemns the killing of the Egyptian overseer as outright murder, neither is it presented as an act of faith but of a reckless vigilante not yet serving the Lord with holiness and faith. In any event, Moses married in the aftermath of the killing, taking as his wife

---

cent spouse freed to remarry. If, however, the criminal spouse subsequently repents of sin, Knox permitted remarriage. John Knox, "Book of Discipline," in *Works*, vol. 2, 248–249.

7. Ulrich Zwingli, "Zurich Marriage Ordinances, 1525," in *Ulrich Zwingli, 1484–1531, Selected Works*, trans. Samuel Macauley Jackson (Philadelphia, Pennsylvania: University of Pennsylvania Press, 1972), 118–122. Robert Kingdon noted how many early Protestants believed: "[Those] who committed adultery deserved to die according to biblical commandment, but if spared by overly lenient modern laws could nevertheless be regarded as legally dead. This, then, left the innocent spouse as free to marry again as if his or her partner had actually died." Robert M. Kingdon, *Adultery and Divorce in Calvin's Geneva* (Cambridge, Massachusetts: Harvard University Press, 1995), 86–87.

a local woman, Zipporah, whom he met during his flight from Egypt. Did Zipporah sin in marrying the slayer of another human being?[8]

In describing actual and allowed marriages for men guilty of bloodshed, what Scripture suggests is that the marital association begins (or ends) for reasons linked explicitly to its essential purposes. A man does not cease to be a husband if he robs a bank or murders a foe, since the laws he breaks are not those that govern marriage. On the other hand, he who violates his oath of fidelity, though provoked by an unaffectionate wife or tempted by months of foreign travel (or years of military service), breaks his marriage vow in a way that a vigilante or persecutor does not. Similarly, a woman does not cease to be a wife because she becomes an alcoholic or an embezzler, yet she who violates her wedding oath in the bed of another man puts her marriage at risk, even though her husband is uncaring and sexually unavailable. In some instances, we (like the Zurich council cited above) may see the adulterer as the better person than many criminals, although this does not change the fact that adultery violates marriage in a way that other sins do not.[9]

Now, it may be that marital desertion is implied, even intrinsic, in any deliberate criminal act that sends a man away for a lengthy prison sentence, just as the fugitive who flees public authorities simultaneously deserts his community and abandons his wife. The issue is not whether criminal activity per se is marriage-ending behavior, but whether an act that voluntarily (becoming a fugitive) or involuntarily (receiving a prison sentence) abandons the marriage bed as an inevitable consequence of freely chosen criminal activity counts as marital desertion, thereby allowing divorce, particularly for sins punished by death in the Mosaic law. To be clear: if crime permits divorce, it seems to impede future marriages; otherwise, such divorces cannot be allowed. But if it is desertion that permits a divorce more than crime per se (unless the crime is intrinsically sexual, such as rape, incest, bestiality, or pedophilia), then crime is not the cause of divorce, but only the trigger for divorce-causing desertion.[10]

---

8. 1 Corinthians 9:5 (ESV); Exodus 2:11–25; Exodus 2:21.
9. One medieval theologian included in his discussion of the impediment of crime not only those guilty of crimes such as incest, priest murder, and killing a spouse ("one who killed his wife ought not take another"), but also adulterers who plot murder against spouses or conspire to remarry in the event of the death of the betrayed spouse. Raymond of Penyafort wrote: "On account of their enormity, there are many crimes… that impede the contracting of marriage." Raymond of Penyafort, *Summa on Marriage*, 49–50.
10. There are prison sentences that do not end a marriage, such as the persecution of polit-

Such reasoning (as indirect as it seems even to me) suggests that converts from criminal lives are permitted to marry, assuming no other impediment to marriage or call to celibacy exists. It is not that God's forgiveness permits every convert to begin life completely anew, without regard or responsibility for past actions, but only that killing a man no more prevents the making of marriage than it dissolves a marriage already made. Scripture itself gives an example of a marriage between a man guilty of two capital crimes and a woman guilty of such sin. The Old Testament hero of faith, King David, impregnated his neighbor, Bathsheba, in an adulterous affair, then sent the pregnant woman's husband on a lethal military mission. After the death of the inconvenient mate, David and Bathsheba married, although both were guilty of capital crimes by the moral law of Moses. David was a murderer before the Lord and married his victim's widow to hide their adulterous affair.

God judged David as the murderer of an innocent husband, even though an enemy army did the actual killing. And while the Lord punished David and Bathsheba for their wickedness, the Bible nowhere invalidated their marriage (and did not annul David's existing marriages). Instead, the once-adulterous couple later conceived a son, Solomon, who was favored by God and made the legitimate heir to the Israelite throne. While David was guilty of murder and adultery, and his bride was guilty of adultery, the Lord accepted their subsequent union as lawful since no impediment to marriage existed; or rather, because the Lord accepted their marriage, we can assess no impediment to marriage to have existed. The Lord graciously blessed their union with a legitimate child who became the king of the land and the wisest man who ever lived. And we must never forget that the God of Israel is the Lord Jesus Christ of the New Testament. The Lord does not change his character or the moral laws reflecting his righteousness. Hence, his blessing of David and Bathsheba seems to represent not an exception or anomaly, but a revealed promise to all believers who share in that couple's repentance and renewing faith. It seems that the Lord included many details of this account in Scripture as a specific comfort for those who repent of similar sins: to reveal to them the depth of the Lord's mercy and the scope of their salvation into the new life that God gives.

---

ical or religious dissenters. The difference is that acts of piety and patriotism are not inherently criminal acts, but are wrongly prosecuted by persecuting authorities. Being unjustly condemned is not an intrinsically marriage-deserting act since it could happen to any persecuted believer.

Contemporary men and women guilty of grave sins and capital crimes may marry and be married, if afforded the opportunity, as they live a new life in Christ. After a complete and transparent confession of previous sins to suitors (and completion of legal punishments), they are free to marry anyone willing to live in patient love with the consequences of their wrongdoing, as well as to build a holy and righteous life filled with the wisdom and love of the Lord. This would include such acts as abortion, which undoubtedly is the killing of an innocent child in the eyes of God. Still, not only did the Lord forgive David's use of legal authority to cover his sin with Bathsheba after the latter became pregnant, but God blessed the repentant David and Bathsheba with a son who would rule the land in great wisdom. It seems not only that Bathsheba had a strong position in David's court to help Solomon secure the throne, but also that she set an example of repentance as her son grew up. Certainly, the taint of the sin of his parents did not follow Solomon through his life, as it often does for those whose repentance proves more tepid and timid than their sin.[11] This was God's gift of faith and new life. In this hope, we, too, may live.

There are many sins left unpunished in the Western world, and many crimes are punished too lightly, including some resulting in the deaths of human beings. Those guilty of terrible crimes and awful sins seem like Paul and David (who sinned within the law) or Moses (who sinned against the laws of Egypt). Like those men, modern men and women may trust in God's gracious blessing, since a pardoned crime or forgiven sin is neither an impediment to marriage nor a hindrance to God's gracious blessing.[12] They are free to marry, and others are free to marry them, only making common judgments regarding faith and good character. I should note, too, that ours is not the first generation in which believers must apply God's grace to a corrupted judicial system that treats human life cheaply and entangles citizens and subjects in the unbelief and sin of lawgivers. Believers faced similar choices during the conversion of the Germanic tribes (whose laws differed from those of ancient Israel by

---

11. 1 Kings 1:28–31.
12. In discussing confession of hidden sins, Martin Luther wrote: "I follow the custom and advice of those who hold that no case of secret sins should be reserved. That is why all those should be absolved whose sins are hidden, whether they are sins of the flesh, or every kind of lust, abortion, and the like." If Luther is right, abortion should be confessed before God, and there may also be a place for the Lord's earthly representatives to pronounce Christ's absolution and forgiveness of its guilt. Martin Luther, "A Discussion on How Confession Should Be Made (1520)," in *Luther's Works*, vol. 39, 42.

allowing financial restitution for the taking of human life) and the Roman Empire (whose toleration of infanticide, abortion, and gladiator fights continued decades beyond the legalization of the Christian faith). In facing the sorrows and sins of this world, we must have faith and trust that the Lord will give his people wisdom to do and live right, insofar as they confess the ways and wisdom of their God.

> *[Bathsheba] conceived; and she sent and told David, and said: "I am pregnant." [Then] David sent to Joab [who] put Uriah at the place where he knew there were valiant men... when the wife of Uriah heard that Uriah her husband was dead, she mourned for her husband. When the time of mourning was over, David sent and brought her to his house and she became his wife; then she bore him a son. But the thing that David had done was evil in the sight of the LORD [and] the child died... Then David comforted his wife Bathsheba, and went in to her and lay with her, and she gave birth to a son, and he named him Solomon. Now the LORD loved him.*[13]

---

13. 2 Samuel 11:5–6, 16, 26–27 (NASB); 2 Samuel 12:18,24 (NASB).

21

LAWFUL ASPIRATIONS IN SELECTING A SPOUSE

Then Rebekah said to Isaac, "I loathe my life because of the Hittite women. If Jacob marries one of the Hittite women like these, one of the women of the land, what good will my life be to me?" [1]

WHEN REBEKAH, the mother of Jacob and Esau, expressed her disgust with the pagan women whom her oldest son, Esau, had married, her younger son, Jacob, responded as an obedient son and a wise believer. He did not allow sexual desire to propel him into rebellion against faith and family, but waited to marry a spiritually suitable wife. As a result, Jacob is commended by Scripture for having obeyed his father and mother as he departed his homeland to find a bride fit to serve in God's household—and it was no mere boy who traveled across the wilderness but a grown man who forsook convenience to please God and parents. Jacob rejected the path taken by his rash older brother Esau, who had several times cast away the blessings of God in exchange for immediate gratification, despising the word of the eternal God for the sake of momentary pleasures. [2] As believers today seek to marry, they must follow Jacob's example by ensuring they pursue the Lord's will rather than their own worldly desires. Not only must they marry a permissible partner (regarding

---

1. Genesis 27:46 (ESV).
2. Genesis 27:46 (ESV); Genesis 28:1–2; Genesis 28:6–9; Genesis 29:1.

biblical impediments to marriage), but they must choose from available partners using discernment rather than marrying from lust and greed.

To be clear, all believers seeking marriage must select a spouse with whom they can build a household based on biblical values. This is the crux of the matter. A man ought not to marry a woman simply because she is physically desirable. Samson made the mistake of selecting a wife because he wanted to sleep with her, and his rash decision cost him his life. Both King David and his son Solomon strayed into unjustified polygamy by marrying for what was sexual desire, with David's grave sin magnified a hundredfold in the faults of his son. Nor should a woman marry a man only because he is wealthy, for Scripture teaches that "those who desire to be rich fall into temptation, into a snare, into many senseless and harmful desires that plunge people into ruin and destruction." In contrast, the book of Proverbs reveals it is better to have "a dish of vegetables where love is than a fattened ox served with hatred."[3]

When making a match, men and women should consider the ability of a potential mate to serve their family and raise children according to biblical criteria and standards, rather than focusing on physical beauty, wealth, or social status. Godliness was the quality Jacob sought as he searched for a wife who would please his parents with reverent piety, and he was right to do so, since it is always foolish to ignore questions of spiritual character and ethical integrity when entering into a marriage. No matter how attractive or wealthy a mate might be, any serious character flaw will bring turmoil and unhappiness to a potential spouse and possible children. Long after hair has grayed and breasts sagged, good character brings joy and delight. What the book of Proverbs declared of women is true for both husband and wife: the supremacy of character over less enduring qualities. After summarizing the godly woman's hard work, devotion to family, good judgment, and temperate lifestyle, one passage in the book of Proverbs observed:

> *Charm is deceitful and beauty is vain,*
> *But a woman who fears the LORD,*
> *she shall be praised.*
> *Give her the product of her hands,*
> *And let her works praise her in the gates.*[4]

---

3. Judges 14:1–3; 1 Kings 11:1–3; 1 Timothy 6:9 (ESV); Proverbs 15:17 (NASB).
4. Proverbs 31:30–31 (NASB).

The Bible teaches that Jacob also considered Rachel's physical beauty—and loved her so much he considered seven years of work to earn her hand as "a few days."[5] With that in mind, it is dangerous to look at marriage merely as a spiritual partnership, as if natural impulses like sexual attraction, intent to raise a family, or prudent management of resources are unimportant when the opposite is true. Marriage is not only a religious partnership or spiritual relationship; its purposes are earthly and temporal, and rightly so since God ordained the moral, affective, and practical purposes of marriage. Because the Lord created the human household to meet a wide range of needs, the wise suitor aspires to marry someone who fulfills as many of these temporal needs as humanly possible (while reflecting God's moral character). It is good to find a spouse who can be an affectionate lover, a kind friend, a prudent householder, a wise parent, and a spiritual partner. Marriage exists to unite body and soul alike and will cease only when our world is filled with the people God planned to create before the world was made.

As such, it is entirely lawful for men and women to marry as much for earthly delights as spiritual experiences. It is spiritually permissible for a woman to marry a man because he will make a good provider, and it is morally right for a man to marry a woman because he finds her physically attractive. The Lord does not require spiritual equality between husband and wife, but does command that both bride and groom profess his name before marrying. It was in this spirit that Moses allowed the Israelites to marry beautiful women captured in warfare, insisting only that such brides be permitted time to mourn their losses and profess their loyalty to the people of God.[6] Similarly, Martin Luther observed that the book of Genesis described Jacob's earthly love for Rachel to "give evidence that God does not reject and condemn those who look at beauty in a wife, and that such choosing is without sin."[7] Even the rigorous John Calvin said the same when commenting on a previous text in Genesis:

> *He who shall be induced to choose a wife, because of the elegance of her form, will not necessarily sin provided reason always maintains the ascendancy, and holds the wantonness of passion in subjection.*[8]

---

5. Genesis 29:20 (NASB).
6. Deuteronomy 21:10–14 (ESV).
7. Luther, "Lectures on Genesis (Chapters 26–30)," in *Luther's Works*, vol. 5, 289.
8. Translated from Calvin's commentary on Genesis 6:1–3. Ioannis Calvini, *Opera Quae*

While the desire for the beauty of a particular woman may be lawful and is not necessarily to be prohibited, the words of John Calvin remind us that sexual passion must be kept under control. The church father John Chrysostom likewise cautioned believers that physical beauty often brings with it vanity and other faults that make marriage with such women difficult. For that reason, Chrysostom advised believers to seek inward beauty more than surface appearances, reminding married men to respect wives who lack good looks and warning the single to marry for character and faith since "familiarity causes [initial] admiration [of physical beauty] to fade." Where good character does not complement attractive looks, Chrysostom warned that love fades during the first months of marriage, and that husbands who select brides primarily for beauty will endure great disappointment once their spouse becomes marred by unanticipated diseases and blemishes.

In contrast to an emphasis on physical appearance, John Chrysostom reminded men to value "affections, gentleness, and humility in a wife," for these are the most enduring "tokens of beauty." Chrysostom emphasized that physical beauty is not something over which women have control and should not be the primary criterion for valuing a woman or selecting a wife. Men are to be patient with the external wrinkles and blemishes of women. Chrysostom called men to focus on repenting of the wrinkles and imperfections in their souls, which are revealed when they desire lesser things, such as physical beauty, over more enduring spiritual attributes, and similarly advised men to avoid the temptation to use marriage as a means to acquire wealth and a high social position. What Chrysostom commanded men also applies to women.[9]

The fact that single men and women must judge the character of a potential spouse gives no one an excuse to avoid marriage based on vague fears for the future or a critical attitude toward others.[10] That a Hebrew was permitted to marry an unknown captive simply because he was attracted to her illustrates the fact that God understands marriage to be an uncertain affair; it is not ethically necessary to have every question

Supersunt Omnia, vol. 23 (Brunsvigae et Berolinae: C.A. Schwetschke et Filium, 1863–1900), 402.

9.   John Chrysostom, "Homily 20," in *On Marriage and Family Life,* 43–44.

10. Critical attitudes of men toward women and women toward men are based both in theory (feminist misandry and historical misogyny) and intrinsic differences between the sexes. Because men and women alike frequently struggle to appreciate persons unlike themselves in core characteristics, we must remember that the Lord created different sexes such that each should glory in their nature and in the opposite (i.e., complementary) sex.

answered (or fear addressed) before committing oneself to marriage—only to exercise reasonable prudence (which may involve truly listening to the assessment and judgments of parents and other believers). Placing faith in a potential husband or wife is like trusting the Lord; it requires a degree of commitment and hope based on sufficient evidence, but does not require exhaustive understanding, and can even be a quick decision when made by mature believers submitting to God's word and common judgment.[11] Of course, some men and women are more prudent and cautious in decision-making and enjoy the fruits of their prudence and patience. More often than not, however, marriages face challenges less because couples misread the character of their future spouse (while seeking to marry according to biblical criteria) than because they prioritize unbiblical criteria, close their eyes to clear warnings, or surrender to immediate physical desire.[12]

The doctrine of original sin serves as a reminder that every suitor must search for a mate in a world of fallen sinners. Therefore, those who seek to marry should be neither naively untroubled with the faults of possible suitors, nor coldly cynical and unsympathetic toward the fellow sinners from whom a mate must be selected. It is no wiser to reject every available mate because of observable personality, character, and physical flaws than to refuse a job because every vocation is filled with waste and toil. Even Sarah, portrayed by the apostle Peter as an ideal believing wife, once laughed at God in scornful unbelief (and given her struggle with infertility, her laughter was more likely a sneer than a giggle). Sarah also recklessly lied to a king that she was her husband's sister and enticed her husband to take a concubine into his bed to conceive an adoptive child for Sarah herself, apparently unwilling to wait on God to fulfill his word at the Lord's appointed time and unconcerned with the consequences of her decision for the servant woman. We must never forget that Sarah was a model of faith and a self-centered sinner at the same time.[13]

Every man and woman is a terrible sinner and will prove to be one in marriage, revealing in themselves serious faults and lesser annoyances. No

---

11. In premodern Europe, courtship could range from two villagers growing up together in the countryside to the arranged marriage of a noble to a foreigner—or even a merchant traveling to a nearby city to spend a few days in identifying (and marrying) a suitable bride.

12. The book of Proverbs provides advice for such decision-making. Proverbs 31:10–31 describes the traits of an ideal wife, thereby providing women with a portrait of who they should become and men with a portrait of who they should seek to marry.

13. 1 Peter 3:3 (ESV); Hebrews 11:11; Genesis 12:10–19; Genesis 16:2; Genesis 18:12.

person or marriage attains perfection in this mortal life. Few women effortlessly accept the leadership of their husbands, for most women would rather demand rights than offer services. Likewise, few men readily assume the self-sacrificing love God requires as the true bride price (i.e., the spiritual cost to marry a woman) as they angle to convince women to serve them for as little cost to themselves as possible. Moreover, even the most carefully planned marriage must bring sorrows, for we live in a world of sin and death. Still, although no spouse guarantees happiness and peace, every husband or wife provides an opportunity for humble and charitable service. If we focus on serving rather than being served (essential not just to marriage but for all human life), even the most sinful spouse will provide an excellent opportunity to imitate the example of Jesus, who came to serve sinners rather than to be served by saints.[14]

Within the parameters of God's holy calling, those seeking marriage are given considerable freedom in selecting a spouse; only they must be led by God's Spirit in doing so, just as with any other matter. While it is liberating to understand that we are permitted to make decisions after reviewing Scripture, praying to the Lord, and seeking godly counsel, we still must be guided by the Lord's Spirit and be exhibiting the fruit of his presence rather than being driven by the lusts of the flesh (not just sexual passion, but all greed and worldliness). Yet, even when we believe we are close to the Lord and listening to his voice, we must also consider the needs of those around us. In the book of Romans, Paul taught how God would have us act in sacrificial love toward believers rather than exercising our freedom solely for our own preferences.[15] As noted earlier, although Moses allowed the marriage of first cousins, John Calvin did not permit Genevan Protestants to engage in such marriages, for fear that such marriages would create a theological scandal that would hurt the Protestant cause and slow the advancement of the gospel of God's grace. Calvin encouraged many marriages previously prohibited by medieval law, but judged the marriages of first cousins to be an unnecessary public scandal best avoided on the grounds of charity. John Calvin wrote:

> It has become accepted by long usage [that] first cousins should not marry, and the refusal to allow such marriages had become a cause for complaint among us. If anyone should ask for a final ruling on

---

14. John 13:12–17.
15. 1 Corinthians 7:17 (ESV); James 4:15; Romans 14:13–15.

this... [we answer] this freedom exposes the gospel of Christ to much abuse, however, and we must remember Paul's admonition that our freedom should not become a stumbling block for someone else and that we should refrain from even permitted acts unless they are free of harm to others.[16]

God ordains marriage to provide sexual intimacy, lawful procreation, and human companionship in establishing a godly household. Assuming no stumbling block to faith or any biblical impediment to marriage, prudent men and women should select spouses based on those purposes as best as they can in a fallen world (although always remembering that we are sinful people courting and marrying equally sinful people). It is lawful to court a woman because she is attractive, of proven fertility (perhaps a widow or a single parent), or a good housekeeper. It is lawful for a woman to choose a husband because he will be a good leader, provider, and father. Still, suitors should not be too infatuated with a slim figure or a fat wallet. A man who marries a beautiful but stubborn wife may find his bride to be like the famous sculpture, the *Venus de Milo.* She has beauty to behold, but her grace is enjoyed without touching—like a museum piece. A woman who marries a wealthy husband may find that she risks being overlooked due to her spouse's greed and uncaring heart. She will learn, to her sorrow, how an impoverished husband rich in love is far better than a wealthy man stingy with affection. Character matters most in making a good and happy marriage, as John Chrysostom wrote fifteen hundred years ago:

I advise, therefore, and exhort those who are about to marry that they should approach the blessed Paul and read the laws which he has recorded concerning marriage. First learn what he bids you to do if your wife happens to be wicked, deceitful, alcoholic, abusive, foolish, or subject to any other such fault. Then discuss marriage with this in mind. If you take a bad wife, you must endure the annoyance. If you are not willing to do this, you incur the guilt of adultery by divorcing her.[17]

---

16. Calvin, *Ecclesiastical Advice,* 121. First-cousin marriage is lawful in nearly one-half of America's states, with a striking lack of consistency and regional diversity in its legal history.
17. John Chrysostom, "How to Choose a Wife," in *On Marriage and Family Life,* 84.

22

THE FALLACIES OF LOVE

It is when the young man begins to fall in love that he must show true nobility of spirit. That he should fall in love is inevitable. But let him be careful not to give way to despairing passion, but to single out as the object of his affection someone whose ways he can always bear with in lawful wedlock.[1]

IN THE PREVIOUS CHAPTER, I did not discuss the idea of romantic love beyond mentioning that Jacob loved Rachel before their marriage. My approach was not accidental. The fact is that the modern world is so enamored with romantic excitement that most people can scarcely bring themselves to marry for any motive except passionate feeling. Many lovers refuse to test the character or examine their aspirations (or those of their beloved), apparently fearing their passion could not withstand scrutiny. For such lovers, as long as the thrills and emotions of love exist, all is said to be well. Still, no one falls in love randomly. People are attracted to one another because of beauty, power, charm, and other qualities that prudence insists must be subordinated to the qualities of goodness and piety. That is why the ethics of selecting a spouse must be examined before discussing romantic love. It is also what Protestant Reformer

---

1. Ulrich Zwingli "Of the Education of Youth," in *Zwingli and Bullinger,* ed. G. W. Bromiley (Philadelphia: Westminster Press, 1953), 112.

Ulrich Zwingli meant (in the passage cited above) when he warned young men to be wise in their *decision to fall in love*.

The Bible neither condemns nor approves of romantic love in every instance, although the story of Jacob's courtship provides a justification for romantic love missing in many ancient non-Christian writings. Jacob moved to a foreign land to find a bride his parents would approve of. There, he fell in love with a beautiful young woman and asked the girl's father for her hand in marriage. The text is straightforward: Jacob was attracted to Rachel because of her beauty and fell in love with her, then entered into a contract with the girl's father so the couple could wed, agreeing to serve his future father-in-law for seven years to marry his bride. For seven years, Jacob seemingly remained chaste in his pursuit of Rachel, with no hints of sexual impropriety. There is no indication he touched Rachel, or any other woman, during the time he worked to earn the hand of his young bride—his passion did not lead him astray. Even when deceived by his father-in-law, he worked another seven years for the woman he loved. Nor is Jacob condemned because he chose to work fourteen years to make one particular girl his own, showing a fondness for one woman far beyond the ordinary.[2]

Still, not every marriage approved in Scripture was preceded by romantic love. David and Abigail married almost at the funeral of Abigail's dead husband, Nabal, with courtship not mentioned at all. David realized that the widowed Abigail would make a good wife and asked her to marry him. Abigail, for her part, recognized David's good character and consented.[3] The marriage of Ruth and Boaz occurred similarly, with the couple marrying after a brief period of secret negotiations during which Ruth approached the older man as if sneaking into his bedroom (without sexually touching him). As for Isaac and Rebecca, they had not even met before their wedding day. Isaac took Rebecca into his tent as his wife on the day he first met her (the bride having been brought by a servant who selected her on Isaac's behalf). Despite their brevity (by modern standards), each of these courtships was considered prudent and fruitful in Scripture, though none of them included what we call romantic love.

---

2. Genesis 29:17–18. Jacob was swindled into a second seven-year contract when he was first married to Rachel's older sister, Leah, with a deceptive wedding.

3. 1 Samuel 25:39–42; Udo Middelmann observed how David's attraction to Abigail was based on his assessment of her character. Udo Middelmann, *Pro.exist.ence* (Downers Grove, Illinois: InterVarsity Press, 1974), 95–97.

Let me repeat this point: there were marriages blessed in the Bible that were not preceded by deep feelings of romance, infatuation, passion, attraction, or friendship. Such unions demonstrate that marriage itself can cultivate passion and affection over time, rather than requiring these qualities prior to marriage. In fact, the marriage that is the model for all subsequent marriages was arranged without the couple's pre-approval: God gave Adam and Eve to one another without first asking their opinion. The first couple fell in love and married, or married and fell in love (it is hard to say which), as soon as they set eyes on each other. Adam sang in joy as he first looked at Eve, with a love neither restrained nor inhibited for having been something less than trial by fire or the result of many years of dating. The opposite is true. Has any more profound love or affection ever been felt for a bride than what Adam experienced when he sang the first love song to his bride, a song (or at least a poem) repeated through many generations of Jewish and Christian weddings?

> *This at last is bone of my bones*
> *and flesh of my flesh;*
> *she shall be called Woman,*
> *for she was taken out of Man.*[4]

The reason that romantic love is not a necessary prelude to marriage is because of the natural compatibility of male and female. In every sense (sexual, emotional, and spiritual), we were made for each other by the specific design of God. It is the same with parenting. Parents do not choose their offspring, but they love their sons and daughters even when grave faults and serious handicaps are found in them. Likewise, children do not choose their parents, yet they love fathers and mothers who are marred by serious flaws and weaknesses. Similarly, respectable and emotionally mature men and women learn to love each other within marriage, if both seek to fulfill their respective marital obligations, even if they never set eyes on one another before their wedding. Commitment to the purposes of marriage creates an unbreakable union of heart and flesh, just as parenthood does. This makes perfect sense, too, since the coming together of man and woman as one flesh is as miraculous as the conception and birth of new life after man and woman physically join together. The birth of a child is a great matter, but no greater than the creation of

---

4. Genesis 2:23 (ESV).

new life in marriage, of which a child's birth is the most tangible sign and essential fruit.

It is the fulfillment of the purposes of marriage that decides the success or failure of a particular marriage, not the length or intensity of courtship or premarital romance. Men and women who choose to live together in patient love will enjoy the fruit of their ways, no matter how they came together, whereas couples who give in to the temptation to live selfishly will produce a failed marriage, no matter how long they courted or how intensely they felt romantic attraction. Passion is no substitute for good character. Moreover, this argument is not theoretical but can be validated from the testimony of previous ages. The following passage from early church history sounds strange to modern ears, yet challenges modern sensibilities with something unexpected, as church father John Chrysostom explained how couples whose marriages had been arranged (and prior courtship minimal or non-existent) frequently love each other from the very outset of marriage. Chrysostom observed:

> *The girl who has always been kept at home and has never seen the bridegroom, from the first day loves and cherishes him as her own body. Again, the husband, who has never seen her, never shared even the fellowship of speech with her, from the first day prefers her to everyone, to his friends, his relatives, even his parents.*[5]

This is not to say that modern Americans must institute arranged marriages or that betrothals should be made randomly, as if by a lottery. Nothing could be further from the truth. Even animals do not mate haphazardly but measure potential mates carefully. Human beings must do no less; they must always choose whom to marry based on the ability of a suitor to fulfill the divinely mandated purposes of marriage. Whether that judgment is made by the involved couple, a parent, a reliable friend, or a marriage broker is less important than that it be made. And as a practical matter, it is plain to see that human affection and sexual desire are such that a blind eye is quickly turned to the faults of suitors by anyone eager to marry or already romantically involved. The prudent, therefore, try to assess character before they become too emotionally involved in a relationship to assess its strengths and weaknesses, or to break it off. And charitable suitors offer this opportunity to anyone they would love.

---

5. John Chrysostom, "How to Choose a Wife," in *On Marriage and Family Life*, 88.

It is possible for people to court for a long time without making this judgment. Many couples date for years without having reasonably assessed how their suitor might handle the trials and temptations of life. It is a sad reality that modern courtship is longer than ever before, even as divorce rates are correspondingly higher. Despite the common advice of parents anxious to delay marriage as the antidote to divorce, extending courtship is not always desirable since prolonged dating often increases sexual sin, with consequent remorse, resentment, and regret. What is needed is for the single to think about marriage with an eye toward its ultimate purposes and true nature. If truly seeking to make wise decisions, those who pursue marriage will be better equipped to date without rose-colored glasses or jaundiced tunnel vision. Not the passing of time but the acquisition of wisdom brings success.

While the Bible neither prohibits nor mandates that couples fall in love before they marry, it absolutely requires that purity, parental authority, and good faith be upheld in the process of selecting a mate. Unfortunately, modern couples often believe their love is the highest law they must obey, perhaps the only law. When a couple burns with love for one another, they think they have the right to come together, no matter what dishonorable acts take place to secure their union. Parents can be deceived, intimacy can be indulged before vows, and faithfulness can be cast aside as new lovers replace former recipients of promises of lifelong fidelity. Even public decency can be undermined by couples who refuse to consider whether their match will benefit the broader community with the children and goods they will produce, or fail to produce. As everyone knows, some men and women have gone as far as to commit treason against their homeland for the sake of a lover.

Many more have betrayed their God. The influential English writer and moralist C. S. Lewis observed that romantic love frequently deceives people into violating every other ethical duty to secure their desire, noting how couples in love have their very own religion—even a god— which requires utter devotion. Lewis wrote that where "a true Eros is present, resistance to his commands feels like apostasy" and "what are really (by Christian standards) temptations speak with the voice of duties." Lewis reminded readers how wrong it is to violate the most minor point of God's law to possess a lover, no matter how fiercely love burns within. What he was saying is that treachery, rebellion, and unchastity are not purified by the fires of romantic love. We must not allow ourselves to become confused and unbiblical in our thinking by allowing romantic passion to cause us to forsake our spiritual, moral, and familial duties. We must desire God before every other desire, and love God above every other love.[6]

Jacob's love for Rachel was holy and noble, but that was because passion itself was ennobled in such an honorable man as Jacob, who sought to practice piety and please his parents rather than to lust for pagan women as did his brother Esau. And though Jacob fell deeply in love with Rachel, he honored her virginity until he could contract a lawful marriage, even though the terms of the contract were exceedingly harsh. No young American asked to complete an education, finish military service, or acquire vocational training before taking a wife was ever asked to do more than Jacob. On the other hand, in a man of deceitful mind and unruled appetite, romantic passion becomes a raging inferno, as it did with Amnon, a son of King David who fell in love with his half-sister, then used a ruse to be alone with her. When the young woman refused her half-brother's advances, Amnon raped her, then cast the poor girl aside with disdain (as seducers often do)—with Tamar's brother, Absalom, eventually murdering Amnon in revenge for his ruined sister. Amnon's passion was the devil's work, which destroyed those personally involved and proved to be a step toward civil war in ancient Israel.

In the end, romantic love can be either high and holy or a treacherous inferno; its character flows from the ethical character and choices of the lover and the beloved, whether in antiquity or today. Romantic love is a legitimate step toward marriage (as are many other approaches that do not involve the knitting of affections before marriage), but it is not the only legitimate approach, and it may not always lead to moral good. At its best, romantic love shares in the impassioned and spontaneous love that Adam and Eve felt for each other. At its worst, it reminds us of the vile and base lust Amnon felt for Tamar. And to be blunt, I suspect that the passionate feelings that modern men and women expect to experience prior to choosing a spouse would just as easily arise after marriage, and for the same causes too (exclusive commitment, sexual intimacy, time spent together). In any event, like every other emotion, romantic love must always be subordinated to the enduring and holy love that comes from the Spirit of God as we submit ourselves to him.

---

6. C. S. Lewis, *The Four Loves* (New York: Harcourt, Brace, and Company, 1960), 156–157. Lewis's discussion of romantic love and eros reaches a height that I cannot begin to match. I strongly recommend this book, as well as Lewis's astute observations found in *Mere Christianity*.

Now it was after this that Absalom the son of David had a beautiful sister whose name Tamar, and Amnon the son of David loved her. Amnon was so frustrated because of his sister Tamar that he made himself ill, for she was a virgin, and it seemed hard for Amnon to do anything to her... [But] since he was stronger than she, he violated her and lay with her. Then Amnon hated her with very great hatred; for the hatred with which he hated her was greater than the love with which he had loved her. [7]

---

7. 2 Samuel 13:1–2, 14–15 (NASB).

23

ETHICAL RITES IN COURTSHIP

The third occasion for lechery is touching; of it is said in Corinthians 7; "It is good for a man not to touch a woman." Since they engaged in kisses and embraces with adulterous passion whenever they could, even though they refrained from unchaste possession of each other's bodies, they are damned.[1]

MARRIAGE WAS ORDAINED to create new life and establish a God-reflecting love between man and woman. Physical intimacy, likewise, is directed toward both of those objectives. The bodies of men and women usually conceive offspring, even as sexual intimacy provides pleasure and emotional closeness for husband and wife alike. Still, many couples promiscuously seek sexual intimacy beyond the bonds of marriage, and others stop short of sexual intercourse while indulging in premarital caresses and touches considered illicit by most Christian teachers. Both medieval Roman Catholic preaching manuals (cited above) and early modern Protestant church courts condemned such acts, denouncing the caresses and petting of an engaged couple as lewd and lascivious conduct. Until recently, the sin of fornication was defined more broadly than as a completed act of sexual intercourse, generally encompassing all forms of

---

1. Siegfried Wenzel, *Fasciculus Morum: A Fourteenth-Century Preacher's Handbook*, 657, 663.

sexual experimentation. Legitimate courtship was not believed to include sexual intimacy of any sort, and the notion of dating apart from a serious intent to marry hardly existed at all.

One of the most distinguished Christians of the twentieth century once implied that the lack of explicit biblical prohibitions against premarital caressing suggests that such activity, at least in select circumstances, might be permissible. Francis Schaeffer always tried to prevent Christians from constructing unscriptural lists of taboos, believing that such lists subverted the authority of Scripture by confusing the prejudices of its commentators and interpreters with the authority of biblical teachings. Although Schaeffer's approach toward biblical forms and freedoms is sound, there is some danger in reading the Bible as if it were written in the modern world and readily understood in a contemporary context. While Francis Schaeffer always understood that Scripture was given to ancient and modern mankind as a universal and absolute revelation presented in a specific historical situation, it seems to me that he may have failed to place this particular biblical teaching in the context of ancient marriage customs. To avoid this mistake, we must understand Scripture within a broader historical context, considering both what it explicitly reveals and what it implicitly requires.

To expand on this thought, we must understand that Moses provided a relatively succinct code of law for guiding life in ancient Israel rather than a comprehensive legal tome covering all possible disputes. Moses expected that a prohibition of fornication established a hands-off position in courtship, even if he did not ordain scores of nuanced regulations to cover every potential scenario or guard against every possible abuse. Moreover, Moses did not provide rules to regulate the dating practices of the modern world (he was a prophet, not a time traveler), but legislated against the idolatry and immorality of his own pagan generation rather than against the atheism and impurity of our own secular age. Moses also wrote commandments that were, for the most part, designed to govern the Hebrew commonwealth. His laws were as much public policy for the Hebrews as personal ethics. We can draw ethics from them, but the laws of Moses were mainly framed to govern criminal acts, public rituals, and property arrangements. For this reason, Scripture nowhere declares *Thou shalt not caress thy girlfriend*. It is why Francis Schaeffer was mistaken to have written the following passage when asked about Christian morality and premarital sexual caresses:

As one passes the point of engagement, other things fall within the proper relationship. The question is [that] sexual intercourse arrive with marriage.[2]

Francis Schaeffer was mistaken—silence does not spell consent. The historical context of the Old Testament law reveals the opposite to be true; the reason God did not speak explicitly against premarital intimacy (which falls short of sexual intercourse) is that reputable Hebrews had few opportunities to commit such sin when the Bible was written. Couples did not *date* in modern fashion, and they certainly were not left free to park their wagons in the backwoods to engage in necking and petting. The ancient Near East was a world of veiled women and absolute chastity; it was also a time of public shame for women suspected of immorality. A seduced girl could not veil her disrepute behind the cover of a wedding dress. At marriage, both she and her father were to be paid a bride price by the groom (a critical economic transaction typically made in public), and the actual amount depended on the girl's value. A girl who was not a virgin would be paid a lesser price, or perhaps none at all, and everyone in the family would have surmised the reason for a reduced bride price. Both families would have haggled for the appropriate settlement based on the bride's character. As a result, a young woman who allowed herself to be seduced threw away the most important insurance policy she possessed to guard against the uncertainties of widowhood or old age; she gambled away her financial security, perhaps for life. Sometimes, such women were unable to find husbands, living out their lives as servants, concubines, or prostitutes. In some circumstances, the penalty for premarital intimacy could be as severe as death, such as when a bride attempted to deceive her groom about her forfeited virginity in order to make a marriage or command a full bride price.[3] And for those women

---

2. Francis Schaeffer, *Letters*, 184. Schaeffer's passage implies that some physical intimacy is permitted prior to marriage. Still, Schaeffer took a strong stance against sexual intercourse outside of marriage and linked all physical intimacy of any sort to movement toward marriage, unlike his contemporary Lewis Smedes—who wrote: "Petting can be a delicately tuned means of mutual discovery... Petting can be an end in itself... The deeper and closer to commitment the personal relationship is, the more heavy the petting properly becomes." While Schaeffer permitted some opening of the package *after* engagement, his error was comparatively venial and a consequence of his devotion to balancing biblical forms and freedoms. In contrast, Smedes discarded biblical injunctions in accommodating church practices to the 1960s sexual revolution. Smedes, *Sex for Christians*, 130–131.

3. Deuteronomy 22:13–21 (ESV).

who became pregnant, there was the prospect of single parenthood without a modern social safety net or widespread social acceptance of women who became pregnant outside of marriage.[4]

With such laws and customs, women needed to prove to the community that they were chaste. This could be done only by two means: character witnesses and the physical proof of virginity. A woman who had been unchaste in any way would have found few reputable people willing to attest that she had behaved chastely. Who could swear an oath that it was only the hands of a suitor that touched her flesh (since everyone knows even the most pious men and women can go too far when playing with sexual intimacy)?[5] A girl known for inappropriate and immoral behavior would be given little leeway in such circumstances. Moreover, a careless woman might also lose the material proof of purity if she allowed herself to be explored by the hands of suitors. The test allowed by Moses was one in which the hymen was to be broken at marriage, under supervision (presumably by respectable matrons). A girl could wave the bloody flag, so to speak, to prove her honor. But since the hymen can be ruptured by contact short of carnal intercourse, a girl could lose her honor from mere caressing. For that reason, a prudent girl would have kept the kisses and caresses of suitors far from her flesh. Moses commanded:

> *If any man takes a wife and goes in to her and then hates her and accuses her of misconduct and brings a bad name upon her, saying, 'I took this woman, and when I came near her, I did not find in her evidence of virginity,' then the father of the young woman and her mother shall take and bring out the evidence of her virginity to the elders of the city in the gate... But if the thing is true, that evidence of virginity was not found in the young woman, then they shall bring out the young woman to the door of her father's house, and the men of her city shall stone her to death with stones, because she*

---

4. While there was no formal groom price for men, this was because men brought labor and property to the marriage. Women and their parents could reject men before betrothal.

5. Michael Rosenberg has thoroughly reviewed biblical and ancient tests for virginity, noting how Cyprian, Ambrose, and (especially) Augustine defined virginity more expansively than as an intact hymen. Ambrose considered the modest disposition of a girl a more reliable test for virginity than physical integrity, and Augustine declared virginity to be a moral and spiritual definition (such that raped maidens remained virgins despite the rupture of the hymen). Michael Rosenberg, *Signs of Virginity: Testing Virgins and Making Men in Late Antiquity, 183–189.*

has done an outrageous thing in Israel by whoring in her father's house. So you shall purge the evil from your midst.[6]

Understanding ancient courtship habits also makes the meaning of Scripture seem far more restrictive than some modern commentators have made it out to be. Francis Schaeffer seems to have considered betrothal to be a time for a couple to become more familiar with one another, seeing engagement as a time to begin to knit together a marriage in both body and soul, only climaxing in sexual intercourse on the wedding day. John Rice, a distinguished fundamentalist preacher, viewed courtship similarly, admonishing young people of his day who married "before they have time to be really in love."[7] Schaeffer and Rice understood courtship as the emotional and moral beginning of a permanent relationship, although modern law and custom do not consider engagement to be legally binding. In previous generations, on the other hand, betrothal was considered a legal agreement that generally could not be broken without a specified cause, even between couples who scarcely knew each other. Betrothals could range in duration from a few days to several years, or could be altogether bypassed with an immediate marriage. Yet, few people demanded that affections be knitted together before marriage, even if couples occasionally experienced a measure of friendship or affection before they wed.[8]

Even when emotions grew warm before marriage, passions were not permitted to heat up, despite betrothals being legally binding. Chastity was the expected norm, and any expression of sexual intimacy was prohibited until after the nuptials were sealed. The ancient Jewish understanding of sexual purity was so strict that men lost the legal right to divorce their wives upon suspicion that she was not a virgin at marriage if

---

6. Deuteronomy 22:13–15, 18–21 (ESV).

7. John R. Rice, *The Home: Courtship, Marriage, and Children* (Murfreesboro, Tennessee: Sword of the Lord Publishers, 1946), 73. Rice advised people not to marry young, based on fear of loneliness or lust, observing that Isaac did not marry until he was forty. This utterly ignores the role of marriage as an antidote to sexual passion, as well as how it is easier for younger couples to conceive babies, raise children, and bless grandparents. If Rice meant that teenagers should delay marriage, he should have been more explicit. Still, the marriages of young men and women do not violate biblical ethics or good judgment, if made in prudence and faith rather than folly and passion.

8. Engagement was legally binding in medieval and early modern Europe. Raymond of Penyafort wrote: "Engagements once contracted always hold and bind in such a way that if an engaged person enters into an engagement afterward with another he must be compelled to return to the first." Raymond of Penyafort, *Summa on Marriage,* 17–20.

there was any doubt that the couple's courtship had been appropriate. A suitor who had been alone in a room with his betrothed was presumed to be her seducer if the man later challenged the fact of her virginity. For being alone with his betrothed before marriage, the prospective groom lost the right to challenge the woman's premarital behavior. For such imprudent behavior, both groom and bride were marked as people willing to put themselves into inappropriate and morally ambiguous situations. The *Mishnah*, an ancient collection of Jewish law and custom, noted:

> *If in Judea a man ate in the house of his father-in-law and had no witnesses he may not lodge a virginity suit against her, since he had [already] remained alone with her.*[9]

Since the customs of the Jews were so strict, how should modern couples behave with one another? Is a couple free to hold hands? May a couple kiss one another? Can they date at all? Here is where Schaeffer's approach becomes useful, for the writings of some Christian teachers provide overly detailed instructions about dating, set up lists of prohibitions (often excessively restrictive), and demonstrate the rule-making that Schaeffer resisted. Consciences cannot be bound by human customs or pastoral preferences, only by divine law. For instance, one contemporary book argues that parents should chaperone the dating of young couples.[10] Though the author grounds his case in the necessity for sexual purity and the need for parental input into the marriages of their children, he goes too far. While the principles being upheld are biblical, the author is absolutizing one of several ways to uphold those biblical values (since chaperoned dating is a custom of a few modern believers rather than a practice observed in Scripture). If contemporary dating practices are to be foregone in favor of biblical courtship habits, both chaperoning

---

9. Danby, *The Mishnah*, 245 (Ketuboth 1:5). John Selden observed how Jewish law mandated "lashes" for betrothed couples who flouted common custom by cohabiting prior to marriage. John Selden, *Uxor Hebraica* (II:8), 162.

10. Jim West wrote that couples should be chaperoned as a moral principle. From my experience, a cinema, a restaurant, or a shopping center provides safety for couples trying to behave chastely. My wife and I attended quite a few movies to reduce time together in our respective apartments. Chaperoning was not realistic since our divorced (and busy dating) parents would not have consented to participate, and we had no other family to substitute on their behalf. Jim West, *Christian Courtship Versus The Dating Game* (Palo Cedro, California: Christian Worldview Ministries, 1993), 9.

and dating should be replaced with arranged marriages and marriage-at-first-sight. Such is the most common example of courtship in Scripture, along with engagements to distant relatives and providential meetings at desert wells.

Yet the Bible (as previous chapters suggest) both depicts and blesses different modes of courtship, from arranged marriages to freely chosen unions. It is not the particular custom of making a marriage that matters most, but whether the approach upholds the purposes for which marriage has been made. What is absolutely required is that men and women choose suitable and lawful mates and maintain chastity, public honesty, and filial reverence, as well as trust in the Lord. Such moral qualities can be sustained amidst a great variety of courtship customs, although it must be acknowledged that contemporary dating practices challenge divine law more often than they support it. Dating prior to readiness for marriage, delayed age of marriage, extended courtship, long engagements, and frequent access to privacy for couples with their own apartments (not to mention frequent travel together and the watching of desire-stirring entertainment) create a system that makes chastity very difficult to achieve. These challenges must be faced by couples, families, and churches to uphold chastity in a reasonable manner.[11]

As for the issue of sexual purity, the apostle Paul (like the medieval preaching manual cited at the beginning of this section) forbade the *touching* of a woman and instructed believers, man and woman alike, to marry if they struggle with sexual temptation. Moses similarly used a broad range of expressions—such as *uncover the nakedness, lie with, take, see her nakedness,* and *commit adultery with*—to show the breadth of the restriction against sexual exposure and intimacy outside of lawful marriage. Even more, Jesus made clear what sexual holiness is in the mind of God, warning how adultery before God is not just a matter of sexual intercourse with a married woman, but also involves sins of the eyes, hands, and heart.[12] Sexual caressing must not be indulged outside marriage, a prohibition undisputed not only among the ancient Jews but

---

11. George Gilder observed that most cultures segregate the sexes and teach them separately, whereas American children are "expected to traffic together intimately for years before they can marry... They are brought up in a society where sex is continuously advertised and propagandized. The result is that American boys and girls are driven into periods of sexual experimentation and stress unparalleled in either length or intensity by any other society." George F. Gilder, *Sexual Suicide* (New York: Bantam Books, 1975), 222–223.
12. Leviticus 20:10–21 (NASB); Matthew 5:27–30 (ESV).

upheld among traditional Christian believers until the advent of our own promiscuous era.

Whether couples are free to hold hands, show affection, and kiss modestly is an open question. Roman custom at the time of the early church perhaps permitted displays of affection between engaged couples, which was accepted by some church fathers. One historian of Roman marriage has noted how Ambrose and Augustine tolerated modest embraces and displays of affection. Susan Treggiari wrote that Augustine may have allowed "kisses between an engaged couple as a sign of love." She also observed how Ambrose, in his commentary on the Song of Solomon, encouraged "gentle wooing," and "sympathetically portrays the aroused passions of the engaged girl." If such tokens of affection can be lawful, then modern Christians need not abolish the custom of dating to ensure modesty in courtship but must subordinate all dating practices and relationships to God's law.[13]

My approach has been to explain biblical ethics and laws as they were understood and lived in the past rather than to defend biblical doctrines against modern challenges. If I were to attempt the latter, I would note how the biblical approach to premarital intimacy prevents a host of natural evils like sexually transmitted diseases, out-of-wedlock pregnancy, emotional trauma (if a partner is deserted following the intimacy of sexual union), and extending courtship beyond the natural age to begin a family. Premarital chastity reflects God's pure holiness, fosters stable relationships, safeguards financial interests, ensures a memorable honeymoon, and leaves couples with a clear conscience. These are significant gains for the loss of sexual pleasure before marriage. Additionally, I would remind readers that many men take pleasure from one woman, then quickly embrace another woman without regard for the first woman's emotional or physical needs: an approach embittering for women and debasing for men. Obedience to the Lord's law protects all women from such philanderers, requiring men to commit to a particular woman via lifelong marriage before asking to enjoy her body for a single hour. And it is the same for men in avoiding women tempted to use sexual intimacy to seek pleasure and profit rather than lifelong love and a holy household. Such is the rightful exchange enjoyed in marriage, with spiritual and

---

13. Treggiari is judicious with her handling of evidence, observing that while courtship customs in the Roman world *may* have permitted display of physical affection, evidence can be read otherwise. Susan Treggiari, *Roman Marriage: Iusti Coniuges from the Time of Cicero to the Time of Ulpian* (Oxford: Clarendon Press, 1991), 160.

emotional protections far greater than a thin layer of defense against pregnancy and disease through the use of protective measures.[14]

Believers not only must do what is right but must do so before the
watching world. This does not allow for self-congratulation if couples
remain chaste, since any such obedience comes directly from God and is
not born of the couple's own righteousness and moral fortitude. Scripture explicitly reveals that no man or woman lives chastely except by a
specific empowering from God, with the difference between piety and sin
resting in God's redemptive work. All of us must be grateful to God, who
saves us from ourselves, and must never consider ourselves better than
others if he does so (whether he keeps us perfectly chaste, limits the scope
of our sin, or spares us the evil of flagrant defiance). We must remember
our particular failures and flaws, whether in the flesh or the heart, matters
not. The difference between a prostitute and a virgin is real enough,
though the seeds of harlotry lie dormant in every virgin: suppressed not
by innate goodness but by God's power to give grace where he chooses to
do so. Jesus explicitly taught that no one is celibate in thought or deed
unless gifted by the Lord to be so.[15]

With this reality in mind, Christians are called to think, talk, and act
in a way that others see us striving to uphold God's law. We must uphold
what C.S. Lewis considered the least popular of Christian virtues—one
that demands "either marriage, with complete faithfulness to your partner, or else total abstinence."[16] A good start to preaching God's laws to
modern men and women would be to confess how unnatural and difficult chastity is, even as we implement rules that uphold chastity. Such
rules may restrict freedoms that worldly couples take for granted (such as
premarital travel, shared hotel rooms, and apartment cohabitation), but
believers must live such that the Lord can use their obedience to lead the
unredeemed to his paths of righteousness, repentance, and forgiveness.[17]

---

14. Francis Schaeffer wrote: "I am convinced that this prohibition from God is one of
God's good gifts to us for two reasons. First, we are all sinners and cannot trust ourselves,
no matter who we are. We are not married until we are married. And it is too easy to leave
one partner brokenhearted [if their partner] walks away. [Also], one knows more of man
and woman as a whole entity by shutting up the whole interplay to one [sexual partner]
[and women] cannot take sexual looseness." Francis Schaeffer, *Letters,* 183–186.
15. Matthew 19:9 (ESV).
16. Lewis, *Mere Christianity*, 94–95.
17. This requirement to avoid the very "appearance of evil" (1 Thessalonians 5:22 in the
King James Version) is not a new problem. Genevan Reformers in the sixteenth century
faced betrothed couples trying to spend nights in the same home or bed. Witte and Kingdon, *Sex, Marriage, and Family in John Calvin's Geneva,* 420.

Christians dare not hide our piety for fear of persecution, mockery, or offending those who do not live as God wills, but must openly testify to the Lord's law and our need for his grace to obey it. Jesus commanded:

> *You are the light of the world. A city set on a hill cannot be hidden. Nor do people light a lamp and put it under a basket, but on a stand, and it gives light to all in the house. In the same way, let your light shine before others, so that they may see your good works and give glory to your Father who is in heaven.*[18]

---

18. Matthew 5:14–16 (ESV).

24

THE MOMENT OF MARITAL UNION

Let us say then that it is consent neither to cohabitation, nor to carnal copula that creates a marriage, but consent to the conjugal society. Then when they come together, so that the man says, "I take you as my wife," and the wife says, "I take you as my husband," the consent, expressed in these words or others signifying the same thing, is not to carnal copulation, not to bodily cohabitation, but to the conjugal society.[1]

SEXUAL INTERCOURSE (and all physical intimacy) does not become morally lawful until a man and woman are married. Before matrimony, sexual relationships conceive bad consciences, bitter remorse, and God's wrath. After marriage, the Lord blesses sexual intimacy with some of the deepest and most enduring joys on earth. For that reason, it is essential for couples to understand what exactly constitutes a marriage, thereby allowing them to recognize when they may join together with the Lord's favor. The above citation reflects medieval church law (accepted by Protestants throughout the Reformation), which holds that it is the consent to marry that matters: what we might call the *vow of marriage*. That is, agreement to be married at a specific moment causes marriage to

---

1.   Peter Lombard's *Sentences* are cited in Theodore Maskin, S.J., *What is Marriage?* (New York: Paulist Press, 1982), 166.

come into being and validates sexual consummation. Does that historical perspective reflect Scripture? That is the question we must answer.

Many years ago, there was an instance in which a Christian couple failed to sign the marriage certificate at their wedding. When they discovered the error following their honeymoon, they became apprehensive that their new marriage had been a time of fornication rather than lawful intimacy. They were afraid they had sinned, albeit unintentionally, by enjoying a honeymoon following a legally invalid marriage. Did they sin? Were they married before the Lord or not? The answer to those questions rests on a simple question: how does marriage come about? Is a marriage made by a wedding ceremony, legal paperwork, public oath, sexual intercourse, cohabitation, or something else? The answer to that question affects not only the couple in question but also men and women touched by various acts of seduction, cohabitation, or betrothal.[2]

Some might argue that it is with sexual intercourse that a marriage lawfully begins, reasoning from the fact that unconsummated marriages can be annulled, as well as from the biblical text found in 1 Corinthians, which states that a man "joined to a prostitute becomes one body with her." By referring to the marital text of Genesis 2 that "they shall become one flesh," the apostle seemed to portray sexual union as equivalent to marriage. But Paul did not intend that reading, which would suggest that prostitutes possess hundreds of husbands and faithless men have harems of legally unrecognized wives. That is to say, if sexual intercourse initiates marriage, the world is filled with unconfessed and unacknowledged polygamy. Men and women do not simply have previous sexual partners with whom they shared a bed, but husbands and wives (who themselves may be married to others with whom they have consorted).[3]

If we simplify the matter by declaring that perhaps a man or woman is married to their first sexual partner, the problem remains—for though a prostitute would be married to her first seducer, dozens of men would be married to that same prostitute (who was their first sexual tryst), which is absurd, for men and women must marry each other at the same

---

2. Historians reviewing various European archives have uncovered many marriage disputes from medieval and early modern records. One woman, from the Constance region of Germany, paid a man to sleep with her, but arranged for neighbors to barge into the room (after the sexual act was completed) to force the man to marry or face the immediate threat of death. Papal lawyers annulled this marriage because the vows were coerced. Ludwig Schmugge, *Marriage on Trial: Late Medieval German Couples at the Papal Court*, trans. Atria A. Larson (Washington, D.C.: The Catholic University of America Press, 2012), 128.
3. 1 Corinthians 6:15–16 (ESV); Genesis 2:24 (ESV).

time. Nor is it the case that marriage exists between two virgins who violate each other at the same time. While Old Testament laws of seduction commanded that seducers of virgins be willing to marry the seduced women (to keep faith with those whom they have wronged), an actual marriage required public ratification, as with any other marriage, particularly by the seduced virgin's father or legal guardian. Something more than coitus is required to create matrimony, even for a seduced virgin.[4] Moses declared:

> *If a man seduces a virgin who is not betrothed and lies with her, he shall give the bride-price for her and make her his wife. If her father utterly refuses to give her to him, he shall pay money equal to the bride-price for virgins.*[5]

Nor is a wedding ceremony always required to establish a marriage. Nowhere does Scripture require that a public ceremony be conducted. Christ participated in the wedding celebration at Cana, but his human ancestors, Isaac and Rebekah, began their marriage by simply living together as husband and wife. At most, they would have said a few words in front of servants and family members to clarify their status as bride and groom rather than man and concubine (and perhaps held a feast). Their wedding was not elaborate, filled with bridesmaids, liturgy, and music. Likewise, the apostle Paul, who was of both Jewish descent and Roman citizenship, nowhere required converted Gentiles to forsake the Roman custom of beginning marriage by making a bridal procession down the street (sometimes without religious ceremony or formal oath). Paul permitted the Corinthians to marry as they were accustomed to do, without requiring a new ritual of faith to separate Christian nuptials from those of unbelievers. What this acceptance of Roman customs reveals is that it is not the wedding ceremony that matters most in the

---

4. One author observed that early Christian emphasis on consent rather than coitus as the moment of marriage represented an effort to counter marriage via abduction, during which men kidnapped and bedded women (sometimes with the woman's consent and sometimes without) as a way to present objecting families with a *fait accompli*. If coitus makes marriage, such marriages remain lawful. However, if consent is required, such marriages become unlawful. This problem existed well into early modern European history. Yifat Monnickendam, *Jewish Law and Early Christian Identity*, 129–134.

5. Exodus 22:16–17 (ESV). Though such a penalty was not necessarily paid to widows, this was not because widows could be abused, but because the financial side of marriage arrangements differed for them.

making of a marriage; it is not necessary to celebrate any particular form of wedding to become married. Lawful marriage is distinct from subsequent wedding celebrations.

Moreover, just as wedding ceremonies have not always existed, marriage licenses have not always been used. These are an invention of the modern state to enforce public morality and family order. Historically, it has been rare to require state consent before initiating marriage. Isaac did not ask for anyone's permission (except his father's) when he took Rebekah into his tent as a wife. Even governments that typically mandate marriage licenses have been required to make concessions in distant territories or on isolated frontiers. Otherwise, settlers and pioneers living on frontiers and in unregulated areas could not marry at all. Such concessions are the rationale for common-law marriages, which allow for the establishment of a legally binding marriage when state officials have not been informed or consulted about the relationship. To be clear: marriages can exist that have not received the prior sanction of the state. While the state rightly regulates morals and property, it does not make marriage. Men and women do so themselves.[6]

This does not mean that couples may secretly be married in their hearts without informing their families and communities. Nor is it to say mere cohabitation (the concubinage of Scripture) makes a marriage. This is most emphatically not the case. For a marriage to be valid, there must be proof that a *marriage* has been solemnized. Lawful spouses must be set apart from illicit lovers, and holy matrimony must be differentiated from base immorality in the eyes of the couple, their society, and the law. Otherwise, a woman could sleep with a man believing their act to be moral while the man's heart was motivated by mere lust, yet no one would know whether a marriage existed. The couple themselves might disagree about whether they were married (a common problem in the past), which brings us back to our question: what signifies marriage?[7]

In religious societies where oaths and promises were taken seriously,

---

6. Past courts enforced promises to marry since engagements (betrothals) could not be broken without cause. One historian has noted how many women involved in such disputes preferred church courts to secular ones because the former did not require the expense of a lawsuit. See Suzanne Lipscomb, *The Voices of Nîmes: Women, Sex, and Marriage in Reformation Languedoc* (Oxford: Oxford University Press, 2019), 202–214.

7. Renaissance historian Gene Brucker documented the case of a Florentine woman who slept with her clandestinely married husband, only to have the man deny their marriage so he could marry up the social ladder. Both confessed to the sexual act, but disputed whether they had first contracted marriage with a private vow. Gene Brucker, *Giovanni and*

simple promises and words created marriage. That was the situation in the Middle Ages, as the words of medieval theologian Peter Lombard make evident in this chapter's introductory quotation. For Lombard and his ecclesiastical heirs, verbal consent makes marriage legitimate. But many societies have required a more verifiable public act, such as giving a ring, taking a public vow, receiving a blessing, signing a document, publishing an announcement, entering a nuptial chamber, or even sleeping with a virgin. Each has been considered a marriage-signifying act in various cultures. We see the same in Scripture with simple vows, legal transactions, wedding receptions, and other marriage-signifying acts. God graciously accepts any of these as sufficient, only commanding everyone to separate legitimate marriage from illicit promiscuity as clearly as the Lord separates light from darkness. As with the vows mentioned by Peter Lombard (and still used in weddings today), the marriage-signifying act must intend marriage on the part of bride and groom alike, as with an oath, a promise, or a vow.[8] Agreeing to be married is indeed marriage. As a footnote, it must be mentioned that while Adam made a verbal vow to his bride, we have no record that Eve responded in kind. Perhaps she said *I do*, or maybe she just responded with a smile, quietly received a kiss, or just bowed to her husband as brides did in at least one medieval English ritual.[9] We do not know, though we certainly have no right to doubt the spiritual legitimacy and moral lawfulness of the only perfect love and holy marriage in human history.

The fact that the act of sleeping with a virgin can signify marriage takes us back to the issue of coitus as the cause of marriage. The Old Testament law required a virgin's seducer to marry the defamed girl, and the woman was required to marry the man whom she had willingly bedded. Under the law of Moses, men and women who enjoyed sexual intimacy with each other understood from the outset that their sexual intimacy created a moral and legal obligation to marry. If the girl's father

---

Lusanna: Love and Marriage in Renaissance Florence (London: Weidenfeld and Nicholson, 1986).

8. Protestant Girolamo Zanchi observed how Adam verbally consented to marriage when he called Eve "the flesh of his flesh." Girolamo Zanchi, *The Spiritual Marriage between Christ and His Church*, 24–26.

9. In an English Missal used in Bury St. Edmunds, the groom placed a ring on the hand of his bride and provided her dowry, at which point the bride fell at the feet of her husband. I suspect this was more a feminine curtsy of affectionate respect, or a vassal-like bow to her feudal lord, than abject prostration. Mark Searle and Kenneth W. Stevenson, eds., *Documents of the Marriage Liturgy* (Collegeville, Minnesota: Liturgical Press, 1992), 151.

concurred, the couple was required to wed. If the father withheld his consent, the bride price was still required of the man as compensation paid to the dishonored woman, although no marriage was enforced. For the law of Moses, it was not coitus per se that made marriage, but the decision to engage in what was recognized as a marriage-obligating act, along with subsequent ratification by a marriage-creating agreement under proper authority. A man who seduced an Israelite woman while not intending to marry her was in the legal position of a modern man who signs a marriage license, participates in a public wedding ceremony, and enjoys a honeymoon with his bride, although his heart is secretly attracted to another woman.[10] Who would pity such a man or doubt the fact of his marriage? Lawful intent is expressed through visible actions more than through hidden hopes and secret aspirations. In all forms of law, actions signify consent. One Puritan explained:

> *For where there hath been a carnal use of each other's body, it is always presupposed that a mutual consent as touching marriage hath gone before.*[11]

Does coitus establish the legal obligation to marry today? Does the law of Moses bind Americans? As a matter of law, it does not. The matrimonial laws of the United States do not require marriage after coitus, and it would be unjust to bind men and women to marry who consented only to sleep together. A man and woman who share a bed after sharing drinks are not to be confused as husband and wife any more than a prostitute and her patron.[12] No Christian legal code has ever obligated women to marry whoremongers or men to marry immoral women. As a general rule, it has been virgins who have been most vigorously protected by law, and even regarding them, laws and opinions have differed. While

---

10. Medieval law did not necessarily recognize preconditions for marriage as negotiated by couples. When John Wyk and Margaret Bele were overheard in York promising marriage on the condition that Margaret was impregnated that night, church authorities voided their illegal restriction (enforcing marriage despite the lack of pregnancy). R.H. Helmholz, *Marriage Litigation in Medieval England (Cambridge*: Cambridge University Press, 1974), 51.

11. William Perkins, "Christian Economy," in Larsen Klein, ed., *Daughters, Wives, and Widows*, 160.

12. The 1546 Marriage Ordinance of Geneva declared: "Let all promises of marriage be made honorably and in the fear of God, and not in dissoluteness or through reckless frivolity, as by merely offering a glass... without previously having agreed in sober discussion." Witte and Kingdon, *Sex, Marriage and Family in John Calvin's Geneva*, 130.

it might be equitable and prudent for American law to defend virginity by pressing seducers to marry their lovers (or otherwise pay for dishonesty and damages), such legal codes are a distant dream.

Because of the amorality of much modern law, I wonder if the elders and pastors of Christian churches should establish appropriate denominational and congregational rules to govern their flocks, using the laws of God as their guide. Christian pastors might consider advising couples to marry if fornication has led to the loss of virginity, or otherwise recommend how satisfaction might be made (something tangible that repairs what has been damaged, replaces what has been lost, and compensates for what has been taken). This is how the law of God can be upheld, and repentance confirmed before the men and women of our society. Such a practice could be a modern version of the penitential and disciplinary codes so evident (and fruitful) not only in early and medieval Christianity, but among many Protestant churches into the modern era.

Moreover, the obligation to consider marriage is particularly pressing when a woman has become pregnant, since both she and her child's father have an undeniable moral (and legal) obligation to provide a home for their flesh and blood, with children requiring both father and mother for the best advantages in life. Moses gave the parents of young couples (especially a daughter's parents) the right to veto an utterly foolish marriage, and modern parents likewise retain the right to protect youthful sons and daughters from seducers, deceivers, predators, and rapists (including date rapists).[13] Parents are also free to morally veto unlawful marriages, such as with unbelievers, the wrongfully divorced, or other miscreants. Still, parents must uphold the glory of God by holding their children accountable for sin rather than subordinating the eternal good of chastity and fidelity to the temporal gain and pleasure of their children, or even a better marriage. Christians cannot pretend to honor God in the abstract while shielding their sexually sinful children from caring for the offspring the latter conceived, whether willingly and wisely or unintentionally and foolishly.[14]

---

13. Deuteronomy 22:28–29 (ESV) commanded: "If a man meets a virgin who is not engaged, and seizes her and lies with her and they are discovered, then the man who lay with her shall give to the girl's father fifty shekels of silver, and she shall be his wife because he has violated her; he cannot divorce her all his days." As previously noted, the penalty for slandering the virginity of a maiden was one hundred shekels, which amounted to twice the penalty for seducing a virgin.

14. Menno Simons, the father of (Anabaptist) Mennonite churches, advised: "If you are a Christian or would be one, and have seduced a poor child with your sensuous approaches, if

The aforementioned letters of Francis Schaeffer contain anguished cries from couples seeking advice about their obligations toward the men and women with whom they experienced premarital relationships. Their choice of a spouse sometimes depended on the answer to this question: did sleeping with one woman preclude the possibility of marriage to another? In large part, this question is answered by determining when a lawful marriage begins, and it seems that marriage begins when a couple willing to participate in a marriage-signifying act does so (whether through a vow, a ceremony, a gift, or even coitus). Using that answer to return to the original case of the couple who failed to sign their license, there is little doubt that a valid marriage before God existed before the couple knew each other sexually. It was the public meaning of their acts that mattered rather than the administrative paperwork. If taking an oath, standing in front of witnesses, wearing wedding apparel, and putting on a marriage band do not signify marriage, what else could? Public promises remain valid even when the administrative paperwork has been inadvertently overlooked or intentionally disregarded. Francis Schaeffer used hypothetical circumstances to make this very point:

> But note that marriage is the declaration before God and then sexual relationship, and not centrally a declaration merely before men either in the state or the church... Think of a situation where two Christians would be shipwrecked on a desert island. They are both Christians, and neither are married... In such a case they do not need to live on the same desert island in agony, while being in love with each other, until rescued. They could simply kneel down and declare their marriage before God who would hear them, and then go on to have sexual relations. They would be married.[15]

---

you would not lose your soul, you are required to marry her and not forsake her." Menno Simons, "The Spiritual Estate of the Christian," *The Complete Writings of Menno Simons*, ed. J. C. Wenger (Scottdale, Pennsylvania: Herald Press, 1984), 378.

15. Francis Schaeffer, *Letters*, 182. Anyone who wonders if I have perhaps become entangled in the nature of marital union should consider how American juries justly send men to prison (and university administrators expel students) after evaluating similar questions of word, deed, and intent when dealing with the line of demarcation between drunken sex and date rape, inebriated passion and post-coital regret, unspoken consent and unvoiced refusal. These complicated matters must be sorted out with fairness and transparency.

25

THE CELEBRATION OF NUPTIALS

The fact that, when people marry, their marriage is blessed by a priest is something established by God at the very beginning of the human race. For it is written: "God made man; in the image of God he made him, male and female he made them, and he blessed them, saying, 'Increase and multiply.'" What happened at that time in paradise is imitated now in the church.[1]

MARRIAGE NEED NOT BEGIN in the church. Otherwise, unbelievers could neither be legitimately married before God nor be judged for their infidelities and divorces. Still, the Christian church has a long tradition of requesting, if not insisting, that believers begin their nuptials with a religious ceremony. In the above quote, Isidore of Seville (from late Roman Hispania) observed that church weddings had a noteworthy beginning, for they are imitations of the first wedding, which God himself officiated. Ignatius of Antioch, a second-century Christian leader, even taught that believers of both sexes should marry only "with the sanction of the bishop." Such ecclesiastical approval would ensure "their marriage will be acceptable to the Lord and not just gratify lust." What these Christian leaders taught is that a religious ceremony serves to remind the involved

---

1.   Isidore of Seville, "De Ecclesiasticis Officiis," in Mark Searle and Kenneth W. Stevenson, eds., *Documents of the Marriage Liturgy*, 117–119.

couple that it is the Lord who sets the rules for marriage, as well as for reproduction and sexual intimacy. In the modern era (when men and women scarcely understand themselves to be more than animals), a wedding celebration also reveals that human intimacy rises to higher and more enduring purposes than the amoral nature of animal mating, and should reflect that eternal reality. Christian weddings can be an act of faith, testimony, and public witness to the truth that human marriage is a specific gift from God for both the couple and their families—and is a prophecy of eternal love and unending joy.[2]

The apostle John recorded how Jesus and his disciples attended a wedding at Cana. His gospel noted that the very first miracle of Christ was turning water into wine during the wedding reception. Because of that miraculous event, many Christian authors have used this story to teach how the Lord blesses marriage. However, the story does not teach that God blesses marriage as much as it reveals how the Lord blesses wedding celebrations. Our Lord demonstrated his approval of wedding festivities by attending one and performing a miracle to continue the celebration beyond what had been prepared. When the master of what was probably a wealthy household ran out of wine for his many guests, Jesus continued the banquet by supplying additional drink, serving wine to guests who had already finished what had been provided. By doing so, Jesus placed his approval on wedding festivities. John wrote:

> On the third day there was a wedding in Cana of Galilee, and the mother of Jesus was there; and both Jesus and His disciples were invited to the wedding. When the wine ran out, the mother of Jesus said to Him, 'They have no wine' [and Jesus turned water to wine]. This beginning of his signs Jesus did in Cana of Galilee, and manifested His glory, and His disciples believed in Him.[3]

Why did the Lord bless the celebration of marriage? The answer is easy to find. As church father Isidore observed, the very first marriage was joyously celebrated. Though no other men and women existed with whom to drink wine or eat cake, Adam celebrated his wedding in the one way possible: by writing a beautiful marriage song that he presented to

2. Ignatius of Antioch, "[Epistle of] Ignatius to Polycarp," in *The Epistles of St. Clement of Rome and St. Ignatius of Antioch*, trans. James A. Kleist (New York: Newman Press, 1946), 98.
3. John 2:1–3, 11 (NASB).

his bride. As the human race increased in number, it became possible to arrange banquets and receptions to celebrate the consummation of new marriages. It is important to understand how the celebration of marriage demonstrates that human mating ought to rise above animal copulation, since birds and wolves (the most monogamous of animals) do not invite kin to celebrate finding a partner. Nor do animals rejoice that something deep has been fulfilled in their souls when they find a mate, at least not in the same way that human beings celebrate the making of a marriage. Receptions and ceremonies do not exist to separate marriage from concubinage (that aim can be achieved far more frugally). People have wedding celebrations because everyone intuitively recognizes that marriage is a great gift from God, which fulfills deep human longings: a woman and a man are joining together to begin what one author calls the wildest of adventures.[4] In this same spirit, one psalmist noted how God provides "wine to gladden the heart of man, oil to make his face shine, and bread to strengthen man's heart."[5] Joy, beauty, and strength are among the most perfect gifts given to mankind. Where are these better experienced and upheld than in marriage? And what better way exists to honor the Lord than to celebrate what he has made? That is why human beings celebrate weddings.

However, just because God blesses nuptial celebrations is no reason to turn holy ceremonies into drunken riots, for the Lord no more blesses overindulgence and drunkenness at weddings than he does anywhere else. It is a commonplace Christian commentary on the story of Jesus turning water into wine to insist that pious couples abstain from the irreverence, drunkenness, immodesty, and ostentation of worldly weddings. Church fathers, medieval clerics, and Protestant Reformers agreed that Christian weddings should be religious celebrations, untainted by boisterous drinking, unchaste dancing, and self-indulgent spending. As one example, because John Chrysostom condemned the marriage ceremonies of antiquity as prodigal affairs, he considered himself disliked by contemporaries for being considered "burdensome and difficult [in] giving advice like this and uprooting ancient customs." Chrysostom observed that Roman

---

4. G.K. Chesterton's essays on the wild adventure that is traditional marriage and family life are collected by Alvaro de Silva in an accessible paperback that I consider the most enjoyable, inspiring, and informative single book on modern family life. What Chesterton wrote a century ago resonates as if written this very hour. G.K. Chesterton, *Brave New Family*, ed. Alvaro de Silva (San Francisco: Ignatius Press, 1990).

5. Psalm 104:15 (ESV).

wedding festivals were often rooted in pagan revelry rather than in the godly moderation shown by Isaac and Rebekah in their simple wedding. Though Chrysostom permitted weddings to be celebrated with feasts and the attendance of relatives, he admonished the foolishness of couples who wasted fortunes to indulge themselves and impress their relatives and friends. Chrysostom particularly censured drunken and lewd merry-making, seeing such revelry as no different than the coarse behavior of idolaters and unbelievers. He wrote:

> *Nowadays on the day of a wedding people dance and sing hymns to Aphrodite, songs full of adultery, corruption of marriages, illicit loves, unlawful unions, and many other impious and shameful themes [and they] accompany the bride in public with unseemly drunkenness and shameful speeches.*[6]

Early Christians did not prohibit the reverent celebration of marriage, nor has any influential Christian tradition since antiquity. A man like Chrysostom was not so parsimonious that he wanted no money spent on nuptial celebrations. Instead, he asked Christians to adopt a new custom of celebrating their marriages in a manner that reflects how their household should be governed. Chrysostom desired modest festivities to impart dignity and piety to wedding participants, with heathen gods and pagan revelry shunned. Rather than purchasing lavish foods to impress wealthy relatives, Chrysostom believed it more pious to provide an abundance of food to be shared with poor neighbors (it seems he was challenging the wealthy to practice appropriate charity). In short, nuptial feasts were to be marked by chastity, sobriety, and generosity rather than lewdness, drunkenness, and ostentatiousness.

Paulinus of Nola taught the same, instructing Christians to celebrate marriage with "sober joys and quiet prayers" so the name of Christ will "resound everywhere on the lips of pious people." Paulinus forbade participation in profane displays, bawdy wedding processions, and "ornate trays heaped high with superfluous gifts." Why? Because he believed that the "proper ornament is good morals, not money."[7] The Christian tradition has long held that marriage should be initiated with the same virtues through which it is to be lived. Such instruction remains

---

6. John Chrysostom, "Sermon on Marriage," in *On Marriage and Family Life*, 76.
7. Paulinus of Nola, "Carmen 25," in *Marriage in the Early Church*, 129–130.

sound, and contemporary couples should celebrate weddings and plan receptions in a more Christian spirit than sometimes is done. A wedding should not be used as a day of indulgence like some booze-fest on the eve of Lent (i.e., Mardi Gras), but to establish a holy and modest commencement to a new couple—now one flesh before God for the remainder of their mortal lives.

For centuries, Christian leaders censured wedding celebrations considered immodest or luxurious. However, another situation has arisen in contemporary society that must be considered: should public ceremonies honoring Christian marriage reflect whether the engaged couple lived in faith prior to their marriage?[8] In Christendom of the past, there were often moral, social, and legal expectations against an unchaste bride wearing the veil of a virgin. The relationship of clothing to status could be so intermingled that virgins wore their hair differently than married women and chaste widows, with hairstyles and head coverings possessing a public significance beyond mere fashion. Prostitutes, for instance, were not permitted to cover their hair in the manner of faithful wives, often as a matter of law.[9] Today, however, neither long hair nor short, natural hair nor fluorescent-dyed, signifies morality. Perhaps there remained some moral significance to hairstyles in the 1960s and 1970s, but the debate about hairstyles during that troubled generation lacked the legal strictures of ancient, medieval, and early modern cultures, which frequently regulated (through strict sumptuary laws) not only women's hairstyles and hair coverings but also men's and women's clothing.[10]

Given the collapse of Christian marriage and sexual morality, contemporary weddings do not possess such moral significance, and few attendees commend the bride as a virgin on account of her veil. Still, I have seen during my life public ceremonies in which ministers blessed

---

8. Modern compromises are not unprecedented. One historian noted how English church courts tolerated some sexual immorality during the later seventeenth century. Martin Ingram, *Church Courts, Sex and Marriage in England, 1570–1640* (Cambridge: Cambridge University Press, 1987).

9. One historian wrote: "Virtually all police regulations concerning prostitutes include a dress code, the earliest of which... prohibited prostitutes from wearing clothing usually associated with honest women. Thus, prostitutes in Arles were not to wear veils, and those in Avignon neither veils nor coats." Leah Otis, *Prostitution in Medieval Society: The History of an Urban Institution in Languedoc* (Chicago: University of Chicago Press, 1985), 79–80.

10. Sumptuary laws (directed against personal expenditures) were common in the premodern world; they regulated dress, hairstyles, and even the consumption of goods. See Giorgio Riello and Ulinka Rublack, editors, *The Right to Dress: Sumptuary Laws in a Global Perspective, c. 1200-1800* (Cambridge: Cambridge University Press, 2019).

with the rites of Christian liturgy couples who had cohabited, birthed children, or unashamedly indulged in premarital sex throughout their courtship, with no thought of repentance. Such flagrant immorality should not be blessed in a Christian church. Sin is common enough, for we all sin. Nevertheless, it is a sad experience to see God's righteousness trampled underfoot by clergymen who equally bless light and darkness. It is distressing to see holy matrimony used as an adornment to the stage play of grooms and brides who have demonstrated little intention of living in holy love before the Lord, yet seek to decorate their wedding with divine prayers and rituals.[11] A Christian ceremony may not prevent couples from immorally using each other outside of marriage, but it ought not to bless them for having done so.[12]

This is not to say weddings should be doleful rather than joyful, with sexually compromised couples receiving rebukes rather than blessings. That would be uncharitable, even malicious and cruel. It is only to argue that the symbols used in a wedding should have meaning, and while God's grace can wash away every sin, no sin can be blessed as righteous conduct. Christians in the past expected moral integrity in their wedding symbols, and contemporary believers are called to uphold the same standard.[13] It is an insult to chaste brides to treat them no differently than if they had been unchaste (the same with grooms). Not everything needs to be said in a wedding ceremony, and the rites of Christian marriage are rightly extended to repentant sinners, but what is publicly declared must be true and holy (to include the holiness of God's grace that forgives and saves each of us). A clear distinction must be made between condoning sin and preserving privacy since the two acts are not the same thing, and neither virtue nor vice should be broadcast with a trumpet. It is not the

---

11. In contrast, one Bavarian custom during the period of the Catholic Reformation (and likely before) had brides adorn themselves with "crowns of virginity" from local churches, imitating crowns depicted on the Virgin Mary. Ulrike Strasser, *State of Virginity: Gender, Religion, and Politics in an Early Modern Catholic State* (Ann Arbor, Michigan: University of Michigan Press, 2004), 40.

12. In ancient and medieval Christianity, churches went so far as to limit the blessing of second marriages (whether by divorce or death) on the ground that these marriages were apostolic concessions rather than religious ideals. I may disagree the theology behind this limitation, but I respect the intent to align religious blessings with church doctrine. Eve Levin wrote of Orthodox second marriages: "As a further mark of ecclesiastical disfavor, the crowning (*venčanice*) was prohibited. Instead, prayers over the newlyweds were recited at vespers." Eve Levin, *Sex and Society in the World of the Orthodox Slavs, 900–1700*, 107.

13. For John Calvin's objections to brides undeservedly donning the symbols of premarital chastity, see Witte and Kingdon, *Sex, Marriage, and Family in John Calvin's Geneva*, 418.

virtue of the marrying couple that should be celebrated first and foremost, but the love and law of Christ which must be preached. Still, if contemporary clergy stopped giving the immoral the same public respect as the pious, young men and women might think twice before surrendering to their passions or living in open sin—or, at least those desiring a church wedding would so restrain themselves.

That said, clergymen should not behave like inquisitors in insisting on moral, medical, and legal proof of virginity during premarital counseling. Even in the Old Testament, that was the place of parents and judges rather than priests. However, ministers can refuse the Christian liturgy for couples whose display of demonstrably immoral behavior has not been repented, or at least modify wedding vows so that ceremonies do not sanction rank hypocrisy on the part of both the pastor and the parishioner. While fewer couples might opt for church weddings under such circumstances, Christian congregations would better understand that the Lord's blessing is not promiscuously given equally to the chaste and the unchaste. As C. S. Lewis observed of marital vows, there is far too much deceit in modern wedding customs. I would add that the sin of the clergy who participate in such hypocrisy may be even greater than that of involved couples, for the clergy are responsible before the Lord to know better. They have willingly assumed this responsibility, trading the rather tedious work of a factory or classroom for the uncompromising responsibilities of pastoral care. It is their duty to stand for God's holy law.

> *Justice, as I have said before, includes the keeping of promises. Now everyone who has been married in a church has made a public, solemn promise to stick to his (or her) partner till death. To this someone may reply that he regarded the promise made in church as a mere formality and never intended to keep it. Whom, then, was he trying to deceive when he made it? God? That was really very unwise. Himself? That was not very much wiser. The bride, or bridegroom, or the "in-laws"? That was treacherous. Most often, I think, the couple (or one of them) hoped to deceive the public. They wanted the respectability that is attached to marriage without intending to pay the price: that is, they were impostors, they cheated.*[14]

---

14. Lewis, *Mere Christianity*, 106. For C.S. Lewis to accuse couples of cheating was serious. Cheating is to a university professor what cowardice is to a soldier or perjury to a judge.

PART III

THE MAINTAINING OF A GODLY HOUSEHOLD

~

The first two sections of this book discussed the meaning and making of marriage. This third segment will examine how a marriage should be maintained once it has been formed. This is the crux of the matter. Theologians may discuss the nature of marriage, and lawyers may define precisely who should or should not marry. Still, it takes real husbands and wives who submit to faith and love to make marriage a thing of beauty in our fallen world as they seek to fulfill its central purpose of revealing and glorifying God. It is not a matter of getting marriage right in theology or theory, but in the moral drama of real life. Like everything else in life, marriage has rules that must be closely followed if it is to be naturally and spiritually productive.

The rules to establish a household of faith are not readily accepted in the modern world. Contemporary men and women are too concerned about their rights, pleasures, and ambitions to subordinate themselves to household, spouse, or love. This is why our generation has reaped such a terrible crop of marital unhappiness and divorce, among other sins. In the Bible, on the other hand, are the rules by which believing Christians may enjoy marriages marked by love, patience, and fruitfulness. Moreover, a biblical understanding of family relationships accurately represents masculinity, femininity, and the family as our Creator intended us to be. Anyone who understands and follows these rules will reap, by God's grace, a crop of the Spirit's fruit: love, joy, peace, patience, goodness, gentleness, and self-control.

This section discusses the duties of Christian matrimony. It begins with discussing the nature of authority in God's creation since family relationships are not strictly egalitarian. The following chapters examine the roles of women and men in marriage and the nature of the love that binds husband and wife together. Next are chapters on the ethics of the marriage bed and marital fidelity, as well as the ethics of divorce and remarriage. The section concludes by discussing reproduction, contraception, and the nature of parenthood, as well as household property. Effort is also made to relate specific duties to their spiritual and eternal objectives in revealing the nature of the Triune God and forming the mind of Christ in individual men, women, boys, and girls.

～

26

HOUSEHOLD AND AUTHORITY

And when the ten heard it, they began to be indignant at James and John. And Jesus called them to him and said to them, "You know that those who are considered rulers of the Gentiles lord it over them, and their great ones exercise authority over them. But it shall not be so among you. But whoever would be great among you must be your servant, and whoever would be first among you must be slave of all. For even the Son of Man came not to be served but to serve, and to give his life as a ransom for many."[1]

No PASSAGE in Scripture better summarizes the Christian notion of authority, power, and glory than the words in the Gospel of Mark rebuking the ambition of disciples John and James. When those two disciples lusted for power and prestige, for the foremost place among the apostles in this life and the next, Christ condemned their sinful attitude. In doing so, he taught lessons with eternal validity, revealing that his servants must follow the example of Christ himself—who came not to be served but to lay down his life in sacrificial love. As a result, the men who once campaigned for heavenly prestige eventually gave up wealth, pleasure, and earthly life itself for the sake of Christ and his church. James was martyred for his faith, and John suffered both torture and exile.

---

1. Mark 10:41–45 (ESV).

In rebuking his disciples, Jesus did not condemn the exercise of authority, but condemned the attempt to exalt self over others: the desire to dominate and be served rather than to be submissive and serve. After all, Scripture reveals that God establishes government in this world and declares how human rule will continue into eternity, with the Son of Man ruling his creation as Incarnate God and human Messiah. Christ will govern the nations with an iron scepter, and his word will be law, as it already is. Scripture suggests that the Lord will make use of lieutenants and subordinates in heaven, just as he does on earth. During a vision recorded in the book of Revelation, the apostle John (one of the two disciples previously chided for craving heavenly authority) observed: "I saw thrones, and seated on them were those to whom the authority to judge was committed." When Jesus chided his disciples for desiring preeminence, he confirmed how positions of authority exist "for those for whom [they have] been prepared."[2] Authority is real; it is just that we are not allowed to crown ourselves rulers (either of empires or households) as Napoleon Bonaparte did, seizing imperial power by force and placing a crown of authority on his head with his own hands. Our hands are meant to serve as Jesus did, while waiting for the Lord to establish authority and power in accord with infinite wisdom and eternal perfection, through which he will bring every chosen person and created quality of his choosing to final redemption and everlasting joy.

This reality is not surprising, for authority flows from the character and nature of the Triune God as surely as justice and love do. Not only does God's slightest word topple empires and bring into being that which once did not exist, but perfect order born of infinite love exists within the divine nature, as the Father eternally *begets* and the Son eternally *submits to his Father,* although Father and Son remain one in mind, will, and essence. The Father begets and the Son is begotten forever, and this by essential nature rather than mutable vote or changing consensus. The mind, will, and being of the One of Israel never change. Nor is there shame in divine subordination, which is eternal love. It is the glory of Christ that he freely does only what he sees his Father do, and it is the humility of the Father to glorify his Son eternally. In this reality, human lord and subject reflect the eternal image and radiance of the Triune God. Moreover, as God Incarnate, Jesus Christ (the Son of Man) revealed how he came to serve rather than to be served. After chastising John and James

---

2. Revelation 20:4 (ESV); Mark 10:40 (ESV).

for selfishly campaigning for heavenly prestige and power, Jesus explained to all of us that those who would be great before God must become servants and slaves of other men and women, just as the Son of Man came to serve and give his life as a ransom. This is the foundation of all biblical doctrine regarding human authority.[3]

Modern men and women do not want to obey anyone, whether it be a human being or Almighty God. Everyone wants to control their destiny and set the parameters of their own life. No one wants to be a servant, and slavery is considered the worst of evils—an unmitigated horror. That is why military service seems burdensome for so many; it irritates them to surrender their autonomy (and perhaps their lives) to the needs of an officer, regiment, or institution. This same instinct against obedience to authority exists in the home. Children defy, ignore, and usurp parental authority, and wives struggle against their husbands. Many, if not most, women insist on equality with or independence from their husbands, and even the most timid of women frequently feel compelled to assert their autonomy. Husbands, for their part, live not to serve their wives but to please themselves, often at the expense of their families. They live as if they are at the center of life, willfully forgetting that Jesus Christ did not live so for one moment, although he was God in human flesh.

Christians are called to a life of willing servitude and self-forgetting humility: to subordinate themselves to parent, spouse, pastor, and ruler, as well as to the Lord. In this subordination, they imitate the Triune God who created our world before becoming a human being to redeem his creation, born into the world not as a prince or celebrity but as a common laborer and itinerant preacher. As Scripture reveals, Jesus Christ, although the eternal Son of God, "emptied Himself, taking the form of a bond-servant," to secure our salvation.[4] Nor is this merely an abstract duty, for it is in day-to-day affairs that humility and love are expressed: in actually submitting to other people for the love of God and man. As Benedict of Nursia (an early and influential monk) wrote:

> *The first degree of humility is prompt obedience. This is necessary for all who think of Christ above all else. These souls, because of the holy servitude to which they have sworn themselves, whether through fear of hell, or expectation of eternity, hasten to obey any command*

---

3. John 15:10 (ESV); John 17:21 (ESV); Mark 10:43–45 (ESV).
4. Philippians 2:7 (NASB).

of a superior as if it were a command of God... [Such] obedience
will be deemed acceptable to God and pleasant to men, only when
commands are carried out without fear, laziness, hesitation, or
protest. The obedience shown to superiors is, through them, shown to
God, who said, He who hears you, hears Me.[5]

The Lord ordains both rule and obedience in human life. One
cannot exist without the other. No kingdom can exist without both lords
and subjects, nor can servants and masters exist without each other. Yet,
everyone is called to both tasks. A man may lead his wife and children,
but he himself submits to his employer and the government. A woman
must submit to her husband, but she governs her children and servants.
Even an unmarried woman may exercise authority in a public service or
professional capacity. For this reason, those who reject male authority in
the home should be challenged for making two mistakes. First, they do
not understand that there is virtue and strength rather than shame and
weakness in servanthood. All of us are in positions of subordination and
are called to serve as Christ did. Second, they fail to understand that all
types of authority are equally grounded in God's word. When people
reject biblical teachings regarding men's authority in the family, they
unwittingly, yet necessarily, undermine the authority of husband and
wife over their children. Why? Because paternal and parental authority
are rooted in the same biblical passages and natural realities.

What I mean is that those who deny that women must heed their
husbands are inconsistent when they command children to obey their
mothers. Like a kingdom, the household divided against itself cannot
long stand. Puritan divine William Perkins once called a married woman
the "goodwife of the house" and observed how she provides assistance
and help "in government to the master of the family." While the husband
is the "prince and chief ruler," his wife is his "associate, not only in office
and authority but also in advice and counsel unto him." Perkins posited
that women govern their homes by "profitable employments for the good
of her charge," as well as by wisely managing children, maids, and
servants. Women are also responsible for providing food to their families
or for arranging for it to be provided. Overall, Perkins linked women's
authority in the household to that of their husbands. Women are deputy

---

5. Anthony C. Meisel and M.L. del Mastro, trans., *The Rule of St. Benedict* (New York:
Image Books, 1975), 54–55.

rulers of the domestic realm (we might say) and stand to their husbands as a deputy commander stands to an army officer or a Vice President stands to the President of the United States: as a confidant, assistant, and replacement in times of need, and with specific roles and duties distinct from those of the President.[6]

Despite the common and complementary purposes to be possessed by husband and wife, the principle of authority must remain undivided. Someone must have the final vote to which others submit. Balancing household power in the vain hope of good intentions, shared interest, and taking turns is a recipe for anarchy and strife, since human beings in close quarters are prone to defend their opinions and interests at the expense of others. Authority is the principle that someone must decide when there is disagreement and a lack of consensus—someone must provide leadership. Not only does authority provide a framework for daily living in which men and women may complete tasks on someone else's terms without feeling wrongly enslaved and personally attacked (just as we do not feel personally singled out every time we submit to a speed limit or pay our taxes), but authority provides the only way to solve otherwise irreconcilable differences. In a household without the proper exercise of authority, sharp differences that remain unresolved after debate and discussion must be addressed in one of three ways: fighting (physical or verbal), separation (abandonment or divorce), or continued stalemate and indecision (leading to stress and quarrels). As John Chrysostom rightly declared, there can be no peace where authority is equal, since "a household cannot be a democracy, ruled by everyone."[7]

Some admit that authority is real enough but qualify that it consists only of moral persuasion rather than bringing with it inherent right to insist on a rightful or prudent course of action, even if that path brings

---

6. William Perkins, "Christian Oeconomy," in *The Works of William Perkins,* vol. 3, ed. Ian Brewer (Berkshire, England: The Sutton Courtney Press, 1970), 439. I use this edition because the very readable version provided by Joan Larsen Klein is not comprehensive.

7. John Chrysostom, "Homily 20," in *On Marriage and Family Life,* 48. C.S. Lewis also observed that households must have a head if marriage is to remain permanent (and discussed why men naturally fill that role). C.S. Lewis, *Mere Christianity,* 112–114. While not addressed by Chrysostom or Lewis, I would note that rotation of power (as with a democratic government) likewise fails in households since many decisions are too consequential for frequent changes. A wife might decide to move the family to Florida during her term of authority, with her husband returning their family to Illinois once he came to office. Similarly, a husband who reduced his family to poverty to purchase fancy automobiles (or fishing trips) would leave his wife spending her term of office repairing the damage. Rotation of power would exacerbate selfishness and frustration for both husband and wife.

stressful or disagreeable consequences to others (or even rightful use of force as with the hand-swatting or spanking of a young child). But we must observe that authority is not limited to influence. Those with authority have the right to insist on biblical guidance to the unwilling, or the idea of authority is nullified. While Christian marriage or parenting must never descend into abuse, neither should the household become a place of anarchy, argument, and disorder. Some decisions must be insisted upon and even enforced for the common benefit and peace. Even before sin entered the world, authority with consequences existed, for the Lord threatened mankind with death for defiance of his authority. And now that the human heart is blinded by its passions and the human mind is dulled by its prejudices, the exercise of authority is all the more necessary, often bringing with it a measure of disagreement, discomfort, or pain.

This is not to say that rulers are allowed to govern by their whims and according to their pleasure. That attitude was the mistake of the disciples rebuked by Jesus for seeking heavenly authority. The Lord commands everyone, great and small alike, to live in sacrificial love and humble service. Scripture instructs rulers everywhere to exercise authority to secure the well-being of their subjects. Jesus is the perfect example of a faithful servant and wise lord. He is God and Messiah, yet laid aside his power to save his subjects. Though there are times when he scourges evil with a whip, it is far more common for our Lord to rule his flock as a gentle shepherd, having laid down his life for his lambs and received the blows we deserve. This is the call of all authority: rulers must lead by sacrificial service. Even military officers should govern with a charity that leads them to secure the good of the lowest recruit (and non-combatants) rather than their personal glory, promotion, or safety, and to treat disarmed enemies with justice and generosity. Men and women who govern in this fashion, whether at the head of a great empire or in a lowly household, will find that gentle government achieves far more than the burdensome commands of a tyrant. Horace Bushnell observed:

> *Is it not well understood that a bawling and violent teamster has no real government of his team [of horses]? Is it not practically seen that a skillful commander of one of those huge floating cities, moved by steam on our American waters, manages and works every motion by the waving of a hand, or by signs that pass in silence; issuing no order at all, save in the gentlest undertone of voice? So*

when there is, or is to be, a real order and law in the house, it will come of no hard and boisterous, or fretful and termagant way of commandment. Gentleness will speak the word of firmness, and firmness will be clothed in the airs of true gentleness.[8]

---

8. Horace Bushnell advised parents regarding bedtimes and feeding of infants and children, making an interesting comparison with modern practices. Horace Bushnell, *Christian Nurture* (Grand Rapids, Michigan: Baker Book House, 1979; 1861 reprint), 325.

27

HUSBANDS AND WIVES

But I want you to understand that the head of every man is Christ, the head of a wife is her husband, and the head of Christ is God. [For] man was not made from woman, but woman from man. Neither was man created for woman, but woman for man... Nevertheless, in the Lord woman is not independent of man nor man of woman; for as woman was made from man, so man is now born of woman. And all things are from God.[1]

[Woman] was formed not from just any part of [man's] body, but from his side, so that it should be shown that she was created for the partnership of love, lest, if perhaps she had been made from his head, she should be perceived as set over man in domination, or if from his feet, as if subject to him in servitude. [Woman] had to be produced from his head, nor his feet, but from his side, so that he would know that she was to be placed beside [him from whose side she] had been taken.[2]

MANY MODERN MEN and women struggle to acknowledge that authority exists in both church and state. They find it more difficult yet

---

1. 1 Corinthians 11:3,8–9,11–12 (ESV).
2. Peter Lombard, *The Sentences, Book 2: On Creation* (Distinction XVIII, Chapter 2), 77.

to accept the authority found in human marriage. As with biblical teachings regarding sexual purity and marital fidelity, apostolic commands detailing the subordination of wives to their husbands are rocks that make modern men and women stumble. However, instructions about the authority of husbands exist in God's word, so it is our duty to uphold and glorify the divine will: to understand and proclaim the wisdom, justice, and love of the Lord's ways. And not only must Christians obey the specific commands found in the Bible, but they are obligated to maintain Scripture's sense of priorities, recognizing how household duties are discussed far more often in God's word than are other social and political obligations. It is more important for believers to order their private affairs rightly than to strive to create a perfect society, for Christ is more interested in nurturing faith and piety in individual souls and homes than in reforming a world in rebellion against his very being.

Passages in 1 Timothy, 1 Corinthians, Ephesians, Titus, Colossians, Hebrews, Malachi, and 1 Peter discuss how men are to order their household affairs. To begin with, men are to provide for their families' material needs. In 1 Timothy, Paul judged as worse than outright infidels those professing Christian men who fail to care for their families. This requires hard work (even at the expense of a man's health, if need be); it also requires men to curtail self-centered spending so they can care for their families and save for future needs. Second, husbands must care for their wives more than for themselves. While English translations and commentaries often use the word *please* when discussing 1 Corinthians 7:33, the original Greek suggests concern and care rather than indulgence. Men also are commanded to sanctify their wives as Christ does his bride, the church. Though men are granted authority in the family, they are sternly reminded to exercise such authority to benefit their entire household in a spirit of peace. Third, the Old Testament makes it clear that God rejects the religious offerings of violent and faithless husbands, while the New Testament similarly requires men to pray to God "without wrath and dissension" in their relationships. The apostle Peter reminded husbands explicitly to be patient and considerate of their wives' weaknesses and faults if they expect to please the Lord.[3] While every man is called to each of these tasks, few will be equally strong in each element, and none will be without sin and fault.

---

3. 1 Timothy 5:8; 1 Corinthians 7:33 (ESV); Ephesians 5:22–31 (ESV); Titus 2:2; Colossians 3:19; Colossians 3:2; Malachi 2:13–16 (ESV); 1 Timothy 2:8; 1 Peter 3:1–7 (ESV).

The fundamental point of marital authority is that husbands are the head of their wives, as Christ is the head of the church. There can be no doubt that Christ rules his flock in accord with God's will, exercising firm and unambiguous authority. That is, Jesus does not apologize for his judgments or hesitate to lead his own. It is essential to realize that the trials and tribulations of this world are ordered by the Lord primarily so that he may bring his church into the fullness of her eternal destiny. Empires rise and fall at the command of Jesus Christ so that his bride may be honored at her eternal wedding, and human husbands must do the same. Their headship should resemble that of Christ as they work out a common salvation with their wives—a salvation that includes the practical government of their household to secure her welfare.[4] Men should take no selfish pride in their authority since women come to them as a gift from God rather than as a right of conquest. Instead, a husband's call is to cleanse and honor his bride rather than to subjugate her, for she is a friend to be loved rather than an enemy to be subdued.[5] It must also be highlighted that Scripture spends more time discussing husbands' duties and obligations than in establishing men's rights. If Jesus did not stand on his authority as God Almighty, husbands must never domineer their wives by standing upon whatever measure of derivative authority they have been granted. In the biblical perspective, husbands are authorized and empowered only to love and serve their wives in humble faith.

Indeed, we must never forget the primary reason for the existence of husbandly authority: men rule their wives and households not simply to scratch a living from the soil (though there exists a sensible division of labor based on physical differences) nor to ensure a level of order amidst sin and dissent. The reason men have been granted authority in their households is to direct their homes toward their heavenly Father and glorify God by representing in their own flesh the toil and suffering through which Christ loved and saved his bride—the church. As Christ's divine power is always exercised in humble service of a sinful world, the derivative and limited power of mortal husbands is intended to serve both virtuous and unworthy wives. Such authority is not a blast of the

---

4. 1 Corinthians 11:3 (ESV); 1 Peter 3:7 (ESV).
5. Herman Bavinck observed: "[Man] received Woman, whom he desired, entirely apart from his own effort, apart from his own knowledge and volition, while in a deep sleep, which God had placed upon his soul and body. Though the woman indeed is *from* the man, she did not come into being *through* him; existence is due entirely to God." Herman Bavinck, *The Christian Family*, 4.

trumpet that all women are subject to all men, but that wives are subject to the care and leadership of their husbands.[6] Following teachings from the earliest days of the church, C.S. Lewis phrased it well when he wrote:

> *The husband is the head of the wife just in so far as he is to her what Christ is to the Church. He is to love her as Christ loved the Church—read on—and gave his life for her (Eph. 5:25). This headship, then, is most fully embodied not in the husband we should all wish to be but in him whose marriage is most like a crucifixion; whose wife receives most and gives least, is most unworthy of him, is—in her own mere nature—least lovable.*[7]

Not every husband attempts this, and few do so consistently. Many men use their authority to please themselves, basing their leadership more on physical strength and emotional dominance than on the word of God. Such men intimidate their wives with threats and rebukes, acting less as shepherds to Christ's flock than wolves who feast on ewes. This attitude has always been a problem, just as drunkenness and adultery are common to every age, and remains a temptation for every husband. For that reason, Edwin Sandys reminded men in the sixteenth century that their authority was to be directed toward God's purposes, warning husbands that their wives' faults should inspire sympathy rather than anger and declaring that a man is an unworthy husband who "brags and boasts that he is the head" of his wife. Such a man, Sandys wrote, does not deserve to "be named that which he is not." Whatever such self-centered rule is, it is not what God intends, for it does not reflect the character of Christ as everything in creation is called to do.[8] Like C.S. Lewis centuries later,

---

6. I am alluding to John Knox's strident attack on the political authority of women (i.e., Roman Catholic queens who persecuted Protestants). John Knox, "The First Blast of the Trumpet Against the Monstrous Regiment of Women," in John Knox, *Selected Writings of John Knox: Public Epistles, Treatises, and Expositions to the Year 1559* (Dallas, Texas: Presbyterian Heritage Publications, 1995), 371–433. In contrast, Douglas Wilson has written: "The Bible does not require submission of women to men, but rather of *a* woman to *a* man. The submission of a woman to a man, far from making her submissive to other men, *protects* her from obligations to other men... She is to be submissive to her own husband, and the Bible teaches clearly that no one can serve two masters." Douglas Wilson, *Reforming Marriage* (Moscow, Idaho: Canon Press, 2005), 38.

7. C.S. Lewis, *The Four Loves* (New York: HarperCollins, 1960), 135.

8. Edwin Sandys, "The Sixteenth Sermon: A Sermon Preached at a Marriage in Stausborough," in *Sermons and Miscellaneous Pieces by Archbishop Sandys*, 317–318. I have edited the text for clarity.

Sandys saw husbandly leadership as Christ-like sacrifice, declaring that husbands are called even to die to defend their wives, writing:

> *As Christ suffered death to redeem his church, so should a husband, if necessity so requires, save his wife at jeopardy of his own life. His life is well spent in saving of her, and by losing her ill-spared.*[9]

Peevish selfishness, emotional abuse, and physical violence are not the only ways in which men fail to be Christ-like in managing their homes. Many husbands and fathers refuse to put their hands to the hard work of leading and tending to their families. Some are so consumed by ambition and greed that they are scarcely present in their homes, let alone intimately concerned with the spiritual, emotional, and practical needs of their wives and children. Others refuse to admit they have the responsibility and obligation to govern their family, perhaps weakened by natural passivity or feminist ideology. Such men are mistaken. A father may be to his family like a shepherd to sheep, but as a shepherd, he must wield the rod and the staff to protect and guide his flock. He must face the summer storm and the prowling wolf. He must endure the lonely watch and the winter cold. Though a wife shares many obligations and much authority in her home, husbands must give an accounting, whether they wish to or not. They must reflect on the needs of their loved ones, pray for their welfare, encourage good character, teach wisdom, correct error, and establish good cheer and happiness. If ever Christ's little flock entrusted to them is scattered among wolves, it is the shepherd's fault, not that of the ewes and lambs—and this includes any scattering from neglect and refusal to work hard enough (no matter the cost to himself) to provide for every morally lawful need for his wife and children. This duty extends to the sacrifice of a husband's life in a physical fight, assuming the risks of dangerous work, or accepting decades of debilitating work and delayed retirement. Husbands have not always assumed this heavy responsibility, even in cultures that granted men obvious (even unbiblical) legal and

---

9.   Edwin Sandys, "The Sixteenth Sermon," in *Sermons and Miscellaneous Pieces*, 317. I have edited the text for clarity. One thousand years earlier, John Chrysostom preached: "Be responsible for the same providential care of her, as Christ is for the Church. And even if it becomes necessary for you to give your life for her, yes, and even to endure and undergo suffering of any kind, do not refuse. Even though you undergo all this, you will never have done anything equal to what Christ has done." John Chrysostom, "Homily 20," in *On Marriage and Family Life*, 42.

social superiority. Weak and timid men have often shirked their duties at home, just as cowards and self-centered men have frequently shirked their responsibilities toward the public good.[10] As John Calvin remarked:

> *How rarely do you find a man who willingly undertakes the burden of governing a wife, for it is a business that involves countless vexations! How reluctantly does a woman, on her side, submit to the yoke.*[11]

The yoke that Calvin refers to is not one of tyranny but the rule of Christ to which all disciples are called. As Jesus said, his yoke is gentle and easy, and comforting for the weary and distressed. This is not easy for men to remember, since the obligations and duties they shoulder often harden many of them toward life. That is one of the reasons men must bear with their wives as the *weaker sex,* as Peter declared in his first epistle. Peter was not suggesting that every man is morally superior or stronger than his wife. The story of Nabal and Abigail in the Old Testament provides a counterexample. In that household, the husband was a churlish fool struck dead for his sin, while his wife was a prudent woman publicly exalted by the Lord. Although there are significant physiological, psychological, and temperamental differences between the sexes that affect marriage, Peter was not observing or theorizing about what they might be in the manner of Aristotle, Galen, or some other ancient philosopher. Peter's aim was far more practical: to remind men to live gently with their wives, even when their wives seem misguided and weak. The apostle wanted husbands to live in kindness and tact with their wives. God's word does not teach men to indulge every whim of an undisciplined, demanding, or anxious wife—only to govern their households wisely. Men are to prudently provide everything necessary to live a

---

10. Martin Luther wrote: "There are many pagan books which treat of nothing but the depravity of womankind and the unhappiness of the estate of marriage... These are the words of blind heathen, who are ignorant of the fact that man and woman are God's Creation. They blaspheme his work, as if man and woman just came into being spontaneously! I imagine that if women were to write books they would say exactly the same thing about men. What they have failed to set down in writing, however, they express with their grumbling and complaining whenever they get together." Martin Luther, "Estate of Marriage," in *Luther's Works,* vol. 45, 36.
11. John Calvin, *Calvin's Commentaries: The Second Epistle of Paul the Apostle to the Corinthians and the Epistles to Timothy, Titus, and Philemon,* trans. T. A. Smail (Grand Rapids: William B. Eerdmans Publishing Company, 1964), 260.

222 UNLESS THE LORD BUILDS THE HOUSE

godly and modest life, but they should not spoil women or assume their wives' share of household responsibilities (unless she is ill or disabled). Nor are men required to indulge luxurious tastes or destroy themselves trying to stockpile more than their daily bread.[12]

While the authority of husbands is real, it has limits. Scripture explicitly teaches that men may not lead their wives away from the Christian faith (including into heretical, apostate, and error-filled denominations) nor command them to do what is wrong. While men rightly exercise authority to do good in the household, they are never free to use their power to promote evil or indulge sin. Moses reminded his fellow Hebrews to hand over to the public authority even loved ones who do evil, and the principle he gave remains binding on Christians, for it is a general principle that limits the exercise of all authority.[13] No government, church, employer, or household may command subjects to do what is wrong or not to do what is right. No subject needs to obey an immoral or unjust order. This point has long been understood, and we can conclude this discussion by pointing to a medieval French law code that compared a wife's right to disobey her sinful husband with a subject's duty to stand against an unjust ruler:

> *Everyone should know that a man should not obey his wife, nor a wife her husband, nor a vassal or an officer his lord, nor should any other persons obey each other in any case or with respect to any order, which is contrary to God, or to morality. [It] is a good reason for a woman to leave her husband when he wants her to sin, and good reason for others not to obey those who give them such orders.*[14]

---

12. Matthew 11:28–30; 1 Peter 3:7 (ESV); 1 Samuel 25:32–35.
13. Deuteronomy 13:6–11 (ESV).
14. *The Coutumes de Beauvaisis of Philippe de Beaumanoir*, trans. F. R. P. Akehurst (Philadelphia: University of Pennsylvania Press, 1992), 598. For one medieval woman's thoughts on the abuse of women, see *Appendix 3: The Testimony of a Medieval Woman.*

28

WIVES AND HUSBANDS

*Likewise, wives, be subject to your own husbands, so that even if
some do not obey the word, they may be won without a word by the
conduct of their wives, when they see your respectful and pure
conduct. Do not let your adorning be external—the braiding of
hair and the putting on of gold jewelry, or the clothing you wear—
but let your adorning be the hidden person of the heart with the
imperishable beauty of a gentle and quiet spirit, which in God's
sight is very precious. For this is how the holy women who hoped in
God used to adorn themselves, by submitting to their own
husbands, as Sarah obeyed Abraham, calling him lord. And you
are her children, if you do good and do not fear anything that is
frightening.*[1]

IN THE EARLIER CHAPTER ON the law of love, it was noted how the
biblical concept of love is closely tied to obedience: those who love God
obey him. This association is evident in the relationship between
husband and wife, as the New Testament makes this reality evident
through the inspiration of biblical words by our Lord. In one epistle,
Paul reminded women to love and to be subject to their husbands, with
the virtues of love and obedience firmly united. Similarly, the apostle

---

1. 1 Peter 3:1–6 (ESV).

Peter portrayed Sarah as the model for believing wives because she called her husband *lord* (a reference to the book of Genesis). However, it is noteworthy that Genesis never shows Abraham barking orders at his wife, for it was not servile fear that led Sarah to obey her husband (and Sarah gives no indication of being a passive person). Rather, in one illustrative passage, Abraham asked Sarah to defer to his wishes as a token of her affection, and she did so. Abraham's exact words were: "This is the kindness you will show to me." My point is that law and love must be as closely joined in human marriage as they are in the eternal nature of the Triune God. Wives prove love by subjecting themselves to their husbands, just as the Son of God loves the Father in perfect and eternal conformity to his Father's will, and the bride of Christ is called to love and obey her eternal husband in everything—even to martyrdom and death.[2]

While living as faithful companions to their husbands, often taking the very names of their husbands, women follow the path trodden by the first woman.[3] As contemporary women dally with feminist ideas about marriage and the family, they must not twist Scripture to escape the clear teaching that woman was created as man's helper, not as his equal or superior in authority. In 1 Timothy, the apostle Paul taught that women should submit to their husbands because Adam was created before Eve and because Eve sinned before her husband did.[4] The subordination of wives is required by natural realities, as well as the need to provide order in a fallen world. Though any particular woman may be stronger, brighter, better educated, or more virtuous than her husband (or most men), authority in the family is not based on superiority of intelligence, goodness, or prowess of men but solely on birth, sex, and the nature of the marital relationship. It is in the office of spouse (or parent) that authority rests, just as it is in the office of the Presidency that authority rests in the United States, regardless of the ability or virtue of any given President. This is how Scripture approaches all offices of authority.

The specific duties of wives toward husbands are spelled out in the

---

2. Titus 2:3–5; Genesis 20:13 (NASB).
3. The discussion of surname use should be handled carefully. Eve received her name from her husband (the Hebrew for *woman* means *taken out of*), and it is suitable for her daughters to do the same. Yet, some women choose to keep their surname as a way to respect the paternal household, which is an honorable gesture. What is not acceptable is to assert independence from a husband by keeping one's *own* name without deference to husband or father. That is to play Peter against Paul to avoid respecting either one.
4. 1 Timothy 2:11–13.

Bible. Women should submit to their husbands as to God, valuing in themselves a gentle and quiet spirit more than expensive adornments and attractive looks. Women must also prove their love for their families by prioritizing family life over personal desires and ambitions. To this end, Paul contrasts pious women who are *child-lovers* with lazy, gossiping busybodies who waste their lives socializing from house to house. Scripture presents Sarah as the model of a reverent and holy woman who respected, even obeyed, her husband as God called the couple to difficult situations and unsettled wanderings. Finally, women must tend to needy relatives, particularly parents and elderly relatives.[5] In short, married women must order their lives to please their husbands and to meet the needs of their children and relatives. This service is more important before the Lord than anything else they might seek to accomplish, whether career or public service.[6] It is critical, however, to recognize how *Scripture discusses the duties of wives in passages directed toward women themselves,* an approach that reminds men that the respect owed by their wives does not proceed from the will, desire, or superiority of husbands but directly from the Lord. Such respectful obedience must never be abused by the selfishness of men, just as the provision and protection of men must never be taken for granted in the self-indulgence of women.[7] To repeat: wives do not obey husbands because men desire and demand power, but because the Lord calls women to such affectionate service. The duties of women do not establish the rights of men, since Scripture is simply explaining to men and women alike what they owe each other. Moreover, the fact that the obligation of wives to obey their husbands is rooted in God's authority also places the matter beyond dispute or negotiation. And, just as wives must be patient with the ordinary faults of men, so, too, husbands cannot expect sinful women (which includes every wife) to be without flaw in the performance of their duties.

This is not to say that women exist only to clean laundry and do

5. Ephesians 5:22 (ESV); Titus 2:3–5; 1 Timothy 5:13; Genesis 12:4–20; 1 Peter 3:1–6 (ESV); 1 Timothy 5:4,10.
6. See *Appendix 4: Dorothy Sayers, Vocation, and Motherhood.*
7. Similarly, passages warning husbands to serve their wives are directed to men and are not cudgels to be used by wives against their husbands. God's holy word is never provided to threaten or nag, for those who preach God's prohibition of divorce while refusing to mend their faults (and demanding to be met on their terms) quarrel not with a particular husband or wife, but with the God who made marriage. To call upon the defense of God's law against divorce is to place oneself under a stricter obligation to serve under his terms (which includes pleasing one's spouse under their terms).

dishes, as if they were domestic servants rather than wives. Wives no more exist for their husbands' convenience than husbands live to indulge their wives' taste for fashion and travel. Modern people must never forget that the biblical notion of a household was far different than what we might initially imagine when discussing family life. In the ancient world, households were the means of making a living, typically through commerce, farming, or public service. There were no supermarkets stocked with food and clothing from distant lands. Each *household* (a better word than *family*, given the broad authority exercised across generations and over servants, as well as the production and storage of provisions on family property) worked to stockpile its own food, clothing, and other provisions, as well as to produce goods to be traded to procure necessities not found at home. To this end, a wife's labor was indispensable for profit and survival, and the book of Proverbs portrays the truly prudent woman as one who produces goods for sale on the market to build wealth in her home. One could almost say that women are born to shop, just not for fashion and frivolities.[8]

It is crucial to remember that, in the biblical world, it was the family that most directly oversaw and supervised the education of children. Although some tasks were subcontracted to tutors, parents determined what their children would learn and how they would be trained for work, culture, and religion. In such a consequential enterprise, the dignity and responsibilities of housewives were hardly insignificant. A woman was no mere adornment, nor was she permitted a life of leisure. A wife's call was to work with her husband to secure the material and spiritual good of her family, servants, and property—and she was called to work as hard as her husband in doing so, even laboring with him in their barns and fields. Of course, it is important to remember that men and women generally worked from their homes and helped each other tend to children (often with older sons assisting and shadowing their fathers), even while earning a living and interacting with the broader community.[9]

The biblical notion of the household permits, if not demands, that women contribute to family finances and teach and exercise authority

---

8. Proverbs 31:13–19.
9. Laura Ingalls Wilder showed the reality of such lives in her *Little House* series of books about growing up on a farm in nineteenth-century America. Her accounts reflect traditional household arrangements of Scripture more than the affluent, church-going families of the 1950s American suburbs do (although the urban households of early modern Europe and the suburban homes of post-World War Two America also seem blessed by the Lord).

over servants, children, and younger women—and it is in this context that the feminist critique of the Bible is best addressed. What the Scriptures expect of family life is no different than what the Bible expects of public life: everyone must seek the interest of others rather than pursue their selfish desires. Household affairs must be directed for the common good instead of private interest, and each man or woman is called to be a humble servant of all. Men and women do have clearly defined and differentiated roles; a husband leads his household while his wife serves alongside him as his helper and second-in-command (whether or not she works outside the home for the benefit of the household). They also have different capabilities and natures: men beget children while women bear them. But despite differences in size, nature, and vocation, men and women must aspire to serve one another as they work together for their common good. Wives must be the kind of women who are child-lovers rather than idle gossips, and men must devote themselves to their families rather than to pubs, stadiums, and fishing trips.[10]

Nor should it be forgotten that Paul did not demand that women stay at home to seclude them from public life (as some cultures do) but insisted, first and foremost, that wives and mothers diligently tend to their domestic affairs. Men and women alike must work hard to secure their common good and raise their children rather than wasting their days in idle conversation. Nothing more and nothing less is required than the government and protection of one's own house. As husband and wife live together for the common good of their marriage and its offspring, they can experience the reality of biblical love more deeply. A woman can learn how her career aspirations and material gain should be secondary to love for her husband and children. She can learn that love is lived through deference and perfected through submission.[11] In the same manner, men

---

10. John Chrysostom observed that it is the oneness of marriage that requires a head. He wrote: "[Paul] does not say 'one spirit' or 'one soul'... but he says 'one flesh.' The wife is a secondary authority, but nevertheless she possesses real authority and equality of dignity while the husband still retains the role of headship; the welfare of the household is thus maintained." John Chrysostom, "Homily 20," in *On Marriage and Family Life*, 51.

11. One author defined submission in discussing the sin of Eve: "The act of disobedience... indirectly involves marriage because the woman makes a unilateral decision when she eats the fruit. She does not pause to consult her husband in mutuality of choice and actions." This gets to the heart of the submission of wives. There is no room for autonomous decision-making in the common life of marriage, except that which Scripture allows or which the couple themselves have negotiated within biblical parameters. It is the same for men, who must live to please their wives not only on the terms of the Lord, but also according to all lawful preferences of their wife. Bromiley, *God and Marriage*, 5.

will discover that their dreams of power and glory must be subordinated to the immediate support of their wives and children: to what their families need today rather than in an ever-distant tomorrow. Husbands will also learn that love for a wife is discovered and demonstrated in exalting and serving women and children above themselves. Together, they will earn a living through the sweat of their brows, learning to work and rest together as they toil in a cursed, toilsome world.[12]

I should add that the biblical ideal of a wife as revealed in Proverbs 31 is one in which women are afforded considerable latitude in making decisions to support their households: a freedom they rightfully retain through prudent decision-making. While operating within biblical parameters and respecting her husband's leadership, and even his preferences, a wife does not need to seek confirmation for every household decision or ratification of every expenditure. Women possess legitimate authority in the home and are free to exercise it on behalf of the common good (consistent with general guidance and agreements they have worked out with their husbands). The woman portrayed in Proverbs 31 was not a modern feminist seeking her happiness or fulfilling selfish ambition, and she certainly respected her husband at home and in public. At the same time, she was active and independent in serving her husband, children, and household with as much energy, focus, and prudence as she could muster. Within the household, she pursued a common purpose with her husband, even as husband and wife divided their labor for the common good and in accord with their distinctive natures and different responsibilities. She respected her husband; her husband honored her; and they together built up their household like a successful business enterprise— not simply for financial success, but also for far greater moral and spiritual objectives.[13]

Because man and woman are called to distinct vocations by God, yet made to reveal in their union the eternal and unalterable love of God, only together in marriage can they provide creation with a glimpse into the nature of the Triune God. This is why the modern confusion of marital roles is so dangerous. Reversing the traditional roles of men and women in the household may or may not lead to confusion and quarrels over temporal concerns (though it usually does), but it always leads to

---

12. Much of the frustration and resentment in contemporary marriage stems from couples comparing their overburdened workloads, then blaming each other rather than the curse of sin (and attempted overachievement) for their exhaustion.
13. Proverbs 31:10–31.

spiritual chaos. Any home ruled by hatred or abandoned to egalitarian anarchy cannot possibly accomplish its divinely appointed purpose.[14] Moreover, such homes often fail to perform well in practical matters. Seventeenth-century Puritan Richard Baxter observed that dissension between husband and wife disorders family affairs, like unequally yoked oxen that slow work because the mismatched animals resist each other (modern people might say, *like a car with a flat tire that makes it difficult to steer*). Baxter noted that nothing is done well or efficiently in disagreeable marriages, and that the children of such couples will either follow the bad example of their parents or come to believe they, too, are at "liberty to do what they will."[15]

In contrast to such spiritual selfishness and moral anarchy, Christian believers are called to reflect the love of the Triune God, which exists within himself and for his creation. Where there is ordered love rather than domestic tyranny and family disorder, couples demonstrate in their own homes how the invisible Father glorifies his eternal Son, how the immortal Son is subject to his eternal Father, and how the Spirit of Love proceeds from Father and Son alike. Just as husband and wife are two persons made one flesh and bound together in holy love, the divine persons of the Holy Trinity are one essence united in eternal love and holy righteousness. Biblical households and marriages also serve as living analogies of Christ's love for his church, his eternal bride. As Charles Hodge observed:

> [None] of the sacred writers speaks in more exalted terms of marriage than [Paul]. He represents it as a most ennobling spiritual union, which raises a man out of himself and makes him live for another; a union so elevated and refining as to render it a fit symbol of the union between Christ and his church. Marriage, according to this Apostle, does for man in the sphere of nature, what union with Christ does for him in the sphere of grace.[16]

---

14. Francis Schaeffer noted: "The world spirit of our age espouses [a] subversive feminist view which teaches that the home and family are ways of oppressing women; that personal fulfillment and careers must come before one's marriage and the needs of children; that housework and child care are demeaning." Schaeffer chided Christian scholars who change "their views about inerrancy [in] trying to come to terms with feminism." Francis Schaeffer, *The Great Evangelical Disaster* (Westchester, Illinois: Crossway Books, 1984), 134.
15. Richard Baxter, *The Godly Home*, ed. Randall J. Pedersen (Wheaton, Illinois: Crossway Books, 2010), 134.
16. Hodge, *Systematic Theology*, vol. 3, 394.

29

MAINTAINING LOVE IN MARRIAGE

By the testimonies of the divine law, we see that the Lord did not only permit, but also expressly and earnestly commanded his people, in whom he willed that all holiness and faith toward the marriage covenant should be observed, that the man who could not induce his mind to love his wife with a true conjugal love be allowed to dismiss her so that she could be married to someone else.[1]

THERE IS a common assumption among modern men and women that some couples cannot be made to live with and love each other. The English poet, John Milton (cited above), was one of the first thinkers in our tradition to preach the gospel of divorce due to incompatibility, believing that some couples are so unable to live with one another in marital love that they ought to part ways to find mates more readily adaptable to their temperaments and personalities. Milton saw divorce as more than an option in such circumstances; he argued it was a religious duty to build an affectionate household. His words suggest that those unable to persuade themselves to love their spouse should seek a more congenial partner. John Milton did not seem to understand or accept the biblical teaching that every spouse is capable (by God's grace and power)

---

1. John Milton "The Judgment of Martin Bucer," in *The Works of John Milton,* vol. 4 (New York: Columbia University Press, 1934), 35.

of fully loving their mate, as well as every other human being on the face of the earth. This is a core truth of Christian doctrine.

God ordains marriage to create and enhance affection. If that were not so, most couples would never learn to love each other more deeply than they do on the first day of their marriage. If marriage does not deepen love, then couples begin marriage at a point of diminishing returns, with their passion fading until they inevitably arrive at reduced ardor and eventual disaffection. Such reasoning contradicts human experience, as nearly everyone understands how marriage strengthens love, just as the body is strengthened by proper nutrition. Who cannot see that it is after the honeymoon that couples cling to each other more firmly than before? Who can deny that the birth of children binds couples together more closely? Who is unaware that the longer a couple is married, the more inseparable they become? That is why remarriage following divorce or death becomes increasingly less likely the longer a marriage has lasted.

While marital love sometimes feels less intense after several years, its transformation reveals not a diminution of affection but a metamorphosis of love: a change into something far quieter and less tumultuous. In contrast to the shallow brook that appears forceful, though its waters unavailingly push against small rocks, a deep river runs quiet as it carries the heaviest boulders downstream by its unstoppable power. Similarly, marriage typically increases affection between husband and wife, soon surpassing the turbulent passions of courtship and honeymoon. When faithful and pious men and women marry, their hearts create love as surely as their bodies create life. This has always been understood, as one medieval guide to household government observed:

> *When two good and honest people are married, all other affections, except their love for each other, are withdrawn, annulled, and forgotten. It seems to me that when they are together they look at each other more than they look at others, they come together and embrace each other, and they would rather talk and communicate with each other than with anyone else.*[2]

---

2. Tania Bayard, ed., *A Medieval Home Companion: Housekeeping in the Fourteenth Century* (New York: HarperCollins Publishers, 1991), 50. While both editions are condensed from the original, Eileen Power's translation is significantly longer than Bayard's version. Eileen Power, trans., *The Goodman of Paris (Le Ménagier de Paris): A Treatise on Moral and Domestic Economy by a Citizen of Paris, c. 1393* (London; Folio Society, 1992).

There are several means by which marriage creates affection. First, the oath of marriage creates love. It is not difficult for a man or woman to love a spouse who has been taken as a lifelong partner and has sworn lifelong love in turn. The permanence of marital vows fosters affection due to the trust and security the vows inspire. Second, living out this association deepens affection. After years of sharing joys, sorrows, and disputes, a couple understands each other better than parents and siblings do— better than the best of friends, since the distinct yet complementary natures of man and woman allow a far deeper appreciation and affection for each other than what is found in the like-minded friendship of man with man or woman with woman. Men and women find worth and joy in what is different from themselves. Third, sexual intimacy strengthens the passion and warmth of marriage. Even illicit lovers find that a casual sexual experience creates an emotional bonding difficult to remove; how much more does marriage create mutual delight and joy! Fourth, the birth or adoption of children brings a couple to a deeper experience of love. Not only is there a mutual interest in securing the good of their children, but couples delight in their offspring in a manner outsiders can scarcely suffer, let alone enjoy. Fifth, shared housing and property arrangements draw couples together in a tangible manner as the material circumstances of their lives become intertwined. Sixth, couples draw together from their shared spiritual experiences before the Lord. Because all of these elements exist in Christian marriages, it can truly be said that marriage is suited to create love by its very nature, regardless of how a given couple feels about each other before getting married.

However, marriage will not produce love if it is misused or abused, just as plants and animals do not grow if they are denied food, light, and water. Anyone who subverts the purposes of their marriage will not enjoy the crop of love that matrimony is designed to produce—and there are several ways by which this typically occurs. First, many couples refuse to bear children, thereby stagnating the maturing of their love in a selfish desire to avoid the responsibilities of parenthood. Second, it is monogamous sexual intimacy that was ordained to deepen marital affection, not celibacy, infidelity, or polygamy. Anyone who neglects conjugal duties or abandons the marriage bed for another lover will reap a crop of indifference or jealousy rather than one of faithful love. Third, not only flesh, but also hearts and minds must be shared. Couples pursuing separate careers and other practical interests often never truly become one flesh in a shared home, as intended for marriage. When a man and woman leave their parents, it is intended that they live a common life. This is why marriages conducted from a long distance seldom prove satisfactory. Nor do those relationships in which practical affairs remain divided. Fourth, many modern people breed needless quarrels and stress by refusing to accept the roles the Lord ordains for husband and wife. Men and women constantly debating their particular place in their marriage have little energy left for the hard work of daily service. Such couples also tend to misunderstand the physical and emotional differences between men and women related to those roles, thereby growing impatient with someone quite unlike themselves (who is naturally unable and rightly unwilling to mirror the personality and preferences of a spouse of the opposite sex). Fifth, many couples strive for the wrong things, hurting their marriages through ambition and greed. Sixth, some couples harbor secret resentment of each other stemming from premarital promiscuity and its aftermath. I suspect that unresolved guilty consciences cause more marital resentment than many couples would care to admit, even to themselves.

The natural bonds of marriage are so strong that many unbelievers can love their spouses, despite a lack of faith and piety. But no one can fully use marriage as intended, namely to glorify the Lord, unless the Spirit of God is with them. In the book of Galatians, the apostle Paul provided instructions that bind every church member, the Lord's household, telling believers to "walk by the Spirit, and you will not carry out the desire of the flesh." Paul even explained the difference between the fruit of the Spirit and the flesh. The flesh conceives acts of "immorality, impurity, sensuality, idolatry, sorcery, enmities, strife, jealousy, outbursts of anger, disputes, dissensions, factions, envying, drunkenness, carousing, and things like these." In contrast, the fruit of the Spirit brings "love, joy, peace, patience, kindness, goodness, faithfulness, gentleness, [and] self-control." Paul made it clear that love is a gift from God, available to all who ask for it, and that every man and woman can love one another if they repent of hatred, discord, and selfishness. Paul commanded believers (to include married couples) to do everything without "grumbling or disputing," thereby proving themselves to be the children of God in this "crooked and perverse generation."[3] That is why John Milton was so terribly wrong regarding his belief in the need for legal divorce to resolve matters of marital incompatibility. No matter how many years of quarreling have existed, a couple may yet learn to love each other with true

---

3. Galatians 5:16, 19–23 (NASB); Philippians 2:14-15 (ESV).

affection, if they will repent of willful selfishness and humble themselves before God and man (or woman). The Lord, who gives his people the ability to love even their persecutors and enemies, can surely enable his servants to care for the husbands or wives with whom they share a common life and bed.

There is a practical reason for this teaching. No matter how much a couple loves each other, their relationship must change over time. No relationship remains unchanged as the years pass. The intense passions of romantic love and new marriage seldom burn long and must be replaced by the warming fire of the hearth, which can provide heat and light to provide for the needs of a household. C.S. Lewis rightly noted that some people wrongly believe that "if you have married the right person you may expect to go on 'being in love' forever." He wrote that when passion dies out, such men and women begin to fear "they have made a mistake and are entitled to a change."[4] Lewis observed that romantic feelings will not remain passionate forever, no matter how intense desire and infatuation once burned between a man and woman. Romantic love is not, and never will be, the glue that binds couples together for life.

A medieval author framed the matter bluntly. Andreas Capellanus wrote that there are men who are "slaves to such passionate desire that they cannot be held in the bonds of love." Such men lust after every woman they see. Their love is "like that of a shameless dog"—they want to change mates with every passing desire.[5] The reality is that every husband and wife will tire of their spouse (if only for a moment) or become attracted to a rival. How people respond to this temptation depends on their understanding of love and marriage, as well as their moral integrity. Those who remain determined by God's help to keep their promise to be faithful will find divine help to fulfill their nuptial obligations, since God gives grace to those who seek it. But anyone who gives in to sinful temptation and desire will never settle down to live happily or productively, for that man or woman will stray at every opportunity. As Pierre Viret noted of godly affection:

If a man loves his wife and children or others for whom he bears affection only for the pleasures and benefits he receives from them,

4. Lewis, *Mere Christianity*, 110.
5. Andreas Capellanus, *The Art of Courtly Love*, ed. John Jay Parry (New York: W.W. Norton and Company, 1941), 33. I use this text only to illustrate a cultural perception since Andreas Capellanus is seldom mistaken for a pious churchman.

he doesn't love them for God's sake but for himself, having no regard for the commandment of God but only for his own beastly sensuality and carnal desires. This is the reason why the love of many is neither steadfast nor constant, but instead often changes. For, if the husband always loves his wife for God's sake and not his own, he will love her no less when she is old than when she is young, sick or healthy, poor or rich.[6]

Spiritually obedient couples will find the duty to love to be joyful since joy itself is a gift of the Spirit of God. When natural means of upholding marital love are found wanting, supernatural grace will enable believers to do what is right and to take delight in doing so. On the other hand, anyone who does not seek God's help or has an otherwise false idea of marriage will be overwhelmed with remorse and regret. Why? Because John Milton is wrong: it is not fruitful to move from spouse to spouse in search of perfect love, for there is no such affection in a fallen world. Not only is modern society filled with the embittered and lonely survivors of infidelity and divorce, but romantic infatuation itself eventually falters if left unsupported by the bonds of marriage: the proper climax of the man and woman relationship. Outside of marriage, there is preparation, impurity, and childish inconstancy. Inside wedlock, there is commitment, chastity, and fulfillment.

This reality is why the great medieval philosopher Peter Abelard and his student, the beautiful and gifted Heloise, were so foolish. Having engaged in a premarital relationship and conceived a child, they rejected marriage as the appropriate solution to their troubles.[7] For a time, they foolishly believed they could preserve their affection by keeping love as a free promise rather than a legal obligation, although the situation degenerated into one in which the uncle of Heloise hired a band of ruffians to castrate the famous philosopher (who proved willing to marry the pregnant woman in secret rather than in public), then separated the disgraced couple and sent them to monasteries for the rest of their lives. Years later, Abelard reflected that he and Heloise had been motivated more by lust than charity and that he had sinned greatly in the matter, even acknowledging how his castration had been an act of God's grace to bring him to

---

6. Viret, *Exposition*, vol. 2, 436.
7. Étienne Gilson explored the complicated motives of Abelard in Étienne Gilson, *Heloise and Abelard* (Ann Arbor, Michigan: University of Michigan Press, 1963).

faith and good sense.[8] Not only had Abelard mistreated the young woman in an illicit affair, but he also rejected the Lord's straightforward remedy for such sin: the use of marriage to convert illicit passion into holy love, no matter the cost to one's reputation and career.[9]

We should learn from the sad experience of this famous medieval affair that the flames of passion are extinguished outside the household hearth. In the quote below, Abelard remembered the foolish words of Heloise: words that showed how she, too, failed to understand that love is maintained through marriage rather than sexual passion and romantic infatuation. Heloise at one point claimed that God was her witness that she would rather have been called Abelard's whore than to be made the wife of "Augustus, Emperor of the whole world."[10] If Abelard were not remembered for having been brutalized by a guardian of the pregnant girl, their relationship would have become just one more cleric-concubine relationship that plagued medieval society, if it lasted at all, for it would have possessed no greater strength than the *free love* unions of the 1960s founded on pop music platitudes rather than divine promises—on impulses not protected through the pledges, restraints, and commitments of holy marriage. In contrast to such worldly wisdom, we must seek our salvation in the laws and word of the Lord.

> *[Heloise said] it would be dearer to her and more honorable to me to be called my lover than my wife so that her charm alone would keep me for her, not the force of a nuptial bond.*[11]

---

8. Abelard wrote: "So when divine grace cleansed rather than deprived me of those vile members from which their practice of utmost indecency are called 'the parts of shame' and have no proper name of their own, what else did it do but remove a foul imperfection to order to preserve perfect purity." Peter Abelard, *The Letters of Abelard and Heloise,* trans. Betty Radice (New York: Penguin Books, 1974), 148.
9. Abelard wrote: "She was a lady of no mean appearance... on fire with love for her, I sought opportunity to enable me to make her familiar with me by private and daily association the more easily to win her over... [Fulbert] put his niece entirely under my control... I was astonished at his simplicity in this matter and would have been no more astounded if he had been giving over a tender lamb to a ravenous wolf." Peter Abelard, *The Story of Abelard's Adversities,* trans. J.T. Muckle (Toronto: Pontifical Institute of Medieval Studies, 1982), 26–30, 37.
10. Peter Abelard, *The Letters of Abelard and Heloise,* 114.
11. Peter Abelard, *The Story of Abelard's Adversities,* 26–30, 37.

30

FULFILLING THE CONJUGAL DEBT

The husband should give to his wife her conjugal rights, and like-
wise the wife to her husband. For the wife does not have authority
over her own body, but the husband does. Likewise, the husband
does not have authority over his own body, but the wife does. Do not
deprive one another, except perhaps by agreement for a limited
time, that you may devote yourselves to prayer; but then come
together again, so that Satan may not tempt you because of your
lack of self-control.[1]

AN ANCIENT COLLECTION of and commentary on Jewish law (the
Mishnah) taught that husband and wife have a mutual duty to fulfill the
conjugal debt consistently, and specified the number of times per month
spouses should seek sexual relations. Even when celibacy was undertaken
to fulfill a religious vow, laborers could deny their wives only for a week,
whereas religious scholars could refrain for up to thirty days. Apart from
religious oaths of temporary celibacy, laborers were required to fulfill
marital obligations twice a week, and vocations that necessitated travel
had their marital debt reduced in proportion to the vocational demands
of work away from home.[2] Though Moses did not explicitly command

---

1. 1 Corinthians 7:3–5 (ESV).
2. Danby, *The Mishnah*, 252 (Ketuboth 5:6).

how frequently couples were required to sleep together, his revelation regarding the origins of marriage indicated that marriage included a sexual component, which should not be neglected. This reality was the premise from which later Jewish commentators drafted more specific codes regarding marital duties. Writings such as the *Mishnah* also built on the wisdom of Solomon in the Proverbs, where we learn that a faithful and affectionate spouse is the best antidote to adultery.[3]

The apostle Paul mirrored Jewish tradition in teaching that frequent conjugal relations are a duty of marriage. Paul differed from Jewish custom, however, in addressing the frequency of coitus by appealing to the law of love rather than to a law of numbers (i.e., a quota system). Because husband and wife are one flesh, their bodies belong to each other: a wife should not refuse the needs of her husband since her body belongs to him as much as to herself, and a husband must not frustrate the desire of his wife since his body belongs to his wife as much as to himself. Moreover, neither one may appeal to manipulation or force to secure their sexual needs—nor should they need to. No one causes his body grief and pain in pursuit of pleasure, and a spouse must be honored in the same way as oneself.[4] Nor does any healthy person deny their body food when hungry, or skip meals to punish a growling stomach (or an annoying spouse). In short, husbands and wives are to live for each other and be willing to lay down their bodies in sacrificial love and humble service. They must love spouses in spirit and flesh, just as they love and care for their own bodies.

When Paul rejected the Jewish numerical solution regarding sexual availability, he insisted on an approach that was far more encompassing rather than less rigorous. It is important to observe how Paul phrased his commands. By reminding husbands and wives they have a *duty* to serve rather than teaching that the married have a *right* to sexual satisfaction, the apostle taught that charity and self-sacrifice (rather than self-indulgence and self-fulfillment) are the aims of piety. Moreover, Paul presented an authoritative rule of faith rather than a personal opinion that churches and individuals are free to ignore. With Paul's rule, the test of adequate conjugal love does not end after a predetermined number of intimate acts per week, since a quota system falls short of what matters most: a loving human heart. It is not enough to concede enough carnal intercourse to

---

3. Proverbs 5:15–20.
4. Ephesians 5:29 (ESV).

deter open adultery. The apostle called spouses to affectionately help each other to resist impure and unfaithful thoughts, which often vex even faithful husbands and wives.

Just as important, by insisting on frequent sexual intercourse within marriage, Paul required Christians to establish their marriages in tenderness and affection. He was not calling men and women to copulate perfunctorily, mechanically, or unaffectionately, nor was the apostle calling married couples to abuse each other's bodies with the impure passion of the pagans. What Paul demanded was intimate marital affection rather than unaffectionate sexual availability. Prostitutes are willing to service a body for a price, but husbands and wives share the priceless touch of physical love. This difference explains why Paul did not take a numerical approach to the conjugal duty. Had he done so, subsequent generations of believers would have considered it sufficient to submit to sexual intercourse a set number of times per week and would not have learned that the rule of charity demands quality of love even more than frequency of intercourse.

The apostle Paul's ancient command requires modern husbands and wives to consider their hidden and open motives in sharing physical intimacy, permitting each couple the freedom to determine the frequency of coitus as their dispositions necessitate. What Scripture demands is that couples help each other to forestall sexual temptation and to grow in charitable and affectionate love. Nor did the apostle Paul (who was a trained Jewish scholar and knew its regulations) follow Jewish tradition in differentiating between vocations. Laborers and scholars alike were called to love and purity, for they are undifferentiated in Christ. Though a man called to be a naval officer may not know his wife intimately as often as a factory worker (who sleeps in the same bed as his wife every night), even the naval officer can govern himself by charity in meeting the physical and emotional needs of his wife, if he devotes himself to her rather than to his career whenever he is on leave or shore duty.

If the naval officer's wife faces persistent or overwhelming sexual temptation in her husband's absence, her husband may need to find a permanent shore assignment or retire from military service altogether, so that he does not sink his family for the safety of his ship. No career, neither of husband nor wife, must be allowed to shipwreck a marriage. Still, if a husband makes this sacrifice, his wife must contentedly accept her husband's love, along with any losses that she and their children must endure from her husband's sacrifice of a prestigious military career. She cannot expect him to give up his career to meet her needs, then expect to live as if no such sacrifice had been made. Rather, she must acknowledge, enjoy, and honor the sacrifice of love made on her behalf. In the book of Galatians, Paul revealed that believers are free from Jewish regulations, but at the same time reminded Christians that their freedom is given to bring forth good rather than self-indulgence and ambition. Paul warned the Galatians:

> For you were called to freedom, brethren; only do not turn your freedom into an opportunity for the flesh, but through love serve one another. For the whole Law is fulfilled in one word, in the statement, "You shall love your neighbor as yourself." [5]

Despite the obligation to prioritize family over career, military service during periods of alarm and war is different than military service as a peacetime posting. War and the peril of war necessitate sacrifices and separations that are generally not justifiable. If the sorrow of death (and cessation of all sexual intimacy) can be justified to save one's country, so much more the distractions and inconveniences of sexual temptation. If, as the apostle writes in 1 Corinthians, a temporary crisis can lead to delaying marriage despite the reality of sexual temptation, there is little doubt that war also requires sacrifices from those already married. After all, it must be remembered that military service keeps the families of one's compatriots free from the threats of the enemy. Moreover, temporary sexual temptation for married recruits is far more palatable than the unsatisfied desire of single soldiers and grieving war widows. If family life is to exist for everyone, *someone* must guard the walls. The writer of Psalm 127, cited at the beginning of this book, explicitly noted that the Lord is the defender of the city and builder of households, showing that both efforts are moral callings under his providential care. The psalmist wrote that unless God himself builds house and city, householders and citizens labor in vain, with their purposes and labors amounting to nothing more than fading efforts. [6]

The apostle Paul, however, revealed that there is a time for husband and wife to deny themselves the use of the conjugal bed for prayer (albeit

---

5. Galatians 5:13–14 (NASB).
6. 1 Corinthians 7:28 (ESV); Psalm 127:1–5 (ESV). Deuteronomy 24:5 exempted men married less than a year from military service.

with mutual consent). Throughout history, many church leaders have stressed that sexual activity ought to be restricted on holy days and church festivals. However, I would note we must be careful with such prohibitions given the apostolic warning that "no one is to act as your judge in regard to food or drink on in respect to a festival or new moon or a Sabbath day."[7] Nevertheless, there are times of celebration, concern, and sorrow during which marital intimacy should be subordinated to earnest appeals to God as a type of fasting, just as with food and drink (practices all too infrequent for many of us contemporary Christians, but accepted custom for believers during the first two millennia of the faith). Still, we must not prioritize such practices over clear biblical commandments. For that reason, church father John Chrysostom placed limits on such spiritual self-restraint, suggesting that periods of abstinence should be limited to "unusually intense prayers" and only by mutual agreement, lest fastidious piety cause marital discord. He wrote:

> *This is what many wives do when they refuse their husbands. They commit a sin that outweighs the righteousness of their abstinence. They are responsible for their husband's licentiousness and the broken homes that result... or on the other hand, [the husband] remains continent but frets and complains, loses his temper, and constantly fights with his wife. Either way, what good is all the fasting and continence? No good at all; it has broken love to pieces.*[8]

Wives must not tempt their husbands into bad behavior, nor must husbands harm their wives. Any use of terror, intimidation, bargaining, or force to secure or deny conjugal obligations is utterly beyond the Spirit of Christ. Sexual intimacy is an obligation of love that is owed, no matter what is given or withheld in return. Still, when a mate is unresponsive in fulfilling the obligation of the marriage bed, the desirous party must patiently endure the loss of intimacy, no matter how much it hurts. Bitter resentment is never tolerable, nor is apathetic unconcern. Love is the

---

7. Colossians 2:16 (NASB). One historian has written: "[Church fathers] of the first three centuries teach that the purposes of marital sex ought to be restricted [and] warned that the times for marital relations should be curtailed. None of the early writers was specific about the precise periods when couples should forego intercourse; they simply stated that it was inappropriate, even sinful, to indulge in sex on holy days and Church festivals." James Brundage, *Law, Sex, and Christian Society in Medieval Europe* (Chicago: University of Chicago, 1987), 67.
8. John Chrysostom, "Homily 19," in *On Marriage and Family Life*, 25–26.

proper response to wrongs suffered in marriage, and enduring unsought and undesired celibacy is a cross that sometimes must be carried for the sake of Christ—though the aggrieved spouse also must speak truth in love, including the sharing of the deep hurt and frustration caused by sexual rejection from the person who should love him (or her) most. Still, patience must never be confused with passivity; there are active steps men and women should take to remedy a frigid marriage, starting with confrontation in Christian charity and moving to counseling and pastoral guidance. A cold heart is as wrong as a hot temper and must be repented, with the aggrieved spouse required to help a sinning spouse to repent and change, just as with addiction, alcoholism, and other obvious vices. Regular sexual intimacy is an expectation for Christian marriage, for it is holy passion that glorifies God by revealing the depths of God's love for his church in a way that passionless love never can.

Finally, the conjugal debt must never be negotiated by bartering or seized by rape. While couples inevitably will discuss the frequency of coitus to arrive at mutual satisfaction, intimacy must no more be bought and sold within marriage than outside of it. Nor must intimacy come with dues to be paid and demands to be met (at least not in earnest, since playfulness and banter are part of a friendly marriage). In the same manner, the use of drunkenness to make a husband or wife more pliable is no more permitted within marriage than without. The apostle Paul commanded: "Do not get drunk with wine, for that is debauchery, but be filled with the Spirit."[9] Assault and rape are utterly beyond the pale since sexual intimacy begins with a freely chosen act of love and must continue in the same spirit. A man is no more permitted to assault his wife than he can rape his own body. Juan Luis Vives, a sixteenth-century church reformer, wrote:

> Love is gotten by love, by honesty and fidelity, and not by violence. Adam did not ravish Eve but received her, delivered unto him by God [that] they should mutually love one another.[10]

---

9. Ephesians 5:18 (ESV).
10. Juan Luis Vives, "Instruction of a Christian Woman," in Joan Larsen Klein, ed., *Daughters, Wives, and Widows*, 124.

31

THE PURITY OF THE MARRIAGE BED

But sexual immorality and all impurity or covetousness must not even be named among you, as it proper among saints... Walk as children of light (for the fruit of light is found in all that is good and right and true), and try to discern what is pleasing to the Lord. Take no part in the unfruitful works of darkness, but instead expose them. For it is shameful even to speak of the things that they do in secret.[1]

Let marriage be held in honor among all, and let the marriage bed be undefiled, for God will judge the sexually immoral and adulterous.[2]

PHYSICAL INTIMACY within marriage does not exist only to beget children. People do not restrict intercourse to a few fertile days of the year, as animals do, since human sexuality also was ordained to reinforce the bond of love between husband and wife (which is why both human males and females are compelled by nature to desire intercourse even when a woman cannot conceive). One Roman Catholic writer long ago

---

1. Ephesians 5:3, 8–12 (ESV). Paul seems to be focusing on sexual ethics, noting that believers must *try to discern* what is right and must avoid *unfruitful* (i.e., *barren*) acts. He is commanding us to separate right from wrong in sexual behavior.
2. Hebrews 13:4 (ESV).

compared sexual intimacy to eating, with sexual intimacy and food both serving to preserve life. While eating food maintains individual lives, sexual intimacy preserves human society. However, beyond sustenance and survival, Francis de Sales observed that God has ordained that men and women may enjoy their food as long as they do not wallow in self-indulgent gluttony. That is, not every morsel of food is eaten to still the pangs of hunger; many banquets and desserts serve higher purposes than physical nourishment.[3]

It is the same with sexual pleasure. Though the procreation of children may be a primary purpose of marital intimacy, husbands and wives are called to strengthen the bond of marital love by the use of sexual intimacy even in those instances when they are not seeking pregnancy. Such intimacy may include more than the bare act of child-making coitus, just as people often satisfy hungry stomachs with more than unbuttered bread. Moreover, because the Lord designed physical love to be passionate, there is no fault in it being so. It is the modern scientist who makes children in loveless test tubes—God joins husbands to wives. What I mean is that sexual reproduction does not exist through biological chance and social convention. The Lord established it for temporal and eternal purposes, pleasures, and joys. We must always remember that the Lord is the one who ordained sexual intimacy to beget children, though he could have chosen differently. We must never forget that God designed intense passion into the experience.

Still, although the Lord creates delightful and tasty food, at the same time, he condemns gluttony and the eating of vile foods. Not every possible bite of food is to be indulged, which is why the restrictions on eating unclean food exist in the law of Moses.[4] Even freed from the regulations of Jewish ritual (what we now call *kosher* foods), some among us eat until the food they have ingested makes them sick and harms their health. Our culture is filled with such people: heart patients gobbling

---

3. Francis de Sales observed how there is "a parity between the pleasures of marriage and those of eating, both being physical, though the former, because more sensual and intense, are referred to as carnal." He explained how both eating and marriage are ordained to nourish life and promote friendship. While observing that the marital debt requires at least the hope for children, de Sales wrote: "[To eat] merely for the pleasure of satisfying our appetite is permissible but not commendable" and "[To eat] immoderately and to excess [is] blameworthy." Francis de Sales, *Introduction to the Devout Life*, ed. Michael Day (Wheathampstead, Hertfordshire: Anthony Clarke, 1990), 195. Augustine of Hippo's *The Good of Marriage* and C.S. Lewis's *Mere Christianity* also compare eating to intimacy.
4. Leviticus 11:2; Deuteronomy 14:3.

down a pound of bacon and diabetics consuming a quart of ice cream. Although such habits are not explicitly condemned in Scripture, we can see how such gluttonous habits are self-indulgent and destructive, even sinfully self-destructive (gluttony has been categorized as one of the deadly sins since Christian antiquity). As previously noted, there are moral limits on human behavior unmentioned in Scripture that remain evident in moral conscience and common judgment.[5] Natural reason and the care of our bodies obligate us to do right.[6]

Perhaps, someone might argue, food analogies permit New Testament believers to enjoy sexual intimacy previously prohibited under the Mosaic law, just as it was revealed to the apostle Peter that dietary restrictions commanded in the Old Testament no longer bind believers in the kingdom of Christ. To that end, the book of Acts recounts how Peter was told (in a vision) to eat foods prohibited under Mosaic ritual, and when he refused to do so, a voice declared: "What God has cleansed, no longer consider unholy." Thereafter, Peter was called to minister to the Gentiles, mixing with people considered unclean by the Jews and eating previously prohibited foods. Are Mosaic regulations regarding sex mere matters of ceremonial cleansing that reached their fulfillment (and subsequent suspension) in Christ? Are passages in Leviticus regarding ceremonial regulations for men and women made unclean through sexual intimacy and menstruation no longer binding on Jews and never binding on Gentiles? Were Mosaic injunctions regarding sexual intimacy the same as these now-suspended regulations? That is what we must determine.[7]

Nothing in Scripture forbids husbands and wives from tearing each

---

5. Whether some foods should be considered *morally unclean* on the grounds of natural law rather than Old Testament dietary restrictions, I cannot say. For examples of what might seem unnatural and immoral foods, see DisgustingFoodMuseum.com
6. A Protestant rival of de Sales wrote: "We must not abuse [marriage] by our sensual desires, [for] though the use of wine is permitted us, yet the abuse of it is always forbidden. Therefore whoever takes it beyond measure and uses it to excess... always offends God." Pierre Viret, *Exposition of the Ten Commandments*, vol. 2, 225. Clement of Alexandria made similar comparisons over twelve hundred years earlier, writing of Paul's comments about the cessation of mortal appetite in 1 Corinthians 6:13, "In this saying he attacks those who think they can live like wild pigs and goats, lest they should indulge their physical appetites without restraint." Clement of Alexandria, "On Marriage," (*Miscellanies, Book III*) in John Ernest Leonard Oulton and Henry Chadwick, eds., *Alexandrian Christianity: Select Translations of Clement and Origen* (Philadelphia: Westminster Press, 1954), 62.
7. Acts 10:15 (NASB); Leviticus 15:2–4, 19–21. Ulrich Zwingli referred to Peter's vision when appealing for the marriage of clergymen. Ulrich Zwingli, "Petition of Certain Preachers of Switzerland to the Most Reverend Lord Hugo, Bishop of Constance, That He Will Not Suffer Himself To Be Persuaded To Make Any Proclamation To The Injury Of

other's flesh with chains and leather whips in sadistic sexual titillation (as the Marquis de Sade enjoyed), even though such perversion is universally condemned based on the ethical principles revealed by the Bible. God's word scarcely mentions a multitude of sexual preferences that modern men and women view on the screen and read about in books every day. The Lord has not given us a long list of explicit commands about such matters, but has provided principles necessary for attaining wisdom and living right. What I mean is that it is not required for God to give mankind a multi-volume encyclopedia of sexual ethics, but to provide laws and principles through which every epoch and culture can judge the propriety of specific acts of sexual intimacy. To exhaustively discuss common ethical problems beyond the need for additional application and amplification, the Bible would have been larger than the twenty-four-volume *Encyclopedia Britannica* of the 1970s (and written in many languages, including some (such as English) that did not yet exist. Such a revelation would have been unusable by everyday Christians and would not have survived centuries of worm and decay, fire and storm, and war and persecution. We would have retained no more than fragments from which we would be applying principles to particulars, just as we now do. Only we would have been reasoning from fragments rather than from a completed and well-ordered written revelation bound as a single, portable book. Rather than taking an impractical and encyclopedic approach, Scripture revealed core truths from which we can judge particular cases, as one medieval preacher observed:

> *God did not give this commandment in a particularized form: 'Do not sleep with this wife or this nun or this widow,' but he gave a general command covering all women when he said, 'Thou shalt not commit adultery.'* [8]

Sexual intimacy involves more than the bare act of beast-like coitus.

The Gospel, Not Endure Longer The Scandal of Harlotry, But Allow The Presbyters To Marry Wives Or At Least Would Wink At Their Marriages," in *Selected Works*, 33–34.

8. Siegfried Wenzel, ed., *Fasciculus Morum: A Fourteenth-Century Preacher's Handbook*, 671. Sixteenth-century Cardinal Cajetan similarly wrote: "[Laws] are never multiplied in view of a mere multitude of cases that can occur. If this were true, we would need an infinite number of laws, according to all possible events. In any commonwealth, the laws laid down are so understood that from one case in a decree one can understand all similar cases under the same decree." Jared Wicks, S.J., ed., *Cajetan Responds: A Reader in Reformation Controversy* (Washington, D.C.: The Catholic University of America Press, 1978), 183.

In fact, it was primarily to differentiate human intimacy from barnyard mating that many past Christian thinkers forbade positions of sexual intercourse that too closely resembled the copulation of brute beasts. Whether Christian missionaries were correct in insisting that non-European converts restrict themselves to face-to-face coitus is far from certain, but it is plain to see that intimacy is meant to be a tender experience rather than a rough and brutal act, which is why the Bible sanctions caresses and kisses in the Song of Solomon. Human love is not to be reduced to the sowing of seed or physiological release, but was established for emotional love and physical tenderness after the example of the Lord's care for his eternal bride, for whom he filled heaven and earth with spiritual and physical joys. Moreover, the book of Proverbs proclaimed a good wife as "a graceful doe," whose husband will delight in her breasts and be "intoxicated" with her love. The imagery of the Bible not only allows but insists that sexual intercourse be a time of kisses and caresses, of passion and play alike. Perhaps this truth is why so many cultures refer to sexual intimacy as acts of *love* and call coitus *love-making*. People intuitively recognize that human sexuality is made to include tenderness and affection; it should not be reduced to the bare engineering of procreation.[9]

However, not everything a couple might do in bed is morally lawful. The word of God unequivocally states that a wife should not be approached during her monthly menstrual flow. In the book of Leviticus, it was decreed that to know a wife carnally during her menstrual flow was punishable by death, with the act condemned along with other serious perversions such as incest, adultery, bestiality, and homosexuality. In a previous passage of Leviticus, the laws read slightly differently. There, Moses ordered a man defiled by his wife's monthly flow to be considered ritually impure for a limited time.[10] What is to be made of this seeming contradiction? Is the prohibition against sleeping with a wife during her period an obsolete law of ritual purity, or is it a rightful moral command that remains binding today? Is the text contradictory or corrupted, as modernist scholars might argue? Did the rule change over time, or does it reflect internal disagreements among ancient Hebrews?

---

9. Proverbs 5:19 (ESV). Douglas Wilson wrote: "The liberated modern, with the furrowed brow of a frustrated technocrat, wants to talk about the various positions of sexual engineering, accompanied by charts, diagrams, and technical manuals—along with stern and graphic lectures to all of us repressed Puritans." Wilson also uses the food analogy for sexual intimacy. Douglas Wilson, *Reforming Marriage*, 107, 111.
10. Leviticus 18:19, 29; Leviticus 15:24.

Scripture does not include contradictions or errors, so we must resolve passages that, on the surface, appear inconsistent. In this instance, what Moses revealed is how intent determines moral responsibility (as with Roman law and modern jurisprudence, both of which distinguish murder from manslaughter by the intent of the criminal). Since the reproductive cycle of women can be unexpected and irregular, Moses made a concession to human ignorance: anyone who realized that his wife was menstruating only after the completion of their intimacy is to be given a slap on the hands for an unintentional ritual violation, whereas any man who deliberately approached his wife during the fullness of her flow was to be put to death. Why? Because the latter would have deliberately and defiantly sought his wife during her ritual separation (according to the law of Moses), prioritizing his passion over public religion. Such a man's sin was a blatant challenge to the Lord's laws of holiness.

The prophet Ezekiel confirmed this restriction against sexual intimacy during menstruation when he named among godly men those who refrain from sexual intercourse with menstruating wives, classifying them alongside those who spurn idols, remain maritally faithful, avoid oppression, feed the poor, judge fairly, and otherwise follow the decrees of the Lord. Ezekiel wrote how the righteous man does not "defile his neighbor's wife or approach a woman during her menstrual period" and "humbled her who was unclean in her menstrual impurity." Given clear revelations by Moses and Ezekiel, it is hard to see this as a matter of ritual, like the eating of pork or shaving a beard.[11] This restriction appears to be one of abiding moral concern. The prophecies of Ezekiel were in accord with the law of Moses, which commanded:

> You shall not approach a woman to uncover her nakedness while she is in her menstrual uncleanness... For everyone who does any of these abominations, the persons who do them shall be cut off from among their people. So keep my charge never to practice any of these abominable customs that were practiced before you, and never to make yourselves unclean by them: I am the LORD your God.[12]

---

11. Ezekiel 18:6 (NASB); Ezekiel 22:10 (NASB). Pierre Viret wrote: "Ezekiel, following Moses, also places [sex with a menstruating wife] alongside incest in the list that he made of the sins and atrocities of the inhabitants of Jerusalem." Viret, *Exposition*, vol. 2, 226.
12. Leviticus 18:19, 29–30 (ESV). Gratian declared Mosaic rituals of purity regarding menstruating women to be inoperative, but believed that the commandment against sexual intimacy with menstruating women remained in effect, writing: "Again, if the man asks the

Moses restrained sexual passion to remind believers that pleasure is not the measure of matrimonial morality. Something greater must govern the marital bed. Moral purity matters, and so do the laws of nature. This was made evident when Moses linked lawful intercourse to the natural rhythms and purposes of the human body. Just as the ears were not made to see nor the eyes to hear, menstruation was not made as a time for sexual intercourse. Certain cultures prohibit carnal relations according to the day, lunar month, or time of the year. In contrast, Moses did not restrict sexual conduct by the time of the day or the day of the year, but allowed the natural purposes of the body to determine what should (or should not) be done in the marriage bed.[13] Nor did he impose any arbitrary rule unrelated to sexual intimacy itself. To determine what is sexually lawful, one must decide how the bodies of male and female are most naturally joined together, for the ethics of sexual behavior flow from the nature of the body and the purposes of marriage. We should neither violate nature nor unnecessarily and unnaturally restrict it.[14]

The fact that sexual ethics are to be determined from the purposes of the body is why the practices of men like the Marquis de Sade must be rejected, despite the lack of explicit biblical commands to keep whips and chains from the bedroom. That infamous pervert provides believers with a lesson to learn, for he had so thoroughly separated pleasure from the function of the body (and Christian doctrine) that the only act that repulsed him was natural sexual intercourse with a woman. He permitted every other perversion—even confusing human intimacy with torture,

woman for the debt during the time of menstruation, the woman should refuse and explain the reason to him." He also wrote: "The sacred law inflicted death on a man who approached a menstruating woman." Gratian, *The Treatise on Laws*, 17–18 (Dist. 5:2).

13. During his readable and modest review of this subject, Clement of Alexandria observed: "Now, not every land is suited to the reception of seed, and, even if it were, not at the hands of the same farmer. Seed should not be sown on rocky ground or scattered everywhere, for it is the primary substance of generation and contains imbedded in itself the principle of nature. It is undeniably godless, then, to dishonor principles of nature by wasting them on unnatural resting places." Clement of Alexandria, *Christ the Educator*, trans. Simon P. Wood (Washington, D.C.: Catholic University Press, 1953), 164.

14. As examples of such improper restrictions, medieval Jewish commentators prohibited men from looking at the specifically female nakedness of their wives, and restricted sexual activity to night hours, lest the couple conceive a "morally illegitimate" child if one of them thought about another person heard outside their window during sex. This went beyond nature, conscience, and Scripture. See Yaakov Shapiro, *Sexuality and Jewish Law: In Search of a Balanced Approach in Torah, vol. 1: Halachic Positions: What Judaism Really Says about Passion in the Marital Bed, An Outline, Analysis and Candid Discussion*, Expanded Edition (Middletown, Delaware: Jonathan Shapiro, 2017), 23–24, 36, 47.

rape, and base acts beyond mention, let alone description, in a book written for public edification. When the Marquis de Sade cut himself off from the natural function of the body, he cut himself off from morality in a deliberately anti-Christian fashion, ignoring every tradition of Christian thought that limited the use of the body to what is natural. Until recently, no one allowed the flesh to be joined in every possible coupling, and acts that appear on television and movie screens were outlawed and anathematized. Medieval theologian Jean Gerson wrote:

> *[Every association [societas] and carnal union of man and woman outside the law of matrimony is forbidden under pain of mortal sin; and to assert the contrary is an error against faith. [The law against adultery] forbids—as much for those bound in matrimony as for those who are single—every erotic stimulation of the genitals in which the natural order imparted by nature is not served or the parts intended by nature for generation are not properly joined. And this sin is the more serious the further it departs from the natural order, whether for single persons or, which aggravates the sin, between those who are joined in matrimony.*[15]

Some pleasures find neither sanction nor prohibition either in Scripture or among Christian teachers, and there have been debates between believers regarding which sexual activities are unnatural acts. By what standard should the acts of the marital bed be measured? There are two key considerations. First, caresses and kisses should be regulated by the law of good conscience. The apostle Paul forbade believers from doing anything (he explicitly spoke of eating meat sacrificed to idols) that seems morally questionable or otherwise shameful. Continuing the theme of eating as an analogy for coitus, it may be argued that what the apostle Paul said of food equally applies to sexual relations when the apostle warned believers that the man is blessed who has "no reason to pass judgment on himself for what he approves" and anyone experiencing scruples should realize that "whatever does not proceed from faith is sin." These are good rules to apply to the bedroom; we should do only what seems pure and honest in our inmost being.[16]

---

15. Cited in Thomas N. Tentler, *Sin and Confession on the Eve of the Reformation* (Princeton, New Jersey: Princeton University Press, 1977), 187.
16. Romans 14:22–23 (ESV). For descriptions of medieval laws regarding various types of

We must, however, remember that the sinful conscience can be rendered spiritually deaf by participation in (and rationalization of) sinful and immoral acts which close the heart to reason and faith. It is not, therefore, enough to appeal to the conscience. Though no one is convicted of sin except through conscience, no conscience refuses and rebukes every sin. For that reason, believers must try to determine the purposes of marital sexuality as determined through the nature and purposes of the human body. In this way, the dullness and weakness of the conscience may be strengthened by something outside of the individual. Nevertheless, we must admit there can be sin on the beds of married couples, as Martin Luther declared when he rebuked "swine" who believed they are "permitted to do anything they please with their wives." Luther wrote against those who "practice shameful and execrable things with their wives in their bedroom."[17]

There will always be debates and disagreements regarding particular acts of marital intimacy. For instance, believers have been divided over the lawfulness of sexual enjoyment between a married couple when a woman is pregnant (though the law of Moses is silent on the subject), or how soon a man might approach his wife following childbirth. Different understandings of the purposes of human sexuality have led to varying opinions regarding that issue. Those who believe procreation is the sole justification for sexual conduct argue against practicing sex with a pregnant wife, while those who consider sexual intimacy within marriage as a means of establishing marital affection and restraining passion are more accepting of sexual activity in at least the early stages of pregnancy. Still, both those who are more restrictive and those who are less so remain bound by the law of love, not only between husband and wife, but also of husband and wife together for the good of their unborn child.

It was in this spirit of charitable restraint that Clement of Alexandria observed that no biblical patriarch *knew* his wife from the time that she was known to be pregnant until the end of breastfeeding, declaring that there is no place in Scripture where "one of the ancients approached a pregnant woman." Only after birth and weaning were marriage relations

non-fertile intimacy (i.e., sins against nature), see John T. Noonan, *Contraception: A History of Its Treatment by the Catholic Theologians and Canonists* (Cambridge: Belknap Press, 1986), 224.

17. Luther, "Lectures on Genesis (Chapters 26-30)," in *Luther's Works*, vol. 5, 37. Luther's mention of the bedroom brings up privacy, which may have been difficult in the past. See *Appendix 5: A Bed of One's Own?*

resumed between husband and wife. Clement reasoned (rightly or wrongly) from the spacing and ages of children born to biblical patriarchs. He noted that the father of Moses must have abstained not only during pregnancy, but through weaning, given the age gap between his children.[18] Similarly, Ambrose of Milan highlighted the reality that animals mate only to procreate and do not approach already pregnant beasts, chiding those who approach pregnant women that they should either "imitate cattle or fear God" by abstaining from such relations.[19] To justify sexual intimacy only on the grounds of procreation is to accept those strictures sometimes observed in the writings of church fathers and medieval clerics.

Early medieval penitential guides did not always take such a restrictive approach to intimacy during pregnancy. The *Penitential of Theodore* declared that a pregnant woman ought to "abstain from her husband for three months before the birth, and afterward in the time of purgation, that is, for forty days and nights."[20] This allowed sexual intimacy through the first six months of pregnancy, which is a significant concession, and prohibited it during the weeks following birth (as modern medicine also recommends). As for Protestant Reformers, most of them did not elaborate on the details of sexual matters while commenting on broader sexual prohibitions. Generally, this was because they commented on biblical passages, and no biblical passage explicitly raises the matter of sexual intimacy during pregnancy. Protestant Reformers also avoided immodest discussions from the pulpit (their written commentaries frequently were revisions of preached sermons) or structured their teachings to bolster public laws rather than to focus on intimate concerns previously resolved in the privacy of the confessional. Martin Luther wrote:

> *I will pass over in silence the matter of conjugal duty, the granting and withholding of it, since some filth-preachers have been shameless enough in this matter to rouse our disgust. Some of them designate special times for this, and exclude holy nights and women who*

---

18. In a world lacking powdered formula and pasteurized milk, a man who impregnated his wife soon after the birth placed the newborn at risk or required use of a wet nurse. Clement of Alexandria, "On Marriage," in Oulton and Chadwick, *Alexandrian Christianity*, 73.

19. Saint Ambrose of Milan, *Exposition of the Holy Gospel According to Saint Luke*, 39.

20. John T. McNeill and Helena M. Gamer, eds., *Medieval Handbooks of Penance: A Translation of the Principal Libri Poenitentiales* (New York: Columbia University Press, 1990), 208.

are pregnant. I will leave this as St. Paul left it when he said... "It is better to marry than to burn with passion." Although Christian married folk should not permit themselves to be governed by their bodies in the passion of lust, as Paul writes to the Thessalonians... each one must examine himself so that by his abstinence he does not expose himself to the danger of fornication and other sins.[21]

Despite disagreements about lesser matters such as the lawfulness of sexual activity during pregnancy, the Christian tradition has stood united against pure hedonism.[22] Catholics, Protestants, and Orthodox alike have insisted that sexual love not be confused with the pursuit of base pleasure. St. Maximus the Confessor, for example, taught that the man who desires "only sensual pleasure uses [sexual intimacy] wrongly."[23] Later Christians generally agreed, believing that the conjugal pleasures of marriage should be subordinated to the virtues of chastity, charity, and modesty: that some of the passions of fallen men and women remain illicit, even within the legitimacy of marriage. When the author of the book of Hebrews commanded believers to keep the marriage bed pure by spurning both adultery and sexual immorality, he appears to be placing restrictions on the use of the marriage bed, although he avoided lewd talk and detailed regulations in providing his instruction.[24]

In contrast to two millennia of church teachings, contemporary Christian authors have written books to diagram and catalog various sexual techniques and positions, teaching the techniques of physical love-making rather than the piety of biblical decision-making. As one example of this unfortunate reality, my wife and I received as wedding gifts two copies of one particular book, whose author began his work by noting that sexual intimacy was ordained to be "very good" in Eden. The author claimed couples are "totally free to do what pleases both of [them] in the privacy of [their] bedroom," and declared restrictions upon sexual intimacy to be little more than "inhibitions" and made no effort to address the broad range of spiritual and moral concerns that most believers have

---

21. Martin Luther, "Estate of Marriage (1522)," in *Luther's Works*, vol. 45, 35–36.
22. Many church codes have restricted coital positions, fearing some positions undermined male superiority and others resembled the loveless mating of beasts. Eve Levin has described Eastern Orthodox customs in such matters. Eve Levin, *Sex and Society in the World of the Orthodox Slavs, 900–1700*, 172–175.
23. Maximus, "Second Century on Love," in *The Philokalia*, vol. 2, ed. and trans. G. E. H. Palmer, Philip Sherrard, and Kallistos Ware (Boston: Faber and Faber Ltd., 1981), 67–68.
24. Hebrews 13:4 (ESV).

considered.[25] Nor did the author remind readers that human nature has fallen and been corrupted from the intrinsic goodness and innocence of Eden: that we now live far outside the paradise of Eden. It is difficult for me to assess this moral blindness as anything less than sin. It certainly stands in stark contrast to every major tradition of church teaching.[26]

More recent authors do the same. One recent book includes a chapter that sweeps away two millennia of Christian morality and commentary with insufficient discussion. Unlike Ed Wheat, its writers at least attempt to bring ethics to bear, although they misguide more than mentor, since their approach ("Is it lawful? Is it helpful? Is it enslaving?") gives an unwarranted appearance of theological insight. Beyond what Martin Luther would have chided as *filthy talk* in their book is the fact that they ignore two thousand years of Christian commentary, as if people born in the 1970s were the first ones to understand Scripture and sex alike. Mark and Grace Driscoll require an unmistakable biblical prohibition, almost at the level of the Ten Commandments, to accept any restriction of sexual activity, while justifying questionable practices on the flimsiest of textual grounds provided by a few modern Christian authors and an ungodly horde of social scientists.

While I appreciate how thoroughly the Driscolls apply the ethic of the sanctity of human life to their extensive discussion of birth control, I wish they had attempted the same for sexual activity within marriage. Instead, they dismiss Mosaic condemnations of sex during menstruation without sufficient review of pertinent biblical passages (or Jewish and Christian commentators), failing to discuss writings by ancient, medieval, and early modern believers. I should note that if pastoral writers attempting to provide guidance to Christ's flock are to be admonished, how much more must we chastise the many theologians and seminaries that have left these topics unstudied and untaught in the face of modern temptations and trials, thereby causing the errors of those busy tending

---

25. Ed Wheat described a plethora of positions and pleasures with clinical terminology: an approach similar to those of secular sexologists like Havelock Ellis, who distinguish sexual acts by individual taste rather than moral status or natural function. Ed Wheat, *Intended for Pleasure* (Old Tappan, New Jersey: Fleming H. Revell Company, 1977), 214.

26. Christian thinkers of the past were no more infallible than modern ones. Clement of Alexandria, for instance, believed that procreation is the primary justification for sexual intimacy, writing that "pleasure enjoyed for its own sake, even within the marriage bonds, is a sin and contrary both to law and to reason." Clement of Alexandria, *Christ the Educator*, 170. For more on Clement of Alexandria and sexual desire, see *Appendix 6: The Holy Desire of Clement of Alexandria*.

Christ's flock to occur. Such judgment should be particularly sharp for those scholars and churchmen who have refused to prophetically witness against contemporary sexual immorality because of their political loyalties, refusal to risk disfavor and persecution, or pursuit of lesser causes than confronting the world-spirit of our age.[27]

Modern believers must not adopt the ethics of modern sexologists and unbelievers. We dare not reflect the image of our corrupt generation but should return to the holiness that has marked Christians since the earliest days of our faith. We must understand that human nature is flawed and acknowledge that every man and woman will be overcome by their infidelities and impurities unless led to the straight path by the holiness and grace of God. We must not rationalize or legitimize every impulse inside us, but must repent our wrong (of which there is much in every single man and woman), confessing with one evangelical author how "fallen human nature enjoys perversion."[28] The marriage bed may be private, but it must be righteous before the Lord—for the Lord will judge and expose what he alone can see. While Christ forgives wayward sinners, he will expose all hypocrisy, defiance, and rebellion.

> *Pleasure is a consequence of honorable works; if they seek it properly, [men and women] are permitted to enjoy right and legitimate pleasure... Just as God did not give us eyes so that we may gaze at and grasp at pleasure, but rather so that we may see and thereby do what is necessary to live, so also we have received that part of the body called the genitals [to] generate offspring, as the very name teaches us. We must obey this divine law... Only right and honorable things should give pleasure, for these are more pleasing to the better people than wicked and ignoble things are to the worse.*[29]

---

27. Mark and Grace Driscoll, *Real Marriage: The Truth about Sex, Friendship, and Life Together* (Nashville, Tennessee: Thomas Nelson, 2022), 177–203.
28. Mary Pride, *The Way Home: Beyond Feminism, Back to Reality* (Fenton, Missouri: Home Life Books, 1985), 29.
29. Lactantius, "Divine Institutes," in *Marriage in the Early Church*, 73–74. I do not read into *Song of Solomon* different types of sexual activity (as is frequently done) for the following reasons. First, Hebrew poetry is not suited for interpretation by those unfamiliar with ancient literature. Second, this book was received into the biblical canon as an allegory of God's love for his people. Third, if we chide church fathers for allegorical flourishes, how much more should we chide modern writers who turn divine allegory into a sex manual.

32

TILL DEATH DO US PART

You shall not commit adultery... You shall not covet your neighbor's wife.[1]

MODERN LITERATURE IS replete with stories of otherwise honest men and women who are tempted to marital infidelity through no fault of their own. In many such accounts, a young woman is forced into a love-less marriage by her ambitious father. Subsequently, she finds herself attracted to a man of her choosing, who likewise cannot be happy unless he possesses a woman who is already committed to another man. The couple finds themselves forced to violate either the formalities of marriage or the integrity of their love. Because romantic love is the end and be-all of modern marriage, it is not particularly difficult to see what such authors are attempting to express: that codes of marital fidelity matter less than the right of couples to change partners in the name of love.

Art often does likewise. When one looks at nineteenth-century paint-ings of the story of Christ and the adulterous woman,[2] the portrait is one of a kindly, soft Jesus standing beside a sobbing woman of sad-faced beauty. Jesus gently reminds the woman to go and sin no more, having driven off the malicious moralists who harshly judged her an adulteress in

---

1. Exodus 20:14,17 (ESV).
2. John 8:3–11.

their thirst for blood. While it is clear from Scripture that Jesus showed little patience with the hypocritical men who wished to cast stones while the God of Israel (namely, himself) forgave the woman's sin, it is also true that Jesus Christ is the Old Testament God and has not changed his mind regarding the pernicious nature of adultery. Christ indeed forgave, but with the voice of God commanded the woman to stop sinning, though neither Scripture nor church tradition mentions how the woman subsequently lived. If the woman obeyed the word of our Lord, his command stands as the beginning of her salvation: a new life for a woman who had violated God's law and wronged her husband, whether he was a good man or bad. If she disobeyed the command of Christ to stop sinning (as with the Pharisees), the words of Jesus stand as eternal judgment against her.[3]

Scripture utterly condemns sexual infidelity, with adultery neither trivialized nor romanticized. The Bible portrays an unfaithful spouse as an "adulteress with her smooth words" who "forsakes the companion of her youth," ignoring the oath she took before God to be emotionally and sexually faithful to her husband. Nor does the Bible portray the motives for adultery as twists of fate, happenstance accidents, and unintended mistakes. Proverbs notes how the "lips of a forbidden woman drip honey, and her speech is smoother than oil," but she proves to be "bitter as wormwood" and "sharp as a two-edged sword."[4] These are images of treachery. No one accidentally commits adultery any more than anyone accidentally betrays her country or embezzles from his employer. Infidelity is a deliberate desertion of the promises, hopes, and obligations of marriage, and no rationalization can make it look good or deaden the pain that it causes to a betrayed spouse and children. In a very real sense, infidelity betrays love itself, violating a wedding oath freely taken before God and man. As G. K. Chesterton explained:

> *[Modern thinkers] appear to imagine that the ideal of constancy was a yoke mysteriously imposed on mankind by the devil, instead of being, as it is, a yoke consistently imposed by all lovers on themselves. It is the nature of love to bind itself, and the institution of*

---

3. Perhaps the Lord left this woman's ultimate choice hidden so that we can focus on our own need to *go and sin no more*. While a case can be made that Jesus's command to *sin no more* was an effective cause of repentance in the woman, I am not knowledgeable enough regarding theology to judge the matter.

4. Proverbs 2:16–17 (ESV); Proverbs 5:3–4 (ESV).

*marriage merely paid the average man the compliment of taking
him at his word.*[5]

I should note, however, that couples do not make their own rules of
marriage. In one of his sermons, Augustine of Hippo mentioned an incident that occurred fifty years earlier in the city of Antioch (circa 345
A.D.), which sheds light on who ultimately establishes the rules of
marriage. In that presumably true incident, the husband of a beautiful
woman was thrown into prison by a Roman prefect for public debt, then
threatened with execution if he did not repay the public treasury within a
set time, which the man lacked the funds to do. Soon, a wealthy citizen
approached the debtor's wife with an offer to pay the debt, a pound of
gold, if the woman would sleep with him for one night. The woman told
her husband of the offer, saying that she was "prepared to do this for him,
but only if he, the master by marriage of her body and to whom all
Chastity is owed, wished it to be done." The husband agreed for his wife
to spend one night with the rich man, considering her act not to be adulterous since "not lust but a great love for her husband demanded it." For
her part, the beautiful woman consented to the arrangement and gave
herself to the supposed benefactor.[6]

We see in this story a couple's misunderstanding that chastity is owed
only to each other: that a husband is the ultimate master of his wife's
body. Perhaps this is true in some human law, but it is not true in divine
law. Chastity is owed to the Lord, and couples are not free to suspend or
otherwise modify its unwavering demands for any reason, neither for
pleasure, procreation, nor protection of life itself. Sixteen centuries later,
it appears that the debtor's wife failed to appreciate this point, as well as
that the debtor failed to appreciate how the virtue and dignity of his wife
were of far greater importance than his own mortal life. Clearly, the
husband was not a man who trusted God in everything (as each of us is
called to do) and was also unwilling to pay the penalty for his profligate

---

5. G.K. Chesterton, "A Defense of Rash Vows," in *Brave New Family*, 51.
6. Augustine, *The Preaching of Augustine: Our Lord's Sermon on the Mount,* ed. Jaroslav
Pelikan, trans. Francine Carman (Philadelphia: Fortress Press, 1973), 55–57 (1:16:50). The
rest of the story is that the wealthy man enjoyed the woman for a night but paid his
promised fee with a bag filled with dirt instead of gold. The woman publicly protested this
deceit, causing the prefect to realize how he had created an intolerable situation through his
severity. In judgment of himself and the wealthy man, the prefect paid the husband's public
debt from his own gold, then awarded the woman the very property from which the rich
man had filled the bag of dirt. This seems to me to have been the justice of Solomon.

spending, risky investments, or restricted circumstances. If this account of adultery committed for the protection of a loved one from strict Roman justice is condemned (as it should be), it is even more difficult to justify a woman who allows her husband to take mistresses because she no longer desires sexual intimacy or a man who permits his wife to take a lover because he is unable to conceive children. The Lord's law allows no exceptions: God's holiness and love are utterly absolute.[7]

When couples promise to marry, they agree to devote themselves to each other for life, not just in the flesh, but from their hearts. Not only is consummated adultery sinful, but so is regard for a rival mate secreted in one's hidden desires. Moses commanded men not to covet their neighbor's wife, and Jesus warned his disciples not to inflame themselves with passion in their inner desires.[8] Though another person is better-looking, better-tempered, more affectionate, more fertile, more virtuous, brighter, wealthier, stronger, or more pious than one's spouse, the obligation to remain content with the husband or wife provided by God remains binding. Any degree of friendship or association that ignores accepted standards of public propriety and rightful marital jealousy (or whose hidden motives are flirtatious or faithless) is strictly forbidden. Not only do such relationships involve sexual temptation, but they also tempt dissatisfied mates to compare their spouses with romanticized ideals, breeding resentment and disappointment. I would also note that if husbands and wives are forbidden from desiring flesh-and-blood rivals to their given spouse, they are equally prohibited from cherishing some imaginary person who never has and never will exist—comparing an imperfect spouse to a compilation of the attractions and virtues (and none of the faults) found in real people. Nor can we draw our expectations from films, novels, romantic mirages, artificial intelligence, and social media.

The apostle Paul made clear that envious comparisons are unacceptable when he warned believers to fulfill the law of Christ by carrying each other's burdens, instructing each believer to "test his own work, and then his reason to boast will be in himself alone and not in his neighbor." Such

---

7. Augustine of Hippo preached: "Another question: if with his wife's permission (either because she is barren or because she does not wish to submit to intercourse) a man should take another woman to himself (not another man's wife, or one separated from her husband), can he do so without being guilty of fornication? [Such] a thought is not to be entertained, lest it seems that a woman too, when her husband permits, can do what everyone's sense prohibits." Augustine of Hippo, *The Preaching of St. Augustine*, 54–55.

8. Exodus 20:17 (ESV); Matthew 5:28 (ESV).

other-centered and sacrificial charity imitates our Savior, who gave up his life to glorify God and save sinful mankind. During an earlier epoch, King Solomon explained that men should be satisfied with and delighted in the wife given to them, the wife of their youth, for she is "a lovely deer, a graceful doe, [let] her breasts fill you at all times with delight; be intoxicated always in her love." This is divine wisdom and consistent with the command of Moses, which plainly warns men not to covet "your neighbor's wife [or] his female servant [or] anything that is your neighbor's."[9]

Solomon not only reminded men and women to love their spouses with delight and devotion but also warned against adultery in no uncertain terms during lengthy passages in the collection of his proverbs—with the book of Proverbs representing the abundance of divine wisdom given to Solomon beyond any other man and the warnings against adultery being set at the beginning of the book, as if to emphasize their importance in establishing a godly life and pious household. I would add, however, that Solomon's wisdom did not fall from the heavens like manna; it was learned as he meditated on the law of the Lord, as well as what had happened within his own family. Solomon would not have forgotten how he lost an infant brother when God rejected David's prayers to spare the newborn child (prayers rejected because of David's sin), nor how the Lord punished David through Solomon's half-brother Absalom: a judgment ordained by God against David for the latter's murder of a husband whose wife David had impregnated during an adulterous affair. In the family quarrels that followed David's sin, the king's children were divided against each other, with sexual assault, murder, and rebellion becoming the backdrop to Solomon's childhood, causing Solomon considerable political trouble at becoming king. Solomon understood what adultery does to a family and warned everyone against it, whether it risked political intrigues or private problems. Per his proverbial writings, men (and women) must keep from all sexual enticement, neither flirting with its temptations nor desiring its illicit pleasures. As for the man who sleeps with another man's wife, Solomon noted that "whoever touches her will not go unpunished."[10]

It is illustrative that the word *touches* is used here, just as in the book of Leviticus, for it is childishly pedantic to imagine that kissing, touching, and texting do not count as adultery, or that charges of infidelity require

9.   Galatians 6:4 (ESV); Proverbs 5:19 (ESV); Exodus 20:17 (ESV).
10.   Proverbs 5:1–23; Proverbs 6:20–7:27; 1 Kings 3:12; Proverbs 6:29 (NASB).

proof of sexual intercourse. Any type of sexual intimacy is adulterous, including kissing and caressing, and an aggrieved spouse can make judgments based on reasonable suspicion and moral probability. Spouses and public officials (church or state alike) can make determinations of guilt based on inappropriate behavior since there is little reason to expect honesty from anyone breaking sacred vows and thereafter trying to escape the consequences of their sin.[11] That is, an undeniable pattern of evasiveness and dishonesty need not be discounted, even if hard evidence seems insufficient to secure a conviction in an American jury trial. As for inappropriate physical intimacy which does not include completed sexual intercourse, we must note that a child who bites from a cookie is not considered innocent of stealing from the cookie jar because he nibbled the edges of a cookie or left behind one last bite.[12]

As a side note, I would also mention that marriage-ending adultery involves improper activity with a real human person. While some contemporary churches appear to allow divorce for the use of pornography, that sin does not seem to violate the person-to-person infidelity that the Bible calls adultery. What I mean is that Christians in ancient Gaul did not commit marriage-ending adultery by casting their eyes on the half-clothed sculpture of the *Vénus d'Arles* or by looking upon a revealing statue of Dionysus. Neither did believers in Pompeii commit marriage-ending adultery by lingering around the pornographic paintings on bedroom walls (paintings that survived the eruption of Mount Vesuvius) or by purchasing vases of Greek wine adorned with lascivious cartoons. That said, a modern spouse engaged in an ongoing, lewd chat stream with another real person may be lawfully divorced since such sin involves a personal relationship, even if physical intimacy was conducted from a distance. Would not a couple found naked in a hotel room stand guilty of infidelity, even if they never touched one another?

Regarding the contemporary problem of artificial intelligence and simulated persons, these would seem to pose the same moral problems as pornography. Computer projections are not real people and never will

---

11. Many Christian magistrates and church officers have allowed circumstantial evidence to establish infidelity. One medieval theologian permitted divorce "where the suspicion is so strong that after it is proven it would rightly seem that the fornication itself is proven, for example, if it was proven that they were alone together, naked, lying in the same bed, in a secret place and time suited for this." Raymond of Penyafort, *Summa on Marriage*, 81.

12. The Hebrew word translated carnal relations in Numbers 5:13 refers to seminal fluid, which suggests completed sexual intimacy is linked to the most serious offenses against marriage. Milgrom, *The JPS Torah Commentary: Numbers*, 37.

be. This is not to say their use is morally acceptable, for it is not. Even if the immoral use of computer images does not justify divorce on the grounds of adulterous acts with another living person, such behavior rightly faces scrutiny by church leaders and is offensive enough to require separation until it has been repented and purged. Biblical principles judge such behavior, in the very least, as spiritually unclean.

Moses warned against adultery and even ordered death as the rightful divine punishment for marital unfaithfulness. Unlike romantic novels and films, Scripture does not idealize adultery but portrays it with images of treachery, lust, and hatred. It is not that biblical writers are unsympathetic toward those caught up in loveless marriages, for the same book of Proverbs that condemned adultery declared an unloved wife to be one of the four unnatural relationships that cause the earth to quake (along with undeserved riches, prestige, and power). Proverbs also taught that it is better for a man to live on the roof of his house than inside with a quarrelsome wife.[13] From God's perfect perspective, love and marriage should go hand-in-hand. Still, while the unloved are treated sympathetically, nowhere does the Bible express sympathy for the adulteress or mitigate the punishment of the adulterer. One of David's wives, Abigail, was praised precisely because she reverently served her churlish husband, despite his stubborn folly. And while no human being has the right to put asunder what the Lord has joined in marriage, God himself struck Nabal dead and freed Abigail to wed a better man. The Lord takes marriage so seriously that he sometimes punishes not simply the unfaithful but also the unworthy (even as he calls husbands and wives to wait for his deliverance rather than to end marriage by their own hand).

Many people use the story of the woman taken in adultery to argue that the Christian attitude toward infidelity must be one of weak-hearted indulgence. This is a mistake. While it is true that repentance and forgiveness typically should be offered to an offending mate by the aggrieved spouse (just as God offers each of us a real opportunity to repent of our spiritual infidelity), it is not true that adultery ought to be left unpunished. The apostle John did not include this story in his gospel to suspend the punishment of adultery by secular and ecclesiastical authorities, and few theologians interpreted the text in that manner before the modern world. In the Sermon on the Mount, our Lord declared that the Mosaic law remains operative and authoritative, though New Testament

---

13. Proverbs 30:23; Proverbs 25:24.

writers did allow Gentile rulers freedom to determine their own laws and how to handle judicial punishments (albeit with the understanding that rulers will give account for ignoring or perverting God's moral law).[14]

The story of Jesus and the adulterous woman does not suspend the prohibition against or punishment of adultery. By including this account in Scripture, God revealed how justice must never proceed from private authority. Neither the religious teacher Jesus nor a tumultuous mob possessed the right to put to death a woman not given a fair hearing in a public court of law. Moses instituted judges to enforce the laws, not prophets and mobs. The story of the adulterous woman also reminds us that public authorities must never punish criminals for malicious motives, for the woman's accusers were less concerned about upholding God's commandment than trapping Jesus with his own words. They hoped to lure Jesus into denying the law of Moses (which punished adultery with death), challenging the rule of Rome (which did not allow Jewish subjects to carry out capital punishment), or blessing a murderous mob (which possessed no right to implement capital punishment). They were using God's law not to enforce righteousness but to destroy a political opponent—and a righteous one at that. Jesus not only eluded their trap but also taught a telling lesson about compassion in the process. He also demonstrated God's authority to forgive sin on earth (and the obligation of the repentant to forsake sin) when he told the adulterous woman that he did not condemn her, although she must immediately stop sinning.[15] Christ spoke at this moment as a compassionate prophet and teacher rather than as a public official. Henry Bullinger explained that: "Our Saviour did not come into the world to be a judge, but a savior; neither did he in any place usurp the right of the sword."[16]

Marital fidelity does have limits, as reflected in the fact that most marriage ceremonies include the clause *till death do us part*.[17] Marriage is

---

14. Matthew 5:17–20.
15. John 8:11.
16. Bullinger, *Decades: First and Second Decades*, 413. Pierre Viret noted that Christ's mercy did not suspend all temporal punishment for adultery, writing: "If Jesus Christ had come to serve in the office of a magistrate, He would have condemned her according to the Law. But, because this was not His office, He did what pertained to the commission which was laid on Him by His Father. He would have done no less with a murderer or some other criminal, as we can see by what He answered in another place to the man who asked Him to prescribe the share of his inheritance that he wished to have from his brother... Must we conclude that it is not lawful to divide inheritances because Jesus Christ did not wish to undertake this when it was requested of Him?" Viret, *Exposition*, 175.
17. The expression "tyll death us departe" (and the vows commonly used for American

binding only in this life, not the next. Not only is it not adulterous to remarry if a spouse dies, but God explicitly instructed believers to do so. Paul was insistent on this point, writing that a married woman is "released from the law concerning her husband" if the husband dies and advising younger widows (and widowers, by implication) to marry. Paul understood how complicated such marriages could be as they merged household resources among children and stepchildren, with ancient property considerations being far more complex than contemporary financial arrangements in a modern world of liquid assets and mobile wealth. Despite practical complications often found in the remarriages of widows and widowers, Paul considered such marriages to be the appropriate place for many to serve God and his church. When describing which widows should marry, Paul specifically called out those still able to conceive children, not exempting widows from the obligation to consider remarriage until they reached the age of sixty.[18]

The apostle Paul's words have been accepted in the Christian world. It has been the Hindu widow who was burned on her husband's funeral pyre to forestall remarriage, not the Christian one. The church father Tertullian, for example, once wrote that his wife's later marriage would not dishonor him (as many contemporary Romans would have insisted). Like Paul (and consistent with Jesus' words regarding the call to celibacy or marriage), Tertullian preferred the celibate life for himself in the event of his wife's death, and similarly advised his wife to follow his planned example if she were widowed due to the freedom that singleness provides in serving the Lord. However, also like the apostle Paul, Tertullian ultimately recognized that remarriage is morally permissible and beneficial. Tertullian observed that the benefit of celibacy for a widow comes not from loyalty to her deceased husband but from the same considerations that guide virgins toward celibacy or marriage: a sense of spiritual propriety and expediency. In the following passage addressed to his wife, Tertullian made clear that marriage is permitted after widowhood, even if he considers celibacy a better path:

> You will confer no benefit on me by [celibacy], other than the good
> you do for yourself. In any case, there is no promise of a restoration

---

weddings) seems to first appear in "The Fourme of Solempniacion of Matrimonye," in the *Book of Common Prayer* of 1559. See Mark Searle and Kenneth W. Stevenson, eds., *Documents of the Marriage Liturgy* (Collegeville, Minnesota: Liturgical Press, 1992), 219.
18. Romans 7:2–3 (NASB); 1 Timothy 5:9–11.

of marriage on the day of resurrection for Christians who have departed this life... Do not think that I have counseled you to remain a widow in order to reserve to myself the integrity of your body because I am afraid that someday I may suffer hardship.[19]

In the above passage, Tertullian acknowledged that his wife would not sin by remarriage, even if he judged it spiritually better for her to remain celibate after his death—a spiritual judgment aligned with the Roman custom of exalting women who married only a single man during their lifetime.[20] That noted, there were church fathers who doubted the legitimacy of remarriage after the death of a spouse and believed that women, in particular, should marry only once. Many subsequent churchmen likewise advised against remarriage, or even enforced rules prohibiting widows and widowers from remarriage.[21] Such restrictions ignored the passage in 1 Timothy advising younger widows to marry to live chaste and productive lives, and are examples of cultural accommodation in which believers subordinate biblical texts to a prevailing cultural ethos.[22] In a related manner, some Christian communities allowed remarriage, although requiring widows to wait a full year following a husband's death to do so (thereby ensuring that the parentage of any subsequent child remained undisputed since genetic tests did not exist and family property necessarily passed to a man's biological children). While their objective was laudable, the biological truth (known in the ancient world as much as today) is that a single menstrual cycle would have proven that such women were not pregnant by their deceased husbands. Perhaps the violation of privacy (in requiring such a test for grieving widows) seemed more onerous than imposing a legal delay for remarriage? [23]

---

19. Tertullian, "To his Wife," in *Marriage and Sexuality in Early Christianity*, 44–45.

20. Tertullian later took a sharper stand against remarriage. See the editor's comments in *Marriage and Sexuality in Early Christianity*, 43–44. P.J. Reynolds discusses the Roman ideal that widows not remarry, writing: "In Roman society, the *univira* (the woman who remained faithful to a single husband) represented the womanly ideal." P.J. Reynolds, *Marriage in the Western Church: The Christianization of Marriage during the Patristic and Early Medieval Periods* (Leiden: E.J. Brill, 1994), 174.

21. Athenagoras wrote: "For a second marriage is veiled adultery. The Scripture says, 'Whoever puts away his wife and marries another, commits adultery.' Thus a man is forbidden both to put away the wife whose virginity he has ended, and to marry again. He who severs himself from his first wife, even if she is dead, is an adulterer in disguise." Athenagoras, "A Plea," in *Early Christian Fathers*, 337.

22. 1 Timothy 5:15 (ESV).

23. Matthew Blasteres provided medieval Eastern Orthodox law: "The widowed woman is

It is interesting how Tertullian rejected the notion that a spouse's remarriage might prove eternally inexpedient in the next life. Accepting the very words of Jesus, Tertullian understood that mortal marriage ends at death and that human beings marry only for this life, not for eternity. Even we admit to this in our marriages when we swear marriage *till death do us part*. That common oath is not simply a matter of human law but reflects what Christ revealed of eternity. Certain Christian sects hold that earthly marriages continue into eternity, with heaven serving as the consummation of earthly passions and relationships, which was the error that Jesus refuted to his Jewish questioners (not simply rebuking their tone, but their assumption that mortal relationships are the basis for eternal ones). Similarly, Muslims view heaven as a time for God's servants to receive harems as their reward for earthly service.

Regarding such beliefs, Jesus reminded all of us that marriage is a feature of this temporal life that will be rendered obsolete in heaven, where presumably there is no longer a need for human reproduction and mortal marriage. No longer will mankind require the moral tutors of childbirth, childrearing, and matrimony, for our toddler-like stumbling toward eternal love will be far surpassed when men and women walk perfectly in the love of God himself. Human beings will be morally and spiritually mature, no longer needing such childish things as children to learn to love.[24] What is prophesied in marriage will become the reality of eternal life, and everyone counted worthy of Christ will enter into joy greater than marriage and parenthood. Scripture states quite plainly:

> *Jesus said to them, "The sons of this age marry and are given in marriage, but those who are considered worthy to attain to that age and to the resurrection from the dead neither marry nor are given in marriage, for they cannot die anymore, because they are equal to angels and are sons of God, being sons of the resurrection."*[25]

compelled to wait the mourning year because of the confusion of parentage, although this does not occur in the case of the husband." Patrick Demetrios Viscuso, *Sexuality, Marriage, and Celibacy in Byzantine Law: Selections from a Fourteenth-Century Encyclopedia of Canon Law and Theology—the Alphabetical Collection of Matthew Blasteres* (Brookline, Massachusetts: Holy Cross Orthodox Press, 2008), 90.
24. Early Protestants took the injunction for the widowed to remarry so seriously that one Protestant woman married several Reformers. The widowed Wibrandis Rosenblatt married Johannes Oecolampadius, Wolfgang Capito, and Martin Bucer. Roland Bainton, *Women of the Reformation in Germany and Italy* (Boston: Beacon Press, 1971), 79–96.
25. Luke 20:34–36 (ESV).

33

MORALLY MAKING A DIVORCE

When a man takes a wife and marries her, if then she finds no favor in his eyes because he has found some indecency in her, and he writes her a certificate of divorce and puts it in her hand and sends her out of his house. She departs out of his house and if she goes and becomes another man's wife. The latter man hates her and writes her a certificate of divorce and puts it in her hand and sends her out of his house, or if the latter man dies, who took her to be his wife, then her former husband, who sent her away, may not take her again to be his wife after she has been defiled, for that is an abomination before the LORD. And you shall not bring sin upon the land that the LORD your God is giving you for an inheritance.[1]

EARLIER, we saw that when Jesus was asked about divorce, he admonished the Jews (including his disciples) for their custom of easy divorce and explained that Moses permitted divorce only for the hardness of men's hearts rather than as an ideal or spiritually acceptable practice. Moses tolerated divorce only because there was little choice in a sinful world, just as the Lord today tolerates a world that turns its back on him, while calling us back to himself. It is crucial to recognize that Jesus does not contradict Moses, but bases his rebuke of easy divorce on the law of

---

1. Deuteronomy 24:1–4 (ESV).

Moses itself. Mosaic law explicitly sanctioned divorce only for indecency (i.e., sexual impropriety), which is what Jesus taught. Beyond that explicit justification, Old Testament law mitigated the reality of divorce without giving its blessing, as with its government of slavery and polygamy.[2] Adam set the pattern for marriage by marrying one woman long before his fallen descendants began to take several wives for themselves. And while Scripture never blesses polygamy, we can see how the Lord extended his grace to men like Abraham and David, who took multiple wives, and judged their children legitimate. The lesson to be learned is not that God condones such relationships, but that he forbears sin in matters of marriage, just as he does in other realms of life. The fact that Moses links divorce to *hatred* of a wife reveals God's hatred of divorce.

In ancient Israel, ending a marriage was like beginning one, only in reverse: a man sent a rejected wife from his house. With no papers to file with the state, such divorces could no more be legislated out of existence than living together could be ended today. For that reason, Moses limited the worst abuse of divorce: the corruption of marriage through adultery. By commanding that a certificate be given to a divorced wife, Moses ensured that temporarily estranged women did not remarry while their first marriages remained intact. Suitors were given an effective means of confirming whether such women were divorced (by requesting the divorce certificate issued by the former husband). Moreover, by forbidding men to return to wives who had taken a second husband, Moses prevented manipulation of divorce laws to permit temporary relationships to satisfy the desire for sex or money. No man would be able to convince (or coerce) his wife into granting him a temporary divorce so he could sleep with a neighbor, or lay hands on a widow's property, before returning to the mother of his children.[3]

Nor would an ordinary falling out between husband and wife lead to marriage-ending sexual trysts following hard words unratified by paperwork in the calm of the next day. Divorce was not to be allowed as an immediate reaction or quick response to the disputes that plague every

---

2. One author has observed: "Divorce first begins to appear as a biblical concept in passages that recognize it as a *fait accompli* over which God (through Moses) exercised a regulating function... God treated divorce in much the same way that He dealt with polygamy and concubinage." Jay E. Adams, *Divorce, and Remarriage in the Bible* (Grand Rapids, Michigan: Zondervan, 1980), 27, 68–69.

3. This is not a theoretical point. There are current Middle East customs that permit temporary marriage (called *Mut'ah*) in which couples *marry* for a few hours or several years.

marriage. Moses explicitly approved of divorce primarily to remedy fornication—a teaching that Jesus subsequently ratified when he revealed that
a man can divorce his wife only for sexual impurity, calling remarriage
(following an unlawful divorce) adultery and declaring that "everyone
who divorces his wife and marries another commits adultery, and he who
marries a woman divorced from her husband commits adultery." Jesus
stated that not every divorce under Jewish law was recognized by God,
and those who engage in marital or sexual relationships after an illegitimate divorce commit adultery. Moreover, the Holy Spirit placed this
restrictive approach to divorce in three of the four gospels.[4]

In like manner, the apostle Paul so forcefully prohibited divorce in 1
Corinthians 7 that he declared marriage to a pagan to remain binding.[5]
Still, the fact that neither man nor woman can lawfully leave marriage
except for adultery does not resolve what to do when a partner does
depart without biblical cause. To address that concern, Paul expanded on
Jesus's teaching, noting that a Christian should accept the inevitability of
divorce when a departing spouse refuses to reconcile. Both Roman law
and Jewish custom allowed men to divorce their wives, leaving the latter
with little legal recourse to enforce marital obligations.[6] In such circumstances, Paul instructed believers to consider themselves free from
marriage rather than to pretend to be married to a spouse who no longer
provides conjugal, material, and emotional support (and has departed).
However, this allowance was intended to cover abandonment and desertion rather than to facilitate legalistic hair-splitting focused on who first
filed a divorce petition. The apostle never excused divorce but accepted
the fact of an ended marriage. He wrote:

> *To the married I give this charge (not I, but the Lord): the wife*
> *should not separate from her husband (but if she does, she should*
> *remain unmarried or else be reconciled to her husband), and the*
> *husband should not divorce his wife. To the rest I say (I, not the*
> *Lord) that if any brother has a wife who is an unbeliever, and she*
> *consents to live with him, he should not divorce her. If any woman*
> *has a husband who is an unbeliever, and he consents to live with*
> *her, she should not divorce him. For the unbelieving husband is*

---

4. Luke 16:18 (ESV); Matthew 19:9 (ESV); Mark 10:11–12 (ESV).
5. 1 Corinthians 7:12–16 (ESV).
6. For a detailed treatment of Roman law, see P.J. Reynolds. *Marriage in the Western Church: The Christianization of Marriage during the Patristic and Early Medieval Periods.*

made holy because of his wife, and the unbelieving wife is made holy because of her husband. Otherwise your children would be unclean, but as it is, they are holy. But if the unbelieving partner separates, let it be so. In such cases the brother or sister is not enslaved. God has called you to peace. For how do you know, wife, whether you will save your husband? Or how do you know, husband, whether you will save your wife?[7]

Building on the words of Moses, Jesus, and Paul, most church leaders have concurred that there are times when divorce is not only permissible but necessary. For just one example, the Shepherd of Hermas, an early Christian writing, taught that a man sins if he "continues to live" with a wife who "persists in her adultery."[8] The relevance of this instruction to our world is simple: a spouse who remains unrepentant in their infidelity (meaning that they continue to commit adultery and refuse to repent) should be divorced rather than indulged. Not only is there no sin in such divorce, but there may be sin in tolerating persistent infidelity that brings unholiness into the household, thereby corrupting children still being raised and polluting the religion of Christ in the household. There can be harm to family and faith in indulgence of infidelity.

Protestant theologians during the Reformation taught the same, advocating forgiveness for repentant spouses, but opposing those spouses who refused to repent or strayed repeatedly. Because Protestant Reformers viewed infidelity as a danger both to individual households and the wider community, they advocated the end of marriages marred by continued infidelity. Representing this position, Puritan theologian William Perkins permitted divorce for adultery since "adultery is such a sin as doth quite break off [the] bond and covenant of marriage." Perkins allowed the aggrieved spouse freedom either to renew the marriage or make a divorce: a right he extended to man and woman alike, for there is "equal right and power in both parties." The Protestant law of divorce is that while it is better to redeem a compromised marriage, innocent spouses retain the right to divorce, being bound only by the duty to forgive from the heart (as God forgives the aggrieved spouse their sins).[9]

---

7. 1 Corinthians 7:10–16 (ESV).
8. Hermas, "Shepherd," in *Marriage in the Early Church*, 29–30.
9. William Perkins, "Christian Economy," in Larsen Klein, ed., *Daughters, Wives, and Widows*, 171. For examples of how John Calvin pressed for marital reconciliation even after adultery, see Robert M. Kingdon, *Adultery and Divorce in Calvin's Geneva*.

Immediately after instructing the Corinthian church regarding the requirement to reconcile if separated, the apostle Paul discussed marriage with unbelievers, writing that anyone married to an unbeliever must continue in their marriage if the unbeliever "consents to live" with the Christian spouse. Paul observed how the believing spouse makes the unbelieving spouse *holy* and enables their children to be raised *holy* rather than *unclean*. That is, the prayers and piety of a believer bring some measure of God's blessing to unbelievers around them. Still, Paul noted that an unbeliever who deserts a believing spouse should not be resisted. Christians are not bound to their marriage in such circumstances, for God has called us to live in peace. To state this plainly: Paul revealed that believers must not make disorderly and destructive efforts to save marriages beyond repair. When Paul explained how believers in such circumstances do not know whether they will *save* the unbeliever, he was not making a plea to maintain dead marriages in hope of conversion, but reminding listeners that pointless sacrifices are not promised success.[10]

Paul was reminding Christians that God is the one who brings faith, not husbands and wives. There is no point in throwing oneself against rocks to restore a marriage with an unbeliever who has departed. The Lord makes no promises either to the restoration of such marriages or the eventual salvation of such unbelievers. Rather, Paul called distressed spouses to implement Jesus's specific instruction not to resist evildoers. A believing spouse is not to resist an unbelieving husband or wife who has abandoned them to a difficult life. If an unbeliever slaps a believing spouse with an unfair and destructive divorce, the believer must make reasonable efforts to save their marriage. But if genuine efforts to restore the marriage fail, the believer is called to turn the other cheek in accepting an undeserved divorce rather than to desperately cling to a relationship that does not exist and has no promise of God's blessing. There is a time to trust God with one's future rather than to fight every injustice with personal rancor and judicial appeal.

The apostle permitted acceptance of divorce if an unbeliever had already abandoned the marriage (physically and emotionally), but demanded that the marriage remain intact if the unbelieving spouse is willing to continue the marriage to the Christian. Such acceptance of marriage between a believer and a non-believer requires further explanation, since it appears to fall outside the Lord's plan for holy households

---

10. 1 Corinthians 7:12–16 (ESV).

dedicated to raising children in his name. In the Old Testament, such unions of believer and unbelief were both forbidden and annulled during periods of religious renewal, such as when Ezra required the Israelites to send away their pagan wives and children (because the women were raising their children in paganism and spoke only their native pagan languages rather than the Hebrew of God's revelation).[11] In the New Testament, the apostles Paul and Peter presented a different model: believers were called to persuade their unbelieving spouses to accept the Christian faith through their piety and love. As previously noted, Paul blessed such spiritually one-sided unions as sanctifying and holy. As for Peter, he said that unbelieving husbands can be converted to faith "without a word by the conduct of their wives, when they see [the] respectful and pure conduct" of their wives. Women who live faithfully and gently with their husbands are apologists for the Christian faith, regardless of whether they are versed in philosophy and theology. According to the Holy Spirit of the Triune God, their humble service and quiet love speak louder than words.[12]

Why did God ordain a change from keeping away from unbelievers to living with them as practical apologetics? The difference between the Old and New Testament approaches is straightforward: the people of God in the Old Testament were called to be a holy nation before all nations, whereas the people of God in the New Testament are called to become a holy people from among all nations. The former is called to show God's law by living in separate holiness, whereas the latter is called to live this previously revealed righteousness among their communities— to make disciples across the earth. These different missions necessitated different rules when the Lord ordained the adoption of Gentile nations into his kingdom. Again, Israel was called to reveal the holiness of God (to be the place on earth where God resides), while the Christian church is chosen to establish the same holiness among all peoples of the world. And just as we can see how Israel was a peculiar nation, one with land and borders, we can see how the Lord has converted to himself ancient

---

11. George Williams documented the Anabaptist religious view of marriage (which permitted divorce from non-Anabaptists and drifted toward polygamy and sexual communism). Anabaptist repudiation of civil authority led to divorce due to religious dissimilarity, as Anabaptists did not necessarily recognize marriages made by civil law. See "Marriage in the Radical Reformation," in George Hunston Williams, *The Radical Reformation* (Philadelphia: Westminster Press, 1975), 505–517.

12. Nehemiah 13:23–24; 1 Peter 3:1–2 (ESV); Exodus 19:6; Matthew 28:18–20 (ESV).

Jews, Roman citizens, Germanic tribesmen, medieval Christendom, Reformation Europe, Victorian England, proselytized Africa, Prohibitionist America, and many other countries, peoples, and tribes. His kingdom is as real now as it was in the ancient world.[13]

Returning to the matter of divorce, when Moses noted that a bill of divorce should be given to an adulterous wife, he declared divorce to be a public matter (like marriage itself). Just as sexual intimacy or private pledges do not automatically create marriage except by law and common custom, so also marriage is not unmade by adultery, but by statute and common custom. If this were not true, the marriage of an undetected adulterer would be null and void, and his innocent wife would fornicate as she enjoyed sexual relations with her seemingly lawful husband, which would be absurd. Still, not every divorce decreed by the state is spiritually valid, and a divorce court judge who declares a marriage ended only ends legal obligations enforceable by the state. Secular judges have no standing to separate men and women bound in God's eyes; it was such judicial presumption that Jesus addressed when he declared *what God has joined together, let man not separate.* If God's word has not confirmed the right to a divorce, the marriage continues in God's sight, and subsequent sexual intimacy is adulterous. As for divorces that the Lord authorizes, the *Westminster Confession of Faith* summarized the biblical position by noting how "nothing but adultery, or such willful desertion as can [in] no way be remedied by the Church or civil magistrate" justifies divorce.[14]

Some might argue (as has been done) that divorce for adultery is no more than a broad generalization encompassing more serious sins and crimes as well. Many Christian states have permitted divorce for insanity, treason, abortion, murder, and other serious offenses. In this matter, Christian churches have sometimes struggled against temporal rulers regarding what is right, with churchmen upholding the traditions of faith

---

13. Wives have often been God's instruments to convert kingdoms through their husbands. Fourteenth-century author Christine de Pizan writes of the conversion of the Franks in the early sixth century: "As for the great benefits brought about by women regarding spiritual matters, just as I told you before, was it not Clotilda, daughter of the king of Burgundy and wife of the strong Clovis, king of France, who first brought and spread the faith of Jesus Christ to the kings and princes of France? [She] never stopped praying to God in tears, fasts, and devotions to enlighten the king's heart." Christine de Pizan, *The Book of the City of Ladies*, trans. Earl Jeffrey Richards (New York: Persea Books, 1982), 151 (II.35.1). For a modern account of Clotilda's life, see Jo Ann McNamara, John E. Halborg, and E. Gordon Whatley, *Sainted Women of the Dark Ages* (Durham, North Carolina: Duke University Press, 1992), 38-40.

14. John Leith, ed., *Creeds of the Churches* (Atlanta, Georgia: John Knox Press, 1982), 221.

and rulers seeking public order and political prudence.[15] We observed earlier (when discussing the impediment of criminality) how Protestant rulers of Reformation-era Zurich allowed divorce for murder and other such crimes, as well as how one historian noted that Reformation-era ecclesiastical leaders often authorized divorce when secular authorities failed to carry out capital punishment for serious crimes. What should a modern husband or wife do if their spouse commits a serious crime that leads to prison or even goes insane? To add a contemporary nuance, what if a wife procures an abortion in defiance of her husband, or a husband refuses to beget children with his wife?

The question we must address is straightforward. Given the explicit words of Jesus that divorce is permitted for the reason of fornication, do we have the authority to extend divorce for other causes or generalize from the particulars of Scripture to expand the justifications for divorce? If we lack such authority and reasoning, then we drift into the position of Jewish leaders condemned by Christ for violating the word of God for the sake of their traditions. We become like those men explicitly judged by the Lord for having made divorce available for unbiblical and selfish reasons (in today's world, these include such pretexts as finding oneself, outgrowing a partner, being attracted to someone else, or just growing restless and bored). The unfortunate reality of life is that marriage does not always bring the happiness couples desire. And even when couples find satisfaction in each other, children are born troubled, harvests fail, jobs are lost, bodies age, and minds lose their edge. As with life in general, marriage frequently brings a cross to be carried. Moreover, each of us is a sinner who would be tempted to grow dissatisfied with our spouse if it were allowed before God to divorce and remarry another.

For the sake of conscience and faith, we must remember that Jesus used the word *fornication* as a lawful reason for divorce, and he meant that word only—just as Moses allowed divorce if a man found *indecency* in his wife. Except for desertion (which is not a reason for divorce but a divorce already in effect) and crimes that imply desertion (such as when a spouse becomes a fugitive or receives a lengthy prison sentence), other sorrows are crosses to be endured rather than justifications for divorce. Each of us is called to lay down our lives for others in many ways, and

---

15. Per the *Alphabetic Collection* of Matthew Blasteres, the Orthodox Church prohibited men with chained, demon-possessed women from divorcing, though Emperor Leo allowed divorce with remarriage for men married to such insane wives. Patrick Demetrios Viscuso, *Sexuality, Marriage, and Celibacy in Byzantine Law*, 139.

those in what they believe to be mismatched marriages have ample opportunity to do so. As for those Reformed cities that authorized divorce beyond the cause of adultery, fellow Protestant Peter Martyr Vermigli openly challenged their reasoning:

> *They are bold to say, that Christ's meaning was to include therein all other evils, which are either equal to or more heinous than adultery. [Nevertheless], Christ excepted only the cause of adultery.*[16]

Our courts allow divorce for reasons Scripture does not approve: divorces that are not lawful before the Lord and should not be accepted as morally valid, meaning that those involved in them have no moral right to remarry. However, even if secular authorities restrict the flood of divorces currently allowed, the government still possesses the right to require couples to behave charitably toward one another. Christians traditionally have been quite clear that the laws of the state should be armed to prevent physical harm, emotional abuse, and lack of material support within marriage. Scripture nowhere sanctions the use of physical force by husbands against wives, and many church laws have judged violence and neglect to be clear violations of Christian marriage, with church leaders frequently at the forefront of protecting women from abusive husbands. Even the dreaded Puritans (as many imagine) held the bonds of matrimony with such affection that men might be fined by Puritan courts simply for calling their wives *servants*. Although insulted wives might dismiss such insults as of little account, church officials did not. I note, too, that a spouse has no right to require a believer to sin or to entangle the believer in an unbeliever's sin. A believing husband has the right and duty to speak for his lost child if his wife procures an abortion

---

16. Peter Martyr Vermigli, *Common Places*, vol. II.10–18 (Reformation Classic/Reformed Retrieval, Independently Published, 2021), 82–83. I have edited this text for clarity. Pierre Viret argued the same, writing: "There are some who go even further than Paul in this matter. For they conclude that if divorce can be justly granted for adultery, with how much greater reason can it be granted for even graver crimes such as murder, poisoning, treason, and other similar crimes? For, if either of the spouses is a murderer, a sorcerer, or is stained by some other egregious crime, it truly seems that the innocent spouse has good reason to demand a divorce. There are also churches which don't hesitate to grant it in such a case, and not only in such a case but also when the husband or wife absent themselves from the other for an extended period of time without mutual agreement and consent... But, on my part, I dare not grant such great license, even though they have very eye-catching reasoning. For there is much greater danger in giving a free rein in such a matter than there is in restraining it." Viret, *Exposition*, vol. 2, 192.

against his will, even if his wife threatens to leave him if he refuses his blessing to her sinful act or biblically brings her sin before church leadership. In like manner, a believing wife has every right to insist that any sexual intimacy with her husband may produce the child she desires and deserves before the Lord. Her husband will face the burden of celibacy if he continues to refuse her lawful desire for children.[17]

Even when suffering from poor marriages and difficult divorces, believers are commanded to imitate the love of Christ, who counsels us to turn the other cheek to those who despise us. We are to wait patiently for the Lord's deliverance, as Jesus did when he stood silent before Pilate and forgave his enemies from the cross. We must love those who wrong us and never give way to resentment, bitterness, greed, and lust—no matter how sorely we are provoked. Still, the Lord who calls us to turn the other cheek also orders governments to protect the innocent. For that reason, abused spouses should use the remedies the Lord provides if they wish to receive his assistance. It is no more prudent for a bruised wife to pray to God without calling the police than it would be for a starving woman to pray for food while refusing to harvest the vegetables in her garden. Public authorities have the duty to protect abused spouses, just like any other citizen. It is possible, by God's grace, for an abused woman to send her husband to jail while praying for him, hoping that he turns toward a better path. Following his release, further separation may be required.

As for temporary or continued separation without formal divorce (and the right to remarry), husbands or wives must remove themselves from households in which they face criminal complicity or physical danger.[18] Paul implied as much in 1 Corinthians 7, when he warned wives who were separated from their husbands either to reconcile or remain unmarried.[19] What I mean is that the Christian prohibition of

---

17. One prominent historian of Puritanism wrote: "When Daniel Eli told his wife Elizabeth that 'she was none of his wife, but his Servant,' his neighbors reported the incident to the authorities, and in spite of the abject Elizabeth's protest, 'that I have nothing Agenst my husband to Charge him with,' the Essex County Court fined him forty shillings." Edmund S. Morgan, *The Puritan Family: Religion and Domestic Relations in Seventeenth-Century New England* (New York: Harper and Row Publishers, 1966), 45.

18. The marriage of mobster Al Capone to his wife Mae is a good example of this problem. They married very young, yet Mae remained with her adulterous, criminal, and murderous husband until he died. While fear may have restricted her options, would she have been biblically free to divorce if Al Capone had been guilty only of crime and murder, but not adultery? She certainly would have been free to separate herself and her children from the danger and criminality of her husband's life.

19. 1 Corinthians 7:11 (ESV). A spouse who has been jailed for abuse will have to decide

unjustified divorce does not require couples to remain together in all situations, but restricts the right of either partner to break the bonds of marriage through remarriage rather than working through their problems.[20] Because extended separation can become an unjustified de facto divorce, the reasons for continued separation must remain biblical. Still, there are times when separation can help settle tempers, prevent criminal conduct, and avert financial ruin, and such separation was allowed even during the supposedly unenlightened Middle Ages. One medieval law code noted:

> *An honest woman should put up with and endure a great deal before leaving her husband's company. But in some cases it is no good for them to stay, and they should be excused for leaving if they do so; for when their husbands threaten to kill or wound them, or when they will not give them, through no fault of their own, anything to eat or drink or wear or when he willfully throws her out without her having committed any offense; or when she leaves because he keeps another woman with him in the house [or if her husband] keeps on committing some other kind of crime for which the punishment is death, or if she knows he is planning some other great crime or some great treachery and he will not abandon it for her sake: in all these cases a woman may be excused if she leaves her husband.*[21]

(after release) whether he (or she) prefers to repent of their criminal acts or to compound violence with desertion. If the abused spouse is unable to trust that the change is real, separation can continue, albeit without a right to remarry.

20. A modern theologian observed that separation is sometimes lawful, even when divorce and remarriage are not, writing: "Naturally, circumstances arise when separation may be advisable and even necessary. Christians, too, can be or become cruel and vindictive and physically or mentally dangerous. Yet even though the victim may have little or no control over events in this unhappy situation, there is no ground for the dissolution of the bond of marriage... the comparatively easy escape of remarriage, which rules out all hope of reconciliation on the basis of future repentance and renewal, runs contrary to the direction of the Spirit." Geoffrey Bromiley, *God and Marriage*, 69.

21. Akehurst, *Coutumes de Beauvaisis*, 593–598. Puritan William Perkins took a very hard stance against marital violence: "If the husband threateneth hurt, the believing wife may fly [i.e., flee] in this case, and it is all one, as if the unbelieving man should depart. For to depart from one and to drive away by threats are equipollent." William Perkins, "Christian Economy," in Larsen Klein, *Daughters, Wives, and Widows*, 169.

34

LAWFUL REMARRIAGE AFTER DIVORCE

So it follows that we should not say—if we wish to be wise with the wisdom of the Apostle—that the adulterous husband is to be reckoned as dead, and that, therefore, it is lawful for his wife to marry another. For, if the marital bond is dissolved by the adultery of either spouse, this perversity follows, that must be avoided, as I pointed out above, that the wife also would be freed from this bond by reason of her unchastity.[1]

Now, we come to the matter of remarriage after divorce. To begin with, the historical Protestant position is that Scripture allows divorce with remarriage for the wronged party in the event of adultery. While some early Christians may have permitted some remarriage following divorce, Augustine's cited passage represents the dominant ancient and medieval position in Latin Christendom, which restricted all remarriage following divorce, regardless of the circumstances. However, despite disagreements with each other, both Protestant and Catholic theologians of the past would have confronted modern churches that allow nearly everyone to divorce and marry at will (contemporary Roman Catholicism tacitly

---

1. Augustine, "On Adulterous Marriages" in *Saint Augustine: Treatises on Marriage and Other Subjects*, ed. Roy J. Deferrari (Washington, D.C.: The Catholic University of America Press, 1955), 56, 106.

permits couples to divorce and remarry via state law with minimal church sanction in what amounts to de facto toleration). A man may have cheated on seven successive spouses, yet he remains free to remarry time and again in the eyes of the modern state—and most churches, too. Despite their disagreements, Augustine and many early Christian leaders would have agreed that the guilty party in such divorces should not remarry, and most traditional Christians would have sided with them.

It is impossible to give a detailed treatment of remarriage after divorce in a few pages, and I do not want to become bogged down in what is probably the thorniest exegetical, historical, and pastoral concern regarding Christian marriage (since this is just one element of a much broader Christian consensus regarding household ethics). As previously noted, Scripture permits divorce for adultery and desertion, at least as far as most Protestants understand the relevant passages of Scripture (best summarized in a document like the *Westminster Confession of Faith*). Such a standard makes clear that many modern divorces are morally invalid, and the Lord has not dissolved the bonds of marriage for many couples who consider themselves divorced. How can believers deal with such matters in their homes, churches, and communities? The answer to this question is not straightforward, as it raises a host of issues that intersect with faith and holiness, as well as forgiveness and repentance. One matter, however, is clear enough: time alone, whether ten days or twenty years, does not unmake a valid marriage. It is also evident that the reality of God's grace and abundant forgiveness does not mean that the consequences of wrongful behavior are to be ignored, eradicated, and dismissed. These two perspectives enable us to navigate some of the complex issues associated with remarriage after divorce.

To begin with, it is best to discuss what is most plain. If a biblically unauthorized divorce has occurred, every effort must be made to restore that marriage (assuming both husband and wife remain single). As previously noted, Paul explicitly taught that a wife "should not separate from her husband," but if she has done so, "she should remain unmarried or else be reconciled to her husband." Paul presented the same rule for husbands: no matter how difficult material circumstances or sexual temptation may be in such cases, remarriage to another person is not permitted. Every effort must be made to salvage the original relationship, and patience is demanded in doing so. Even celibacy and sexual frustration must be endured when necessary, for marriage is spiritually more critical than the gratification of the sexual impulse. Moreover, charity matters even more than chastity, for (as Paul says of the virtues) "the greatest of these is love." In a sense, there is no need for marriage to be restored in cases of unlawful divorce since the bonds of marriage never really ended. Though such husbands and wives live apart, they remain married before the Lord. Did not Jesus declare what "God has joined together, let not man separate." For separated couples, marriage vows are not necessary to restore their union, even if paperwork might be required to regularize their union in the eyes of the state and their insurance provider.[2]

This stands true as long as both partners have merely separated and not indulged in a subsequent sexual liaison or remarried. If one of the pair has enjoyed sexual intimacy without the benefit of marriage, the case should be treated as adultery, for that is what it has become. The guiltless spouse has the right to repudiate the marriage for the sake of adultery, although any guiltless party in such circumstances should demonstrate more than the ordinary willingness to forgive if sustained denial of conjugal rights tempted the separated spouse to sin. I should add that while separation sometimes must occur in a fallen world to prevent violence and other abuses, no believer should manipulate separation to intentionally tempt an undesired mate to commit adultery, thereby providing a pretext for divorce with the right to remarry. No one should deliberately place their spouse in a position to be overwhelmed by sexual temptation to allow themselves the freedom to take another spouse. The Lord knows the hidden desires of the heart, and Jesus taught how it is better for a tempter to be cast into the sea with a stone tied to his neck than to lead another person into sin. God will not be mocked, and such manipulation will be exposed in the next world—and often in this one.[3] As for a guilty partner who has brought about a separation through wrongdoing, that person is responsible for their own temptations.

Simple divorce without consequent sexual sin should be reconciled whenever possible, and unlawful divorce followed by extramarital sexual relationships should be treated as adultery, just like an adulterous act during marriage (which sometimes is forgiven and sometimes leads to divorce). But what is to be done if an additional step has been taken: if one or both of the original pair has remarried? At that point, it is not only inconvenient to restore the original union but morally unlawful to do so. The text of Deuteronomy 24 reveals that the Lord forbids a spouse

2. 1 Corinthians 7:10–11 (ESV); 1 Corinthians 13:13 (ESV); Matthew 19:6 (ESV).
3. Mark 9:42.

from returning to a former mate after either of them has remarried. Moses declared such an act to be "an abomination before the LORD." Such couples are explicitly forbidden to remarry, whether after another divorce or the death of the second mate. Even if the couple was wrongly divorced in the first place, they are forbidden to hold marriage in such contempt as to return to each other after marrying someone else. Why? Probably because of the confusion that such reunions would bring. How would children ever learn to treat marriage as a holy thing if their parents were using it as a carousel? How would the world understand the holiness of the believing life? How would marriage represent God's love?[4]

Medieval Roman Catholic (and some later Protestant) law frequently violated Scripture at this point, where those traditions annulled what they considered adulterous marriages and required remarried couples to return to their marriage, if there was a wrongful annulment, divorce, or declaration of death.[5] This attempt to enforce strict monogamy appears to be a clear violation of the law of Moses, which explicitly stated that a man whose wife has lost his favor should provide a "certificate of divorce" when he sends the woman away. Moses continued that if a subsequent husband divorced the woman (or died and left her free to remarry as a widow), "her former husband, who sent her away, may not take her again to be his wife, after she has been defiled, for that is an abomination before the LORD." Based on this clear passage from Moses, a woman (or man) who has been divorced may not return to their spouse after any subsequent remarriage. If they have only lived with another person or engaged in wrongful sexual intimacy outside marriage, it seems that their sin is to be treated like adultery (with greater guilt and fewer restrictions), but if marriage vows have been made, obligations become absolute and unconditional. There is to be no return to the first marriage under any circumstances.[6]

---

4. Deuteronomy 24:1–4 (ESV).
5. Medieval theologian Raymond of Penyafort wrote of marriages annulled when men proved unable to consummate the union: "Therefore, when divorce is proclaimed by reason of [male] frigidity permission is not granted the man to marry another and if he should marry, the second marriage is to be separated and the first restored since it seems the Church was deceived. It is the same if there is separation on account of the woman's constriction, if she married another." Raymond also wrote of men whose wives remarried in a mistaken belief her husband was dead, noting that first husbands are "bound to take her back notwithstanding such adultery unless she remained knowingly with the second husband when the first came back." Raymond of Penyafort, *Summa*, 66, 81.
6. Deuteronomy 24:1–4 (ESV).

While previous marriages cannot be restored, are illicit spouses permitted to keep what they have wrongly taken? While it is clear that a man cannot return to his first wife if he has wrongly divorced his wife and remarried, what of his second wife? Can he keep her as a lawful wife, or must their marriage be dissolved as adulterous once the man comes to understand his sin? Robbers, after all, are not allowed to keep stolen goods after confessing to a crime but must return stolen money and jewels. Nor are embezzlers permitted to retain stolen funds. Moreover, our Lord commended the corrupt, yet repentant, tax collector Zacchaeus primarily because the latter repaid his ill-gotten gains fourfold upon his conversion. Is it required for a man to return stolen money, but permissible to keep a stolen wife? Do the words of John the Baptist given to Herod regarding the monarch's incestuous marriage ("It is not lawful for you to have her") apply in these circumstances? Would not repentance for Herod have meant repudiation of his ongoing marriage to the wife of his living brother, regardless of the laws of his kingdom? As for Herodias, she would have been in a difficult situation since biblical law did not allow a divorced and remarried woman to return to her first husband, and it would have been dangerous for the queen to marry anyone outside the royal family. Perhaps recognition of what biblical obedience meant in her circumstances (seclusion and celibacy) is why she conspired to murder John the Baptist?[7]

I do not claim certainty, but it seems acceptable to keep such a spouse for several reasons. First, it must be remembered that wrongful remarriage is more like murder than theft—and spilled blood cannot be restored, at least not in this life. Second, it is doubtful that divorce in such circumstances would teach the penitent anything about the virtues of loyalty and fidelity. However, the strongest argument for permitting an illicitly married couple to continue in wedlock is that even Moses and Paul seem to make that concession. Moses allowed lawful remarriage only after a spouse's infidelity, but nowhere commanded the Israelites to annul (or punish) all wrongful remarriages as adultery. All he insisted on was that priests not marry divorced women. In like manner, Paul demanded that polygamists and the adulterously married be denied positions as church elders and kept such women off the welfare rolls of pious widows,[8] but nowhere ordered illicit unions to be dissolved (both Jewish

---

7. Luke 19:8–9; Matthew 14:4 (NASB).
8. 1 Timothy 3:2; 1 Timothy 5:9.

and Roman law permitted biblically invalid remarriages following divorce, so such instances surely existed among believers). Certainly, of all men, Paul and Moses would have made the duty to dissolve a marriage clear if necessary; they were not men to mince words and were inspired by the Spirit of God to reveal the fullness of divine truth. Unlike incestuous and gay marriages, which are never morally valid (and therefore must be dissolved at repentance), wrongful divorce and remarriage bring together couples who might have rightly married had they not already been married. This is not to deny temporal government its right to impose secular punishments or churches the authority to mandate reasonable sanctions against adultery.[9]

The Bible seems clear about the following: broken marriages should be reconciled if at all possible, but no one may return to an earlier spouse after either party has remarried following their divorce. Nor should *adulterous remarriages* (as they have been called) necessarily be annulled because of their initial taint.[10] Paul and Moses penalized such marriages but did not altogether eradicate them. Whether such prohibitions extend to common-law marriage or extended cohabitation seems uncertain. This leaves one last situation: if an innocent partner has remarried following a divorce, does the unfaithful mate who caused the divorce through adultery possess the right to remarry after the aggrieved party has done so (or if the aggrieved party refuses over an extended period to reconcile or remarry)? One author used this very point to deny the right of either party to remarry, noting that either the marriage has been dissolved or it has not, writing: "If indeed the 'innocent party' is free to remarry, this can only be because the original marriage bond has been dissolved." For David Engelsma (and others who restrict remarriage after divorce),

---

9. Marital sin is not singled out because it is worse than all others, but because the ongoing association frames such marriages in some sense as *adulterous*.

10. Phillip L. Reynolds observed: "One should distinguish here between two aspects of the normative Western position that are sometimes confused. They are certainly closely related but they are distinct nonetheless. One aspect is the prohibition of remarriages in all circumstances: not only the wife but also the husband must remain "unmarried" after divorce, and this even after licit divorce on the ground of adultery. The other is the doctrine that remarriage while one's spouse is alive is not only forbidden but invalid. In other words, it is not marriage at all, but adultery in a strict and egalitarian sense. Since liceity and validity are not the same, the crucial question is what the person who had been excommunicated for having remarried had to do to be received back into the Church. It seems to me unlikely that this other aspect of the normative Western position (namely, the annulment of remarriage) prevailed in any province of the church before the late fourth century." Phillip L. Reynolds, *Marriage in the Western Church: The Christianization of Marriage*, 177.

neither the guilty nor the innocent party can remarry since the bonds of marriage continue until the death of a spouse.[11] In contrast, Protestant theologian Charles Hodge represented traditional church law in allowing the innocent to marry while inflicting a penalty upon the guilty:

> *It has been earnestly objected to the doctrine that divorce dissolves that marriage bond, that both parties, the guilty as well as the innocent become free, and either may contract a new marriage... But it is to be remembered, that adultery is a crime in the sight of man as well as in the sight of God, and as such it ought to be punished. Under the old dispensation it was punished with death; under the new, it may be punished by imprisonment, or by prohibition of any future marriage.[12]*

For Charles Hodge, the end of a marriage for adultery allows divorce for the aggrieved party, but temporal and spiritual penalties might still be imposed on the guilty, including loss of the right to remarry. Whether the church can and should impose sanctions beyond those of the temporal authorities has been a point of contention between churchmen and secular powers for nearly two thousand years, and I will not resolve it here. But when remarriage has been allowed, the betrayed partner must be protected in every instance, even at the expense of the unfaithful husband or wife. Protestant Reformer Pierre Viret hoped for reconciliation in such circumstances, yet pointed out that because it was Jesus Christ who gave the innocent the right to divorce, no one can deny that right. Viret judged that no one (neither church nor state officials) can rescind the right to divorce, "which is granted by Jesus Christ in such a case." And while Viret advised the wronged partner not to remarry too quickly (hoping that reconciliation might sometimes occur), this guidance was not to advantage the adulterer, against whom Viret thought more serious penalties should be used, as well as additional deliberation in permitting subsequent remarriage.[13]

---

11. David Engelsma, *Better to Marry* (Grand Rapids, Michigan: Reformed Free Publishing Association, 1993), 76.

12. Charles Hodge, *Systematic Theology*, vol. 3, 393.

13. Pierre Viret wrote: "Concerning the guilty, it's very reasonable to use a greater severity against them and, if they are permitted to remarry, this shouldn't be done quickly or easily, lest many seek an opportunity for divorce because of this fact so that they can enjoy this liberty." Viret, *Exposition*, vol. 2, 196–197.

As noted, many early Christian church leaders did not permit remarriage following divorce. Still, Christian Roman emperors who lived before and after Augustine disagreed, passing laws allowing remarriage following divorce as a matter of public necessity.[14] Sixteenth-century Protestant Reformers likewise were divided, with some Protestant states simply making the point moot by exiling the guilty party from their jurisdiction, leaving the theological issue unresolved while achieving a practical solution that restored a measure of peace to now-divided households. Reformation scholar Robert Kingdon said of Protestant practices that there was "reluctance among Protestants of the [Reformation] period to permit a guilty party to marry again." Kingdon also observed that there was a "rather strong general rule that marriage to the person with whom adultery had been committed would not be permitted." Dr. Kingdon did write that the Franco-Swiss city of Neuchâtel allowed the innocent to remarry six months after divorce and the guilty to petition to marry after a year (if they had lived chastely), while Calvin's Geneva denied all petitions of women guilty of adultery to remarry, though "it did not reject the legality of a marriage such a woman contracted elsewhere."[15]

When used, banishment was a simple, if somewhat harsh, solution. I should note that larger countries, such as Scotland, did not have the luxury of such an approach, as the laws of their churches and states covered a much broader geographical territory than a comparatively small Swiss or German city-state. Scottish Reformer John Knox, who was by no means a moral compromiser, believed that the "guilty offender may be remarried after reconciliation" with the church if that man or woman "cannot remain continent."[16] This was a definite break from the medieval Augustinian position, which held that no remarriage was permitted after

---

14. Jesuit scholar Theodore Mackin commented on Justinian's allowance of some remarriage following divorce: "Perhaps Justinian did what many other Christians did: he took to be just as authentic as any of the Gospel texts on divorce and remarriage the exceptive clause in Matthew 5:32 and Matthew 19:9—'But I say to you, whoever dismisses his wife, except in the case of her *porneia,* and marriages another, commits adultery.' And trusting the authenticity of the phrase, he worked a logical excursus from it as follows: Jesus never meant that there are no causes warranting a man's dismissing his wife. Her unchastity he himself says is such a cause; and there are other delinquencies in marriage as grievous as unchastity, and some of them worse. Therefore by the rule of equivalence there must be other causes warranting dismissal. And if this dismissal is available to husbands, then by the same law of equivalence and in virtue of fairness, it ought also to be available to wives." Theodore Mackin, S.J., *Divorce and Remarriage* (New York: Paulist Press, 1984), 108–109.
15. Kingdon, *Adultery and Divorce,* 89.
16. Knox, *Works,* vol. 2, 249.

divorce, as Knox conflated Paul's injunction to maintain chastity through marriage with the fact that a dissolved marriage is ended for both parties. Knox might ask, "How can one spouse be married but not the other?" Yet, as compelling (and convenient) as this approach is, the explicit words of Jesus must be heeded, regardless of whether they fit into our doctrinal confessions—and John Knox perhaps went beyond those words.

We must never forget how Jesus taught that men should neither divorce their wives, except for marital infidelity, nor marry any woman so divorced.[17] While Scripture does not explicitly command annulment of all such marriages, Christ plainly stated that marrying a woman wrongly divorced is an act of adultery—similar to engaging in an extramarital affair. The matter must be taken seriously in a modern world where even orthodox theologians may be tempted to excuse the many divorces in their families, churches, and communities. But we must start with the words of our Lord that many of the divorces among the Jews (who likely divorced and remarried far less than we do) were unlawful before God.[18]

It is undoubtedly true that Jesus forbade at least some remarriage after divorce. His words were (and remain) plain that those who marry a divorced woman themselves commit adultery and cause the woman to commit adultery, just as with an extramarital affair. For Christ, unlawful remarriage after divorce is as culpable as an adulterous affair during marriage. In the book of Matthew, Jesus allowed lawful divorce (the Jewish audience would have presumed this to include the right to remarry) for adultery, but otherwise made clear that whoever divorces and remarries or marries someone unlawfully divorced commits adultery. While dealing with the aftermath of affairs and immoral marriages sometimes is not perfectly clear, no one should miss the main point that many modern divorces are unauthorized before the Lord, and those involved in them are called by the grace of God to return to repent for the sin of adultery.

However, there remains the problem of unauthorized remarriages (perhaps a man married a woman divorced without biblical justification,

---

17. Matthew 5:31–32 (ESV).

18. Biblical commentators have struggled to explain God's patience with the polygamy of Abraham, David, and other early fathers of the faith. While I do not have answers, I believe whatever answer exists is similar to why the Lord tolerates many wrongful remarriages after divorce today, sometimes blessing men and women who sinned in marrying. As with the woman taken in adultery (John 8:1–11) or David's adulterous affair with Bathsheba, Christ forgives sins on earth (as he does for each of us). Those of us trying to systematize Scripture must remember that the Lord is not beholden to our interpretations and explanations.

or an adulterous couple divorced their betrayed spouses and remarried each other). While there have been disagreements among believers over these, most Christian churches have been unafraid to uphold the Lord's laws by means of penances, annulments, and refusal of church blessings (not just of the remarriage itself, but by disallowing communion and public church rites for the sinner who remains in defiance of God). This is where a crucial New Testament teaching comes to bear: the words of Jesus to Peter that what the Lord's church binds and looses on earth is also bound and loosed in heaven, as well as Paul's reminder that believers someday will judge angels and therefore should also judge matters "pertaining to this life?"[19]

Based on this teaching, Christian churches must seek, through God's Spirit, to uphold God's law by using the written word of the Lord as their rule of faith. While a review of how other believers have understood Scripture is critical (since the Lord's Spirit is given to all generations rather than to one denomination or tradition, let alone to a single generation, congregation, or individual), identifying God's will is not to be based on "traditions, councils, and decrees." This is because, as Protestant Reformer Pierre Viret observed, no one can "prove to us by clear testimonies that those who are the authors of the tradition and decrees which we reject were inspired by the Holy Spirit, as we are certain that Paul was and that he said nothing except by [God]."[20] Viret rightly observed that while God works among believers through the ages, the testimony of fallible men, no matter how valuable their opinions, does not outweigh infallible and inerrant Scripture. Nonetheless, Scripture reveals that the Lord works through the weak and sinful vessels that each faithful member of his church remains, just as he previously worked through the fallible and limited judges appointed by Moses to implement divine law.

In that spirit, it appears that our Lord providentially established a Christian core in Western civilization when he led his churches to prohibit polygamy, challenge double standards of sexual morality,

---

19. Matthew 5:31-32 (ESV); Matthew 16:19; 1 Corinthians 6:3 (NASB).

20. Viret, *Exposition*, vol. 2, 191–192; Gratian wrote: "Do not treat my writings as if they were the canonical Scriptures. When you find something you did not believe in the latter, believe it without hesitation; in the former, do not take as fixed what you did not think to be certain unless you know it to be certain." Gratian, *Treatise on Laws*, 29 (Dist. 9:1:3). Just as church fathers, medieval theologians, and Protestant reformers made errors in many matters, so do believers of our era. But when I compare the sexual and marital purity of previous generations to what I have seen during my lifetime, I remain convinced that the fruit of God's Spirit is more evident in past generations than in our era).

proscribe abortion and infanticide, and otherwise bring a measure of holiness and humanity into the household: compassion and morality that did not always flourish among ancient barbarians and pagan Romans. But we must not stop with doctrinal confessions since the Lord gave his holy laws to rule and redeem us in real life. For that reason, we must not discuss these matters as if they were academic exercises, religious history, or political polemics, but should confess that the Spirit of Christ is working among us to redeem our lives for God. The law of Moses was at the heart of the people of Israel, but it did not exist as an abstraction— only as the living work of God leading his people to righteousness.

What I mean is this: when the apostle Paul learned that a church member had married the man's stepmother, he did not dispassionately detail doctrinal error, but handed the man's flesh (the body once joined in unholy union with the wife of the man's father) to Satan for destruction. He did not simply publish a commentary on Moses or consult with Peter. He did not even write an essay or a book, nor did he preach a sermon or appeal to the elders of the churches in Jerusalem. Instead, Paul acted decisively to cleanse God's church from what seems to have been the *sin leading to death* mentioned by the apostle John. In the same manner, we must boldly uphold the Lord's holy law amidst the unholy couplings of our generation. While I cannot resolve every complicated issue in this short book, the Lord is always with his people. He will lead them to righteousness as they seek his will in true piety, heartfelt obedience, and humble study of his holy Scriptures. In this promise, many difficult questions may be resolved.[21]

> *It is actually reported that there is immorality among you, and of a kind that is not tolerated even among pagans, for a man has his father's wife. And you are arrogant! Ought you not rather to mourn? Let him who has done this be removed from among you... When you are assembled in the name of the Lord Jesus and my spirit is present, with the power of our Lord Jesus, you are to deliver this man to Satan for the destruction of the flesh, so that his spirit may be saved in the day of the Lord.*[22]

---

21. 1 John 5:16–17 (ESV). For additional thoughts on remarriage after divorce, see *Appendix 7: Reflections about Divorce and Remarriage.*
22. 1 Corinthians 5:1–5 (ESV).

35

THE PURPOSES OF PROCREATION

Judah said to Onan, "Go in to your brother's wife and perform the duty of a brother-in-law to her, and raise up offspring for your brother." But Onan knew that the offspring would not be his. So whenever he went in to his brother's wife he would waste the semen on the ground, so as not to give offspring to his brother. And what he did was wicked in the sight of the LORD, and [God] put him to death. [1]

THE STORY of Onan shows us that the ancients knew how to avoid begetting children. Human beings have always figured out means of contraception, though some methods have required limitation of coitus itself. [2] Motives for doing so have ranged from pure lust to apparent charity. For instance, before the invention of pasteurization, women sometimes avoided pregnancy while nursing a newborn, out of rightful concern that their milk might dry up (and the child starve). For that reason, many theologians permitted postponement of the conjugal debt

---

1. Genesis 38:8–10 (ESV).
2. John M. Riddle has written that contraception of some effectiveness existed in the ancient, medieval, and early modern worlds. John M. Riddle, *Contraception and Abortion from the Ancient World to the Renaissance* (Cambridge, Massachusetts: Harvard University Press, 1992) and *Eve's Herbs: A History of Contraception and Abortion in the West* (Cambridge, Massachusetts: Harvard University Press, 1997).

in such circumstances. Still, whenever the matter of contraception was discussed, the story of Onan was sure to be mentioned, for by refusing to father a child with his sister-in-law, Tamar, Onan wronged both Tamar and her dead husband. Onan enjoyed sexual intercourse without giving Tamar her due, subverting his culture's customs in hateful lust and spilling to the ground Tamar's hope for a child and his family's need for an heir. Consequently, God struck him dead. Procreation is never simply a woman's choice, nor is it a matter between a man and a woman; it is a concern between man, woman, and the Lord God.[3]

The first point to be made in discussing birth control is that children are a gift from God, not an inconvenience or a burden. The duty to bear and raise offspring was (and remains) nothing less than one of the first *blessings* with which the Lord graced mankind, and Scripture continues this theme throughout its pages, portraying a large family as a reward and a barren womb as a misfortune. Nevertheless, it is essential to remember how the blessings of God are not given as guarantees of ease or comfort. God ordains human life for greater purposes than achieving human happiness in this sinful world. In this light, the Sermon on the Mount declared the *blessedness* of those who are poor, despised, and persecuted. Jesus did not pretend that the afflicted should be *happy* about their suffering, but declared them to be *blessed* through their trials.[4] God uses the suffering of men and women to purify their hearts, enrich their souls, and glorify his name. Jesus once observed how a woman remains in anguish through childbirth but forgets her pain as soon as her baby is delivered. And we should note that when the Father sent his own Son to become man, he sent him into the most difficult and humble of circumstances, born into a feed bin for farm animals.[5]

To that end, parents are blessed with children so that they can learn to love patiently and serve humbly, imitating the suffering and sacrifices of our Lord Jesus Christ. Sleepless nights, dirty diapers, thankless carpools, and troubled teenagers enable them to grow in patience and overcome the selfishness into which we were all born. Even the act of

3. Regarding intimacy during breastfeeding, medieval theologian Gratian wrote that there should be no sexual relations between husband and wife until the child is weaned (although he may have meant an earlier time than modern weaning). Gratian, *Treatise on Laws*, 17 (Dist. 5:2).

4. Genesis 1:28 (ESV); Psalm 127:4–5 (ESV); Matthew 5:1–12; John 16:21.

5. Fort Wayne bishop John Francis Noll authored a primer on birth control (in the later 1930s) that cites this text. J.F.N., *A Catechism on Birth Control* (Huntington, Indiana: Our Sunday Visitor Press, n.d.), 29.

delivering a child (a dangerous matter in the ancient world, where women frequently died from childbirth) was described by Paul as a means of sanctification. In 1 Timothy, the apostle Paul revealed how God protects those women who face childbirth in pious faith, stating that women will be "preserved through the bearing of children" if they live in "faith and love and sanctity with self-restraint."[6] Paul's promise did not guarantee an uncomplicated pregnancy to every Christian woman, but revealed how faith and love increase as pious women obey God's command to reproduce. Still, his revelation suggests that some women will be spared their lives as they bring forth the very children who share in Christ's sufferings and spiritual triumph, as prophesied to Eve against the tempter who had ruined her and her offspring: a promise fulfilled primarily in the virgin Mary and her eternal Son, but also shared with her daughters of faith as they give birth to sons and daughters through whom the living Christ fulfills the divine prophecy by continued triumph over sin and evil:[7]

> *I will put enmity between you and the woman,*
> *and between your offspring and her offspring;*
> *he shall bruise your head,*
> *and you shall bruise his heel.*[8]

Parenthood is often risky and painful, but it is seldom joyless tribulation. Most of the time, those who spurn immediate satisfactions and pleasures for an investment in children gain far more than they lose. What excitement is greater than pregnancy? What earthly joy is greater than a child? Marriage itself finds its greatest satisfaction in the mutual

---

6. 1 Timothy 2:15 (NASB). Modern childbirth mortality is 33 deaths for every 100,000 births, while ancient and medieval mortality likely numbered between 1000 and 10,000 maternal deaths per 100,000 births. For a history of childbirth in early modern Europe, see Jaques Gélis, *History of Childbirth: Fertility, Pregnancy, and Birth in Early Modern Europe*, trans. Rosemary Morris (Boston: Northeastern University Press, 1991), 238–254.

7. Anselm wrote: "Just as the sin of mankind and the cause of our damnation originated from a woman, correspondingly, the medicine of sin and cause of salvation should be born of a woman. [Since Eve first brought sin to mankind] it is right that an equivalent great good should proceed from a woman, so as to rebuild their hope." Anselm, "Why God Became Man," in *Anselm of Canterbury: The Major Works*, 323.

8. Genesis 3:15 (ESV). Christ defeated sin and the devil at the cross, thereby fulfilling this prophecy many generations after giving it to Eve, and involving many women in its completion. The prophecy also seems fulfilled in every mother whose descendants become co-heirs in the suffering and conquest of the risen Christ.

love that husband and wife share in making and rearing children. And while artists may spend their entire lives perfecting one self-expressing masterpiece, parents are blessed to create and raise several living likenesses of themselves (both of them together). If the painted image of a human being hanging in a museum is good (which it is), then a living person dwelling among mankind is nearly divine. If it is glorious to make a marble bust that might endure (at most) a millennium or two, what sheer joy it is to create a human being who will live forever! The most humble of fathers and mothers are blessed to be greater artists than Michelangelo and Monet, Rembrandt and Rodin, Chagall and Cassatt, Vermeer and Van Gogh, and a collection of every piece of great art through human history would not compare to a single human child. Every painting and sculpture would be little more than an ill-made forgery of the eternal art of parenthood: a cheap counterfeit of human life, a dead and lifeless icon.

The very act of making and raising a child is godlike. Just as God created the world from nothing, so parents bring forth a human being who did not previously exist. Thereafter, they care for and instruct their child just as the Lord in his providence guides the entire human race. The insightful writer, G. K. Chesterton, observed how "the creation of a new creature [is] an immeasurably more grand and godlike act" than even the joy of marital love.[9] It is the most incredible work and joy of human life, and any discussion of procreation must begin with recognizing the fundamental truth that the most remarkable and enduring work of humanity is to make more human beings. Such discussions must also acknowledge that parents do not conceive children solely for themselves, as if the entire cosmos revolves around their home (whether a small cottage or a grand mansion does not matter), but also raise children for their families, communities, churches, and countries as part of God's redemptive plan. Peter Martyr Vermigli observed how we must "endeavor within our power to leave very many children unto the church."[10]

The world, however, does not consider the begetting and caring for children in this divine light. Couples pursue sex without its fruit and seek rest without toil, unwilling to participate in any eternal good that might strip them of more immediate pleasures and pursuits. Titus, a church leader in late antiquity, once observed how his contemporaries avoided

9. G. K. Chesterton, "Blasphemy and the Baby," in *Brave New Family*, 171.
10. Peter Martyr Vermigli, *Common Places*, vol. II.10–18, 27. This passage was edited for clarity.

the "dangerous and difficult" labor of pregnancy so they could "indulge in pleasure more frequently." Likewise, Caesarius of Arles chided those who limit their household to just two or three children from "fear lest perhaps if they have more children they cannot be rich."[11] That same warning was made by Martin Luther, a thousand years later, when he wrote that those who delay marriage too long or refuse to bear large families are like pagans who "trust in God as long as they know that they do not need him [and] are well supplied." Luther called upon Christians to marry while still young and to have children, even if this meant that they would be "poor and despised, and [do] insignificant work." Luther warned believers not to be wrongly anxious that their offspring might starve, noting how: "God makes children; he will surely also feed them."[12] English Reformer Thomas Cranmer wrote the same:

> *Furthermore, mark this well, that the Lord says, "Grow, increase, replenish the earth and till it." Many abstain from marriage because they are anxious about how they shall live if they were married. Therefore, our Lord God plainly shows that he will plentifully give to married folks everything necessary to the maintenance of life, if they put their trust in him and apply their labors diligently.*[13]

Faith that God will feed the children of those who pray is seldom found in the modern world. A campaign of population limitation has grown strident during my lifetime, and many of its proponents are professed unbelievers who do not trust the providence of God to feed the nations in accord with the Lord's mercy and judgments: people who do not see poor people of destitute countries to be of greater value than their hunger and disease. Even today, many doubt that the lives of impoverished Asians and Africans are worth living since the latter often lack the material comforts of advanced nations, yet fail to comprehend how Western countries face a destructive depopulation that is causing suicidal

---

11. John T. Noonan, Jr., *Contraception: A History of Its Treatment by the Catholic Theologians and Canonists*, 147–149.
12. Luther, "Estate of Marriage (1522)," in *Luther's Works*, vol. 45, 48. Luther judged it best for men to marry at twenty and women at eighteen. For comparison, this was only slightly younger than the average age of marriage for men and women in the United States during the 1950s.
13. Cranmer, *Catechism*, 67.

self-collapse. While it is true that some peoples need to manage their resources more carefully to avoid famine and catastrophe, it is wrong to believe a lower birth rate should be enforced or accepted so that people can purchase additional video games, automobiles, and cell phones. It must be remembered that population pressures and threats of wide-spread impoverishment exist neither in Europe nor the United States, the lands where birth control is so prevalent that families average two children (or less). Some might argue that the average family size should be limited due to a declining standard of living, but this is sheer nonsense. No prior age has ever been blessed with the present generation's spacious homes, luxurious automobiles, home entertainment, and secure finances. Never have there been so few children amidst so much health, leisure, and abundance.

At a personal level, I knew a man who hurried to the doctor within days of having his second child: too anxious to let a few weeks pass before receiving a vasectomy. Simple prudence would suggest ensuring that a newborn lives beyond infancy (or that there will be no change of mind). While I have heard some rationalize, "God will overrule the vasectomy if he intends for us to have another child," the apostle James required believers to seek God's will in all decisions. We must not imitate Jewish authorities who blasphemed by demanding that Jesus perform miracles to convince them to submit to his authority. Believers must never for a moment test God as Satan tempted Jesus, to which Jesus replied that no one should put the Lord "to the test." A demand for divine miracles to overrule human preferences is wrong; in some instances, it may rise to the level of blasphemy.[14]

Moreover, modern calls for a reduced population amidst a Western population decline sound like the shrill cries of the monk Jerome, who advised Christians of antiquity not to marry or have children because "the world is already full and does not hold us" (a statement made as the depopulation of the Roman Empire was accelerating and there were too few citizens to staff the legions of the Roman army or work the farms of the Roman provinces).[15] Like modern depopulation advocates, Jerome incorrectly assessed that the Roman population could support no more people, wrongly seeking the end of God's creative work on earth well before the Lord's salvation had been brought to all peoples and nations.

---

14. James 4:13–17; Matthew 4:7 (NASB).
15. Cited in Noonan, *Contraception*, 83.

Similarly, many modern polemicists claim that the earth's resources are running out and most countries are overpopulated—even though couples are having fewer children than ever before, labor shortages are becoming acute, Western society is steadily aging, a population decline has begun, and modern technology is finding new ways and additional resources to support human society.

One modern Anglican church commission even declared that men and women should curtail "the drive toward parenthood" for "the well-being of the species." No parent, the report stated, has the right to "as many children as they desire for themselves." Why? Because God's word does not give an "unlimited license to procreate large families" and thereby overfill the earth. This is to turn God's specific command to reproduce into a command not to do so.[16] It is a preposterous perversion standing in stark contrast to a Puritan who wrote the following while serving in the same Church of England (several centuries earlier): "Children are the gift of God, and therefore married folks are not only to use the means but also to pray for the obtaining of them."[17] What motivates the modern mistake is the same fretful desire that prompts couples to unreasonably restrict the size of their families, showing a preference for pleasure, comfort, security, and abundance over life, love, faith, and humility. As previously noted, this temptation has existed from antiquity and must be resisted with the utmost vigor since the mere hope for infertility leads to self-destruction.

On the other hand, men and women who prefer large families must guard their hearts just as carefully. To be willing to tend a large family in obedience to the word of God is good, but some multiply their children from wrong motives. Such men and women take arrogant pride in their fertility and pour scorn on the barren, forgetting that God alone makes new life in the womb, and does so for his purposes and on his timetable. Others build up large families in a competitive spirit, not for God's glory but for their own. Rachel and Leah (sisters and polygamous wives of Jacob) were involved in a baby-making race to earn the love of Jacob and prove the blessing of God: a contest that grew truly pathetic as they named children in spiteful pride, manipulated their marriage beds, and

---

16. *Marriage, Divorce, and the Church: The Report of a Commission appointed by the Archbishop of Canterbury to prepare a statement on the Christian Doctrine of Marriage* (London: SPCK, 1971), 112.

17. William Perkins, "Christian Economy," in Larsen Klein, ed., *Daughters, Wives, and Widows*, 170.

encouraged Jacob to father adoptive offspring through female servants. The lust, envy, and vainglory portrayed in the book of Genesis are as wrong as any modern idealization of infertility. Everyone is called to reproduce with an attitude of faith and gratitude for what God has declared to be a blessing, not in pursuit of self-centered glory or selfish comfort. No one is exempt.

> *[Leah] conceived again and bore a son, and said, "Now this time my husband will become attached to me, because I have borne him three sons." Therefore he was named Levi. And she conceived again and bore a son, and said, "This time I will praise the* LORD.*" Therefore she named him Judah. Then she stopped bearing. Now when Rachel saw that she bore Jacob no children, she became jealous of her sister... [Rachel] said, "Here is my servant Bilhah, go in to her that she may bear on my knees, that through her I too may have children." So she gave him her maid Bilhah as a wife, and Jacob went in to her. Bilhah conceived and bore Jacob a son... Rachel's servant Bilhah conceived again and bore Jacob a second son. Then Rachel said, "With mighty wrestlings I have wrestled with my sister and I have indeed prevailed." And she named him Naphtali... When Leah saw that she stopped bearing, she took her maid Zilpah and gave her to Jacob as a wife.*[18]

---

18. Genesis 29:34–30:9 (NASB).

36

A REASONABLE REPRODUCTION

Unlike many acts on which moral judgment has been passed, contraception requires a knowledge of technique. Even the most elementary contraceptive behavior calls for the possession of some biological information; mechanical methods rest on some awareness of physiology; chemical preparations require a further mastery of pharmacology. If those kinds of technical information were non-existent, there would be no acts of contraception for moralists to judge. The effectiveness of existing technique, and the distinction between it and means used to control birth by producing abortions, are also germane to the moral evaluation, as are the extent and diffusion of the practice, and the motives of those who employ it.[1]

No INFLUENTIAL CHRISTIAN authority has ever argued that a couple must make as many children as biologically possible. Rather, couples are called to reproduce with an attitude of service and a willingness to bear a cross (which may require some couples to conceive more children than they would otherwise be inclined to do). After all, Jesus blessed the little children, and his followers should likewise bless their homes with an abundance of babies. However, because human beings were not made to mate like rabbits and because they possess the means and intelligence to

---

1. Noonan, *Contraception*, 9.

avoid doing so, the issue of birth control exists. No Christian tradition has ever required human beings to have as many children as they can conceive, regardless of the consequences. Believers have always permitted couples to conceive only as many children as they can feed. Not every farm in ancient Palestine, medieval France, or early modern England could support a dozen children, and every branch of the Christian tradition has desired the marital bed to build up the households of the godly rather than ruin families through irresponsible reproduction. Nearly a century ago, conservative Roman Catholic Bishop Noll addressed the biblical command to "increase and multiply":

> *Many entertain a prejudice against these words of the Almighty addressed to Adam, and again to [Noah], and still again to Abraham. In fact, they are very much misunderstood [since they do not intend] everybody to marry and become the parents of as many children as is possible. Such is not the meaning of Almighty God's words.*[2]

The traditional Christian position on contraception and birth control has been relatively straightforward. Until the advent of the modern age, nearly all authors agreed that chemical (i.e., organic) and mechanical contraceptives were to be rejected.[3] Contraceptives of varying effectiveness existed before the modern world (as did medical opinions about inducing or avoiding pregnancy). These generally were condemned by church leaders, who also restricted the use of *coitus interruptus,* arguing that Christian husbands should not repeat Onan's sin against Tamar with their wives. The primary method of birth control allowed by churchmen was self-restraint (which is indeed quite effective). Parents unable to feed additional children were allowed to deny themselves sexual intimacy that might produce hungry bellies they could not feed. It is essential to recall that ancient, medieval, and Reformation-era believers shared a common understanding of this doctrine. And while Protestants generally did not categorize the various types of sin to the extent that

---

2. Bishop Noll observed that sterility is God's "greatest temporal punishment." J.F.N., *A Catechism on Birth Control*, 28-29.
3. Charles D. Provan (who held some objectionable views early in life) listed early Protestants who objected to the use of birth control. Provan's analysis is flawed, but he effectively cataloged historical Christian objections to birth control. Charles D. Provan, *The Bible and Birth Control* (Monongahela, Pennsylvania: Zimmer Printing, 1989).

Roman Catholics developed guides for use in the confessional, Protestant commentaries on Genesis did discuss Onan's sin.

One Protestant who openly preached against birth control was English poet and preacher John Donne, who found traditional Christian teachings (from antiquity and the Middle Ages) to be authoritative as he chided believers of his generation who as much as hoped for infertility. Donne may even have gone beyond ancient and medieval opinions, which permitted couples to separate from each other as a legitimate means of birth control, when he declared self-denial as a means of contraception to be wrong. For John Donne, merely planning to avoid pregnancy was to be condemned. This is not to say that Donne opposed all forms of self-restraint to prevent impoverishment of a family (I have not read enough of his writings to understand all of his nuanced beliefs). Still, in one wedding sermon, he emphasized the obligation to bear children and admonished common reasons for not doing so, preaching:

> *As Saint Augustine puts the case, "To contract before, that they will have no children, makes it no marriage but an adultery. To deny themselves to one another is as much against marriage as to give themselves to another. To hinder it by Physik, or any other practice, nay to hinder it so far, as by a deliberate wish, or prayer against children, consists not well with this [use] of marriage.*[4]

Since antiquity, it has been understood that conception is not equally possible at all times of a woman's reproductive cycle. Though ancient medicine could be mistaken in determining exactly when fertility peaked, the ancients understood that intercourse was more productive at certain times of the month than at others. For instance, the ancient natural philosopher Soranus believed that "intercourse was most fruitful just as menstruation was ending" and "in humans not every time is suitable for conception of the seed discharged during intercourse."[5] While I am unsure whether Soranus properly timed the reproductive cycle, what matters for our present discussion is not the accuracy of his science but the fact that he claimed knowledge upon which reproductive decisions could be based. This is the core requirement for the use of birth control

---

4. John Donne, *The Sermons of John Donne*, vol. 3, ed. George R. Potter and Evelyn M. Simpson (Berkeley, California: University of California Press, 1957), 245.
5. Owsei Temkin, trans., *Soranus' Gynecology* (Baltimore: Johns Hopkins University Press, 1956), 34.

in any form. It should be noted that possession of such information can be used either to enhance or restrict fertility, depending upon what couples do with such understanding, and many Christian teachers (most notably, Augustine) opposed efforts to use such insight to avoid pregnancy, just as some contemporary couples use improved understanding of reproductive cycles to enhance their chances of conception.[6]

As the rise of modern medical science led to a more precise understanding of ovulation and fertility, a purely natural method of birth control (restricting coitus to infertile periods) grew more effective and received the sanction of many believers, including the Roman Catholic church. A recent Roman Catholic catechism allowed parents "for just reasons" to "space the births of their children."[7] Similarly, the fundamentalist preacher John Rice wrote that there is "nothing against decency and morals" when a married couple decides to have intercourse only during infertile periods. Conservative Protestant and Roman Catholic theologians have permitted the use of natural family planning, provided it is used to space children rather than to prevent the birth of a good-sized family altogether.[8] This may extend beyond what was previously allowed, but modern medicine generally enables a more precise understanding of biological reality and more effective reproductive responses to the nature of our physical bodies.

I should add that there is another historical position that approached birth control from an altogether different perspective. Ancient Jews believed the best way of dealing with this issue was not to center the discussion on the procreative possibilities inherent in any given act of sexual intercourse but to ensure that involved couples complete their particular obligation to replenish and fill the earth. This approach to the ethics of reproduction restricted most forms of birth control, including natural family planning and self-denial, until a couple had fulfilled God's

---

6. Ancient, medieval, and early modern medical knowledge often was in error. For instance, it was wrongly believed by many that a rape victim could not conceive a child since it was thought that man and woman equally contributed to conception through willing sexual intimacy. One historian viewed this as a socially convenient mistake necessitated by the strictures and realities of property and title succession. Eric Jager, *The Last Duel*, 118.

7. *Catechism of the Catholic Church* (Mahwah, New Jersey: Paulist Press, 1994), 569–570.

8. John R. Rice, *The Home: Courtship, Marriage, and Children* (Murfreesboro, Tennessee: Sword of the Lord Publishers, 1946), 165. John Noonan once observed of natural family planning: "Evidently, there was no one who recalled St. Augustine's opinion that [daring] intercourse only on sterile days was a prime way of doing something to prevent conception." Noonan, *Contraception*, 439.

command to multiply. Still, it also seemed to permit couples to grow their families according to resources, although it is unclear whether Hebrews openly allowed the use of either *coitus interruptus* or natural family planning to do so (some Jewish texts suggest such freedom, while others imply not). The collection of the ancient Jewish oral tradition, the *Mishnah*, taught that no couple should abstain from sexual relations until an appropriate number of children has been born, implying that couples might be free to space births once they had conceived their quota of offspring. The means and timing of birth control seem less important than the duty to replenish the human race. The *Mishnah* noted:

> *No man may abstain from keeping the law "Be fruitful and multiply," unless he already has children: according to the School of Shamai, two sons; according to the School of Hillel, a son and a daughter.*[9]

Modern debates frame my understanding of contraception, so I share my thoughts only as an opinion since I may have been too compromised by modern practices to view the issue with moral clarity. Anyone who wants to be safe should accept the strictest historic position of Christendom by denying themselves coitus when they can afford no more children, or otherwise accepting as many sons and daughters as their desire for sexual intercourse produces. Scripture provides no explicit permission to restrict conception beyond these principles; every other approach is an attempt to balance principles and practicalities. Even the acceptance of natural family planning is a recent doctrine rejected during antiquity, the Middle Ages, and possibly the Protestant Reformation. At the same time, I believe that piety is found in the hopes and intentions of the inner heart more than in the use or disuse of external contraceptives, and that we must begin our discussion with the hidden desires of our hearts. There is no virtue in either using or avoiding the use of contraception if our souls are sterile and barren toward the beauty of life in God's world.[10]

Nor will it suffice to argue that modern technology has opened the debate to new issues, since natural family planning is little more than the

---

9. Danby, *The Mishnah*, 227 (Yabamoth 5:6).
10. Non-Christian cultures and civilizations disagree in many instances with Christian morality. For a book that describes Islamic medicine and birth control practices during the Middle Ages, see B.F. Musallam, *Sex and Society in Islam: Birth Control Before the Nineteenth Century* (Cambridge: Cambridge University Press, 1983).

use of the sterile period, an act known and condemned by all camps in the Christian tradition. Even mechanical and chemical (organic) means of contraception (albeit far less effective than modern variants) existed and were condemned in the past. As noted, John Donne rebuked the bare hope to delay conception when motivated by an illicit desire (such as the hope to preserve a woman's figure), writing that while God would not have the beauty of women marred by intemperate behavior, neither would he have "care of that comeliness, and handsomeness frustrate his purpose of children in marriage."[11] Modern technology and medicine have made effective birth control readily available, but they have not changed the core moral concerns that arise from such knowledge and techniques. Contemporary life has not changed the discussion one iota, except in making a cleaner distinction between proper contraception and various abortifacients that destroy life already begun.[12]

As previously observed, no theologian has required every possible child to be conceived; most have allowed at least the use of abstinence.[13] Still, focusing the discussion on the negative command (what not to do) seems somewhat misguided for several reasons. First, the Bible insists that marriage has been ordained to create love and restrain lust as much as to reproduce offspring. Nature hides the fertility of women so that copulation is desired during infertile periods, which means that human sexuality (unlike that of animals, who mate primarily during fertile periods) is ordained to generate a pregnant crop of love and affection as well as of babies. Second, the apostle Paul commanded couples to refrain from carnal relations only for the purpose of prayer. Now, unless some type of birth control is morally permissible (natural or otherwise), this command would obligate believers to conceive as many children as biologically possible unless they are in constant prayer—an implication potentially inconsistent with Paul's insistence that parents must support their children. Third, if abstinence is the only legitimate form of birth control, an absolute absurdity arises, for couples who abstain entirely from marital relations to avoid having children are morally justified, while those who use natural or artificial birth control to space their conceptions are sinning. Yet, which couple better fulfills God's explicit command to reproduce: a frigid and loveless couple hoping for barrenness through

11. Donne, *Sermons*, vol. 6, 270.
12. Various birth control pills sometimes prevent the implantation of a conceived ovum, and the I.U.D. necessarily leads to the destruction of nascent life.
13. Augustine of Hippo, *The Preaching of Augustine*, 43–44.

abstinence, or the hard-pressed and sexually passionate parents of four or five children who believe they have contributed what they can to the building of God's eternal household?[14]

For these reasons, I believe the ancient Jews rightly focused on fulfilling the duty to reproduce rather than restricting the use of birth control (natural or artificial). God's command was to have children rather than not to use birth control. It was a positive rather than a negative directive. Couples who have obeyed this command by having a reasonable number of children possibly are free to slow the further growth of their families, while those who have not fulfilled God's command to reproduce are not free to forestall pregnancy even through sexual abstinence (except, perhaps, as part of short-term planning required to establish a large household). When the Lord first established marriage, he commanded couples to reproduce, and his plain commandment has not been rescinded. As Bishop Noll observed in an earlier citation, the Lord reiterated his command after the flood of Noah, doubling down on the moral parameters he had ordained at the creation.[15]

Such an approach to the ethics of birth control allows couples to balance family size with factors such as fertility and food availability, as long as they are actively striving to fill the earth with their share of children. This understanding coincides with that of the fundamentalist John Rice and the Roman Catholic Church, both of whom allow the spacing of children. There remains only the matter of family size. As noted earlier, some Jews believed each parent should be replaced by a child. Modern demographers might argue that an *increase* over two parents is three children (so that married couples can make up population losses incurred by infertility, celibacy, and early death), and a comedian might joke that two *multiplied* by two is four. I am not qualified to dispute about numbers since my objective here is to remind everyone that the duty to have children must not be limited for worldly motives. Married

---

14. James T. Burtchaell dissented from Roman Catholic teaching when approving of contraception "within an overall commitment to children." Burtchaell wrote how it is the "entire course of childbearing, not the individual acts of contraception, that is crucial to the life of a marriage." Still, he demanded a generous desire to bear and love children, agreeing with Pope Paul IV that modern parents "feed their children cake and live in fear of a bread shortage," whereas the real hunger is children "starving in a famine of love." James Tunstead Burtchaell, *Rachel Weeping: The Case Against Abortion*, xvi.
15. Genesis 9:1. For ancient and medieval interpretations of the command to reproduce, see Jeremy Cohen, *"Be Fertile and Increase, Fill the Earth and Master It": The Ancient and Medieval Career of a Biblical Text* (Ithaca, New York: Cornell University Press, 1989).

couples should seek to serve as many children as possible, without rendering themselves unable to fulfill their obligation to provide daily bread.[16]

This allowance is grounded in the notion that fathers and mothers should care for the children they conceive. The apostle Paul taught that a man who does not provide for his family is worse than an unbeliever, which suggests a measure of prudence may be required in marrying and begetting children. Parents must have no more children than they can truly love.[17] Moreover, such daily provision should not be reduced to food and shelter at minimal levels, for man does not live by bread alone. Because it is a parent's duty to provide adequate attention and care for children so that the latter grow up in the fear and love of God, it is senseless to have so many children that the biblical duty to raise them in piety cannot be accomplished. Similarly, to place a couple under such strain that they will be ruined does not make a reasonable use of procreative abilities, just as the right to self-defense exempts a woman from bearing children if doing so would kill her. Such an exemption probably should be extended to causing insanity, though it seems to me that few parents crack up from having too many children. Sober, hard-working parents with large families generally flourish and learn how to live humbly before the Lord. Only if anxiety, ambition, arrogance, alcoholism, addiction, infidelity, illness, indolence, or other serious problems are added to a large family do problems typically start to emerge, or even prevail.

The obligation to choose prudently must be measured according to biblical thresholds, as some people would fear for their finances if they had a chest of gold buried in their backyard and a second fortune of stocks and bonds in their grasp. Anxious and faithless fear is not a valid reason to bear fewer children, but a temptation to overcome. God blesses large families, would have children raised with several brothers and sisters (in most instances), and even takes special care of the poor who trust him. There is no biblical call to limit the size of one's family to provide wealth and leisure. It is enough to gratefully receive our daily bread from our

---

16. No clear biblical passage permitting birth control exists, so it must be stated outright that there is no *right* to birth control. John Warwick Montgomery wrote how this decision must be "made by faith and in prayer," though couples should not permit "the number of children to reach a point where they cannot be taken care of properly." John Warwick Montgomery, *How do we know there is a God?* (Minneapolis, Minnesota: Bethany House Publishers, 1973), 70–71.

17. 1 Timothy 5:8.

heavenly father. Still, I would add that some selfish parents fail to provide for their children what their heavenly father calls them to give of themselves and their property. It is not enough to ensure that children are fed with table scraps or clothed with rags, for that is not how God tends to our physical and spiritual needs—or how we pray to God to treat us. The Lord provides sacrificially and bountifully for his loved ones, while leading his sons and daughters to behave with equal generosity toward children entrusted to their care. In the Lord's house, the father does not serve snakes to children who ask for a meal of fish, and so it must be in our families.[18]

It must be added that parents are responsible for *all* their children, whether young or grown, from a current or previous marriage, legitimate or illegitimate. A man who has sired children outside of marriage must provide for each one of them, whether his relationship with their mother is healthy, troubled, or non-existent (just as the mother of children must surrender her desires and dreams to bring good to each child she bears, as well as those stepchildren belonging to the man she willingly married). This may entail a crushing burden on the man's plans and opportunities, and perhaps even limit his chance to marry and raise a large family—or more likely, to enjoy himself with conveniences, pleasures, and luxuries. It may also restrict many opportunities for his eventual wife and their children, but these obligations remain absolute and immediate.[19] In all such matters, we have a simple, but effective, rule of faith given by Jesus, who commanded us to do to others as we would have them do to us. This summarizes the entire Law and Prophets.[20]

While some Christians have regulated birth control by the natural function of the human body, it seems equally prudent to regulate fertility by the natural needs of children. This is not to say that couples may limit the size of their families to maximize leisure opportunities or to ensure prosperity. That would be to spoil children rather than to provide for

---

18. Luke 11:11–13.
19. One historian wrote: "Calvin and other Reformed leaders strongly affirmed that men were, by divine decree, the heads of households and responsible for the welfare of all members of their families, including children they fathered outside of marriage. Consistories, in conjunction with secular authorities, made much more aggressive efforts than their Catholic counterparts to oblige men to support all the children they produced. At times this meant that they raised their illegitimate offspring in their own households, at others that they provided financial support to the mothers of their children born out of wedlock." Jeffrey Watt, *Consistory and Social Discipline in Calvin's Geneva,* 104–105.
20. Matthew 7:12 (ESV).

their daily bread. Instead, it is to advise that couples should intentionally conceive no more children than those for whom they can provide necessary material, emotional, and spiritual provisions daily. We must also remember that the apostle James made it clear that poverty is not an unbearable burden for believers, and Jesus called (and still calls) his disciples to trust God for their necessities rather than to stockpile wealth to mitigate the risks of life. Having children when it is difficult to do so is a very real act of faith in the fact that God exists and provides for his sons and daughters, just as men and women provide for their own children. The Lord's Prayer specifically calls us to seek our daily bread, rather than an abundance that renders such prayer unnecessary. Parents must plan their families while anticipating that they will need to call on the Lord for their daily bread: the spiritual, emotional, and physical support upon which their households are founded.[21]

When prophesying the coming destruction of Jerusalem, Jesus called believers to pray for the circumstances around pregnancy (that judgment would not fall on the Sabbath or in the winter), adding still another dimension to this discussion: the reality of God's providential care for those who persistently pray to him. This adds resources far greater than what human diligence and planning can ever achieve. What Jesus instructed believers to pray for God's protection during his coming destruction of rebellious Jerusalem equally applies to our family planning: namely, that we understand that our prayers will impact our lives. The promise of God to take care of his children if we so pray to him should be factored into our own concern to provide for our sons and daughters. Even today, Jesus calls us to trust our Father in heaven, which is the spirit in which Martin Luther spoke when he observed that God makes children and will, therefore, provide for them. Because this is true, couples should dare to raise larger families with faith in the Lord's daily provision.[22] We should pray to God as Jesus specifically told us to pray. Jesus said:

> *And alas for women who are pregnant and for those who are nursing infants in those days! Pray that your flight may not be in winter or on a Sabbath.*[23]

---

21. James 2:5; Matthew 5:31–32.
22. James 1:9–11; Matthew 6:11.
23. Matthew 24:19–20 (ESV).

Though we are called to trust in the Lord, a sound faith in God is not rash foolishness. When Jesus himself was tempted in the desert, he did not expect God to turn stones into bread. Faith in that situation meant humbly waiting for God to provide food at the right hour, and generally through natural means. If a couple has more children than they can feed based on their station in life, they must not presume that God will turn stones into bread for them or send manna from heaven every morning. Though they must trust in the Lord's providential care amidst the struggles of life, they cannot expect to find bags of money in their backyard or be inspired to select winning lottery numbers. Scripture, which openly praises large families as a blessing, simultaneously reveals the importance of wisdom and foresight in caring for a family. While Jesus portrayed birds as the epitome of trust in God, we can see that most of them are wise enough to build nests before they lay eggs. Only the ostrich does not do so, and Scripture describes her as the epitome of heartless folly. It is not fitting for mankind to imitate such short-sighted stupidity.

> *[The ostrich] leaves her eggs to the earth*
> *and lets them be warmed on the ground,*
> *forgetting that a foot may crush them*
> *and that the wild beast may trample them.*
> *She deals cruelly with her young,*
> *as if they were not hers;*
> *though her labor be in vain, yet she has no fear,*
> *because God has made her forget wisdom*
> *and given her no share in understanding.*[24]

---

24. Job 39:14–17 (ESV).

37

THE DUTIES OF CHILDREN

Honor your father and your mother, that your days may be long in the land that the LORD *your God is giving you.*[1]

Children, obey your parents in the Lord, for this is right. "Honor your father and mother" (this is the first commandment with a promise), that it may go well with you and that you may live long in the land.[2]

THERE IS a movement in the modern world to rewrite children's rights under the law. Modern reformers seek to end not only actual child neglect and abuse but also to establish the state as the most immediate and relevant ruling power over individual children, thereby restricting the traditional and natural rights of parents. Some believe the government ought to determine what children should be taught and how they are to be disciplined, and do not believe parents have been ordained by God and nature to rule their offspring, or are competent to do so—seeing parental authority as selfish, untrustworthy, and traditionalistic. These counter-culture radicals prefer supposedly disinterested observers like themselves at the helm of our nation's families. This mindset is directly opposed to

---

1. Exodus 20:12 (ESV).
2. Ephesians 6:1–3 (ESV).

divine law. Not only does Moses, but the entire Bible reveals that fundamental obligations exist between parent and child. Common experience also reveals the misfortune that befalls everyone (child and parent alike) who undermines the duty to maintain a respectful relationship between parent and child.

Parenthood does not exist simply to see offspring to maturity, as many people, including some Christian thinkers, assume. It is mistaken to identify sonship and daughterhood with mere youth, as something to be outgrown. Just as our parents remain our parents through our entire lives, so the doctrine of the Trinity indicates that eternal fatherhood is at the core of divine reality, reflecting how God conceived the creation in his mind from nothing (as men and women make children who did not previously exist from an act that began as a mere thought). It was Arian heretics who claimed the Son of God was created by (and less than) God; orthodox Christians taught, and continue to teach, that the Son of God is eternally begotten of his Father (with whom the Son shares the fullness of the divine essence). Christ's eternal sonship will never be outgrown since God exists outside of creation's mutability.[3]

Similarly, human sonship and daughterhood continue through this mortal life (and would also have existed in a world without sin).[4] While the exercise of parental authority changes as a child moves from infancy and childhood to youth and adulthood (to gain something of that equality with a parent that the Son shares with his Father), it does not cease altogether. Just as the Father always honors the Son and the Son does what his Father wills, so parents and children never reverse their roles. Children never outgrow sonship or daughterhood, and parents never retire from the authority and obligations of parenthood (though we can see that decay brought on by disease and old age often limits parental power to perform their natural duties). When grown sons and daughters challenge the authority of their aging parents, they necessarily

---

3. The Bible also emphasizes the importance of respecting all older people. The young are called to intentionally and consistently honor those superior to them in authority and experience, just as they will want to be so recognized when they themselves age. Moreover, the biblical world (like many non-Western cultures today) was one in which multi-generational households (and nearby relatives) were common, so the need for such respect was required in close-quarters living that involved the full range of human sins, faults, and disagreements. Moses commanded: "You shall stand up before the gray head and honor the face of an old man, and you shall fear your God: I am the LORD." Leviticus 19:32 (ESV).
4. Peter Lombard envisioned what childhood might have been like in a sinless world. Peter Lombard, *The Sentences, Book 2: On Creation*, 86–92 (Distinction XX, Chapter 3).

undermine their right to receive such deference when their own children are grown, as well as their claim on any support (even inheritances) from the same parents whose parenthood they spurn. The complementary rights and responsibilities associated with parenthood and childhood are mutually reinforcing and ever-enduring. It was with this thought in mind that the insightful G. K. Chesterton observed how it is inconsistent to claim that parents owe support to their children while being owed nothing in return. Chesterton wrote of the matter as one of reciprocity:

> *If the child is free from the first to disregard the parent, why is not the parent free [to] disregard the child? If Mr. Jones, Senior, and Mr. Jones, Junior, are only two free and equal citizens, why should one citizen sponge on another for the first fifteen years of life?*[5]

Because Moses included a command to honor parents in the Ten Commandments, we should begin there: children must honor their parents, both father and mother. Martin Luther explained that while siblings, neighbors, and enemies are owed charitable love, only parents are owed honor. The relationship of child to parent is unlike any other human bond and must always be held in affectionate esteem.[6] It is the one human relationship everyone will experience in one fashion or another. A person may lack siblings, spouse, offspring, compatriots, or friends, but everyone (even an orphan) is born to a father and mother. Regarding the respect and reverence due to parents, Luther wrote that honor requires both courtesy and respect toward parents, even to those who "go too far" or are otherwise flawed and sinful. Children must honor even those parents whose sins exceed ordinary bounds, and their respect must be paid in word and deed alike. Luther observed that parents are not to be "deprived of their honor because of their ways or their failings."[7] It is for this reason that Jesus, God Incarnate, submitted

---

5. G.K. Chesterton, "The Drift from Domesticity," in *Brave New Family*, 55. Intriguingly, G.K. Chesterton saw emancipation at age fifteen in his day, and was not wrong to do so. My grandfather lived in this era and quit school after the eighth grade to take a job.

6. Scripture makes plain that we also must honor public authorities, albeit not with the affection due to parents.

7. Luther specified that children (including adults) are to "esteem and prize [parents] as the most precious treasure on earth," as well as to "behave respectfully toward them, and not address them discourteously, critically, and censoriously, but submit to them and hold your tongue, even if they go too far." Theodore G. Tappert, ed., *The Book of Concord: The Confessions of the Lutheran Church* (Philadelphia: Fortress Press, 1959), 379–380.

to the authority of Joseph and Mary, despite being born sinless, divine, and destined to rule all mankind, while his parents were sinful, mortal, and subject to his Messianic authority. Moreover, Joseph was not his biological father but an adoptive one.

In stark contrast to honoring one's parents is the account of Noah and his sons in the book of Genesis. When Noah became despondent following the great flood and threw off his clothes in drunken inebriation, his son Ham told his brothers about their father's folly. For mocking his father's nakedness and sin, the descendants of Ham were cursed (a fitting punishment in that a cursed son was to beget cursed children). The other brothers showed far more prudence by walking backward toward their father, holding a blanket in their hands to cover his naked body, and were blessed for having done so.[8] Few will face this situation during their lives, but many will deal with other parental sins: rage, theft, murder, adultery, drunkenness, drug addiction, betrayal, selfishness, jealousy, miserliness, neglect, ambition, adultery, cruelty, and greed. While men and women must never justify or excuse any evil act, they must always honor their parents by turning their backs to parental shame and sin. In some instances, there may be a need to point out a parental sin so that we might honor the law of our divine Father. In other instances, children will need to remain respectfully quiet about a living (or even a deceased) parent's foolish choices rather than pouring contempt on a sinful parent as Ham did with Noah. In all instances, children must support their parents with prayer, kindness, honor, and good deeds— even when sinful parents prove unworthy of such pious support.

Children must obey their parents in everything that is not sinful or illegal, even when the moral judgment of the said parent is poor. Since the Lord values a humble and obedient attitude more than success and prosperity, there are times when children must accept foolish parental commands rather than adopt a rebellious or defiant attitude. Nor may they ignore their parents or speak to them as if they were equals, for they are not. Of course, since Paul limited parental authority to commands *in the Lord,* children are not permitted to sin at their parents' behest. While there must be obedience, there cannot be sin. John Calvin observed that parents who tempt their children to sin should be considered "strangers who are trying to lead us away from obedience to our true Father."[9] Nor

---

8. Genesis 9:20–25.
9. Calvin, *Institutes,* vol. 1, 403–404.

can a parent forbid a child to do what God has called that man or woman to do, such as marry, pursue a particular vocation, or preach judgment against an open injustice. God's will must be obeyed first and foremost, though it must be stressed that the Lord's will often is found only as sons and daughters humbly follow the authority established over them.

To illustrate this obedience, we should review the life of the Genevan reformer, John Calvin. When young, Calvin studied law at his father's direction, despite his own preference for letters and theology. Only at his father's death was Calvin free to choose his path. John Calvin's obedience, however, did not derail God's plans for Calvin's place in intellectual life and church leadership, but enhanced the Genevan reformer's impact through superb legal training that he applied throughout his ministry to reform the laws and churches of Geneva, as well as to comment on Scripture and guide pastoral work. Calvin's superb legal training, which came from his filial obedience despite the young man's scholarly preferences, was crucial for the growth of Reformed Protestantism. It may be that Calvin's profound trust in God's providence (a central tenet of his faith) was rooted in his experience of God's shaping human affairs for a young man who trusted him to do so, with the Lord overriding and overruling the plans of father and son alike to achieve higher purposes than either one of them could have imagined. As for parents, we must realize that if we become roadblocks to the Lord's plans for our sons and daughters, the Lord may remove the roadblock (namely, us) from this mortal life. Parents must never seek to wrest control of their children from God. It is not a contest they can win.

Nor does the duty to honor parents end when a child grows up and establishes their own household, even though Scripture is clear that the primary focus of parental authority is to raise children in the "discipline and instruction of the Lord."[10] Elderly and infirm parents must be materially assisted if they are too "old, sick, feeble, or poor" to tend to themselves, and good children will cheerfully endure any hardship involved in doing so, even when parents are "lowly, poor, feeble, and eccentric."[11] Paul's words in 1 Timothy reveal that God expects children to provide for elderly parents as a matter of course and sharply rebukes those who fail to do so, declaring that men who do not care for their households are to be

---

10. Ephesians 6:4 (ESV).
11. Martin Luther, "Larger Catechism of Martin Luther," in Tappert, *The Book of Concord*, 379–380.

regarded as worse than unbelievers. Every ancient reader of this text would have understood Paul's command to care for elderly parents and young children, both in providing material assistance and giving visible tokens of affection that demonstrated gratitude and respect. Paul's initial readers would have recognized parental rights throughout their lives (not ending once a child establishes their own home).

While a parent's authority over grown children is not as direct as over young children, it nevertheless remains real. Parents retain authority in their households just as grown sons and daughters possess authority over their own children. As parents of young children rightly protest the intrusion by grandparents on their rights, so they must not usurp the rights that their aging parents possess over themselves and their siblings. There must be a consistent respect for parental rights based on principle and piety rather than on personality and the will to power: a respect that includes a measure of deference and obedience in matters related to parents and their leadership of their own family. Respect for parental authority is readily discernible throughout Scripture and has long been recognized, even to the doorstep of the modern age. Pierre Viret illustrated how sixteenth-century Protestants navigated this instruction, particularly for adult children with families living on common property and under the leadership of their aged parents.[12] Viret wrote:

> *There are also husbands who are angry at always being in submission to their fathers and mothers. And, if the husbands are always angry at being submissive to their fathers and mothers and for this reason prefer to remain separated from them than live with them,*

---

12. 1 Timothy 5:8. Modern writers tend to reduce the scope of parental authority. Ranald Macaulay and Jerram Barrs provide a well-reasoned example of this tendency with the following: "The independence of the child should be a goal to which the parents aim. And it should be fostered deliberately so that with each succeeding year, quietly and perhaps imperceptibly, because of its gradual nature, the child moves from being under the parents to being alongside them. The Bible gives no age at which this is to be achieved, but it is clearly the whole intention of the parent/child relationship... God alone is the child's permanent parent. Therefore, they are to aim at withdrawing gradually from their position of authority." While the authors are absolutely right about the need for maturity and emancipation, their statement about the withdrawal of parental authority goes too far. It applies to temporal life a reality reserved for eternity and places biblical teachings in a strictly Western social context. In many non-Western cultures, property arrangements lead to shared lives in which parents exercise decision-making authority over grown children until their deaths. Even in Western societies, active parental leadership is required to impart wisdom and resolve disputes over grown children who sometimes require an arbitrator. Macaulay and Barrs, *Being Human: The Nature of Spiritual Experience*, 184.

it also often happens that their wives are even angrier at this
submission and are even more desirous of freeing themselves from
it, and incite their husbands against their own fathers and mothers.
In this, both of them have very poorly fulfilled their roles. [13]

Jesus' rebuke of the Pharisees for ignoring the needs of their parents
by devoting their money to religion reminds modern believers how
parents must be cared for materially, often before supporting church
responsibilities. By devoting money to the temple, Jewish custom allowed
people to free themselves from the obligation to care for infirm parents—
since the gift subsequently belonged to Jewish religious institutions (gift
givers continued use of such property during their lifetime, suggesting
the practice served as a religious tax shelter to prevent the spending down
of wealth to assist aging parents).[14] Christ excoriated this abuse,
reminding his followers that God demands children care for their parents
beyond the sending of an occasional greeting card. Jesus made it clear
that religious duties must not interfere with the care of parents, repri-
manding Jewish leaders for nullifying God's word for the sake of their
traditions. And if hypocrites neglecting parents for ostensibly pious
purposes are judged with severity, how much more the Lord will judge
sons and daughters who ignore their parents to pursue pleasure, cater to
their own children, seek worldly success, take vacations, or enjoy quiet-
ness in their spacious homes.[15]

Jesus taught that even obligations to God do not negate the duty to

---

13. Viret, *Exposition*, vol. 2, 72. Pierre Viret implied arrangements in which married sons
lived with their parents. For a description of such household structures in premodern
France, see Jean-Louis Flandrin, *Families in Former Times: Kinship, Household, and Sexuality in Early Modern France* (Cambridge: Cambridge University Press, 1991).
14. These duties can be sacrificial and burdensome in a modern world where jobs and
careers separate parents and children from each other far beyond the typical experience
found in the ancient world, or even in the modern society into which many of us were born
during the 1960s and 1970s—for distances between parents and grown children previously
were shorter than they are in today's mobile world. Nevertheless, God's commandment
stands above every social custom, perceived necessity, and personal preference. It cannot be
doubted that the Lord calls grown children to take care of their aging parents exactly as they
themselves want to be treated by their own children once they, too, grow old—and no one
wishes to be ignored, isolated, or exiled to the care of strangers without regular face-to-face
visits from their sons, daughters, and grandchildren. Such filial love will bring glory to God,
for it will be deep love in a rapidly aging world filled with the isolation and loneliness of the
elderly. Such charitable affection will meet a very real need for an aging society and be the
true light of Christ amidst the darkness of the modern world.
15. Matthew 15:5–6.

care for one's parents. If this is so with public religion, it also remains true for household relationships. While duties toward a spouse and children are very high priorities, it is seldom the case that the care of one's spouse and children precludes taking care of one's parents and grandparents. I have seen it argued that duties toward parents are vacated at marriage since Genesis reveals that "a man shall leave his father and his mother and hold fast to his wife," but such reasoning ignores Paul's specific admonitions in 1 Timothy 5 that parents must care for their aging family members rather than to send them to the provision of the church, with those who fail to do so considered worse than unbelievers.[16] Scripture likewise commends affectionate regard for aging in-laws and links the piety of the impoverished widow Ruth to her willingness to look after her mother-in-law rather than to seek Ruth's own welfare.

The parent-child relationship is one of the most important in all creation since it reveals a dimension of the divine nature not readily seen elsewhere. God the Father begets his eternal Son while God the Son is begotten of his Father. In the same way, fathers and mothers beget children, and children are begotten of parents. Yet, the biology of this relationship (the physical begetting) is its least important feature. What matters most is its spiritual and moral quality: the Son submits to his Father, and the Father honors his Son. In like manner, the Lord promises long life to children who resemble him so perfectly as to honor and respect their parents, letting their fathers and mothers live within their hearts just as they once drew life from their parents' love. This applies to all, whether good Christian parents or selfish unbelievers. It applies to parents at their best, as well as in their weakness and sin. In honoring any parent, there is good and glory, both now and forevermore. Martin Luther wrote:

> [Honor] requires us not only to address [our parents] affectionately and reverently, but above all to show by our actions, both of heart and of body, that we respect them very highly and that next to God we give them the highest place.[17]

---

16. Genesis 2:24 (ESV); 1 Timothy 5:3–8.
17. Martin Luther, "Larger Catechism of Martin Luther," in Tappert, *The Book of Concord,* 379–380.

38

THE OBLIGATIONS OF PARENTS

[Jesus] said to his disciples, "Temptations to sin are sure to come, but woe to the one through whom they come! It would be better for him if a millstone were hung around his neck and he were cast into the sea than that he should cause one of these little ones to sin." [1]

JUST AS CHILDREN have a father and mother who rule them, adults have a heavenly father to whom they are responsible and who is the model for every human parent. Men and women are called to imitate and share in the patience, love, and fairness of the Lord God, who loves his children such that he became a mortal man who gave up his life to secure their good and to exalt them before the entire creation. Harsh and cruel parents must realize that the verbal and physical blows by which they afflict their children will not go unanswered. Those who humiliate, scorn, bully, neglect, or forsake their offspring must not believe that a government child protection agency is their worst foe. The Lord himself has given life to every boy and girl and will bring vengeance on all who harm his young: a revenge that will be as pitiless as that of a human father whose child has been murdered or molested. Surely, many suffer poverty, shame, and disease in this life because of their cruelty toward and neglect

---

1. Luke 17:1–3 (ESV).

of their flesh and blood; and many will face the anguish and terror of eternal damnation for having sinned against their sons and daughters.

Parents must tend to their children. As previously noted, the apostle Paul's first epistle to Timothy teaches that believers must care for their children's material needs.[2] Moreover, Moses spelled out in the law how inheritances were to be administered in ancient Israel, thereby ensuring that sons and daughters would be protected against parental favoritism or capriciousness—no one would be disinherited or otherwise deprived of the opportunity to make a living by the negligence, inadequacy, or evil intent of a parent. Parents were required to provide dowries for virgin daughters and inheritances for sons (or educate sons to make an honest living as the Lord's gifts dictated); they were to provide food, clothing, medical attention, and a basic education for young children. Parents were also to ensure that older children learned an honest trade and prepared for the responsibilities of adulthood. Every parent was bound to these duties, no matter the cost to themselves.

In our society, such care typically requires parents to plan for sons and daughters to receive a formal education, vocational training, military service, farmland, or participation in a profitable (for the child and the parent alike) family business.[3] Parents have the duty to foster their children's gifts and opportunities with both encouragement and whatever material assistance is prudent and possible to share. It is pure negligence to allow young men and women to drift into adult life without direction in the most important choices of their lives, or to permit guidance counselors the final say in a young person's plans, or to indulge children with entertainment and amusement rather than readying them for adult obligations and opportunities. The Lord has delegated the responsibility of raising children to the affection of parents rather than to governments and schools, so parents must not abdicate their responsibilities (although it is God's call for the child which must be supported rather than the parents' dreams and aspirations). Moreover, parental direction, assistance, and sacrifice should continue into adulthood, just as sons and daughters must honor their parents long after they marry and are blessed with offspring. This is not to say that parents should emotionally and

---

2. 1 Timothy 5:8.
3. Pierre Viret noted how Athenian lawgiver Solon required all children to support their elderly parents, except those whose parents were "negligent in instructing their children in a profession by which they might earn their own living and provide for their fathers and mothers." Pierre Viret, *Exposition of the Ten Commandments*, vol. 2, 33.

socially cripple their children by failing to foster independence and maturity at an early age, only that parental obligations continue until death.[4]

Most importantly, God's law is to be taught in the home. Moses explicitly warned his fellow Hebrews to teach God's laws "diligently to your [children]," teaching godliness inside the house and outside during walks, even marking the Lord's laws on their apparel and in their homes. The apostle Paul did the same in the book of Ephesians, commanding fathers to raise their offspring "in the discipline and instruction of the Lord."[5] One Puritan writer observed that this is a key responsibility of Christian parents, for "atheists, yea, Turkes, and Infidels" can be as adept as Christian householders in securing temporal advantages for their families, but cannot provide what the author calls "christian care."[6] Nor are parents allowed to leave this task to churches, Sunday school classes, or expensive private schools. It is the responsibility of parents to train for and implement a coherent plan for their children's spiritual growth, even if that training is as simple as reading Scripture and praying daily.

The Bible discusses several principles for such training, which can be summarized as follows. First, parents must be models of faith and virtue; they must work and sacrifice for the good of their children so that sons and daughters grow up with a settled understanding of parental love deeply imprinted on their hearts and minds, knowing from experience what Jesus meant when he declared that God is like a good father. Second, parents must teach their children sound biblical doctrine and wisdom. This requires that parents devote time to prayer and Bible meditation, as it is not possible to teach what they do not know. Fathers and mothers must have their own hearts and minds formed in the image of

---

4. Henry Venn wrote: "For what can be more contrary to the feelings of parental love than, by idleness or extravagance, to expose their offspring to poverty, or to force them to settle in a station of life beneath that in which they were born—a cause frequently of much vexation to them, and a bitter disappointment which few are able to bear." Gary Ezzo, ed., *The Godly Family: A Series of Essays on the Duties of Parents and Children* (Pittsburgh, Pennsylvania: Soli Deo Gloria Publications, 1993), 95. Modern authors Elton and Pauline Trueblood observed how parental support for children is lifelong, writing: "The idea that parents should support their children until marriage, and then do no more, is as absurd as it is widespread." Elton and Pauline Trueblood, *The Recovery of Family Life* (New York: Harper Brothers Publishers, 1953), 107.

5. Deuteronomy 6:7–9 (NASB); Ephesians 6:4 (ESV).

6. Robert Cleaver, "A Godlie Form of Household Government: For the Ordering of Private Families According to the Direction of God's Word," cited in James Turner Johnson, *A Society Ordained by God: Puritan Marriage Doctrine in the First Half of the Seventeenth Century* (Nashville, Tennessee: Abandon Press, 1970), 55.

Christ if they are to impart divine knowledge to their sons and daughters. Third, parents should pray that the Spirit of God will dwell within their offspring from birth, just as the Holy Spirit descended upon John the Baptist in his mother's womb, and the Lord granted Timothy knowledge of Scripture (leading to salvation) from infancy. Finally, children must be raised in the fear of the Lord through inducements and corrections. Appropriate discipline must be used to chastise the faults and reward the virtues of children lovingly. However, because discipline is not the same as hateful cruelty, Paul warned fathers not to exasperate their children, indicating that parents can be too hard or go too far. The author of the epistle to the Hebrews suggests that proper chastisement is discipline respected by a mature child (most commonly a grown child raising his or her own children and now looking at discipline from the perspective of running a household rather than from the view of a child annoyed to be told what to do).[7] No one thanks a parent either for harsh treatment or for having been left without support and direction.[8]

Still, the pain of a particular chastisement (even if fair) may linger into adulthood when children nurse resentment or otherwise fail to confess that their parents were exercising rightful, discretionary authority in their families—and were not obligated to bow to the preferences of the young. Moreover, children who create difficult situations in their families through willful disrespect and resistance to reasonable demands have no just complaint if their persistent noncompliance or direct disobedience leads to unwanted and uncomfortable consequences. Parents are not required to remain quiet in the face of their children's provocations, but are given authority to set the family standard for scheduling routines, leisure time use, and religious obligations. Parents have the right to forbid tattoos, prohibit piercings, approve clothing, take away video games, require regular chores, set homework standards, prohibit unwise friendships, set rules for driving, require part-time work, and restrict dating by

---

7. Ephesians 6:4 (ESV); Deuteronomy 6:7–9; Matthew 7:9–11; 2 Timothy 3:15, Ephesians 6:4 (ESV); Hebrews 12:7–11.

8. One Puritan preacher wrote against those who deny the utility of physical discipline: "No parent may hope to weaken and destroy the corruption that is in his child's heart, though he teaches him never so well, and uses all the allurements he can to draw him to goodness, if he does not also correct him and use the rod sometimes. The Lord Himself, who is both the wisest and the best father, and who loves his children a thousand times more than any of us can love ours, takes this course with His children; yes, in this way He gives Himself as a model for all wise parents." Portions of Arthur Hildersham's sermons are found in Gary Ezzo, ed., *The Godly Family*, 119–120.

minor children. Children must obey their parents in all things, while parents are required to love their children by seeking the good of their sons and daughters over their own needs, to the point of laying down their lives. They must provide prudent and consistent guidance for living in a fallen world, while nurturing the specific gifts God has given their children and loving their offspring, even when the latter prove self-centered and truly unlovable.[9]

In the previous chapters, I noted that the eternal sonship of Christ serves as a model for honoring our parents. Scripture also makes it plain that parents must honor their children and that the biblical model for a household includes significant parental authority, although the family is neither a military hierarchy nor a business administration. Fathers (and mothers) are called to reflect the image of the Triune God in their parent-hood. We must always remember how the Father honored his eternal Son during the Transfiguration, declaring: "This is My beloved Son, with whom I am well pleased; listen to Him." Likewise, Christ himself revealed that the Father loves the Son, shows him all things, and the Son does whatever the Father does. Indeed, the Father gives authority and power to his Son so that "all will honor the Son even as they honor the Father."[10] This is the holy call of every parent: to imitate our eternal Father in honoring our sons and daughters (just as the Lord commands children to honor their parents) by directing them toward honorable lives. Any failure to so honor a son or daughter (whether a toddler, a young adult, or a mature parent with their own family) is a grave sin that violates the biblical model of parenting. Just as I started this chapter with God's threat of judgment for those who harm his little ones, so each of us must reflect on the accountability every parent faces whenever we fail to honor (and make honorable) our children as God the Father honors the God the Son.

Children must equally honor their parents, or they will face the same judgment, for the Son always does what his Father does. The Lord has ordained that parents guide their children into maturity, and any child who rebels against good parents will stumble, as will those who persis-tently ignore their parents by favoring friends, church associates, and

---

9. C.S. Lewis observed: "All who have good parents, wives, husbands, or children, may be sure that at some times—and perhaps at all times in respect of some one particular trait or habit—they are receiving charity, are loved not because they are lovable but because Love Himself is in those who love them." Lewis, *The Four Loves*, 170.

10. Matthew 17:5 (NASB); John 5:19–23 (NASB).

their own children over that relationship specifically called out by the Lord for honor. Entitled children (even an entire generation of disrespectful sons and daughters) must not imagine that they are allowed to arrogantly set their own rules or demand honor from their parents, for it is their place to show obedience and humility. Nor can they expect to be coddled and spoiled, or allowed to seize rightful parental authority from their fathers and mothers. The relationship between parent and child is bound by the full scope of biblical ethics that require Christians to humble themselves, forgive wrongs, forsake worldly lusts, and carry a Christ-like cross: to pursue every duty of piety summarized in the Sermon on the Mount. Children who push their parents to go beyond biblical teachings, demand that parents submit to their preferences, or require exaltation beyond the humility of Jesus, are tempting their fathers and mothers to ignore God's true religion and disrespect their parents' rightful authority. In doing so, they are rebelling against their Father in heaven even more than they are resisting their earthly parents. Such children should prepare themselves for divine displeasure and discipline against their sin: a discipline that may go far beyond the comparatively weak rebukes and chastisements meted out by mortal parents.

The duties of parents and children toward each other exist for both natural and adopted children—equally and without qualification. What else is adoption but a covenant between parent and child to live in lawful parenthood? The levirate custom in ancient Israel, by which a man married his deceased brother's wife and adopted their firstborn to the deceased brother (to inherit the deceased brother's name and property), was an ancient form of adoptive practice. We also see in the book of Exodus how the daughter of Pharaoh adopted the foundling Moses, and in the book of Esther how Esther's uncle raised his orphaned niece as his daughter. In the New Testament, we see authoritative language revealing how believers are the very children of God, having received "a spirit of adoption as sons by which we cry out, 'Abba! Father!'"[11] The Lord's adopted children are his beloved children, as seen in the best of human families, only more so, and without nuance or qualification. And so it must be for those made in the image of God who adopt sons and daughters in the flesh: they must model divine adoption to show everyone how believers are called into eternal life in the household of the Lord.[12]

---

11. Deuteronomy 25:5–10 (ESV); Exodus 2:10; Esther 2:7; Romans 8:15 (NASB).
12. Western churches did not allow modern forms of adoption when social and political

When a household is established in righteousness, it reveals the love and wisdom of God. Sons obey their fathers with trust and hope, and fathers exalt sons with honor and blessing. Every family member sacrifices their own interests for the good of others and is supported in turn by the rest of the family. It is essential to recognize that such homes embody what men and women aspire to: bringing delight, affection, and life.[13] By humbling themselves, family members exalt others and are themselves blessed in turn. No family is perfect, and every family member is fatally flawed, so these principles are always worked out imperfectly and incompletely. Still, as with God's church, we are called to strive for the Lord's calling, whether or not we can fully attain it.

Not everyone, however, accepts this divine reality or God's call. Many parents resent the years spent nursing babies and tending to toddlers, wishing instead to satisfy their desire for comfort, ease, security, enjoyment, entertainment, and recognition. They bitterly complain about the restrictions on their freedom when assisting teenagers and adult children, and view their children as rivals rather than as heirs. Sons and daughters, for their part, disobey parents from cradle to the grave, seldom thanking parents and grandparents for the many sacrifices through which their needs have been met and their achievements supported: forgetting decades of sacrifices made on their behalf, while remembering every parental failure as if it had just occurred. Such ungrateful and selfish children express as little respect for broader society as for their own families. Just as the reverent are promised long life, so, too, the rebellious often end their days far too early. Martin Luther observed:

> *Why do we have so many criminals who must daily be hanged, beheaded, or broken on the wheel if not because of disobedience? They will not allow themselves to be brought up in kindness; consequently, by the punishment of God they bring upon themselves the misfortune and grief that we behold, for it seldom happens that such wicked people die a natural and timely death.*[14]

---

legitimacy was based on blood-based inheritances. What the West developed was godparentage. For a survey of Western adoption practices, see Chapter 2 ("Adoption Laws from Antiquity to the Early Modern Period") in Kristin Elizabeth Gager, *Blood Ties and Fictive Ties: Adoption and Family in Early Modern France* (Princeton, New Jersey: Princeton University Press, 1996).

13. Medieval motherhood is reviewed in Clarissa W. Atkinson, *The Oldest Vocation: Christian Motherhood in the Middle Ages* (Ithaca, New York: Cornell University Press, 1991).

14. Luther, "Larger Catechism," in Tappert, *Book of Concord*, 384.

39

OECONOMICS: MANAGING THE SOUL OF THE HOUSE

The directions which God has given us, touching the use of our worldly substance, may be comprised in the following particulars: provide things needful for yourself [and] provide these for your wife, your children, your servants. If, when this is done, there be an overplus left, then "do good to them that are of the household of faith." If there be an overplus still, "as you have the opportunity, do good unto all men." [1]

"Therefore do not be anxious, saying, 'What shall we eat?' or 'What shall we drink?' or 'What shall we wear?' For the Gentiles seek after all these things, and your heavenly Father knows that you need them all. But seek first the kingdom of God and his righteousness, and all these things will be added to you." [2]

SEVERAL ANCIENT AUTHORS wrote manuals on proper household government, with many such treatises being little more than guides for accumulating wealth and preserving property. Household manuals by noted pagan authors such as Xenophon, for instance, taught readers how

1. John Wesley, *John Wesley's Fifty-Three Sermons*, ed. Edward Sugden (Nashville, Tennessee: Abingdon Press, 1983), 643–644.
2. Matthew 6:31–33 (ESV).

to manage their produce, farms, and commerce properly. Moreover, some of these treatises were titled *oeconomics* (the study of the *oikos*, or household)—a word from which it is easy to see that the modern study of *economics* originated—and resemble modern books advising families how to make profitable investments and accumulate wealth.[3]

Scripture, too, discusses the maintenance of the individual household and the accumulation of riches, but provides a radically different emphasis than its ancient or modern rivals. Jesus explicitly revealed how it is a particular temptation for unbelievers to live for material wealth, and reminded his followers how their heavenly Father provides for his loved ones as they obey their Lord's word with faith and zeal. As cited above, Jesus revealed that our mortal life is far more than accumulating material goods and financial security. We are not to run after such things, for God will surely care for our needs as a human father provides for his offspring. For that reason, Christians have no more right to worry about necessities than an anxious child might spend her day fretting whether her mother might forget to cook dinner. Just as children should play heartily and trust their parents to provide for their needs, believers must work diligently and trust God to provide for their needs.

The book of Proverbs, a biblical version of an ancient household manual, does not mention cultivating gardens or storing crops. Nor is there guidance about canning vegetables, curing meat, laying down fertilizer, or shearing sheep. In contrast, the book of Proverbs teaches us how to cultivate a godly household and preserve the fruits of virtue. It provides readers with the sayings and insights of wisdom useful for cultivating piety and sowing love, rather than accumulating wealth and preserving possessions. What every household must remember is that families are not made merely to secure livelihoods, accumulate goods, or increase pleasures (as pagans wrongly believed). Mankind has been created to reflect the good and glory of God. As Jesus declared: "Man shall not live on bread alone, but by every word that comes from the mouth of God." We are to trust in the God who created the world rather than in the things of the world itself.[4]

Proverbs reveals several principles necessary for establishing a godly

---

3. Russ Crosson has written a helpful book on Christian stewardship that balances the accumulation of property with investment in family and God's kingdom. Russ Crosson, *Your Life... Well Spent: The Eternal Rewards of Investing Yourself and Your Money in Your Family* (Eugene, Oregon: Harvest Books, 1994).
4. Matthew 4:4 (ESV).

household. All who ignore such divine wisdom forfeit the promises and provisions of the Lord, for God blesses only those who obey his revelation. In contrast, those who trust God to provide for their households will accept the following maxims, and their heavenly Father will protect them as faithful and favored children. To that end, the principles summarized in Proverbs are as follows: First, it is wisdom, not wealth, that protects from sin and destruction. Second, God and his people must be honored with material goods, since it is hypocritical to pray for the Lord to be open-handed toward us if we are selfish toward the Lord and tight-fisted toward the needy (both God's servants and the poor). Third, work must be performed in a diligent and timely fashion. Skill is required to succeed in life. Fourth, men and women must care for the goods and opportunities placed in their hands since there is no justification for carelessness and waste. Fifth, God's blessing requires consistent hard work rather than hasty get-rich-quick schemes or chance lotteries. Sixth, men and women must labor where God has called them and where they are skilled. We should seek to understand the type of life the Lord would have us live and develop our talents rather than pursue money alone. Seventh, those who use their goods in a risky manner may lose what the Lord has entrusted to them. The Lord blesses wisdom, not folly. Eighth, necessities must be sought before luxuries. Finally, people must understand when to attend to their families' higher needs once basic material needs have been met. There is a time to be content with one's daily bread.[5]

When the teachings of Proverbs are examined, it becomes clear that the Bible is less interested in showing us the road to riches than providing us the path to wisdom. What God intends for us is not wealth and ease but orderly and diligent habits of life. He wishes for us to be prudent and wise and good and generous because it is the worth of our souls that matters more than the poverty of our purse or the wealth of our estates. Nor are we allowed to mistake *prosperity* for *blessing* since many diligent households suffer poverty and ignominy despite their moral worth and spiritual productivity. Jesus himself was a dirt-poor teacher (and former laborer) during his public ministry, and his chief disciples included mere fishermen. Moreover, many unbelievers and evildoers prosper for a time

---

5. Proverbs 2:12–22; Proverbs 11:28; Proverbs 11:24–25; Proverbs 10:4–5; Proverbs 12:27; Proverbs 13:11; Proverbs 1:5; Proverbs 22:29; Proverbs 20:16; Proverbs 24:27; Proverbs 23:4.

as a direct result of greed and theft, while otherwise good providers suffer poverty as a result of base injustice, oppressive taxation, or limited opportunity.[6] In sum, it is simply wrong to see the blessing of God more in the market value of a house than in the spiritual worth of its inhabitants. The true blessing of God is the joy and peace of a household, not foreign travel, swimming pools, or expensive automobiles. The writer of the book of Proverbs observed:

> *Better is a little with the fear of the LORD*
> *than great treasure and turmoil with it.*
> *Better is a dish of vegetables where love is*
> *than a fattened ox served with hatred.*[7]

While riches do not indicate value, the qualities of prudence and industry reflect a person's moral worth, whether the person is the owner of a grand estate or a small tent. This is important: a person may possess only limited money to give away, but still share what they have, no matter how much or little it might be. Even a poor man can teach his children to care for their lives by setting a good example, such as caring for a small yard or an old car. Nor is there ever a good reason for a woman to let the filth and squalor of laziness overrun her house, since even wild animals keep dung and decay from their dens and nests. In contrast to slovenliness and filthiness, every father and mother must understand how the tidiness of their home surely affects the tidiness of their children's spirits (children will learn more from the routines of the home than what they are taught with words).[8] Moreover, parents who refuse to keep their house free of filth are unlikely to adequately instruct their children in the true faith—their offspring are likely to have dirty faces and disordered souls alike. Nor can a man who loses and mistreats his tools be expected to care for his children as he ought. Carelessness is a habit of the soul. Of course, it does no good for a parent to keep a child clean-faced and nicely dressed if the child's soul becomes filled with impiety and impurity.

Those who doubt this should remember how the importance of stewardship in both small and great matters is stressed throughout the Bible (including Christ's parables). Paul used such reasoning to forbid

---

6. Ecclesiastes 5:8–9.
7. Proverbs 15:16–17 (NASB).
8. In Leviticus 14:34–42, Moses commanded that certain types of uncleanness in a house should be considered ritual impurity—and resolved.

heads of unruly households from governing the church of God, requiring every elder to "manages his own household well, keeping his children under control with all dignity." Why? Because anyone who cannot properly rule his family well is not qualified to "take care of the church of God." That is to say, those with disordered habits at home should not be entrusted with the far more difficult task of ruling God's household. Can a man who is unable to manage his own finances govern a community of human beings? Probably not. The Lord himself confirmed this point in his parable of the talents: those persons who break trust and fail with small things in mortal life (like money) will not be entrusted with the far greater treasures of eternity.[9]

In contrast to those with unruly families and untidy households, those who govern their households well, including the material goods thereof, learn true wisdom and experience something of how the Lord governs and cares for his creation. Udo Middelmann rightly reminded us that man is called to reign wisely and creatively as "vice-regent of God" over the Lord's creation.[10] In caring for the goods of this world, mankind is enabled to experience a greater measure of divine wisdom. And while understanding how to change a diaper or paint a house may seem trivial matters, they are not. God himself has ordained not only cosmic matters, such as the Creation and the Incarnation, but also trillions of lesser concerns, like feeding sparrows and clothing the flowers of the field. It is the Lord's care that feeds young lions, brings rain to a thousand streams, and provides rocks for the very insects of the world to dwell in.[11] By attaining wisdom in their stewardship of material creation, believers can share in the Lord's wisdom, who cares for every living creature on the earth. Believers can possess a share of the wisdom that creates and governs the entire world.

Moreover, the government of property is not a matter of individual taste and consumption, as if generations live only for themselves. Just as children are obligated to care for their parents even at a significant financial and emotional cost, parents are required to ensure that family property (provided to them by their parents in some instances) is passed to their heirs after they die. Inspired by the Spirit of the Lord, Solomon noted that "a good man leaves an inheritance to his children's children."

---

9. 1 Timothy 3:4–5 (NASB); Matthew 25:14–30.
10. Middelmann, *Pro.exist.ence,* 36.
11. Psalm 104:11–12,14,18,21,27,30.

Prudent men and women save not only for their own needs but also to assist their children and grandchildren. It does not matter whether such assistance is a fortune left by the wealthy, a car shared by a middle-class grandparent, or a meaningful keepsake left by the humble of estate. What matters is that men and women not consume, spend, or waste everything they earn and inherit, but work to influence and support future generations. Everyone must remember that life neither begins nor ends with one generation; we are neither nihilist philosophers, godless thugs, nor self-centered individualists. Believers understand that just as parents are a biological link between generations, so, too, they should be a financial link between generations to whatever extent the Lord allows. We must ask ourselves whether taking a world tour or purchasing an expensive sports car is more important than educating our children or equipping our grandchildren to serve the Lord. There must be a place for charity in death, just as during life.[12]

However, before we discuss the biblical ethics of inheritance, it is essential to review how inheritances generally worked before modern times. In much of the ancient, medieval, and premodern world, the inheritance of property (typically land) was determined by legal and moral customs—just as noble titles were so established (in fact, noble titles often accompanied land). Parents did not have the right to select their heirs in violation of common customs unless a potential heir proved unworthy, committed treason, or was lawfully disqualified through some egregious or treacherous action.[13] We see this reality in the parable of the prodigal son, in which the prodigal son requested his share of the family property before his father's death. The portion he received truly was his to inherit, just as what was left truly belonged to his brother, so his request was legitimate, even if his objective was not.[14]

In traditional societies, property arrangements could become complicated after remarriage following divorce or death, particularly when men and women held property to be passed to their children and grandchildren. We see the shadow of this former system in our own system of

---

12. Proverbs 13:22 (NASB).
13. A great introduction to this subject can be found in Jack Goody, Joan Thirsk, and E.P. Thompson, eds., *Family and Inheritance: Rural Society in Western Europe, 1200–1800* (Cambridge: Cambridge University Press, 1976). For an excellent review of medieval canon law regarding legal rights in marriage, household, and inheritance, see Charles J. Reid Jr., *Power over the Body, Equality in the Family: Rights and Domestic Relations in Medieval Canon Law* (Grand Rapids, Michigan: William B. Eerdmans Publishing Company, 2004).
14. Luke 15:12, 31.

intestate inheritances, in which states divide property according to set formulas when property owners die without a valid will and property is divided among children and other heirs (though modern law generally favors spouses and permits disinheritance of children in a manner traditional societies did not). The premodern world often resembled one in which most people faced obligatory intestate inheritance.

The point of my digression is straightforward: Scripture provides laws to address situations as complex as any modern dilemma. Just as Moses provided specific statutes and general principles for determining inheritances despite any preferences of the deceased, we, too, are not allowed to do as we please with our property either preceding or following our deaths—no matter what civil law authorizes. We have all seen grown children shocked and embittered to find they have been disinherited by a devoted or beloved parent, with newcomer stepparents inheriting generations-held family property and eventually passing it to the stepparent's children. Or perhaps the stepparent has been enabled to live in comfort and ease while disinherited children and grandchildren struggle to make ends meet. This is unfair, unjust, and ought not to be. It represents a flaw in our legal system that often favors second marriages over first ones and spouses over children. Often, it is the final aftershock following the betrayal, infidelity, and lust of a parent who marred his or her children's youth through adultery and divorce, or results from the complications of remarriage after the death of a spouse.[15]

To avoid such evils, Scripture stresses fairness and equity in inheritance laws. A summary of Mosaic inheritance law includes the following principles to frame our planning. First, children should be treated equitably, regardless of whether they have different mothers or fathers. Whether a marriage is ended by divorce or death does not matter; whether children take an opposing side in a divorce does not matter (unless, perhaps, children assisted an adulterous conspiracy against the betrayed spouse). Parents must treat their children equally, regardless of

---

15. One historian wrote: "Testamentary freedom is assumed by many to be a cardinal principle of the American law of wills and estates. The idea that one who drafts a will should be free to dispose of his or her property as it seems best, without regard to ties of natural affection, has had a strong hold on the American legal imagination... In modern American law, testators are generally free to disinherit their children. Various statutory and judicial doctrines have developed to mitigate the harsher aspects of this rule, but it remains the case that in most American jurisdictions, 'a child or other descendant has no statutory protection against disinheritance by a parent.'" Charles J. Reid Jr., *Power over the Body, Equality in the Family: Rights and Domestic Relations in Medieval Canon Law*, 153.

how bitter or hateful the situation may be. Second, there should be parity among all children, without favoritism, and each child should be given an equal—rather, a generous—share of parental love. While there may be a prudent reason to assist a struggling or disadvantaged child more than a successful one, all children must experience their parents' remembrance and love. Moreover, while Moses allowed firstborn sons a double portion, this was because the oldest son was expected to care for his aging mother and unmarried sisters. There must be no unfair favoritism based on success, beauty, personality, or any cause beyond the Lord's providence and the obligation to care for dependent family members (for which effort the caretaker should be recompensed). Third, an inheritance received from a relative who dies without heirs should, in some sense, be used to sustain the memory and name of that heirless man or woman. No man or woman should die forgotten, especially if they lived uprightly. This can be as profound as remembering the deceased by building a charitable institution in their name or as simple as cherishing a family memento in their honor.[16] Fourth, both sons and daughters must be treated with respect. Moses gave women rights that they often lacked in the ancient world; it must also be remembered that the dowry of a Hebrew woman represented her share in family property, being sufficient to enable her to start life with her husband. In today's world, there may be a need to ensure that sons are honored as much as their sisters. Whether these principles are reflected in civil law or not, they provide direction for believers managing the transfer of property to the next generation in a manner that honors the Lord and causes their children to bless them rather than weep bitter tears over parental betrayal.[17]

It should be noted that children who do great wrong can (and often should) be disinherited. Parents have an obligation to treat their children with generous equity. At the same time, children have an equal responsibility to respect their living parents and to prepare to receive the labor and savings of a previous generation with humble gratitude and affection.

---

16. For instance, my family preserves the handcrafted furniture and Second World War keepsakes inherited from my wife's great uncle, Lewis Elliott—a Seabee veteran who fought in the Pacific and a master carpenter, whose decades of labor and savings helped fund the educations of many family members.

17. In the biblical system of property, parents could not cheat the system by passing property to a favored child prior to death, so the above principles apply to sharing in life as well as in death. I would add that in many systems of inheritance the property of the deceased might pass to a man or woman's children rather than to a living spouse, which prevented many difficulties associated with remarriage by a widow or widower.

Ungrateful and unworthy children cannot lay moral claim to what they have not earned. As the book of Proverbs noted, rebellious offspring will "inherit wind." Why? Because the harvest of good works should not be used to support profligate and criminal lives. Moreover, it may also be necessary to disinherit selfish and unaffectionate children who fail to honor their parents with appropriate respect, attention, and support. Those who distance themselves from their parents for years, or even decades, should not be treated the same as brothers and sisters who diligently and compassionately tend and care for aging and ailing parents and grandparents. Equity demands differentiation.[18]

Adam and Eve foolishly sought the knowledge of good and evil by sinning, trying to shortcut the attainment of wisdom as God intended it to be acquired through making good moral and spiritual choices over time. Like lazy, dishonest students trying to earn good grades without studying, the first couple did not wait to grow wise through months, years, and generations of patient care for their own people and property, but tried to cheat. In contrast to their foolish cheating, the redeemed are to imitate our Creator (whose infinite wisdom is revealed over many years in a human life, many centuries in human history, and many eons in the universe's history). Scripture makes clear that the unfolding of our world is the unveiling of God's eternal wisdom and love, as well as the truth that by living in such wisdom we receive the greatest of gifts: the opportunity to become like God in his providential care of all things.

> *"The LORD possessed me at the beginning of his work,*
> *the first of his acts of old.*
> *Ages ago I was set up,*
> *at the first, before the beginning of the earth...*
> *When he established the heavens, I was there...*
> *when he marked out the foundations of the earth,*
> *then I was beside him, like a master workman,*
> *and I was daily his delight,*
> *rejoicing before him always,*
> *rejoicing in his inhabited world*
> *and delighting in the children of man."* [19]

---

18. Deuteronomy 21:15–17; Deuteronomy 25:6 (ESV); Numbers 27:6; Proverbs 11:29 (NASB).
19. Proverbs 8:22–23, 27–31 (ESV).

PART IV

SIN AND SALVATION IN THE CONTEMPORARY HOUSEHOLD

∼

It is evident that the modern household does not live up to the ideas and ethics presented in this book, falling far short of God's eternal, immutable, and absolute standard. Therefore, as contemporary believers pursue a Christian marital ethic, they must consider both the world in which they live and the world that lives in them. Moreover, they must go far beyond patiently understanding the sins that accompany every gathering of fallen human beings, whether in or outside the family. The fact is that Western households are being remade in a most unchristian way and are drifting far from the divine purposes that they are called to reflect. Believers must understand and reject the temptations of modern immorality. We must repent of our sins.

However, seeing the drift toward immorality as a uniquely modern phenomenon would be a serious mistake. Contemporary academics often make this error when they attribute the disruption of the Christian household to social factors such as industrialization, mass society, consumer culture, modern telecommunications, or other impersonal influences. The reality is that familial and sexual relationships are profoundly personal in their very nature. Anyone who seduces a virgin, commits adultery, or deserts a spouse is motivated by sinful desires in their own heart and flesh, not by external forces and influences. In human experience, what is most personal and concrete are sexual desires, marital hopes, and failed dreams rather than the impact of the broader structures of society (since the individual person matters more than their circumstances and situation). This has always been the case; every generation has had to decide whether to uphold morality and charity in its public and private behavior. God blesses those generations that choose right and condemns those that do wrong.

This final section of my book aims to accomplish several objectives. First, it reminds believers that God remains at work among our families through all generations. Second, the section notes how family life requires the exercise of patience for its best fruits, a need aggravated by the bitter legacy of the sexual revolution. Third, the section explores the relationship between believers and the modern world, emphasizing the need for Christians to reject evil while nurturing God's creation and reforming marital life in our culture. There are also chapters regarding the nature of modesty between the sexes and the sanctity of human life, followed by a reminder that while it is laudable to strive to protect the Christian household, no one should love God's gifts more than their giver. That is, the love of family must be subordinated to the love of God.

This section also discusses how the Lord will judge the sins of our generation, as he has always punished wicked societies and civilizations. Modern men and women will not be exempted from divine wrath, and God's fury is not dependent on our concurrence, even regarding politically accepted evils like abortion. The section concludes with reminders of what marriage and family life are ultimately about and how God blesses men and women in this life and the next, both those believers long devoted to him and newly repentant Christians alike.

∼

40

PATIENCE AND FORBEARANCE IN THE CHRISTIAN HOUSEHOLD

[As soon as some men and women begin to live together and find that their spouse opposes them], they bawl and cry, "You were not sent to me by a human being but by the devil himself!" These people are like a man who bought a vineyard and then went into it before the time of harvest to test the grapes which were still hard and sour, unseasoned and unripe. Because of this, the man plucked up the grapes and destroyed the entire vineyard. Just as in such a case the proper time must be understood, so also must a man and woman be patient with one another in beginning to live together. And even when the grapes are ripe, still the juice is not immediately turned into wine at the beginning. Indeed, in many wines aging and the passing of years makes it even better and more pleasant. But those who will not wait for the proper time cast the juice out because it is not wine at the very beginning, and will always lack the wine that they need. Likewise, those who cannot endure human infirmities and blemishes must not marry, for every person is tempted and has not only the weakness and imperfection inherited from our first father Adam, but also his or her own particular blemishes and faults.[1]

---

1.   H. Bullinger, *The Christen State of Matrimonye* (reprint; 1541, Norwood, New Jersey: Walter Johnson, Inc., 1974), 52-54. Please note that I have edited this passage for clarity, and

HENRY BULLINGER, one of the most important Protestant Reformers, provided an illustrative and effective analogy when he compared marriage to a good wine: grapes must be picked at the right time and allowed to age. Only foolish vinesmen destroy their crops because the grapes have not ripened early, or dump their wine because it has not matured in a few weeks. It is the same for attaining a vintage marriage: a couple should not expect their relationship to be as harmonious at the outset as the marriages of those who have lived together for decades, who have spent years in prayer and toil to work through weaknesses and develop strengths. Newlyweds must not imitate foolish vinesmen who destroy crops because they are not prematurely ripe, but should wait patiently for the best fruits of marriage. Nor should couples trample the vineyard of marriage with adultery, desertion, and divorce, or nurse critical and dissatisfied attitudes. There must be patience and a willingness to let marriage ripen over the years.

No marriage is perfect. Though it is easier to see the faults of some couples more than others, no marriage is without its sins and sorrows. The reason for problems in marriage is not deficient courtship customs or inadequate premarital counseling; nor is it mistaken modern ideas and customs of marriage, though these do not help the situation. No, every marriage has its particular problems because every generation of human beings is born as sinners. While most couples, both today and in the past, avoid aimed gunfire and vicious verbal abuse, no marriage lives up to the perfect standard of selfless love reflective of God's goodness. What the apostle Paul declared of human beings in general remains true of human beings in marriage and family life: "All have sinned and fall short of the glory of God." For this reason, each of us must daily recognize and remember that we live among fallen human beings in our households, communities, and countries. We must not be sharper in our judgments and attitudes toward these fellow sinners than we would have others be toward our faults, public and hidden alike. Jesus made it clear that we must treat others as we would like to be treated, and Paul, in the same spirit, warned against being judgmental toward others while falling short of God's law in our own lives.[2]

For those who doubt they and their loved ones are filled with such

---

the original pagination is challenging to follow. The text is located between Roman numerals lii–liiii, as marked in the original.

2.   Romans 3:23 (ESV); Romans 2:1; Matthew 7:12.

faults, let me note how the apostle John revealed the high standard of love demanded of each man and woman, teaching that every person must love every man and woman and boy and girl in their path with perfect charity since the person "who does not love his brother whom he has seen, cannot love God whom he has not seen." Still, while John preached perfection, he also understood that everyone is born into sin, insisting that human beings acknowledge the reality of their imperfection when he declared that we are "deceiving ourselves" if we claim to be without sin, but the Lord will "forgive us our sins [and] cleanse us from all unrighteousness," as we confess our sins.[3] The apostle John set the standard for all human relationships by recognizing that everyone is flawed, yet calling believers to a divine standard of perfect love. Lest anyone consider John naive or rash, we must remember that the apostle lived with our Lord's perfection on earth, learning exactly what righteousness looks like and understanding in real life how all mortals necessarily fall short of the divine standard. Still, John equally understood the promise of Christ (in whom there is neither error nor lie) to empower his people through his Spirit to follow his example and live in love.

Because there is no perfect husband, wife, father, mother, sister, brother, or child, people should be gentle and patient with the faults and weaknesses of family members, not expecting ideal behavior that is unattainable in a sinful world. Men and women should not expect perfection from themselves or others, falling into despondency when they fail to realize some utopian ideal fashioned not from God's revelation (or common experience), but from fiction portrayed in novels and films. Every household is the dwelling place of sinners, whether or not its inhabitants confess (or even recognize) all of their faults. Therefore, people must expect neither to give nor to receive a full measure of love in their families. Every household will have difficulties and quarrels, just as every physical house will have leaks and cracks—and every family will have serious faults and flaws in many matters. There will be problems with irreligion, pride, anger, lust, laziness, dishonesty, disrespect, greed, jealousy, ingratitude, and envy in every household, even in homes of one or two people. Remembering this truth will help cultivate patience toward others, as we focus more on the troubles we cause than the difficulties that are made for us. As Gregory the Great wrote nearly fifteen hundred years ago:

---

3. 1 John 4:20 (NASB); 1 John 1:8–9 (NASB).

*[The married] are also to be admonished to consider not so much
what each has to endure from the other, as what the other is made
to endure. For if one considers what is endured from oneself, that
which is endured from another is the more easily borne.* [4]

Patience must not, however, be confused with indulgence. The
prophet Hosea married a prostitute who eventually became such a
trollop that she was rendered repulsive and valueless even to her lovers: a
harlot on the lowest rung of the ladder. As she sat at the slave market to
be sold for a petty sum, her husband obeyed the Lord's command to
redeem his wife from her self-made shame and sin-imposed slavery.
Subsequently, Hosea brought his wife home, but sternly warned her not
to be intimate with any other man. It is implied that she was told to
become faithful or risk utter destruction. This is the model of patience to
which we aspire. We must be as loving and forgiving as God and, at the
same time, uphold the Lord's law and authority as Hosea sought to do.
Those who defile the most fundamental laws of God in the household
must be taught to do what is right, not only to instruct children to differentiate right from wrong, but also because it is the right thing to do. [5]

As an example of the balance to be kept, Protestant Reformers generally requested that adulterers and adulteresses be given a second chance
by their aggrieved spouse—if the former have repented of their marital
infidelity—while equally insisting that Christians be unaccepting of
unrepentant wickedness and rebellion. Church leaders from John Calvin
to Martin Luther upheld the divine standards of forgiveness and holiness,
rebuking those who indulge in ungodliness and condemning those who
do not forgive human weakness. Calvin spoke against husbands who too
readily endured the infidelity of their wives, and quickly accepted a
return from infidelity "with a smiling countenance." Calvin believed any
such man wrongly sets aside his authority and "ruins his wife" by his
leniency. In addition to uncompromising moral integrity, Martin Luther
reminded his hearers of a corresponding need for mercy and forgiveness
when he observed that it is sometimes better to forgive a wayward spouse
(after restitution and repentance) rather than to divorce the guilty partner. Luther wrote:

---

4.   Gregory the Great, *St. Gregory the Great: Pastoral Care*, ed. Henry Davis, S.J. (Westminster, Maryland: The Newman Press, 1955), 188.
5.   Hosea 3:3.

There is no command of God that would enjoin [a husband] to keep the unchaste woman, [but] if he is a good man, he may let himself be persuaded to accept damages for it and keep her in the hope that in the future she might conduct herself honorably; this would be a good deed and better than being divorced.[6]

This is not to say that men and women should harshly uphold the law of God. Nothing could be further from the truth. God is both loving and holy, and his servants must be the same. Especially in the family, gentleness must be exercised toward lifelong faults and weaknesses since those who rule their houses or speak truth to loved ones in an overbearing manner do the work of the devil rather than the will of the Lord. In 2 Timothy, the apostle Paul warned us to correct "with gentleness" those who fall into the "snare of the devil" so the latter could come to "repentance leading them to a knowledge of the truth."[7] The early preacher John Chrysostom likewise observed that "nothing will persuade [a wife] to admit the wisdom of your words as the assurance that you are speaking to her with sincere affection."[8] Similarly, the medieval friar Francis of Assisi warned his followers to avoid anger when disappointed with their fellows since the devil is pleased to "ensnare many others through one man's sin." Most importantly, the Lord redeems our world by preaching his hatred of sin from the cross of Christ rather than proclaiming judgment without mercy.[9]

People must be patient with the inevitable trials and sacrifices of family life. Men and women who desire to honor God with a holy and loving household must enter family life seeking humble service and preparing themselves to become common servants to bawling babies and ungrateful spouses. Family life brings many responsibilities and burdens that pious people should undertake as willing servants. Those who do so learn that the yoke of marriage and parenthood is not a chain of slavery, but a fitted harness that enables couples to harvest a crop of everlasting love and delight. In contrast, those who resent the servanthood of family

---

6. John Calvin, *Commentaries on the Twelve Minor Prophets*, vol. 1, trans. Rev. John Owen (Grand Rapids, Michigan: William B. Eerdmans, 1950), 126–127; Martin Luther, "Estate of Marriage (1522)," in *Luther's Works*, vol. 46, 300.

7. 2 Timothy 2:25–26 (ESV).

8. John Chrysostom, "Homily 20," in *On Marriage and Family Life*, 54. I also like the version of this sermon in David G. Hunter's *Marriage in the Early Church*.

9. Francis of Assisi, *The Writings of St. Francis of Assisi*, trans. Benen Fahy, O.F.M. (Chicago: Franciscan Herald Press, 1963), 31, 36.

relationships, preferring lives of comfort and glamour, poison even the sweetest joys of God's creation. Such people mistake babies for burdens and faithful marriage for a prison sentence. Negligent fathers flee from their own homes, holing up in bars, gyms, and forests to drink, play, and hunt. Embittered women remain with their offspring from necessity but spit out bitter venom toward unloved husbands and unwanted children. Often, ungodly men and women desire for life to be an unbroken succession of dances, movies, and vacations, spurning household obligations as the cause of their dissatisfaction, when it is their insatiable desire for recognition, pleasure, and comfort that makes them unproductive and unhappy. They view family life, especially the care of children, as a burden that limits their self-indulgence and pleasure-seeking, and stubbornly refuse to subordinate their desires to the needs of other human beings.[10]

Beyond learning patience, we must consider every trial and sorrow of family life as a potential source of divine blessing (along with temporal burdens). While Scripture speaks of God's blessing of family life (for instance, Psalm 128 praises the godly and happy family), Christ reminded believers that those who mourn are most truly blessed before God.[11] Only when we consider family life with this divine perspective does mistreatment by a loved one become an invitation to Christian love rather than a temptation to hateful retaliation. Only with such faith does God enable believers to give thanks for sharing in the pains of the cross to which Christ was nailed: a cross where Jesus revealed the full extent of divine and human love. Why? Because it is in responding with humility and generosity to wrongdoing by parents, spouses, siblings, and children that we come to resemble our Father in heaven—who gives light and life to good and bad people alike. It may be that the Lord sometimes subjects us to undesired, difficult, and painful family circumstances in order to cultivate this God-like response in us: to remake us in his morally and spiritually perfect image. For that reason, when God gives us demanding parents, difficult siblings, domineering spouses, or disrespectful children,

---

10. Nineteenth-century writer Horace Bushnell observed: "[Sometimes a mother] submits to the maternal office and charge, as to some hard necessity. This charge is going to detain her at home and limit her freedom. Or it will take her away from the shows and pleasures for which she is living. It will burden her days and nights with cares that weary her self-indulgence. Or she is not fond of [children] and never means to be fond of them—they are not worth the trouble." Bushnell, *Christian Nurture*, 257–258.
11. Matthew 5:4.

we must understand and rejoice that we can grow more like Christ in accepting our suffering than we could in seeking an easy, undemanding life. I do not enjoy writing this any more than my readers enjoy hearing it, but it is true. God's redemptive work is to conform each believer to the perfect image of Christ, and loving a difficult family member can teach us the patience, humility, and charity required for such spiritual maturity and moral perfection. A difficult relative may be God's means of redemption in our lives.

As God patiently endures our frailty and sin, so we must grace our families with love, even when they prove as unworthy as we ourselves are before the Lord, and particularly when they repay our labor, love, and gifts with contempt, disrespect, and ingratitude. Everyone who approaches marriage and family life with a servant's attitude will learn both to give and receive love. When human employers often pay their workers a fair wage, will not the Lord reward faithful and patient men and women with a harvest of love, piety, and joy? Nevertheless, no master pays his servants before they have done their work, which is why men and women cannot glean the choicest fruits of human love until they have laid down their lives for others (often for long periods of time). As noted at the beginning of this chapter, patience is required to accomplish that task, and the wine of marriage (and all family life) should not be dumped down the drain after its first intoxication has worn off. As Puritan leader Richard Baxter wrote several hundred years ago:

> *Remember that both of you are diseased persons, full of infirmities. Therefore, expect the fruit of those infirmities in each other. Did you not know beforehand that you married a person of such weaknesses, who would daily provide trial and offense? If you could not bear this thought, you should not have married. If you had resolved that you could bear this cross, you are obliged to bear it now. Resolve, therefore, to bear with one another in recognizing that you married one another as sinful, frail, and imperfect persons, not as blameless and perfect angels.*[12]

---

12. Richard Baxter, *The Practical Works of the Reverend Richard Baxter,* vol. 4 (London: James Duncan, 1830), 125.

41

BROKEN HOMES AND REPENTANT HEARTS

The triumph of Christian teaching is when a man and a woman marry without either having had previous sexual experience. In nine cases out of ten where this occurs, the results are unfortunate.[1]

A SEXUAL REVOLUTION has swept across American culture. Bertrand Russell's attack on chastity is an intellectual and idealized specimen of a disease common to all classes of men and women in this culture: sexual immorality and promiscuity. Russell scorned virginity as the cause of marital maladjustment, implying that couples would enjoy better sexual experiences during marriage if only they behaved more promiscuously before marriage. Chastity finds few public defenders in our land and almost no support from important opinion givers and policy makers, so it is not surprising that half of our young men and women have lost their chastity before they have earned their high school diplomas. Entire generations of men and women have played (and continue to play) sexual roulette, swapping spouses and lovers in a gamble for new pleasures. Only as STDs, abortion, and lonely regret consume their lives do people

---

1. Bertrand Russell also wrote: "The more civilized people become, the less able they seem of lifelong happiness with one partner." Bertrand Russell, *Marriage and Morals* (New York: Bantam Books, 1968), 91, 93. Ironically, the growth of Western civilization seems to have been founded on a Christianized monogamy that converted the lusts of uncivilized barbarian tribes and pagan Romans alike. Russell's definition of *civilization* is incomplete.

realize that sex is no toy—that they have been playing Russian roulette with a loaded pistol.

Bertrand Russell could not have been more wrong when he advocated premarital promiscuity as the cure for lackluster sexual intimacy in marriage. The opposite is true, for it is the promiscuous who bring to their relationships a variety of troubles and memories that impact their emotional and physical adjustment to the rigors of close-quarters living. It is not the virgin who finds her groom's touch dangerous and threatening, but she whose bridal veil covers wounds and scars. Anyone who looks at the pain of men and women suffering from their own sinful choices knows this to be true, although the sexual revolution is so pervasive that there can be little thought of quickly remedying its evils: families have been divided, adulterers remarried, and significant numbers of children born without the committed love of father and mother. As believers respond to this morass of immorality and sorrow, they must seek God's wisdom in understanding how to witness to the Lord's love and holiness. Scripture provides absolutes that cannot be violated, but the Spirit of God also leads his people with prudence and freedom, insisting only that a full measure of wisdom and spiritual maturity guide every choice. To that end, the apostle Paul reminded the Corinthians to judge their choices by what is not only lawful, but also helpful and valuable.[2]

Let me give an example of what Paul intended. Earlier, it was noted how both men and women are free to marry, even if they are not virgins. This biblical principle must never be restricted, since no one can lawfully place a burden on the repentant that the Lord would not have them bear. This freedom exists because virginity is not morally necessary to make a marriage and because a person truly becomes a new creation in Christ when the Lord forgives, indwells, and sanctifies a convert's heart. Moreover, various psalms remind believers how God leads many such converts to the enduring joys of family life. Consider how seven demons possessed Mary Magdalene before Christ freed her from the grip of evil.[3] While the causes and effects of her possession are not clear, most accounts of demon possession described in the New Testament indicate crazed and unrestrained behavior, which are not the most attractive qualities in a wife. Yet, Mary presumably would have made a fine Christian wife for a believing man of her time, and only a hard man would have scorned a

---

2. 1 Corinthians 10:23 (ESV).
3. Psalm 107:41; Luke 8:1–3.

woman so favored by the Lord himself. In many instances, converts to the Christian faith from grossly immoral lives prove to be more devout than those who grow up in church. A born-again prostitute with zealous piety may be a more fervent believer (and more suitable wife) than a virgin of tepid piety. Gregory the Great observed:

> For often there are those who, returning to the Lord after their sins of the flesh, evince themselves the more zealous in doing good works, as they realize they were worthy of condemnation for their evil deeds. And often certain people who persevere in the integrity of the flesh, on perceiving that they have less to deplore, think to themselves that the innocence of their lives is sufficient, and do not arouse themselves by zealously striving to be fervent in spirit.[4]

It is vital that the repentant understand that they are free to marry if granted the opportunity. Converts should strive toward marriage or celibacy only in obedience to the call of the Holy Spirit, and no one must withdraw into solitude because of past sin and shame. As previously discussed, God does not call people to either marriage or celibacy through such means. Nor is anyone rendered unworthy of marriage or human love by their sin. The most immoral sinner and the most passionate saint alike must realize that they are saved only by God's grace, and thereby included in every provision of the Lord's salvation for this life and the next. Unless specific impediments to marriage or an actual call to celibacy exist, marriage is permitted, even encouraged, to stave off sexual temptation and selfish singleness. It is not enough that churches welcome repentant sinners into their congregations as the adopted children of God, which they have become. Those previously promiscuous, unfaithful, and impure must now be seen (by others and themselves) as new creatures, not clinging to a former life fully atoned for by the sacrifice of Christ on the cross (though believers will struggle with the old nature of sin until their death).[5] God's justice and judgment are to be feared and respected, but his mercy is greater yet.

---

4. Gregory the Great, *Pastoral Care*, 197. John Chrysostom wrote two centuries earlier: "Have you not heard how that prostitute, who once surpassed all in her wanton immorality, now overshadows all in her moral scruple? I am not talking about the prostitute in the gospels, but the one in our own time, hailing from the most lawless city of Phoenicia." Cited in Kyle Harper, *From Shame to Sin*, 192.
5. Peter Abelard observed (even following his castration) how difficult repentance is for

To repeat: no one is permitted to isolate themselves into lifelong single-ness as a self-imposed penance for sin. Christ forgives freely, and it is the devil's trap to deceive converts who previously scorned chastity to spurn matrimony afterward, thwarting God's desire for holy children in both instances. If Satan cannot conceive illegitimate children, sometimes he is content to block the birth of babies altogether. But the Lord so favors marriage that he called sinful humanity to marry even in the days following the flood: the most terrible period of human history. Though the Holy Spirit revealed how "the intention of man's heart is evil from his youth," the Lord still commanded all mankind to "be fruitful and multiply and fill the earth."[6] Using such reasoning, the apostle Paul instructed previously promiscuous Corinthian believers to marry and be given in marriage, despite the sins and troubles of this mortal life.

Moral evil, however, does have consequences. A prostitute is not a virgin by any definition of the word. She may have emotional and phys-ical scars (such as infertility, disease, or addiction) that render her unable to love a husband, run a household, or raise children. She may be so distressed and distorted in her inner being that she cannot handle the responsibilities of parenthood and marriage. As a result, a prudent suitor may decide to marry another woman from a legitimate concern that the converted prostitute will prove to be a poor wife and inadequate mother, weighed down by the memories of her sins and bearing the scars of her former life (as some such women can be for a time). The same holds true for other sins, as the wise consider the consequences of marriage for themselves and any potential children. Just as suitors must choose between possible mates based on the criteria of temperament, family, and character, so, too, the chaste are free to select potential mates who do not bring to the marriage bed lifelong troubles stemming from sexual immorality. The freedom of one person to marry does not necessitate an obligation on the part of another person to marry that person. If a man

---

sexual sin, writing: "For if I truthfully admit to the weakness of my unhappy soul, I can find no penitence whereby to appease God, whom I always accuse of the greatest cruelty in regard to this outrage [i.e., Abelard's castration]. By rebelling against his ordinance, I offend him more by my indignation than I placate him by making amends through penitence. How can it be called repentance for sins, however great the mortification of the flesh, if the mind still retains the will to sin and is on fire with its old desires? It is easy enough for anyone to confess his sins, to accuse himself, or even to mortify his body in outward show of penance, but it is very difficult to tear the heart away from hankering after its dearest pleasures." Peter Abelard, *The Letters of Abelard and Heloise*, 132.

6. Genesis 8:21 (ESV); Genesis 9:1 (ESV).

or woman prefers not to wed a particular suitor because of the former's sexual experimentation, the repentant convert has no just grounds for complaint since God's grace does not promise exemption from every consequence of sin.[7]

The single are not the only ones who must wisely deal with the consequences of modern immorality. Married couples also must do so. A family wrongly brought together after a biblically unjustified divorce and subsequent remarriage faces a genuine dilemma, with its children trapped between the obligation to honor their natural parent and the fact that a stepparent would possess no rightful place in their life apart from grave parental sin. Still, despite the unnaturalness of the situation, children must be taught to honor stepparents for God's sake. Parenthood as an institution must be respected, just as Jesus honored the institution of the state when he deferred to the unjust decrees of Pontius Pilate and the oppressive power of Roman military authorities.[8] Even standing before the ungodly King Herod, Jesus showed such deferential respect that a wicked tyrant found no fault in him. Of course, natural parents and step-parents responsible for confused and unjust circumstances must be careful to wield their authority fairly and gently, remembering how they are responsible for the establishment of unnatural and unholy circumstances that God hates. They must remember that, like Pontius Pilate and King Herod, they have no authority over their subordinates except what God has granted for his purposes. Such parents must be as generous toward children who have lost the primary birthright of every person— namely, rightful parents—as God is in his patient government of our confused and rebellious world. If natural parents are called to self-sacrificial love for their sons and daughters, old or young alike, how much more those who subject children to unnatural situations? To be blunt, all of those who assume the title and authority of parent bind themselves to its

---

7. Many of the repentant live exemplary lives, though some struggle to recover. Josh McDowell and Dick Day told of a young woman so wounded by previous choices that she lashed out in her distress at a believing young man who respected parental wishes against dating her because of her background (to include an abortion), then intentionally got pregnant with a man who looked like a second boyfriend (who ended their relationship for the same reason)—hoping to blame the man for her pregnancy. She miscarried that child. To read the actual text is to feel trauma and pain almost beyond description, but also to see a young woman unsuited for marriage before deeper repentance and healing. Josh McDowell and Dick Day, *Why Wait? What You Need to Know about the Teen Sexuality Crisis* (San Bernardino, California: Here's Life Publishers, 1987), 420.
8. John 19:11.

self-denying obligations. Just as parents are called to serve in sacrificial love, stepchildren must return love and respect.

Henry Smith, who lived during a time when stepparents were common due to high mortality rates, reminded readers that the very name of a stepmother signifies "a stead-mother."[9] What Smith meant is that all parents (natural or otherwise) must conform to the divine standard and the reality of parental love, putting the needs of children ahead of their own aspirations and interests. In this spirit, the divorced should remember that any parent who tries to build up personal authority by casting down a rival makes a terrible mistake. Just as military officers maintain a common front against enlisted soldiers and conscripts, parents must honor each other to preserve the sanctity of parenthood, even after they divorce. They are bound to treat ex-husbands or ex-wives, even selfish and sinful ones, with a generous measure of forgiveness and love, just as they want to be treated by our Lord (though without the modern twist of pretending that divorce and remarriage are less than unholy tragedies). They must uphold the sanctity of parenthood, even when a particular father or mother fails to be the person God calls them to be. They must be charitable and humble even toward a former spouse.

Children who find themselves in spiritually and morally mixed households, whether from death or divorce, should not despair that they live in less-than-ideal circumstances. After all, the moral laws that govern family life are based more in eternal reality than in fallen human nature. God's character alone is the perfect standard that all human fathers must imitate, yet his children are all spiritually adopted: none of us becomes a true believer through biology and birth. None of us is born into a perfect family. Nor should men and women who convert to the Christian faith while married despair if they find themselves attached to a spouse who lives anything but a Christian life, but must trust God to bring good from evil and salvation from sin, as he is already doing in their lives. Although children born of spiritually mixed marriages frequently face burdens that the offspring of two godly parents do not, no one should doubt how the Lord is willing and able to bless such children. As in every other realm of human life, the grace and blessing of the Lord are not limited by the nature and extent of human sin. God's power is made perfect not in our strength but through our sins and failures.

---

9. Henry Smith, "A Preparative to Marriage," in *The Works of Henry Smith*, vol. 1 (Edinburgh: James Nichol, 1866), 37.

Indeed, the apostle Paul explicitly mentioned God's blessing on children with a single Christian parent. Paul also discipled and mentored his close co-worker Timothy (likely born of a pagan father and a believing mother), who became one of Paul's most trusted associates and the recipient of two New Testament epistles (the first of which is a veritable treatise on the Christian household).[10] And Augustine of Hippo grew up to become one of the most influential Christian teachers and philosophers in Western civilization, as well as a church leader overflowing with knowledge and love of God, despite being born into a mixed marriage (or perhaps because he was born into such a home). Born of a pagan, maritally unfaithful father and a devoted, pious mother, Augustine worked through the strictures and sorrows of his once profligate and unbelieving life (which included an illegitimate child) to help establish and guide the churches of Christ for the next thousand years, and well beyond. Augustine was not only a serving bishop preaching to his congregants as the Roman Empire collapsed around him, but also wrote influential books on the holy Trinity, God's providence, divine grace, an autobiography of his conversion, and treatises discussing various challenges to God's churches. Nearly every branch of Christianity has roots in Augustine's theology and writings—and ultimately in the piety, prayers, and persistence of his mother Monica in her once unholy household.[11]

When given a second chance, the repentant must not let shame for their previous sin destroy their condemnation of wrongdoing. Those once guilty of adultery and fornication must not fear teaching their children about marital fidelity and sexual purity from worry about awkward questions. It is possible, perhaps probable, that sons and daughters being taught about chastity and fidelity will question their parents about their own premarital intimacy or post-marital fidelity.[12] Answering awkward

---

10. 1 Corinthians 7:14 (ESV); 2 Timothy 1:5.
11. Augustine of Hippo recounted in his *Confessions* the piety of his mother, Monica, whose prayers won over her pagan husband and profligate son.
12. Charles Williams wrote that true forgiveness reminds us of our own sins: "Guilt is in all; it is the guilty who forgives. Entreated to forgive, by another as guilty, it is his whole duty to restore reconciliation by any and every means, forever and ever, without condition... The entreaty for forgiveness does not, among mortal creatures, abolish the sin, but... provokes a shy humility on the part not only of the pardoned but of the pardoner. The awful consciousness (in any serious matter) that he is necessarily exercising, in his proper degree, the conceded prerogative of Christ, prevents pride, prevents anything but shame. Must the lecherous forgive the malicious? The slothful the arrogant? It seems no less. But not, surely, without a keener sense of lechery or sloth, a renewed entreaty on his own part, a confessed exchange of guilt. Not perhaps, vocally... it is sometimes a solecism to intrude one's own

questions may not be enjoyable, but it is better than avoiding humble sharing altogether, for the example of King David warns us against masking our shame in silence. When confronted with his son Amnon's rape of a half-sister, Tamar, David grew angry, yet failed to punish Amnon either for rape or incest (likely paralyzed by the shame of his own adulterous affair with Bathsheba and responsibility for her husband's death). Because David refused to punish Amnon, Tamar's full brother, Absalom, took justice into his own hands, culminating in a bloodbath of vengeance, murder, and rebellion.[13]

A few years later, David came to understand better how God's law must be upheld, even if doing so led to a fear of hypocrisy and the blush of shame. We know this because David taught Solomon (his son by the once-adulterous Bathsheba) to hate adultery above every other sin. Discussing such a sensitive subject must have been troubling to father and son alike, especially since Solomon's older brother died as a newborn in God's judgment of the affair. Still, the book of Proverbs records Solomon as saying when he was still an only child, a mere boy, his father taught him that he who "commits adultery with a woman is lacking sense; he who would destroy himself does it." By confessing his grave sin to his son, David humbled himself before God and his own family. It is no wonder the Lord so favored him despite his terrible wrongdoing—for the Lord loves a contrite heart. If only the king had expressed that quality earlier, tragedy might have been avoided for his family and country.[14] Francis Schaeffer observed of the shame that previously paralyzed David from dealing with the sin of his son:

> *Because people knew about [David's] sin with Bathsheba, he was in a poor position, both as king and father, to do anything about [Amnon's rape of Tamar]. And he did not jump over this difficulty; he became angry but did nothing. If David had punished the sin rightly, perhaps Absalom, another of David's sons, would not have taken it upon himself to punish it wrongly.*[15]

sins, though hardly to remember them." Charles Williams, *The Forgiveness of Sins* (Grand Rapids, Michigan: William B. Eerdmans Publishing Company, 1984), 73–74.

13. 2 Samuel 13:1–2, 10–14; 20–22, 28–29.

14. Proverbs 4:3–4; Proverbs 6:32 (NASB). The sad conclusion is that Solomon avoided adultery but embraced polygamy, taking hundreds of wives and drifting from God. In this, Solomon followed the bad example of his father (who also took several wives).

15. Francis Schaeffer, "No Little People," in *The Complete Works of Francis A. Schaeffer: A Christian Worldview*, vol. 3 (Westchester, Illinois: Crossway Books, 1982), 94.

42

LOT AND THE FLIGHT FROM
PERVERSION

*Lot went up from Zoar and stayed in the mountains, and his two
daughters with him; for he was afraid to stay in Zoar; and he
stayed in a cave, he and his two daughters. Then the firstborn said
to the younger, "Our father is old, and there is not a man on earth
to come in to us after the manner of all the earth. Come, let us make
our father drink wine, and let us lie with him that we may preserve
our family through our father." So they made their father drink
wine that night, and the firstborn went in and lay with her father;
and he did not know when she lay down or when she arose. On the
following day, the firstborn said to the younger, "Behold, I lay last
night with my father; let us make him drink wine tonight also;
then you go in and lie with him, that we may preserve our family
through our father." So they made their father drink wine that
night also, and the younger arose and lay with him; and he did not
know when she lay down or when she arose. Thus both the daughters
of Lot were with child through their father.* [1]

LOT WAS SPARED the fate of the wicked and perverse inhabitants of
Sodom and Gomorrah. Unfortunately, he seems to have fallen into
anxious fear or a moral stupor following the deaths of his neighbors,

---

1. Genesis 19:30–36 (NASB).

betrothed sons-in-law, and wife. Leaving the stricken cities of the plains, Lot fled with his daughters to a nearby cave, where he lingered for what may have been a long while. Over time, it became apparent to his daughters that their father had little intention of providing them with husbands, while Lot must have grown apathetic about finding husbands for his daughters and a wife for himself, and did not seek the protection of his wealthy kinsman Abraham (who undoubtedly would have arranged marriages for his beleaguered relatives). In what seems to have been self-pitying despondency, Lot languished around the cave until his daughters twice got him so drunk that he could not afterward remember sharing a bed with them. The book of Genesis tells this story to condemn Lot's sin rather than to mitigate his responsibility, and Lot's descendants were judged as a cursed people because of their forefather's sin. Scripture presents Lot as a man both saved by God's grace from terrible judgment and one who committed acts as wicked as those of the destroyed cities of Sodom and Gomorrah.

It is important to recognize that though God physically destroyed Sodom and Gomorrah, the vices of those wicked cities lived on in the persons of Lot and his daughters, demonstrating how *the world* exists in each individual, not merely among defiantly unbelieving people, for sin cannot be destroyed by brimstone alone.[2] At the very least, Lot was guilty of extreme drunkenness (just like Noah after the destruction of the world by flood), and it seems possible that Lot had demonstrated sexual interest in his daughters before the women took the initiative to seduce their father, since it is otherwise difficult to imagine how they dared such a wicked scheme.[3] As for the two daughters, they were guilty of incestuously enticing their father, then rationalizing that they had followed the custom of women bearing children. Even if they believed themselves to be the last three people on God's earth as they claimed (ignoring the facts that the small city of Zoar had survived the apocalypse and their kinsman Abraham retained the Lord's protection), Lot and his daughters should have considered that the Lord had miraculously spared their lives for a

---

2. Lot's daughters were unmarried, likely still teenagers, showing how sin is in each of us from our youth. While we must repent of the sin that we recognize, no one should be surprised at the manifestation of sin from an early age. The fact that even elementary school children become caught up in such wrongdoing is not a result of sexual education in the schools, but of fallen human nature.

3. Among the Romans was the expression: "In vino veritas" ("In wine, there is truth"). An English variant is found in the common proverb: "A drunk man's words are a sober man's thoughts"—which may have been popularized in a play written by William Butler Yeats.

purpose and would care for them in all that they required. But lacking faith and decency, the women insisted they had the immediate *right* to have offspring, seemingly by whatever means were available. Still, when the Lord told mankind to increase and multiply, he never intended them to do so with their parents.

The warning in this story is that the thinking and practice of the world around them must not infect God's people. By living in Sodom, Lot made compromises that cost him much of what he should have held dear. His family was perverted by the sinful environment in which he chose to live. While Abraham guarded his soul in the countryside, Lot chose to live in a rich and luxurious city overrun by perversion and filth. This story reminds contemporary readers that wicked lusts must be resisted entirely. When possible, we should build our homes where our families and we can serve God in piety rather than remaining in an ungodly environment that will lead our households astray.[4] Lot's daughters were influenced by their sinful surroundings—thereby adopting the evil ways of Sodom and Gomorrah, corrupting their souls, and eventually defiling their bodies. We must seek to live among the godly, and when called by the Lord to live among the unbelieving and immoral, we must do so as holy prophets preaching the judgment and grace of God. As the apostle Paul warned all believers in his first epistle to the Corinthians:

> *Do not be deceived: 'Bad company ruins good morals.' Wake up from your drunken stupor, as is right, and do not go on sinning. For some have no knowledge of God, I say this to your shame.*[5]

Even removed from the immediate surroundings of Sodom, Lot and his daughters sinned as terribly as the homosexual rapists of Sodom. Sin flourished in Lot's family as much as in Sodom, and it equally exists in each of us. Long before the outside world has an opportunity to poison our souls, we are born into selfish corruption. Babies do not lash out in hatred and jealousy because they have learned to do so from watching television, reading ungodly books, browsing the Internet, watching the bad examples of older siblings, or being impacted by the flaws of their parents and grandparents. No, *I-want-what-I-want-and-I-want-it-now* is

---

4. How many of us risk our households in wealthy suburbs filled with opportunity and unbelief rather than move to pious towns and neighborhoods that might have lesser schools and worldly opportunity?

5. 1 Corinthians 15:33–34 (ESV).

born into each of us, whether during a baby's self-centered impatience for her mother's breast or a grown man's self-centered desire for a stranger's beauty. We are born (and remain) selfish creatures, guilty before God and in need of redemption. In the epistle of 1 John, the apostle John reminded believers that we deceive ourselves and blaspheme God if we deny that we are sinners. In the book of Romans, the apostle Paul declared that none of us are righteous or naturally seek God. Paul observed how mankind overflows with deceit, venom, violence, and ruin; no one fears God. Paul also explained that sin comes to all men through Adam, a teaching consistent with David's lament that mankind is conceived in sin and "brought forth in iniquity."[6] As with the incestuous daughters of Lot, there is self-justifying and God-denying wickedness in each one of us. The Christian philosopher Blaise Pascal observed:

> *Larceny, incest, infanticide, parricide, everything has at some time been accounted a virtuous action. There no doubt exist natural laws, but once this fine reason of ours was corrupted, it corrupted everything.*[7]

Whereas Lot toyed with sin and let himself be seduced by his daughters, the example of the patriarch Joseph shows a better way. When his master's wife, Potiphar, attempted to seduce the young man, Joseph fled from her house. After the woman invited the handsome young man into her bed, Joseph fled so swiftly that his cloak remained clutched in the woman's hand. The woman subsequently covered her wrongdoing (and retaliated against her rejection) by accusing Joseph of attempted rape, with the wrongly accused Joseph subsequently suffering years of imprisonment as a result.[8] What is significant about the incident is Joseph's refusal to dally with sin. He did not allow himself to be seduced. A weaker man might have bantered with the woman until the persuasion of desire became so strong that he faltered and sinned, but Joseph left himself no opportunity to weaken. I suspect it was his godly example that inspired the apostle Paul many centuries later to warn Christians in Corinth to "flee youthful passions."[9] Had Lot resisted sin with the resolute and determined attitude of Joseph, he might have fled to the moral

---

6. Genesis 19:4; 1 John 1:8–10; Romans 3:9–12; Romans 5:12; Psalm 51:5 (ESV).
7. Blaise Pascal, *Pensées*, trans. A. J. Krailsheimer (New York: Penguin Books, 1966), 46.
8. Genesis 39:6–8; 11–12, 19–29; Genesis 41:1.
9. 2 Timothy 2:22 (ESV).

protection of Abraham's house, where his uncle could have provided appropriate housing and lawful mates for everyone involved.[10]

These two accounts should remind readers of three essential truths. First, the world lives within each man's heart. Sodom was destroyed as a city, but its temptations and wickedness continued to live in the hearts of its only refugees: Lot and his daughters. As long as fallen humanity lives, vices and iniquities will be passed down from generation to generation, even in the churches of Jesus Christ—and some generations openly war against the Lord. Those of us raised in the 1960s and 1970s will carry the temptations and sins of our generation to the grave, and our children and grandchildren will face the lifelong temptations into which they were born. Second, though a man or woman repents of the evil in their own heart, the people of the world will tempt the godly to join them in the latter's evil plans. No matter how good a person might be, they will be pushed and drawn toward sin, even tricked and forced into sin. Only those willing to forsake their selfish desires and immoral companions will prevail in righteousness. For that reason, prudence sometimes requires physical separation from the worst evildoers, lest we be drawn into their ways. Third, the example of Joseph reminds believers that there is a God to whom every human being will give account. Joseph denied himself the bed of his master's wife and exchanged illicit pleasure for years of unjust suffering. Why? Because he understood that there is a God to whom everyone must give an account and thought it better to suffer a life of unjust punishment than to share in sin's pleasures for an hour. Joseph was honored in this life for his faith and will be exalted in eternity.

Sin lives in us, and we live in a sinful world. There is no easy escape, and the only path to God's blessing is the way of the cross of Christ: self-denial to the point of spiritual and even physical death. No one chooses this for the pure enjoyment of self-sacrifice, but only because we are convinced that God is in control not only of our eternal salvation but also of our temporal destiny, both ours and that of our children. By the leading and power of the Lord in our lives, feeble as we may be, we must

---

10. One ninth-century Frankish noblewoman (whose handbook for her son, William, reflected a serious education and an understanding of Scripture) wrote: "[Joseph] feared and avoided fornication with women, maintaining chastity of the mind for God's sake and of the body for his earthly lord's sake. Thus he was worthy to be loved more than all the other servants of his lord." Dhuoda, *Handbook for William: A Carolingian Woman's Counsel for Her Son* (Washington, D.C.: The Catholic University of America Press, 1991), 24.

choose wisely (like Joseph) to flee sin (unlike Lot). We may submit to the Lord that his word and law may live in us. By God's grace and love, we must show regard to the spouse we now have (or may someday be given), as well as our children and even the man or woman whom we would wrong in our sin, be it sexual, financial, or something else altogether. We must confess with the early church father, Athenagoras, the truth about our lives:

> *If we did not think that a God ruled over the human race, would we live in such purity? The idea is impossible. But since we are persuaded that we must give an account of all our life here to God who made us and the world, we adopt a temperate, generous, and despised way of life. For we think that, even if we lose our lives, we shall suffer here no evil to be compared with the reward we shall receive from the great Judge for a gentle, generous, and modest life.[11]*

---

11. Athenagoras, "A Plea," in Hunter, *Early Christian Fathers,* 310.

43

THE CONTEMPT OF THE WORLD

Do not love the world or the things in the world. If anyone loves the world, the love of the Father is not in him. For all that is in the world—the desires of the flesh and the desires of the eyes and pride of life—is not from the Father but is from the world. And the world is passing away along with its desires, but whoever does the will of God abides forever.[1]

It is evident that Christians are called to *hate* both the world and the evil desires of the heart and the flesh. This means (before anything else) that every believer must actively resist the sinful impulses that exist within. Each individual must, with God's help, crucify the sin that so easily defiles. The Bible also warns against compromise with the sins of others since temptation is intrinsic to human society. Even an individual who wishes to do right is dragged down into the gutters by neighboring sinners who labor day in and day out to entice the godly to destruction. Now, the fact that temptation comes from within the human heart, whether of oneself or others, makes it quite evident that sin cannot be eradicated by external forces. Passing laws, fleeing to monasteries, or scourging the flesh will not eliminate sinful temptations and evil choices. Only the Spirit of God can accomplish that righteous work as he recreates

---

1. 1 John 2:15–17 (ESV).

us in his perfect image. The battle against sin is one waged in the soul; it will not be won in the flesh or through human law and effort.

Yet, this struggle is not directed against human nature itself—only against the sinful perversion of the human heart and mind.[2] The Lord calls his people to live quiet and gentle lives rather than to corrupt themselves by the pursuit of glory and gold, fortune and fame, pleasure and power. This makes perfect sense since God never intended for mankind to degenerate into a society of tyrants, celebrities, and millionaires, but to become his own dear children who live through eternity: perfecting and enjoying the virtues of holiness, humility, and love. When believers stand against the temptations of the world, they stand for their own truest nature as made in the divine image.[3] Their call is less to desert their rightful home than to abandon the ranks of a malevolent stepfather who lies about and plots against their true father. We are to remain steadfast in the Lord's ways amidst the evil around us. Jesus interceded to his Father for each one of us in this regard, praying:

> *I do not ask that you take them out of the world, but that you keep them from the evil one. They are not of the world, just as I am not of the world. Sanctify them in the truth; your word is truth.*[4]

Heaven will not be a realm of riches, pomp, pleasure, and domination. It is the Muslim, not the Christian, who desires a heaven of harems and preeminence; Christians aim to spend an eternity in righteousness, charity, and humility: worshipping and enjoying the glory, greatness, and authority of the God who became a human child rather than exalting himself. For that reason, anyone who desires to pursue passion and privilege is hardly fit to live in Christ's heaven as revealed by his servant John, and would despise the kingdom of God if admitted. Only those who agree that the point of human existence (indeed, of the entire cosmos) is to glorify God can enjoy a world where such behavior is reality. Only those who confess that Jesus Christ, the eternal Son of God, is the only way to his Father know the true God of Israel rather than a pagan idol, a

---

2. Moses commanded Israel to: "Love the LORD your God with all your heart and with all your soul and with all your might" (Deuteronomy 6:5) (ESV). Even in its corrupted and disordered state, mankind is called to serve God rather than to renounce human nature.
3. For a helpful book showing spiritual experience is rooted in our human nature, see Ranald Macaulay and Jerram Barrs, *Being Human: The Nature of Spiritual Experience*.
4. John 17:15–17 (ESV).

misleading icon (distorting the image of Christ as revealed in the Bible), or false philosophical ideal. All confessing Christians have agreed on this essential point, whether early martyrs, medieval monks, Protestant Reformers, or modern evangelicals. Jesus calls every believer to the self-denial of the cross to crucify selfish passions that prioritize oneself over God.

However, we must exercise caution since it is the sinful cravings of fallen mankind that are judged rather than human nature per se.[5] Christians are not called to withdraw from the world any more than God himself withholds his blessing from his creation, bringing good to his servants and sinners alike. That would be selfish and unspiritual, reducing piety to spiritual self-centeredness and ignoring God's call to a life of other-directed charity. From the law of Moses to the letters of Paul, Scripture reveals that godliness has both private and public consequences. Moses gave laws to govern the Hebrews in their hearts and houses, in their communities and countries, and Paul provided public commands to govern the churches scattered throughout the Roman Empire from the generation of Nero to our own. To this day, there remain Christian congregations that Paul and Peter helped to establish in Greece and Rome. What is called the Great Commission at the end of the Gospel of Matthew settled the matter, insisting that believers not merely repent of their own sins but also make disciples of the nations. In fact, the latter is explicitly commanded.[6]

No believer may indulge in a quiet life of contemplation and prayer without seeking to bring others to the knowledge of God. To crucify the flesh is not to forsake family and neighbor but to follow the example of Jesus as he cared for both strangers and family members (even helping his mother with her earthly needs as he died on the cross). It should be remembered that Christ portrayed the Good Samaritan as the essence of virtue, and that parable shows a man tending to human needs in the course of everyday life—even those of an ethnic rival and political foe.[7] Moreover, it must be observed that the Good Samaritan would not have

---

5. John Calvin wrote: "Let believers accustom themselves to a contempt of this present life that engenders no hatred of it or ingratitude against God. Indeed, this life, however crammed with infinite miseries it may be, is still rightly to be counted among those blessings of God which are not to be spurned. Therefore, if we recognize in it no divine benefit, we are already guilty of grave ingratitude toward God himself." John Calvin, *Institutes of the Christian Religion*, vol. 1, 714.

6. Matthew 28:18–20 (ESV).

7. John 19:26–27; Luke 10:29–37.

encountered the wounded traveler alongside the road if he had been living as an ascetic hermit in the Judean desert rather than going about the business of life. Churches that segregate leaders from everyday life by making ascetic isolation and renunciation of marriage a requirement for piety display an unfortunate contempt not for worldliness but for God's created world itself. Such unbiblical restrictions sometimes lead to evil prayers and uncharitable dispositions.[8]

Just as hatred of the world is not contempt for mankind, so also the denial of the flesh is not the same as the hatred of the body. As noted, there have been believers who thought it best to turn away from marital intimacy, scorning the body itself as the source of temptation.[9] Even today, some denominations forbid priests from marrying (or remarrying after the death of a wife), reasoning that celibacy helps clerics avoid the distractions of marriage and sexual desire.[10] From the Protestant optic, this is both counterproductive and unbiblical. Of all men, would not an unmarried or widowed clergymen bring good to a lonely virgin, a repentant convert, an abandoned wife, or a needy widow? When the apostle John rebuked the worldliness of this life, he condemned the sinful cravings of the heart and the eyes, but did not tell men and women to pluck out their eyes in an overzealous application of Jesus' words. Natural faculties are made to be used, and it is entirely proper for God's people to find delight in what the Lord has created, whether the marital bed or parental affection. To be frank, no one can progress in piety unless he (or she) uses all means ordained by the Lord to do so, and marriage is revealed in the Bible to be the appropriate safeguard against sexual impurity. It is only sinful desires that must be crucified, not lawful longings.[11]

---

8. Ancient Frankish churches so idealized celibate clergy (even among priests already married) that one bishop prayed for the deaths of his wife and daughter to become a celibate clergyman. To pray for the death of one's family is hardly Christian charity; such religion is either deluded or demonic. Dyan Elliott, *Spiritual Marriage: Sexual Abstinence in Medieval Wedlock* (Princeton, New Jersey: Princeton University Press, 1993), 89, n. 158.

9. Clement of Alexandria vigorously opposed an early heresy that openly despised marriage. He wrote: "But those who, from a hatred for the flesh, ungratefully long to have nothing to do with the marriage union and the eating of reasonable food, are both blockheads and atheists, and exercise an irrational chastity like the other heathen. For example, the Brahmans neither eat animal flesh nor drink wine." Clement of Alexandria, "On Marriage," in Oulton and Chadwick, *Alexandrian Christianity*, 68.

10. See *Appendix 8: A Woman Sacrifices Her Son.*

11. Matthew 5:29–30 (ESV). Early church father Origen made himself into a eunuch by taking the words of Jesus too literally. Still, Jesus did not say to castrate oneself but to remove offending hands and eyes—something no monk-scholar would have dared since he would have lost the ability to read and write (skills critical to much of monastic life). Origen

Moreover, it is open sacrilege to despise what God has made in unbiblical rejection of the physical world, as Paul warned:

Now the Spirit expressly says that in later times some will depart from the faith by devoting themselves to deceitful spirits and teachings of demons... who forbid marriage and require abstinence from foods that God created to be received with thanksgiving by those who believe and know the truth.[12]

Because we must not mistake the society of sinful mankind for the glory of God's creation, believers are called to hold *the world* in contempt, spurning evil desires and submitting to the word of the Lord. The lusts of the flesh and the desire of the sinful heart for worldly approval cling so firmly to the soul that believers cry out with Paul against the evil they can never completely eradicate. And aside from the struggle in each individual soul and body, there also is an inescapable moral battle at the social level since unbelievers often persecute God's holy prophets and faithful servants. Nearly all of the apostles were murdered for their faith, and the one survivor was tortured and exiled to a remote island. Likewise, King Herod executed John the Baptist for publicly rebuking the former's incestuous marriage to Herodias. Moreover, the apostle John forewarned all churches that many antichrists and heretics would enter among them, with the apostle warning believers to refuse all support to such heretics and apostates (even if the latter falsely claim the name of Christian).[13]

The same warning holds true today. Not since the paganism of the Roman Empire has the world witnessed such an unashamed and destructive flourishing of sexual promiscuity and moral perversity as we see in contemporary society. To be sure, many Christian communities have struggled throughout history with the sinful deeds of individuals or even countries, and there was serious sexual sin among believers even within the churches of the holy apostles. Sometimes, the poor have been prone to ignore Christian marriage in favor of concubinage; at other times, the rich have idealized adultery or tacitly accepted homosexuality. At all

was non-literally literal in his error. Eusebius, *The History of the Church from Christ to Constantine*, trans. G.A. Williams, 186.

12. 1 Timothy 4:1–3 (ESV).
13. Romans 7:21; 2 John 7, 10–11.

times, there have been immoral sects and vile cults.[14] But not since pagan antiquity has an entire society given itself over to base lust as the modern West has done, and sorrow will come of it. If we continue down our current path, we will end up like Sodom and Gomorrah, for whom Abraham boldly prayed for God's mercy if only ten righteous men could be found among those condemned cities. But no one (except Abraham's morally flawed kinsman, Lot) could be found, so both Sodom and Gomorrah were destroyed through divine intervention.[15]

In the first chapter of his letter to the Romans, Paul rebuked those cultures who surrender themselves to spiritual apostasy and moral license, warning that unbelief leads to the climax of cultural decadence: open idolatry and unrepentant homosexuality. Paul declared that such sinners will receive the "due penalty of their error."[16] For centuries, Christian lands have condemned not only homosexuality but also adultery and the seduction of virgins. However, the decadent spirit of pagan Rome has been resurrected, and it is again stylish to live immorally, perhaps even worse than among pagans, since Greeks and Romans generally expected chastity from wives and daughters. The words of one ancient Christian writer sound as if written today, setting Christ and morality against the spirit of the age and the fashions of higher learning. Arnobius of Sicca observed:

> *And all who by writing books attack in many forms public morals with biting criticism; who slash, scorch and scourge your luxurious lives; who hand down to posterity through the permanence of writings the stigmas of their own times; men who seek to persuade us that marriages should be held in common; who cohabit with boys all these with wonder and approval you raise to the stars of heaven, place them in secret places at libraries, endow them with chariots and statues, and as far as in you lies, grant them a certain kind of immortality, by the witness of immortal titles. Christ alone you wish to reproach, to tear in pieces, if you can do so to a god.*[17]

---

14. For a review of medieval cults, see Norman Cohn, *The Pursuit of the Millennium: Revolutionary Millenarians and Mystical Anarchists of the Middle Ages* (Oxford: Oxford University Press, 1957).

15. Genesis 18:32.

16. Romans 1:18–29 (NASB).

17. Arnobius of Sicca, *The Case against the Pagans*, trans. George E. McCracken (Westminster, Maryland: Newman Press, 1949), 110–111.

44

MORALS AND MODESTY IN MODERN SOCIETY

Adam and Eve, for this is the name of the woman, "were naked and were not ashamed," since there was in them an innocent and childlike mind and they thought or understood nothing whatsoever of those things which are wickedly born in the soul through lust and shameful desires, because, at that time, they preserved their nature intact, since that which was breathed into the handiwork was the breath of life. [Because] 'they were not ashamed,' [Adam and Eve were] kissing and embracing each other in holiness.[1]

SINFUL MANKIND IS ashamed of who and what we have become—hiding not simply our bare bodies but also the shame of our hearts and minds. After sinning, the first couple immediately understood how they were naked, while the rest of us come to comprehend our shame as we grow from being babies and toddlers to teenagers and adults. And we must be thankful for our shame, for it reveals the pangs of conscience and a recognition that we are not who we are meant to be: we are not righteous before the Lord. Far better to be ashamed of who we know ourselves to be than to be given over to a shamelessness that does not care what anyone else thinks, man or God alike. Beyond a handful of exhibitionists

---

1. St. Irenaeus of Lyons, *On the Apostolic Preaching*, trans. John Behr (Crestwood, New York: St. Vladamir's Seminary Press, 1997), 48.

and nudists, few of us would dare walk the beach naked, and not just because our physiques lack muscle and tone but mostly because we know ourselves to be sinful and corrupted. Even then, most of us would rather expose our physical nakedness to the mockery and jeers of strangers than reveal the full wickedness of our moral shame to those who know us.

Regarding the clothing of human nakedness in the Garden of Eden, it would be an error to read the story of how mankind came to wear clothes like some silly pagan myth. What Adam and Eve sought to do with clothing was not to warm themselves in the cold or protect themselves from the heat of the sun, but to cover (with plant-made clothing) the shame and guilt that they could not ignore. The first couple corrupted themselves, then responded to their subsequent moral guilt with an irrational, superficial, and unsatisfactory effort to mask the shame they felt, rather like each of us does from the time we are very young until the day we die.[2] We, too, feign that innocence we do not possess, refuse to look deeper than the surface of our hearts, and imagine we can justify the terrible consequences of our sinful selfishness with the slightest of pretexts and excuses. Sometimes, we even pretend to be better people than we are by adorning ourselves in wool suits and silk scarves, not much different than the fig skirts of the first couple. In rightly condemning their childish simplicity, we judge ourselves.[3]

Nevertheless, the Lord took pity on Adam and Eve. He covered them with the atoning skin of an animal: an innocent who died in their place as a prophetic sacrifice to foreshadow the death of Jesus Christ to cover their naked sin and shame with his righteousness. In this spirit, the apostle Paul revealed how we are "clothed [with] Christ," if we have been baptized into Christ and follow the Spirit of the Lord rather than gratifying the desires of the flesh, which he lists as "immorality, impurity, sensuality... envying, drunkenness, carousing and things like these." The book of Revelation later prophesied how a great multitude of people will stand before God "clothed in white robes"—for "they have washed their robes and made them white in the blood of the Lamb." Our naked shame can be covered no other way than by the forgiveness and new life found

---

2. Francis Schaeffer noted how Scripture speaks of true moral guilt (i.e., judicial guilt) rather than guilt feelings, which may or may not be aligned with true moral guilt (some people despair over trifles, while others murder without compunction). See "True Spirituality," in Francis Schaeffer, *Complete Works*, vol. 3, 199 ("The Law and the Law of Love").
3. I should add that while we often feel our shame before other men and women, ultimately our shame is before God himself, the true judge of every man and woman.

in Christ. This must never be forgotten: Christ's naked shame and sacrificial death are our holiness.[4]

That deeper meaning understood, we must remember how Scripture calls sinful mankind to live modestly as the shamed and naked children of Adam and Eve, neither exposing our corrupt desires for everyone to see nor living to inflame others to sin through how we present ourselves. In this spirit, the apostle Paul warned women to "adorn themselves in respectable apparel, with modesty and self-control, not with braided hair and gold or pearls or costly attire but with what is proper for women who profess godliness—with good works." The apostle Peter wrote the same, noting how women should not let their "adorning be external—the braiding of hair and the putting on of gold jewelry, or the clothing [they] wear." Peter commanded that the beauty of women be the "hidden person of the heart with the imperishable quality of a gentle and quiet spirit, which in God's sight is very precious."[5] Both apostles instructed women to lead quiet lives of service rather than indulging in vanity and immodest dress. Protestant Reformer Pierre Viret observed:

> It isn't easy [to] hold a good opinion of the chastity and modesty of a woman who lives so pompously and shamelessly and who is excessive and lewd in her clothing and makeup. [Even] if it were possible for this pride and boldness to be joined with a chaste, modest, and meek heart (which is a most difficult thing), yet even so the fleshly and excessive clothing can't be anything but wicked. For, besides the unnecessary expense lavished on this which ought to be employed in works of charity, another very great evil still exists, which is that such adornments provoke and inflate the wicked lust for fornication in the heart of those who see it."[6]

The prophet Isaiah declared the same thousands of years earlier, condemning the prideful women of Israel who "walk with heads held high and seductive eyes, and go along with mincing steps, and tinkle the

---

4. Genesis 3:21; Galatians 3:27 (NASB); Galatians 5:19, 21 (NASB); Revelation 7:9, 14 (NASB).
5. 1 Timothy 2:9–10 (ESV); 1 Peter 3:3–4 (ESV).
6. Viret called out women (frequently procuresses and prostitutes) who dressed shamelessly in church, noting that "hardly anything reveals the heart of a woman more than her attire and adornments, through which a man can see and know (just like in a mirror) and read like a book what is in her heart." Pierre Viret, *Exposition*, vol. 2, 229–230.

bangles on their feet." For their immodest ways, Isaiah prophesied that the Lord would strip from such women all bangles, headbands, earrings, necklaces, bracelets, veils, anklets, shades, perfume bottles, signet rings, robes, cloaks, capes, purses, mirrors, and other finery. He would even shave the women bald.[7] The Lord who created the beauty of women calls women to be humble and modest. He will tolerate no immodesty, no matter what the world's fashion may be. By his fierce judgments, the Lord will bring forth through painful troubles and diseases the humility that should come from willing piety. God never indulges sin, and his wrath upon a society irretrievably given over to evil is unsparing, just like human judgment against persons and cultures who do evil without the least sign of remorse.[8]

Nor should we deceive ourselves that vanity is a fault restricted to women. The ancient poet Prudentius, a Christian believer, complained of men whose love of finery was such that they wore "flowing robes [made] of the spoils taken from branches of trees and fetched from the eastern world." He observed how some men were seen "chasing hot-foot after luxuriant tunics, and weaving downy garments with strange threads from many coloured birds," as well as how strong men took to effeminate dress.[9] We cannot limit vanity to tailoring either, for is it not vanity to wear a timepiece costing thousands of dollars or to wrap oneself in a sports car to look good? Or to choose any house, hairstyle, or hobby because it is prestigious? Or to favor physical conditioning over spiritual service? In the book of Ecclesiastes, King Solomon lamented the vanity of life: a breath wasted on the pursuit of wealth, pleasure, acclaim, and everything the sinful heart foolishly desires at the expense of eternal life.[10] We must not live for mortal and fleeting pleasures.

In contrast to such vanity, Scripture commands us to reflect the image of God, who values good character and faith over superficial traits such as appearance, status, and reputation. In the book of 1 Samuel, the Lord explained why he chose the young David as king to replace Saul, revealing to the prophet Samuel: "Man looks at the outward appearance, but the LORD looks at the heart." Jesus said the same when reminding

---

7. Isaiah 3:16–24 (NASB).
8. I speak of cultures devoted to child sacrifice, cannibalism, and genocidal slaughter of the innocent. For such evildoers, even sinful humanity shows little tolerance.
9. Prudentius, *Prudentius,* vol. 1, ed. Jeffrey Henderson and trans. H.J. Thomson (Cambridge, Massachusetts: Harvard University Press, 2006), 223–225.
10. Ecclesiastes 2:11.

believers not to toil and worry about their clothes, declaring: "And why are you worried about clothing? Observe how the lilies of the field grow; they do not toil nor do they spin, yet I say to you that not even Solomon in all his glory clothed himself like one of these."[11] Moreover, the apostle James tied vanity to a lack of charity, declaring by God's Spirit that favoring the fashion and beauty of the wealthy over the modest rags of the poor is both uncharitable and worldly. James provided the following warning and reminder to all of us:

> *If a man comes into your assembly with a gold ring and dressed in fine clothes, and there also comes in a poor man with dirty clothes, and you pay special attention to the one who is earning fine clothes and say, "You sit here in a good place," and you say to the poor man, "You stand over there, or sit down by my footstool," have you not made distinctions among yourselves, and become judges with evil motives?*[12]

Christian preachers have often warned against the vanities of life, especially when preaching on the passages noted above. However, Christian churches generally have not required congregants to live as if they were Amish, demanding plainness and simplicity in dress as a fundamental religious practice.[13] While many church leaders and even some denominations have been strict about the use of cosmetics or jewelry, few believers outside of monastic institutions have demanded that the rich live like paupers or that believing women veil themselves with burkas. Even in epochs when clergymen were required to take vows of chastity and poverty (and to dress as such), such pledges were not demanded of the laity. Since Scripture does not expect every believer to become a self-denying ascetic, how can we grasp the principle behind biblical strictures against immodest dress? How can we know what is authoritative and binding upon all of us? How can we practice the modesty demanded by

---

11. 1 Samuel 16:7 (NASB); Matthew 6:28–32 (NASB).
12. James 2:2–4 (NASB).
13. For the transformation of the radical and militant Anabaptist movement of the sixteenth century into more peaceful and quietist communities (from which the Amish emerged) following the disastrous Anabaptist effort to establish a cultish, theocratic kingdom at Münster, see George H. Williams, *The Radical Reformation* (Philadelphia: Westminster Press, 1975. For an account of the theocracy (and polygamy) practiced at Münster, see Anthony Arthur, *The Tailor-King: The Rise and Fall of the Anabaptist Kingdom of Münster* (New York: St. Martin's Press, 1999).

the Lord? We must pay careful attention to every apostolic injunction and implement all biblical teachings within our churches.

The apostles Paul, Peter, and James focused on core teachings. Men and women must first and foremost focus on faith and good character, as evidenced in good works rather than frivolities and vanities. Clothes, hairstyles, watches, and automobiles must not be sought at the expense of God's eternal kingdom, and we should not live for style and status, but use our possessions and our bodies to build Christ's church, both now and forevermore. And not just things external to the body, but the body itself must be subordinated to godliness. While the apostle Paul admitted that "bodily training" is useful, he subordinated the value of physical conditioning to that of godliness, which "holds promise for the present life and also for the life to come."[14] No matter how conditioned an athlete may grow or how trim a model may keep herself, both the strong athlete and the beautiful woman will decay and die, whereas godliness endures forever: to be resurrected to eternal strength and perfected beauty far beyond what can be imagined in this mortal life.

Beyond living for eternity, we must avoid provoking others to unchastity or using our possessions (including our bodies) uncharitably. Perhaps the most significant passage in Scripture for addressing modesty is not any explicit teaching against ornate or seductive adornment, but rather the instruction in the book of Romans, in which Paul subordinates every Christian to the rule of charity in handling sensitive issues arising from coming to faith in an unbelieving and immoral society.[15] In that passage, the problem was the eating of food slaughtered at pagan temples, then sold in the marketplace as everyday food—with the apostle Paul declaring pagan rituals to be of little consequence since pagan gods were not real, and consequently did not restrict the eating of meat once dedicated to them. However, other believers (either of Jewish heritage in strict opposition to pagan ritual or pagans converted from such practices) were scandalized by what they perceived as Christian support for pagan sacrificial rites (since pagan priests and temples profited from the sale of such meat on the market). Responding to this disagreement, Paul warned both sides to allow each other freedom and to let God judge each individual by that person's faith and love. Both sides were bound by the law of love for the spiritual well-being of other believers. The handling of

---

14. 1 Timothy 4:7–8 (ESV).
15. Romans 14:1–3, 13-21.

modesty requires similar charity and humility as Christians institute God's eternal truth in their particular place and time.

C.S. Lewis provided excellent direction regarding the virtue of modesty in his book *Mere Christianity*, in which he defined modesty as the rule of propriety that "lays down how much of the human body should be displayed and what subjects can be referred, and in what words, according to *the customs of a given social circle*" (emphasis mine). Lewis distinguished modesty from chastity, observing that the rule of chastity is eternal and binding for all believers in all cultures, whereas the rule of propriety changes over time and place. In that light, Lewis observed how a girl on a Pacific island "wearing hardly any clothes" and a "Victorian lady completely covered in clothes" might be equally modest according to the standards of their societies. What matters is how they are perceived by and influence those around them.[16] For the record, it should be noted that Polynesian women of the mid-twentieth century were not necessarily the half-naked pagans depicted in a Paul Gauguin painting. Period photographs show women and girls alike wearing long dresses and modest wraps, though there remained considerable differences between a covered Victorian woman and a more simply dressed Polynesian.[17]

Historically, I would note that ancient sculptures and paintings suggest differences in clothing between the lightly dressed Egyptians and the well-covered barbarians of Germany and Gaul, some of which are based on cultural norms and some related to climate (a German woman would have suffered frostbite across her body had she worn the clothing of desert Egypt during a cold European winter). Yet the New Testament neither prescribes nor proscribes exactly how men and women are to dress (there are no Amish regulations restricting clothing to homespun or coarse material), only that all believers in all churches must spurn vanity and luxury. The Victorian lady might need to forego ornate and

---

16. C.S. Lewis, *Mere Christianity*, 94–95. Lewis was no moral relativist (or temporizer), and his works frame modern Christian apologetics. Moreover, Lewis made his astute observations during a period of relaxing standards of propriety for dress. His was an era in which more formal Victorian standards were relaxed for casual clothing, whereas ours is one in which naked unchastity has become utterly unrestrained.

17. Paul Gauguin's paintings did not portray actual Tahitian culture, which was under strong French cultural influence. Rather, they reflected vile instincts found in the artist: a man who married three very young teenagers during his stay in Polynesia. Though more than forty years old, Gauguin married girls of fourteen or younger. By today's understanding, Gaugin was a pedophile—so we dare not use his paintings to portray the norms of Tahitian society, but only the deep depravity of the artist's vile heart.

expensive plumage in her hat to remain modest, whereas the Polynesian girl might need to spend less time braiding her hair or obsessing over her sandals. Just as words have different meanings in different languages, so, too, with modesty. God's truth must be translated, so to speak, into every culture, and each of us is responsible for making that translation effort. Is this not the gift of Pentecost to make Christ known among the nations in their tongues and customs? Is this not the power of the Spirit of the Lord who lives in each of us who confesses Christ?[18]

Modesty may be a question of dress as Lewis defines it, but there is also the related matter of propriety in speech. C.S. Lewis observed that "some of the language which chaste women used in Shakespeare's time would have been used in the nineteenth century only by a woman completely abandoned."[19] The apostle Paul, living in a Roman world filled with the same impurity we face, warned believers of all generations not to let any "unwholesome word proceed from your mouth, but only such a word as is good for edification according to the need of the moment, so that it will give grace to those who hear." Jesus spoke with divine authority when he declared that people will give an accounting on the day of judgment for "every careless word that people speak," noting that "by your words you will be justified, and by words you will be condemned."[20] Cultural standards may change over time, but the Lord's judgment never wavers, and everyone will be judged by the divine command to practice and uphold chastity and charity in speech. In some fashion, this commandment must be obeyed by every believer.

Likewise, decency is required in entertainment, which is a significant problem in contemporary society. While we do not have time to review this matter in detail, I would like to share a few thoughts from the perspective of a Protestant Reformer who lived several hundred years ago, and whose words remain applicable today. Like us, Pierre Viret lived during one of the great cultural revolutions of human history: the growth of a book culture that began with the invention of the printing press and spread with the expansion of literacy and education.[21] And though Viret wrote many books himself, he still objected to those "pictures and books containing lewd and lascivious things."

18. Acts 2:42.
19. Lewis, *Mere Christianity*, 94.
20. Ephesians 4:29 (NASB); Matthew 12:36–37 (ESV).
21. See Elizabeth L. Eisenstein, *The Printing Revolution in Early Modern Europe* (Cambridge: Cambridge University Press), 1983.

Viret's complaint, however, was not limited to books, for he also objected to traditional songs and dances, writing how it is "difficult to imagine anything more suitable to give an opening to all immorality and to all debauchery than dances, no matter what type they are." Viret protested that "shameless, filthy, and lewd songs [that cause women to] stir themselves up to even more lewdness and sexual immorality, as well as the men who hear them insomuch as, by the words they speak and what they insinuate, they express the debauchery within." He considered it worse yet "if young men are mixed with them." While Viret's opposition to dancing may or may not be biblical, his objection to immoral lyrics is consistent with biblical teachings that unwholesome talk must never come from the mouth of the believer. Moreover, it is not difficult to understand how sexually suggestive dancing crosses moral boundaries.[22]

Though modesty is not a virtue primarily for women, there can be little doubt that it is tied to the relationship of the sexes: to the ability of men and women to befriend each other apart from sexual impulses. For that reason, if a culture lacks an appropriate sense of shame, both sexes will be consumed by their sexual appetites, and far too many interactions between men and women will be tempted toward base sensuality, not only in social and professional relationships, but also in spiritual and familial ones. To avoid this, Scripture demands an exacting and absolute standard between the two sexes, requiring Christian believers to treat each other as brothers and sisters: a sacred and holy relationship unlike any other. In just one of many passages, the apostle Paul explicitly called believers to treat "younger men as brothers, older women as mothers, and younger women as sisters, in all purity."[23]

While we cannot discuss all the differences between men and women in this book, it is essential to note that Scripture distinguishes how we treat brothers and sisters in Christ, providing rules of behavior that are consistent with the needs of each. Paul provided detailed guidance in 1 Corinthians, offering advice on dress and behavior in public worship, while distinguishing between the attire and conduct of men and women. Paul equally demanded respectful behavior from both sexes, grounding his teaching in creation. And while this passage has led to considerable discussion regarding the role and attire of women during worship, one

---

22. Viret, *Exposition*, vol. 2, 140–141.
23. 1 Timothy 5:1–2 (ESV). While Jesus never called any woman *sister* in the Gospels, he did treat women as such. He also declared that "whoever does the will of my Father in heaven, he is My brother and sister and mother." Matthew 12:48–50 (NASB).

obvious point is often overlooked: that Paul judged propriety within the Greco-Roman culture of Corinth rather than imposing Jewish law on a Gentile congregation. The apostle did not require Christian converts to grow beards, as the Hebrews were required to do, nor did he forbid them from adopting the short haircuts of the Romans.[24] Moreover, while I have seen numerous discussions regarding the covering of women's hair, I have seen fewer discussions regarding the uncovering of men's heads—a point that struck me during a worship service in Fort Worth at which I observed numerous Texans wearing cowboy hats into the church building, only to set them aside for the worship service. Is this what Paul intended? That men expose their shameful balding and women hide their glorious beauty so they together might worship the Lord in modest reverence, undistracted by each other's physical appearance. Paul wrote:

> *Every man who prays or prophesies with his head covered dishonors his head, but every wife who prays or prophesies with her head uncovered dishonors her head, since it is the same as if her head were shaven... For a man ought not to cover his head, since he is the image and glory of God, but woman is the glory of man. For man was not made from woman, but woman from man... Nevertheless, in the Lord woman is not independent of man nor man of woman; for as woman was made from man, so man is now born of woman. And all things are from God... Does not nature itself teach you that if a man wears long hair it is a disgrace for him, but if a woman has long hair, it is her glory? For her hair is given to her for a covering. If anyone is inclined to be contentious, we have no such practice, nor do the churches of God.*[25]

Whatever Paul meant by women being veiled (and he certainly intended that the Christian worship to be conducted in modest attire), he did not impose Mosaic restrictions requiring the separation of women from public life during menstruation or the removal of men from priestly

---

24. Leviticus 19:26.
25. 1 Corinthians 11:4–16 (ESV). John Calvin published a commentary on the Roman writer Seneca's *De Clementia* in which Calvin noted that Seneca used the expression *with an uncovered head* as a proverb for something without shame. *De Clementia* was written several years after 1 Corinthians, suggesting that Paul and Seneca may have drawn from common cultural roots in their writing. It appears to me that Paul was using a common expression to advocate for modesty among believers. Calvin, *Ecclesiastical Advice*, 87.

duties for the sake of diseased or damaged genitals. The apostle did, however, make clear that duties of modesty were related to the interaction of men with women and women with men. The Lord intends a differentiation and distinction of the sexes in conformity to Scripture, natural law, and chastity in honoring each other as brothers and sisters. Whether or not there is a contemporary application of head coverings, veils, and hairstyles, there can be no doubt that the apostle is teaching both sexes to honor the Lord by publicly celebrating and enjoying the differences God created between man and woman (while upholding chastity and modesty). Additionally, there is an indisputable Old Testament commandment that men and women not wear each other's clothing (referring to efforts to cross the distinctions of sex by dressing like the other). Moses declared: "A woman shall not wear man's clothing, nor shall a man put on a woman's clothing."[26] Whatever else these commands intend, they make clear that believers must acknowledge, respect, and rejoice in man as man and woman as woman—distinct and complementary.

Mankind lives in shame—and rightly so, for we are not who we ought to be. Our shame must be covered, first and foremost, in the righteousness of Christ and by good deeds and modesty in dress and speech, so that we do not stir unchastity or provoke uncharity. As the book of Ecclesiastes observed, our lives are brief, temporary, and uncertain (what different versions of the Bible translate as *breath, vanity,* or *meaningless).* King Solomon, who elsewhere preached against adultery based on the sorrows that came from the adulterous affair of his parents, examined his failures from living for worldly success and mortal pleasures: for dedicating himself to wealth, art, power, work, and far too many women. Only near the end of his life did Solomon recognize how the vanities of his earlier years were empty and fruitless. Advising the wise among his readers to avoid his mistakes, he instructed believers to remember the Lord in their youth and to "enjoy life with the wife whom you love, all the days of your vain life that he has given you under the sun, because that is your portion in life and in your toil at which you toil under the sun." Ultimately, King Solomon noted, we are born of shame and need redemption, just as Adam and Eve did following their sin. We will go to

---

26. Leviticus 12:1–6; Leviticus 15:16, Leviticus 15:19–30; Leviticus 21:17–21; Deuteronomy 23:1; Deuteronomy 22:5 (NASB). For a brief discussion regarding Old Testament laws of ritual purity regarding menstruation and other impurities, see *Appendix 9: Ritual Cleanliness and the Church.*

our graves in naked death to await what Scripture reveals as the eternal clothing of righteousness, restoration, and renewal that we shall receive in Jesus Christ.[27]

> *As he came forth of his mother's womb,*
> *naked shall he return to go as he came,*
> *and shall take nothing of his labour,*
> *which he may carry away in his hand.*[28]

---

27. Ecclesiastes 1:1; Ecclesiastes 2:1–11; Ecclesiastes 12:1; Ecclesiastes 9:9 (ESV).
28. Ecclesiastes 5:15 (KJV).

45

THE SANCTITY OF LIFE

He took to himself a body, a human body even as our own... Thus taking a body like our own, because all our bodies were liable to the corruption of death, He surrendered His body to death in place of all, and offering it the Father. This He did out of sheer love for us, so that in His death all might die, and the law of death thereby be abolished. [1]

IF THERE IS anything that establishes the sanctity and value of human life, it is the birth of Jesus Christ in Bethlehem. In his profound *On the Incarnation*, church father Athanasius presented a conundrum that resulted from the fall of mankind into sin, corruption, and death—which required ultimate resolution. Mankind sinned in Adam, and sin always merits death (because sin is a denial of God, who is the source of life). Because of this reality, the Lord was faced with what Athanasius called a divine dilemma: God could deny his righteous character, or he could uproot the human race such that mankind "fell back into non-existence through corruption." That is to say, the Lord could abort the sinful human race at the outset of its history and just start again—precluding and preventing all of the evils and injustices that God foreknew would come from corrupted human nature: genocide, war, slavery, oppression,

---

1. Athanasius, *On the Incarnation*, 34.

murder, massacre, rape, pedophilia, impurity, theft, treason, infidelity, adultery, tyranny, poverty, ignorance, incest, riot, hatred, malice, jealousy, and pollution, along with every other corporate and individual evil that would ever occur.[2]

Athanasius judged the first option to be a denial of God by God, which is impossible since God is not only eternal life but also eternal love and righteousness. The Lord can no more condemn his condemnation of human evil than a good man can justify the Holocaust, excuse slavery, or ignore sex trafficking—or limit his response to empty verbal protests, like Neville Chamberlain's hollow objections to Adolf Hitler's occupation of Czechoslovakia. Righteousness cannot make peace with unrighteousness, or it ceases to be righteousness and becomes collaboration with evil. Like the unavailing appeasement of Neville Chamberlain, or even the terrible treachery of Vichy France, heaven itself would have been fatally compromised if God had ignored, excused, or tolerated the reality of human sin. As with Occupied France, resistance and war are the rightful response to evil, not cowardice and compromise. The Lord is holy and must fight the evil that has brought about not only sin and death, but every tyranny, betrayal, and infidelity that has ever occurred among human beings, family and neighbors alike. The infinite God is eternally and immutably holy and righteous, and his response to human evil must reflect who he is now and forevermore. If this were not so, not only would God be a moral relativist, making peace with wickedness, but he would not be there to defend us when wrongdoing strikes us down. He would not be the savior of the downtrodden and the avenger of the oppressed. He would not be our righteous Father in heaven.

Regarding the second option, Athanasius considered what would have been an abortion of humanity to be "unworthy of the goodness of God that creatures made by him should be brought to nothing through the deceit wrought in mankind by the devil." Athanasius was declaring

---

2. Anselm of Canterbury also posited this divine dilemma, writing: "With regard to the nature of mankind, there are two alternatives: either God will complete what he has begun, or it was to no avail that he created this life-form. [But] it is foreign to him to allow any rational type of creature to perish utterly... It is necessary, therefore, that, with regarding to the nature of mankind, God should finish what he has begun. However, this cannot be done, as we have said, except through the paying of complete recompense for sin, something which no sinner can bring about." Anselm observed that the devil stole from God everything that God "planned to do with regard to the human species"—a theft I see repeated in every abortion, which ends both a life and a human lineage. Anselm of Canterbury, "Why God Because Man," in *Anselm of Canterbury: The Major Works*, 308, 317.

that God would not have been good if he allowed evil to abort the human race at its inception, for the Lord would have accepted the triumph of wrong over right and allowed an eternal wound in his creation. Though no one else in all creation understood that a miscarriage (i.e., an abortion) of the human race had taken place, God would have remembered what had been lost: all of the persons and possibilities of human life. Moreover, even if the Lord had destroyed the human race and attempted a do-over with a different Adam and Eve, the loss would not have been any less. If God had created a second human race in all ways like us, except it was a different Adam in whose loins was a different human race, the first wound would have remained unhealed and unredeemed—even if the Lord made the second race our identical twin (including identical children and grandchildren), with its own William Shakespeare and Mother Theresa living their lives in an unfallen world. The first world would have remained a blotted thought in the mind of God. Heaven forbid that we imagine for one moment that the Lord could resemble our evil spirits by aborting the billions of people to be born into the human race.[3]

Rather than these unacceptable options, Athanasius observed how our Lord chose a third option: a divine solution to the divine 'dilemma. God became man and took the guilt and sin of all men and women on himself, so that humanity could regain its lost innocence and gain eternal life. To this end, the Son of God became God Incarnate (God in the flesh). While Athanasius never used the word abortion, his third option at its core represented a wholehearted repudiation of abortion, for the Lord's solution was not to destroy our misbegotten race in the hope of creating a better one at a future date (which is what abortion tries to do with an individual child). Rather, God joined himself to our fallen race by becoming an unborn child, living as one of us, and growing to redeem his spiritually dead brothers and sisters. This solution ensured that each of us was born into this mortal world as purposed from the beginning of time, but with a means of restoring us to the favor of the Lord. The Lord allowed our sinful birth to occur, then saved us from the illegitimacy and corruption in which we were conceived and born through the baptism of Christ, calling each of us to the blessing offered to our first parents.[4]

Though there is much that could be said about both the reality and

---

3. Athanasius, *On the Incarnation*, 32–33.
4. As we discuss this particularly sensitive and painful subject, we must remember that only the Lord is sufficiently wise and good to deliver mankind into new life rather than death. If any of us avoids the sin of abortion, it is because God has delivered us from wrong

the implications of the Incarnation, I will restrict myself to several salient points regarding the sanctity of human life (more specifically, of unborn life). To begin with, we must remember how the infinite God became a human being in all that humanity encompasses. Ancient and medieval medicine made many mistakes in its understanding of how human beings are conceived, and modern perceptions of the historical ethics of abortion have been clouded by premodern misconceptions of how and when pregnancy occurs. However, we (the modern world, since the discovery of the genetic code and the development of in utero imaging) understand the beginnings of human life in a way that no ancient philosopher, medieval theologian, or Renaissance scientist ever could. We know how each man possesses several billion sperm inside himself and leaves as many as one billion of them inside a woman to fertilize her typically single egg (from the one or two million present at her birth and the many hundreds she ovulates during her life). We understand how the fertilized egg divides and grows as a self-building person according to the genetic blueprint hidden in the new human life from the instant of conception. While there is still much to learn, the understanding that modern people have gained in recent decades is considerable.

How this worked in the virgin Mary is a mystery, as mysterious as the fact of a virgin conception in which the fatherhood of God brought life to the baby Jesus, and the reality that a woman (whose eggs included only female chromosomes) conceived a child with male chromosomes miraculously provided by God himself. Still, it is a necessary Christian confession (as the Apostles' Creed states) that Jesus was "conceived by the Holy Spirit, born of the Virgin Mary." What this confession of the humanity of Christ signifies is that Almighty God subjected himself to being born a human baby: to having human DNA, becoming a human zygote, then growing as an embryo and a human fetus. Of course, Christ is Almighty and Everlasting God—and was worshipped as such in his mother's womb, we may say, by John the Baptist—who leaped for joy during his sixth month in Elizabeth's womb at the presence of the newly pregnant Mary (with Jesus in his first trimester of life when this occurred).[5] Not only John the Baptist, but we, too, should leap for joy that God shared in our flesh and blood. As one psalmist wrote:

---

choices through his love and sovereign grace rather than by our own wisdom and virtue. All alike are enslaved to ignorance and sin apart from God's providence and saving grace.

5. Gabriel announced Mary's impending pregnancy when Elizabeth was in her sixth month, so John would have been born before Mary ended her first trimester. Luke 1:36–42.

For you formed my inward parts;
you knitted me together in my mother's womb.
I praise you, for I am fearfully and wonderfully made.
Wonderful are your works; my soul knows it very well...
Your eyes saw my unformed substance;
in your book were written, every one of them,
the days that were formed for me,
when as yet there were none of them.[6]

In light of the reality that our God became an unborn child, the Christian church, from its outset, valued unborn life. The second-century *Didache* condemned abortion and infanticide, noting: "You will not murder offspring by means of abortion. And you will not kill [them] having been born." A few years later, the apologist Tertullian wrote: "Since murder is altogether forbidden for us, it is not permissible even to destroy what has been conceived in the womb... What will be a human is human; the whole fruit is already in the seed." Clement of Alexandria observed that women who "resort to some sort of deadly abortion drug" kill "all human kindness," along with the embryo.[7] Additionally, the Council of Ancyra condemned abortion in 314 A.D. (during the same period when the Nicene Creed was decreed and the New Testament canon finalized), requiring those guilty of abortion to do penance for ten years. Subsequently, the eminent church father Ambrose condemned "the murder of an unborn human" (through organic poisons and potions) as *parricide,* and sixth-century Caesarius of Arles condemned women who killed children recently conceived or already born, noting how such women must appear before the judgment of Christ for their sin.[8] Throughout the history of the early church, Christian opposition to abortion was unquestioned, consistent, and public.[9]

---

6. Psalm 139:13–14, 16 (ESV).
7. Clement of Alexandria, *Christ the Educator*, 174. Clement also chided genteel women who favored exotic birds, puppies, and other pets over the children born to them, writing: "Even worse, they abandon to exposure the children born to them, yet lavish care on their brood of birds." Clement of Alexandria, *Christ the Educator*, 224. Are these not like those modern activists who save the eggs of eagles while advocating human abortion?
8. In Roman law (including codes revised by Christian Emperors Theodosius and Justinian), *parricide* involved killing a close relative and was considered a heinous crime.
9. Michael J. Gorman, *Abortion and the Early Church: Christian, Jewish, and Pagan Attitudes in the Greco-Roman World.* Eugene, Oregon: Wipf and Stock Publishers, 1982; Zubin Mistry, *Abortion in the Early Middle Ages, c. 500–900* (York: York Medieval Press, 2015), 40, 45, 57, 59.

Building on the teachings and writings of the church fathers, medieval Christians codified opposition to abortion in penitential codes, ecclesiastical law, and secular courts—with some penances and laws appearing relatively light in modern eyes and others appearing quite severe, but opposition to abortion remained universal among Christian churches. Though penances for abortion differed by historical epoch, particular culture, and even stage of pregnancy, Christian churches consistently condemned abortion itself. Theologically, perhaps one of the most significant theologians and church lawyers of the High Middle Ages linked the Incarnation of God to human experience in the womb. While some of the science of the Middle Ages was inaccurate and incomplete, what is undeniable is that the first recognizable moments of human life were valued and protected. Peter Lombard wrote:

We say most truly and without any ambiguity that, from the moment that God took on human form, he took on the whole man, and joined to himself soul and flesh together.[10]

Moreover, churches not only passed penitential codes against abortion and glorified nascent human life, but they also acted to protect many of the unborn and newborn children at risk of abandonment due to parental poverty or moral desperation (with parents sometimes abandoning or even killing burdensome babies). As Latin Christendom grew in population and wealth, it developed previously unknown institutions to care for children abandoned due to parental death, poverty, or illegitimacy—namely, hospitals and orphanages. These represented a practical investment in Christian mercy that institutionalized the kindness for which God's churches had been known since antiquity. Over time, individual and church support for unwanted children grew from taking in children abandoned in a public place (often a church) to the construction of hospitals with medical staff, wet nurses, and budgets. The repurposed buildings for some of these medieval orphanages and hospitals remain intact to this day.[11]

The strict Christian condemnation of abortion continued into the

---

10. Peter Lombard, *The Sentences, Book Three: On the Incarnation of the Word*, trans. Giulio Solano (Toronto: Pontifical Institute for Medieval Studies, 2008), 9 (Dist. II, 3).
11. For a history of an institution used for orphaned and illegitimate children in Renaissance Italy, see Philip Gavitt, *Charity and Children in Renaissance Florence: The Ospedale degli Innocenti, 1410–1535* (Ann Arbor, Michigan: University of Michigan Press, 1990).

Reformation. Martin Luther wrote of unborn life: "Yet we were certainly alive even during the first year, when the fetus is carried in the mother's womb... Thus I have lived for 60 years. I also lived in my mother's womb." Luther condemned violent men who beat their wives to the point of harming "the tender fetus." Such men, Luther observed, are "murderers and parricides."[12] Within Reformed churches, John Calvin commented on Exodus 21:21–25 (a passage in which a woman miscarries after being struck during a fight between two men).[13] While at first observing how the Hebrew text appears "ambiguous" in applying the *lex talionis* (i.e., *eye for eye*) to any death that results from injury to a pregnant woman during such a brawl, Calvin soon affirmed that Mosaic law protected mother and unborn child alike, writing:

> *[If] the word death only applies to the pregnant woman, it would not have been a capital crime to put an end to the foetus, which would be a great absurdity; for the foetus, though enclosed in the womb of its mother, is already a human being and it is almost a monstrous crime to rob it of the life which it has not yet begun to enjoy. If it seems more horrible to kill a man in his own house than in a field, because a man's house is his place of most secure refuge, it ought surely to be deemed more atrocious to destroy a foetus in the womb before it has come to light. On these grounds I am led to conclude, without hesitation, that the words, "if death should follow," must be applied to the foetus as well as to the mother.[14]*

---

12. Martin Luther, "Lectures on Genesis, Chapters 26–30," in *Luther's Works*, vol. 5, ed. Jaroslav Pelikan (Saint Louis: Concordia Publishing House, 1968) 75, 382.

13. Hincmar of Rheims discussed this passage during the divorce trial of Queen Theutberga (died 875), differentiating between formed and unformed children—and penalizing the loss of the latter as "life for life." Hincmar of Rheims, *The Divorce of King Lothar and Queen Theutberga: Hincmar of Rheims's De Divortio*, translated and annotated by Rachel Stone and Charles West (Manchester: Manchester University Press, 2016), 199–200.

14. John Calvin, *Commentaries on the Four Last Books of Moses Arranged in the Form of a Harmony*, vol. 3, trans. Reverend Charles William Bingham (Oxford: Oxford University Press, 1845), Christian Classics Ethereal Library. Calvin commented as follows on Psalm 139:16: "The embryo, when first conceived in the womb, has no form; and David speaks of God having known him when he was yet a shapeless mass, το κυημα as the Greeks term its for το εμβρυον is the name given to the foetus from the time of conception to birth inclusive." John Calvin, *Commentary on the Book of Psalms*, vol. 4, trans. Rev. James Anderson (Grand Rapids, Michigan: Baker Books, 2005), 217. Eastern Orthodox medieval theologian Matthew Blastares cited Basil the Great in considering abortion murder, although Blasteres noted that Basil had reduced punishment for this sin because abortion could be committed

It is critical to remember that the sanctity of unborn life is not restricted to lives deliberately conceived in purest love, for none of us was so created. David wrote in one psalm: "Behold, I was brought forth in iniquity, and in sin did my mother conceive me."[15] David confessed how he himself is a sinner born of a sinner—a son of Adam. As for those born into what we might call accidental, unplanned, immoral, or illegitimate circumstances, the early church father Methodius of Olympus observed that "many who are begotten of unrighteous seed are not only numbered among those who are gathered into the flock of the brethren, but are often called even to preside over them." Methodius noted: "[Those] who are so begotten, even though it be in adultery, are committed to guardian angels."[16] Moreover, we must remember that even if our parents hoped and planned for pregnancy, we ourselves were not specifically desired, for each of us was only one of hundreds of millions of possibilities in that hour. God alone creates specific (and eternally known) people. Recognition of God's hand in the making of every human child, even the accidental and ill-begotten, underpins Christian condemnation of abortion, as well as church efforts to rescue abandoned children. Finally, each of us must be honest about our beginning. In the long lineage that created each of us (no matter our class, race, or nationality), there were murderers, rapists, adulterers, perverts, seducers, prostitutes, thieves, traitors, slavers, cowards, and thugs, along with the honorable men and women whose names and ancestry we more willingly claim.

Unborn life is sacred, no matter one's parentage or lineage. Scripture is clear that ancient practices of abortion, infanticide, child sacrifice, and child abandonment were judged by God. But what does the Christian tradition say about modern legal and scientific practices regarding adoption, surrogate pregnancy, and in vitro fertilization? While each of these requires its own book, I would note several key (and succinct) points. To begin with, adoption has long been practiced, as previously observed, with the levirate custom of legally assigning a firstborn child to a dead brother following marriage to the man's widow. God ordained that the orphaned Esther be raised by her cousin Mordecai in faith and piety, as

---

less from a "savage" disposition than from "shame or ignoble fear" of parents or masters. Blasteres, *Alphabetical Collection*, 141.

15. Psalm 51:5 (ESV).

16. Methodius, "Discourse II, Theophilia" in Schaff, Philip, ed., *Ante-Nicene Church Fathers, Volume 12: Fathers of the Third Century* (Grand Rapids, Michigan: Aeterna Press, 2014), 343–346.

well as that the daughter of Pharaoh raise Moses. More significantly, throughout the New Testament, the Spirit of the Lord frequently used Roman adoption practices to reveal God's spiritual adoption of the elect into the household of faith, placing God's blessing on adoption as an act of love. There is a sense that all of us are spiritually adopted into God's household: a reality we can best understand by observing the many adoptions around us.[17]

Surrogate pregnancy is more difficult to assess but resembles, in an unfortunate manner, Sarah's use of her handmaiden to foster a child through her husband, Abraham. Although the Lord showed great mercy to the handmaid, Hagar, in the Genesis narrative, the event is portrayed as unfortunate and wrong, suggesting a lack of faith in God's provision and promises, potentially leading to Hagar's ruin. Moreover, Moses placed limits on slavery to help those forced to sell daughters into servanthood, with the linkage to the enslaved woman's family never completely severed and restrictions placed on the enslaving household. More critically yet, Christian behavior must always be motivated by faith and love, and it is simply impossible to believe that any woman would choose to become a surrogate as an act of piety. Surrogacy goes so far beyond the natural order that it is hard to imagine women being motivated by anything except an illicit desire for money, thereby prostituting their wombs just as harlots sell their breasts and hips. Admittedly, there may be rare instances of altruistic surrogacy in which the surrogate woman receives no compensation. Such women generally appear to act on behalf of friends, family, and ideological associates rather than from God-inspired, charitable motives.[18]

Finally, we come to the matter of in vitro fertilization. Given the clear teaching that the Lord makes children and that human life begins at conception, it does not seem to me that using medical science to assist infertile couples differs in essence from many other types of medical treatment that did not exist one hundred years ago (assuming no embryo is intentionally and callously aborted, destroyed, or discarded in the process of rendering treatment—as sometimes occurs). Destruction of an embryo returns us to the Christian objection to abortion from the moment of conception. We also must remember how abortifacients destroy fertilized eggs and embryos, some a couple of days old and others

---

17. Esther 2:7; Exodus 2:10; Romans 8:14–17.
18. Genesis 16:1–16; Genesis 21:8–21; Exodus 21:7–11 (ESV).

a few weeks after conception. Given the sanctity of human life and the church's opposition to poisons used to abort pregnancies, any procedure that intentionally discards an embryo (as some in vitro fertilization and some birth control pills do) is morally objectionable in a manner that prevention of conception or implantation of an embryo is not.

Because I believe the principle of the sanctity of human life to be self-evident, I will not discuss the specifics of genetic selection (abortion directed against a specific gender or handicap), euthanasia, and medical infanticide. All of these stand condemned under the prohibition against taking innocent life and have been condemned throughout the history of the church (or the motives behind them have), and not only condemned, but resisted by laws of charity and charitable laws. Whether abortion itself, the Roman exposing (abandoning) of unwanted babies, or even widespread female infanticide in India during the nineteenth century, Christians have acknowledged that God is the giver of life and mankind is obligated to protect every life given by God, no matter how unwanted by other individuals or an entire society.[19] As for life-ending euthanasia, this dangerous evil will lead Western nations to destruction when God judges our medical violence and selfish greed. Why? Because every talking point about conducting mercy killing for the benefit of ailing patients is a lie declared for the convenience and cost to the living. Putting the elderly and afflicted to death is heartless and ignores terrible lessons from human history. There is little doubt that the euthanasia ethics of the Weimar Republic and National Socialist Germany stoked the fires of the Holocaust, adding a social Darwinian rationale and approach to anti-Semitic pogroms of the past.[20]

The sanctity of life is one of the more difficult issues Christians face in our world, and even the cause of persecutions. Abortion is a grave moral evil and must be condemned not only as wrong but also as destructive of God's blessing to mankind. As Martin Luther once observed, the

---

19. When the British ruled India, there were villages lacking a single girl, with the bones of daughters buried beneath their houses. British evangelicals who led efforts to abolish slavery also worked to end widespread female infanticide. See Lalita Panigrahi, *British Social Policy and Female Infanticide in India* (New Delhi: Munishiram Manoharlal, 1972), 24.

20. See Michael Burleigh, *Death and Deliverance: 'Euthanasia' in Germany, 1900–1945* (Cambridge: Cambridge University Press, 1994). One Nuremberg prosecutor described how Nazi euthanasia fed into the Holocaust. See Leo Alexander, "Medical Science under a Dictatorship," *New England Journal of Medicine,* Vol. 241:2 (July 14, 1949), 39–47. See also: Virgil C. Blum and Charles J. Sykes, "The Lesson of Euthanasia," in Jeff Lane Hensley, ed., *The Zero People: Essays on Life* (Ann Arbor, Michigan: Servant Books, 1983).

devil "would kill you in your mother's womb," if possible, so much does the evil one begrudge mankind "every kernel of grain in the field... every cherry or apple, or any happy experience."[21] Luther rightly traced the impulse to murder men and women in the womb (rather than to let the good fruit in God's creation blossom and grow) back to demonic evil. Still, modern abortion is not a matter of one child threatened in the womb, for it is practiced at scale, with an industry of death rooted in the fabric of contemporary society and entire political parties dedicated to defending the right to kill unborn children. Whether one abortion or millions, believers face the same ethical concerns that Christians have faced since antiquity, and which have resulted in significant efforts by believers to assist and save the unwanted and ill-conceived.[22]

Moreover, scale matters since the death of one child does not make a massacre. In that spirit, a fourteenth-century Franciscan friar preached how sexual immorality must be resisted because, among other reasons, women who become unlawfully pregnant frequently suffocate their offspring, if they are unable to "provide for their children [and] get no help from their fathers." At the same time, the friar observed how much worse matters would be if "everybody could sleep with anyone." He feared that "frequent struggles would arise... strife, hatred, homicide, and many more evils than are now in the world."[23] The friar could see even from the more limited sexual immorality that existed in fourteenth-century Europe how many evils would result from the spread of sexual license, and prophetically envisioned from the sin of a few during his generation to what might result if sexual immorality became widespread. He saw what sin did among those of his generation who found themselves in unholy and desperate circumstances and judged that such evil would multiply if widespread sexual immorality led to more undesired pregnancies and children.

The fourteenth-century friar proved correct, for we do live in a world where anyone can sleep with anyone else, and we see the very problems he feared, including numerous children discarded through abortion. In response to this flood of destruction, believers must preach God's holy

21. Martin Luther, "Sermons on the Gospel of St. John, Chapters 6–8," in *Luther's Works*, vol. 23, ed. Jaroslav Pelikan (Saint Louis: Concordia Publishing House, 1958), 256–257.
22. For a book that includes primary texts regarding church efforts to save abandoned children, see John Boswell, *The Kindness of Strangers: The Abandonment of Children in Western Europe from Antiquity to the Renaissance* (New York: Vintage Books, 1988).
23. Wenzel, *Fasciculus Morum*, 669.

law, reveal God's great mercy, and live out God's tireless compassion. We must keep our hands clean of innocent blood, not only by what we do, but also through what we consent to, approve, or tolerate in our attitudes and priorities. By God's grace and wisdom, we must seek solutions that save everyone involved, and each of us must do something to stem the tide of evil. Believers must seek the good of the unborn (and their sorely tempted parents) over social and political issues of far less importance than saving unborn life from death. Too many lives have been lost, and we must not pretend this matter is less than the atrocity it is.[24] And the example of historical Christianity is not simply condemnation and legal restrictions of abortion, as necessary as this might be, but practical assistance to those so overwhelmed by poverty, shame, or fear that they are being tempted to make a very wrong and destructive, even self-destructive, decision. We must preach and help the tempted so that they can understand how parenthood is a far greater joy than any other achievement or pleasure found in human life.

In the book of Deuteronomy, Moses declared that if the corpse of a murdered man was found in the countryside, public authorities of the nearest city were to conduct a ritual sacrifice and swear publicly before everyone that their "hands did not shed this blood, nor did [their] eyes see it [shed]." Only with that public declaration of innocence was the land purged of the "guilt of innocent blood."[25] Given this rather demanding law of righteousness, we moderns stand condemned as a people, for most of us understand what abortion is and how it takes a nascent life—violently and often painfully. As with the Holocaust or American slavery, there are few men or women (even older children) who do not realize that innocent blood is being spilled, even if some remain unaware of the horrible details, and others do not care.[26] Who among us dares to swear the oath Moses required of the Hebrews? And even if we

---

24. For the record, I was a pro-life activist in deed during my youth and remain one in spirit to this day. I find no moral justification for abortion, except to save the life of the mother. Even then, I knew a woman (like canonized Roman Catholic pediatric physician and mother of four children, Gianna Beretta Molla), who continued her pregnancy after a diagnosis of cancer, thereby sacrificing her life for that of her child and demonstrating courage and valor as heroic as any soldier awarded *The Medal of Honor*.

25. Deuteronomy 21:1–9 (NASB).

26. Pierre Viret commented on Deuteronomy 21: "How then could a land be considered pure and clean in which known murderers and manslayers are tolerated? For the shedding of human blood bears with it such a staining and pollution that it can scarcely ever be effaced and the land purged from it, and even less the hands which have been sullied and stained by it." Viret, *Exposition*, vol. 2, 107.

believe our hands are clean, our eyes are not, for we see the bloodshed and do not prevent it. Every one of us stands guilty in some measure, for the sin belongs to our people as a whole.

What Protestant Reformer Pierre Viret said of the fierce persecutions suffered by his co-religionists, so we must say of those who persecute (or fail to rescue) the unborn: every word, act, and vote will be scrutinized, and the Lord will accept no excuse that we are not our brother's keeper. God made that duty clear at the beginning of human history (after the first murder of a man by his brother), and he has not retracted the moral responsibility of each man or woman for those near them. For that reason, we stand as Christians did in the United States before the Civil War, or as confessing believers in Germany during the 1930s and 1940s.[27] Like it or not, abortion is the issue of the day, and we must give an accounting for the spilled blood of our unborn brothers and sisters. God has demonstrated great forbearance to date, but a day of reckoning must come when the Lord's wrath will strike down those who spearheaded the prochoice movement and supported their damnable efforts to murder the unborn, as well as everyone who assisted their efforts, accepted their arguments, voted for their candidates, profited from their funding, or stood by in silent acquiescence. We must actively protect the unborn, just as early, medieval, and early modern believers did, and lead those who have sinned to life-giving repentance.[28] Regarding our duty to save those persecuted in our midst, Protestant Reformer Pierre Viret observed:

> *Those who give counsel to kill the innocent and anyone whom it is not lawful to kill, kill by their words; as Herodias killed that holy man John the Baptist when she counseled her daughter to request his head... We can say the same of all those today in the counsel of rulers who by their counsel persuade [others] to persecute [the] inno-*

---

27. That many Germans understood something horrible was happening to Jewish people is made plain in Eric A. Johnson and Karl-Heinz Reuband, *What We Knew: Terror, Mass Murder, and Everyday Life in Nazi Germany, An Oral History* (Cambridge, Massachusetts: Basic Books, 2006). As for American slavery, political debates at the founding of the republic, acts of emancipation, observations by travelers, and details presented in Harriet Beecher Stowe's *Uncle Tom's Cabin* demonstrate how its evils were known.

28. A tenth-century Benedictine monk (Regino of Prüm) wrote a book for bishops (*De synodalibus*), which suggested discreet adoption of unwanted children. Regino wrote: "[If] any woman corrupted in secret has conceived and given birth, she should absolutely not kill her son or daughter... [but] should carry and expose her offspring before the doors of the church, so that brought to the priest the next morning, it can be adopted and nourished, and she will avoid the guilt of homicide." Zistry, *Abortion in the Early Middle Ages*, 203.

cent. We could add to these [those persons] who, being counselors or assistants and judges of justice, condemned them by their sentence of judgement even as Pilate condemned Jesus Christ... We can add to these all those who by betrayal deliver men to death, as Judas delivered Jesus Christ... We can include under this type of murder not only those who kill in secret either by sword or poison, but all false witnesses and all those who obey the murderous commands of tyrants to testify and pronounce a sentence of death against the life of the innocent.[29]

---

29. Viret, *Exposition*, vol. 2, 103–104. Medieval canonist Gratian similarly wrote: "They are dangerously deceived who believe that only those who kill a man with their hands are murderers and not rather those through whose counsel and deceit and urging men's lives are extinguished. [Let] those by whose counsel blood is poured submit themselves to repentance if they should desire to be promised mercy." Atria A. Larson, ed. and trans., *Gratian's Tractatus de Penitential: A New Latin Edition with an English Translation* (Washington, D.C.: The Catholic University of America Press, 2018), 13 (Distinction 1, c. 23).

46

THE REFORMATION OF FAMILY LIFE

Emperors Constantius and Constans Augustuses to the People:
When a man "marries" in the manner of a woman, a "woman"
about to renounce men, what does he wish, when sex has lost its
significance; when the crime is one which it is not profitable to
know; when Venus is changed into another form; when love is
sought and not found? (Milan and Rome, 342 A.D.) [1]

LONG BEFORE MOSES gave God's law on Mount Sinai, the brother of
a deceased Hebrew slept with his childless sister-in-law for the ostensible
purpose of carrying on his dead brother's name—a practice Onan abused
to his destruction by enjoying the physical relationship while avoiding
conception of a child. He also may have feared that his deceased brother's
property would pass to the conceived child rather than to himself.[2] Yet
even the honest use of this ancient custom was problematic, sometimes
involving extramarital sexual relationships with in-laws. Therefore, when

---

1. Clyde Pharr, ed., *The Theodosian Code and Novels and the Sirmondian Constitutions: A Translation* (Princeton, New Jersey: Princeton University Press, 1952), 231–232.

2. One author noted: "[Onan] had nothing to gain and possibly a great deal to lose by providing his sister-in-law with an heir, for the child born of the union would inherit the property which he would otherwise have possessed, since the deceased's estate normally passed to the surviving brothers." Eryl W. Davies, "Judah, Tamar, and the Law of Levirate Marriage," in Hilary Lipka and Bruce Wells, eds., *Sexuality and Law in the Torah* (London: T&T Clark, 2020), 116.

Moses (in truth, the Lord) established levirate marriage laws for the Hebrew commonwealth, he found a way to modify this custom in a more godly fashion, commanding men to marry a deceased brother's widow and thereafter share the couple's firstborn son with the deceased brother through adoption. No longer would Jews allow men to impregnate sisters-in-law outside of marriage. Nor would young widows be permitted to find motherhood in the bed of a father-in-law (as with Judah and Tamar).[3] Moses purged one of the most essential and intimate Hebrew customs of its sinful elements. Early Christian rulers did likewise. Christian Emperors of the Roman Empire outlawed homosexual weddings (in which Emperor Nero once participated), believing it their God-given duty to uphold pious standards of conduct. They legislated not only from the New Testament ethics but also from Old Testament laws.[4]

This was not done to establish a theocracy by instituting Old Testament judicial law and its punishments, but to enforce the truth that the moral law binds everyone—Gentile and Jew alike. Of course, the book of Hebrews, as well as the whole tenor of the New Testament, frees Jewish and Gentile believers from the obligation to participate in Jewish theocratic ritual and ceremonial law (which were fulfilled in Christ). Christians are also freed from the multiplication of Jewish regulations, which unduly bound the conscience and stifled the exercise of charity. In the Acts of the Apostles, the Council of Jerusalem framed the flow of church history by instructing believers to follow the Old Testament law in several key matters (to include abstaining from sexual immorality), indicating that the moral law of Moses had not been altogether suspended, only adapted to Gentile cultures.[5] In a like manner, contemporary believers are called to uphold those principles of the Old Testament which reflect God's unchanging character, even though we are neither allowed nor

---

3. Sleeping with a father-in-law was not the levirate ideal, which was for a brother to impregnate the childless widow of his deceased brother. The incident between unwitting Judah and his conniving daughter-in-law occurred because Judah's first son was put to death by God, and Judah's second son withheld from Tamar out of fear (Genesis 38:1–30).

4. The Roman historian Tacitus wrote: "Nero, who polluted himself by every lawful or lawless indulgence... stooped to marry himself to [a man], with all the forms of regular wedlock. The bridal veil was put over the emperor; people saw the witnesses of the ceremony, the wedding dower, the couch and the nuptial torches; everything in a word was plainly visible, which, even when a woman weds darkness hides." Tacitus, "*Annals,*" in Moses Hadas, ed., *The Complete Works of Tacitus*, trans. Alfred John Church and William Jackson Brodribb (New York: The Modern Library, 1942), 376, 380–381.

5. Acts 15:19–21.

obligated to mandate legal codes intended for Jews living in ancient Israel before the coming of Christ. While Christians are neither called nor permitted to reestablish an Old Testament theocracy, they must uphold natural law, common morality, and public order. Protestant Reformer John Calvin explained the difference:

> *For there are some who deny that a commonwealth is duly framed which neglects the political system of Moses, and is ruled by the common laws of nations. Let other men consider how perilous and seditious this notion is; it will be enough for me to have proved it false and foolish. We must bear in mind that common division of the whole law of God published by Moses into moral, ceremonial, and judicial laws. The moral law [is] the true and eternal rule of righteousness, prescribed for men of all nations and times, who wish to conform their lives to God's will.*[6]

It is unnecessary to discuss the exact use of the Mosaic law in every instance, only to point out that the moral law has not been suspended for the contemporary state any more than it has been annulled for modern individuals. God's will neither shifts nor evolves as the generations pass since his character remains eternally constant. Still, particular human beings and finite societies alike can reflect only a few rays of God's infinite glory, and none share in the full measure of his goodness. Just as the separate sexes show different facets of God's character, so, too, different human communities (European and African, ancient and modern, monarchical and republican) reveal unique dimensions of the infinite God's character: different facets of his authority and dominion over the peoples of the earth. Monarchies reveal God's divine majesty and personal authority, as well as the direct nature of human subjection to

---

6. Calvin, *Institutes of the Christian Religion*, vol. 2, 1502–1503; Calvin's contemporary, Henry Bullinger, likewise wrote: "Therefore the judicial laws do seem to be abrogated... because no christian commonweal, no city or kingdom, is compelled to be bound and to receive those very same laws which were by Moses in that nation. [Every] country hath free liberty to use such laws as are best and most requisite for the estate and necessary of every place, and of every time and person; so yet that the substance of God's laws be not rejected, trodden down, and utterly neglected. For the things which are agreeable to the law of nature and the ten commandments, and whatever else God hath commanded to be punished, must not in any case be either clean forgotten, or lightly regarded [that] honesty may flourish, peace and public tranquility be firmly maintained, and judgment and justice be rightly executed." Bullinger, *The Decades of Henry Bullinger: The Third Decade* (The Parker Society), trans. H.I. (Cambridge: The University Press, 1850), 280.

legitimate lordship, whereas republics and other confederations suggest the rightful authority of God's eternal law and his rule through the willing consent of virtuous people. All types of government are bound by constitutional order, political legitimacy, and natural law, all of which reflect God's righteous character and unchanging justice.

This limitation upon human government is why modern rulers are not obligated to pass laws as if they lived in ancient Palestine but are called to adapt the eternal principles of morality to their circumstances (as the godly rulers of Israel did in their own time). Pious leaders are called to the wisdom found in the book of Proverbs and the reforms expressed in Old Testament accounts of godly rule. Jesus commanded believers to be "shrewd as serpents" and "innocent as doves." Rulers and citizens are to exercise prudence as long as they do not become base pragmatists implementing amoral laws and customs. Cultures can manifest their particular values, as long as they do not despise universal codes of morality that govern male and female, black and white, dead and living alike. We all reflect a different glory from God, but it must be the same God to whom our lives testify. Similarly, each of us may display a different color of refracted light from the spectrum of the rainbow, but the light we refract must be to the Lord God's eternal glory. Additionally, the rainbow we celebrate must be the holy covenant of God's terrible judgment against all idolatry, violence, and sexual immorality in this sinful world—as well as the Lord's restorative redemption and divine forgiveness.[7]

The notion that God's will must be discovered and obeyed amidst the varied and specific cultural conditions becomes evident in a close reading of the Old Testament. As noted with the custom of levirate marriage, Moses passed laws for Israel that preserved Jewish customs while subordinating them to the will of the Lord. The ancient Hebrews, as with many Semitic tribes, accepted the notion of family lineage as the basis for ordering society and thus believed it necessary for men to impregnate the widows of close relatives. Why? Because this was the only way for a family to ensure its solidarity and to keep household property

---

7. Matthew 10:16 (NASB). The apostles Paul and Peter were under no illusions regarding the Roman state: both would be executed under Nero. The apostles gave the state a place in public morality and order, not in the establishment of God's eternal kingdom. State authority is real, but limited, per Romans 13:1–2 (ESV) and 1 Peter 2:13–14 (ESV). For an overview of state authority, see Glenn S. Sunshine, *Slaying Leviathan: Limited Government and Resistance in the Christian Tradition* (Moscow, Idaho: Canon Press, 2020).

intact, not dispersing family allegiances and inheritances among strangers (it also ensured a son for the sonless widow). Moses did not rebuke this Semitic custom any more than the Bible rebukes moderns for ensuring that our marriages are freely chosen rather than arranged by parents, as we uphold our most important value of freedom. What Moses condemned was the incestuous and promiscuous manner by which the Hebrews were choosing to protect their economic and social needs, just as he might chide contemporary couples for exercising modern freedoms that defy divine law.

God's solution to this problem was simple, yet profound. Moses ordained that Hebrew men take their brother's widow as a wife rather than as a paramour: a cultural revision with two dimensions. First, widows were forbidden to defile the bed of their husband's father. All such incest, as explained elsewhere by Moses, was outlawed. Even if maintaining morality meant property might fall into the hands of rivals or strangers, a man could not sleep with his dead son's widow as Judah did with Tamar. The children of such marriages would be deemed illegitimate and unable to inherit any property. What was previously upheld only in conscience (the fact that Tamar used subterfuge against Judah shows how she knew such intimacy to be wrong) was made a matter of written law. Second, the sanctity of marriage was upheld. Moses permitted Hebrews (indeed, he required the men of Israel) to impregnate the childless wives of dead brothers, but required marriage rather than extramarital promiscuity. Hebrew men were commanded to marry their deceased brother's widow and to adopt the couple's firstborn male to the deceased husband. This honored the deceased brother, allowed practical control of resources to the living brother, secured the property interests of the broader family (allowing the patriarch with more than a single line of descent), and guarded an otherwise vulnerable widow against ill-treatment or the disgrace of being returned to her father's house. Even the adopted child benefited, as he gained his biological uncle's property while retaining the companionship of his genetic father and the kinship of siblings born to the latter. Everyone benefited from a new law that reformed an incestuous and promiscuous custom. Moses wrote:

> *If brothers dwell together, and one of them dies and has no son, the wife of the dead man shall not be married outside the family to a stranger. Her husband's brother shall go in to her and take her as his wife and perform the duty of a husband's brother to her. And*

the first son whom she bears shall succeed to the name of his dead brother, that his name may not be blotted out of Israel.[8]

It took more than common human understanding for Moses (rather, the Lord through Moses) to draft such an excellent law amidst a terrible and degrading social custom. Divine wisdom alone enabled Moses to uphold God's standards while protecting the legitimate interests and aspirations of people trapped within the hardships and constraints of a fallen world. And the demonstration of such skillful prudence in legislating and judging remains the standard for rulers and subjects today. Although God permits every culture to glory in its distinctive traits, every people must order their laws according to the divine pattern, using the principles of godliness drawn from Scripture. Moreover, it requires study and prayer to determine what is right, as particular aspects of the Mosaic law are far from simple to understand (as the prophets and apostles attest). If God had intended the application of his moral will to be simple and easy, he would have revealed himself in nursery stories and children's books. But because the Lord revealed himself in parables and mysteries, mankind can learn to be wise as well as good. In this fullness, we better reflect the image (i.e. the infinite wisdom) of our heavenly Father.

Moses acknowledged the need for wisdom in interpreting God's law when he established a system of judges, courts, and appeals to handle the more contentious cases that were bound to arise. He did not think every legal issue could be easily resolved by a surface reading of the laws of God: interpretation and application would be required. As just one example, Moses demanded that anyone who seduced a virgin must be willing to marry the dishonored woman, while commanding that rapists be stoned to death. What he did not decree was precisely what is to be done to an evildoer whose crime straddles both sins.[9] What should be done with the man who seduced an adolescent girl, committing what modern judges and juries would punish as statutory rape? Is such a man a rapist or a seducer? This becomes a particular problem if the girl refuses to testify out of fear of what public authorities will do to the man she cares for, which has been an unfortunate (yet common) historical occurrence.[10]

---

8. Deuteronomy 25:5–6 (ESV).
9. Deuteronomy 1:15-17; Exodus 22:16-17; Deuteronomy 22:25–27 (ESV).
10. David Nicholas observed of late medieval abductions of women: "Although kinsmen were involved in bringing the abductor to justice, only the victim was legally competent to bring charges, and in most cases she refused. In 1376 Jan Van den Berghe and his party were

Moses's silence does not indicate that such sins were to be tolerated. Rather, the great lawgiver established principles on which future judges could build opinions, arguing that consensual sexual intercourse should lead to marriage and non-consensual intercourse should be punished. Subsequent generations of judges were called upon to determine when (and at what ages) consent existed and when it did not, allowing for shifts in society and culture while striving for a fixed standard of justice. Modern judges, too, struggle with the same question of intent. As just one example, consider the matter of sexual consent and inebriation: at what point is a woman too drunk to consent to lawful sexual activity? While it is clear that a woman passed out (or staggering drunk) can give no legal consent to anything (though the same woman will be held legally responsible if she stumbles to her automobile, then kills someone in an automobile accident), it is also evident that a woman of average build who drank no more than one glass of wine remains in full possession of her faculties. But what of a woman who has consumed two, three, or four drinks? Should she be judged legally competent to consent to sexual intimacy (though not to drive an automobile to meet her consort), or should she be evaluated and judged based on her physical size, liver function, genetic makeup, and drinking experience?

To consider the matter further, how can this variation be set in law so that judges and juries can provide consistent verdicts? The Hebrews themselves understood that Moses delivered only broad parameters of moral law rather than a comprehensive system intended to address every difficulty, which is why they developed a detailed legal tradition that applied the principles drawn from the law of God to crimes and sins not directly discussed by Moses. Like the United States Constitution (or any founding legal code), the law of Moses provided a framework for subsequent legislation and legal interpretation.[11]

---

accused of raping Adelise Van Crabbingen. [There] had been a cry for help and the girl's friends had rescued her. But she refused to press charges despite the bailiff's express urging." David Nicholas, *The Domestic Life of a Medieval City: Women, Children, and the Family in Fourteenth-Century Ghent* (Lincoln, Nebraska: University of Nebraska Press, 1985), 54.

11. In commenting on the role of the law in Christian life, Geoffrey Bromiley noted how God uses law to "protect the life of the people from disintegration through self-interest, force, and violence." He noted that "even if the particular rules of the Old Testament need not (all) be adopted, social stability demands legislation for marriage—preferably the best legislation—as a matter of public concern... Christians must ask themselves whether... they should not work to establish the best laws for the safeguarding of marriage. Even if they neither can nor should try to legislate the Christian view and practice of marriage, does not law still have a protective function and should they not join with others who have a concern

There are two temptations that modern believers must resist. To begin with, indulging the evil desires of the ungodly is prohibited.[12] When progressive activists press for the religious blessing of now-legalized gay marriage, Christians must uphold uncompromising standards that protect traditional marriage, purity, and charity while resisting modern perversion, infidelity, and promiscuity. It is never permitted to be weak-willed toward the wicked. We must show God's charity and compassion toward every same-sex couple in our family, neighborhood, or workplace (just as we must demonstrate charity and compassion toward adulterers, drunkards, gamblers, and drug addicts who live among us), but we absolutely cannot call wrong right, or suggest tacit consent to sin through silence. We can no more bless same-sex marriages than we should excuse, justify, or bless adulterous affairs, alcoholic abusers, reckless gamblers, and manipulative drug addicts. Believers cannot take half-measures that involve us in compromise with moral evil and unbiblical behavior. Sin is sin, and we must call it out.[13]

At the same time, Christians sometimes must practice righteousness in circumstances in which the law itself has drifted, accepting practices once prohibited (sometimes as a result of imperfect and ungodly reforms).[14] As we noted before, Lot's toleration of his evil neighbors nearly cost his life, and it did ruin his family: his wife was put to death by God, and his daughters were disgraced. For as long as this mortal life endures, these women will stand as examples of unbelief and immorality.

---

for social cohesion... [or] are Christians committed exclusively to a more distinctive and specific mission?" Bromiley, *God and Marriage*, 19

12. Still, we must not accept sinful cultural customs. To that end, the Christian apologist Lactantius, in his *Divine Institutes,* observed how Christians of his day parted from Roman tradition over the issues of infanticide and the double standard of sexual morality (by which men were allowed to engage in extramarital sex with slaves, prostitutes, and women of low social status). Judith Evans Grubbs, *Law and Family in Late Antiquity: The Emperor Constantine's Marriage Legislation* (Oxford: Clarendon Press, 1995), 90.

13. We must not implement morally compromised laws such as those of early modern Seville, which restricted prostitution to known brothels and made prostitutes more religiously pious without abandoning their profession. One historian observed: "Since the late fifteenth century, laws had required legal prostitutes to attend mass and rest from work on Sundays and feast days... A desire to constrain prostitution within a socio-religious order may have motivated these regulations as much as a wish to protect the souls of the prostitutes and provide them some days of rest." Mary Elizabeth Perry, *Gender and Disorder in Early Modern Seville* (Princeton, New Jersey: Princeton University Press, 1990), 139–140.

14. In *Prostitution in Medieval Society*, Leah Otis observed how prostitution was explicitly prohibited in select areas in medieval cities, but left unprosecuted in what became unregulated red-light districts—a neglect that grew into de facto toleration of vice. We see a similar dynamic with many types of sin in the United States.

We must not imagine that our marriages and families will be spared if we side with the unruly crowd of evildoers in whose cities we dwell.

Nevertheless, while believers must preach and practice the righteous of God, they must never pretend to live in cultures other than their own. It is right and honorable to preserve the customs and traditions of one's own culture insofar as those traits are godly and moral. We need not overthrow the laws of our land in the name of Moses. The example of Christianized Roman law cited in the introduction of this chapter makes this very point. Christian rulers honored their tradition by operating within the (harsh to modern sensibilities) principles of Roman jurisprudence that governed the ancient world. Still, they honored God by framing laws to outlaw acts Moses condemned as sinful, as well as to save fellow men and women from abominable exploitation and abuse.[15] Contemporary Christians must likewise subordinate our laws to the moral principles revealed in Scripture, as we live among unbelieving people, even though we need not always institute the harsh punishments found in Mosaic or Roman law. The baptism of the nations, which we are called to perform, sometimes necessitates an adult dunked in a deep river, and other times involves the sprinkling of water on an infant's head—only there must be a baptism of repentance and faith.[16] Still, even in discipline, we must uphold the dignity of God's law and the love of Jesus Christ.[17] Such is the command of the Lord God.

And Jesus came and said to them, "All authority in heaven and on earth has been given to me. Go therefore and make disciples of all nations, baptizing them in the name of the Father and of the Son and of the Holy Spirit, teaching them to observe all that I have commanded you. And behold, I am with you always, to the end of the age."[18]

---

15. Kyle Harper wrote about Clement of Alexandria (Egypt): "In Alexandria Clement had a disturbing front-row seat to the most brutal machinery of the Roman sexual economy. He could watch the giant slave ships at dock, bringing 'fornication like wine or grain,' selling girls wholesale to procurers throughout the empire. Sexual moralism inspires Clement's discomfort, but he is one of the most striking observers of the realities of the Roman slave trade." Kyle Harper, *From Shame to Sin*, 115.

16. For a review of how C.S. Lewis suggested dealing with the divorces of unbelievers, see *Appendix 10: C.S. Lewis and Dechristianized Marriage.*

17. For an example of a culture that did not treat sinners with dignity in their judicial process, see *Appendix 11: Welsh Mistreatment of Sinful Women.*

18. Matthew 28:18–20 (ESV).

47

FORSAKING FAMILY IDOLS AND HOUSEHOLD GODS

Rachel and Leah said to [Jacob], "Do we still have any portion or inheritance in our father's house? Are we not reckoned by him as foreigners? For he has sold us, and has also entirely consumed our purchase price"... When Laban had gone to shear his flock, then Rachel stole the household idols that were her father's. [Laban] did not find them. [Rachel hid the idols under her skirt while sitting on a camel and] said to her father, "Let not my lord be angry because I cannot rise before you, for the manner of women is upon me." [1]

IN ANTIQUITY, many men and women possessed their own household gods. Many idols were portable and could be carried about on an ass or hidden under the skirt of a menstruating woman. Men and women fashioned some of these gods after the desires of their hearts, so the idols could be used to procure what an individual wanted most. Some ancient religions even honored gods whose duty was to protect home and hearth. While it is difficult to know what Rachel intended to do with her father's idols, it is much easier to uncover her motives; Rachel was so determined to get a fair share of her father's inheritance that she stooped to idolatry, theft, and deception to do so, then tried to hide her impure motives by staking her claim in the name of her children and family rather than

---

1. Genesis 31:14–16, 19, 34–35 (NASB).

confessing her greed and presumption against her father's property (although Rachel may have had a just claim on the dowry which Laban had consumed). In short, Rachel used religion and family obligations to seek wealth for herself and her family, as well as revenge against her father. But it was a false religion to which she appealed, for the worship of the God of Israel does not allow piety to be manipulated for personal benefit. The apostle Paul wrote of such abuse when he condemned corrupted men who "suppose that godliness is a means of gain."[2] Neither the law nor worship of God should be used to achieve worldly objectives, even legitimate aspirations to strengthen one's household and family life.

During the 1980s, a popular bumper sticker proclaimed *the family that prays together stays together*. This is not necessarily true. God is not a household idol, useful primarily to secure the bliss and interests of a family. Families indeed exist to lead children to their heavenly Father, but the Lord does not exist to serve the human family as if he were a housemaid or hired hand. If family obligations are established so that members prioritize one another over God, the family becomes a source of temptation and must be resisted, even repudiated in some instances. Because the glory of God is the final call of every human being, as well as the ordained purpose of every facet of human life, there are times when believers must ignore, disobey, forsake, or rebel against an unbelieving heritage. Parents must be defied, and children put aside. Brothers may be fought, and sisters turned away. This is what the Bible means by insisting that men and women turn from the ways of their fathers to the paths of the living God. Each person must love God beyond everything they have been raised to think and be, especially if their heritage was not pious. True religion must sometimes be disruptive in any particular family since not every loved one serves God. Christ explicitly stated that he would bring strife into many households when he prophesied:

> *Do you think I have come to give peace on earth? No, I tell you, but rather division. For from now on in one house there will be five divided, three against two and two against three. They will be divided, father against son and son against father, mother against daughter and daughter against mother, mother-in-law against her daughter-in-law and daughter-in-law against mother-in-law.*[3]

---

2. 1 Timothy 6:5 (NASB).
3. Luke 12:51–53 (ESV). C.S. Lewis wrote of the even stronger statement by Jesus that to

The duty to love God more than family has several implications. One of the most obvious ways men and women must prioritize God over family is by living to please God, even when that life brings grief and suffering to their loved ones. A man should not readily cause pain to his wife and children, or children to their parents, but sometimes the kingdom of God requires such sacrifice (although not as cults attempt when they prevent members from contacting their families). For example, the apostle Paul was called to the rigors of a celibate life as he worked tirelessly to bring forth spiritual progeny. Still, so were the married apostles—and Paul admitted the right of apostles to marry and have children.[4] Not only did married apostles need to balance family responsibilities with the needs of the church, but it is probable that their deaths (and nearly all of the apostles were martyred) left wives and children without appropriate human protection and affection in an extremely hostile environment. I suspect their families suffered for the martyrdom of the married apostles.

Execution by the state is not the only form of sacrifice. Although few are called to martyrdom, everyone is obligated to put the Lord before family, living in such a way that the glory of God is more important than temporal happiness. Believers who dedicate time, money, and focus to the service of God do so at the expense of their families, who must lack something (and someone) good beyond common expectation. To that end, William Wilberforce, who spent much of his life campaigning to abolish slavery in the British Empire, reminded his listeners how middle-aged people are "tempted to be supremely engrossed by worldly cares, by family interests, by professional objectives, and by the pursuit of wealth and ambition."[5] There is a strong temptation for Christian householders to become so engrossed in the worldly success and comfort of their families that they deny the cross of Christ and grow slow to offer themselves and their children to the service and suffering of the Lord.

Lest anyone deceive himself that he is exempt from such sacrifice, we have the example of the Old Testament sacrificial system requirements in

---

love God, we must hate not only our own lives, but also our parents, siblings, and children: "Older theologians were always saying very loudly that (natural) love is likely to be a great deal too much. The danger of loving our fellow-creatures too little was less present to their minds than that of loving them idolatrously. In every wife, mother, child, and friend they saw a possible rival to God. So of course does Our Lord (Luke 14:26)." Lewis, *The Four Loves*, 153.

4. 1 Corinthians 9:5 (ESV).

5. William Wilberforce, *Real Christianity* (reprint; 1829, Portland, Oregon: Multnomah Press, 1982), 119.

which every household was called to sacrifice (*destroy unto the Lord*) a portion of its wealth, as well as the explicit words of Christ and various epistles that each of us is to become a living sacrifice before God. The book of Exodus made clear that not only the wealthy, but also the poor must share in such offerings of gratitude, piety, and atonement—with some gifts offered to support God's priests and the needy, and others burned before God without human gain. It was with this completeness of calling that Paul urged believers to offer their entire lives as sacrifices, alluding to the still-active sacrificial system of Moses and ultimately to the sacrifice of Christ, whom we are to imitate in all things. And it was the clear teaching of Jesus that each of us must take up his or her cross that makes the matter most plain: our lives are to include service and sorrows accepted for the sake of the Lord.[6]

Beyond sacrifice, God must be honored in the family by insisting that every household live by his law. This means that the word of God must be respected and taught, and rebellion against God must be held accountable. Parents must rebuke their children's sins rather than coddle misbehavior or indulge them for fear of being disliked or rejected. Moses went as far as to command Jews to hand over every idolater to public authorities for capital punishment, even a beloved spouse or adored child. It was not Moses's intent to turn parents against children, or children against parents, by fashioning a network of spies like communist youth behind the Iron Curtain—only to insist that believers have such regard for true religion that they would rather lose their loved ones than betray the Lord. This is no easy matter. King David could scarcely forsake his son Absalom when the latter was in armed rebellion against God, king, and father alike. Yet, Moses was clear that parents must not defy God's word by opening their arms to unrepentant sons and daughters (who stain themselves with the guilt of selfish ambition, open promiscuity, or unjust violence). The law of God must be preached with gentle compassion, but it must be preached. Moses commanded:

> *If your brother, the son of your mother, or your son or your daughter or the wife you embrace or your friend who is as your own soul entices you secretly, saying, 'Let us go and serve other gods,' ... you shall not yield to him or listen to him, nor shall your eye pity him, nor shall you spare him, nor shall you conceal him... your hand*

---

6. Exodus 12:3–4; Romans 12:1; Matthew 16:24-26.

shall be first against him to put him to death... because he sought to draw you away from the LORD your God, who brought you out of the land of Egypt, out of the house of slavery.[7]

It is relatively easy to see that duty comes before family. Our difficulty is not one of knowledge but of will. It is not easy to give someone up to God, whether for good or evil, who is cherished as much as life itself. Truly offering a loved one to God is one of the most sorrowful duties.[8] However, there is a right and a wrong way to offer sacrifice to God, and the Old Testament prophets frequently denounced the evil custom of Moloch worship in which pagan couples offered their firstborn child as a human sacrifice to that pagan god in a terrible, fiery ritual. The cruel custom of the pagans was to sacrifice a firstborn child in exchange for good weather and crops. Moses and other Hebrew prophets condemned this as a most heinous and unnatural sin, and its priests and practitioners were given no quarter, but were judged with the same unsparing justice that Allied armies ordered against Nazi perpetrators of the Holocaust.[9] This was eye-for-eye justice against one of the most evil practices in human history: the intentional sacrifice of one's firstborn child to gain security and wealth from a god who did not exist (with a sacrifice that would have tainted one's household with the evil of murder for the rest of one's days). How could anything be worse?[10]

In contrast to the detestable human sacrifice of firstborn children, the Lord called his people Israel only to circumcise every male born into the community. Such circumcision devoted children to the Lord and made it evident that every child belongs to God as the Lord's spiritual son or daughter (girls were adopted into the Jewish community without such

---

7. Deuteronomy 13:6–10 (ESV).

8. Even contemporary civil society insists that public obligations are more important than family happiness: sons are drafted for war over the protests of their parents, taxes are levied for common benefit despite hardships they inflict on struggling households, and parents are expected to turn over fugitive children to public authorities.

9. Deuteronomy 18:10; Ezekiel 16:20–21.

10. G.K. Chesterton argued that the struggle between Carthage and Rome was ultimately about the soul of the ancient world, given the inhuman child sacrifices of the commercial empire of Carthage compared to the more human and approachable gods of Roman households. Chesterton wrote: "It is not for us to guess in what manner or moment the mercy of God might have rescued the world; but it is certain that the struggle which established Christendom would have been very different if there had been an empire of Carthage instead of an empire of Rome." G.K. Chesterton, *The Everlasting Man* (New York: Image Books, 1955), 154.

ritual), yet entrusted to human parents through natural birth. Likewise, when God takes a man from his family to be anointed as a prophet, sets a daughter apart for martyrdom, or calls a man to a mission field far from his home, it is only right since the Lord is the true father and God of everyone—he is more to each of us than the entire cosmos. With that in mind, we should note that the biblical approach of using circumcision to symbolize deeper obligations was far more humane than murdering a baby in a cruel ceremony, for it involved only a slight cut that brought with it the benefit of cleanliness. The way of the Lord was kinder to parents, though it required its own type of sacrifice as parents watched their baby cut at a most delicate part of his body (we can assume the baby screamed, mothers wept, and fathers flinched as the newborn was cut before their very eyes).[11]

Spiritually, a far greater sacrifice is signified than a few cuts of the knife. The spiritual meaning of Jewish circumcision is that every child belongs to God rather than to the child's parents. This indicates that parents should use their authority to do something most unnatural in the sinful and selfish human heart: they must teach their children to love God more than anyone else, including themselves. This is not to say that parents should be unfeeling toward or detached from their offspring. No, mere detachment would be far too simple a task. It is far more difficult to devote oneself to loving a child so the child can grow up to love the Lord more than parent and kin. As a side note, we should observe how it was newborn boys who faced this painful covenant ritual, not baby girls. From the outset of life, male leadership is called to be one of bleeding sacrifice rather than the pursuit of power or pleasure.[12]

The ancient rite of circumcision signified that obedience to God requires men and women to endure many trials and tribulations for his sake, some of which are almost unnatural in their ferocity. By cutting sensitive flesh rather than marking children with a tattoo or piercing a

---

11. Genesis 17:9–13; Jeremiah 1:5. These are hard teachings, but we must put them in context. Did not the French rightly condemn, often to death, their countrymen who collaborated with the Nazi oppressor? Did not the United States justly condemn, even to death, the Stalinist agents who treasonably delivered to the Soviet Union plans for a nuclear weapon—a weapon whose possession made subsequent wars in Korea and Vietnam far more likely? And if we rightly judge those who sided with particular manifestations of evil, how much more must we judge those who betray ultimate good to final evil.

12. Some countries practice female circumcision (which substantially reduces pleasure for women during sexual intimacy). Unsurprisingly, such customs are associated with cultures in which men wrongly dominate and abuse women.

lobe of the ear, the Lord made clear how we are to be subordinate to him where it matters most: in our deepest desire for love and intimacy (a desire we enjoy in many different forms from infancy through old age) and in our willingness to suffer pain and loss for God's glory. In such a life of faith, parents must watch patiently while their children suffer far worse fates than cuts to the flesh. Like Mary, whose son Jesus was taunted, tortured, and executed on a cross, we must accept the sufferings God has appointed for each of our children, without growing bitter toward God or trying to dissuade our offspring from accepting the burdens of a God-centered life.

Anyone who questions whether they are duty-bound to subordinate their love for a family member to their love of God must look carefully at the intended sacrifice of Isaac. Isaac was guilty of no sin or crime, nor was his father Abraham living idolatrously or sinfully. In short, the boy did not deserve to die, and his father did not deserve to lose a son. Still, God demanded that Abraham be willing to give up the very child whom the Lord had miraculously conceived a few years earlier. In response to God's demand that the child ultimately belonged to the Lord, Abraham determined to put his only son to death by his hand and led the boy to a mountain for sacrifice. The drama played out to the end, as the Lord called Abraham to prove his love for God was more than idle talk by waiting until Abraham's knife was raised over Isaac before God intervened. Only then did the angel of the Lord stop Abraham's hand with a blessing, as he declared: "Now I know that you fear God, since you have not withheld your son, your only son, from Me."[13]

Abraham was not engaging in a pagan-like human sacrifice; he was not offering Isaac in exchange for better crops or good weather, as with Moloch worship. As the New Testament reminds us, Abraham understood that the Lord was both just and powerful, and trusted the Lord to raise the boy from the dead, perhaps that very day. Abraham remembered the Lord's leading to Canaan, various visions and appearances of God, the explicit promise of a great progeny, and God's conception of Isaac from the womb of an elderly and barren woman. With these clear signs and wonders in mind, it makes perfect sense that the patriarch believed the Lord could raise Isaac even from death. This is the example we must follow in our lives and with our families, remembering that we and our loved ones who (literally or figuratively) lay down their lives in this world

---

13. Genesis 22:12 (NASB).

will gain a better resurrection in the next, and encouraging them to do so. We are called to share Abraham's faith that the Lord can and will raise the dead from the grave, and to act upon that faith.[14]

The reason the Lord called Abraham to contemplate the terrible sacrifice of his son was that the Lord intended the story to illustrate what he himself would actually do to redeem fallen man. When Abraham offered up Isaac, he revealed a dimension of God's character and love that was prophetically fulfilled at the cross of Christ—where Jesus was the Isaac struck dead by his eternal Father. God does not seek to please himself or secure his own interests, but shares a love so great that it flows from the holy Trinity into all creation, even blessing rebellious and sinful mankind. The Lord's love is so great that the Father sent his only Son to die on a cross so that a race of juvenile delinquents might become divinely adopted sons and daughters who will flourish in his household forever. Human households illustrate this divine love by sending forth their offspring to endure various trials to glorify God and serve humanity, thereby attaining the perfection of Christ's love. If and when this is accomplished, the human household will not be perverted toward selfish and greedy purposes as it was by Rachel and the devotees of Moloch, but will fulfill its deepest purpose by teaching men to love after the example of the Lord. This is the disciplined Christian love we must live and teach in our households. As the preacher Henry Smith wrote:

> *Before we teach parents to love their children, they must be taught not to love them too much, for David's darling was David's traitor; and this is the manner of God, when a man begins to set anything in God's room, and love it more than him who gave it, either to take away it before he provoke him to much. Therefore, if parents would have their children live, they must take heed not to love them too much: for the giver is offended when the gift is more esteemed than he.*[15]

---

14. Hebrews 11:17–19. In a sermon on 6 April 2025, Pastor Ryan Laughlin of McLean Presbyterian Church noted that Isaac's offering ultimately condemned ancient rites of human sacrifice—for the Lord refused this offering and stopped Abraham's hand.
15. Smith, "A Preparative to Marriage," in *Works,* vol. 1, 35.

48

THE JUDGMENTS OF GOD

And the LORD *God commanded the man, saying, "You may surely eat of every tree of the garden, but of the tree of the knowledge of good and evil you shall not eat, for in the day that you eat of it you shall surely die."* [1]

HUMAN SIN IS NOT ONLY wrong; it is also deadly. God has ordained that those who sin shall die. Life is neither a child's game nor an academic exercise, but a deep drama with temporal and eternal consequences flowing from decisions regarding right and wrong, wisdom and folly, good and evil. Daily life itself is filled with lethal possibilities: an act as simple as crossing the street is a dangerous adventure, since no one knows when a simple mistake will cost them their life. Just because people are accustomed to making significant daily choices does not mean such actions are inconsequential, any more than the courage of a single soldier should be disdained because he fought alongside many thousands and his entire regiment proved courageous. The reality of human choice reveals the significance of human beings in God's sight. Every man and woman, boy and girl, has been given the opportunity to choose between good and evil, life and death, heaven and hell. Those who do right will be blessed forever, but those who sin will be cursed and damned. Evil brings the

---

1. Genesis 2:16–17 (ESV).

inevitable judgment of God, and no one can escape the consequences of their misdeeds. Anyone who looks at life in this unjust world will see how destruction and servitude often crush the immoral and faithless.

There are several means by which the Lord punishes evil. First, God established nature such that evil brings futility and pain. Choosing wrong brings inevitable suffering to the soul and body alike. A man who divorces his wife is not spared the anguish of loneliness for the sons and daughters he betrayed, or longing for the woman he deserted. Nor is a woman who defies God through promiscuity spared the shame that follows her sins. She will not grow old with the good conscience given to chaste virgins and faithful wives. There are also physical consequences that nature inflicts on the immoral, including modern plagues such as incurable sexually transmitted diseases, that testify to the fact that God made nature to bless purity and curse promiscuity. In his letter to the Romans, Paul explicitly warned believers that those who commit indecent acts with members of their own sex will receive the "due penalty of their error."[2] When human beings try to uncover the root causes of such matters as sexually transmitted diseases, they must never forget that whatever the biological origin or transmission of a disease, the wrath of God may be its ultimate cause. When medical attempts to resolve such an epidemic prove futile, it is sometimes best to address the disease by repentance rather than striving against the Lord's inexorable judgment.[3]

Second, the Lord ordains government as an agent to reward good and punish evil. If wickedness is not to destroy a community (whether a small town or a great country), public leaders must diligently uphold God's moral law. Every government sanctions certain sexual norms and marital codes, and no state or community can remain neutral. The issue is to decide which moral laws will be enforced. Even modern America restricts date rape, outlaws incest, and punishes child molestation. Still, God demands that his eternal character be our standard of conduct, even when contemporary governments fail to implement the divine law in matters of adultery, divorce, and abortion. In all such circumstances,

---

2. Romans 1:26–27 (NASB).
3. In Leviticus 26:14–16 (NASB), the Lord declared of those who break, ignore, or fail to comply with his commandments: "I will appoint over you a sudden terror, consumption and fever that will waste away the eyes and cause the soul to pine away; also, you will sow your seed uselessly, for your enemies will eat it up." Human prudence and medical remedies should be pursued, just as the ancient world dealt with God's judgment of famine by purchasing grain from foreign merchants. However, when human remedies fail, mankind must pray for God's forgiveness and restoration.

believers are called to prophesy against contemporary moral indulgence, just as John the Baptist cried out against Herod's incestuous relationship with his sister-in-law. Such prophetic witness is a matter not only of right but also of survival. Why? Because God gives land and life to nations and peoples as a sacred trust, while revoking his gifts from the sinful and rebellious. The pious Pilgrims and Puritans of colonial America were given a fertile land for themselves and their descendants, but that gracious gift will be forfeited if their heirs continue to sell themselves to unbelief and immorality. The Lord Almighty will prove himself the righteous ruler of the kings and countries of the earth. As early Lutheran theologian and leader Philip Melanchthon noted:

Worldly authorities are to earnestly punish adultery and incest; if they are lax, and allow it, God himself punishes, as he did at Sodom... removing both the evildoer and the authorities.[4]

Third, God instructs his church to discipline its sinful members. The Lord's assembly exists not simply as a brotherhood of love but also as a holy community. In 1 Corinthians, Paul reminded believers that 23,000 Hebrews died in a single day because of their sexual immorality, strongly suggesting that Christians will suffer a similar fate if they tolerate such sexual immorality. Paul elsewhere commanded churches to excommunicate notorious sinners, including men and women who sin in sexual and marital matters. The apostle required public censure of sin and demanded that the faithful avoid associating with professing Christians who live scandalous lives. Paul instructed the Corinthian church to excommunicate one particular man who went beyond the pale by involving himself in an affair "of a kind that is not tolerated even among pagans." The Corinthian church was called to hand over to Satan a congregant who dared possess "his father's wife" (that is, his stepmother), thereby saving themselves from God's judgment and saving the sinner's spirit on the day of the Lord. Only if churches judge themselves will they escape Christ's wrath.[5]

Lest anyone wrongly argue for differences between Paul and Christ,

4. Melanchthon, *On Christian Doctrine*, 114.
5. 1 Corinthians 10:8 (ESV); 1 Corinthians 5:1–5 (ESV). Both the early church and the medieval church required penance for premarital intimacy, with the penalty extended if the couple did not marry. Fornication was considered a public matter rather than a private concern. James A. Brundage, *Law, Sex, and Christian Society in Medieval Europe*, 205.

the book of Revelation reveals that Jesus strikes down sinners linked to false worship and sexual immorality, distinguishing between those who tolerate such evil and those who do not. Jesus castigated one church leader who brought her congregation into sexual immorality, saying that the Lord will throw those "who commit adultery with her into great tribulation, unless they repent of her deeds." Jesus further revealed that he will strike "her children with pestilence" and give "to each of you according to your deeds." To be plain: in judgment of what appears to be an apostate and cultish church, Jesus threatened death to leaders, followers, and their dependents (possibly the children born of immorality and adultery).[6] It must be emphasized that these are the authoritative words of Jesus Christ to a New Testament church. There is no denying them without denying Christ and the authority of the book of Revelation—a book that curses those who reject it and is the basis of most Christian doctrine regarding the afterlife. The only way to circumvent this clear teaching is to allegorize both the Old and New Testaments, or to diminish the Bible's binding authority to the teachings of the Sermon on the Mount (as some in the Anabaptist tradition do). Otherwise, contemporary believers must understand that God continues to judge churches and nations to this day: an understanding common among God's people until recent generations.

Many contemporary Christian churches indulge the sins of a host of unrepentant violators of sexual chastity and marital fidelity, from unwed mothers to wrongly divorced couples. For just one example of modern apostasy, an official Methodist book of church law from recent decades allowed ministers to "solemnize the marriage of a divorced person," provided the minister is satisfied that the divorced person understands why their previous marriage failed. While there are far too many examples of ecclesiastical unbelief to catalog in this book (from mainline Protestant to Roman Catholic to Orthodox to Evangelical churches), it is evident that modern churches do not discipline marital and sexual morality as Christian churches in the past commonly did. Such sinful indulgence

---

6. Revelation 2:20–23 (NASB). When I read this passage, I do not think about moral failure by church leaders (visiting prostitutes or seducing parishioners), but of the cultish Children of God who emerged in southern California during the 1960s and 1970s under the leadership of David Berg. Also called The Family International and Teens for Christ, this sect became utterly corrupted as they confused religious faith with perversion, pornography, and pedophilia—sinning far beyond the hypocrisy and sexual immorality of ordinary sinners and unfaithful clergymen. Upon such reprobates, God's judgment will fall.

does not follow the apostolic word or the historical example of the churches, which have proven hotbeds of moral fervor against all sorts of sins (including divorce, adultery, and abortion). The cited Methodist church law made insufficient use of moral judgment from biblical values and church tradition as the modern approach drifted into apostasy and unbelief, refusing to uphold the specific teachings of the word of God.[7]

While Paul spoke for the apostolic example, medieval clergyman Peter Damian represented the practice of later churches. Damian believed that churches should prohibit sinners "degraded by a crime deserving death" from receiving ecclesiastical office, no matter how zealous their faith later became (Damian was referring primarily to men guilty of sexual fornication and homosexuality).[8] This same strictness was seen in the early church, with Basil of Caesarea forbidding women separated from their husbands from attending communion services, declaring that wives who have abandoned marriage "without prior cause" must be "excluded forever" from the Lord's Supper (presumably until they returned to their husbands in repentance). For these believers, sin led to public and visible separation from the sanctified church community. Basil was similarly severe with adulterous men, writing:

> *The man who commits adultery will be excluded from the sacred rites for fifteen years. During the first four years, he will weep; for the next five he will be a hearer; for the next four years he will kneel; and for the next two he will stand [with the congregation] without communion.*[9]

The type of public repentance and penance practiced in early and medieval Christianity (and even in Reformation churches) is seldom found in contemporary Christian churches. While this book is not one regarding ecclesiastical structure, and I dare not share any thoughts on church government, I will make one statement: many of the texts drawn from Christian history in this book were written to govern Christian churches or influence those who governed them. Whether in the early

7. *Doctrines and Discipline of the Methodist Church* (Nashville, Tennessee: The Methodist Publishing House, 1964), 159.
8. Peter Damian, *Book of Gomorrah*, ed. Pierre J. Payer (Waterloo, Ontario: Wilfrid Laurier University Press, 1982), 34.
9. Basil the Great, "Letter 217 to Amphilochius," in David Hunter, ed., *Marriage and Sexuality in Early Christianity*, 244.

church, through penitential codes of medieval Christianity, or in church courts during the Reformation, Christian congregations have historically taken discipling and discipline (we can see the linkage in the very words) earnestly. While I will not attempt to describe what this should look like in contemporary Christianity, I highlight that Jesus's commands to the seven churches in Asia Minor remain authoritative. If we do not discipline ourselves, the Lord will do so: with blessing or curse in his hand of judgment.

Finally, those who evade God's judgment through nature, state, or church must not believe they have escaped his sword altogether. Such men and women should fear that God will turn from them as they have turned from him. To begin with, God turns a deaf ear to the prayers of godless men and women. As we previously discussed, both the Old and New Testaments reveal that the Lord does not answer the prayers of unrepentant sinners. If an adulterer appeals to God to spare his life from a mortal disease, he should not expect the Lord to answer the pleas of a man who has been deaf to the divine law, unless the man repents. Entire communities endure cold silence from heaven once the weight of collective sin has reached the level where God must judge, which is why the book of Malachi revealed how Jews of the period appealed in vain to God for relief from their afflictions. God's wrath occurs even when public authorities and church leaders tolerate, or even bless, such wrongdoing. Malachi prophesied against the prevalence of infidelity, divorce, and abuse in his time:

> You cover the LORD's altar with tears, with weeping and groaning because he no longer regards the offering or accepts it with favor from your hand... Because the LORD was witness between you and the wife of your youth, to whom you have been faithless, though she is your companion and your wife by covenant. [The] man who does not love his wife but divorces her, says the LORD, the God of Israel, covers his garment with violence, says the LORD of hosts. So guard yourselves in your spirit, and do not be faithless.[10]

Among other reasons, God was punishing the Israelites for divorces unjustified in his sight. Because the Israelites were wrongly divorcing the brides of their youth, the Lord was standing as a faithful witness (almost

---

10. Malachi 2:13–16 (ESV).

as the best man) to the sanctity of marriage and avenging himself on infidelity and faithlessness. The prophet Malachi revealed how God turned his back on the prayers and offerings of his people because he was "witness between you and the wife of your youth." On an individual level, it should be remembered that the Lord turned his back to the prayers of David on behalf of the stricken child born of David and Bathsheba's adulterous affair, refusing to heed David's plea for mercy. The situation was complicated by the fact that the child would have had a claim to the throne of Israel, thereby polluting the religion of God before the pagan peoples of antiquity.

There are acts of God even more direct than unanswered prayer. Often, the Lord brings destruction upon the wicked. The Old Testament declares that sometimes, though not always, a barren womb can be the Lord's judgment against sin. Michal, the wife of David, was one such woman who died without children precisely because of her arrogant attitude toward the Lord and her husband. However, the text of the Bible does not reveal whether her barrenness came more from the providential act of God or separation from the bed of her husband. Sometimes, the Lord goes beyond the curse and tragedy of infertility to bring about the far worse tragedy of death. Onan, as noted earlier, was put to death by the Lord for his impiety and faithlessness in sexual matters.[11]

As previously mentioned, Jesus punishes with death some of those who sin defiantly, although he remains gentle and full of mercy to those who seek him and his ways. Just as there are soldiers who fight enemies while remaining men of compassion to enemies who lay down their arms, so the Lord is holy and filled with mercy. As previously noted, the church at Thyatira fell into idolatry and sexual immorality, such that the Lamb of God threatened the sinners and their children with death if the congregation did not repent. Apparently, some believers were committing what the apostle John called the "sin that leads to death" (an act for which even prayer is forbidden by Scripture). The apostle John quoted Jesus as saying he would cast the heretical leader of the church at Thyatira on "a bed of sickness" and make those who commit adultery with her suffer "great tribulation," unless they repented of their sins. Christ threatened to "kill her children with pestilence" so the churches would know he is the one who searches minds and hearts and repays men according to their deeds. Scripture makes clear that God can and does judge sin through many

---

11. 2 Samuel 12:13–19; 2 Samuel 6:16, 20–23; Genesis 38:8–10 (ESV).

types of punishment: famine, plague, war, depression, infertility, rebellion, natural disaster, and many other ways.[12]

While God's judgment is real, it would be negligent not to mention how God delights in forgiving and healing repentant sinners. Both the Old and New Testaments reveal his abundant grace, and even the harsh warnings against the church at Thyatira offered forgiveness for those who "repent of [Jezebel's] deeds." Those who sin may have their iniquity removed as they turn from their evil ways. And though David and Bathsheba lost their infant son conceived in sin, David consoled himself with the hope of seeing the child in heaven, and the couple subsequently married and were blessed with Solomon. Moreover, both David and Bathsheba (referred to as "the wife of Uriah" as a reminder of her sin) were specifically honored as named ancestors in the genealogy of Jesus Christ. Though our Lord will destroy for eternity all who persist in their wickedness, we must never forget how the Lion of Judah is the Lamb of God who died on a cross from love for sinful mankind: bearing in his flesh every type of sin from idolatry and apostasy to adultery and murder, every sin of every sinner who cries for mercy. If anyone accepts the Lord's freely offered gift of atonement, Christ's sacrifice will purify their sin and bestow eternal life, no matter how sordid the sinner's past. And, I must add, each of us will know ourselves to be sinful and despicable at the core of our being if we examine ourselves in light of who Christ calls us to be: to resemble and reflect the divine righteousness and love revealed in the law, prophets, histories, wisdom, gospels, and epistles of the Lord God.[13]

Though the unfaithful and immoral have much to fear if they persist in their impure ways, everyone who admits to moral guilt and forsakes sin has nothing to fear from God's mercy.[14] The grace of God truly is greater than all of our sins and will bring redemption and healing if we call to God with empty hands and repentant faith. Converts have much to hope

---

12. 1 John 5:16 (ESV); Revelation 2:22–23 (NASB). Christians traditionally have confessed that God uses sinners as instruments of his wrath. Gregory of Tours, living among disorderly Frankish tribes, assessed that the violent death of one contemporary king came from God's judgment, writing: "There lived in Cambrai at this time a King called Ragnachar who was so sunk in debauchery that he could not even keep his hands off the women of his own family... [King Clovis] raised his axe and split Ragnachar's skull." Gregory of Tours, *The History of the Franks,* trans. Lewis Thorpe (New York: Penguin Books, 1974), 156–157.

13. Revelation 2:22 (NASB); 2 Samuel 12:15, 19, 24; Matthew 1:6 (NASB).

14. In 1 John 2:1, the Lord reveals that he forgives all repented sin, while Matthew 18:21-22 and Luke 17:3-4 show how God's mercy forgives sins that follow one another quickly, even for our entire lives.

for, as they have become the adopted sons and daughters of the eternal God and are promised restoration in heaven to an everlasting righteousness that makes the wedding white of a virgin bride look like filth-stained menstrual rags. Why? Because even the purest virgin flesh, undefiled by any human touch, veils a lustful and faithless heart, while the redeemed of the Lord will be perfect both in heart and body as they live in eternity as the bride of Christ, devoted and faithful to their God and his righteousness forever. As such, they will experience and enjoy, both men and women together, the eternal love of which mortal marriage will be considered to have been no more than a pale reflection.[15]

> *"Sing, O barren one, who did not bear;*
> *break forth into singing and cry aloud,*
>   *you who have not been in labor!*
> *For the children of the desolate one*
>   *will be more than the children*
> *of her who is married," says the* LORD.

> *"For your Maker is your husband,*
>   *the* LORD *of hosts is his name;*
> *and the Holy One of Israel is your Redeemer,*
>   *the God of the whole earth he is called.*

> *"For the* LORD *has called you*
> *like a wife deserted and grieved in spirit,*
> *like a wife of youth when she is cast off,"*
>   *says your God.*[16]

---

15. Francis Schaeffer reminded us that sexual sin is no worse than other sins, noting how Paul "carefully breaks up the lists of the sins so that sometimes one is in the first place and sometimes another." Schaeffer considered this "deliberate in the inspiration of the Holy Spirit, to demonstrate that one sin is not greater than another, and that all sins are forgiven by the blood of Christ." Schaeffer, *Letters,* 205.

16. Isaiah 54:1, 5–6 (ESV).

49

THE BLESSING OF THE LORD

And because you listen to these rules and keep; and do them, the LORD your God will keep with you the covenant and the steadfast love that he swore to your fathers. He will love you, bless you, and multiply you. He will also bless the fruit of your womb and the fruit of your ground, your grain and your wine and your oil, the increase of your herds and the young of your flock, in the land that he swore to your fathers to give you. You shall be blessed above all peoples. There shall not be male or female barren among you or among your livestock. And the LORD will take away from you all sickness.[1]

ISRAEL WAS CALLED to be God's holy people and promised a *blessing greater than any other people* if they served the Lord with all of their heart and strength. Though the people of God would have remained subject to the ordinary troubles found in mortal life (disease, natural destruction, and death), theirs would have been a blessed land if they had fully obeyed the Lord. This same promise extends to God's people today: to all Gentile peoples who are adopted into the Lord's kingdom and made heirs of his eternal household. If we fulfill our divine calling—our very nature as human beings made in the image of God—by living according to the laws and love of the Lord, we will find peace, joy, and love, even in

---

1. Deuteronomy 7:12–15 (ESV).

the troubled and sorrowful world in which we must live our lives. This is a promise for now and forevermore.

The specific promises of God to the people of Israel offer a clear understanding of what the blessing of God entails in this mortal life. While we must be very careful to serve the Lord by taking up our cross and living for eternity as he calls us to do (for the Beatitudes declare as *blessed* those who live for God's kingdom rather than an earthly one), we rejoice that the blessings of the Lord manifest themselves in this temporal life, as well as in the eternal one. When Paul wrote of peace and joy in God's Spirit, he described the deep emotions each of us long to share, here and now.[2] Paul's revelation was not the hollow assurance of a cult leader begging his misguided followers to endure *just a little while longer till the end* (meaning just long enough for the cult leader to profit more from his gullible followers). No, the apostle who spoke for the Lord God, or rather, through whom the Lord God spoke (and still speaks), was calling men and women to share in the promises once delivered to the custodianship of Israel and now given to all Gentile peoples who call upon Jesus Christ.

As we review the promises of God above, what do we see for those who serve the Lord, keep themselves from unbelief and false religion, and remain faithful to the laws and people of the Lord in their marriages, households, and churches? What I see is something extraordinary: families abounding with children and grandchildren raised in love and good order; material wealth carefully managed to support the rising generation (rather than selfishly wasted on drugs, drink, and vanities); jobs and careers made fruitful; peace and security protected from the ravages of crime and war; and blessing on childbearing so that women are spared the sorrows of infertility and miscarriage. I see peaceful love between parents and children—a divine blessing that surpasses any other in mortal life, as well as Christian peace between brothers, sisters, aunts, uncles, and cousins. I see neighbors helping each other (young and old alike) to provide comfort and support amidst the inevitable troubles of life. I see faith rooted and growing over many generations, as people work together to serve God and support one another.[3]

What can be a greater blessing than a woman content with her

---

2. Galatians 5:22.
3. John Calvin wrote of the blessing of children: "Among earthly blessings, Scripture speaks in the highest terms of the gift of offspring... It is no small or mean honor, that God, who alone is entitled to be regarded as a Father, admits the children of the dust to share

husband and a man devoted to his wife? Or an aging couple looking back at years of life lived together and children raised? Or children safe in their parents' home, unafraid of abuse and crime, for they do not know such things? What can be more blessed than a young man remaining chaste to bring pure joy to his bride without a trace of shameful remorse? Or a young woman remaining pure so she protects her ability to bear the children she desires? What can be better than a kiss between a man and a woman, confident they will remain together for decades? Or a man working with every ounce of his strength to support the woman who has loved him for decades? Or a woman honoring the man whom she serves with affectionate diligence? What can be better than children born to parents bound to each other by a sacred oath and committed to their offspring? What is more peaceful than a mind untouched by the sorrow of abortion? Or never troubled by a disease that cannot be cured? What is more enjoyable than playing with brothers and sisters on a newly mowed lawn? Or piling into an old car for a long vacation? Or into a new automobile for a short trip to the ice cream parlor? What can be greater than a family of several generations living in love and sacrifice day and night for the fear of God and love of each other? Or celebrating a family reunion of many branches and generations at a picnic in a public park? What can be better than children spared the trauma of divorce? Or a woman spared a heart broken by her husband's infidelity? What is more satisfying than looking back to see godly grandparents and ancestors? Or looking forward to the hope of descendants who might someday serve the Lord? What can be better than all of these gifts of God for us, our children, and our grandchildren? What can be greater than life, joy, and peace?[4]

The law of Moses was not given as human law: arbitrary, irrational, and capricious. Instead, the Lord knows who man is and what blesses us, male and female alike. He created us in his image to share in his joy and peace, yet we are sinners departed from his ways and prone to take our selfish path toward loneliness, shame, and death. Jesus calls us to build our houses (meaning our families and lives) on the solid foundation of

---

with him this honor." John Calvin, *Commentary on a Harmony of the Evangelists, Matthew, Mark, and Luke,* vol. 1 (Grand Rapids, Michigan: Baker Books, 2005), 30.

4. I intentionally emphasize the broader blessings of the household over the relationship of husband and wife. While many marriage books are written to enable couples to achieve deeper intimacy and sexual satisfaction, that narrow objective reflects a response to the modern culture of small families and broken marriages. Scripture exalts the intimacy of marriage as a symbol of Christ's love, but grounds marriage in the wider context of household authority, expectations, and lineage.

God's word rather than on sand that is washed away when winds and storms (the hurricanes of life) come. While we all must face the accidents, cancers, wars, unemployment, and other sorrows of this world, it matters whether God is with us through our suffering. Despite our sin and folly, our Lord gives grace to redeem us, and an essential aspect of that grace is his revelation of who we are and how we ought to live—even repairing our broken lives. This is the joy of the law of Moses, the prophets, and the apostles: of the revelation of Jesus Christ. If we follow the ways of the Lord, we will be led back step-by-step to the house and family of the Lord, where our loved ones and we will be blessed.

> *Blessed shall you be in the city, and blessed shall you be in the field. Blessed shall be the fruit of your womb and the fruit of your ground and the fruit of your cattle, the increase of your herds and the young of your flock. Blessed shall be your basket and your kneading bowl. Blessed shall you be when you come in, and blessed shall you be when you go out.*[5]

This great blessing is not simply for those who live well from infancy, but is for everyone who calls on the name of the Lord. The thief on the cross (who I suspect was more brigand than pickpocket) repented and was eternally blessed in the final hour of his life. But the Lord's redemption is not just an escape pod into eternity like some science fiction movie or the emaciated desires of a life-denying ascetic. The Lord's blessing is given to heal lives once ruined by unbelief, apostasy, and rebellion. Our Lord looks on the terrible aftermath of our marital and sexual sins (and all sin) and understands the disappointment, loneliness, despair, and disease that darken our days, particularly when we consider the full blessings that might have been ours had we and our loved ones and we completely obeyed the Lord God from our youth. We must place our faith in Christ's finished work and living hope, trusting and hoping that he will restore joy and peace to those who call on him, no matter how wrong our lives have been or how old we have grown. It is never too late to be blessed by God in this mortal life—and for all eternity.[6]

---

5. Deuteronomy 28:3–6 (ESV).
6. In discussing the prayer of Abraham's servant for God's help in providing a wife for Isaac, John Chrysostom shared the type of prayer that we ought to offer to God, one that is based not on our good deeds but on God's good grace. He wrote: "Even if we have done many righteous deeds, we ask to be saved by grace. We ask to receive our request from thy

In the book of Deuteronomy, Moses listed the severe punishments by which the Lord swore to chastise his people if they departed from his ways, including military defeat, oppression, enslavement, cannibalism, poverty, pestilence, infertility, and many other evils. Having previously promised blessing for obedience, the Lord also described the consequences of unbelief and made clear how sin would drive the rebellious to madness and despair. Still, the very passages that damn those who rebel against the Lord include God's promise to restore those same sinners, as they return to him following their disobedience. For those who repent of their sins, the Lord promised (and still promises) to return them from exile to their homeland and "prosper and multiply" them more than their forefathers. God promised to protect his repenting people from their enemies, bless their work, and build their lineage as they returned to him with all of their heart and soul. The Lord swore to "rejoice over [the repentant] for good, just as He rejoiced over [their] fathers." If we confess that God punishes sin with death, then we must equally confess how the Lord blesses repentance with restored life—and both oaths equally come from the word of the Lord, from the very same passages of the Bible. The Lord rejoices in our repentance.[7]

We have described God's blessing for the faithful, but what of the repentant? What does God's favor look like for those returning to the Lord after sinning in bitter and shameful ways: for those whose sins include promiscuity, abortion, divorce, drunkenness, drugs, and other such sins? From what I have seen during my life, I confess how the Lord can place such penitents in good marriages, bless them with homes and stability beyond their hopes, restore them to loving relationships with children and families, raise them as church authorities and spiritual leaders, redeem them from drinking and drugs, and provide them wisdom, compassion, and holiness to bless others and bring honor to their names. The Lord can heal the trauma of divorce, bring comfort to the lonely, and restore health to the sick. He can overcome mental illness and cure addictions, making the promiscuous chaste and the hateful kind. He can bring order from chaos and blessing from nothing at all. The Lord can provide new friends and establish new families late in life: households filled with piety and joy. God can comfort the childless by welcoming

---

love and not as a debt or an obligation." John Chrysostom, "How to Choose a Wife," in *On Marriage and Family*, 94.

7.   Deuteronomy 28:14–64 (NASB); Deuteronomy 30:1–3, 5, 9–10 (NASB).

them into loving families. He can forgive sins and grant grace to those who have caused suffering and sorrow. He can settle the disquiet of the anxious heart and nurse the health of the stricken. The Lord can release the convict from prison to do good in her community and lead a forlorn man to a rewarding and useful job. God allows sinners to make amends and grants parents who have led their children astray after their first birth to become spiritual parents, guiding their natural sons and daughters through the pangs of the second birth: a birth that spares children the worst evils of mortal life and prepares them for unending joy. God can grant those who once suffered grievous sins the utter joy of knowing that their own children, born of faith into God's church, will not so suffer.

Even more than all of these mortal blessings, the Lord gives each of us hope that the death and decay in which we live our lives will not triumph over his promised resurrection. For some, repentance will not bring repair of damaged relationships and despoiled bodies, nor will faith heal every broken heart, restore all lost fertility, or reunite every broken family. Sometimes due to age and other times due to sin's severity, there are consequences for wrongdoing that must be patiently endured until the end of one's days. Such men and women (all of us in some manner) must rejoice that God's restoration is only dimly prophesied in the joys of mortal life, for the Lord is creating a world for his children that far exceeds whatever is lost in this life, if only we will trust in his resurrection, life, and love. We must not for one moment forget that there are mansions enough for every resurrected man and woman to enjoy their God and his redeemed sons and daughters (for who else requires spacious dwellings but the many men and women whom we will befriend for eternity?). To be clear: what is lost in this life will be no more than the rice and seed thrown away at a large wedding—seized by the birds and beasts of the earth as a great feast, but of no consequence to the joy and passion of the married couple. That wedding is the union of Christ to his bride, his eternal people who have called to the Lord for forgiveness and have been redeemed for eternity.

Scripture warns believers not to ask, "Why is it that the former days were better than these?"[8] Nevertheless, I will venture to say that our world is different from the one in which I was conceived near the beaches of Malibu at the heyday of California surfer culture. There was plenty of sin in those days, both in Malibu and Inglewood, where I was born to a

---

8. Ecclesiastes 7:10 (NASB).

Korean War veteran (and Illinois farm boy), along with his small-town wife of just nineteen years. But something terrible changed during the 1960s with the spread of the countercultural drug and sexual revolutions, and there now are entire neighborhoods given over to addiction, homelessness, and illegitimacy (from which Inglewood itself has suffered). Millions of men and women face the regret of promiscuity, the loneliness of divorce, the remorse of abortion, and the sorrow of infertility. Our land is filled with broken hearts and broken minds, trying to blot out their sin and shame with alcohol, drugs, and sex, but managing only to make the situation worse and regrets greater. We see in this escalating sin how God seems to have withdrawn his full blessing from our people, leaving us to our selfishness and sin.

The blessing of the Lord is needed today, just as chemotherapy is required to treat a cancer that is growing fast and is dangerous. Our world is lost, as the world always is, and many of us find ourselves in lives that have not worked out as we hoped in our youth (being filled with brokenness, loneliness, and shame). Still, each of us can receive the favor of the Lord if we return to God to serve him with all our heart, soul, and strength: a truth preached by Moses and confirmed by Christ.[9] This is a promise equally for all races, classes, neighborhoods, nationalities, and generations. All people will be equally blessed by it, just as they will be equally cursed if they turn their backs on the Lord, since God is no respecter of persons, platforms, or parties. Those people, whether a vast empire or a small neighborhood, who do good will be blessed, and those who sin will be cursed, without exception or exemption. For that reason, we ought not to seek the blessing for ourselves alone, but should seek God's grace that we might share it with others: with strangers, rivals, enemies, and people different than ourselves, both in our own neighborhoods and on distant continents (and everywhere in between).[10]

This choice is not new. Moses gave the people of Israel a choice, and they often chose wrong. The prophets called Israel back to the Lord, and Israel frequently proved unrepentant. Likewise, Jesus called the Jews of his day (as well as each of us born of either Jew or Gentile) to repent, as did the apostles in their letters to the churches. One of the most perfect

9. Deuteronomy 6:5 (ESV); Mark 12:30.
10. It must be emphasized that we do not save ourselves in either eternity or our mortal lives. If we are to have a legacy of godly heirs, the Bible clearly reveals that it is the Lord who will call this into existence. In contrast, if the Lord curses us for our sins, our lineage will fade and fail both to do good and prosper and eventually die out.

and memorable responses to God's call for mankind to serve him was found among the Hebrews as they neared the promised land after decades of wandering (imposed for their spiritual idolatry and sexual immorality).[11] In this passage, Joshua (the successor to Moses) declared for himself and his household how they would serve the Lord. If we, too, show the single-minded devotion to the Lord that Joshua did, we can be blessed in the same manner, and not only we ourselves but our children and grandchildren after us. Let us confess as Joshua did when he and the people of God renewed their covenant with the Lord:

> *Now therefore fear the* LORD *and serve him in sincerity and in faithfulness. Put away the gods that your fathers saved beyond the River and in Egypt, and serve the* LORD. *And if it is evil in your eyes to serve the* LORD, *choose this day whom you will serve, whether the gods your fathers served in the region beyond the River, or the gods of the Amorites in whose land you dwell. But as for me and my house, we will serve the* LORD.[12]

---

11. Do we not see many among us who live out their lives in toilsome and aimless wandering, as they must endure the sins of their youth and middle age? Such men and women must repent of their wrongdoing and call on the Lord, lest they end their days like the lost generation of Israel.

12. Joshua 24:14–15 (ESV).

50

THE GOOD OF THE HOUSEHOLD

Surely we must see that God gives us some goods which are to be sought for their own sake, such as wisdom, health, friendship; others, which are necessary for something else, such as learning, food, drink, sleep, marriage, sexual intercourse. Certain of these are necessary for the sake of wisdom, such as learning; others for the sake of health, such as food and drink and sleep; others for the sake of friendship, such as marriage or intercourse, for from this come the propagation of the human race in which friendly association is a great good.[1]

EARLIER, the nature of the household and the good it was created to produce were discussed. By now, it should be clear that family life was ordained for several purposes. Marriage intimately reveals the nature and love of God, and parenthood reveals his providential concern for his creation. Because human beings are born into families, they have a real opportunity to experience and understand profound truths about the Triune God. Living with the infirmities of a sinful family also serves as a type of true penance, enabling men and women to live quiet and humble lives in sacrificial service to other human beings. Family life serves as a

---

1. Augustine, "The Good of Marriage," in *Treatises on Marriage and Other Subjects*, 21–22.

type of cross by which men and women, as well as boys and girls, can better learn to obey the Lord and serve one another. The family is one of those things which, as Augustine rightly said, serves a greater purpose than itself. No one must expect that family life has been ordained merely for the emotional and sexual pleasures of individuals. Such an attitude is pure hedonism; whether primarily psychological or sensual matters not.

The world does not believe this. Sociologists, historians, anthropologists, and many others believe that the family exists merely for temporal purposes (such as reproduction) or is a holdover from history, now rendered obsolete by evolutionary, social, or technological advances. They explain the origins and nature of family life without reference to divinity or eternity alike. Even more commonly, the good of the human household is measured by a single criterion: its ability to provide physical pleasure and emotional satisfaction. Modern hedonists justify domestic arrangements that make individuals happy and condemn those that do not. Such men and women do not try to measure the household by its ability to give birth to either physical life or moral good. Why not? Because most men and women of our culture consider only their most immediate pleasures and desires, taking little thought of future generations or eternal life. Only the whim of the individual seems to matter.

Almost every recent theory of marriage or sex stresses one concern: the desire of the individual. In contrast to such self-centered ethics, Jude (likely the brother of Jesus) prophesied against men and women who blaspheme and are destroyed as they live in their dreams, pollute the flesh, and defy God's authority through their base instincts, "like unreasoning animals." Jude compared such people to the wicked and condemned inhabitants of Sodom and Gomorrah, who gave themselves over to "gross immorality and went after strange flesh."[2] In the same manner, as modern people give themselves over to an orgy of sexual promiscuity, they become increasingly less able to separate their base lusts from the amoral mating of the animal kingdom. While it is true that mankind and the animal kingdom share many physical traits, it is not true that the human household is an offspring of the courtship and parenthood that exist among birds and apes. Human beings share certain biological and chemical processes with animals. Still, people are more than their flesh, having souls fashioned in the divine image and a spiritual nature displayed in the corporeal body itself. Male and female together are made

---

2. Jude 7–8, 10 (NASB).

in the image of God (did not Eve exist in Adam when he was created, just as men now carry chromosomes to conceive both male and female offspring?) and reflect the morality and reason which separate mankind from beasts of the field.

Modern humanity ignores this truth and forgets where the human household originated and why it was established. As a result, modern thinkers neither understand how the human family differs from the broods of beasts nor why unrepentant human beings cannot fulfill the most basic moral purposes for which family life was ordained. In his letter to the Romans, the apostle Paul declared that generations of men and women given over to sexual immorality and perversity become foolish in their understanding of creation and refusal to give God glory. The sexually immoral not only conflate good and evil but also come to confuse the divine and the natural as well.[3] This confusion does not come only from scientific theories regarding the origin of humanity but is rooted in a failure to understand the nature of mankind: one's own nature, we might say. It is in this spirit that the Christian philosopher and scientist Blaise Pascal observed how man, apart from God, is mistaken not only about spiritual truth but about his humanity, writing:

> It is dangerous to explain too clearly to man how like he is to the animals without pointing out his greatness. It is also dangerous to make too much of his greatness without his vileness. It is still more dangerous to leave him in ignorance of both, but it is most valuable to represent both to him.[4]

Man's moral nature must be explained in thought and deed. Anyone who wishes to please God must think about and live their private life as if eternity matters, never forgetting that human love and marriage must never be reduced to the amoral and base acts of mere animals. People do not resemble dogs in heat, or at least they should not. In addition, the Lord provides every person with an opportunity to make a difference in

---

3. Romans 1:18–27.
4. Pascal, *Pensées*, 60. Francis Schaeffer brought out this thought better than nearly every other Christian thinker since C.S. Lewis (although often in the context of the fear of reducing mankind to a machine as much as to an animal). He observed: "It is important to note that fallen man still retains something of the image of God. The Fall separates man from God, but it does not remove his original differentiation from other things. Fallen man is not less than man." Francis Schaeffer, *Genesis in Space and Time*, 35.

human history (perhaps not in the history of empires and nations, but in the far more important and impactful history of religion, morality, and family). While William Shakespeare's *The Tragedy of Romeo and Juliet* is a fictional story, there are thousands of young couples whose lives resemble the predicament of that hapless couple. Such couples have one chance to make the right choice and to do so in real life rather than in literature. Those couples who choose to honor their parents and remain chaste will reap an eternal harvest of good, even if they must drink of self-denial in this life. But those couples who follow their blind impulses will be destroyed not just on earth but for eternity unless they repent, no matter what momentary pleasures they might find before death. In the same way, Shakespeare's *King Lear* shows us the temptation of cruelty, neglect, and ingratitude that we face when dealing with our aging parents and the passing of generations, as well as the peevish folly that the aged sometimes embrace as they flail against their own mortality.

What I mean to say is that every human household has the ingredients of a William Shakespeare drama, and every man, woman, boy, or girl must choose between sacrifice and selfishness, wisdom and folly, life and death. All of us are Romeo or Juliet, Lear or Regan, Cordelia or Kent. We are allowed to choose our character in life's play and decide what part we will play on the stage. This is a great privilege and responsibility not given to birds, bees, and bears. Every thought and deed in our lives, including household and sexual ones, is a spiritual test like that of Adam and Eve in the Garden of Eden. Will we serve the Lord or indulge our appetites? Will we trust God's holy wisdom and perfect love or fall victim to our foolish opinions and selfish fears? Will we seek to become God by giving way to the temptation to choose our path, or love God by accepting our place as the Lord's obedient children? How we choose determines whether our play ends as a tragedy of terror or a comedy of joy and mirth. Family life is the real-life setting in which our play is staged.

This brings us to an important truth. Though it is legitimate for citizens and states to change laws to strengthen family life, God is not for *the family* in the abstract any more than he is for *the state* in general. In one form or another, family life and government must exist among all mankind; there must be order, and there will be reproduction. Any society that denies this undeniable reality will find itself outnumbered and overwhelmed by its neighbors who do value discipline and fertility.[5]

---

5. One historian documented how early Bolshevik revolutionaries and Soviet authorities

What God is concerned with are specific families and particular rulers. Just as in Israel, the Lord does not bless every household but only the houses and homes of the godly, even as he judges the wicked and the ungodly—as we can see in the depopulated countries and minuscule families of the secularized West (which seems to lose strength corresponding to its loss of religion and faith). There appears to be divine judgment at work in Western culture, with curses from the Lord being freely chosen and actively promoted by contemporary men and women, and made into core values for both public policy and the political polity. It appears that the Lord is judging us with death by suicide, which may be the most avoidable and, therefore, the most terrible of his judgments.[6]

No matter what happens to the modern family, believers must not despair, for the godly have the Lord's explicit promise that he will be with them and their descendants. On Pentecost, Peter proclaimed how the promise of forgiveness and the gift of the Holy Spirit are for "you and your children and for all who are far off, as many as the LORD our God will call to Himself." On the other hand, the house of the evildoer (whether abortionist, media mogul, unbelieving politician, street thug, or unfaithful spouse) will be pulled to the ground, even as the humble abode of the godly survives fire and storm, depression and war, poverty and disease—and even death. Though God's work is generally hidden because it takes place at the passing of generations, it remains real and effective as the meek inherit the earth, even in this temporal life. It is inescapable that believers will produce fruitful heirs while the vine of the ungodly withers. To repeat: God blesses good families and curses evil ones, something most clearly revealed in his words to the Hebrew soldier-king Jehu. For instance, because the believing warrior Jehu obeyed the word of God by judging the household of Ahab according to God's

---

sought to abolish traditional family life and sexual morality but found it necessary to return to pro-family policies. Wendy Z. Goldman, *Women, The State, and Revolution: Soviet Family Policy And Social Life, 1917–1936* (Cambridge: Cambridge University Press, 1993). For the perspective of a pro-Soviet apologist (who published her 400-page work at the height of Stalin's Great Terror), see Fannina W. Halle, *Woman in Soviet Russia,* trans. Margaret W. Green (London: Routledge, 1933). Halle's book includes a tragic and ironic photograph (p. 138) of what appears to be a wet-nurse factory or a breastfeeding collective farm.

6. In 1978, Alexandr Solzhenitsyn delivered a speech that challenged the weakness of the secularized West and Jacques Ellul wrote a book that similarly explored the roots of spiritual decay. Alexandr Solzhenitsyn, *A World Split Apart: Commencement Address Delivered at Harvard University, June 8, 1978* (New York: Harper and Row, 1978); Jacques Ellul, *The Betrayal of the West* (New York: Seabury Press, 1978).

explicit command, Jehu's own family was exalted.[7] The Lord declared to Jehu:

> *And the LORD said to Jehu, "Because you have done well in carrying out what is right in my eyes and have done to the house of Ahab according to all that was in my heart, your sons of the fourth generation shall sit on the throne of Israel."*[8]

The house of Ahab was destroyed; that of Jehu was raised. It is difficult to determine where this process originated. Ahab's ancestors allied themselves to iniquity for years, culminating in the king's marriage to a wicked foreign woman—Jezebel. That entire family was perverted by terrible sins, ranging from idolatry and greed to murder and religious intermarriage. On the other hand, Jehu's lineage was honored. Perhaps Jehu was converted from an evil line and honored by God after his conversion, but it seems more likely he had been raised to regard the Lord with fear and awe. When Jehu was a young military officer, he heard with his own ears the Lord's prophecy that the house of Ahab would pay for the murder of Naboth. This word impressed the young man, suggesting he had been taught from his youth to respect the word of God. After all, not every warrior heeded the warnings of God's servants, with the prophet Elijah striking dead a number of soldiers who followed their king rather than God. Moreover, when Jehu destroyed the house of Ahab, he demonstrated considerable zeal by going beyond the specific command of the prophet (to destroy the family of Ahab) by purging the child-sacrificing cult of Baal in accordance with the law of Moses. Jehu's faith was not a merely complacent attitude, even if he was far from a perfect man. Was it Jehu's parents and relatives who taught him the zeal of the Lord? Possibly. In any case, pious zeal pleased God and established the house of Jehu on the throne of Israel for several generations.[9]

God will bless the righteous as he directs human affairs according to

---

7. Acts 2:39 (NASB). Horace Bushnell noted that the kingdom of God is extended by propagation, entitling one of his chapters: "The Out-Populating Power of the Christian Stock." Bushnell's theological liberalism and doubts about original sin are troubling, but he recognized a profound truth: that God blesses his people with fertility to build his heavenly kingdom on earth. While every child of pious parents must be individually converted to Christ, God today remains as interested in the progeny of the faithful as when he promised Abraham the blessing of many descendants. Bushnell, *Christian Nurture*, 195–223.

8. 2 Kings 10:30 (ESV).

9. 2 Kings 1:10, 12; 2 Kings 9:25–26.

his purposes. But that is not the whole story, for the servants of the Lord also enjoy the wine their master gives them to drink, for God both vindicates his people and brings them lasting joy. We must remember that the Lord is the creator of sexual intimacy, childbirth, and brotherhood. It is the Triune God who makes babies coo, toddlers babble, children play, youth court, and married couples embrace. Although believers must be careful to live for the Lord and not fall into a blind pursuit of pleasure, it is also important to remember that the Lord is the maker of every lasting joy and is always concerned with the fate of his handiwork. As previously observed, the power of God is significant enough to transform pain into pleasure, disease into health, and death into life. The God who made the world good remains utterly and supremely good in himself.

When the Lord cursed mankind for our sin, he made human childbirth more dangerous and painful, but simultaneously promised to use its sufferings to bring forth a blessing greater than mankind's original state of paradise.[10] How? By using the children of women to defeat evil and to redeem the world. God used the suffering of many women in childbirth to bring into the world one specific child who would deliver mankind into eternal life and joy—and it is the same with us. Remember how often the Lord transforms our trials into delight and joy that endures for eternity! Even in common childbirth, the suffering of women brings forth the children who grow into the men and women who bring God's good to this broken world, including the making of more men and women destined for eternal life and everlasting joy. Henry Smith noted:

> Paul sheweth how, by [marriage], the curse of the woman was turned into a blessing; for the woman's curse was the pains which she should suffer in her travail, Genesis iii. 16. Now, by marriage, this curse is turned into a blessing; for children are the first blessing in all the Scripture, Gen. i. 27. For, first, she shall have children and after, she shall have salvation. What a merciful God have we, whose curses are blessings![11]

Though the Lord blesses men and women in this life, God's salvation is not for this earth alone. It would not be *salvation* at all if the Lord just made mortal life a little less difficult, a little more enjoyable, or a few years

---

10. Genesis 3:15–16 (ESV).
11. Smith, "A Preparative to Marriage," in *Works*, vol. 1, 7.

longer, yet still subjected mankind to death and damnation without hope of eternal redemption. In the end, we would suffer for our sins and rot in our graves, cursed before God for eternity. For those blessed with good families and Christian homes ended by death, this would be despair enough, for they would lose everything good in this world of sorrow and pain. Still, the loss would be far greater for those forced to look on the blessedness of others without having shared in life's joys: those whose years included unsought celibacy, loneliness, childlessness, betrayal, divorce, disease, shame, and every other sorrow coming from the sins of men against women, women against men, and parents and children against each other. For these, salvation that makes life a little better, yet does not bring ultimate redemption and restoration, would be of little value since they never experienced the joys of mortal life. God's redemption would be little more than the adorning of a bleak and lonely prison cell with a fading and dying flower.[12]

Jesus warned us to store our treasure in heaven rather than in earthly bins and banks, where thieves steal and rust destroys, and also tells us to use our wealth to make friends who will welcome us into heaven.[13] In a similar vein, we must remember that the eternal love of mankind for God and for one another in heaven is the only love that will survive the sins and frailties of mortal life and inescapable death. The Lord's salvation promises the eternal resurrection of the physical body for every man and every woman who believes. Though we cannot comprehend what Paul meant when he declared that "flesh and blood cannot inherit the kingdom of God" and told of being caught up in the "third heaven" (i.e., deep heaven) where he heard "inexpressible words, which a man is not permitted to speak," we can be certain that God who imagined into existence the strength of men and beauty of women will not let those glories shine brighter in this sinful world than in his eternal kingdom.[14] The city of God revealed in the book of Revelation is far beyond comparison with mortal cities such as Athens, Rome, Constantinople, New York, Venice, Vienna, London, Los Angeles, Tokyo, and Paris. God's eternal Jerusalem

---

12. Geoffrey W. Bromiley wrote: "Marriage, for all of its high significance, has an eschatological limit. Married partners need not be afraid that they will lose the precious thing they already have. They will no longer be married, but in God they will have a more wonderful relationship that transcends the very best that marriage could ever offer, let alone what it can now offer in the sinful situation after the fall." Bromiley, *God and Marriage*, 41.
13. Matthew 6:19; Luke 16:9.
14. 1 Corinthians 15:50 (ESV); 2 Corinthians 12:2,4 (NASB).

is beyond all of their greatness, bound together and multiplied by itself trillions of times. So it will be with men and women raised in the body to the glory of the eternal God. In heaven, men and women will shine together beyond what we can imagine in this mortal life. With a joy that cannot now be fathomed, men and women will laugh at the cessation of marriage like newlyweds having first shared sexual passion, giggling at their previous enjoyment of childish pleasures through which they naively thought themselves blessed beyond measure.[15]

The prophet Isaiah revealed how the day will come when true righteousness is returned to the earth, such that wolves, leopards, lions, bears, and adders shall dwell with lambs, calves, and goats. Isaiah also prophesied that tamed nature will be led by little children, with no harm done by one to the other.[16] What perplexes me about this prophecy is not so much the transformation of nature as the reference to children in a redeemed world that presumably lacks marriage (since Jesus prophesied a heaven that lacks marriage and presumably childbirth). What the prophet hints at is a redemption of human life that perfects mankind in all of its desires and dimensions, even as mortal life blossoms into immorality. The apostle Paul, citing the prophecies of Isaiah, revealed that no eye can see or ear hear or heart imagine "what God has prepared for those who love him."[17] Those who have lacked marriage and family in this life are promised everything that marriage dimly prophesies but will never overshadow. Those who enjoyed marriage and parenthood are promised something greater than the enjoyments they must lose at death. Something far greater than marriage is planned for man and woman in eternity, and those who serve the Lord are being prepared for it. Such is God's holy promise to all of his spiritual children, whether they are married or divorced, parents or childless, aged or young. We can even trust that those who died in the cradle or womb will share in Christ's victory over death.

As noted earlier, the Lord ordained childbirth through the virgin Mary to bring forth a sinless Savior, Jesus Christ, to redeem mankind not only from the sin of Adam and Eve but from the sin each of us adds to the cumulative guilt of mankind. As Messiah, Jesus judges with perfect truth and righteousness those who reject him, regardless of religion or

---

15. For a brief discussion of gender in eternal life, see *Appendix 12: The Resurrection of Man and Woman*.

16. Isaiah 11:6–10.

17. 1 Corinthians 2:9 (ESV); Isaiah 64:5. The citation in Isaiah is soon followed by another prophecy of transformed nature in Isaiah 65:20, 25.

ethnicity, and gives his righteous kingdom to those who call his name in faith. To rephrase the matter: each of us has a choice to become the bride of Christ or to reject God's proposal of eternal love and joy. The Spirit of Christ inspired the apostle Paul to write that the marriage of man and woman as one flesh prophesies Christ and his church, declaring, "This mystery is profound, and I am saying that it refers to Christ and the church."[18] Whatever good marriage is intended to bring in mortal life, it has an even greater divine purpose to represent in immortal life: the marriage of Jesus Christ to his eternal bride—the Christian church.

To that end, Protestant theologian Girolamo Zanchi wrote a book in the sixteenth century that discussed many parallels between a man marrying a woman and Jesus marrying his bride, the church. For Zanchi, as with the apostle Paul in the letter to the Ephesians, earthly marriages "fulfill their truest purpose by drawing our attention toward the real thing: the spiritual marriage between Christ and His church." According to Zanchi, earthly marriage and Christ's heavenly marriage resemble each other in many ways, including betrothal, consent, exclusiveness, and cele-bration. Zanchi noted how the Son of God is the church's bridegroom, for the Father has given the church to his Son. As one passage of many, Zanchi wrote: "The Father betroths the church to none but Him from whose side she was also taken and, through regeneration, made flesh of His flesh and bone of His bones, that is, to Christ." Zanchi found paral-lels not simply in marriage but in the creation of the church from the life of Christ, just as woman was taken from the life of man.[19]

What I mean is that the good of marriage is not restricted to the mortal joy of man and woman for each other in courtship and matri-mony, nor to the charitable service and self-sacrifice found in family life. The good of marriage is limited neither to filling the earth with billions of new people (each of whom will live forever) nor to shaping human history in mercy and judgment. All of these things are true enough, but what marriage ultimately provides is a window into eternity: the eternity of those men and women made one as God's eternal bride. Marriage prophesies eternal joy that transcends mortal marriage, a joy to be lived in redeemed spirit and resurrected flesh for all eternity. It promises the final consummation of everlasting love with God and with each other—which

---

18. Ephesians 5:32 (ESV).
19. Girolamo Zanchi, *The Spiritual Marriage between Christ and His Church and Every One of the Faithful*, xxxi, 22–28.

is the mystery we anxiously await. The Lord gives this promise to every man and woman who calls to him for mercy and a share of God's holy love: for a place in God's eternal family.

> *And I heard as it were the voice of a great multitude, and as the voice of many waters, and as the voice of mighty thunderings, saying,*
>
> > *Alleluia: for the Lord God omnipotent reigneth.*
> > *Let us be glad and rejoice, and give honour to him:*
> > *for the marriage of the Lamb is come, and his wife*
> > *hath made herself ready.*
> > *And to her was granted that she should be arrayed*
> > *in fine linen, clean and white:*
> > *for the fine linen is the righteousness of saints.*
>
> *And he saith unto me, Write, Blessed are they which are called unto the marriage supper of the Lamb. And he saith unto me, These are the true sayings of God.*
>
> > *And the Spirit and the bride say, Come.*
> > *And let him that heareth say, Come.*
> > *And let him that is athirst come.*
> > *And whosoever will,*
> > *let him take the water of life freely.*[20]

---

20. Revelation, 19:6–9 (KJV); Revelation 22:17 (KJV). I have slightly adjusted the formatting of the King James Version original for the sake of clarity.

POSTSCRIPT: TRADITION AND TODAY

It is not necessary for a good marksman always to hit the bulls-eye; one must also concede that he who comes close to it or hits the target is a good shot.[1]

I believe that I have followed biblical ethics in framing and writing this work, though several issues have been challenging to resolve, and I do not pretend to have ironed out every wrinkle in the discussion. Hopefully, other Christians can build on my arguments and approaches. I pray the Lord will send teachers and scholars who can chide my faults and correct my mistakes. For centuries, indeed millennia, there was an unbroken stream of teaching about sexual ethics and marital law among Christian teachers: a river of wisdom now dammed by modern immorality and infidelity. Still, the Holy Spirit yet speaks to us from the past, and in listening to the wisdom of the ages, I hope that I have at least hit the target—even if I have not scored a bull's-eye. If Martin Luther is correct in the above passage, this makes me a good shot. While my work remains incomplete

---

1. In this passage, Martin Luther observed how some atypical marriage problems "cannot be decided on the basis of a writing or book" and are increasing at a pace "faster than one could make laws or rules." For that reason, he believed the counsel of good, pious men should be sought since too much legislation to cover every nuance would lead to oppression, noting how: "Strict justice is the greatest injustice." Martin Luther, "On Marriage Matters (1530)," in *Luther's Works,* vol. 46, 287–288.

and certainly includes mistakes and errors flowing from my faults and sins (as well as discussions missing due to my ignorance and limitations), I pray my book is good enough to be helpful to God's people, if only a few of them.

To be genuinely comprehensive, this book would have required its author to be fluent in Greek, Hebrew, and Latin, and to be trained in theology, church history, legal history, and social history across all epochs of Middle Eastern and European history, from ancient Israel to modernity. Because there will never be a scholar so trained, and there is a pressing need for insight drawn from ages more faithful to biblical law than ours is proving to be, I will share my best effort, despite my conviction that I am inadequate to this task. I should note that this is not a pretended humility, but a genuine concern that I am operating in the realm of theologians, of which I am not one—for I am a sinful and limited amateur operating where only those with a sacred calling should work. My plea is that of necessity: that I have written this book because those who ought to have done so have remained silent or busy with tasks far less urgent. I will not cite any source establishing their failure beyond what I have seen with my eyes during the past fifty years. From my perspective, many Christian churches tolerate a level of immorality, infidelity, and immodesty (not to mention abortion and other grave sins) that demonstrates that many of our ordained leaders are failing us.

Despite my personal limitations, it seems significant to me that the Lord provided me with an excellent education, a tremendous personal library, and the leisure to revise my original book after decades of my own marriage and family life. God also led me to experience family life at its best and at its worst throughout my life, and gave me a mind to remember what I have observed and experienced. I have known delights and joys that I do not want to lose at death, and I have suffered sins and sorrows during which a Christian death might have come as a friend. Still, in all of these things, I have seen salvation in the wisdom, righteousness, and love of God. With that salvation in mind, I hope to share a historical perspective on Christian marriage and family life that has been overlooked, thereby helping theologians to accomplish the work they are called to do. I would be overjoyed to learn that some of them are correcting my errors, provided they do so in the name of the broad Christian tradition rather than to justify a narrow-minded, immodest, and faithless modernity.

It must be stated that many contemporary men and women who

might disagree with much of what I have written do not have a complaint merely with me, but with the traditional doctrines and consensus of nearly all Christianity and with the confession that our Lord is the one who brought such teachings to his churches and people. Such doubters must deny that the Spirit of Christ redeemed and inspired Clement of Alexandria, John of Chrysostom, Augustine of Hippo, Gratian, Peter Lombard, Martin Luther, John Calvin, John Wesley, and nearly everyone who professed the Christian faith before the last century. Such contemporary schismatics and dissenters (even if they are highly placed in evangelical or other denominations, seminaries, and editorial boards) should be required to support their arguments with an honest examination of both the Bible and centuries of biblical exegesis and common piety, rather than mishandling Scripture to cover their preferences and sins. If Adam and Eve were reproved for hiding their nakedness behind a fig leaf, how much more will modern men and women be judged for hiding infidelity and promiscuity behind the misuse of biblical authority?

As noted earlier, the tradition of the church is not infallible, unlike the written word of God. But it still seems far safer to bow before the consensus of Christians from a variety of cultures and epochs than to view marital and sexual mores only from a modern perspective, which is false to authority, fidelity, and purity. The modern age is one of promiscuity, divorce, and abortion, not exactly a template for how to order household and sexual ethics. Nevertheless, if believers carefully review how ancient, medieval, and early modern Christians understood key biblical passages cited in this book, they will more easily escape the shortsightedness of our faithless, barren, and perverse generation. Students will uncover questions and debates about marital and sexual ethics that are seldom mentioned in modern newspapers, university lectures, or marriage books. After all, journalists write for an hour, and professors lecture for a semester, but Christian doctrine reflects the nature of the eternal God. Tapping into the Christian tradition is a means of touching eternity itself, producing work whose value extends beyond a fleeting fad.

Consideration of the Christian tradition cuts both ways. Just as the church's opinion is valuable, so too is the church's silence. Where consensus has not been achieved regarding the interpretation of biblical texts, teachers should be wary of binding the consciences of their charges with their private understandings (a humility I pray is found in my work, although I confess to several musings in the footnotes and some expository writing that go beyond bare presentation of church texts and biblical passages). To that end, John Donne (cited previously for his sharp repudiation of birth control) preached about the need to respect not only ecclesiastical authority but also church silence, declaring: "Where the Church is silent, let me be silent too."[2]

Still, there is much about which the church has not been silent, and the long-established Christian consensus must be reviewed so that modern believers can appreciate the faith of previous generations. Early, medieval, and Reformation-era believers disagreed about many things of importance (even eternal significance), but they never disputed that marriage and family life were ordained to reflect the divine qualities of fidelity, purity, and charity. Eastern Orthodox, Roman Catholic, and Protestant Christians shared a framework regarding the definition and duties of godly marriage. The plain fact is, as an influential modern historian has noted, believers have spoken in chorus concerning the fundamental truths of marriage. Roland Bainton observed how Christian churches have taken "an undeviating and undivided stand about the fundamentals of marriage, however much they have diverged on points less crucial."[3] In like manner, contemporary Lutheran scholar John Maxfield challenged modern critics who have chided Martin Luther for being trapped in an Augustinian understanding of human sexuality. He wrote:

> *Such characterizations of Luther as preserving far too much of the medieval mentality tend to assume that modern sexual ethics have arrived at a maturity and freedom unknown not only in the patristic and medieval traditions but also in the Reformation and early modern Protestantism. It is debatable whether sexuality in the highly secularized and modern West should be the standard against which views on sexuality of earlier Christians are evaluated, especially since Luther's views were, in general, similar to the views of most Protestant Christians of his own time.*[4]

Some may fault me for quoting Francis of Assisi alongside Clement

---

2. Donne, *Sermons*, 6:249.
3. Bainton also observed that Christian tradition has held marriage to be "good" and "sex is not defiling." Roland Bainton, *What Christianity Says about Sex, Love, and Marriage* (New York: Association Press, 1957), 9.
4. John Maxfield, *Luther's Lectures on Genesis and the Formation of Evangelical Identity* (Kirksville, Missouri: Truman State University Press, 2008), 117.

of Alexandria, Cardinal Cajetan, and John Calvin. I am perfectly aware of the significant differences that men like these had among themselves and that I myself have with some of the men whom I have cited. For instance, it is doubtful that many Protestant Reformers sympathized with celibate friars such as Francis of Assisi or with Papal spokesmen such as Cardinal Cajetan. Yet my rationale is simple: until recently, all professing believers insisted that Christ's disciples are bound to crucify the flesh, forsake the pursuit of worldly goods, and humble themselves after the manner of Christ, even though there has been debate about how best to achieve these objectives. Even when Christians drew ecclesiastical, political, and military swords to fight with one another over matters like the reality of the Incarnation, the nature of the Triune God, justification by faith, ecclesiastical structure, or the authority of the Papacy, few disagreed about the purposes of the human household—and all similarly drew faith and practice from Scripture and church fathers. This is why I have cited early fathers, medieval believers, Protestant and Catholic Reformers, and modern churchmen. It is also why I have endeavored to draw my sources and ideas from various Christian traditions, including Roman Catholics, Lutherans, Calvinists, Puritans, Fundamentalists, Anglicans, Anabaptists, Methodists, Evangelicals, and the Orthodox. This broad Christian tradition stands as a prophetic witness against modern thinkers, even those ostensibly bearing the name Christian, who weave together sinful philosophies to rationalize and justify self-indulgence and shameful sin.[5]

Let me, then, reiterate my main points in closing. Most believers from Africa, America, Europe, and Asia have agreed about the essential purposes of human sexuality until fairly recently. Everyone would have agreed that marriage was divinely instituted, binding until death, tied to reproduction, governed by modesty and charity, and reflective of natural sexual differences. Protestants and Catholics may have disagreed over whether remarriage was permissible following divorce. Still, they would have stood arm in arm to refute the modern heresy that an individual

---

5. The modernist theologian Paul Tillich not only strayed from traditional Christian doctrine but also possessed loose sexual morals beyond the temptations common to most of us. At his death, his wife found his desk filled with pornography and letters documenting infidelity. See Alexander C. Irwin, *Eros Toward the World: Paul Tillich and the Theology of the Erotic* (Minneapolis: Fortress Press, 1991), 99–120. For a review of Western legal trends, see Mary Ann Glendon, *The Transformation of Family Law: State, Law, and Family in the United States and Western Europe* (Chicago: University of Chicago Press, 1989).

may marry and divorce as often as he or she pleases. The infidelity of a modern woman like Elizabeth Taylor, who possessed eight husbands (outdoing even the Samaritan woman at the well), would have been denounced in every great center of Christian thought: Aachen, Alexandria, Antioch, Boston, Cambridge, Canterbury, Constantinople, Geneva, Jerusalem, Oxford, Paris, Rome, Wittenberg, and Zurich. Until recently, Christian opinion kept immorality on the streets where it belonged. Moreover, pious thinkers of all denominations agreed that matrimony is ordained to help men progress in charity and faith, not to please the flesh. Everyone agreed that moral and temporal law is needed to discipline passion, lust, and infidelity.

This nearly universal consensus regarding the meaning of human marriage presently is being assaulted by a vast horde of sexual barbarians, and the ideals of chastity and charity are being raped and left desolate. It is unclear whether the problem is that the people of Western civilization have become more perverse and faithless or whether the amoral lawlessness of the modern state regarding sexual affairs has allowed intrinsic evil to become less restrained and more openly practiced.[6] In either case, it is clear enough what is to be done: individuals must live in purity and love, and households must govern themselves by the laws of God. Christian colleges and seminaries must study and teach codes of church law, while denominational hierarchies and individual congregations must work to uphold standards of sexual purity and marital fidelity through explicit teaching and appropriate spiritual punishments. In this way, holiness will become a quality preached and lived among Christians. What the learned sixth-century statesman, scholar, and monk Cassiodorus Senator said of a church father who preceded him should be noted by all orthodox and pious Christians who write about marriage:

Let us therefore take pains, and after the introductory books let us read the authority and its expositors assiduously, and let us follow with pious zeal the paths of knowledge discovered by the labor of the Fathers, and let us not aim with a greedy superfluity at exceedingly empty questions. Let us consider as divine beyond doubt that which is found to be said rationally in the most excellent commentators; if

---

6. Gertrude Himmelfarb discussed the moralization and demoralization of society in her comparison of nineteenth-century Great Britain and contemporary America. Gertrude Himmelfarb, *The De-Moralization of Society: From Victorian Virtues to Modern Values* (New York: Vintage Books, 1994).

> *anything happens to be found out of harmony and inconsistent with the rules of the Fathers, let us decide that it should be avoided.*[7]

Additionally, believing citizens and public servants must strive to return honesty, faithfulness, and modesty to community morals and law codes at all levels of government. Christian magistrates must formulate public policy to protect purity and fidelity, and (at the very least) government should require as much honesty in marital and sexual transactions as it does in economic ones. A man in the United States may sue a car dealer who fails to complete a promised car repair, but a virgin girl seduced under an unfulfilled promise of marriage has no recourse against her deceiver. Her loss and tears allow no legal redress. Additionally, no-fault divorce laws treat good and bad spouses the same, substituting legal expediency for real justice. The philanderer who betrays his wife is treated the same as the wife who suffered for his sin. Are cars and convenience more valuable than character and conscience? The perversion of our legal system is even more obscene than the daily flood of pornography that pollutes our land. It must be changed sooner rather than later.

Even more important than adhering to specific biblical commandments regarding marital and sexual ethics is upholding what this book began with: the biblical rule of faith. The Lord demands that Scripture be the rule of faith and life for believers, and humility requires us to review the judgments of previous generations since the Lord's Spirit is given to all of his people rather than to a few prophets, priests, and pastors of our generation. We are not allowed to compromise with modern immorality and unbelief, especially with a postmodern ethic in which every man or woman is allowed not simply to define and redefine

---

7. Cassiodorus Senator, *An Introduction to Divine and Human Readings*, trans. Leslie Webber Jones (New York: W.W. Norton and Company, 1946), 123–124. In addressing heresies regarding the Holy Trinity, Hilary of Poitiers observed how false teaching arises when men refuse the gospel faith, nothing: "The chief and lasting cause of irreligion [is that we refuse the gospel faith as we] publicly defend our impieties [with] newfangled chatter, deluding the ears of the simple with bombast and deceptive words, as we avoid believing about [what Christ] taught us to believe, as we surreptitiously unite under the specious name of peace, claim to reject novelties while rebelling... against God with new terms, and use the text of the scriptures to invent things that are not in the scriptures. Errant, impious spendthrifts, we all the while change things abiding, waste the gifts received, and venture things irreligious." Hilary of Poitiers, "Letter to the Emperor Constantius," in Hilary of Poitiers, *Conflicts of Conscience and Law in the Fourth-century Church: Against Valens and Uracius: the extant fragments, together with his Letters to the Emperor Constantius*, trans. Lionel R. Wickham (Liverpool: Liverpool University Press, 1997), 107.

marriage and gender as they prefer, but to establish the individual as a law unto himself (or herself). Such thinkers posit that marital and sexual matters are rooted not in revelation or nature but in the imagination, appetite, and preferences of the individual (or an always evolving social consensus).

In contrast, what must be remembered and systematically taught in Christian churches is that the Lord reveals the nature and purpose of marriage in Scripture and expects all people to accept his laws. Readers of this book have seen with their own eyes how often Scripture discusses marital and sexual morality; these are essential aspects of God's revelation to fallen mankind that must be taught and lived. From the first marriage presented in the book of Genesis through the commands of Moses, the judgments of the prophets, and the directives of the apostles, and especially in the words of the Lord Jesus Christ, God revealed his will regarding matters of marriage and sexual intimacy. The Lord also wrote his moral law into the laws of nature. Divine revelation in Scripture and common judgment found in nature make it evident that matters of marriage and sex are governed by fixed standards rather than mutable opinions and fads. To ignore such divine laws is to risk judgment.

The rebuilding of the fabric of love and purity will not be a one-night stand or the work of a single election; this is work for an entire generation. House by house, the Christian family must be reconstructed. Change will not occur simply through government programs, church activism, or legal reform, as necessary as each of these may be.[8] Such reforms would be fair and right, and glorify the wisdom and law of the Lord. Still, lasting reform will come when the majority of this perverse generation forsakes their evil ways and humbles itself in the sight of God. Every household must make the Lord God its center, forsaking the idols and values that tempt its inhabitants to false ideals and ill-gotten pleasures. If this is done, the Lord will bless pious families with a rich crop of marital fidelity, sexual chastity, and humble service by which they and their children will be blessed—even for many generations.

---

8. During the 1960s, I saw one of my grandfathers divorced by my grandmother due to his philandering, with my maritally faithful grandmother receiving all household and family business property, and alimony payments as well. Grandma lived her life in modest comfort while my grandfather (after being jailed for refusing to pay alimony) rebuilt his wealth with a (young) second wife. Grandpa wronged his first wife, but the state of Illinois did not aggravate his wrong through unfair public laws that treated the guilty and the innocent without distinction.

As petitioners, let us call upon the Lord, pleading for him to cleanse us of our many sins so that he might reveal himself to our neighbors and countrymen through us. Let us take our place as the legitimate children and adopted heirs of God's house, forsaking everything that entangles us with the father of illegitimacy and lies. Let us also show the world that real love comes from the tender love of God, not from the unfeeling touch of strangers. Let us fight to save our families and glorify our God. Let us rebuke sin and punish abandonment and abuse. As Nehemiah declared when he led the Jews to rebuild the city of Jerusalem following the Babylonian exile of the Jews, so we must arm ourselves for spiritual conflict as fierce as any persecution and as costly as any war. We must bring the received revelation, wisdom, and love of God to the modern world so that our generation may know the Lord's blessing and peace.

So in the lowest parts of the space behind the wall, in open places, I stationed the people by their clans, with their swords, their spears, and their bows. And I looked and arose and said to the nobles and to the officials and to the rest of the people, "Do not be afraid of them. Remember the LORD, who is great and awesome, and fight for your brothers, your sons, your daughters, your wives, and your homes." [9]

---

9. Nehemiah 4:13–14 (ESV).

APPENDICES

APPENDIX 1: CHARLES HODGE AND SLAVE MARRIAGES

WHATEVER PRIVATE ARRANGEMENTS were made on slave estates in the United States before the Civil War, slaves generally could not marry in any manner recognized by public law, at least not with the rights that marriage brought to every other couple. Prominent Presbyterian theologian Charles Hodge (born in 1797; died in 1878) practiced his theology amidst the American debate over slavery, and while Hodge was no radical abolitionist (coming slowly to emancipation), he did attempt to apply biblical doctrine to marital law: an effort that cut at the deepest and most pernicious roots of American slavery when he set the sanctity of marriage above laws of race.[1]

In his influential *Systematic Theology,* published shortly after the Civil War, Hodge tells the story of a man who married a young woman only to discover that she possessed African blood (despite her white appearance) and consequently was deemed a slave. Upon this discovery, her husband purchased his wife, emancipated her, then divorced her and remarried another woman. Hodge objected that the Presbyterian Church had accepted this divorce as morally valid, writing how "the law of God

---

1. For a discussion of Charles Hodges' efforts to reconcile biblical inerrancy, church unity, abolitionist ideals, and the American republic, see Richard Reifsnyder, "Charles Hodge: A Conservative Theologian Finds His Way to Emancipation" (National Archives of the PC(USA): Presbyterian Historical Society, 17 April 2018), https://www.history.pcusa.org/blog/2018/04/charles-hodge-conservative-theologian-finds-his-way-emancipation.

was thus regarded as a mere nullity."[2] Hodge found no rightful, biblical impediment to a mixed marriage (of race or enslavement alike) and admonished Presbyterian authorities for having ignored the teachings of Jesus regarding the prohibition of divorce. Moreover, Hodge published his protest during a period when interracial marriages were being debated and outlawed following the Civil War. For a man slow to support slave emancipation, this seems a surprisingly radical perspective, though I suspect that both positions are rooted in Hodge's acceptance of the book of Deuteronomy as God's inerrant word (a book that severely curtailed the practice of slavery and legitimized marriage between free men and enslaved women but did not outright abolish all slavery).

Charles Hodge similarly condemned Prussian military authorities for prohibiting enlisted soldiers from marrying without an officer's permission. In observing that civil legislatures "can no more annul the laws of God than the laws of nature," Hodge essentially placed Christian marriage above the laws of the state, thereby challenging military customs that had existed for centuries in some locations. As a side note, what Hodge challenged was the Prussian militarism that (along with broader German nationalism) would bring war and suffering, even slavery, to Europe for many decades. While some American military leaders, such as Civil War General Sheridan, admired Prussian military efficiency, Charles Hodge upheld Scripture against a militarist nationalism that would challenge Western democracies for several generations, culminating in the rise of Hitler, the Second World War, and the Holocaust. Hodge stood for a biblical ethic of marriage even when his understanding clashed with the preferences of temporal authorities.

This is not to declare Hodge a leading abolitionist regarding slavery, for he was not. It is only to suggest that as God's word is obeyed, it will prove to be curative even in a fatally flawed institution like American chattel slavery.[3] If the Lord's law is obeyed, it will overcome evil. Not

---

2. Charles Hodge, *Systematic Theology*, vol. 3 (Grand Rapids, Michigan: William B. Eerdmans Publishing Company, 1981), 379.
3. Had Moses been obeyed by American slaveholders, as he should have been by a Christian people, the virulent racism of American slavery would have been softened, if not ended, in a generation or two. Moses freed slaves who were physically injured (even for the damaging of a tooth), gave enslaved women the rights of wives if seduced (with children inheriting the property of their father), and freed enslaved women without cost if divorced. He also limited slavery to seven years for fellow believers. We must never confuse the servanthood found in the Old Testament with the brutality of much slavery found in antebellum America.

only was the blatant racism and suspension of the teaching of Jesus regarding divorce and remarriage immoral and unbiblical, but the whole tenor of Moses and church tradition castigated men who abused enslaved women by exploiting them outside marriage. There was also the matter of hypocrisy in slave owners separating slave families in a manner that slave owners would have drawn weapons to resist if attempted against their own households. Hodge took a cautious approach to the abolition of American slavery, but nevertheless offered biblical protections to those caught in such a terrible institution. This seems the very intent of Moses: not to bless the evil of slavery but to alleviate the sufferings, sorrows, and indignities of an institution never designed by God for any person or people.[4]

---

4. Before contemporary men and women, myself included, try to wipe too much dust and dirt from the eyes of antebellum Americans (some of whom truly did evil in their practice of slavery), we need to understand how we ourselves support slavery with purchases of Chinese-made products and turn a blind eye to the slavery of sex trafficking. We also must understand that our toleration of legalized abortion is worse than many forms of slavery.

APPENDIX 2: THE LEGITIMACY OF ILLEGITIMACY?

In his book *The Sins of the Fathers: The Law and Theology of Illegitimacy Reconsidered,* John Witte Jr. summarizes what he calls the doctrine and law of illegitimacy, providing a succinct historical overview of the topic. While I do not wish to review Witte's book as a whole, I do think he raises an important point: namely, that the traditional concept of illegitimate birth has become problematic in modern Western societies plagued with extremely high rates of extramarital births.[1] Witte employs modern concepts of individual rights to critique former laws and customs, generally unfavorably and with the sharp eye of a lawyer scrutinizing what he considers unnatural, oppressive, or ungrounded law. That noted, we must consider several salient facts that Witte's analysis does not highlight. While I will not challenge Witte point by point (since I am unqualified to do so), I will raise several conceptual matters, pertinent facts, and modern realities that Witte and others must explain before disparaging past generations and traditions.

What troubles Witte is the legal and social practice of distinguishing between illegitimate and legitimate children. Considered superficially, the desire to establish a holy people seems alien to modern democratic values, which focus on individual rights and decision-making. Still, taking a

---

1. John Witte, Jr., *The Sins of the Fathers: The Law and Theology of Illegitimacy Reconsidered* (Cambridge: Cambridge University Press, 2009).

deeper look suggests that modern democracies similarly draw lines between those born lawfully and those born unlawfully. To this day, Western societies distinguish between the rights of citizens and non-citizens: between those born to lawful citizen parents and those not born of a legally legitimate bloodline. What else is this but to draw a line between those of lawful birth and those not of such birth? Moreover, European countries grant citizenship to the children of emigrants who have long departed, while frequently denying citizenship to immigrants living among them (in countries that do not consider every inhabitant a citizen for having been born within their borders). The United States is more generous with naturalized citizenship than most, but it requires a citizenship education and a loyalty oath for those not born into a family with a history of American citizenship or born on American soil. To serve on a jury, vote in an election, or be elected to office requires citizenship by birth or naturalization (i.e., adoption), and those lacking such citizenship are not granted membership in the American assembly, if we can use the verbiage of ancient Israel.

Every society, even the most modern and egalitarian, has membership rules that reflect its structure and values and categorize who has citizenship rights and who does not. Europeans value blood lineage (and limited naturalized citizenship), while Americans also allow for soil birth into citizenship (with the European model being more common worldwide).[2] God's purpose for ancient Israel was to build a holy people to reveal his law to pagans and immoral Gentiles: to use rules of citizenship to establish a sacred community—repudiating and rejecting the sexual immorality, false gods, and human sacrifices of infidels. Because Israel was called to be the land where the holy God of Abraham lived among mankind, a call to holiness was not xenophobia intended to keep foreigners at a distance, but a God-mandated effort to build a holy commonwealth into which neighboring and distant Gentiles could become naturalized citizens once they turned to the living God of Israel and his righteous ways.

This call to holiness required separation from outside pagan practices (as well as internal evils). Just as the New Testament excommunicates and bans heretics and apostates, so did Israel. And just as the children of excommunicated heretics and apostates suffer for the sins of their fathers and mothers, so, too, children of criminals and sinners suffered in ancient

---

2. Europeans, except for the United Kingdom and Ireland, follow the *jus sanguines* (law of blood), while the United States practices the *jus soli* (law of soil).

Israel. We can say that their citizenship rights were restricted, though no more so than those of many non-naturalized immigrants living in modern European countries. Both represent a type of second-tier resident: a status codified into law.[3]

Still, although I am discussing birthright and legitimacy in terms of legal customs and social practices, ultimately, Christians must ground the matter in theology, as with every marital practice. Believers must not begin with mortal bloodlines (whether to preserve a noble lineage or a middle-class household), but rather must discuss the eternal legitimacy of perfect love and the holiness of the Triune God—remembering that the Father eternally begets the Son in holiness and love. Is this not what human legitimacy is called to represent: a father conceiving his child in the beauty of lifelong marriage rather than through the ugliness of momentary lust? A good and honorable beginning for a human life? Blessings for what reflects God's image and curses for what does not?

To repeat my point: illegitimacy is simply the obverse of legitimacy—of what is holy, charitable, and righteous. If the notion of legitimacy is legitimate, so is the concept of illegitimacy (which represents the failure of sinful parents to honor God by giving their children a life conceived in faith, hope, and love). Illegitimacy is the sad reality of abandonment, neglect, and failure, and no rebranding or renaming will make its moral or social reality any different. God designed men and women to marry, establish a home, and then give birth to wanted and beloved children, and children born into a crisis pregnancy lack this rightful beginning, even if repentance and maturity eventually lead to an equally loving home. Even when ill-conceived children are adopted into good families, they often feel abandoned by the biological parents they never knew. Moreover, no single mother can change the reality that her children were raised fatherless, no matter how much she tries to replace him. God can and does redeem sinful and forlorn situations (with the good news being that he promises to do so for all who turn to him), but such circumstances remain evils to be redeemed rather than ideals to be accepted.

The concept of legitimate and illegitimate children should lead us back to who God is and who he calls us to be, even if divine attributes such as mercy, charity, and grace equally apply when considering children

---

3. The reduced rights of the illegitimate in the holy commonwealth of Israel established something of a moral caste system, in which the virtuous maintained government for themselves (as in colonial New England). Still, the problem of divergent groups of people with different rights living in a single commonwealth is the same as in the modern world.

made in unholy circumstances. We may receive God's mercy from the punishments of the law, but we must not suspend God's law altogether as moral antinomians and religious skeptics. Believers must not deny the idea of legitimate birth (of God's ideal plan for families) from fear of persecuting those born into illegitimacy. Christians must not cast out the legitimacy of all children born of a married father and mother for the sake of the dirty bathwater in which some of their more unfortunate peers have been baptized at birth. There are far better ways to fix the problem of mistreating the illicitly born than altogether denying the concepts of legitimate and illegitimate birth.

As a final note, modern men and women often find unfairness and injustice in the fact that one person's life is to a great extent determined by the sins of a parent, grandparent, or even great-grandparent. While I sympathize with their complaint, this is the dilemma of human life in general, and we cannot wish it away except by giving up what is most treasured in our lives: parenthood, sexual reproduction, heritage, and human significance. The fact that the sin of my grandfather impacted his children and (through them) me is no more morally troubling than the reality that a man left an innocent family desolate for decades after raping and murdering their young sister, or that a drunk driver left an aging woman to linger alone for many years after killing her husband. Whether we like it or not, the sin of one person affects many people beyond his or her deliberate intention, for each of us resembles Adam and Eve in our ability to choose either good or evil, for ourselves, our descendants, and everyone around us.

APPENDIX 3: THE TESTIMONY OF A MEDIEVAL WOMAN

WHILE I CITE medieval law regarding women's rights, this does not mean such laws were universally applied or fully implemented. They were not, and the Middle Ages was a mixed bag regarding the rights of women, which often depended on local circumstances, church leaders, and political authorities. Medieval Europe also encompassed a diverse range of cultures, from the hard-nosed warriors of the Frankish kingdom and the chivalric knights of the High Middle Ages to the wealthy and often educated guildsmen of late medieval Italy and various orders of clergy officially devoted to celibacy. Christian de Pizan, who lived in Italy and France during the fifteenth century, observed that many wives suffered at the hands of their husbands, while she was fortunate to have married a good man. She wrote:

> *How many women are there [who] because of their husbands' harshness spend their weary lives in the bond of marriage in greater suffering than if they were slaves among the Saracens? How many harsh beatings—without cause and without reason—how many injuries, how many cruelties, insults, humiliations and outrages have so many upright women suffered, none of whom cried out for help? And consider all the women who die of hunger and grief with a home full of children, while their husbands carouse dissolutely or go on binges in every tavern all over town, and still*

the poor women are beaten by their husbands when they return, and that is their supper.

Although there are bad husbands, there are also very good ones, truly valiant and wise, and the women who meet them were born in a lucky hour... You know this perfectly well from your own experience, for you had such a good husband that if given a choice, you could not have asked for better, whom no other man in your judgment could surpass in kindness, peacefulness, loyalty, and true love.[1]

I added this explanation to prevent any misunderstanding from the passage I cited. All human generations are sinful, and all mankind will remain sinful for as long as we remain subject to sin and death. While I indeed find fault with the immorality of modernity, mankind fell into wickedness and violence long before the sexual revolution of the 1960s or the birth of modern culture a century ago. Before our era, Western society possessed numerous strengths and virtues, but it also included terrible flaws, as does every culture and generation in a fallen world. Our task is neither to condemn the past cynically nor to romanticize previous generations foolishly. Instead, we are to uphold the Lord's law, which judges the sin of all ages and brings divine blessing to every culture that follows Jesus Christ.

---

1. Pizan, *The Book of the City of Ladies*, 119.

APPENDIX 4: DOROTHY SAYERS, VOCATION, AND MOTHERHOOD

CARE MUST BE EXERCISED in discussing the balance of women's lives in the public and private spheres; extremes must be avoided. On the one hand, we dare not deny that men and women share many common pursuits. To that end, the great thinker and writer Dorothy Sayers (in her essay *"Are Women Human?"*) *makes a convincing case for men's and women's shared vocational and intellectual life, noting that some women possess what were traditionally* called male interests and aptitudes rather than typically female ones. On the other hand, because men and women differ in body and temperament (and in human reproduction), there are as many differences as similarities that require deeper exploration and explanation. And, I would note, as provocative and insightful as Ms. Sayers's essay is, it lacks discussion of pregnancy and motherhood, which seem to be the core discussion in the relationship between the sexes.

I cannot speak to her other writings, but in *Are Women Human?* Dorothy Sayers is so focused on the question of the vocational equality of men and women (and the right of women like herself to pursue careers in the arts and letters) that she fails to provide a nuanced counterpoint regarding the distinctive female temperament required for motherhood, as well as the nature of the female body and specialization of labor in the household. Ms. Sayers is so devoted to the vocational rights of women (that is, the right to pursue a literary career of her choosing) that she neglects, even dismisses, a long tradition of Christian thinking regarding the requirements for successfully making, raising, and loving a human child—which is a far more important task than the making, editing, and publishing of a book. And while I admit that my own writings are a child's scribblings compared to Ms. Sayer's creativity, productivity, and insight, I believe that no book that either Ms. Sayers or I have written, or ever will write, possesses a fraction of the value that each of my four children has before God and man. I would not trade any of my children (even on my worst day and the worst day of the child) to become as prolific as Dorothy Sayers, or even William Shakespeare, for the simple reason that I would not trade a human being destined to live in eternal joy for a mortal reputation that endures a few centuries—and a mere millennium for the greatest poets and playwrights. It is bad math. Even one small child of any race, nationality, or class is worth more than all the books and libraries in the world.

What is especially troubling about the vocational focus of Ms. Sayers (of her advocacy of the notion that women have the right to choose any vocation if they are so interested and skilled) is how she was unable to effectively balance career aspirations and parenting in her own life after having conceived a child during a short affair with a married man. Ms. Sayers gave birth to a son whom a foster mother initially raised before being adopted by Ms. Sayers, without subsequently notifying the boy of their biological relationship as mother and child. Ms. Sayers seems to have lived her entire life hiding from her child the fact of her biological parenthood—the reality that she was far more than his adoptive mother. Dorothy Sawyers achieved her vocational aspirations with a prodigious literary and theological corpus, but at the expense of a truly respectable family life (rather than a pretense) and honest motherhood. She made her son bear the burden of his mother's sin, possibly leaving the boy to wonder why his biological mother had abandoned him when she, in fact, had not done so. His sorrows and stresses must have been significant.[1]

In my opinion, a common laundress raising her illegitimate child in humble confession of sin, yet openly sharing the depth of maternal affection, lived a better life than Ms. Sayers, where it matters most: in her relationship to God and other people rather than in her vocation or career. The laundress accepted the limits placed on her life by her sin and never

---

1. Dorothy L. Sayers, *Are Women Human?* (Grand Rapids, Michigan: William B. Eerdmans Publishing Company, 1971); Colin Duriez, *Dorothy Sayers, A Biography: Death, Dante, and Lord Peter Wimsey* (Oxford: Lion Hudson Limited, 2021), 96–99.

UNLESS THE LORD BUILDS THE HOUSE

left her child feeling abandoned by his mother. Nor did the laundress leave her son feeling like the victim of an unsolved crime mystery in his own home, confused as to why his mother never claimed him as her own flesh and blood. The laundress who repented of her initial sin thereafter provided a life of toil, honesty, humility, and love to her child—which is as much as any child can expect from a parent, no matter how the child was conceived. The story of the laundress was more sacrificial in real life (and therefore a better story than anything Ms. Sayers ever imagined in a book), even though the laundress's tale must wait for eternity to be told.[2]

In *Are Women Human?* Ms. Sayers complains, with more than a hint of scorn, about how the ancient duties of women were taken away in the modern world (namely, the business enterprises and estate management of noble and bourgeois women), with women expected to cram children into small flats—a seemingly unfair way of life. While this difficult reality may have been actual for the urban poor, I would note there were plenty of houses in rural and urban England that were far larger than small flats, and women birthing many children to fill them during the years when Ms. Sayers lived. Women of the 1920s and 1930s frequently raised children in the same types of houses, if not the very same house, that their grandmothers once tended during the Victorian era.

Moreover, I wonder if that small flat so scorned by Ms. Sayers (when considered with modern lighting, plumbing, and social welfare) might have appeared an object of envy to an Elizabethan housewife raising her brood of children in the ramshackle cottage of a remote village or amidst the feces- and flea-filled streets of a premodern city. I suspect that the mother in that modern flat may have lived a far easier life than many of her foremothers and lost fewer children to disease along the way. It seems that Ms. Sayers set up a straw man (or should I say straw woman?) to portray social circumstances in her day as having antiquated customs, thereby emancipating modern women like herself from the difficulties of common motherhood to pursue literary careers. From a more traditional perspective, raising a family in humble faith and quiet service is always pleasing to the Lord, whether or not the world values it.

People sin, and God forgives—of that there is no doubt. The fact that Ms. Sayers conceived a child during an affair (after breaking up with a

---

2. The Internet indicates that one of the great pop singers of the 1950s and 1960s struggled after learning (when grown) how his mother and sister were really his grandmother and mother.

man who forswore children) is far less troubling to me than the polygamous and extramarital affairs of several biblical patriarchs. Still, we must incorporate the breadth of our experiences into our thinking, and *Are Women Human?* proves inadequate at this point, not only failing to draw lessons but even hiding the discussion as completely as the author hid her own motherhood. For Ms. Sayers to claim a special place for herself in the world is one matter, since it is easy to see she was gifted above nearly everyone else. Perhaps she truly deserved consideration as a God-inspired prophet like Deborah or the prophesying daughters of Philip the Evangelist?[3] I would not object to that proposition in principle, for Ms. Sayers surely was gifted by God. But for Ms. Sayers to press society to accommodate the vocational interests of women without discussing how this should be balanced with parental duties is less than forthright. At the very least, Ms. Sayers should have acknowledged that children are human, just as women are, and that society has as much interest in accommodating their needs as those of their more literary and philosophical parents, men and women alike.

---

3. Judges 4:4; Acts 21:9.

APPENDIX 5: A BED OF ONE'S OWN?

PRIVACY during marital intimacy was one of the more perplexing matters of ethics and etiquette in the world before our own. Most modern men and women live in homes with private bedrooms, which means that marital intimacy is generally enjoyed in seclusion, even in small cottages and apartments that house several children. Consequently, marital privacy is usually taken for granted: rarely discussed, yet always expected. It is unclear whether this was equally true in ancient, medieval, and early modern worlds, raising the question of how private marital intimacy was expected. What were the ethics and etiquette for hiding sexual intimacy from the eyes of one's children? How this is addressed also has implications for the practice of modesty in our era.

What stands out to me in the historical literature is not anything I have read, but what is not commonly observed. I have not encountered many sermons preached against unseemly, immodest behavior before one's children. Perhaps mention is occasionally made in discussions of the parable found in the Gospel of Luke that poor people sometimes sleep in bed with their younger children.[1] However, few clergymen have taken the opportunity to preach a broader message about the need for parental privacy. While evidence is limited, there are references to children sleeping with their parents and the use of shared beds in inns and

---

1. Luke 11:7.

family homes alike. Still, even these references give few hints of sexual exhibitionism or gross immorality, and available texts often suggest a standard of moral judgment against such exposure, at least by church officials and clergymen. Texts imply a strict modesty regarding marital privacy.

One recent historian cites two Roman Catholic bishops who used the confessional to oppose improper bedroom etiquette. One of the bishops complained about widespread moral corruption that occurred when parents permitted children to share their beds after the latter had attained the use of reason. A second bishop instructed his clergy to teach the laity to segregate by sex at bedtime after the age of seven. This testimony, along with details from rape trials, suggests at least some use of communal beds among rogue and impoverished underclasses: beds in which a naked woman might sleep with her husband alongside other men, albeit without reported sexual activity (per the testimony of witnesses). When questioned, one witness testified that communal beds used innocently in his youth could no longer be used since the world had degenerated during his lifetime—which suggests to me how the man had become better aware of wrongdoing to which he was previously blind. I also wonder if those who mentioned communal beds may have preferred to deny the presence of immodest sexual activity that would have led not simply to shame but also to penitential requirements from priests and bishops receiving their confession.[2]

The most direct evidence I found regarding the ethics of marital intimacy and bedroom privacy is found in the ancient writings of the pagan writer Plutarch and the church father Clement of Alexandria. Plutarch's essays were widely published in early modern Europe, and observed that it was "indecent for people to caress and kiss and embrace each other in the presence of others." Plutarch also discussed whether a man should approach his wife during the daytime or after dark, with the latter act being perceived as indecent and inappropriate. Because Plutarch's treatises were read only by the educated and literate, the impact of his prescriptive writing cannot be readily ascertained. However, the widespread publication of his writings suggests a shared sensibility with early

---

2. Jean-Louis Flandrin, *Families in Former Times*, 98–101. We should note that sleeping children might not notice or identify sexual activity around them. Drunken spouses might also sleep through intimacy occurring on a large bed of straw. Moreover, it is possible that those interviewed by church officials would have had good cause to lie about legally culpable acts of adultery, perhaps feigning an innocence that did not exist.

modern Christian writers, and Plutarch's treatises possibly served as an indirect and occasional vehicle for discussing the etiquette associated with such matters.[3] As for Clement of Alexandria, he wrote that the married should not "celebrate the mystic rites of nature during the day," but only in the evening. Clement also noted that intimacy should not be enjoyed after church services or upon returning home from the market—all of which suggest a regard for privacy.[4]

Social history suggests that many families lived in small, crowded homes in the premodern past, and modern beds did not become widespread throughout society until the sixteenth century. We have all seen intact (or replicated) buildings from the ancient, medieval, and early modern worlds, as well as beds (or paintings thereof) from the same periods. This evidence suggests that wealthy individuals had private rooms for married couples (just as today), with beds in the medieval and early modern periods often enclosed by drapes to enhance warmth, privacy, and protection from vermin. At the same time, there were one-room, thatched cottages for poor peasants and crowded city apartments for common laborers: housing in which it is hard to imagine privacy being attained in any manner at all, at least when older children slept nearby (especially when the only bed in the house was a straw bed on which the sexes and ages were mingled). While beds with posts and drapes became far more common by the sixteenth and seventeenth centuries (being inventoried in wills and probate records), what strikes me as interesting is how many early prints and paintings of beds suggest use by couples rather than entire families. Whether this reflects an ideal or actual reality is uncertain, but it suggests, in the very least, that artists did not desire to suggest or idealize immodest and indecent circumstances.[5]

Despite cramped quarters and a lack of private beds for many couples

---

3. Plutarch was not preaching privacy, but using the unquestioned reality of such marital privacy to declare that if couples hide intimacy from the eyes of others, they certainly should hide fault-finding and quarrels even more. Plutarch, "On Marriage Counsel," in Moses Hadas, trans., *On Love, the Family, and the Good Life: Selected Essays by Plutarch* (New York: Mentor Books, 1957), 82; Plutarch, "Book IX, Question VI: Which is the Fittest Time for a Man to Know His Wife?" in *Symposiacs*, accessed January 6, 2025, https://catholiclibrary.org/library/view?docId=/Antiquities-EN/Antiquities.plutarch-symposiacs.html&chunk.id=00000005.
4. Clement of Alexandria, *Christ the Educator*, 174.
5. Norman Pounds, *Hearth and Home: A History of Material Culture* (Bloomington, Indiana: Indiana University Press, 1989), 184–218 (Chapter 6: The Privacy of the Home). A. Roger Ekirch, *At Day's Close: Night in Times Past* (New York: W.W. Norton and Company, 2005), 191–197; Annik Pardailhé-Galabrun, *The Birth of Intimacy: Privacy and*

before the sixteenth century, few sermons, writings, paintings, prints, or church codes addressed the etiquette of parental intimacy in front of their children, suggesting at least five possible explanations. First, children may have been sent from their parents' room as required, perhaps to sleep near the hearth or in an attic (as with some log cabins on the American frontier). Second, parents possibly arranged for older children to stay with relatives and neighbors on occasion or met furtively when they could break free from their children for a short time. Third, people may have been less concerned with modesty than their descendants. This is not to say that premodern peoples had a hippie-like lack of modesty or sexual perversity, but that they were earthy men and women who lived close to the couplings of animals on their farms and estates and possessed an openness that modern city dwellers lack. Fourth, it is possible that some couples restricted intimacy to those times of the year when children spent less time outside the family home.[6] Fifth, perhaps houses were primarily used for sleeping, and most time was spent in public and other communal spaces, as some cultures still do today, permitting a measure of privacy during the day. Sixth, perhaps sons and daughters, in some instances, moved from the family home as they passed into puberty (and thereby better understood the nature of parental intimacy).[7] The fact that many people reportedly slept naked in the past also adds a layer of moral complexity to the matter (regarding parental modesty before children).[8] There is also the question of having sexual relations in sacred places, which I will not address in this book. It has long been believed that it is sacrilege to defile a church or other holy place with sexual intimacy.[9]

Domestic Life in Early Modern Paris (Philadelphia: University of Pennsylvania Press, 1980), 73–83.

6. Noted historian Fernand Braudel challenged Lewis Mumford on this latter point, noting that birth records dispute Mumford's claims that intimacy became a year-round event only in the eighteenth century. Fernand Braudel, *Civilization and Capitalism, 15th–18th Century, vol. 1: The Structures of Everyday Life: The Limits of the Possible*, trans. Sian Reynolds (Berkeley, California: University of California Press, 1992), 308.

7. One historian notes that New England Puritans often raised their children in the homes of other people, even apart from customary apprenticeship arrangements. See Edmund S. Morgan, *The Puritan Family*, 76,

8. One historian wrote: "In the Middle Ages, it was customary for people, including lords and ladies, to sleep naked." Jager, *The Last Duel*, 73.

9. Peter Abelard wrote of his affair with Heloise: "After our marriage, when you were living in the cloister with the nuns at Argenteuil and I came one day to visit you privately, you know what my uncontrollable desire did with you there, actually in a corner of the refectory, since we had nowhere else to go. I repeat, you know how shameless we behaved on

Whether the truth is found in one (or more) of these, I cannot say—
only that modern bedrooms and beds allow a more easily acquired
privacy than many couples in the past possessed, even though people in
the past were raised with an expectation of moral and religious discipline
that modern men and women can scarcely imagine. Maybe it is in that
very discipline that our answer can be found, just as the few hints I have
seen are drawn from Roman Catholic confessional instructions. I suspect
that the etiquette of modesty remains hidden in the records of church
courts, diaries, and biblical commentaries and may be uncovered by a
scholar with a keen eye and probing questions. Indeed, some of the truth
may already be available through existing scholarly studies that I have not
discovered.

---

that occasion in so hallowed a place, dedicated to the most holy Virgin. Even if our other
shameful behavior was ended, this alone would deserve far heavier punishment." Peter
Abelard, *Letters of Abelard and Heloise,* 146.

APPENDIX 6: THE HOLY DESIRE OF CLEMENT OF ALEXANDRIA

Our general argument concerning marriage, food, and other matters, may proceed to show that we should do nothing from desire.[1]

WHILE I DO NOT PRETEND to be a trained philosopher, the drafting of this second edition has exposed me to many ancient, medieval, and early modern texts that struggle with the notion of desire in the Christian life. For one obvious (and easy-to-access) instance, readers might review Clement of Alexandria's *On Marriage* (*Miscellanies, Book III*), in which a very astute and orthodox Christian teacher struggled with the place of desire in the Christian life, as cited above. In any case, this matter warrants a brief review, so I would like to make an attempt.

The desire for food and sexual intimacy is so rooted in human life that we cannot imagine life without them. In refuting an ancient heresy so opposed to sensuality that heretical teachers attacked marriage as inherently corrupt, Clement of Alexandria separated licit physical desire from illicit sensual desire as a means of upholding marriage as a lawful calling. Unlike Tatian and the heretical Encratites, who despised marriage as intrinsically corrupt and unspiritual, Clement honored marriage and

---

1. Clement of Alexandria, "On Marriage," in Oulton and Chadwick, *Alexandrian Christianity*, 67.

the marriage bed itself as a lawful calling before the Lord (who created both marriage and reproduction). In particular, Clement noted that lawful sexual intimacy exists for the undeniably charitable purpose of making new human beings rather than fulfilling base lust. In this, Clement sanctified the act of sexual intimacy by noting its ultimate other-centered purpose. This was both an astute observation and a compelling argument, and in making it, Clement took an uncompromising stand against the ascetic spirit of heresy and rejection of physicality that frequently troubled the early church (see Clement's work for examples). I will throw no sharp stones at one of the great fathers of our faith: a church father who upheld the sanctity of natural fatherhood (and motherhood).

However, I would make two observations to qualify Clement of Alexandria's wording (which has proved influential for centuries). First, reading the bare text without the aforementioned Encratite heresy in mind poses problems, since Clement was focusing on key points rather than presenting an encyclopedic and balanced account of biblical revelation. As with a physical fight, a defender may need to become off-balance to land a decisive blow against his opponent, at least for a moment. It is possible that the main points made by Clement were telling blows against Tatian and the Encratite heresy, but represent a decisive point of attack rather than the nuanced truth of Scripture. Second, and far more critical, is the fact that the desire for children as the rightful objective of sexual passion does not solve the problem of desire. Both men and women can desire (even lust for) children for uncharitable reasons. As just one instance, Henry VIII's insatiable and ungodly lust for a royal heir led him to seek a son by divorcing or executing several of his wives (on false charges). In refusing to submit to the will of his heavenly father regarding his dynastic desires, Henry VIII sinned as much as any man who ever desired the bed of his wife without a prayer for offspring.[2]

Regarding the lawful desire for a child, do we not get caught up in the lawful enjoyment of parenthood as much as we become tangled in the sensuality of sexual desire? What I mean is that the natural desire to become a parent and to enjoy being a parent can be just as distracting

2. Henry VIII of England (1491–1547) fathered multiple daughters, but sired only one son (whose mother died from complications of childbirth). Previously, Henry had annulled one long-lasting marriage, executed one wife for false charges of adultery, annulled a marriage when the bride proved to be a poor match and plain of appearance, and executed another wife for actual adultery.

from piety as the desire for sexual intimacy. After all, most couples spend far more time pleasing children than enjoying sexual intimacy. The fact that sexual intimacy seems more troubling to many suggests that it is sensuality that they consider the real temptation, more than other natural desires, suggesting that they may be tainted with the asceticism found in ancient heresies. However, God created sensuality to make children, and it is not possible for us to separate sensuality and lawful desire in the sanitary manner that Clement attempted, for he left his readers with an understanding that licit sexual passion is that desire which intentionally seeks offspring. But how can any man purge sensual desire from his embrace of a wife? How can any man even want to? Is a man supposed to be thinking about making a child while embracing his wife? The near impossibility of differentiating moral objectives and sensual desire during sexual passion is at the root of our moral limitations. Speaking for myself, even when I desired a child with my wife at the initiation of a specific instance of sexual intimacy, the making of a child seldom remained my primary desire. Perhaps it never was.[3]

Not only is sexual passion often beyond deliberation and rational decision, but human beings are also morally corrupted, such that human desires are inescapably tainted with selfishness. This taint is a particular problem with sexual intimacy because, of all things human, the act of physical love was intended not only to (sometimes) bring children, but also to be a union of flesh and spirit that reflects Christ's divine love for his church: an objective that sexual intimacy most emphatically does not consistently accomplish in sinful, mortal life.[4] At our best, and for mere moments of our lives, we actually reflect the radiance of Christ's passion for his people. More often, we reflect selfish and sordid desires that are far from divine. Along with the Protestant Reformers, I confess that we are more than our concupiscence. Yet, with decades of marriage behind me, I also confess that mankind's sexual instinct is as fatally flawed as every other element of human nature. We must not expect a perfection of soul and body that can come only when sin and death are no more, which is

---

3. My wife was so fertile (and regular in her cycle) that three of our four children were conceived during the first month of trying. While we both believed that conception might occur each time we tried to conceive, our passion was more than the dutiful sowing of seed.

4. On one hand, pregnancy is the objective of sexual intimacy, with pleasure as a second-order effect. In another sense, the love of a husband for his wife is the objective of sexual intimacy, with pregnancy as a second-order effect. The problem is that human beings are finite in their understanding of God's multiple purposes for many events in mortal life.

why theologians have ascribed to marriage a remedial purpose for the subjugation of our disordered desires.

In reading Clement, one gets the sense that Tatian and his associates took an ascetic approach toward food, which brings us back to the apostle Paul's teachings in the book of 1 Corinthians—where the apostle noted that food and the stomach are meant for each other, but that God will someday change the body to another form.[5] This observation served as a preamble to subsequent teaching about marriage and sex, for the apostle reminded us that the perishable life of eating and reproducing is not eternal. Still, we must not get ahead of ourselves, for none of us lives long in this life without food, and no community survives without human reproduction. And if it remains lawful in mortal life to desire chocolate cake instead of barley bread, or a glass of wine rather than tasteless water—as well as to snack between life-giving meals—we face the same question of pleasure in eating that we face with sexual intimacy. Ascetics of ages past may have been heretical and wrong, but they were consistent in renouncing marriage and restricting their table fare to plain foods, for the principle of sensual pleasure remains the same.

The ascetic spirit of the ancient world is not a temptation of modernity. We so instinctively seek pleasure that we feel no need to justify our desire, just as Clement implied that sensuality was evil unless legitimized through the charitable desire for a child. Still, I wonder whether modern believers should use Clement's writings to help us reevaluate the nature and evaluation of desire. As we review our thinking, perhaps we should consider whether we too instinctively justify pleasure even as we attack raw hedonism, and whether we might lose our own balance at times as we fight the excesses of sensuality. I suspect that we give as much ground to the spirit of hedonism as ancient churchmen gave to the practice of asceticism. Like Clement, we fight the good fight but may give ground where we ought not.

Incidentally, anyone who doubts that we are tainted by the sensuality we claim to forsake should consider the many sermons preached against gluttony in the United States: sermons that remind us that we must be temperate in our desire for food, warning us to treat our bodies as sacred temples, and detailing the sin of gluttony as it has been condemned for nearly two thousand years of church history. The fact that none of us has heard one such sermon despite so much gluttony among us proves how

---

5. 1 Corinthians 6:14 (ESV).

instinctively modern Americans justify pleasure, whether of eating or sexual intimacy. May the Lord return us to the holy feasts and regular fasts of the Christian tradition: feasts and fasts that blessed the physical nature of God's creation without blessing unbridled appetite.

APPENDIX 7: REFLECTIONS ABOUT DIVORCE AND REMARRIAGE

REMARRIAGE AFTER DIVORCE IS, without doubt, the most controversial ethical concern regarding Christian marriage. Review of historical Roman Catholic theological works, as well as contemporary studies such as A. Andrew Das's recent *Remarriage in Early Christianity*, suggests that church fathers generally restricted remarriage following divorce and set the foundation for church law in the Latin-speaking churches of the West. This approach to divorce inspired medieval Roman Catholic doctrines challenged by Lutheran and Reformed churches during the sixteenth century and continued into the modern era. The following is the critical point of contention: do the words of Jesus that it is adulterous to remarry following divorce allow an exception if a man divorces his wife because of her adultery? Would such an exception also apply to women?[1]

While I am not a Greek scholar and cannot speak authoritatively to the details of the New Testament texts (which ultimately reveal the biblical rule of faith), I would like to point out several nuances that contextualize the writings of the Latin church fathers: limiting the scope of their authority in establishing current doctrine. To that end, there are three main areas of concern: the use of incomplete historical evidence, the

---

1. A. Andrew Das, *Remarriage in Early Christianity* (Grand Rapids, Michigan: William B. Eerdmans Publishing Company, 2024).

need to arrive at a systematic biblical system of ethics, and the improper use of exactitude when discussing biblical texts. Review of these factors suggests a far more complicated case than what is seen in the pastoral instructions of bishops in the Western churches during the centuries leading up to the synthesis of Augustine's views on Christian marriage—an approach codified into medieval law and followed by many believers to this day.

To begin with, we should examine the writings of the Latin fathers themselves. Perhaps the best book I have found that includes early church texts regarding divorce (in Latin and English translation) is E. Christian Brugger's study of marriage at the Council of Trent (which represented Roman Catholic reform attempted in light of Protestant challenges regarding multiple points of doctrine). Brugger's *The Indissolubility of Marriage and the Council of Trent* includes an appendix with translations of pertinent ancient and medieval authorities consulted during debates about marriage at Trent, presenting the best possible case for Roman Catholic doctrine prohibiting remarriage following divorce.[2] Simply perusing the translated sources confirms how many Western church fathers did not permit remarriage after divorce, even for adultery.

A Protestant response to such Tridentine texts can be found in the works of Reformer Peter Martyr Vermigli, who discussed divorce and remarriage in his commentary on the seventh commandment in his *Loci Communes* (available as *Common Places* in English in the reprint of a sixteenth-century translation). Not only did Vermigli place the Latin fathers in a broader historical context than a limited number of passages from leading church fathers, but he also included passages unmentioned by Brugger (and presumably ignored at Trent), as well as reviewing Roman law as promulgated by Christian emperors in late antiquity (who permitted remarriage following divorce, despite the objections of church leaders). Vermigli observed that some medieval church texts and practices were inconsistent with doctrines emphasized at Trent.[3]

Similar to Vermigli's observations that ecclesiastical and temporal authorities conflicted over divorce, I would note that divisions regarding divorce existed within Christian churches during late antiquity. This can be seen in the fact that church councils and leaders, whose decrees form

---

2. E. Christian Brugger, *The Indissolubility of Marriage and The Council of Trent* (Washington, D.C.: The Catholic University of America Press, 2017).
3. Peter Martyr Vermigli, *Common Places,* vol. II.10–18, 81–103.

the foundation of Latin Christian marital law, were proponents of more rigorist approaches to divorce and remarriage than were some of their peers—and sometimes seemed to be imposing order on what they considered morally lax church practices. Even penitential guides show a range of responses to divorce and remarriage, ranging from strict to less severe penalties for such sin.

What I mean to say is that the most restrictive texts prohibiting remarriage after divorce were the ones that were preserved and emphasized by medieval theologians and lawyers, whereas the writings of their opponents have sometimes been downplayed or lost. In highlighting the struggle between secular and ecclesiastical authorities regarding divorce, P.J. Reynolds similarly suggests that early Christian opinion was less than monolithic: an increasingly unmarried clergy restricted remarriage following divorce, even for the cause of adultery, though church law seems inconsistent, permits exceptions, and varies its penalties. Temporal law sometimes enforced different codes altogether, even for believers. The question for God's people is this: who speaks on behalf of Scripture when clergymen and public authorities disagree about the teaching of the Bible? Or when one church tradition overwhelms its rivals? We must never forget that while Scripture itself is inerrant, its clerical spokesmen are not.[4]

The second problem with a primary focus on the Latin church fathers is that this approach differentiates the Old and New Testaments more sharply than I do as a Reformed Protestant. When I consider the authoritative passages in Matthew 19, I follow Protestant efforts to harmonize New Testament texts with the divorce laws found in the book of Deuteronomy. The best way to state this is to note that both the Old and New Testaments provide a consistent ethic: that Moses and Jesus reveal commands from the God who does not shift or change. With that in mind, I am far less interested in arriving at a consistent church ethic than at a consistent biblical one. Many church fathers lived three or four hundred years (or longer) after Christ and relied on the same apostolic authority as the rest of us. They were as far removed from Christ as our generation is from the Puritans of the seventeenth century. Such churchmen and we face the same perplexing questions rooted not simply

4. See P.J. Reynolds, *Marriage in the Western Church: The Christianization of Marriage during the Patristic and Early Medieval Periods.*

in the Greek language and apostolic explanation, but in the commands and texts of the Old Testament.

Those who use church fathers who lived hundreds of years after Christ appeal to an authority that is no more valid than ours, except through proper biblical exegesis and cultural awareness. And, I would note, some church fathers do not explain the teachings of Jesus in light of Moses but wrongly divide the Old and New Testaments from each other. This is a fatal error since every biblical word is part of a comprehensive and internally consistent divine revelation. Sometimes this division seems to be less an articulated theological statement than a vague sense that the church fathers of the Roman Empire seem more like us than do the tribal believers of ancient Israel, so we defer to Roman and Greek insight and authority, while ignoring Jewish commentary and customs. Because the modern West is rooted in ancient Greece and Rome far more than we generally recognize, elements of Old Testament culture and society sometimes feel foreign and distant to our sensibilities.

Third, I would address what I will call *unwarranted exactitude* in understanding New Testament texts. Because some of the most important New Testament texts appear to be addressed only to men (i.e., males), many find in them no right for women to divorce, even for adultery. While nothing in the New Testament explicitly permits a woman to remarry after a divorce, it is misguided to apply different rules of divorce to men and women, given the *one flesh* connection of marriage. When scholars remind us how Jesus spoke only to men regarding divorce and remarriage, I would highlight that Jesus also spoke only to men about not lusting after women, and never specifically placed women under similar restrictions.[5] Does that mean that women are free to sexually desire men other than their husbands because Jesus did not explicitly warn them not to do so? Similarly, in Exodus, Moses commanded men not to covet their neighbor's wife, but said nothing about women envying the property, looks, or charm of a neighbor's husband. Were Hebrew women, therefore, allowed to lust for the husbands of their neighbors?

Such an interpretation would violate every rule of common sense in human speech. While modern scholars err when they erase all distinctions of sex in the churches, bending the knee to modern egalitarianism (for there have been and always will be rightful differences in law and custom between men and women) in the matter of divorce, there is and

---

5. Matthew 5:27–28 (ESV).

should be equality between the two sexes. The reasons for which a man may morally divorce a woman are the same reasons for which a woman may morally divorce a man: both because of the oneness of the flesh in marriage and equality in receiving biblical rights and responsibilities. Additionally, Peter Martyr Vermigli observed that the words of Jesus (and Paul) are to "be understood of the usual divorce among that people," which allowed divorce with the right to remarriage.[6]

The above arguments do not establish a right to remarriage after divorce. Only proper exegesis of the New Testament Greek can do so— and I confess that I must rely upon the interpretation of the Protestant tradition, which I find convincing and which I confess. What my arguments suggest is that church tradition from the earliest centuries was divided, that it is more important to arrive at a consistent biblical ethic of marriage than a consistent early church approach, and that some very particular interpretations of New Testament texts (that restrict the remarriage of women following divorce) lead to absurdities when such methodologies are applied consistently across Scripture. For those reasons, while contemporary believers should respect church tradition, we need not fear differing from church leaders who lived hundreds of years after Christ, for we, too, are promised God's help in understanding Scripture. Disagreeing with elements of one epoch is not the same as abandoning the entire church tradition.

---

6. Vermigli, *Common Places*, vol. II.10–18, 86.

APPENDIX 8: A WOMAN SACRIFICES HER SON

NOTED historian Natalie Zemon Davis detailed the life of a seventeenth-century Roman Catholic sister, Marie de l'Incarnation, who *sacrificed* her eleven-year-old son to God in exchange for life in a convent and as a missionary to the indigenous people of Canada. Marie became convinced that she had to choose between the worldly love she felt for her son and the true charity found in a religious life. Planning to take the veil (that is, to become a nun), Marie raised her son in a detached manner and was unwilling even to hug the boy. Her brother (who eventually raised the child) assessed that his sister had abandoned her child.[1] We can recognize Marie's zeal and firm principles while also seeing how she refused to accept an obligation imposed on her by God's providence, namely, her son's welfare. From the account we have before us, Marie de l'Incarnation proved to love strangers across the ocean more than her own child.

From my perspective, this account shows the temptation we all face to exalt principles over people, spirituality over the secular life. Such wrongdoing can be found in all of us and is a sin to be repented. It is a temptation just as common (if less obvious) for Protestant clergymen with wives and children as for Roman Catholic celibates who forsake family in favor of a convent or mission. One can also see this fault in

---

1. Natalie Z. Davis, *Women on the Margins: Three Seventeenth-Century Lives* (Cambridge, Massachusetts: Harvard University Press, 1995), 63–83.

secular reformers and unbelieving advocates of secular causes (who place political parties and ideals above the families and neighbors that God gave them). Among both religious and irreligious people, there is a temptation to care for the cause or the crusade more than individual people who happen to be family members and neighbors, whom one did not even choose but were foisted into one's life by so-called chance and providence.

In contrast to such misplaced idealism, the Lord would have us wash the feet of those presently standing before us. Christ would have us serve the people given to us rather than seeking great causes and grand crusades. While the ministry of Jesus culminated in the salvation of the entire world (at least of those who would be saved), most of his life was spent serving and loving a more intimate group of family, friends, and neighbors. Christ perfected his humility and love while tending his family and neighbors in Nazareth (and the surrounding region), and preached to his own community before taking his message to greater Israel. That is our call, and perhaps we are not worthy to preach God's gospel among distant nations until we have done so at home.

APPENDIX 9: RITUAL CLEANLINESS AND THE CHURCHES

IN A PREMODERN WORLD lacking modern plumbing, deodorants, and tampons, menstruation was discussed more openly than in a contemporary world where men seldom realize when the women around them are menstruating. For that reason, Old Testament laws of ritual separation and purity seem capricious and humiliating to us, almost heartless, mainly because it is so difficult for moderns to contextualize those laws given the significant changes that have taken place in material culture and public hygiene. While I will not write a history of the matter, I would like to share a few thoughts about a concern frequently addressed in epochs preceding our own.[1]

During the ancient and medieval epochs, even to the doorstep of modernity, some church traditions segregated women during what they considered the physical uncleanliness and ritual impurity of menstruation and childbirth. Such separation seemed so evident to the church father Dionysius that he judged it a "superfluous inquiry" even to discuss whether menstruating women ought to enter the house of God since he was convinced no Christian woman would be "rash enough in such a condition either to approach the holy table to touch the body and blood of the Lord." Historian Eve Levin has confirmed similar restrictions in medieval Orthodox churches. Such traditions were also present in the

---

1. Leviticus 15:2, 13, 16, 19, 20.

Latin churches, though some Western church leaders objected to such restrictions.[2] Gregory the Great, for instance, declared that women should be free to enter the church to give thanks to the Lord immediately after giving birth. Similarly, medieval theologian and church lawyer Gratian pointed to a gospel miracle to challenge the customs of his day that denied menstruating women access to churches.[3] Gratian spoke against the prejudices and customs of his era when he wrote:

> If it was praiseworthy for her with the issue of blood to touch the garment of the Lord, why should a woman suffering menstrual bleeding not be allowed to enter the Lord's church?[4]

Both Gregory and Gratian also mentioned the sexual impurity and uncleanliness of men, with Gratian discussing male nocturnal pollution and Gregory forbidding men from entering a church after coitus unless they have "washed with water."[5] While I cannot judge whether these leaders were importing Old Testament ritual purity into the Christian church or just demonstrating their preference for Roman cleanliness, it is clear that matters of hygiene were an essential aspect of church custom and that the matter was far greater than a simple *please wash your hands after you eat because your fingers are dirty.* Moreover, it seems that Gregory and Gratian may have been stricter with the sexual pollution of men following sexual intercourse than with the impurities associated with the reproductive cycles of women. I suspect this strictness toward men came from the fact that both theologians justified sexual intimacy primarily for its reproductive purposes, which seems more direct in the reproductive cycles of women than in the emissions of men. It may also have come from efforts to defend women from mistreatment and apply a consistent biblical ethic in their churches.[6] That is, they may have been

---

2. Dionysius, "Canon II," in Philip Schaff, ed., *AnteNicene Fathers,* vol. 232: (Grand Rapids, Michigan: Aeterna Press, 2014), 27; Levin, *Sex and Society,* 171; Pierre J. Payer, *Sex and the Penitentials: The Development of a Sexual Code, 550–1150* (Toronto: University of Toronto Press, 1984, 35–36.

3. To review these customs, one would need to understand the separation of Jewish Christians from Jewish ritual during the early centuries of the church, as well as the proper relationship of the Old and New Testaments and the reality of material culture and sanitation among the Romans and barbarians.

4. Gratian, *Treatise on Laws,* 18 (Dist. 5:2).

5. Gratian, *Treatise on Laws,* 18 (Dist. 6:1).

6. Peter Lombard, *The Sentences, Book 4: On the Doctrine of Signs,* trans. Guilio Solano (Toronto: Pontifical Institute of Medieval Studies, 2010), 185 (Distinction XXXI, Chapter

attempting to ensure that Christian freedom was not wrongly restricted by a wrongful application of Old Testament law, which is the very point Clement of Alexandria had made hundreds of years earlier, when he wrote the following:

> *The providence of God does not order now, as it did in ancient times, that after sexual intercourse a man should wash. For there is no need for the Lord to make believers do this after intercourse since by one Baptism he has washed them clean for every such occasion.*[7]

Although I see few direct applications of these teachings in the modern world, given our access to cleanliness in a way that no ancient person could have imagined, I consider it worthwhile to expose readers to this aspect of the past that seems so different from the practices of the modern world. Nevertheless, before condemning the past as superstitious or oppressive, we should consider where we have deeply rooted customs that color our understanding of marriage, intimacy, and sexual differences. What common assumptions do we have that go beyond Scripture or blind us to unquestioned prejudices? Have we adopted Old Testament laws of cleanliness as unconsciously as we have adopted Old Testament laws of circumcision? Do we doubt the piety of those with uncombed hair and unwashed faces in our churches?[8] Would we judge as spiritually disrespectful a man who came to church in filthy clothes and smelling of dried urine and sweat—defiling the sanctuary with the filth, fleas, and stench of an unwashed and unconverted barbarian? Do we wrongly see no ethical significance in a man fasting from (and cleaning himself after) physical intimacy? Perhaps our blindness is not in what we look like, but in how we speak and listen to each other (i.e., modern communications)?

While I am not prepared to provide answers I do not have, there may be yet unarticulated questions worth considering. I certainly see neither reason nor charity in mocking past customs simply because previous churchmen lacked modern plumbing and sanitary products (meaning

---

8). It could be argued that Gratian was adapting Old Testament ritual law when he allowed that men with mutilated genitals should not be promoted to higher ecclesiastical rank, as well as that violated [raped] women cannot be consecrated virgins. Gratian, *The Treatise on Laws*, 17–18 (Dist. 5:2).

7. Clement of Alexandria, "On Marriage," in Oulton and Chadwick, *Alexandrian Christianity*, 79.

8. James is clear that discrimination in churches against the poor and unwashed is prohibited. James 2:2–4 (NASB).

that menstruation may have been experienced differently by women than it now is, just as men were subject to more filth, fleas, and disease than they are in the modern West). Menstruating women without modern sanitary products and practices faced different issues than the same women in contemporary society and material culture. At the very least, cultures that used public baths to maintain cleanliness might have faced the same challenges I vaguely remember my mother and sisters facing with public swimming pools in the 1970s—they did not swim for short periods each month. So, before judging the past, we need to imagine what life was like in a world that was far less sanitary and healthy than our own (even if it was not an open cesspool). Perhaps certain customs, which may be offensive to modern ears, had legitimate purposes that we cannot recognize because we possess advantages that our forefathers lacked. Maybe we are too far removed from the reality of a world without plumbing, toilets, and sanitary napkins to pass an accurate judgment.

APPENDIX 10: C.S. LEWIS AND DECHRISTIANIZED MARRIAGE

IN *MERE CHRISTIANITY*, which the author initially delivered as radio broadcasts during the Second World War, C.S. Lewis discussed the problem of enforcing Christian marriage in a secular society. What Lewis argued was that the people of Great Britain had ceased being Christian in any meaningful sense by his day and ought not be held to standards of Christian morality regarding divorce. Lewis wrote that secular law should allow divorce for unbelievers while church law upholds a higher standard of conduct for professing Christians. As with the early church, believers are to enforce higher standards of conduct in their churches, while permitting secular governments to adopt laxer practices in civil law and across society as a whole. This approach essentially reverses the Christianization of law as instituted by Roman emperors such as Constantine, Theodosius, and Justinian. C.S. Lewis observed:

> *A great many people seem to think that if you are a Christian yourself you should try to make life difficult for every one. I do not think that. At least I know I should be very angry if the Mohammedans tried to prevent the rest of us from drinking wine. My own view is that the Churches should frankly recognize that the majority of the British people are not Christians and, therefore, cannot be expected to live Christian lives. There ought to be two distinct kinds of marriage: one governed by the State with rules enforced on all citi-*

zens, the other governed by the Church with rules enforced by her on her own members.[1]

While I see some merit in Lewis's arguments and incorporate aspects of his approach into my book (i.e., enforcing morality in churches that is not necessarily lived among unbelievers), certain difficulties must be noted. To begin with, for churches to implement specifically Christian doctrine only on Christians makes good sense since there is no biblical call for churches to include among their congregants those who do not bear the name of Christ and who have not been baptized into the Spirit of Christ (who alone enables men and women to attain true piety). While Christians should prophetically preach against sin and warn unbelievers of God's coming wrath (which unbelievers must face if they do not confess Christ, place themselves under church rule, and repent of their particular sins), church order is for those who have been baptized into the faith. In this, I agree with Lewis and with nearly every churchman who has upheld our common faith.

It is more difficult for me to bifurcate (as Lewis suggests) ecclesiastical and secular approaches to marriage: to allow two distinct confessions of marriage rather than one confession of what marriage is and ought to be. Even in a matter such as divorce (the subject of Lewis's discussion), this leads to confusion, since divorces obtained under secular law do not always have rightful standing under church doctrine. It seems to me that Lewis rightly professed the very impulse that the apostle Paul expresses in 1 Corinthians regarding divorce: where the apostle allows pagan-initiated divorces to stand without undue wrangling on the ground that God has called us to live in peace. Believers are to accept wrongful divorces by unbelievers for the reason that believers are a religious minority before a powerful, non-Christian state. This certainly was the case in the ancient world, and may yet become the reality for modern Christians. Insofar as Lewis is accepting of this reality, he is both in the right and providing practical advice.[2]

At the same time, the moral laws of marriage apply to believers and unbelievers, just as with the Ten Commandments and other biblical principles of morality, and it is wrong to establish differing codes of conduct. For instance, it would hardly be suitable for Christians to restrict fellow

---

1. Lewis, *Mere Christianity*, 112.
2. 1 Corinthians 7:15 (ESV).

believers from owning slaves while refusing to impose abolitionism on unbelievers. Would this not be to make peace with injustice, cruelty, and oppression? How could Christians advocate God's saving laws for themselves but not for the wider world? Are we not our brother's keeper? Should Christians place themselves in the position of declaring moral superiority to other people by positing a sub-level morality for common mankind and a higher morality for God's children? It is one thing to argue that unbelievers lack the power to obey God's holy commandments apart from his grace, but another altogether to present unbelievers with a lower set of expectations and standards, as if they can never repent and rise to God's holy image or are more beast-like than human. There is one moral law reflecting God's eternal character, and it must be preached to each and all of us, whether or not we wish to accept it.

Moreover, whatever the merits of Lewis's position in classical antiquity or 1940s Great Britain, the contemporary state would file lawsuits and criminal prosecutions, even persecutions, against churches for enforcing historical Christian standards against believers for even the simplest refusal of blessing—let alone the force of excommunication (which is the primary means of church discipline when Christians lack state power). Church history makes it clear that kings punish troublesome clerics who chide kings or their close allies (in today's world, this means a core voting constituency rather than a favored duke or noble faction) for their sexual and marital sins. Modern states possess powerful tools to monitor dissent and have a clear interest in maintaining order on their own terms, and would soon cry out with the exasperation of a murderous medieval monarch: "Who will rid me of these meddlesome priests?"[3] That is to say, if churches allow the secular realm to establish its marriage laws while believers sidestep a role in the public arena, Christians will face raw state power in short order, unless they choose to separate themselves from modern society more thoroughly than have the Amish communities of the United States.[4]

Additionally, the stakes today are far higher than issues of the past,

---

3. In martyring the Archbishop of Canterbury, Thomas Beckett, in 1170, English King Henry II reportedly cried out, "Who will rid me of this meddlesome [i.e., turbulent or troublesome] priest?"

4. The Scottish government has declared exclusionary zones in which believers are restricted from conducting observable prayer against nearby abortion clinics, even from porches on their property. Likewise, the French left demanded action against French Christians who held a prayer vigil to atone for the blasphemous opening performances during the 2024 Olympics held in France. Secularists demand the silencing of all opposition—even

which were often restricted to divorce, clerical celibacy, and cousin marriage. In our generation, it is polygamy, pedophilia, and incest that are being litigated as the next phase of the struggle for public morality, even as modernists consolidate their gains regarding divorce, abortion, and gay marriage. To step aside at this time would be to allow polygamy to become tolerated and perhaps legalized in the West for the first time since the barbarian tribes converted to Christianity following the collapse of the Roman Empire. Women will be exploited far more than with serial divorce, and children of unfavored wives will be abused and ignored, as they are everywhere polygamy is practiced. Moreover, plain-looking and poor men will lose access to wives as rich and handsome ones claim several women for themselves. To abandon the struggle for public life is also to allow pedophiles to stalk children, particularly those unfortunate boys and girls who lack the defensive walls of a robust Christian household. To walk away from this public dispute is tantamount to closing one's eyes to the plight of child slavery, for that is what sexual exploitation involves. As for incest, it is clear what inevitably happens to families in which familial affection and sexual passion are not diligently segregated and separated: vile lust and raw passion destroy bonds of innocent love that the Lord intends between close family members. Everything becomes corrupted and defiled.

Tolerating such evils is not what the apostle Paul taught, nor is it the objective C.S. Lewis sought. It is illustrative that Lewis used the example of alcohol in discussing the relationship of faith to society. While he presented his argument against imposing religious belief as a problem of Islamic prohibitions restricting the drinking of alcohol, I wonder if his objective included a backhanded slap at the temperance movement in the United States (which outlawed alcohol during a significant portion of Lewis's life). I suspect Lewis doubted the theological basis of prohibition and objected to abstinence being imposed on the unwilling (himself being fond of British pub life). Instead, Lewis encouraged men and women to decide for themselves how to handle such disputable matters. However, marriage belongs to the realm of natural law (to what Lewis elsewhere calls the *Tao*) in a way that drinking alcohol does not. It is the relationship of natural law to Christian and secular society that Lewis should have used to ground his thinking about divorce rather than

---

prayer to the Lord. The god of the left is a jealous god, vying against the Lord God for power and authority over heaven and earth.

simply classifying marriage doctrine as an ecclesiastical matter. The law of marriage is as grounded in natural law as is the prohibition of murder, rape, and robbery. Prohibition of sexual immorality and marital infidelity is far more necessary than the prohibition of alcoholic beverages.[5]

Treating marriage like temperance is an error since laws regarding sexual conduct restrict terrible violations of natural law: rape, incest, child abuse, sexual deviancy, bigamy, polygamy, and many other sins of public importance (such laws formerly restricted adultery, homosexuality, pornography, and fornication). Whatever one believes about the relationship of church and state, these are not inconsequential matters—and the public pays moral, social, and economic costs for the pleasures of those who sin: public welfare for illegitimate children, public health costs for sexually-transmitted diseases, and public prisons and psychiatric wards to house persons ruined in broken homes. Unless there are laws against marital and sexual sins, an orgy is set loose, and those not participating in the immorality become the ones who pay the price for sinners too hungover by their misdeeds to take care of themselves and the children they produce. For that reason, I do not believe Christians can desert the struggle to maintain what we can call Christian marriage; we are not imposing church ceremonies, pious blessings, or clerical control of marriage, but defending what marriage truly is and what it must remain. We are protecting the notion of civilization founded upon the human household: a notion found in Moses and classical philosophy alike.[6]

In her book *The Mind of the Maker,* Dorothy Sayers addressed the same topic (she explicitly mentioned the failed experiment of American Prohibition), observing a difference between natural law and those codes enforced by human opinion (and, I would add, human authority), which may or may not be rooted in natural law. Ms. Sayers noted that laws consistent with natural law lead to blessings across generations, as they reflect human nature as it is, whereas codes unrooted in natural law lead to what she called *catastrophe*—fatal misalignments in human society. In particular, Ms. Sayers hinted that the codes of unbelievers lead to sorrow

---

5. For his view on the *Tao* (natural law), see C.S. Lewis, *The Abolition of Man* (New York: HarperOne, 1971), 83–101.

6. Aristotle wrote: "In the first place there must be a union of those who cannot exist without each other; namely, of male and female, that the race may continue... When several families are united, [the] first society to be formed is the village... When several villages are united in a single complete community, [the] state comes into existence." Aristotle, "Politics," in *Basic Works of Aristotle*, 1127–1129 (Book 1, Chapter 2)..

and loss, not because God is the enforcer of some arbitrary code, but because the laws of human nature have an internal logic we dare not ignore. In this, Ms. Sayers attempted to argue for the continuing relevance of natural law (i.e., moral law) in a modern democracy founded on common judgment and public opinion. As Ms. Sayers wrote:

> *Societies which do not share Christian opinion about human values*
> *are logically quite justified in repudiating the code based upon that*
> *opinion. If, however, Christian opinion turns out to be right about*
> *the facts of human nature, then the dissenting societies are exposing*
> *themselves to that judgment of catastrophe which awaits those who*
> *defy the natural law.*[7]

As for the natural law, while C.S. Lewis discussed natural law throughout his works (particularly at the beginning of *Mere Christianity* and throughout *The Abolition of Man*), he often stressed common morality and natural law as a statement of apologetics: as a defense of moral value that intellectually establishes, or at least suggests, the existence of Supreme Value, namely God. Lewis also pointed out that gutting the idea of natural law is a self-refuting and self-destructive philosophy (if we may call it a philosophy, given its cynical origins), which leads to selfish behavior that no one admires, even when it surprises those responsible for undermining the natural law in the first place. For her part, Ms. Sayers took matters a step further in observing how ignoring natural law does not simply set an individual in the direction of an unhappy afterlife or make for flawed human beings ("men without chests" is the expression Lewis used to describe them) but brings temporal consequences in just a few generations: the self-destruction of human society and civilization.[8] She wrote:

> *Defy the commandments of the natural law, and the race will*
> *perish in a few generations; co-operate with them, and the race will*
> *flourish for ages to come. That is the fact; whether we like it or not,*
> *the universe is made that way. This commandment is interesting*

---

7. Dorothy Sayers, *The Mind of the Maker* (New York: HarperCollins Publishers, 1987), 11.
8. C.S. Lewis, *Mere Christianity;* C.S. Lewis, *The Abolition of Man* (New York: Harper Collins Publishers, 1974). I do not believe that Lewis and Sayers disagree in fundamentals, so much as the objective of their apologetics differed in secondary matters.

because if specifically puts forward the moral law as the basis of the moral code: because God has made the world like this and will not alter it, therefore you must not worship your fantasies, but pay allegiance to the truth.[9]

This self-destruction seems to describe what is happening in our culture aptly. There is a moral degeneration taking place that may indeed trigger God in his providence to punish and judge by edict and providential judgment through war, famine, disease, or depression. Still, even if such open calamity does not occur, there is undoubtedly a self-destructive violation of natural law that is causing Western societies to falter in the face of their foes beyond any specific hardship imposed by God or nature. Already, Europeans who have turned away from traditional families find themselves without sufficient offspring to sustain their own cultures and struggle with the hostile customs of increasing numbers of immigrants who bring hostile customs and values. It is the same with the sexual revolution, which has left a wake of sorrow and catastrophe that uproots and wrecks households that prospered for many generations. In this way, the dechristianization of the West is little more than a stepping stone to the suicide of the West. There is no path forward to blessing except repentance and a return to the ways of the Lord. If the great cathedrals of Europe are to survive as more than relics, museums, or repurposed mosques, they must once again become sanctuaries filled with pious Christians worshipping the Lord Jesus Christ and preaching our Lord's laws to the nations and peoples of Europe.[10]

Finally, given comments by C.S. Lewis and Dorothy Sayers on Islamic abstention from alcohol and the failure of the temperance movement in the United States, I would like to conclude with an unrelated observation on American Prohibition. While the American temperance experiment is generally considered an enormous failure, that harsh judgment overlooks the complete picture. Whatever Prohibition was unable to accomplish and whatever organized crime it fostered, it still led to less drinking, less violence (inside and outside the family), and less disease and

---

9. Sayers, *Mind of the Maker*, 12.
10. The greatest church in the Christian world, the *Hagia Sophia (Holy Wisdom)* in Istanbul, was repurposed as a mosque after Constantinople fell to Islam in 1453. It is now called *Ayasofya-i Kebir Cami-i Şerifi*. Must Notre Dame of Paris and the magnificent cathedral at Chartres someday face a similar fate? Will cathedrals at Canterbury and Cologne become isolated islands of a former faith, like quaint Amish villages in Pennsylvania and Indiana?

death than previously existed. Moreover, critics of Prohibition fail to consider how it was the generation of church-attending teetotalers who passed a constitutional amendment to outlaw alcohol (by clear majority vote) who at the same time raised what we subsequently named the Greatest Generation of Americans: a demographic cohort which endured the Great Depression without revolution, courageously and honorably fought the Second World War, defeated the Communist threat, built a previously unknown level of material prosperity, and made significant headway against the evil of racism entrenched in American society. Any one of these accomplishments would have been a generational achievement, but to complete them all shows greatness of a rare sort.

I suspect that the Greatest Generation rose to greatness precisely because it was shaped for public and private virtue by the upbringing and example of its prohibitionist parents, who represented a solid majority of American voters. While the shared sacrifices of depression and war certainly marked that generation and taught lessons in leadership, service, and sacrifice that endured long after prosperity and peace had returned, the men and women of this generation possessed a strength and dignity beyond the good character forged in suffering; or rather, they possessed the good character that allowed their trials and suffering to bring forth patriotism and decency rather than bitter resentment. One can never prove ultimate causes regarding such matters, for such knowledge of contingencies belongs to God alone, but it seems likely that being raised without ready access to beer, wine, and liquor mattered in the forming of the Greatest Generation. While temperance per se might not make individual men and women better than fellow citizens who share in an occasional bottle of beer or glass of wine, abuse of alcohol certainly makes them worse as citizens, spouses, parents, congregants, and neighbors. And where there is no alcohol, there can be no alcohol abuse. For men and women to focus on faith and family rather than losing their souls to booze and beer is to build several virtues and avoid many vices.

In contrast, will current generations raised in an era of legalized drugs, permissive sex, and state-sponsored gambling raise sons and daughters prepared for great sacrifice and subsequent honor? I fear not. Already, we can see public chaos stemming from their private addictions, as well as the terrible cost in homelessness, poor health, and child neglect. Rather than becoming a great generation, we live in the midst of an ignominious one, at least for a large portion of our fellow citizens. I fear that it may take a generation of suffering and subsequent revival for us to consider the strictures of temperance with a little more empathy than we now possess. But once our lessons are learned, perhaps even C.S. Lewis (in my opinion, the most significant Christian thinker and apologist of the twentieth century, and rivaled in practical theology over the centuries only by Augustine of Hippo and John Calvin) might offer a toast to his teetotaling cousins across the ocean? I certainly hope so.

In the very least, we might convince C.S. Lewis that his beloved England was better off hosting hundreds of thousands of American troops raised by a generation of majority teetotalers than it would have been with a comparable number of the drunken Soviet troops who brutalized and raped their way through Eastern Europe. American soldiers committed many sins (many soldiers rejected the temperance in which they were once raised) and crimes (nearly one hundred men were hanged for murder or rape by U.S. military authorities). Still, few armies the size of U.S. forces in Europe during the Second World War have behaved as well as American troops did—and such uncommon decency comes from causes far deeper than the leadership of a few commanders and the preaching of politicians. Such fundamentally decent soldiers reflected the households and communities into which they had been born and raised. Of that, there can be little doubt.[11]

---

11. For short biographies of Americans executed for crime, see French L. MacLean, *The Fifth Field: The Story of the 96 American Soldiers Sentenced to Death and Executed in Europe and North Africa in World War II* (Atglen, Pennsylvania: Schiffer Military History Publishers, 2013). To the point of this essay, I would highlight that many of the executed were inebriated when they committed the capital crime for which they were subsequently put to death. As for American soldiers, many were far from sexually chaste, but comparatively few indulged in the rapes of the Nazi and Soviet armies.

APPENDIX 11: WELSH HUMILIATION OF DISHONEST BRIDES

As we attempt to implement God's law, we must never drift into self-righteousness or humiliation of those who sin, no matter how distasteful or evil their wrongdoing. An examination of medieval Welsh custom reveals unbiblical, perhaps pagan, cruelty that should never have soiled those who bear the name of Jesus Christ. That is, Welsh authorities subjected women who falsely claimed virginity at marriage to a cruel ritual that fused financial ruin, personal shame, and public ridicule into one terrible ordeal. Per the medieval Welsh *Laws of Hywel*, the following was done to the woman who married under the pretense of virginity:

> *Her shift [was to be] cut off as high as her genitals and let a year-old steer with its tail greased be put into her hand. And if she can hold on, let her take its place of share of the argyfrau. And if she cannot hold it, let her have nothing.*[1]

The young woman accused of falsely claiming virginity had her smock cut to expose her nakedness and was allowed to retain her dowry only if she could hold on to the greased tail of a calf, which was a nearly impossible task. Financial loss alone would have sufficed to deter sin,

---

1. Dafydd Jenkins and Morfydd E. Owen, eds., *The Welsh Law of Women* (Cardiff: University of Wales Press, 1980), 9, 167.

without the need for gratuitous humiliation, impossible tasking, and public ridicule. None of this was done in the spirit of Christ, who gently told an adulterous woman to *Go...sin no more*. Jesus did not expose the guilty woman's nakedness nor did he chide her before a hostile crowd, or mock her with an impossible physical task in a vain attempt to retain any dowry rights following the woman's broken marriage.

Rather than subjecting the guilty woman to ridicule, our Lord commanded the adulteress to repent and expected her to do so, just as he does with each of us every day. And this was not just a New Testament approach, for the Mosaic laws for the holy commonwealth of Israel, which could be strict and severe, never subjected the accused to such gratuitous ridicule and mockery. I would also add that the exposure of the woman's nakedness to the community likely caused others to stare and sin in their thoughts, thereby degrading the woman in the eyes of her peers and the onlookers in the eyes of God. For many women, such humiliation may have been the gateway to a life of immorality and prostitution, both to drag others into her shame so that she might justify herself and to seek a moment of solace amidst her sorrows.

While this Welsh custom was abusive, my objective in reciting such a lurid custom is not to mock our ancestors as ignorant or oppressive, but to make contemporary men and women understand that we must reflect on our own abuses. We, too, practice ungenerous and cruel customs—whether we recognize them or not. Because all mankind is made of the same flesh as the Welsh, all of us must seek to identify our uncharitable callousness, arrogant ignorance, and evil customs. Many of us have Welsh blood in our veins, and all of us share in the sin we and the medieval Welsh together inherited from our fallen parents, Adam and Eve. So let us look at ourselves and repent of what is wrong and evil, even in the chiding of sin. Let us be toward sinners as Jesus was, holding sin accountable and upholding the law of the Lord, while showing gentle mercy toward those who should *Go... sin no more*.[2]

---

2. John 8:11 (NASB).

APPENDIX 12: THE RESURRECTION OF MAN AND WOMAN

Jesus said to them, "The sons of this age marry and are given in marriage, but those who are considered worthy to attain to that age and to the resurrection from the dead neither marry nor are given in marriage, for they cannot die anymore, because they are equal to angels and are sons of God, being sons of the resurrection." [1]

THE QUESTION of sexual identity after the resurrection has often been discussed among Christians, being framed by biblical portrayals of Christ and his church in the book of Revelation, the doctrine of the resurrection of the body, and explicit teaching by Jesus that there will be no marriage following the resurrection. While a complete discussion of this matter is beyond the parameters of this book, it seems prudent to share a few thoughts for review, at least for those readers as curious about and unsettled by these matters as I find myself to be. As a man who desired marriage long before I knew what it meant and who finds great satisfaction in being a husband and father after decades of marriage, living without a wife seems a lesser paradise than I presently enjoy. I confess that I am sometimes tempted to side with native tribesmen (fictionally portrayed in an old film) who scoffed at a missionary's mention of a heaven without women (i.e., sexual intimacy). Moreover, I suspect that

---

1. Luke 20:34–36 (ESV).

men and women who have suffered undesired singleness, disappointing marriages, or lifelong childlessness feel even stronger about the matter than I do as a blessed husband of a lovely wife and father of four great children—just as starving men suffer greater pangs of hunger than those who have eaten three meals each day.

To begin our discussion, we must note how the book of Revelation reveals the unapologetic masculinity of Jesus Christ and the undisguised femininity of his bride, the church of Christ, as eternal realities.[2] Christ was raised from the grave as a man and remains a man (i.e., a male) in appearance and temperament: the Son of Man whose image every son of man is called to reflect. Given that mankind was created as male and female and that we are raised in the very bodies that die, it is to be anticipated that men will live eternally as men and that women will live eternally as women. The church itself is represented as the bride of Christ, suggesting the eternal reality of feminine qualities. What wives are to husbands in mortal life, the church of Christ will be to Jesus in eternal life: obedient, deferential, and loving. My point is that male and female spiritual qualities and differences are not transient and temporary features of human life needed only for mortal marriage and human reproduction, but are rooted in eternal life.

Now, the traditional emphasis on eternal life teaches that mankind will be spiritually completed in God's love, transcending the flesh-and-blood desires of mortal life: an idea consistent with Paul's teaching in 1 Corinthians, where the apostle revealed that mortal desires shall be resurrected as incorruptible ones and mortal life be replaced by immortality.[3] While the Lord is Spirit and we shall know him as such, we shall be raised in the body and face the risen Christ in the body. And while we will see God face-to-face (that is, know him directly), we will do so with hearts, minds, and bodies differentiated by masculinity and femininity (albeit in a world where there is neither marrying nor giving in marriage). Of course, this immediately raises questions about those parts of the body related to earthly marriage and procreation. Is it bull and cow to build the herd, but gelded steer for eternity? Are we to be physically neutered like cats and dogs living in city apartments? Will we become spiritually degendered in our souls? Are the cultural radicals morally wrong but prophetically right? Will mankind ultimately transcend gender?

2. Revelation 1:13–14; Revelation 21:9.
3. 1 Corinthians 15:50–54 (ESV).

Whatever God has in place for redeemed mankind will be perfect, and there will be no regrets at losing the momentary joys of mortal life. Such pleasures and satisfactions as the return of health after a near-death experience, or the vanquishing of a tyrant, will be transcended in a perfectly righteous world from which all sin, disease, oppression, and death have been vanquished. Any cause for such momentary triumphs will no longer exist. Still, I must confess that I am troubled by the idea of an eternity without a wife to love or children to raise. I must confess how I become as agitated as the tribesmen mentioned above, although I simultaneously confess that I am profoundly wrong to question the notion of eternal joy with God simply because it lacks marriage: as if the touch of women (a pleasure that inevitably decays into ugliness, impotence, and death as mortal life draws to an end) is a greater good than eternal life.

To be frank, we learn in this earthly life that temporal blessings, no matter how bright they shine, do not bring happiness like the knowledge and love of God do, or at least we should be learning this truth in preparation for eternity. To be even blunter, we should also be learning that our bodies and souls are made to grow from the first moments after conception into the power and wisdom of human maturity. And along the way, we grow to understand that our desire deepens with maturity, moving from lesser to deeper experiences. While young boys and girls imagine playground teasing to be the epitome of fun between the sexes, and seek each other out for such sport, puberty soon stirs them to desire the profound and passionate intimacies of marriage—those very intimacies (emotional and physical) we later fear losing in an angelic eternity. Still, we should no more fear losing the glory of the relationship of man and woman in eternity than children should fear that puberty will end the fun of the playground. Change will come, but only as preparation for greater goods and more profound joys than what preceded it. Such is prophesied in the flesh itself.

A passage from Protestant Reformer Myles Coverdale draws together several points of doctrine regarding this matter. In a treatise on death, Coverdale praised Jerome of Stridon (i.e., Saint Jerome) for objecting to the errors of the Christian philosopher Origen regarding the resurrection of the body (an interesting approach, given frequent Protestant objections to some of Jerome's teachings against marriage). Origen had contrasted believers who believed that the physical parts of the mortal body are resurrected with those who doubted a bodily resurrection, splitting the difference by claiming that the resurrected will receive a body, albeit a heavenly one that cannot be seen with the eyes. Against this ghost-like claim, Coverdale cited Jerome, who observed that the resurrected Christ displayed his hands and side and ate food with his disciples, having been raised in the same body in which he had been born and crucified. What Jerome was arguing (and Coverdale positing through his citation of Jerome) is that our mortal body is the basis (we might say the seed, skeleton, DNA, or form) of our immortal one, meaning that differences of sex will be retained for eternity since every human body is born male or female. Women will not be transitioned into men, and men will not be spiritually gelded for eternity. Myles Coverdale wrote:

> *Where flesh, bones, blood, and members are, there must needs be a difference of kind, as of man and woman, and where these both are distinct the one from the other, there John must be John, and Mary must be Mary.*[4]

Coverdale was declaring that if the apostle John and the virgin Mary are to be raised in the body as man and woman (and what believer would dare deny that Mary, mother of God, will be in heaven as a woman?), so shall every other John and Mary—and every Jeff and Pam and Juan and Maria, too. In her excellent review of the history of Christian thought on the body, historian Caroline Walker Bynum similarly noted that the medieval theologian Bonaventure observed that mankind will be resurrected in both genders, with genitals and other bodily organs perfected rather than removed. Bynum Walker also points out that belief in post-Resurrection sexual differences was observed in the writings of Jerome and Augustine, categorizing this understanding as orthodox doctrine rather than heresy and novelty.[5] My point is this: the belief that men and women shall be raised as men and women for eternity reflects long-standing Christian tradition, even among believers who fully accept the words of Jesus that heaven will not include marriage and sexual intimacy as these now exist.

Although we must not be tempted to put the eternal relationship between men and women above the relationship that each person (man and woman) will have with God, this teaching remains a great comfort.

---

4. Myles Coverdale, "Treatise on Death," in *Remains of Myles Coverdale, Bishop of Exeter*, ed. Rev. George Pearson (Cambridge: Cambridge University Press, 1846), 186–191.
5. Caroline Walker Bynum, *The Resurrection of the Body in Western Christianity, 200–1336* (New York: Columbia University Press, 1995), 90–91, 98, 254.

The idea of a beatific vision (of spiritually knowing God face-to-face in holiness and love) makes clear that our ultimate joy comes from knowing and loving God above all else. Still, human beings are not (and never will be) solitary creatures or ungendered spirits: we will know and serve God in resurrected bodies as men and women, together glorifying God and enjoying his immense and intimate creation. Our senses will exist in heaven, as the book of Revelation makes clear in its discussion of music, precious stones, and feasts. God's heaven will be a place with musical splendor, physical beauty, and excellent food. We can take comfort in the reality that the essence of our humanity (reason, morality, creativity, physicality, and sexual identity) will remain intact forever, though raised from a mortal body to a spiritual one and purged of all sin.[6] In this spiritually mature state, man and woman will live forever as brother and sister: knowing, serving, and enjoying each other with a depth of love not experienced for a single hour in this fallen world. We will be like a great choir of baritone and soprano voices singing their distinctive parts to God's eternal praise—only this music will echo from every aspect of redeemed human life, and not only in song.[7]

I would continue with this rejoinder: these teachings should be studied, taught, and preached. While believers must avoid sinful accommodation with mortal life, illicit sensuality, and human sin (the types of speculation that lead us down the paths of deceivers who seek to retain, for eternity, our mortal experiences and relationships), we must still preach the resurrection and transformation of the flesh to resolve two contemporary problems. First, we must make clear that male and female exist (and are distinguished from each other) for eternity, thereby refuting current transgender fears and fantasies. Second, we must share

---

6. I wonder if even those physical features that seem created for reproduction contain undisclosed hints at far greater purposes and joys between men and women than mortal marriage and procreation presently provide (just as the innocent bodies of young children contain in some undeveloped and immature sense the post-puberty passions of adult life). Still, whatever shall be is a mystery hidden from sinful mankind.

7. What serving means in a world without sorrow and limits is difficult to imagine, but sacrificial love and eternal subordination are at the heart of God's nature (even in the blessed Trinity), so it is a joy to consider that we shall have the opportunity to deny ourselves much in the service of God and love of others. To that end, I suspect that the lifelong sacrifice of husband for wife will appear like child's play compared to the profound sacrifices men will make for women in God's eternal kingdom. In like manner, the fealty of women to their husbands for a few decades may appear a moment of light duty—no more than wiping dishes for a few minutes or brewing a pot of coffee—compared to a deferential, devoted, and dedicated friendship toward men lived through an unending eternity.

God's promises with those who have been disappointed in earthly love and family life. Preaching the hope of eternally perfect love between man and woman is an effective way to prevent marital and sexual sins rising from apprehension that heaven might not measure up to earthly life (tempting some to take what they can get now). Why? Because many infidelities and impurities seem to rise from an anxious fear in the minds of aging men and women that every act of sexual intimacy spurned in this life is a pleasure forever lost (instead of a seed planted for eternal delight). I confess that I myself would struggle to make peace with the loss of youth, strength, and beauty that I see around me (and in myself) as I enter old age, if it were not for trust in Christ's promised resurrection of the body and realization that God does not dangle the pleasures of mortal marriage before us prior to an eternity lacking the delight of men and women in each other—like a teasing uncle reminding his nieces and nephews that their candy is gone and they can have no more.

Indeed, Christians insist that every believing man who lacks a wife in this life is promised something far better than marriage in heaven. Any believing woman (whether baptized as a child into a Christian family or converted at the end of a sinful life) who lacks children on earth will gain an eternal inheritance superior to motherhood in fulfilling her desire to give and nurture life. Even happily married couples blessed with children are promised an eternal home beyond mortal comparison, and this in a resurrected body (which is a great comfort as we grow old, face the decay of marriage, and lose the joy of parenting young children). Amidst decline and loss, we can console ourselves that we are not to become spiritually gelded in heaven but will become more perfectly masculine or feminine than we now are, with a fruitfulness between the sexes that will exceed mortal marriage and human parenthood. How could it be otherwise? God does not order his creation so that we will forever waste away in wistful melancholy regarding mortal years buried in the grave. We will not suffer in heaven like old women separated from their offspring as they wait to die. We will not endure the pitiful reminiscing of retired athletes aching for the lost vigor of their youth.[8] No, the Lord does not play cruel tricks on his children, but blesses heaven with eternal *life* rather than everlasting barrenness and unending infertility.

---

8. C.S. Lewis provides an imaginative account of how men and women might be in the afterlife in Chapters 11 and 12 of *The Great Divorce*. C.S. Lewis, *The Great Divorce: A Dream* (New York: HarperOne, 1973), 97–123.

Contemplation of the resurrection rightly focuses on the beatific vision (the direct knowledge of God's infinite love and goodness) as the ultimate good of mankind. Still, it also makes clear that mankind was created as both man and woman for purposes greater than procreation. The traditional approach to this matter is that the end of sex is linked to the completion of the human race, sometimes reducing mankind to ghost-like souls (more in implication than direct doctrinal declaration), in direct spiritual experience of God. The book of Revelation teaches otherwise, noting the existence of a great city and a perfected nature in which God dwells as eternal man among redeemed mankind. This should be emphasized: when God revealed to the apostle John what eternity will be, the Lord showed humanity redeemed from sin and glorified, not human nature transcended or transformed into pure spirit. The eternal city of God will not be a world of ghost-like spiritual experiences, but a Christ-like resurrection of the bodies of men and women (just as Jesus was raised as male and so dwells in heaven at this hour). It will be the restoration to mankind of that Paradise lost when our first parents fell into sin.

Though we are not told what the joys and delights of the next world will be, men will live in righteousness and women in chastity rather than as androgynous spirits. We must not chatter about our sexual identity (as perfected as it will be), what some mistakenly said about eating: reasoning that since men will transcend death like angels (per the words of Jesus) and angels do not eat food (since food is the source of mortal life), mankind will not eat food in heaven. While drawing from the epistle to the Corinthians (which teaches that God will destroy the stomach and food), such teachers overlooked passages in Scripture indicating that Jesus ate food in his resurrected body and that he promises to hold a grand wedding banquet for his bride, the church.[9] Whatever the state of man and woman will be (and it seems that sinful mankind either cannot absorb or be trusted with that revelation), we should consider our food analogy yet again. It would seem that heavenly food and human digestion will be perfected rather than abolished. Biological life as we now know it will be raised to a far greater physical and spiritual good.

In discussing these matters, we must heed a valid warning from Protestant Reformer John Calvin. In chiding those who speculate too far on the nature of resurrected life (to include those like myself tempted to "go still further and ask what better estate remains for man, since the

---

9. 1 Corinthians 6:13 (ESV).

blessing of offspring will them be at an end"), Calvin observed that Scripture reveals how "the blessing of offspring applies to the increases whereby God continually advances the order of nature toward his goal; but in perfection itself, we know, there is another reckoning." Just as the fertilized egg matures to become a grown man or woman, so, too, the procreative impulse is building a human race that will outgrow the need for human procreation for man and woman to enjoy each other before the face of God. To that end, Calvin also warned how "each one is pleased by his own opinions [and] there is no end of disputing." Calvin reminded believers that the escape from the trap of disputable and unprovable opinions is to remain content with the dim nature of our mortal vision until that day when we see God. He also observed how few "out of a huge multitude care how they are to go to heaven, but all long to know beforehand what takes place there." Calvin warned believers that many are "lazy and loath to do battle" while already "picturing to themselves imaginary victories." What he wanted was for believers to live their faith in preparation for eternity rather than to speculate about eternity while living for the world.[10]

I want to conclude with a personal story that brings together human marriage and God's eternity. When my wife, Pam, and I were married several decades ago, we used Johann Sebastian Bach's *Jesu, Joy of Man's Desiring* as our wedding processional, hoping to impart a joyful solemnity to our special day. Recently, I listened to the English translation of lyrics that helped inspire this chorale—and now find the piece to be a kind of prophecy of the union of human love and eternal joy, being at the same time my marriage anthem and God's call to everlasting passion. The lyrics speak of Christ in the flesh and the joy of his redeemed people, impassioned with the fire of eternal love and life. Heaven is revealed as more than superficial pleasures, for it is a place of profound happiness, beauty, and joy. Christ in eternal flesh is praised as the center of all that is joyful and good. This is the blessedness that marriage prophesies, but can never attain. Even the most joyful weddings and enjoyable marriages are dim prophecies of such utter and immortal joy.

Indeed, I wonder if our many divorces and infidelities are rooted in this holy promise—in the prophecy of marriage that stirs the soul toward eternal love? That is to say, does the taste of immortal joy promised in every beautiful wedding turn to dust in the mouths of those couples who

---

10. John Calvin, *Institutes of the Christian Religion*, vol. 2, 1007.

fail to realize that the joy of heaven is reserved for eternity and will never be found on this earth? Do some married couples seek on earth what can never be found among sinful men and women, eventually becoming disappointed, frustrated, and embittered when their mortal spouse fails to fulfill the promise of their wedding day? Do they respond to unfulfilled and incomplete joy with impossible demands of their spouse, or even seek rival persons to press for what was prophesied? Do they seek in imperfect men and women what can be found only in Jesus, the true desire of every human heart? Do they mistake the dying reality of sinful and mortal human life for divine prophecies of everlasting joy?

Bach's chorale is stirring music to be remembered not only by those who seek in mortal life what cannot be found, but also by those, like myself, who fear that the beatific vision of God means the loss of mortal pleasures that we now enjoy. Why? Because this magnificent piece captivates us in a rapture of emotion that surpasses some trite and shallow love song, and even the best romantic ballad ever written. By worshipping God on our wedding with this song, Pam and I confessed, even unwittingly, that our wedding had greater purposes than lawful intimacy and legitimate procreation. We confessed how our marriage testified to a grander purpose than marriage itself. After all, the chorale that bound the congregation together in song did not acknowledge the desire of Jeff or honor the radiance of Pam, but praised Jesus Christ as the true joy of man's desiring. The chorale celebrated how immortal love and life will be given to redeemed man and woman in our resurrected bodies, each of us known to the depth of our soul by our God, and each of us bound together as man and woman in the holy joy of God's gathered people.[11]

It is for this reason alone that all of us, including me, can disregard silly fears found in old films and our anxious hearts alike. We can rise

---

11. As usual, C.S. Lewis adds profound depth to the discussion, writing: "We may hope that the resurrection of the body means also the resurrection of what may be called our 'greater body'; the general fabric of our earthly life with its affections and relationships. But only on a condition; not a condition arbitrarily laid down by God, but one necessarily inherent in the character of Heaven: nothing can enter there which cannot become heavenly. 'Flesh and blood', mere nature, cannot inherit that Kingdom. Man can ascend to Heaven only because the Christ, who died and ascended to Heaven, is 'formed in him'. Must we not suppose that the same is true of a man's loves? Only those into which Love Himself has entered will ascend to Love Himself. And these can be raised with Him only if they have, in some degree and fashion, shared His death; if the natural element in them has submitted—year after year, or in some sudden agony—to transmutation." Like John Calvin long before him, C.S. Lewis focuses on preparing for heaven more than speculating about heaven's joys. That is what our Lord demands. Lewis, *The Four Loves*, 174–175.

above the base pleasures of pagan natives and amoral filmmakers when we pray—willingly and with great gladness—that the Lord's perfect and eternal salvation will come soon, for God is the true joy that all men and women seek. And in finding God for eternity, we will receive as gifts whatever rightful and delightful arrangements our Lord will establish between redeemed man and woman. The Lord shall be our desire, but there may also be an eternal reflection of that desire in the everlasting love of man for woman and woman for man, just as with every other element of our Lord's restored and perfected creation—now filled with grandeur, brilliance, and pure passion. The book of Revelation is clear: God's heaven will be the maturing and completing of the life first given in Eden. This is the great hope of the believer: that we will be given Christ and the entire creation with him.

> *Jesu, joy of man's desiring,*
> *Holy wisdom, love most bright;*
> *Drawn by Thee, our souls aspiring*
> *Soar to uncreated light.*

> *Word of God, our flesh that fashioned,*
> *With the fire of life impassioned,*
> *Striving still to truth unknown,*
> *Soaring, dying round Thy throne.*

> *Through the way where hope is guiding,*
> *Hark, what peaceful music rings;*
> *Where the flock, in Thee confiding,*
> *Drink of joy from deathless springs.*

> *Theirs is beauty's fairest pleasure;*
> *Theirs is wisdom's holiest treasure.*
> *Thou dost ever lead Thine own*
> *In the love of joys unknown.*[12]

---

12. *Jesus, Joy of Man's Desiring:* Words by Martin Janus; Translated into English by Robert S. Bridges; Music by Johann Schop; Arrangement by Johann S. Bach in his Cantata 147. See http://www.hymntime.com/tch/htm/j/e/s/u/j/jesujomd.htm. I suggest that readers spend a moment to find an Internet video of this chorale (in which the words are sung to the music) to appreciate how this music suggests a prophecy of eternal joy.

SUPPLEMENTARY
MATERIAL

~

GLOSSARY OF CITED AUTHORS

Peter Abelard was a twelfth-century philosopher and theologian in France who became involved in a tragic love affair with his paramour, Heloise, about which they later corresponded.

Ambrose of Milan was a late fourth-century contemporary of Augustine of Hippo, who served as bishop of Milan and was instrumental in guiding Augustine in the Christian faith.

Andreas Capellanus was a French medieval writer whose *Art of Courtly Love* was discussed for centuries. Though it is sometimes difficult to fully understand the meaning of "Andrew the Preacher," it is plain to see that he disliked any concept or practice of love that degenerated into base sensuality, even if he did not preach complete chastity.

Anselm of Canterbury was an eleventh-century philosopher and theologian who served as Archbishop of Canterbury. He was most noted for his discussions of the Incarnation, the Atonement, and the existence of God.

Thomas Aquinas was probably the most prominent and influential medieval theologian. His works summarized the doctrines of the Christian faith, attempting to reconcile Christian learning with insights from classical philosophy (especially Aristotelianism). Aquinas lived in thirteenth-century Italy.

Arnobius of Sicca was a third-century Christian convert from North Africa. He wrote an important defense of Christianity against pagan criticism.

Athanasius of Alexandria was a fourth-century bishop and theologian whose works included *On the Incarnation,* which examined the Incarnation and crucifixion of Jesus as the crux of the Christian faith.

Athenagoras of Athens was a second-century Christian apologist from Greece.

Augustine of Hippo lived in Roman Africa during the late fourth and early fifth centuries (in the closing days of the Roman Empire after Christianity had been legalized). Augustine wrote on a host of doctrinal and moral subjects.

Roland Bainton was a prominent twentieth-century historian of Christian thought and culture. He specialized in the Protestant Reformation.

Basil of Caesarea lived in the fourth century. He reformed the church, cared for the poor, and established schools.

Herman Bavinck contributed to the maturation of modern yet orthodox Dutch Calvinism in the late nineteenth and early twentieth centuries.

Richard Baxter preached the Puritan message during the English Civil War (mid-seventeenth century) and wrote extensively on theological and practical piety.

Benedict of Nursia was an early Christian monk who lived and prayed in the sixth century. He founded a crucial religious community in Italy, whose codes influenced subsequent Western monasticism.

Bernard of Clairvaux was a twelfth-century European monk, writer, and theologian. His work on the love of God and the nature of spiritual experience was enormously influential.

Matthew Blasteres was a fourteenth-century Byzantine monk who attempted to reconcile civil and canon law.

Dietrich Bonhoeffer was a German Protestant known both for his numerous writings on Christian belief and his execution for his involvement in the German resistance against Adolf Hitler.

Geoffrey W. Bromiley was an influential American evangelical theologian (and translator of theological works) of the twentieth century.

Martin Bucer was an early Protestant Reformer in Strasbourg. Bucer was one of the first Protestant clergymen to marry, and his work permitting divorce was quite radical.

Henry (Heinrich) Bullinger was a peer of Ulrich Zwingli in Zurich. Upon Zwingli's death in battle, Bullinger took leadership of the Reformed churches. His *Decades* was a series of sermons widely read in England by both Anglicans and Puritans. Bullinger rivaled John Calvin for early leadership of Reformed churches.

Horace Bushnell was a nineteenth-century religious thinker from New England. Although his ideas were not always perfectly orthodox, his book on family life compares favorably with modern efforts.

Caesaria of Arles was a sixth-century bishop from southern France who wrote apologetic and theological works. He resisted the Pelagian heresy.

Cardinal Cajetan was a Roman Catholic opponent of the Protestant Reformation known for (among other things) his arguments against the divorce of Henry VIII and Catherine of Aragon, a divorce that spurred the English Reformation.

John Calvin was a Protestant Reformer and influential theologian. Though a Frenchman, Calvin did most of his work in Geneva, whose churches became a model for future Presbyterians and were influential during the sixteenth century.

Edward John Carnell was an American twentieth-century evangelical apologist and philosopher of the Christian religion.

Cassiodorus Senator was a sixth-century Roman statesman, scholar, and monk who cataloged the church fathers and secular writers, describing what had been written and how it was received.

G. K. Chesterton was an early twentieth-century Roman Catholic writer and British social critic. He wrote extensively on marriage and family life, and his essays read as if they were written for today.

John Chrysostom worked in Asia Minor in the late fourth and early fifth centuries. Nicknamed "the Golden Mouthed," John was a famous preacher and writer whose works circulated widely.

Clement of Alexandria, born in the second century, was converted from a heathen background. He worked in the crucial intellectual center of Alexandria (Egypt), and his works were influential in establishing Christian doctrine.

Myles Coverdale was a sixteenth-century Protestant Reformer whose translation of the English Bible was a significant milestone in the development of English Protestantism.

Thomas Cranmer played a significant role in introducing Protestant thought to England during the sixteenth century. Cranmer was one of the fathers of the Church of England, now known as the Anglican Church (whose American branch is the Episcopal Church).

Cyprian of Carthage was a third-century bishop in North Africa who was involved in defending and guiding the church amidst persecutions and discord.

Peter Damian was an eleventh-century monk and church official who sought to purify ecclesiastical life. His treatise, *Book of Gomorrah*, argued for tightening the laws and practices of celibacy in the early medieval church.

Dhuoda was a ninth-century Frankish noblewoman who wrote a handbook for her son. This book shares lessons of Christian piety within the hard-pressed world of Carolingian factions and rebellions. This is the only surviving book written by a woman from the period.

Dionysius of Alexandria was a third-century bishop involved in defending Christianity, both in its teachings and amidst fierce pagan persecutions.

John Donne was a seventeenth-century English Protestant. Most noted for his poetry, Donne was also an ordained clergyman.

Ephrem the Syrian was a fourth-century theologian and a writer of many hymns. He is an important figure in Syrian Christianity.

Eusebius of Caesarea was a fourth-century Roman historian and government official who documented the history of the Christian church from its founding through its legalization under Constantine the Great.

Francis of Assisi lived in the twelfth and thirteenth centuries. He was an Italian friar who required simplicity and poverty from his followers and prohibited the accumulation of wealth among ascetic communities.

Francis de Sales lived in the sixteenth century. He sought to reconvert Protestant churches to Catholicism and reform Roman Catholic piety.

Jean Gerson was a fifteenth-century French church official who wrote on political, theological, and moral topics. He wrote an essential guide for parish priests to instruct their congregations.

Gratian was a twelfth-century medieval church lawyer and philosopher of Bologna, Italy. He compiled various church codes into a single work, aiming to revive the authority of the early church fathers.

Gregory the Great became bishop of Rome in the late sixth century.

His effective administration and influential writings helped cement the papacy's power.

Gregory of Tours was a sixth-century bishop in southern France who chronicled the tumultuous religious life of the late Roman Empire. Gregory's work reveals the significant amount of missionary work required among the violent tribes of ancient Europe.

Hilary of Poitiers was a fourth-century bishop in what is now western France. He was noted for his alliance with Athanasius during the Arian controversy.

Charles Hodge was a nineteenth-century American Calvinist theologian associated with Princeton College. His *Systematic Theology* remains in print.

Ignatius of Antioch, one of the earliest and most prominent church leaders, was martyred early in the second century following a long life as a bishop and pastor.

Irenaeus of Lyons was a second-century theologian who knew Polycarp (who knew the apostle John). *On the Apostolic Preaching* is a simple yet profound book. Irenaeus made clear by the message and genealogy of the faith that the message of Christ was accurately handed down to the saints.

Isidore of Seville was a late sixth- and early seventh-century church leader from Spain, whose collections of definitions (or words) served as an essential encyclopedic guide for medieval thinking about various topics.

Justinian was one of the greatest Christian Emperors of the late Roman Empire. He was also known for reorganizing Roman law into several volumes incorporating reform (and Christian ethics)—a masterpiece that remained a critical work of jurisprudence into modernity. He lived during the sixth century.

John Knox helped introduce Reformed thought into Scotland during the mid-sixteenth century, particularly the ideas of John Calvin and the practices of the Reformed Church in Geneva.

Lactantius was an educated late-third- and early-fourth-century North African writer (who assisted Emperor Constantine), whose apologetic works defended Christianity and attacked pagan religion.

C.S. Lewis was a noted English scholar and lay religious writer who wrote extensively on a range of topics. His work on marriage ranged from an influential treatise on the medieval idea of courtly love to an account of his emotions at his beloved wife's death. Lewis wrote before, during, and after the Second World War.

Peter Lombard was a crucial twelfth-century theologian. His handbook of theology was used for generations. One of its four sections contained key ideas that helped define the medieval concept of marriage, both as a sacrament and as a legal institution.

Martin Luther was the most influential sixteenth-century Protestant theologian regarding marital doctrine. His treatises on marriage challenged Roman Catholic beliefs concerning the celibacy of priests, definitions of incest, parental rights over the marriage of younger children, and the spiritual superiority of celibacy over marriage. Though an ordained Roman Catholic monk and priest, Luther married former nun Katherine von Bora, serving as an example of clerical marriage throughout Europe.

Walter A. Maier was a twentieth-century Lutheran theologian associated with the more conservative element of the Lutheran churches.

Philip Melanchthon was Martin Luther's most critical compatriot. Melanchthon's *Loci Communes* (*Commonplaces*) was one of the sixteenth century's most published and read works.

Methodius of Olympus was a third-century Christian thinker whose works represent a philosophical and detailed clarification and defense of the Christian faith.

John Milton, the famous English poet, also wrote on religious, social, and political subjects. He lived during the English Civil War and sided with the Puritans, who overthrew King Charles I in the 1640s.

John Warwick Montgomery was a contemporary apologist and Christian thinker whose works encompass a range of issues and debates. He was best known as a staunch defender of Scripture's inerrancy and evidentialist apologetics.

Blaise Pascal was a seventeenth-century Catholic thinker and scientist who developed key scientific and mathematical ideas. He also studied religion and philosophy.

William Perkins was an early and very influential Puritan theologian whose works were widely read in England.

Philo of Alexandria was a Jewish thinker who was born about two decades before Jesus and died nearly two decades after Christ was crucified.

Christine de Pizan was an Italian-born writer who served in the medieval French royal court.

Raymond of Penyafort. Raymond was a thirteenth-century canon lawyer whose laws of marriage were quite influential during the High Middle Ages.

John Rice was one of the best-known American fundamentalist leaders and thinkers. He lived and worked in the mid-twentieth century.

Edwin Sandys was an English Protestant bishop in the sixteenth century who helped shape the Elizabethan Church of England until he died in 1588.

Dorothy Sayers was a twentieth-century British writer and Christian apologist, as well as a contemporary and associate of C.S. Lewis.

Francis Schaeffer was an essential twentieth-century Christian writer and thinker. He wrote about the relationship between Christianity and modern culture and thought.

John Selden was a seventeenth-century English lawyer and writer. Associated with the cause of Parliament during the English Civil War, Selden's book on the Hebrew household is an extraordinary effort of exegesis and commentary.

Shepherd of Hermas is a very early Christian writing whose author remains unidentified. It was one of the most detailed early church writings.

Menno Simons, the father of modern Mennonites, was a sixteenth-century Anabaptist whose practical theology emphasized good works and the authority of the New Testament.

Henry Smith was a popular Protestant preacher, writer, and church official in England. He lived during the sixteenth century.

Tertullian of Carthage was one of the most critical Latin-writing church fathers. He died in the early third century, having lived a life that included writings on apologetics, orthodoxy, and pastoral concerns.

Titus of Bosra was a fourth-century church father during the reign of Julian the Apostate. He labored in what is now Syria.

D. Elton Trueblood was an American Quaker, educator, author, and thinker. His work on marriage is an excellent critique of the pitfalls of modern familial customs.

Francis Turretin was a seventeenth-century Calvinist theologian from the Netherlands who systematized the teachings of the Reformed tradition.

Henry Venn was an eighteenth-century Anglican rector and theologian who lived and worked in England.

Peter Martyr Vermigli was one of the most important Reformed theologians of the sixteenth century. His *Common Places* was a theological textbook used for many generations.

Pierre Viret was a mid-sixteenth-century Protestant reformer associated with Calvin's Geneva and the French Reformed churches.

Juan Vives was a Spanish Catholic reformer who lived during the sixteenth century. Both Catholics and Protestants read his writings on the proper ethos of the household.

B.B. Warfield defended Reformed theology at Princeton Theological Seminary until he died in 1921. He was known as a staunch defender of historical Christianity against modernist challenges.

John Wesley founded the Methodist movement in the late eighteenth century. The Methodist and Wesleyan churches bear his imprint in the United States.

William Wilberforce was an English political leader during the French Revolution. He led the movement to abolish slavery in England a generation before the American anti-slavery movement gained momentum.

Charles Williams was a twentieth-century British novelist and scholar who addressed Christian topics in works of fiction and non-fiction.

Girolamo Zanchi was an Italian-born Protestant Reformer who ministered in Strasbourg (and elsewhere) and wrote numerous works of theology.

Ulrich Zwingli was one of the first Protestants. Operating from the Swiss city of Zurich, he defied his vows of celibacy (taken as a Roman Catholic) in the early 1520s by taking a wife. Zwingli helped draft some of the first Protestant marriage ordinances in Zurich.

∽

FOR FURTHER READING

Author's Note: Although I am not competent to draft a comprehensive bibliographic essay on the understanding of marriage, household, and sex in Christian history, I would like to catalog several works that are useful for personal study, as well as for enhancing the library of a Christian college, university, or seminary. While far from exhaustive, this list provides a starting point for further review of Christian marital, familial, and sexual ethics through translated primary sources and noteworthy secondary sources. Both primary and secondary sources focus on writings most critical to understanding the premodern family, particularly those that include core religious texts and commentary, as well as secondary sources that provide religious, cultural, social, legal, and medical background to make sense of primary texts and commentary. Footnotes will provide additional works of interest for particular topics and inquiries.

Recommended Primary Works

Aquinas, Thomas, *Summa Theologica.* The comprehensive discussion of ethical issues surrounding marriage in the *Summa Theologica* represents a harvest of medieval theology, incorporating numerous references to sources from antiquity and the Middle Ages. Aquinas's *Summa Contra Gentiles* deals with marriage in a natural law setting and is also valuable.

Augustine, Saint, *Treatises on Marriage and Other Subjects.* This book includes two of Augustine's most important discussions on marriage—his writings *The Good of Marriage* and *On Adulterous Marriages.* For over fifteen hundred years, all branches of Christianity have read, cited, and incorporated these into Christian thought. I also recommend *The Preaching of Augustine: "Our Lord's Sermon on the Mount."*

Bavinck, Herman, *The Christian Family.* Bavinck offers an early twentieth-century theology of family life, examining its role in the social order and in the Christian life. The book serves as an excellent starting point for gaining a general understanding of what Scripture teaches about family life in the face of modern challenges. It feels contemporary, but reflects the thinking of a Christian consensus that was still prevalent when it was written.

Baxter, Richard, *The Godly Home.* Baxter offers a valuable introduction to mature Puritan perspectives on family life, providing a marriage manual that stands in sharp contrast to modern ones.

Blastares, Matthew, *Sexuality, Marriage, and Celibacy in Byzantine Law: Selections from a Fourteenth-Century Encyclopedia of Canon Law and Theology—the Alphabetical Collection of Matthew Blastares.* A century before the fall of the Byzantine Empire, Matthew Blastares compiled a compendium of civil and canon law, including sections on marriage and sex. The codes indicate where the Orthodox churches diverged from Latin Christianity in their views on remarriage after divorce and on clerical marriage, as well as where the two branches remained in agreement.

Bromiley, Geoffrey W., *God and Marriage.* This is a succinct and masterful summary of biblical teachings regarding marriage—from its creation through its eschatological completion in Christ's marriage to his bride. Bromiley provides an orthodox and coherent theology of marriage that is accessible to every reader and ought to be read by those who teach God's people.

Bullinger, Henry (Heinrich), *The Decades.* While I used a mid-nineteenth-century edition when I first wrote this book, modern editions of these collected sermons by the Zurich Reformer are available. These make an excellent supplement to John Calvin's commentaries on various books of the Bible, providing insight into Protestant thought in the mid-sixteenth century. If it becomes available in a modern edition, I would also recommend Bullinger's *Christian State of Matrimony* (1541).

Calvin, John, *Commentaries.* John Calvin's commentaries on various books of the Bible provide insight into how Scripture was understood in an era much closer to the world of the prophets and apostles than our own. Calvin covers the doctrine and law of marriage in his *Institutes.* Readers interested in understanding how Reformed pastors treated marriage should also examine the now-published records of the Genevan Consistory and Company of Pastors.

Chesterton, G. K., *Brave New Family.* This collection of essays, written a century ago on women, sex, and family life, reads as if it were written to address today's issues. Chesterton brings a sharp analytical mind and an indescribable imagination as he looks behind the veil of contemporary ideologies and presuppositions. Chesterton also understands the grand adventure and daring risks that underlie every promise of love, marriage, and conception of a child. These essays stir body and soul like few others ever written about marriage and family life.

Chrysostom, John, *On Marriage and Family Life.* This short book includes several sermons by Chrysostom and offers a more comprehensive treatment of his teachings than my frequent citations. The work is filled with humanity, insight, and compassion, and is well worth examination. I suggest using the cited edition since it offers a good translation and an excellent introduction.

Clement of Alexandria, *Miscellanies, Book III ("On Marriage").* Clement both strove to defend marriage as God's creative act and to keep believing couples from base sensuality. His discussion of zoology as a comparison for human behavior is fascinating, especially his discussion of unusual hyena reproductive anatomy (also reported by modern scientists).

Danby, Herbert, ed., *The Mishnah.* This written collection of the oral tradition referred to by Jesus in the New Testament reflects ancient Jewish customs and interpretations of Scripture. It also provides context for understanding parts of the Old Testament. However, the opposition of Jesus to Jewish additions to Mosaic law makes it clear that elements of the Mishnah may be inconsistent with the law of Christ.

Hincmar of Rheims, *The Divorce of King Lothar and Queen Theutberga: Hincmar of Rheims's De Divortio.* This book presents both an exhaustive introduction to early medieval culture and politics and a significant divorce case that pitted ecclesiastical authorities against royal power. The translation of *De Divortio* also includes many citations from the church fathers regarding a host of sexual practices and sins.

Hodge, Charles, *Systematic Theology, Volume Three.* In his effort to discuss the Seventh Commandment in a high-level exposition of marriage and associated ethics, Hodge provides a detailed account of the historical differences between Roman Catholic and Protestant marriage doctrine, contrasting them with those of unbelievers. While not a typical source for the history of marriage, Hodge offers theological insights that are frequently lacking in legal and social history. Hodge also discusses issues of marriage and slavery in American life.

Hunter, David G., ed., *Marriage and Sexuality in Early Christianity.* This sourcebook of translations includes numerous church fathers, ecclesiastical legislation, and marriage blessings. It provides direct access to translations of important texts in a single volume.

Lewis, C. S., *Mere Christianity.* C. S. Lewis was a great writer of the mid-twentieth century and contributed scholarly work on love in medieval literature. He also brought his learning to his concept of "mere Christianity" (i.e., what has been believed across denominations), in which he discusses core Christian teaching regarding marriage, love, and sex. Among Lewis's more effective writings *on* marriage and love are *Mere Christianity*, *The Screwtape Letters*, and *The Four Loves*. His novels *Perelandra* and *That Hideous Strength* also include intriguing discussions of gender. Toward the end of his life, Lewis married and subsequently reminisced about his deceased wife in his autobiographical *A Grief Observed*.

Lombard, Peter, *The Sentences, Books II and IV.* Lombard was one of the most significant medieval theologians, particularly regarding the doctrine of marriage. His discussions of creation and marriage cite numerous church fathers and reveal medieval Christendom's approach to marriage.

The translation by Giulio Solano makes Lombard accessible to the modern reader.

Luther, Martin, *Luther's Works, Volumes 45–46 (The Christian in Society II–III)*. These two volumes of Luther's works include one treatise objecting to monasticism and four treatises on marriage, which reveal early Protestant doctrine and marriage laws. Additionally, Luther's comments regarding the family lives of Isaac and Jacob in his *Lectures on Genesis* affectionately discuss the place of marriage in the life of faith.

McNeil, John T., and Helena M. Gamer, *Medieval Handbooks of Penance: A Translation of the Principal Libri Poenitentiales*. This translation of key penitential guides for clergy to use with both laity and clergy is a compendium of sources regarding sin and repentance in the medieval church (covering both earlier and later periods). While reflecting different periods and regions, this collection does provide primary texts used to govern Christian morality.

Perkins, William, *Christian Oeconomy*. Perkins' guide to household and marriage ethics presents a systematic exposition of mature Protestant marriage doctrine in the seventeenth century, making a notable point of comparison with that of the medieval theologian Raymond of Penyafort. While I used an academic (but abridged) version for this book, a complete reprint is available as a self-published edition through online booksellers. See William Perkins, *Christian Economy: The Ordering of a Family According to Scripture*.

Raymond of Penyafort, *Summa on Marriage*. This medieval work represents the details of medieval canon law, yet proves surprisingly straightforward and readable. I recommend it to anyone who wants to understand medieval canon law better (as it is short and fascinating, with much of its reasoning tracing back to biblical anecdotes and injunctions).

Schaeffer, Francis, *Letters of Francis Schaeffer*. This collection of Francis Schaeffer's letters includes many on marital and sexual matters, expressing the type of balance between love and holiness that churches must uphold in their pastoral implementation of Christian doctrine.

Selden, John., *The Uxor Hebraica.* This seventeenth-century review of Jewish, pagan, and early Christian texts and marriage codes is comprehensive. It provides an ideal reference for understanding both ancient texts and subsequent discussions about them. The book is a veritable compendium of ancient texts on marriage and women, offering modern readers unfamiliar with ancient traditions and languages access to these texts.

Searle, Mark, and Kenneth W. Stevenson, eds., *Documents of the Marriage Liturgy.* Searle and Stevenson provide a reference guide that includes marriage ceremonies, customs, and liturgy. Stevenson also wrote a history of Christian marriage rites titled *Nuptial Blessing: A Study of Christian Marriage Rites.*

Vermigli, Peter Martyr, *Common Places.* While recent translations exist of the theological elements of Vermigli's *Loci Communes* (*Common Places*), the only complete translation of the work's exposition of the Ten Commandments is found in a sixteenth-century edition. Given the grammar and spelling of Elizabethan English, mastering it takes some effort (though considerably less than mastering Latin to read it in the original). However, it is worth the effort, as Vermigli brings an intellectual depth unmatched by his peers, particularly in his reading of the Roman law context of early Christian doctrine.

Viret, Pierre, *Exposition of the Ten Commandments.* This translation of Viret's dialogue-format commentary provides a window into the mind of an earlier era and a rather comprehensive review of the commandment against adultery, which was taken to summarize all teachings regarding household, chastity, and modesty (the fifth commandment also includes household implications, since it summarizes duties of authority). This translation is eminently readable, though it is not a scholarly critical edition with explanations and annotations.

Zanchi, Girolamo, *The Spiritual Marriage between Christ and His Church and Every One of the Faithful.* While this work of theology is filled with allegory, often foreign to Reformation-era writings, Zanchi presents a convincing argument that human marriage intentionally parallels, in many ways, the marriage of Christ to his church.

Recommended Secondary Works

Bainton, Roland, *What Christianity Says about Sex, Love, and Marriage*. While dated and lacking input from modern scholarship, Bainton's book introduces Christian ideas about marriage and sex. Bainton should be one beginning (though not the end) of study for the various epochs, since later generations of the twentieth century witnessed the publication of numerous excellent books on marriage based on meticulous archival research.

Boswell, John, T*he Kindness of Strangers: The Abandonment of Children in Western Europe from Late Antiquity to the Renaissance*. Though a controversial book, this work has value in discussing the practice of "exposing" (i.e., abandoning in a public place) children and how that problem was addressed during late antiquity and the Middle Ages. This book includes invaluable translations of church teachings and law.

Brucker, Gene, *Giovanni and Lusanna: Love and Marriage in Renaissance Florence*. This microhistory examines marriage during the Renaissance by investigating a breach of promise to marry in a legal system where engagement was considered a binding commitment. Brucker discusses marriage and class, man–woman relationships, and the inner workings of ecclesiastical courts.

Brugger, E. Christian, *The Indissolubility of Marriage and the Council of Trent*. This book provides a clear account of the discussions on marriage at the Council of Trent (which was convened to reform the Roman Catholic Church in response to the Protestant challenge). It includes translations of critical documents cited at Trent.

Brundage, James A., *Law, Sex, and Christian Society in Medieval Europe*. This book is essential reading. It traces the history of laws related to marriage and sex from pagan and Hebrew antiquity through the Middle Ages. It effectively describes and details canon law.

Clark, Stephen B., *Man and Woman in Christ: An Examination of the Roles of Men and Women in Light of Scripture and the Social Sciences*. Stephen Clark situates the New Testament teachings on men and women within an appropriately nuanced social, cultural, and historical context.

Cohen, Jeremy, *"Be Fertile and Increase, Fill the Earth and Master It"*: *The Ancient and Medieval Career of a Biblical Text.* This scholarly work examines the biblical text in Genesis 1:28 and the Jewish and Christian interpretations of the passage through the Middle Ages. While some biblical scholarship represents a modern approach that may be problematic for evangelicals, the author provides invaluable scholarship on the historical interpretations of the Genesis passage.

Gies, Frances, and Joseph Gies, *Marriage and the Family in the Middle Ages.* Although more of a popular history than an academic monograph, this book provides a broad survey of the cultures, issues, and ideas surrounding marriage and the household during the Middle Ages. The authors provide a solid introduction to traditional sources on medieval family life, though the book is somewhat dated and overly accepting of controversial ideas (later disproved by archival work and other historical review).

Gorman, Michael J., *Abortion and the Early Church: Christian, Jewish, and Pagan Attitudes in the Greco-Roman World.* Gorman reviews texts and customs in Judaism and early Christianity regarding abortion, as well as pagan thought, law, and medicine. This is an excellent introduction to abortion and early Christianity.

Gottlieb, Beatrice, *The Family in the Western World from the Black Death to the Industrial Age.* This summary of modern scholarship provides an excellent introduction to the religious, social, and legal history of family life in early modern Europe, encompassing legal and theological disputes, as well as demographic and economic realities. The author provides the historical context in which Reformation-era doctrines and controversies can be understood. For a similar review focused on England (rather than Western Europe as a whole), see Alan Macfarlane, *Marriage and Love in England: Modes of Reproduction 1300–1840.* While not cited in my book, both of these works are great introductions to the structure and study of early modern family life.

Grubbs, Judith, *Law and Family in Late Antiquity: The Emperor Constantine's Marriage Legislation.* Grubbs provides a detailed review of the laws governing marriage during Constantine's reign, as well as the relationship between Christian teaching and the emperor's reforms.

Hanawalt, Barbara, *The Ties That Bound: Peasant Families in Medieval England*. This historian examines the lives of peasant families in medieval England, framing the social context in which church laws were implemented. Hanawalt challenges contemporary historiography that claims the modern affective family did not exist until recent generations.

Harper, Kyle, *From Shame to Sin: The Christian Transformation of Sexual Morality in Late Antiquity*. Harper provides a well-written, engaging, and comprehensive review of early Christian discussions of marriage, situating them in the context of pagan Roman civilization, internal church debates, and the conversion of the Roman Empire to an enforced Christian ethic.

Helmholtz, R. H., *Marriage Litigation in Medieval England*. R. H. Helmholtz offers a detailed yet highly readable review of medieval marriage laws and their implementation in England.

Herlihy, David, *Medieval Households*. Whereas Barbara Hanawalt discusses the medieval peasant family and R. H. Helmholtz writes about medieval marriage laws, David Herlihy examines patterns of kinship and law during the Middle Ages.

Ingram, Martin, *Church Courts, Sex, and Marriage in England, 1570–1640*. This book examines the ecclesiastical courts in early modern England, from the Elizabethan settlement until the English Revolution. It is a detailed study of church structure, marriage disputes, and social morality.

Kingdon, Robert M., *Adultery and Divorce in Calvin's Geneva*. Robert Kingdon reviews Protestant marriage practices through several cases brought before the Geneva Consistory, providing insight into Genevan law and legal practices. Additionally, Kingdon and John Witte Jr. published *Sex, Marriage, and Family in Calvin's Geneva: Courtship, Engagement, and Marriage*, which weaves together Genevan marriage ordinances and Calvin's theology. This work is complemented by Jeffrey R. Watt's *The Consistory and Social Discipline in Calvin's Geneva*.

Levin, Eve, *Sex and Society in the World of the Orthodox Slavs, 900–1700*. Eve Levin surveys marriage and sex among the Orthodox churches during the medieval and early modern periods. Her book opens a window into Eastern Christianity that is often closed in discussions focused on Latin churches and Reformation-era controversies.

Mackin, Theodore, S.J., *What Is Marriage?* and *Divorce and Remarriage.* Jesuit scholar Theodore Mackin wrote two monumental surveys of marriage from a Roman Catholic perspective: the first discussing the nature and purpose of marriage, as well as its establishment under ecclesiastical jurisdiction as a sacrament; and the second providing a comprehensive review of divorce and remarriage in Scripture, the church fathers, the medieval canonists, and beyond. This second book includes ambiguous texts, Eastern Orthodox practices, and challenges to medieval Roman Catholic law.

McGuckin, John A., *The Ascent of Christian Law: Patristic and Byzantine Formulations of a New Civilization.* John A. McGuckin presents a survey of the laws of the patristic fathers and church councils, particularly in the Eastern Roman Empire.

Mistry, Zubin, *Abortion in the Early Middle Ages, c. 500–900.* Zubin Mistry surveys Christian attitudes toward abortion, as demonstrated in a wide range of historical sources and religious texts. This masterful book covers the breadth of Western discussions and practices regarding abortion and provides translations of numerous historical documents of significance.

Monnickendam, Yifat, *Jewish Law and Early Christian Identity: Betrothal, Marriage, and Infidelity in the Writings of Ephrem the Syrian.* Monnickendam explores the work of Ephrem the Syrian, a fourth-century Syrian Christian whose writings show the influence of Roman and Jewish law. This work includes fascinating sections on the rules of betrothal and Eastern Christian customs.

Morgan, Edmund, *The Puritan Family: Religion and Domestic Relations in Seventeenth-Century New England.* In this insightful book, Edmund Morgan examines the Puritan household, including marriage, parenting, education, servants, and the household's relationship to broader society.

Müller, Wolfgang P., *Marriage Litigation in the Western Church, 1215–1517*. While broader in scope than many archival studies recommended in this review, Müller's work merits attention for its focus on the uneven application of canon law across Christendom, with several regional studies forming its core.

Nicholas, David, *The Domestic Life of a Medieval City: Women, Children, and the Family in Fourteenth-Century Ghent*. While many works on medieval marital life have been drawn from legal archives in recent decades, I find this one of the most compelling. The book utilizes legal archives to explore the underlying realities for women, households, and children.

Noonan, John T., *Contraception: A History of Its Treatment by the Catholic Theologians and Canonists*. Noonan details the history of contraception, tracing the development of Catholic doctrine from antiquity to the modern world. This is an essential book that includes details of medieval theological objections to various types of non-reproductive sexual intimacy.

Ozment, Steven, *When Fathers Ruled: Family Life in Reformation Europe*. Steven Ozment examines changes to family life brought about by the Protestant Reformation. This is an excellent introduction to the basic legal, theological, and social premises for studying the household in Reformation-era Europe.

Payer, Pierre J., *Sex and the Penitentials: The Development of a Sexual Code, 550–1100*. Payer reviews the transformation of penitential codes into medieval canon law from late antiquity to the High Middle Ages. This instructive book provides many passages from penitential guides and church law.

Reid, Jr., Charles J., *Power over the Body, Equality in the Family: Rights and Domestic Relations in Medieval Canon Law*. While a study of medieval legal theory rather than a history of marriage, this book provides a starting point for reviewing how traditional Christians approached the law of marriage and family.

Reynolds, Philip L., *How Marriage Became One of the Sacraments: The Sacramental Theology of Marriage from Its Medieval Origins to the Council of Trent.* This comprehensive review of the development of the theology of marriage from late antiquity to the Council of Trent is an essential read for understanding how the doctrine of marriage evolved during the Middle Ages. The author's *Marriage in the Western Church: The Christianization of Marriage during the Patristic and Early Medieval Periods* provides a history of the concept of marriage in the West as Roman and Germanic societies converted and transformed their laws and customs, covering both ecclesiastical and civil laws.

Riddle, John M., *Contraception and Abortion from the Ancient World to the Renaissance* and *Eve's Herbs: A History of Contraception and Abortion in the West.* In these two works, Riddle discusses contraceptive practices and abortifacients from antiquity through the Renaissance. His work provides the academic, philosophical, and folk medicine contexts that frame biblical, medieval, and early modern legal codes, penitential guides, and religious texts discussing the use of herbs inducing abortion.

Safley, Thomas Max, *Let No Man Put Asunder: The Control of Marriage in the German Southwest—A Comparative Study, 1550–1600.* This book presents a comparative study of Protestant and Roman Catholic laws and practices within a southwest German political culture characterized by division between rival religious confessions.

Schmugge, Ludwig, *Marriage on Trial: Late Medieval German Couples at the Papal Court.* Schmugge uses German petitions to the Papacy during the late fifteenth century to discuss the nature of ecclesiastical law. This work not only explains Roman Catholic marital law but also its use, misuse, and abuse, as couples appealed to church officials for assistance in making, repudiating, and living Christian marriages.

Treggiari, Susan, *Roman Marriage: Iusti Coniuges from the Time of Cicero to the Time of Ulpian.* Susan Treggiari provides a definitive discussion of Roman marriage law during the period when the Christian faith was shaping the Roman Empire and, in turn, was being shaped by Roman culture.

∾

SELECT BIBLIOGRAPHY

Abelard, Peter. *The Letters of Abelard and Heloise*. Translated by Betty Radice. New York: Penguin Books, 1974.

———. *The Story of Abelard's Adversities*. Translated by J.T., Muckle. Toronto: Pontifical Institute of Medieval Studies, 1982.

Adams, Jay E. *Marriage, Divorce, and Remarriage in the Bible*. Grand Rapids, Michigan: Zondervan, 1980.

Adams, Kirk. *Measures of Insight: Moral Reflections for Daily Life*. Kirk Adams Books, 2021.

Akehurst, F. R. P., Translator. *The Coutumes de Beauvaisis of Philippe de Beaumanoir*. Philadelphia: University of Pennsylvania Press, 1992.

Ambrose of Milan, Saint. *Exposition of the Holy Gospel According to Saint Luke, with Fragments on the Prophecy of Esaias*. Translated by Theodora Tomlinson. Etna, California: Center for Traditionalist Orthodox Studies, 2003.

Anselm of Canterbury. *Anselm of Canterbury: The Major Works*. Edited by Brian Davies and G.R. Evans. Oxford: Oxford University Press, 1988.

Anselm of Canterbury. *St. Anselm: Basic Writings*. Translated by S. N. Deane. La Salle, Illinois: Open Court Publishing Company, 1962.

Aquinas, St. Thomas. *Summa Theologiae of St. Thomas Aquinas*. Translated by the Fathers of the English Dominican Province. Second and Revised Edition. 1920. Published online in New Advent by Kevin Knight, 2017.

———. *The Summa Theologica*. Two Volumes. Translated by Rev. Daniel J. Sullivan. Chicago: Encyclopedia Britannica, Inc., and William Benton, 1952.

Ariès, Philippe. *Centuries of Childhood: A Social History of Family Life*. Translated by Robert Baldick. New York: Vintage Books, 1962.

Aristotle. *Basic Works of Aristotle*. Edited by Richard McKeon. New York: Random House, 1941.

Arnobius of Sicca. *The Case Against the Pagans*. Translated by George E. McCracken. Westminster, Maryland: Newman Press, 1949.

Arthur, Anthony. *The Tailor-King: The Rise and Fall of the Anabaptist Kingdom of Münster*. New York: St. Martin's Press, 1999.

Athanasius, Saint. *On the Incarnation: The Treatise De Incarnation Verb Dei*. Translated by C.S.M.V. and Introduced by C.S. Lewis. New York: St. Vladimir's Seminary Press, 1993.

Atkinson, Clarissa W. *The Oldest Vocation: Christian Motherhood in the Middle Ages*. Ithaca, New York: Cornell University Press, 1991.

Augustine of Hippo. *Basic Writings of Saint Augustine*. Two Volumes. Edited by Whitney Oates. Grand Rapids, Michigan: Baker Book House, 1980.

———. *On Christian Doctrine*. Translated by D. W. Robinson, Jr. Upper Saddle River, New Jersey: Prentice Hall, 1958.

———. *The Preaching of Augustine: "Our Lord's Sermon on the Mount."* Edited by Jaroslav Pelikan. Philadelphia: Fortress Press, 1973.

———. *The Rule of Saint Augustine: Masculine and Feminine Versions*. Edited by Tarsicius J. Van Bavel. London: Darton, Longman, and Todd, 1984.

———. *Saint Augustine: Treatises on Marriage and Other Subjects*. Edited by Roy J. Deferrari. Washington, D.C.: The Catholic University of America Press, 1955.

Bainton, Roland. *What Christianity Says about Sex, Love, and Marriage*. New York: Association Press, 1957.

———. *Women of the Reformation in Germany and Italy*. Boston: Beacon Press, 1971.

Bavinck, Herman. *The Christian Family*. Translated by Nelson D. Kloosterman. Grand Rapids, Michigan: Christian's Library Press, 2012.

Baxter, Richard. *The Godly Home*. Edited by Randall J. Pedersen. Wheaton, Illinois: Crossway Books, 2010.

———. *The Practical Works of the Reverend Richard Baxter*, Twenty-eight Volumes. London: James Duncan, 1830.

Bayard, Tania, ed. *A Medieval Home Companion: Housekeeping in the Fourteenth Century*. New York: HarperCollins, 1991.

Benedict, Saint. *The Rule of St. Benedict*. Translated by Anthony C. Meisel and M. L. del Mastro. New York: Image Books, 1975.

Bernard of Clairvaux. *The Love of God and Spiritual Friendship*. Edited by James M. Houston. Portland, Oregon: Multnomah Press, 1983.

Blamires, Alcuin, Editor. *Woman Defamed and Woman Defended: An Anthology of Medieval Texts*. Oxford: Clarendon Press, 1992.

Bonhoeffer, Dietrich. *Creation and Fall/Temptation*. Translated by John C. Fletcher. New York: Macmillan and Company, 1959.

Boswell, John. *The Kindness of Strangers: The Abandonment of Children in Western Europe from Late Antiquity to the Renaissance*. New York: Vintage Books, 1988.

Bower, Jacinta. "What Are the Odds You Exist?" *ScienceAlert*, December 17, 2015.

Braudel, Fernand. *Civilization and Capitalism, 15th—18th Century, Volume One: The Structures of Everyday Life: The Limits of the Possible*. Translated by Sian Reynolds. Berkeley, California: University of California Press, 1992.

Bromiley, Geoffrey W. *God and Marriage*. Grand Rapids, Michigan: William B. Eerdmans Publishing Company, 1980.

Bromiley, G. W., ed. *Zwingli and Bullinger*. Philadelphia: Westminster Press, 1953.

Brown, Peter. *The Body and Society: Men, Women, and Sexual Renunciation in Early Christianity*. New York: Columbia University Press, 1988.

Brucker, Gene. *Giovanni and Lusanna: Love and Marriage in Renaissance Florence*. London: Weidenfeld and Nicholson, 1986.

Brugger, E. Christian. *The Indissolubility of Marriage and the Council of Trent*. Washington, D.C.: The Catholic University of America Press, 2017.

Brundage, James A. *Law, Sex and Christian Society in Medieval Europe*. Chicago: University of Chicago Press, 1987.

Bullinger, Heinrich. *The Christen State of Matrimonye*. 1541. Reprint, Norwood, New Jersey: Walter Johnson, Inc., 1974.

———. *The Decades of Henry Bullinger*. Four Volumes. The Parker Society. Cambridge: University Press, 1849–1850.

Burleigh, Michael. *Death and Deliverance: 'Euthanasia' in Germany, 1900-1945*. Cambridge: Cambridge University Press, 1994.

Burtchaell, James Tunstead. *Rachel Weeping: The Case against Abortion*. San Francisco: Harper and Row, 1982.

Bushnell, Horace. *Christian Nurture*. 1861. Reprint, Grand Rapids, Michigan: Baker Book House, 1979.

Cairncross, John. *After Polygamy Was Made A Sin: The Social History of Christian Polygamy.* London: Routledge and Kegan Paul, 1974.

Calvin, John. *Calvin's Ecclesiastical Advice.* Translated by Mary Bath and Benjamin W. Farley. Louisville, Kentucky: Westminster John Knox Press, 1991.

———. *Calvin's Commentaries: The Second Epistle of Paul the Apostle to the Corinthians and the Epistles to Timothy, Titus, and Philemon.* Translated by Rev. T. A. Smail. Grand Rapids, Michigan: William B. Eerdmans Publishing Company, 1964.

———. *Commentaries on the First Book of Moses Called Genesis.* Two Volumes. Translated by Rev. John King. Grand Rapids, Michigan: Baker Books, 2005.

———. *Commentaries on the Four Last Books of Moses Arranged in the Form of a Harmony,* Volume Three. Translated by Reverend Charles William Bingham. Oxford: Oxford University Press, 1845, Christian Classics Ethereal Library.

———. *Commentaries on the Twelve Minor Prophets.* Five Volumes. Translated by Rev. John Owen. Grand Rapids, Michigan: William B. Eerdmans, 1950.

———. *Commentary on the Book of Psalms.* Volume Four. Translated by the Reverend James Anderson. Grand Rapids, Michigan: Baker Books, 2005.

———. *Commentary on a Harmony of the Evangelists, Matthew, Mark, and Luke.* Volume One. Grand Rapids, Michigan: Baker Books, 2005.

———. *Concerning Scandals.* Translated by John W. Fraser. Grand Rapids, Michigan: William B. Eerdmans Publishing Company, 1978.

———. *Genesis.* Translated by John King. Grand Rapids, Michigan: William B. Eerdmans, 1948.

———. *Institutes of the Christian Religion.* Two Volumes. Edited by John T. McNeill. Translated by Ford Lewis Battles. Philadelphia: Westminster Press, 1960.

———. *Opera Quae Supersunt Omnia.* Fifty-Nine Volumes. Brunsvigae et Berolinae: C.A. Schwetschke et Filium, 1863–1900.

Campbell, Ken M., Editor. *Marriage and Family in the Biblical World.* Downer's Grove, Illinois: InterVarsity Press, 2003.

Capellanus, Andreas. *The Art of Courtly Love.* Edited by Frederick W. Locke. New York: Continuum Publishing Company, 1989.

Carnell, Edward John. *A Philosophy of the Christian Religion.* Grand Rapids, Michigan: Baker Book House, 1952.

Cassiodorus Senator. *An Introduction to Divine and Human Readings.* Translated by Leslie Webber Jones. New York: W.W. Norton and Company, 1946.

Catechism of the Catholic Church. Mahwah, New Jersey: Paulist Press, 1994.

Chesterton, G. K. *Brave New Family.* Edited by Alvaro de Silva. San Francisco: Ignatius Press, 1990.

———. *The Everlasting Man.* New York: Image Books, 1955.

Chrysostom, John. "Homily 20 on Ephesians," in *Nicene and Post-Nicene Fathers, First Series,* Volume Thirteen. Edited by Philip Schaff. Buffalo, New York: Christian Literature Publishing, 1889. Revised and edited for New Advent (online) by Kevin Knight.

———. *On Marriage and Family Life.* Translated by Catherine P. Roth and David Anderson. Crestwood, New York: St. Vladimir's Seminary Press, 1986.

Clark, Stephen B. *Man and Woman in Christ: An Examination of the Roles of Men and Women in Light of Scripture and the Social Sciences.* Ann Arbor, Michigan: Servant Books, 1980.

Clement of Alexandria. *Christ the Educator.* Translated by Simon P. Wood. Washington, D.C.: Catholic University Press, 1953.

———. *Miscellanies (Stromata).* United States of America: Beloved Publishing, 2014.

Cohen, Jeremy. *"Be Fertile and Increase, Fill the Earth and Master It": The Ancient and Medieval Career of a Biblical Text.* Ithaca, New York: Cornell University Press, 1989.

Cohn, Norman. *The Pursuit of the Millennium: Revolutionary Millenarians and Mystical Anarchists of the Middle Ages.* Oxford: Oxford University Press, 1957.

Coverdale, Myles. *Remains of Myles Coverdale, Bishop of Exeter.* Edited by Rev. George Pearson. Parker Society. Cambridge: Cambridge University Press, 1846.

Cranmer, Thomas. *A Catechism Set Forth by Thomas Cranmer.* Introduction by D.G. Selwyn. Oxford: Sutton Courtenay Press, 1878.

Crosson, Russ. *Your Life... Well Spent: The Eternal Rewards of Investing Yourself and Your Money in Your Family.* Eugene, Oregon: Harvest Books, 1994.

Damian, Peter. *Book of Gomorrah.* Edited by Pierre J. Payer. Waterloo, Ontario: Wilfrid Laurier University Press, 1982.

Danby, Herbert, Editor. *The Mishnah.* Oxford: Oxford University Press, 1991.

Darmon, Pierre. *Trial by Impotence: Virility and Marriage in pre-Revolutionary France.* Translated by Paul Keegan. London: The Hogarth Press, 1985.

Darwin, Charles. *The Descent of Man and Selection in Relation to Sex*. Princeton, New Jersey: Princeton University Press, 1981.

Das, A. Andrew Das. *Remarriage in Early Christianity*. Grand Rapids, Michigan: William B. Eerdmans Publishing Company, 2024.

Davis, Natalie Zemon. *The Return of Martin Guerre*. Cambridge, Massachusetts: Harvard University Press, 1983.

———. *Women on the Margins: Three Seventeenth-Century Lives*. Cambridge, Massachusetts: Harvard University Press, 1995.

Dhuoda. *Handbook for William: A Carolingian Woman's Counsel for Her Son*. Washington, D.C.: The Catholic University of America Press, 1991.

Doctrines and Discipline of the Methodist Church. Nashville, Tennessee: The Methodist Publishing House, 1964.

Donne, John. *The Sermons of John Donne*. Ten Volumes. Edited by George R. Potter and Evelyn M. Simpson. Berkeley, California: University of California Press, 1953–1962.

Driscoll, Mark, and Grace. *Real Marriage: The Truth about Sex, Friendship, and Life Together*. Nashville, Tennessee: Thomas Nelson, 2022.

Duby, Georges. *Medieval Marriage: Two Models from Twelfth-Century France*. Baltimore, Maryland: Johns Hopkins University Press, 1978.

Duriez, Colin. *Dorothy Sayers, A Biography: Death, Dante, and Lord Peter Wimsey*. Oxford: Lion Hudson Limited.

Eisenstein, Elizabeth L. *The Printing Revolution in Early Modern Europe*. Cambridge: Cambridge University Press, 1983.

Ekirch, A. Roger. *At Day's Close: Night in Times Past*. New York: W.W. Norton and Company, 2005.

Elliott, Dyan. *Spiritual Marriage: Sexual Abstinence in Medieval Wedlock*. Princeton, New Jersey: Princeton University Press, 1993.

Ellul, Jacques. *The Betrayal of the West*. New York: Seabury Press, 1978.

Engelsma, David. *Better to Marry*. Grand Rapids, Michigan: Reformed Free Publishing Association, 1993.

Eusebius. *History of the Church from Christ to Constantine*. Translated by G.A. Williamson. Revised and Edited by Andrew Louth. London: Penguin Books, 1965.

Ezzo, Gary, ed. *The Godly Family: A Series of Essays on the Duties of Parents and Children.* Pittsburgh, Pennsylvania: Soli Deo Gloria Publications, 1993.

Fildes, Valerie. *Breasts, Bottles, and Babies: A History of Infant Feeding.* Edinburgh: Edinburgh University Press, 1986.

———. *Wet Nursing: A History from Antiquity to the Present.* Oxford: Basil Blackwell, 1988.

Fisher Drew, Katherine. *The Burgundian Code: Book of Constitutions or Law of Gundobad, Additional Enactments.* Philadelphia: University of Pennsylvania Press, 1949.

Flandrin, Jean-Louis. *Families in Former Times: Kinship, Household, and Sexuality in Early Modern France.* Cambridge: Cambridge University Press, 1991.

Fletcher, Joseph. *Situation Ethics: The New Morality.* Philadelphia: Westminster Press, 1966.

Flinn, Michael W. *The European Demographic System, 1500–1820.* Baltimore: Johns Hopkins University Press, 1981.

Francis of Assisi. *The Writings of St. Francis of Assisi.* Translated by Benen Fahy, O.F.M. Chicago: Franciscan Herald Press, 1963.

Francis de Sales. *Introduction to the Devout Life.* Edited by Michael Day. Wheathampstead, Hertfordshire: Anthony Clarke, 1990.

Friesen, Garry. *Decision Making and the Will of God: A Biblical Alternative to the Traditional View.* Sisters, Oregon: Multnomah Publishers, 2004.

Gager, Kristin Elizabeth. *Blood Ties and Fictive Ties: Adoption and Family in Early Modern France.* Princeton, New Jersey: Princeton University Press, 1996.

Gavitt, Philip. *Charity and Children in Renaissance Florence: The Ospedale degli Innocenti, 1410–1535.* Ann Arbor, Michigan: University of Michigan Press, 1990.

Gélis, Jacques. *History of Childbirth: Fertility, Pregnancy and Birth in Early Modern Europe.* Translated by Rosemary Morris. Boston: Northeastern University Press, 1991.

Gies, Frances, and Joseph. *Marriage and the Family in the Middle Ages.* New York: Harper and Row, 1989.

Gilder, George. *Sexual Suicide.* New York: Bantam Books, 1975.

———. *Men and Marriage.* New York: Bantam Books, 1986.

Gilson, Étienne Gilson. *Heloise and Abelard.* Ann Arbor, Michigan: University of Michigan Press, 1963.

Glendon, May Ann. *The Transformation of Family Law: State, Law, and Family in the United States and Western Europe.* Chicago: University of Chicago Press, 1989.

Goldman, Wendy Z. *Women, The State, and Revolution: Soviet Family Policy And Social Life, 1917—1936.* Cambridge: Cambridge University Press, 1993.

Goody, Jack, Joan Thirsk, and E.P. Thompson, Editors. *Family and Inheritance: Rural Society in Western Europe, 1200–1800.* Cambridge: Cambridge University Press, 1976.

Gorman, Michael J. *Abortion and the Early Church: Christian, Jewish, and Pagan Attitudes in the Greco-Roman World.* Eugene, Oregon: Wipf and Stock Publishers, 1982.

Gottlieb, Beatrice. *The Family in the Western World from the Black Death to the Industrial Age.* New York: Oxford University Press, 1993.

Gratian. *Tractatus de Penitential: A New Latin Edition with an English Translation.* Edited and Translated by Atria A. Larson. Washington, D.C.: The Catholic University of America Press, 2018.

———. *The Treatise on Laws (Decretum DD. 1–20) with the Ordinary Gloss.* Translated by James Gordley. Washington, D.C.: The Catholic University of America Press, 1993.

Gregory the Great. *Gregory the Great: Pastoral Care.* Edited by Henry Davis, S.J. Westminster, Maryland: The Newman Press, 1955.

Gregory of Tours. *The History of the Franks.* Translated by Lewis Thorpe. New York: Penguin Books, 1974.

Grubbs, Judith Evans. *Law and Family in Late Antiquity: The Emperor Constantine's Marriage Legislation.* Oxford: Clarendon Press, 1995.

Hadas, Moses, ed. *The Complete Works of Tacitus.* Translated by Alfred John Church and William Jackson Brodribb. New York: The Modern Library, 1942.

Halle, Fannina W. Halle. *Woman in Soviet Russia.* Translated by Margaret W. Green. London: Routledge, 1933.

Hamilton, Edith. *Mythology: Timeless Tales of Gods and Heroes.* New York: Black Dog and Leventhal Publishers, 1942.

Hanawalt, Barbara. *The Ties that Bound: Peasant Families in Medieval England.* Oxford: Oxford University Press, 1986.

Harper, Kyle. *From Shame to Sin: The Christian Transformation of Sexual Morality in Late Antiquity.* Cambridge, Massachusetts: Harvard University Press, 2013.

———. *Plagues Upon the Earth: Disease and the Course of Human History.* Princeton, New Jersey: Princeton University Press, 2021.

Harris, Marvin. *Our Kind: Who We Are, Where We Came From, Where We Are Going.* New York: Harper Perennial, 1989.

Helmholz, R.H. *Marriage Litigation in Medieval England.* Cambridge: Cambridge University Press, 1974.

Henderson, Jeffrey, Editor. *Prudentius*, Volume One. Loeb Classical Library. Translated by H.J. Thomson. Cambridge, Massachusetts: Harvard University Press, 2006.

Hensley, Jeff Lane, Editor. *The Zero People: Essays on Life.* Ann Arbor, Michigan: Servant Books, 1983.

Herlihy, David. *Medieval Households.* Cambridge, Massachusetts: Harvard University Press, 1985.

Hilary of Poitiers. *Conflicts of Conscience and Law in the Fourth-century Church: Against Valens and Uracius: the extant fragments, together with his Letters to the Emperor Constantius.* Translated by Lionel R. Wickham. Liverpool: Liverpool University Press, 1997.

Himmelfarb, Gertrude. *The De-Moralization of Society: From Victorian Virtues to Modern Values.* New York: Vintage Books, 1994.

Hincmar of Rheims. *The Divorce of King Lothar and Queen Theutberga: Hincmar of Rheims's De Divortio.* Translated and Annotated by Rachel Stone and Charles West. Manchester: Manchester University Press, 2016.

Hodge, Charles. *Systematic Theology.* Three Volumes. Reprint. Grand Rapids, Michigan: William B. Eerdmans, 1981.

Holy Bible, American Standard Version. United States: RJ&WC Press, 2017.

Holy Bible, English Standard Version. Wheaton, Illinois: Crossway, 2001.

Holy Bible, King James Version. Iowa Falls, Iowa: Riverside Books and Bible House, 1971.

Holy Bible, New American Standard Bible. La Habra, California: Lockman Foundation, 1995).

Hunter, David G., Editor. *Marriage and Sexuality in Early Christianity.* Minneapolis, Minnesota: Fortress Press, 2018.

———, Editor. *Marriage in the Early Church.* Minneapolis, Minnesota: Fortress Press, 1992.

Indiana Code, Titles 31 to 35. Indianapolis, Indiana: Indiana Legislative Council, 1993.

Ingram, Martin. *Church Courts, Sex and Marriage in England, 1570–1640.* Cambridge: Cambridge University Press, 1987.

Irenaeus of Lyons. *On the Apostolic Preaching.* Translated by John Behr. Crestwood, New York: St. Vladimir's Seminary Press, 1997.

Irwin, Alexander C. *Eros Toward the World: Paul Tillich and the Theology of the Erotic.* Minneapolis, Minnesota: Fortress Press, 1991.

Jager, Eric. *The Last Duel: A True Story of Crime, Scandal, and Trial by Combat in Medieval France.* New York: Broadway Books, 2004

Jenkins, Dafydd and Morfydd E. Owen, Editors. *The Welsh Law of Women.* Cardiff: University of Wales Press, 1980.

Johnson, Eric A., and Karl-Heinz Reuband, *What We Knew: Terror, Mass Murder, and Everyday Life in Nazi Germany, An Oral History.* Cambridge, Massachusetts: Basic Books, 2006.

Johnson, James Turner. *A Society Ordained by God: Puritan Marriage Doctrine in the First Half of the Seventeenth Century.* Nashville, Tennessee: Abingdon Press, 1970.

Kingdon, Robert M. *Adultery and Divorce in Calvin's Geneva.* Cambridge, Massachusetts: Harvard University Press, 1995.

Klein, Joan Larsen, Editor. *Daughters, Wives, and Widows: Writings by Men about Women and Marriage in England, 1500–1640.* Urbana, Illinois: University of Illinois Press, 1992.

Kleist, James A., Translator. *The Epistles of St. Clement of Rome and St. Ignatius of Antioch.* New York: Newman Press, 1966.

Knox, John. *Selected Writings of John Knox: Public Epistles, Treatises, and Expositions to the Year 1559.* Dallas, Texas: Presbyterian Heritage Publications, 1995.

———. *The Works of John Knox.* Seven Volumes. Edited by David Laing. Edinburgh: Bannatyne Club, 1848.

Krause, Harry. *Family Law.* St. Paul, Minnesota: West Publishing Company, 1986.

Kreeft, Peter. *The God Who Loves You.* Ann Arbor, Michigan: Servant Books, 1988.

Kühl, Stefan. *The Nazi Connection: Eugenics, American Racism, and German National Socialism.* Oxford: Oxford University Press, 1994.

Lacey, W.K. *The Family in Classical Greece.* Ithaca, New York: Cornell University Press, 1968.

Lacroix, Paul. *History of Prostitution among All the Peoples of the World, from the Most Remote Antiquity to the Present Day.* Translated by Samuel Putnam. New York: Civici Friede Publishers, 1931.

The Larger Catechism of the Westminster Assembly. Philadelphia: Presbyterian Board of Publication and Sabbath-School Work, 1912.

Laven, Mary. *Virgins of Venice: Broken Vows and Cloistered Lives in the Renaissance Convent.* New York: Penguin Books, 2002.

Leith, John, ed. *Creeds of the Churches.* Atlanta, Georgia: John Knox Press, 1982.

Le Roy Ladurie, Emmanuel. *Times of Feast, Times of Famine: A History of Climate Since the Year 1000.* New York: Farrar, Straus & Giroux, 1988.

Levin, Eve. *Sex and Society in the World of the Orthodox Slavs, 900–1700.* Ithaca, New York: Cornell University Press, 1989.

Lewis, C. S. *The Abolition of Man.* New York: HarperOne, 1971.

———. *The Four Loves.* New York: Harcourt, Brace, and Company, 1960.

———. *The Great Divorce: A Dream.* New York: HarperOne, 1973.

———. *Mere Christianity.* New York: HarperOne, 1980.

———. *Perelandra.* New York: Scribner Classics, 1996.

———. *That Hideous Strength: A Modern Fairy-Tale for Grown-Ups.* New York: Scribner Classics, 1996.

Lipka, Hilary, and Bruce Wells, Editors. *Sexuality and Law in the Torah.* London: T&T Clark, 2020.

Lipscomb, Suzanne. *The Voices of Nîmes: Women, Sex, and Marriage in Reformation Languedoc.* Oxford: Oxford University Press, 2019.

Lombard, Peter. *The Sentences, Book Two: On Creation.* Translated by Guilio Solano. Toronto: Pontifical Institute for Medieval Studies, 2008.

———. *The Sentences, Book Three: On the Incarnation of the Word.* Translated by Guilio Solano. Toronto: Pontifical Institute for Medieval Studies, 2008.

———. *The Sentences, Book Four: On the Doctrine of Signs.* Translated by Guilio Solano. Toronto: Pontifical Institute of Medieval Studies, 2010.

Luther, Martin. *Luther's Works: American Edition.* Fifty-five Volumes. Edited by Jaroslav Pelikan and Helmut T. Lehmann. Philadelphia: Fortress Press, 1955–1986.

———. *Luther's Works*. Fifty-five Volumes. Edited by Jaroslav Pelikan. St. Louis, Missouri: Concordia Publishing House, 1955–1986.

———. *Martin Luther's Basic Theological Works*. Third Edition. Edited by Timothy F. Lull and William R. Russel. Minneapolis, Minnesota: Fortress Press, 2012.

Macaulay, Ranald, and Jerram Barrs. *Being Human: The Nature of Spiritual Experience*. Downers Grove, Illinois: InterVarsity Press, 1978.

MacFarlane, Alan. *Marriage and Love in England: Modes of Reproduction 1300–1840*. New York: Basil Blackwell, 1986.

Mackin, Theodore, S.J. *Divorce and Remarriage*. New York: Paulist Press, 1984.

———. *What is Marriage?* New York: Paulist Press, 1982.

Maier, Walter A. *For Better, Not for Worse: A Manual of Christian Matrimony*. St. Louis, Missouri: Concordia Publishing House, 1939.

Mäkinen, Virpi, ed. *Lutheran Reformation and the Law*. Leiden: Brill, 2006.

Marriage, Divorce, and the Church: The Report of a Commission Appointed by the Archbishop of Canterbury to Prepare a Statement on the Christian Doctrine of Marriage. London: SPCK, 1971.

Maxfield, John A. *Luther's Lectures on Genesis and the Formation of Evangelical Identity*. Kirksville, Missouri: Truman State University Press, 2008.

McDowell, Josh, and Dick Day. *Why Wait? What You Need to Know about the Teen Sexuality Crisis*. San Bernardino, California: Here's Life Publishers, 1987.

McGuckin, John A. *The Ascent of Christian Law: Patristic and Byzantine Formulations of a New Civilization*. Yonkers, New York: St. Vladimir's Seminary Press, 2012.

MacLean, French L. *The Fifth Field: The Story of the 96 American Soldiers Sentenced to Death and Executed in Europe and North Africa in World War II*. Atglen, Pennsylvania: Schiffer Military History Publishers, 2013.

McNamara, Jo Ann, John E. Halborg, and E. Gordon Whatley. *Sainted Women of the Dark Ages*. Durham, North Carolina: Duke University Press, 1992.

McNeill, John T., and Helena M. Gamer, Editors. *Medieval Handbooks of Penance: A Translation of the Principal Libri Poenitentiales*. New York: Columbia University Press, 1990.

Melanchthon, Philip. *Melanchthon on Christian Doctrine*. Edited by Clyde Manschreck. New York: Oxford University Press, 1965.

Middelmann, Udo. *Pro.exist.ence*. Downers Grove, Illinois: InterVarsity Press, 1974.

Milgrom, Jacob. *The JPS Torah Commentary: Numbers*. Philadelphia: Jewish Publications Society, 1989.

———. *Leviticus 17-22: A New Translation with Introduction and Commentary*. New Haven, CT: Anchor Yale Bible, 2000.

Milton, John. *The Works of John Milton*. Eighteen Volumes. New York: Columbia University Press, 1934.

Mistry, Zubin. *Abortion in the Early Middle Ages, c. 500–900 A.D.* York: York Medieval Press, 2015.

Monnickendam, Yifat. *Jewish Law and Early Christian Identity: Betrothal, Marriage, and Infidelity in the Writings of Ephrem the Syrian*. Cambridge: Cambridge University Press, 2020.

Montgomery, John Warwick. *How Do We Know There Is A God?* Minneapolis, Minnesota: Bethany House Publishers, 1973.

Morgan, Edmund S. *The Puritan Family: Religion and Domestic Relations in Seventeenth-Century New England*. New York: Harper and Row Publishers, 1966.

Moxey, Keith. *Peasants, Warriors, and Wives: Popular Imagery in the Reformation*. Chicago: University of Chicago Press, 1989.

Müller, Wolfgang P. *Marriage Litigation in the Western Church, 215–1517*. Cambridge: Cambridge University Press, 2021.

Musallam, B.F. *Sex and Society in Islam: Birth Control Before the Nineteenth Century*. Cambridge: Cambridge University Press, 1983.

Newman, Paul B. *Growing Up in the Middle Ages*. Jefferson, North Carolina: MacFarland and Company, Inc., Publishers, 2007.

Nicholas, David. *The Domestic Life of a Medieval City: Women, Children, and the Family in Fourteenth-Century Ghent*. Lincoln, Nebraska: University of Nebraska, 1985.

Noll, John Francis. *A Catechism on Birth Control*. Huntington, Indiana: Our Sunday Visitor Press, n.d.

Noonan, John T. *Contraception: A History of Its Treatment by the Catholic Theologians and Canonists*. Cambridge: Belknap Press, 1986.

Otis, Leah. *Prostitution in Medieval Society: The History of an Institution in Languedoc*. Chicago: University of Chicago Press, 1985.

Oulton, John Ernest Leonard, and Henry Chadwick, Editors. *Alexandrian Christianity.* Philadelphia: Westminster Press, 1954.

Palmer, G. E. H., Philip Sherrard, and Kallistos Ware, Editors. *The Philokalia.* Two Volumes. Boston: Faber and Faber Limited, 1981.

Panigrahi, Lalita. *British Social Policy and Female Infanticide in India.* New Delhi: Munishiram Manoharlal, 1972.

Pascal, Blaise. *Pensées.* Translated by A. J. Krailsheimer. New York: Penguin Books, 1966.

Pauck, Wilhelm, ed. *Melanchthon and Bucer.* Philadelphia: Westminster Press, 1969.

Payer, Pierre J. *Sex and the Penitentials: The Development of a Sexual Code, 550–1150.* Toronto: University of Toronto Press, 1984.

Perkins, William. *Christian Economy: The Ordering of a Family According to Scripture.* Independently Published: Reformed Retrieval, 2022.

———. *The Work of William Perkins.* Volume Three. Introduced and Edited by Ian Brewer. Berkshire, England: The Sutton Courtney Press, 1970.

Perry, Mary Elizabeth. *Gender and Disorder in Early Modern Seville.* Princeton, New Jersey: Princeton University Press, 1990.

Pharr, Clyde, Editor. *The Theodosian Code and Novels and the Sirmondian Constitutions: A Translation.* Princeton, New Jersey: Princeton University Press, 1952.

Philo of Alexandria. *The Works of Philo.* Translated by C. D. Yonge. Peabody, Massachusetts: Hendrickson Publishers, 1993.

Pizan, Christine de. *The Book of the City of Ladies.* Translated by Earl Jeffrey Richards. New York: Persea Books, 1982.

Pounds, Norman J.G. *Hearth and Home: A History of Material Culture.* Bloomington, Indiana: Indiana University Press, 1989.

———. *A Historical Geography of Europe.* Cambridge: Cambridge University Press, 1990.

Power, Eileen, Translator. *The Goodman of Paris (Le Ménagier de Paris): A Treatise on Moral and Domestic Economy by a Citizen of Paris, c. 1393.* London: Folio Society, 1992.

Pride, Mary. *The Way Home: Beyond Feminism, Back to Reality.* Fenton, Missouri: Home Life Books, 1985.

Provan, Charles D. *The Bible and Birth Control.* Monongahela, Pennsylvania: Zimmer Printing, 1989.

Raymond of Penyafort. *Summa on Marriage*. Translated by Pierre Payer. Toronto: Pontifical Institute, 2005.

Reid Jr., Charles J. *Power over the Body, Equality in the Family: Rights and Domestic Relations in Medieval Canon Law*. Grand Rapids, Michigan: William B. Eerdmans Publishing Company.

Reifsnyder, Richard. "Charles Hodge: A Conservative Theologian Finds His Way to Emancipation." *National Archives of the PC(USA)*: Presbyterian Historical Society, 17 April 2018. https://www.history.pcusa.org/blog/2018/04/charles-hodge-conservative-theologian-finds-his-way-emancipation.

Reynolds, Philip L. *How Marriage Became One of the Sacraments: The Sacramental Theology of Marriage from its Medieval Origins to the Council of Trent*. Cambridge: Cambridge University Press, 2016.

———. *Marriage in the Western Church: The Christianization of Marriage during the Patristic and Early Medieval Periods*. Leiden: E.J. Brill, 1994.

Rice, John R. *The Home: Courtship, Marriage, and Children*. Murfreesboro, Tennessee: Sword of the Lord Publishers, 1946.

Richardson, Cyril R., Editor. *Early Christian Fathers*. Philadelphia: Westminster Press, 1953.

Riddle, John M. *Contraception and Abortion from the Ancient World to the Renaissance*. Cambridge, Massachusetts: Harvard University Press, 1992.

———. *Eve's Herbs: A History of Contraception and Abortion in the West*. Cambridge, Massachusetts: Harvard University Press, 1997.

Riello, Giorgio and Ulinka Rublack, Editors. *The Right to Dress: Sumptuary Laws in a Global Perspective, c. 1200-1800*, Cambridge: Cambridge University Press, 2019.

Rivoire, Émile, and Victor van Berchem, Editors. *Les Sources du Droit du Canton de Genève*. Four Volumes. Genève: H. R. Sauerländer & Cie., 1927–1935.

Roche, George. *A World Without Heroes: The Modern Tragedy*. Hillsdale, Michigan: George Roche and the Hillsdale College Press, 1987.

Romney Wegner, Judith. *Chattel or Person? The Status of Women in the Mishnah*. New York: Oxford University Press, 1988.

Rookmaaker, Hans. *Modern Art and the Death of a Culture*. Wheaton, Illinois: Crossway Books, 1994.

Rosenberg, Michael. *Signs of Virginity: Testing Virgins and Making Men in Late Antiquity*. New York: Oxford University Press, 2018.

Rowley, H.H. "The Marriage of Hosea." *Bulletin of the John Rylands Library* 39, no. 1 (September 1956): 200–233. Reprinted in *The Marriage of Hosea*. Manchester, 1956.

Ruggiero, Guido. *The Boundaries of Eros: Sex, Crime, and Sexuality in Renaissance Venice.* New York: Oxford University Press, 1985).

Russell, Bertrand. *Marriage and Morals*. New York: Bantam Books, 1929.

Safley, Thomas Max. *Let No Man Put Asunder: The Control of Marriage in the German Southwest: A Comparative Study, 1550–1600.* Kirksville, Missouri: The Sixteenth Century Journal Publishers, Inc., 1984.

Saletan, William. "Incest Is Cancer—The David Epstein Incest Case: If Homosexuality Is OK, Why Is Incest Wrong?" *Slate*, December 14, 2010. https://www.slate.com/id/2275994/

Sandys, Edwin. *The Sermons of Edwin Sandys, D.D.* Edited by Reverend John Ayer. The Parker Society. Cambridge: The University Press, 1842.

Sayers, Dorothy. *Are Women Human?* Grand Rapids, Michigan: William B. Eerdmans Publishing Company, 1971.

———. *The Mind of the Maker*. Introduction by Madeleine L'Engle. New York: HarperCollins Publishers, 1987.

Schaeffer, Francis. *The Complete Works of Francis A. Schaeffer: A Christian Worldview*. Five Volumes. Westchester, Illinois: Crossway Books, 1982.

———. *The Great Evangelical Disaster*. Westchester, Illinois: Crossway Books, 1984.

———. *Letters of Francis Schaeffer*. Edited by Dennis. Westchester, Illinois: Crossway Books, 1985.

Schaff, Philip, trans. *Ante-Nicene Church Fathers. Volume Twelve. Fathers of the Third Century*. Grand Rapids, Michigan: Aeterna Press, 2014.

———. *History of the Christian Church*. Eight Volumes. Grand Rapids, Michigan: William B. Eerdmans, 1950.

Schmugge, Ludwig. *Marriage on Trial: Late Medieval German Couples at the Papal Court*. Translated by Atria A. Larson. Washington, D.C.: The Catholic University of America Press, 2012.

Searle, Mark, and Kenneth W. Stevenson, Editors. *Documents of the Marriage Liturgy*. Collegeville, Minnesota: The Liturgical Press, 1992.

Selden, John. *John Selden on Jewish Marriage Law: The Uxor Hebraica*. Translated by Jonathan R. Ziskind. Leiden: E. J. Brill, 1991.

Shapiro, Yaakov. *Sexuality and Jewish Law: In Search of a Balanced Approach in Torah, vol. 1: Halachic Positions: What Judaism Really Says about Passion in the Marital Bed, An Outline, Analysis and Candid Discussion*, Expanded Edition. Middletown, Delaware: Jonathan Shapiro, 2017.

Shorter, Edward. *A History of Women's Bodies*. New York: Basic Books, 1982.

Simons, Menno. *The Complete Writings of Menno Simons*. Edited by J. C. Wenger. Scottdale, Pennsylvania: Herald Press, 1984.

Smedes, Lewis B. *Sex for Christians*. Grand Rapids, Michigan: William B. Eerdmans Publishing Company, 1994.

Smith, Henry. *The Sermons of Henry Smith*. Two Volumes. Edinburgh: James Nichol, 1866.

Solzhenitsyn, Alexandr I. *A World Split Apart: Commencement Address Delivered at Harvard University, June 8, 1978*. Harper and Row: New York, 1978.

Sommerville, Margaret R. *Sex and Subjection: Attitudes to Women in Early Modern Society*. London: Arnold, 1995.

Stevenson, Kenneth. *Nuptial Blessing: A Study of Christian Marriage Rites*. New York: Oxford University Press, 1983.

Stone, Lawrence. *Family, Sex, and Marriage: 1500–1800*. New York: Harper and Row, 1979.

Strasser, Ulrike. *State of Virginity: Gender, Religion, and Politics in an Early Modern Catholic State*. Ann Arbor, Michigan: University of Michigan Press, 2004.

Sunshine, Glenn S. *Slaying Leviathan: Limited Government and Resistance in the Christian Tradition*. Moscow, Idaho: Canon Press, 2020.

Tappert, Theodore G., ed. *The Book of Concord: The Confessions of the Lutheran Church*. Philadelphia: Fortress Press, 1959.

Temkin, Owsei, Translator. *Soranus' Gynecology*. Baltimore: Johns Hopkins University Press, 1956.

Tentler, Thomas T. *Sin and Confession on the Eve of the Reformation*. Princeton, New Jersey: Princeton University Press, 1977.

Tolstoy, Leo. *Works of Leo Tolstoy: Anna Karenina I*. New York: The Century Company, 1911.

Treggiari, Susan. *Roman Marriage: Iusti Coniuges from the Time of Cicero to the Time of Ulpian*. Oxford: Clarendon Press, 1991.

Trueblood, Elton, and Pauline Trueblood. *The Recovery of Family Life*. New York: Harper Brothers Publishers, 1953.

Turretin, Francis. *Institutes of Elenctic Theology*. Two Volumes. Edited by James T. Dennison Jr. Phillipsburg, N.J.: Presbyterian and Reformed Publishers, 1994.

Vermigli, Peter Martyr. *Common Places*. Three Volumes. Reformation Classic; Reformed Retrieval. Independently Published, 2021.

———. *The Common Places of the Most Famous and Renowned Divine Doctor Peter Martyr*. London: n.p., 1583.

Viret, Pierre. *Exposition of the Ten Commandments*. Two Volumes. Translated by R.A. Sheats. Monticello, Florida: Psalm 78 Ministries, 2020.

Viscuso, Patrick Demetrios. *Sexuality, Marriage, and Celibacy in Byzantine Law: Selections from a Fourteenth-Century Encyclopedia of Canon Law and Theology—the Alphabetical Collection of Matthew Blasteres*. Brookline, Massachusetts: Holy Cross Orthodox Press, 2008.

Walker Bynum, Caroline. *The Resurrection of the Body in Western Christianity, 200–1336*. New York: Columbia University Press, 1995.

Warfield, Benjamin Breckinridge. *Biblical and Theological Studies*. Edited by Samuel G. Craig. Philadelphia: Presbyterian and Reformed Publishing Company, 1968.

Watt, Jeffrey R. *The Consistory and Social Discipline in Calvin's Geneva*. Rochester, New York: University of Rochester Press, 2020.

Wenzel, Siegfried. *Fasciculus Morum: A Fourteenth-Century Preacher's Handbook*. University Park, Pennsylvania: Pennsylvania State University Press, 1989.

Wesley, John. *John Wesley's Fifty-Three Sermons*. Edited by Edward Sugden. Nashville, Tennessee: Abingdon Press, 1983.

West, Jim. *Christian Courtship Versus The Dating Game*. Palo Cedro, California: Christian Worldview Ministries, 1993.

Wheat, Ed. *Intended for Pleasure*. Old Tappan, New Jersey: Fleming H. Revell Company, 1977.

Wicks, Jared, S.J., Editor. *Cajetan Responds: A Reader in Reformation Controversy*. Washington, D.C.: The Catholic University of America Press, 1978.

Wilberforce, William. *Real Christianity*. 1829. Reprint, Portland, Oregon: Multnomah Press, 1982.

Williams, Charles. *The Forgiveness of Sins*. Grand Rapids, Michigan: William B. Eerdmans Publishing Company, 1984.

Williams, Florence. "A House, 10 Wives: Polygamy in Suburbia." *New York Times*, Thursday, December 11, 1997.

Williams, George Hunston. *The Radical Reformation*. Philadelphia: Westminster Press, 1975.

Wilson, Douglas. *Reforming Marriage*. Moscow, Idaho: Canon Press, 2005.

Witte, Jr., John. *From Sacrament to Contract: Marriage, Religion, and Law in the Western Tradition*. Louisville, Kentucky: Westminster, John Knox Press, 1997.

———. *The Sins of the Fathers: The Law and Theology of Illegitimacy Reconsidered*. Cambridge: Cambridge University Press, 2009.

Witte Jr., John, and Gary S. Hauk, *Christianity and Family Law: An Introduction*. Cambridge: Cambridge University Press, 2017.

Witte, John Jr., and Robert M. Kingdon. *Sex, Marriage, and Family in John Calvin's Geneva: Courtship, Engagement, and Marriage*. Volume One. Grand Rapids, Michigan: William B. Eerdmans Publishing Company, 2005.

Zacharias, Ravi. *I, Isaac, take Thee, Rebekah; Moving from Romance to Lasting Love*. Nashville, Tennessee: Thomas Nelson Publishers, 2004.

Zanchi, Girolamo. *The Spiritual Marriage between Christ and His Church and Every One of the Faithful*. Translated and Introduced by Patrick J. O'Banion. Grand Rapids, Michigan: Reformation Heritage Books, 2021.

Zwingli, Ulrich. *Ulrich Zwingli, 1484–1531: Selected Works*. Translated by Samuel Macauley Jackson. Philadelphia: University of Pennsylvania Press, 1972.

≈

SELECT INDEX OF CITED AUTHORS
AND SOURCES

The following index lists cited sources rather than all names, topics, or places, since the table of contents should suffice for subject searches. This index does not include references found in the Supplementary Material.

ABOUT THE AUTHOR

Jeffrey E. Ford is a trained historian and writer living in Virginia who earned his Ph.D. in European History from the University of Wisconsin–Madison and an M.A. in European History from Indiana University Bloomington, with his doctorate dissertation being on marital law in sixteenth-century France. Jeffrey and his wife raised four children and are evangelical Protestants who have practiced the Christian faith since their teenage years.

Jeff has self-published fiction and nonfiction under the pen name Kirk Adams, including the following titles: *Left on Paradise, The Electronic Mother, The Trouble with Girls, Hundreds of Reflections: 100 Psalms Explored in 100 Words, Measures of Insight: Moral Reflections for Daily Life,* and *Husbandry.* In his true name, Jeffrey has previously published essays in *First Things* (both print and online), as well as academic book reviews and the original version of this book.

www.ingramcontent.com/pod-product-compliance
Lightning Source LLC
Chambersburg PA
CBHW071944110426
42744CB00030B/239